North Macedonia

the Bradt Travel Guide

Thammy Evans
Updated by Philip Briggs

www.bradtguides.com

Bradt Travel Guides Ltd, UK
The Globe Pequot Press Inc, USA

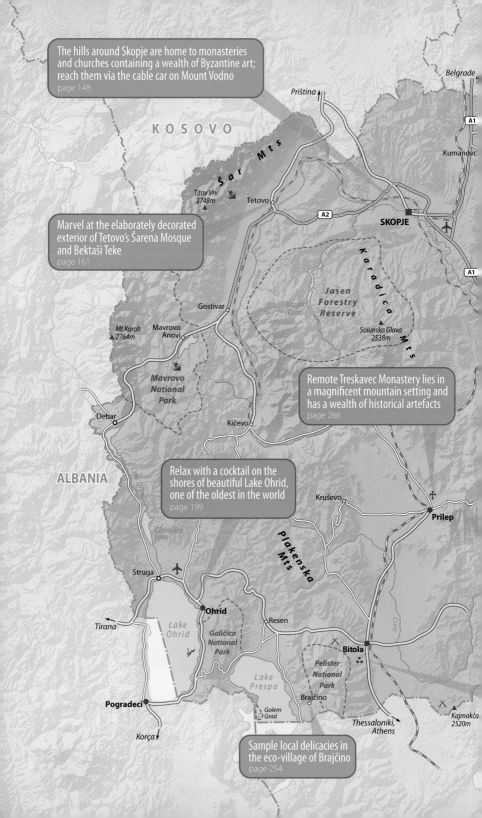

The hills around Skopje are home to monasteries and churches containing a wealth of Byzantine art; reach them via the cable car on Mount Vodno
page 148

Marvel at the elaborately decorated exterior of Tetovo's Šarena Mosque and Bektaši Teke
page 161

Remote Treskavec Monastery lies in a magnificent mountain setting and has a wealth of historical artefacts
page 266

Relax with a cocktail on the shores of beautiful Lake Ohrid, one of the oldest in the world
page 199

Sample local delicacies in the eco-village of Brajčino
page 254

KOSOVO

Belgrade

Priština

Kumanovo

A1

Šar Mts

Titov Vrv
2748m

Tetovo

A2

SKOPJE

A1

Jasen
Forestry
Reserve

Karadica Mts

Treska

Kozjak
Ezero

Vardar

Solunska Glava
2538m

Gostivar

Mt Korab
2764m

Mavrovo
Anovi

Mavrovo
National
Park

Debar

Kičevo

Crn Drim

ALBANIA

Kruševo

Prilep

Plakenska Mts

Globočica
Lake

Struga

Ohrid

Resen

Crna

Tirana

Lake
Ohrid

Galičica
National
Park

Pelister
National
Park

Bitola

Lake
Prespa

Brajčino

Pogradeci

Golem
Grad

Kajmakča
2520m

Korča

Thessaloniki,
Athens

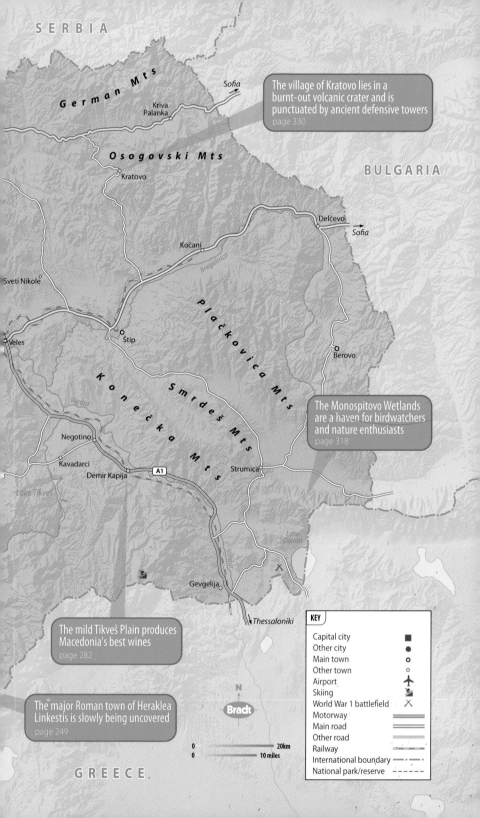

SERBIA

German Mts

Kriva
Palanka

Sofia

The village of Kratovo lies in a
burnt-out volcanic crater and is
punctuated by ancient defensive towers
page 330

Osogovski Mts

BULGARIA

Kratovo

Delčevo

Sofia

Kočani

Bregalnica

Sveti Nikole

Plačkovica Mts

Štip

Veles

Berovo

Vardar

Smrdeš Mts

Konečka Mts

The Monospitovo Wetlands
are a haven for birdwatchers
and nature enthusiasts
page 318

Negotino

Kavadarci

Demir Kapija

A1

Strumica

Lake Tikveš

Lake Dojran

na

Vardar

The mild Tikveš Plain produces
Macedonia's best wines
page 282

Gevgelija

Thessaloniki

The major Roman town of Heraklea
Linkestis is slowly being uncovered
page 249

N

Bradt

0   20km
0   10 miles

GREECE

North Macedonia

Don't miss...

Wineries
The rich Tikveš Plain
running from Veles
along the River Vardar
to Demir Kapija is
renowned for its wines
(PM/S) page 274

People and culture
The future mother-in-law hosts a
dance in traditional dress with the
closest relatives at the Galičnik
wedding festival (SL) page 184

Ohrid
Lake Ohrid is the jewel of the Macedonian crown — the lake and town are a UNESCO World Heritage site
(t/S) page 199

Art and architecture
The new Sv Kliment, completed in 2002, stands amid the ruins of the early 5th-century basilica at Plaošnik
(z/S) page 213

Hiking
North Macedonia is brimming with beautiful countryside that makes splendid hiking for a range of fitness and experience levels
(o/S) page 92

North Macedonia in colour

above Skopje's Cathedral of Sv Kliment of Ohrid was built in the 20th century (DH/D) page 145

left The views from the walls of Kale Fortress are quite magnificent (s/S) page 144

below The River Vardar flows beneath the late 15th-century Kamen Most in Skopje (Si/S) page 139

above left   *Warrior on a Horse* is one of the monuments that was constructed for the Skopje 2014 restoration project (PB) page 137

above right   Home to the ornate Mustafa Pasha Mosque, the old Turkish quarter of Čaršija is one of Skopje's most atmospheric areas (SS) page 140

below   Housed within one of Skopje's most impressive buildings, the Archaeological Museum of Macedonia shares its home with the Supreme Court and National Archives (AL/S) page 139

above   Heraklea Linkestis (left) and Stobi (right) are two of the country's most impressive Roman sites, although only parts of the former have been uncovered, meaning that future visits will prove even more fruitful (SS and PB) pages 249 and 282

left   The Ilinden Monument in Kruševo was erected in 1974 to commemorate the 71st anniversary of the Ilinden Uprising and 30th anniversary of the town's liberation from Nazi occupation (PB) page 272

below   Almost 2,000 years old, the Roman theatre in Ohrid remained undiscovered until the early 20th century (CM/S) page 212

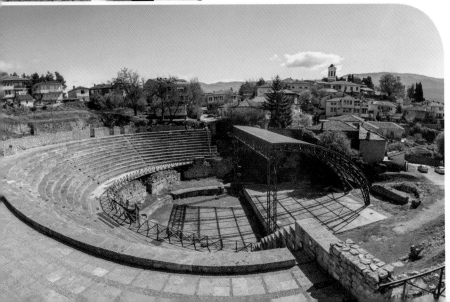

AUTHOR

Born in London, of Welsh and Malay Chinese parents, **Thammy Evans** has travelled and lived abroad for over 20 years. Professionally, her career lies in the field of political analysis. Her first overseas trip was to Malaysia at the age of eight, and she has been dabbling in numerous foreign languages ever since. Among her many other travels, her most memorable are the Trans-Mongolian Railway from Tianjin to Moscow in 1991, mountaineering in Bolivia in the summer of 1999, and doing the field  research for her second Bradt travel guide *Great Wall of China* in 2005. Despite many forays to far-off lands, she feels most at home in the southern climes of wider Europe and has lived and worked in Macedonia for five years. She and her family now have a small stone house by the sea in Istria.

CONTRIBUTING AUTHOR AND UPDATER

Philip Briggs (e philip.briggs@bradtguides.com) has been an inveterate traveller since he first backpacked between Nairobi and Cape Town in 1986. His association with Bradt dates to 1991, when wrote the first internationally published guidebook to South Africa following the release of Nelson Mandela. Philip has since written Bradt guides to Tanzania, Uganda, Ethiopia, Malawi, Mozambique, Ghana, Rwanda, Gambia, Somaliland, Suriname and Sri Lanka, all of which are still regularly updated for several subsequent editions.

DEDICATION

To my mother

A NOTE ON THE NAME CHANGE

Following years of conflict with Greece, the Former Yugoslav Republic of Macedonia was scheduled to formally change its name to North Macedonia in early 2019, shortly after this book went to press. Consequently, while the book itself is called North Macedonia, all references to the country within the text and on the maps remain as 'Macedonia'.

PUBLISHER'S FOREWORD *Hilary Bradt*

Macedonia is the Cinderella of the former Yugoslavia, attracting fewer visitors than its high-profile neighbours. Readers are fortunate to have Thammy Evans and updater Philip Briggs to guide them – they are two of our most enthusiastic and conscientious authors. Users of this new edition have a treat in store.

Sixth edition published June 2019
First published 2004
Bradt Travel Guides Ltd
31a High Street, Chesham, Bucks HP5 1BW, England
www.bradtguides.com
Print edition published in the USA by The Globe Pequot Press Inc,
PO Box 480, Guilford, Connecticut 06437-0480

Text copyright © 2019 Thammy Evans
Maps copyright © 2019 Bradt Travel Guides Ltd; includes map data © OpenStreetMap contributors
Photographs copyright © 2019 Individual photographers (see below)
Project Manager: Laura Pidgley
Cover research: Pepi Bluck, Perfect Picture

ISBN: 978 1 78477 084 6

British Library Cataloguing in Publication Data
A catalogue record for this book is available from the British Library

Photographs Alamy Stock Photos: FO Travel (FOT/A); Philip Briggs (PB); Julian Cartwright (JC); Dreamstime.com: Darko Hristov (DH/D), Mrotchua (M/D), Nace Popov (NP/D), Nehru Sulejmanovski (NS/D); Getty Images: DaveLongMedia (DLM/G); Samir Ljuma (SL); Shutterstock.com: Thomas Dekiere (TD/S), The Visual Explorer (VE/S), BrankoG (BG/S), jordeangjelovik (j/S), Jane Josifovski (JJ/S), Zoran Karapancev (ZK/S), Andrii Lutsyk (AL/S), ColorMaker (CM/S), mbrand83 (m/S), milosk50 (m50/S), Petar Milevski (PM/S), ollirg (o/S), saiko3p (s/S), silverjohn (Si/S), Ljupco Smokovski (LS/S), trabantos (t/S), vlas2000 (v/S), Predrag Vasilevski (PV/S), zefart (z/S); SuperStock (SS)
Front cover Ohrid town (DLM/G)
Back cover Mavrovo Lake (BG/S); Mustafa Pasha Mosque, Skopje (m50/S)
Title page Sv Jovan Kaneo, Ohrid (s/S); Cave church of Sv Stefan (PB); Archaeological Museum of Macedonia, Skopje (AL/S)

Maps David McCutcheon FBCart.S

Typeset by Ian Spick, Bradt Travel Guides
Production managed by Jellyfish Print Solutions; printed in India
Digital conversion by www.dataworks.co.in

I ended up back in the Balkans (which is another story), with my husband in Macedonia. Not good at twiddling my thumbs, I had already sought advice from a travel writer friend (Cam Burns) about doing some freelance travel writing. 'Why don't you update a travel guidebook on Macedonia?' he suggested. 'What a brilliant idea!' I replied; and off I went to Stanford's, the biggest map and travel bookshop in the UK, to survey the many guidebooks on Macedonia and to choose the one closest to my style of writing to update. After about 5 minutes of research in the Europe section, I quickly came to the conclusion that there was a grand total of zero guidebooks on Macedonia, and that *ipso facto* I myself would be writing the very first one! Another 5 minutes of research led me to the further deduction that the only publishing house crazy enough to tackle such a proposition would be Bradt Travel Guides.

I contacted Bradt, and to cut a very long story short, the then chief editor, Tricia Hayne, wrote back and said 'Yes!' Bradt was looking to expand its Balkan titles and I was very lucky to be in the right place at the right time.

Gathering accurate information on Macedonia, however, was not easy. In 2003 there was little published in English, and what was on the internet was sparse, outdated and contradictory. More was available in Macedonian, but was hyperbolic and did not meet the needs of an independent traveller. If you asked a Macedonian at the time about travelling independently in Macedonia, they would look at you as if you were crazy for such an idea 'and what could a foreigner possibly write about Macedonia?' they would cry. Undeterred, armed with tip-offs, mostly from the international community there at the time, I set off every weekend to conduct primary research. I remember sending the resulting first edition to the then Macedonian Ambassador to the US, a certain Nikola Dimitrov – he recounted to me in a future meeting his surprise that somebody would write a travel guide for his country. Now, as Minister of Foreign Affairs, he is promoting Macedonia as a tourist destination, a friend in the region, and open for business. Several editions later and with much fact-checking by some very knowledgeable Macedonians, is the guide you have in your hands today. Enjoy!

HOW TO USE THIS GUIDE

AUTHOR'S FAVOURITES Finding genuinely characterful accommodation or that unmissable off-the-beaten-track café can be difficult, so the updater has chosen a few of his favourite places throughout the country to point you in the right direction. These 'author's favourites' are marked with a ✳.

PRICE CODES Throughout this guide we have used price codes to indicate the cost of those places to stay and eat listed in the guide. For a key to these price codes, see page 85 for accommodation and page 87 for restaurants.

MAPS
Keys and symbols Maps include alphabetical keys covering the locations of those places to stay, eat or drink that are featured in the book. Note that regional maps may not show all hotels and restaurants in the area: other establishments may be located in towns shown on the map.

Grids and grid references Several maps use grid lines to allow easy location of sites. Map grid references are listed in square brackets after the name of the place or site of interest in the text, with page number followed by grid number, eg: [103 C3].

WEBSITES Although all third-party websites were working at the time of going to print, some may cease to function during this edition's lifetime. If a website doesn't work, you might want to check back at another time as they often function intermittently. Alternatively, you can let us know of any website issues by emailing e info@bradtguides.com.

Foreword

It has always struck me – in a good way – that Europe, a continent of 750 million people, still has so many little-known yet remarkable places. Mountainous, landlocked Macedonia is one, hidden away in the Balkans yet within easy reach from elsewhere in Europe.

This is a young country, founded in 1991 with the break-up of Yugoslavia, and yet it has a history and cultural depth as rich as anywhere. Ancient towns like Stobi and Heraklea are a legacy of the region's importance as a crossroads on a main route between East and West in the Roman Empire. Ohrid's influence as a centre of learning and of the Orthodox Church left its mark across central and eastern Europe in the Cyrillic alphabet used by Slavonic languages. The impact of the Ottomans, who ruled this region for 500 years, is everywhere in the food, the customs, the music, the language. Macedonia feels strongly like a place where Europe and Asia meet.

The people of Macedonia further reflect the region's turbulent history. Alongside Macedonians, many others – Albanians, Turks, Roma, Bosniaks, Vlachs, Serbs – make up the highly diverse population, and each group contributes its own character to the country. The art and architecture of their religions, Orthodox Christianity and Islam, are ever-present, some of which – notably the fresco of the Lamentation of Christ at Sv Pantelejmon – was extremely influential on the development of painting in Europe.

Macedonia's natural beauty is the perfect setting for all this. The mountains, wild and rugged, are everywhere, the backdrop to every town, and offer superb walking, cycling, horseriding and ski-touring. And being still relatively untrammelled, they are a haven for wildlife, such as bears, wolves, lynx, eagles. The lakes, huge, beautiful and remarkably unspoilt, are the equal of any in Europe.

Macedonian history since independence has not been an easy ride. The political crisis of 2015–17 was a particularly difficult time for many. In some ways this is a country still finding its feet as an independent state. But there is clear determination to push ahead with the reforms needed to strengthen democracy and the rule of law. And it is a country steadily and sensitively developing its own unique and fascinating allure to foreign visitors.

Charles Garrett
British Ambassador to Macedonia 2014–18

Acknowledgements

THAMMY EVANS So many people have helped with this book, especially all the friendly people of Macedonia who have willingly or unwittingly helped me.

For previous editions I would like to thank (any mistakes in the text are purely my own) Mimoza Gligorovska for her contribution to the education section and for chasing endless questions; Gerard and Sonja McGurk for the section on travelling with children, and for hosting me in Skopje; Lucy Abel Smith for the box on Renaissance art; Ray Power for the section on business; Eric Manton for the box on *rakija*; Aubrey Harris for the box on traditional medicines; Samir Ljuma, Goran Miševski, Zoran Bogatinov, Ana Novakova, Silvana Boškovska Georgievska, Beni Arjulai, Sally Broughton, Jennifer Arnold, Luke Hillier, Kim Reczek, Andriana Dragovič, Paško Kuzman; Sašo Dimeski of SAGW for help with the maps; Romeo Drobarov, Bingo, and John Durance for succeeding in getting to Dojran battlefield; Pece and Renata at Villa Dihovo; Stevče, Valentina and Jakim from Kratovo Rock Art Centre.

I am particularly thankful to all those readers who have found the time to write in with corrections – please continue to do so – and to Philip Briggs for taking on updating this edition and bringing a fresh perspective. I'm also dearly grateful to all of the Bradt team for their help and understanding throughout the writing and sale of the book.

Finally I must once again thank my mother for her tireless care of my affairs and family, and my husband, Vic, for conducting last-minute secondary research; it brings back many fond memories, and we look forward to going back to Northern Macedonia in future years.

PHILIP BRIGGS Many thanks to Thammy Evans for the opportunity to update her guidebook and to explore Macedonia so thoroughly. On the ground, I'm grateful for the support of the following: Mihael Dimitrovski, Stevče and Valentina Donevski, Christina Ristovska, Ljubica Musulanova Ristevska, Lence Nedeva, Jordan Trajkov, Borche Manev, Ema Fildishevska, Filip Risteski, Goran Andonov, Oliver Stefanovski, Zoran Tuntev, Viktor Lazarevski, Niko Bojadjiev, Mihael Misevski and the friendly folk at Unity, Urban and Vertical hostels.

Contents

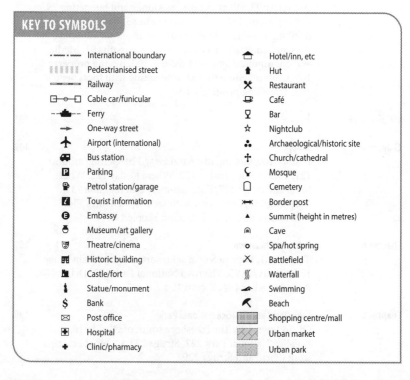

KEY TO SYMBOLS

⸺ ⸱ ⸺	International boundary	🏠	Hotel/inn, etc
▌▌▌▌▌▌	Pedestrianised street	⬧	Hut
⊏═══⊐	Railway	✕	Restaurant
⊟—o—⊟	Cable car/funicular	⬚	Café
--🚢--	Ferry	ⵈ	Bar
⟶	One-way street	☆	Nightclub
✈	Airport (international)	⦙⦙	Archaeological/historic site
⛢	Bus station	†	Church/cathedral
℗	Parking	☾	Mosque
🛢	Petrol station/garage	⬭	Cemetery
ⓘ	Tourist information	⤬	Border post
Ⓔ	Embassy	▲	Summit (height in metres)
👁	Museum/art gallery	◠	Cave
♺	Theatre/cinema	○	Spa/hot spring
⌗	Historic building	✕	Battlefield
⬛	Castle/fort	⦚	Waterfall
⬧	Statue/monument	⬳	Swimming
$	Bank	⬔	Beach
✉	Post office	▨	Shopping centre/mall
⊞	Hospital	▨	Urban market
✚	Clinic/pharmacy	▨	Urban park

LIST OF MAPS

FEEDBACK REQUEST AND UPDATES WEBSITE

At Bradt Travel Guides we're aware that guidebooks start to go out of date on the day they're published – and that you, our readers, are out there in the field doing research of your own. You'll find out before us when a fine new family-run hotel opens or a favourite restaurant changes hands and goes downhill. So why not write and tell us about your experiences? Contact us on ☏ 01753 893444 or e info@bradtguides.com. We will forward emails to the author, who may post updates on the Bradt website at w bradtupdates.com/macedonia. Alternatively, you can add a review of the book to w bradtguides.com or Amazon.

Introduction

There is so much in this small land. It is not a place of extremes, but it is an area filled with intoxicating untold stories. Its outdoors is its jewel – bijou, pristine and almost untouched. Long lost in the battles of neighbouring states, the tangible evidence of previous rulers is only now being unearthed. Most people don't even know where Macedonia is and it was once described to me as the greatest 'non-destination' country. But if you care to scratch the surface, you will find a Macedonia brimming with history, artefacts, rich local culture and beautiful scenery.

This guide, however, is just a starter kit, leaving plenty to be discovered and much to be created. Geographically and historically there is much more to Macedonia if you veer off the tarred and hardened road, and you will only ever be rewarded for taking the bumpy side track. A Macedonian friend is invaluable to help you find your way around and introduce you to your own adventure, especially once you wander off the edges of this book. You will pick up many of these friends along the way who will go out of their way to help as if it is really nothing at all, and many of whom will speak excellent English or German. Talk to the people and you will find them a fount of knowledge on the region, happy to give you their version of events – for what is written here is certainly not the last word on the subject.

Part One

GENERAL INFORMATION

MACEDONIA AT A GLANCE

Country name Republic of North Macedonia (FYROM)
Constitutional name Republika Makedonija (Република Македонија)
Status Independent republic since 1991 through referendum
Languages Macedonian (Cyrillic alphabet), Albanian, Turkish dialects, Roma, Serb dialects
Population 2,084,367 (2017 estimate, Macedonian State Statistical Office): ethnic Macedonian 64.2%, Albanian 25.2%, Turkish 3.9%, Roma 2.7%, Serb 1.8%, other 2.2%
Religion Orthodox Christian, Sunni and dervish Muslim, Roman Catholic, Methodist
Government Parliamentary democracy
Main political parties Governing coalition: SDSM (Social Democratic Party of Macedonia), DUI (Democratic Union of Integration) and the SPM (Socialist Party of Macedonia); in opposition: VMRO-DPMNE (Internal Macedonian Revolutionary Organisation-Democratic Party of Macedonian National Unity), NDR (National Democratic Revival) and DPA (Democratic Party of Albanians)
President Gjorge Ivanov
Prime minister Zoran Zaev
Municipalities 80, of which 10 constitute the City of Skopje
Capital Skopje
Other major towns Bitola, Kumanovo, Ohrid, Prilep, Štip, Strumica, Tetovo
Border countries Albania, Kosovo, Serbia, Bulgaria, Greece
Area 25,713km^2
National parks Mavrovo, Galičica, Pelister
UNESCO protected area Ohrid Lake and town
Total length of roads 10,591km (surfaced: 6,000km)
Total railway 922km
Airports 17 (international airports are Skopje and Ohrid)
Time GMT+1
Currency Denar (MKD)
Exchange rate £1 = 71.5MKD; US$1 = 54.6MKD; €1 = 61.5MKD (March 2019)
GDP Official: US$10.9bn (World Bank, 2016); Purchasing Power Parity (PPP): US$31.55bn (World Bank, 2017)
Average annual income US$5,015 (GNI Atlas Method, World Bank, 2016); GNI per capita PPP US$14,500 (World Bank 2016)
International telephone code +389
Electricity 220 volts AC. Sockets are round two-pin.
Flag A yellow oval at the centre emanating eight yellow segments against a red background
National anthem 'Today above Macedonia' (Денес над Македонија)
National flower Poppy
National animal Lion (*Panthera leo*); Balkan lynx; Ohrid trout
National holidays 1–2 January (New Year), 7 January (Orthodox Christmas), April (usually) (Easter), 1–2 May (Labour 'Day'), 2 August (Ilinden), 8 September (Independence Day, also referred to as Referendum Day), 11 October (National Day, also referred to as Revolution Day)

1

Background Information

And she, Deucalion's daughter,
of Zeus, the thunderer,
bore two sons:
Magnet and Macedon – a cavalryman, a warrior …

Hesiod, Catalogue of Women, 7BC

GEOGRAPHY

Geographically speaking, Macedonia is bounded by the Šar and Osogovska mountains to the north, Lake Ohrid and the Pindus Mountains to the west, the Rhodope Mountains to the east, and by Mount Olympus and the Aegean Sea to the south. This area was divided into four parts after the Berlin Treaty of 1878: Vardar Macedonia in the northwest; Pirin Macedonia encompassing the Pirin Mountains in the northeast (now part of Bulgaria); Aegean Macedonia to the south as part of Greece; and a tiny sliver of land north and south of Debar and part of Lake Ohrid, which now belong to Albania. Although Vardar Macedonia in particular (the land around the upper reaches of the River Vardar) may have changed hands several times since then, the division of the four parts has largely stayed the same.

Vardar Macedonia is divided from Pirin Macedonia in the east by the peak of Mount Ruen and the Vlaina Mountains above the River Struma in Bulgaria, while

GEOGRAPHICAL MACEDONIA

the mountain ranges of Kožuf and Nidže divide the northern Vardar region from the southern plains. This area is completely landlocked and is split almost in half by the River Vardar, which runs south to the Aegean Sea. Only the River Crni Drim, which starts in Lake Ohrid and ends in the Adriatic, and the Strumica, which drains into the Struma in Bulgaria, also lead to a sea port.

As is already evident, there are numerous small **mountain ranges** in Vardar Macedonia, and in fact 80% of the country is considered mountainous. This is due to the fact that three tectonic plates, African, Asian and European, meet in this region. It is mostly the work of the African plate sliding beneath the Eurasian plates under Greece that caused the geographic formation of the Macedonia that we see today, and it is also the reason why there are frequent earthquake tremors in the region and many hot springs.

The friction between the plates has brought about a number of fault-lines that run across Macedonia approximately along the course of riverbeds. The one under Kočani along the River Bregalnica contributed to the 1904 earthquake, and the Skopje fault-line along the Vardar contributed to the 1963 earthquake that destroyed most of the city. Minor tremors, though frequent, are well below the surface. The earliest well-recorded earthquake in the region was in AD518 when Heraklea was destroyed. Scientists claim that these earthquakes are moving eastwards in intensity, which doesn't bode well for Macedonia.

The highest peak in Macedonia and one of the highest in the Balkans, at 2,764m, Mount Korab is on the border with Albania. The highest peak wholly within Macedonia is Titov Vrv at 2,748m in the Šar Planina range, which is surpassed in the former Yugoslav states only by Mount Triglav in Slovenia. The lowest point in Macedonia is where the River Vardar exits into Greece at 45m above sea level.

There are eight well-developed **hot springs** in Vardar Macedonia and dozens more that are undeveloped. The former have all been developed for medicinal purposes,

CASTLE BAGGING

Macedonia has over a thousand ruined castles and forts. As a constant front over the millennia – between the Paeonians and the ancient Macedonians, then the Romans and the ancient Macedonians, then from marauding Gauls, Slavic tribes and crusaders, later between the crumbling Byzantine Empire and the Ottomans, and finally the crumbling Ottoman Empire and the new nation states of the 19th century – the southern border of Macedonia in particular has repeatedly seen strong fortification.

Sadly, Macedonia's position on the cusp of the European and African tectonic plates means that its regular earthquakes have all but destroyed Macedonia's castles. The remains of a few are undergoing archaeological excavation and renovation, such as the Kale (castle) at Skopje, Ohrid, Strumica, Prilep, Tetovo, Štip and Gradište. The Carevi Kuli (towers) at Strumica form part of a very clear fortification line along the border, while Markovi Kuli in Prilep were once the pinnacle of an entire fortified town.

Many castles, such as at Otunje and Stenje near Tetovo, Kozle and Veles along the River Vardar, and at Kičevo, have little to show and can be quite hard to find. Others, such as the once mighty Paeonian castles of Cyclopean masonry at Varoš near Oktisi, Prosek near Demir Kapija, and others at Matka and in Mariovo, are but scars in the ground unless you know what you are looking for.

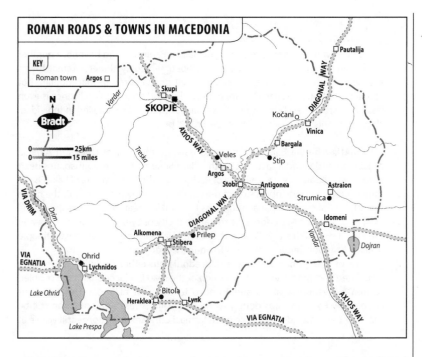

ROMAN ROADS & TOWNS IN MACEDONIA

KEY
Roman town   **Argos** □

although moves are afoot to open them up for recreational use. The medicinal qualities of the water depend on the mineral deposits beneath the spring, which the water has been forced through in order to reach the surface. Yugoslavia put a lot of research into understanding the medicinal properties of these hot springs and Macedonian doctors will frequently prescribe a sojourn at a particular hot spring for its healing qualities in relation to all sorts of malady, from broken bones to pneumonia. The border of Vardar Macedonia shares three tectonic **lakes**, Ohrid, Prespa and Dojran, with its neighbours Albania and Greece. As their names imply, these lakes were formed millennia ago from movements in the tectonic plates. Lake Ohrid in particular is so old and its life forms so unique that it is comparable to Lake Baikal in Russia and Lake Titicaca in Peru/Bolivia, and it is under UNESCO protection. There are also ten manmade lakes, which were formed to create a hydro-electric production capability under Yugoslav Macedonia, and a number of glacial lakes high up in the mountains of the Baba, Jablanica and Šar ranges.

The longest **river** in Macedonia is the Vardar, which starts in the mountains above Gostivar and drains out at Thessaloniki in Greece, and collects 80% of the water run-out of Macedonia. The next-longest rivers are the Bregalnica and Crna, both of which empty into the Vardar.

CLIMATE

Macedonia has a relatively dry Mediterranean climate with the full array of four seasons, although spring can be quite short, and each season is tempered by the altitude. In the Vardar Valley, Ovče Polje and the lower Pelagonia plains, temperatures are roasting hot in the summer and relatively mild in the winter. Skopjites tend to empty out of the capital during the hottest months of July and August, when temperatures can reach 40°C. These summer highs are infrequently

As Rome advanced its empire across the Balkan Peninsula and beyond, a number of key trade and military routes were developed, served by numerous small towns and settlements. Their whereabouts are well documented in Macedonian, but little information is available on them in English and their full significance is even less understood (see box, page 12). Key ancient towns are detailed in individual chapters of this book, but roads are described below.

VIA EGNATIA The Via Egnatia connected Italy via the port of Durres in Albania to Elbasan and Ohrid, mostly along the River Shkumbin on the Albanian side. It entered Macedonia near the village of Radožda on the western side of Lake Ohrid, then went around the north side of the lake to Ohrid town and around the north side of the Galičica and Baba mountains to Heraklea near present-day Bitola. The road exited Vardar Macedonia via the ancient city of Lynk on the River Crna and then went on to Edessa, Pella and Thessaloniki, and eventually to Constantinople (today's Istanbul; Carigrad or 'Tsar's Town' in Macedonian).

Most of the Roman surfaces in Macedonia are either buried or have been resurfaced. The most well-known section of the road in Macedonia is the cobbled section between Magarevo and Turnovo to the west of Bitola. This road was cobbled by French troops during World War I offensives. Some of it can still be seen but the remainder has since been tarmacked. A small section is still visible at

punctuated by summer storms, but they do occur, especially in the mountains. Favourite summer retreats to the cool and welcoming mountains are Mavrovo and Pelister national parks, Popova Šapka, Kriva Palanka, Berovo and Kruševo. Bitola, a mere 380m above Skopje, is usually a good 10–12°C lower in temperature year round than the city itself.

Although the winters are mild in the low areas along the River Vardar, rarely getting below freezing, there are occasionally freak winters, such as in 2001–02, which saw Skopje come to a standstill when snow and ice blocked the roads for weeks. The mountains, however, regularly see 1–2m of snow. This makes for decent skiing, limited only by the standard of facilities or a skier's own abilities to go off-piste. Regions above 2,000m will see pockets of snow as early as August, and the peaks are certainly dusted with a light coat of snow by early November.

September and April may see longer spells of cloud and rain. In general though, the weather is warm and sunny from March through to November and perfect for outdoor sports. October to November is when the mountain trees turn colour before they shed their leaves, and this is the time to take a drive or hike through the ravines of Mavrovo, the Radika, Treška, Babuna and Maleševo. Skopje can get caught in fog during this time, but 20 minutes outside of the capital usually reveals bright sunny weather.

NATURAL HISTORY AND CONSERVATION

Due to Macedonia's location between the Mediterranean and Euro-Siberian regions, the variety of flora and fauna is extensive. During the 1970s and 1980s, research and records were made of all the animals and plants in the Yugoslav Federation. Since then, however, Macedonia has had few resources to spend on maintaining these records and so even approximate figures on how many of each type of animal

the back of Radožda (page 230). The Via Egnatia Foundation aims to reinvigorate the Via Egnatia and some of its work has helped to mark the Via Egnatia trail. The Macedonian section of the Via Egnatia was marked in 2012, and a detailed new guidebook to the 475km section of the route between Durres and Thessaloniki, with maps and GPS logs, was published in 2014 (page 356).

There are claims that sections of the Via Egnatia are visible between Oktisi and Gorna Belica at a stopping point called Vajtos, which some believe is the eighth stopping point on the road. But this location would be a complete dog-leg off the Radožda to Ohrid route and it is more likely that this section of ancient Roman road belonged to the route that followed the River Crni Drim from Enchelon (now Struga) via Debar to the mouth of the Crni Drim in present-day Albania.

VIA AXIOS AND THE DIAGONAL WAY The Diagonal Way linked Heraklea with Stibera (which lies halfway between Bitola and Prilep), Stobi, Bargala near Štip and Pautalija (now Kustendil) in present-day Bulgaria. It was an important road linking the Vardar Valley with the Struma Valley (now in Bulgaria) and crossed other important roads along the way. At Stibera it met the road from the mining town of Demir Hisar which followed the River Crna. At Stobi it crossed the Via Axios (the ancient Greek name for the Vardar River), which ran along the Vardar, and at Bargala it crossed the road from Strumica to the Ovče Polje plains around Sveti Nikole.

there are in Macedonia are few and far between. Macedonia has worked jointly with other countries, such as Greece, to try to establish approximate numbers of wolves for instance, but more research needs to be done in order to confirm these figures.

A number of hotels and travel agencies can arrange wildlife observation trips by jeep if you are interested. Lake Dojran and Golem Grad Island in Prespa Lake are havens of water wildlife, insects and birds, and there are dedicated wetlands at Ezerani (near Resen) and Blato (near Strumica). If you take a guided tour in one of the national parks, such as from the village of Brajčino, your guide will be able to show you the tracks and beds of the local animals. Bats can often be seen in the evening around many of Macedonia's caves, such as at Leskoec, Matka and Treskavec.

If you just want a quick overview of Macedonia's wildlife then the Macedonian Museum of Natural History in Skopje (page 145) houses everything (stuffed) in one convenient location. Although the museum is in desperate need of attention and a good English brochure, it is quite interesting and also houses the skeletons of prehistoric animals that used to roam through Macedonia.

MAMMALS There are several protected mammal species in Macedonia, including brown bears, jackals and Balkan lynx.

A study in 1997 on **brown bears** (*Ursus arctos*) assessed their figures at somewhere between 160 and 200, of which there were around 70 in Mavrovo National Park, 30 in Pelister and only three or four in Galičica. Although brown-bear hunting became illegal in 1996, the bear population does not appear to have increased – the estimated population in 2010 (when the last count was carried out) remained at 160–200.

For the **golden jackal** (*Canis aureus*) there are no available numbers. The **Balkan lynx** (*Lynx lynx martinoi*) is the national animal, depicted on the back of the five denar coin. Despite being illegal, it is still poached for its

If you leave early for a hike in the Macedonian mountains, you will definitely meet a couple of old folk collecting whatever the season offers. Macedonians still use a wide variety of herbs and teas for their medicinal properties and most people will be able to inform you about the characteristics of these plants, where to find them and how to use them.

The pleasure of collecting nettle in early spring, wild strawberries in high summer and chestnuts in autumn creates an intimate relationship with nature, enriching the experience of walking in the mountains. Collecting herbs must be done in agreement with existing regional and national laws for protection and sustainable usage of plant species. Always pick only small parts from each plant to make sure that it is still able to grow.

An excellent book on collecting edible wild plants and mushrooms is Richard Mabey's *Food for Free* (HarperCollins, 2012, available in the pocket-sized Collins Gem series). The overview below (courtesy of the Berovo Hiking Trail map) provides a list of the most common herbs in Macedonia and their uses. The Berovo map is published by the Tourism Information Point. They offer programmes on rural and ecotourism and can arrange activities such as hiking, walking, biking and camping.

Latin name	Common name in English and Macedonian	What and how it is collected	Uses
Thymus spp.	Thyme *Majčina dušica*	Young, green parts of the stem with leaves and flowers	Pneumonia, bronchitis and sore throat, nervousness, insomnia
Rosa canina	Rose hip *Šipka, diva roza*	Mature and hard fruits without stem, clean or sift out the centres which contain sharp hairs	In jams and tea, rich in vitamin C
Primula veris	Primrose *Jaglika aglička*	Flowers in dry, sunny weather; the plant is rare and should only be collected in small batches	Cough, runny nose, cleaning of the blood
Chamomilla vulgare	Chamomile *Kamilica, vrtipop*	Flower and section above ground from spring until end of the summer	Inflammation of the mouth, dry lips, sore throat

gorgeous spotted golden-brown fur, and its habitat is also under continuous threat from illegal logging. In continuing decline, its numbers are believed to be fewer than a hundred across Macedonia and Albania, with even fewer in Serbia and Kosovo. In an effort to reverse this phenomenon, the Balkan Lynx Recovery Programme has been established across the Balkans to monitor and assist with protection. Thirty cameras have been set up in Galičica National Park alone, where the programme is monitored by Dime Melovski of the Macedonian Ecological Society.

Wolves, on the other hand, are not protected as they are considered a pest, preying on sheep and other farm livestock. Hundreds are killed every year, but

Latin name	Common name in English and Macedonian	What and how it is collected	Uses
Origanum vulgare	Wild marjoram Planinski čaj, rigjen	Section of plant above ground and the flower	For the throat, pains in the kidney, and stomach
Urtica dioica Kopriva	Nettle	Leaves and herb are collected in July and August; roots are collected in the autumn and in the spring	Cleaning of the blood, a homeostatic and for kidney disorders
Sambucus nigra	Elder Bozel	Collected when blossoms begin to open in May and June	Given for colds, flu, pneumonia and other respiratory illnesses
Achillea millefolium	Common yarrow Bela rada, ajdučka treva	Above-ground section collected when it blossoms from May to September	Pains from diabetes and in the liver
Juniperus communis	Juniper Cmreka	Fruits are collected when they become dark blue from the end of August to September	Improving appetite, pains in gastro-intestinal tract and respiratory illnesses
Plantago lanceolata	Narrowleaf plantain Tesnolisten tegavec	Leaves are collected from May to October when the plant blossoms	Cold, diarrhoea and ulcers
Viscum album	Mistletoe Bela imela	Leaves and the stem are collected from November to March; plant grows very slowly and large collections are tough on the plant	Regulation of blood pressure, makes blood vessels more elastic, increases metabolism and processes in the digestive tract
Rubus idaeus	Raspberry Malina	Leaves are collected in summer from June/July to September	Nervousness, premenstrual tension, diarrhoea and dysentery
Mentha piperita	Peppermint Nane	Leaves are collected before blossoming in May	Used against gastro-intestinal pains and gases
Erythraea	Centaury/ red gentian Crven kantarion	The upper section is collected before blossoming	Increasing appetite and gastro-intestinal pains
Hypericum	St John's wort Kantarion	Leaves and flowers	In tea and as an oil; an all-round immune booster, antiseptic and antidepressant

their population remains stable at around 700. Since the government decreased the amount paid for a wolf skin (now about 700MKD), it has been assumed that the wolf population will increase.

The national parks and Jasen Forestry Reserve are home to many of the hunted species in Macedonia such as wolf, marten, wild boar, chamois, roebuck and other deer, and their numbers are meant to be regulated through the use of a hunting licence system.

REPTILES AND INSECTS Macedonia has a few poisonous insects and reptiles, including some snakes and a couple of species of **spider**, including a rare fish-eating spider which lives in the wetlands near Strumica. Like most wild creatures, these will go in the opposite direction of a human being if given enough chance to do so. Many types of **lizard** will be seen scurrying from footpaths as you walk through the mountains, and **frogs** are abundant at Lake Prespa. **Mosquitoes** are common in marshy areas in the lowlands, but these areas are few and far between. Watch out also for **tortoises** or **turtles** crossing the roads – these are as much of a hazard and victim here as hedgehogs are in Great Britain.

Among Macedonia's 17 different types of **snake** are the common (and poisonous) adder, field viper and the more poisonous nose-horned viper (known as *poskog* or 'jumping snake' in Macedonian), as well as non-venomous water snakes and other more unusual species. The javelin sand boa, found in sandy areas around Lake Dojran, can reach up to 70cm in length and is one of the smallest of the boa and python family usually found in warmer parts of the world. The largest European snake, which can be found in the lowlands of Macedonia, is the large whip snake (*Coluber caspius*), which reaches up to 3m in length. Although non-venomous, it will bite in captivity or when frightened.

Two 'semi-venomous' snakes also live in Macedonia. The Montpelier snake (*Malpolon monspessulanus*) is found up to 2m in length in rocky limestone areas with dense vegetation. The cat snake (*Telescopus failax*) reaches up to 1m in length and prefers dry rocky lowlands, old walls and ruins. Both snakes are semi-poisonous because their venom produces only localised swelling and numbness and is difficult to eject from the small mouths of these snakes into a human arm or leg. Fingers might be tempting, though.

FISH Macedonia's freshwater fish include carp, bream, catfish, barbell and perch. Dojran bleak, Strumica bleak and Macedonian dace are some that are peculiar to Macedonia, as is the Dojran roach (*Ratilus ratilus dojrovensis*) and Ohrid trout (*Salma trutto letnica*). The latter are now endangered and fishing for them is illegal. Ohrid trout is one of four protected fish species in Macedonia. Another type of Ohrid trout, *S.t. belvica*, is also served in restaurants and is a tasty alternative for a law-abiding tourist.

Eel (*jagula* in Macedonian) is common in Macedonia and a favourite dish of the locals. The eel from Lake Ohrid used to spawn in the Sargasso Sea until dams were built along the River Crni Drim. It is not yet clear how this is affecting their population, but they still seem abundant. Of the many small fish in Lake Ohrid, the *plašica* is the most famous, for its scales are used to make Ohrid pearls, using a painstakingly intricate technique the secret of which is fiercely guarded by the artisans of Ohrid.

BIRDS There are over 330 kinds of bird in Macedonia, and almost a hundred migratory bird species that spend some of the year in the country. Of Macedonia's native birds, 56 are protected, including vultures and eagles. Despite this status and efforts to increase numbers, **vulture** populations have halved over the past 20 years or so. In 2010 there were estimated to be 19 or 20 pairs of griffon vultures, 26–28 pairs of Egyptian vultures, and only one solitary male bearded vulture and one male black vulture. Having not been seen for ten years, a sighting of a black vulture was made again in 2015. Black and bearded vultures are monogamous creatures, so it is extremely unlikely that a solitary sighting will find new mates. Three black vultures have been released by the Vulture Conservation Foundation to neighbouring Bulgaria as of 2018, and so in due course further sightings might be seen in the region.

Although **eagles** used to be abundant in Macedonia, only a dozen or so pairs can be found now around Mount Korab and the Šar mountain range. Storks, both white and black, are also on the decline, but you will still see them nesting in a number of villages and towns. Macedonian folklore claims they bring luck, especially with regard to childbearing.

Pelicans and cormorants are quite common and fishermen use cormorants to catch fish on Lake Prespa. A wetland reserve at Ezerani is home to many of Macedonia's birds. Imported birds include peacocks, to be found at the Monastery of Sveti Naum; swans, introduced to Lake Ohrid in the early 1970s; black turkeys at the Monastery of Zrze; and ostriches farmed near Tetovo and Gostivar.

PLANTS AND BUTTERFLIES There are over 3,500 different plants in Macedonia, which include alpine flowers, such as gentian and furry alpine bluebell, as well as imported stocks of kiwi, pomegranates and rice, usually the preserve of more tropical climates. The great variety of flowers here also attracts an incredible number of different butterflies and moths. Look out particularly for the hummingbird hawk-moth (*Macroglossum stellatarum*), which is not commonly found in northern Europe.

Over 35% of the country is forest, most of which is deciduous. Less than 10% of Macedonia's forests are evergreen, but among that 10% is the Molika pine, which is unique to the greater Macedonia region, Bulgaria and Albania. In Macedonia the Molika pine is mostly found in Pelister National Park.

ENVIRONMENTAL EFFORTS Despite views to the contrary, the communist period of Macedonia's history had gone a long way, both deliberately and inadvertently, towards helping preserve Macedonia's rich wildlife and unspoilt natural environment. All three national parks, Pelister (1948 – one of the first to be established in the Balkans), Galičica (1949) and Mavrovo (1958), were set up during this time, as well as Jasen Forestry Reserve (1958), and 48 natural monuments were designated for protection. Inadvertently also, Macedonia's poor economy, low levels of tourism and lack of urbanisation have helped to preserve many areas of natural beauty.

Industrial pollution has been and is still a problem, as is the Macedonian disregard for litter, especially the non-biodegradable kind. The Macedonians may try to blame the government for a lack of litter bins and anyone to take the litter away (which is true), but Macedonians don't help themselves. As every responsible hiker knows, if you pack it in with you, then pack it out with you, and get rid of your rubbish through the waste-disposal service rather than leave it as an eyesore and health hazard. There are efforts under way by NGOs to move the government towards better waste management, but it may be a few more years before the effects are seen.

Macedonia does have some environmental groups that date back to the communist era of social awareness, and even more are springing up now in the wake of international money earmarked for building civil society and civil participation. Although these groups do good work, and go some way towards educating local communities about environmental concerns in their area, to be effective a nationwide effort really needs to be led by the government.

Macedonia's environment is at a critical point in its development and so now is the time to ensure that it is saved for the likes of you and me to enjoy when we come to visit another day. If you would like to find out more about how you could get involved with environmental protection in Macedonia, contact one of the following groups:

Andriana Dragovic and Nikica Korubin

Macedonia has a rich and varied archaeological resource. Of all the periods to be found in the country (from the Mesolithic to the more recent archaeology of the cold war) it is the Roman sites that are the most monumental and most visible in the landscape. Remarkably little archaeological research has been undertaken, however, and the management, curatorship and presentation of archaeological sites are universally poor. Nevertheless the situation is changing (though maybe not for the better) and a great deal of state funding is pouring into excavation campaigns. Conversely, work in the realms of heritage management and resource quantification is being undertaken largely by the NGO sector, with geophysical surveys at sites such as Skupi, Bargala near Štip and Konjuh near Kumanovo.

Macedonia sits astride the land routes from western Europe into Asia, and indeed the conquest of Macedonia was the key to the spread of Roman influence and later military occupation in the east. The ancient territories of Macedonia and Alexander the Great were of particular significance to the Romans because the emulation and surpassing of the feats of Alexander were a visible testament, both in the wider world and more importantly at home in Rome, to the greatness of Rome, the Senate (and later the emperor) and Roman civilisation.

The Romans were extremely familiar with the Hellenic way of life, thought, architecture and urban living, and claimed much of it as their own. Hellenic colonies were interspersed in the western Mediterranean and much of southern Italy was influenced by Macedonian colonies, the most famous of which being the city of Pompeii. Much of the design of Roman houses aped Greek or Hellenic forms. As a result, the Hellenistic world created by the Macedonian military campaign might have appeared familiar to the Romans, as if Macedonia itself was a part of Rome's backyard. When Augustus conquered the modern-day areas of Serbia and Bulgaria, establishing the province of Moesia, the frontier of the Roman world in the Balkans became the River Danube. Macedonia in the hinterland of this important frontier was thus one of the keys to military and civilian control of both the northern frontier of the Balkans and a gateway to the ancient Mediterranean world.

Ekosfera w www.ekosfera.mk. Regularly seeks volunteers to help with clean-up days & other larger projects.
Vila Zora w vilazora.org.mk. Involved in preserving & presenting natural habitat & trails, educational projects, & in the promotion of sustainable development. Has also been a stalwart advocate of remediating soil around the Veles area that has been contaminated by local industry, & is involved in an initiative to declare the Veles area a GMO-free zone.

HISTORY

The Republic of Macedonia achieved independence from Yugoslavia on 8 September 1991. The word 'Macedonia', however, has been associated with a much larger area than that represented by today's republic. 'Macedonia' has meant many things and had a multitude of changing boundaries across the millennia, but at its core is a geographical area upon which most historians and geographers are united. Geographical Macedonia, covering a large swathe of land from the source of the

The significance of the archaeology in Macedonia is global, not least because the historical region of Macedonia was Alexander's manor and he still occupies a pre-eminent role in the psyche of northwest Europe and the US.

Funding for archaeological research is derived entirely from the Ministry of Culture. In a country with serious economic problems, the realisation of the potential of the archaeological resource to entice the tourist dollar is growing, but as yet lacks the sophistication of approach found in many other European countries. Local archaeological organisations and NGOs are trying to build international co-operation with foreign institutions, with some success. There are a number of examples of collaborative archaeological excavations with foreign (usually American) and Macedonian teams working in tandem.

Looting of archaeological sites is a big problem in Macedonia but identifying the scale is difficult for two reasons. First, looted artefacts are whisked away to foreign markets in Europe, America and the Far East and secondly, the precise provenance of any artefacts can seldom be established because so many of the sites of discovery are unknown to the archaeological community in Macedonia and thus cannot be policed. There is a robust legal framework to protect the archaeological sites of Macedonia, but the actual process of enumerating, identifying and characterising where the undiscovered archaeological sites are is yet to commence with any seriousness and the possibility of state provision for such a process has been called, from within the archaeological community of Macedonia itself, a 'science fiction'. There are, however, many iconic archaeological sites to visit, with excavations under way at Plaošnik in Ohrid; Markovi Kuli, Visoka and Stibera in the Prilep region; Stobi near Veles; Heraklea in Bitola; and Skupi outside Skopje.

Opportunities to excavate at Stobi (Macedonia Secunda) in Macedonia can be arranged through the **Balkan Heritage Field School** (e balkanheritage@ gmail.com; w bhfieldschool.org), which also offers workshops in conservation and documentation of Roman mosaics, murals and pottery. If you come across an archaeological find, by law it must be reported to the **Cultural Heritage Protection Office** (e contact@uzkn.gov.mk; w uzkn.gov.mk). The Law on Protection of Cultural Heritage, Official Gazette 20/04, and changes and updates to this law, can be downloaded from the CHPO website.

River Vardar (Axios in Greek) to its estuary at Solun (Thessaloniki in Greek), has a very rich and varied history, which is reflected in the present-day political climate and division of the geographical region.

Macedonia had its heyday during the build-up of its ancient empire, ending with the sudden death of Aleksandar III of Macedon (also known as Alexander the Great). Macedonia's claim today to this period of history is hotly disputed by the Greeks (page 32). As a recognised state, Macedonia rose for a short while again in the 11th century during the reign of Tsar Samoil (hotly disputed by the Bulgarians, see box, page 20). The region exerted an influence variously through its status as the Archbishopric of Bitola and Ohrid but, as an independent state, Macedonia did not emerge again until the ten-day Kruševo Republic of 1903.

Geographical Macedonia is now made up of four political entities: Vardar Macedonia, which is the Republic of Macedonia; Pirin Macedonia, which is in Bulgaria; Aegean Macedonia, which is in Greece; and a tiny sliver north and south of Debar, which is in Albania.

CHRONOLOGY

Pre-9500BC	Palaeolithic (Old Stone Age) findings yet to be confirmed at Cocev Kamen
9500-6000BC	First traces of human existence in northern Macedonia date back to the Mesolithic (Middle Stone Age) period
6000-4000BC	Neolithic (New Stone Age) period, Gorlevo seal and Golemata Majka found near Skopje
4000-2200BC	Aneolithic (Bronze Age), including the use of Kokino observatory
2200-600BC	Iron Age and rock paintings in Cocev Kamen
600-217BC	Paeonian kingdom
Mid 4th century BC	Paeonia becomes a vassal state of the Macedon royal dynasty
294-168BC	Antigonid dynasty
168BC-AD395	Roman period
AD395-1204	Byzantine period
5th century	Invasion of Goths, Huns and Avars
7th century	Beginning of Slavic immigration
976-1014	Reign of Tsar Samoil
1018-1767	Archbishopric of Ohrid
1096-97	Crusaders cross Macedonia
1371-94	King Marko's Kingdom of Macedonia
1392-1912	Ottoman rule
1877-78	Russo-Turkish war
March 1878	Treaty of San Stefano gives most of Macedonia to 'Big Bulgaria'
July 1878	Treaty of Berlin returns Macedonia to the Ottoman Empire
1893	Formation of the Internal Macedonian Revolutionary Organisation (VMRO) separatist movement
3 September 1901	Kidnapping of American missionary Miss Ellen Stone
3-10 August 1903	The Kruševo Republic
1912	First Balkan War sees Serbia, Greece and Bulgaria defeat Turkey; Macedonia is divided between Serbia and Greece
1913	Second Balkan War – Bulgaria tries to retake Macedonia
1914-18	Macedonia ruled by Bulgaria during World War I in return for supporting Axis
1918-41	Came under the rule of the Kingdom of Serbs, Croats and Slovenes
1920	Ruled for six months by the Yugoslav Communist Party
1941-44	Ruled again by Bulgaria
1944-91	Socialist Republic of Macedonia (within Federal Republic of Yugoslavia)
1991-present	Independent (former Yugoslav) Republic of Macedonia
2001	Six-month internal conflict between the National Liberation Army (ethnic Albanian) and state security forces
13 August 2001	Signature of the Ohrid Framework Agreement ends the conflict
15 December 2005	Macedonia receives EU candidacy status
April 2008	Greece vetoes Macedonia's accession to NATO due to their name dispute

| 5 December 2011 | The International Court of Justice declares that Greece violated its 1995 Interim Accord with Macedonia by vetoing Macedonia's accession to NATO |
| June 2018 | Greece and Macedonia agree to a name change for Macedonia |

STONE AGE PREHISTORY Information on this period of Macedonian history is sketchy. However, there is increasing speculation and some evidence that prehistoric Macedonia (6500–3500BC) may have had a matriarchal society worshipping female lineage and deity until their demise through the arrival of male-dominated Vinca-Turdas Neolithic tribes around 4500BC (established through pottery findings). The discovery of the Golemata Majka (Great Mother, not to be confused with the much later Magna Mater worship of the Romans from around the 2nd century BC) statue of 6500BC in Tumba Madžari in southeast Skopje in 1981 is cited as evidence of this.

The Aneolithic stilt water village, the Bay of Bones (page 220), near Gradište, Ohrid, is another example of human settlement in Macedonia from prehistory.

Paeonia According to Homer's rendition of mythical times in the Iliad, before Macedonia and the Macedonians came Paeonia and the Paeons. This land stretched from the source of the River Vardar to its estuary at Thessaloniki and across the River Struma to the Rhodope Mountains in the east. The legend goes that the Paeons themselves were direct descendants of the river god Axios. They were culturally quite close to their Illyrian, Thracian and Greek neighbours, and even took part in the siege of Troy around 1200BC. Later, other Greek historians such as Herodotus, Livius, Strabo and Thucydides described Paeonia and the Paeons in their writings.

It is now known that the Paeonian tribe existed from at least the late 6th century BC when the tribe started to issue its own coins, some of which are on display in the Museum of Coinage (page 145) in Skopje. The first known capital of the Paeonians was Vilazora (today's Veles), and this was later moved to Stobi. By that time (mid 4th century BC) Philip II (Alexander the Great's father) brought Paeonia under his rule as a vassal state. It was completely subsumed into Macedonia by 217BC. Traces of their walled towns can still be found around Macedonia, where tumbled piles of limestone blocks tell of the Cyclopean masonry techniques used to build their mighty fortresses. Vajtos, Matka, Mariovo and Demir Kapija were four such sites.

There is also mention during this time that in the southwest of the land lay an area called Pelagonia. Named after Pelagon, the son of Axios, this land was located around the River Crni Drim, which runs from Struga at Lake Ohrid through Debar into present-day Albania.

Further descriptions are made of other tribes bordering on, and fighting with, the ancient Macedonians who came to dominate the region. These tribes include the Lyncestis, who used to live in the area around Heraklea (now Bitola); the Brigians, who spread out in pockets all over Macedonia, modern-day central Albania and northwest Greece; the Enhelians centred around southeast Macedonia; the Dassaretians settled around Ohrid (then Lichnidos); the Illyrians who moved into present-day Albania and therefore bordered on western Macedonia; and finally the Dardanians who originated from a similar area to the Illyrians, and who some believe may have been related to the Illyrians. All these tribes are mentioned by Thucydides in his *History of the Peloponnesian War*, a war fought between Athens and Sparta in 431–404BC.

1

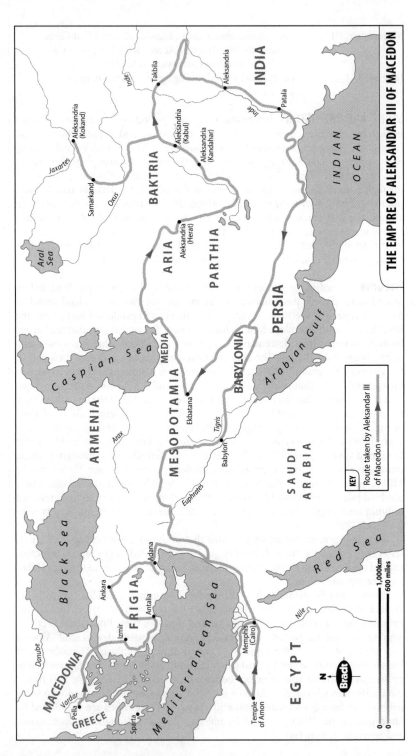

THE EMPIRE OF ALEKSANDAR III OF MACEDON

KEY

Route taken by Aleksandar III of Macedon

INDIA

INDIAN OCEAN

Patala

Aleksandria

Takbila

Inde

Indus

Aleksandria (Kabul)

Aleksandria (Kandahar)

BAKTRIA

Aleksandria (Kokand)

Jaxartes

Samarkand

Oxus

Aral Sea

Aleksandria (Herat)

ARIA

PARTHIA

PERSIA

Arabian Gulf

Caspian Sea

MEDIA

Ekbatana

Tigris

MESOPOTAMIA

BABYLONIA

Babylon

ARMENIA

Arax

Euphrates

SAUDI ARABIA

Red Sea

Black Sea

Adana

Ankara

Antalia

FRIGIA

Izmir

MACEDONIA

Danube

Vardar

Pella

GREECE

Sparta

Mediterranean Sea

Memphis (Cairo)

Nile

EGYPT

Temple of Amon

N

Bradt

1,000km
600 miles

0
0

HOUSE OF MACEDON Legend says that the Macedonians came from Macedon, the grandson of Zeus (the Greek god of thunder) by his first daughter. Hesiod's epic, *Catalogue of Women*, says that Zeus's second daughter bore two sons: Graecian and Latin. Thus the Greeks and the Romans, according to legend, were brothers, and cousins to the Macedonians. Some might say this is the origin of the animosity between the Greeks and the Macedonians. Indeed, at the time, the Greeks had gone to some lengths to keep their 'barbarian' cousins out of the Delphian Amphyctionic Council and from participating in the Olympic Games. Only in the early 5th century BC was the Macedonian royal family finally permitted into the Olympics, having

ALEKSANDAR III OF MACEDON (THE GREAT)

Born in Pella (in modern-day Greece) in 356BC, Aleksandar III of Macedon was the son of King Philip II and his wife Olympias, a Molossian princess from neighbouring Epirus. Although both of the royal houses of Macedon and Molossia were probably begrudgingly accepted as Greek by ancestry by the time Aleksandar was born, it remains much debated in today's Hellenic Republic and the Republic of Macedonia as to whether Aleksandar was half Macedonian and half Epirian/Molossian or truly Greek. In either case, his father Philip II, who learnt to highly appreciate the Greek military and diplomatic education he was given as a hostage in Thebes, passed his love of Greek culture and education on to the young Aleksandar.

Aleksandar became famous for continuing his father's dream of a united and expanded pan-Hellenic empire. Philip was assassinated in 336BC before he could realise his plans. But, at the age of 20, Aleksandar continued to strengthen his father's gains. A fearless fighter and far-sighted tactician, he spoke both Greek and his native Macedonian, and had been taught in his early years by Aristotle. In the name of spreading Hellenic culture and practices, Aleksandar's empire stretched all the way to the River Jhelum in the Punjab. In his reign of 12 years his victories were numerous and are legendary:

336BC	Wiped out all remaining contenders to the Macedonian throne from within Macedon
335BC	Destroyed the town of Thebes in Greece
334BC	Defeated the Persians in Asia Minor
333BC	Defeated Darius III, King of Persia, at Issus
332/1BC	Conquered Egypt and founded the town of Alexandria
331BC	Defeated Darius III again at the Battle of Gaugamela in northern Mesopotamia and made Babylon capital of his empire
327BC	Defeated King Pora, thereby acquiring the Punjab
325BC	Died on 10 June on his return to Babylon

His body was eventually interred in Alexandria in Egypt. However, his tomb has since disappeared without trace. Some believe his body now lies at Idomena near Gevgelija in Macedonia, but it has yet to be discovered.

The 2004 Oliver Stone movie, *Alexander*, and the 1998 Michael Wood BBC documentary, *In the Footsteps of Alexander*, are two succinct, popular sources on the man and his achievements, and Robin Lane Fox's book *Alexander the Great* is an excellent, accessible and gripping account of the man and his exploits.

been ordained 'sufficiently' Greek because of their common ancestry and worship of the same Greek gods. Common Macedonians were not allowed to compete until another century later.

How much the Macedons mixed with the Paeonians after they were made a vassal state by Philip II is not known. Philip II, who ruled 359–336BC, did found the city of Heraklea, near Bitola, and this probably brought with it a certain amount of associated Hellenic city culture.

Compared with other tribes in the Balkans, the Macedonians, allegedly by virtue of being mountain people, were renowned hunters and fighters, who also took a liking to drink and dance. These traits were equally matched by their desire for political power, which allowed the Macedonian dynasty to expand its empire gradually over the course of almost seven centuries. At the pinnacle of its existence during the reign of Aleksandar III of Macedon (known to Hellenites as Alexander the Great), the former Macedonian dynasty had gone forth in the name of spreading Hellenism and encompassed geographical Macedonia, most of the Hellenic city-states under the League of Corinth, the Aegean islands, Egypt, Asia Minor, eastern Iran and western India. In 331BC, Babylon (now in modern-day Iraq) was made the capital of Aleksandar's vast pan-Hellenic empire.

In the course of his ambitious campaigning, Aleksandar had squandered the previously good relations with the Greeks won by his father Philip II. Aleksandar's sudden death from fever left behind a weak and unprepared heir, and without the mighty backing of the Greek city-states the empire soon crumbled as a result of fighting between Aleksandar's generals. Eventually divided into four main territories, Aleksandar's empire was already in the care of the Regent Antipater. Antipater's son, Cassander, ruled after him, but on his death the empire fell into civil strife.

ANTIGONID EMPIRE With the ancient royal house of Macedon long in tatters and the kingdom in civil war, another of Aleksandar III's generals, Antigonus I Monophthalmus, tried to retake Macedon. He had been ruler of Syria and Asia Minor after Aleksandar III, but was not able to recapture Macedon and died fighting for it at the Battle of Ipsus in 301BC. His son, Demetrius, did succeed in taking Macedon a few years later and thereby established the Antigonid Empire over Macedon and many of the Hellenic city-states for the next 125 years.

294–277BC	Demetrius I Poliorcetes
277–239BC	Antigonus II Gonatas
239–229BC	Demetrius II
229–221BC	Antigonus III Doson
221–179BC	Philip V of Macedon
179–168BC	Perseus of Macedon

ROMAN RULE The Antigonid dynasty was no match for the emerging empire of Rome. Three devastating Macedonian–Roman wars ensued over a 50-year period: 215–205BC, 200–197BC and 171–168BC. On 22 June 168BC, Perseus, the last Macedonian king, was finally defeated at the Battle of Pydna. The land of ancient Macedon was incorporated into the Roman prefecture Macedonia, which also included Epirus, Thessaly, Vetus and some of Thrace and Illyria. Pondering how to rule over the unruly Macedonians, the Amphipolis Council of the Roman Empire declared that Macedonia would be divided into four regions (*meriden*) but that each region would be free to elect its own magistrates and laws. It was forbidden, however, for the regions to co-operate at any level.

Unused to, and unhappy with, these limited freedoms, Andriskos, also known as Phillip the False, led a rebellion of Macedonians against the Roman dictators in 149BC. The rebellion was resolutely put down and Macedonia's former freedoms were revoked. The Macedonians themselves were largely left alone, but a garrison of soldiers was permanently stationed there in order to fight off marauding neighbours.

As the Roman Empire grew bigger, so did the importance of various towns in Macedonia that lay on key trading routes. The most famous route was the Via Egnatia, which joined the Illyrian port of Durres (now in Albania) with Pelagonia on the Crni Drim, Heraklea near Bitola and on to Thessaloniki on the Aegean coast. Later the road extended even further to Constantinople. The section of the Via Egnatia between Durres and Thessaloniki has now been waymarked as a long-distance hiking route (see box, page 6). Another important route, the Diagonal Way, linked Heraklea with Stibera near Čepigovo (Prilep), Stobi, Bargala and on to Pautalija (now Kustendil in Bulgaria). There was also the Via Axios linking Skupi near Skopje with Argos south of Veles, Stobi and Dober near Valandovo (see box, page 7). These important trade and military routes developed significant garrison and trading depots which soon morphed into an intricate system of towns and villages throughout Macedonia, the stories of which remain largely untold. See the box on page 12 for more on Roman archaeological sites and page 5 for a map of Roman roads and towns in Macedonia.

The expansion of the Roman Empire under Illyrian-born Diocletian (who killed St George, see box, page 191) reduced the size of the prefecture of Macedonia to make way for the new prefectures of Thessalia and Novus Epirus. Later, Macedonia was divided into Macedonia Prima, covering most of present-day Macedonia, and Macedonia Secunda, which covered Heraklea and Dober and the land to the south of these cities.

BYZANTINE MACEDONIA In AD395, the Roman Empire was divided into west and east, with the Greek-language-dominated eastern empire becoming commonly known as the Byzantine Empire. At this time, Macedonia became part of the Byzantine Empire and was ruled from Constantinople.

After Diocletian's death in AD305, Christianity slowly settled in Macedonia. Early in the 4th century, Skupi became the seat of the bishopric for the province of Dardania. In the year AD325, Stobi also acquired its own bishop at the Council of Nicea. Finally, Heraklea was also appointed a bishop later in the century. The ruins of their early Christian basilicas can be found now in Heraklea, Stobi, Skupi and Ohrid.

After over 800 years of Roman and Byzantine rule, the orderly life of the Roman towns in Macedonia fell victim to the Huns, the Goths and the Avars. Attila the Hun and his men ransacked almost a hundred towns in the year AD447. Stobi and Heraklea survived these attacks fairly well, but a few decades later they fell to the Goths of Theodorik the Great. What the Huns and the Goths hadn't destroyed, the Avars (tribal brothers of the Mongolian hordes) finished off. And then, as if to add fate's final signature, the earthquake of AD518 undermined any attempt by the formerly great Roman towns to re-establish themselves.

SLAVIC MACEDONIA After the Huns, Goths and Avars had left the land in ruins, life in Macedonia fell to subsistence farming around small mountain towns and churches. Into this unguarded territory towards the end of the 6th century roamed the Slavic tribes from beyond the Carpathian Mountains (today's Poland, Ukraine and Moldova). The Draguvite and Brysak tribes of the south Slavs settled in the northern Macedonian and western Bulgarian regions. Over the next three centuries

By the end of the 10th century AD, one family's aspirations for their own state were such that the four sons of the Brysak Duke Nikola started to rebel against the feudal rule of the Bulgarian authorities that were also ruling over Macedonia. Embroiled in its own fight with Byzantium, Bulgaria had little time for the four brothers, Aron, David, Moses and Samoil. But Bulgaria fell to Byzantium in 971 and with it Macedonia came under Byzantine rule. Five years later in 976, the Byzantine emperor John I Tzimisces died, and the four sons succeeded in taking Bulgaria and Macedonia back.

After David was killed by Vlach travellers and Moses was killed in the Battle of Serres, Aron and Samoil quarrelled. Soon Samoil had Aron and his family killed, leaving Samoil as the sole ruler of an expanding empire. He brought most of Bulgaria under his rule and most of Macedonia minus Thessaloniki, as well as large parts of Greece, Albania, Dalmatia, Bosnia and Serbia as far as the Danube.

Samoil was crowned king by Pope Gregory V at Golem Grad on Lake Prespa. For many Macedonian historians this symbolises the official break with the Bulgarian, quasi-Russian, Orthodox Church, and marks the start of a Macedonian branch of the Church headed by the archdiocese of Ohrid. Others see Samoil and his achievements as the first of many attempts at Bulgarian domination. Weighing slightly more in favour of the argument that Samoil was seen by himself and others as Bulgarian is the evidence of the Bitola inscription (found in 1956, see page 247) and the fact that Samoil's arch-enemy, Emperor Basilius II, was known by the nickname Bulgar Slayer, 'Boulgaroktonos'.

Tsar Samoil later moved his capital to Ohrid, where he built the great fortress being rebuilt today. But by 1014, the new Byzantine emperor Basilius II had had enough of this young upstart and sent troops to take back Samoil's empire. At the Battle of Belasica on 29 July 1014, Samoil's troops were resoundingly crushed by the Byzantines. Basilius (also written as Vasilius, Vasilie and Basil) then ordered that the 15,000 troops remaining should be blinded, leaving only one eye per 100 soldiers so that they could make their way back to Samoil (who had escaped during the battle) and he could see their defeat. The battle was at present-day Vodoča near Strumica. Vodoča means 'plucked eye'.

It is believed that when Samoil saw his blinded troops returning to him at Prilep on 6 October, he collapsed from a heart attack and died shortly afterwards. Macedonia then fell under Byzantine control and the people had to pay severe reparations to Constantinople for several decades to come.

they integrated with the local Greek-speaking tribes and eventually adopted Christianity, which had already taken a strong hold on the indigenous population. Some Macedonian historians claim that Macedonia's Slavs came from a unique Slav tribe and had their own language and aspirations for a nation state. There is little evidence, however, to back this.

Shortly after the fall of Tsar Samoil's empire (see box, above), the Normans came riding into Macedonia under Robert Giscard (1016–85) to plunder and loot. The crusaders followed in 1096–97 on their way to pit the strength of Christ against that of Muhammad in the Middle East, levying war taxes as they went. Later on, Giscard's son, Boemund of Tarent (1050–1111), returned in 1107, replaying the plundering and looting of his father.

All the while, the locals tried repeatedly to rise up against their Byzantine rulers. Late Byzantine art flourished in the churches in the area (see box, page 62) and, carried by traversing crusaders, ushered in the 12th-century Renaissance in western Europe. In 1204, the Norman crusaders succeeded in sacking Constantinople and the Byzantine Empire fizzled into a few renegade dukes in Epirus and Nicea. The new states of Bulgaria and Serbia moved in to try to reconquer parts of Macedonia.

FIVE HUNDRED YEARS OF OTTOMAN RULE The fall of Byzantium was eventually replaced by another empire, this time the Ottoman (for more on the Ottoman rulers, their rules and the ruled see box, page 49). Despite King Marko of Prilep's brave attempts to keep back the Turks (see box, page 264), his defeat at their hands in 1394 signalled the completion of Ottoman victory over Macedonia. Skopje had already been taken, in 1392. Debar regained some independence under Gjergj Kastrioti's Albania from 1444 to 1449, but then fell to Ottoman rule along with all Albania.

With the Ottomans came Islam and the building of mosques, covered markets, balconied houses, an increase in trade and eventually clock towers and railways. As when the Romans arrived all those centuries earlier, Macedonians did not take kindly to these new foreign rulers and many fled the country. While the Ottomans encouraged the rule of the Orthodox elite over its millet (see box, page 49) and even

THE FIVE VILAYETS OF THE OTTOMAN EMPIRE IN 1880

KEY TO BOUNDARIES
1880 Vilayet bdy
1880 Historic bdy
1991 International bdy

SERBIA
Novipazar
MONTE-NEGRO
Peč
Priština
Prizreni
BULGARIA
Shkodra
Üsküb (Skopje)
Debar
Durrësi
Elbasan
Manastir (Bitola)
Drama
Serres
Berati
Korça
(Thes)Saloniki
Gjirokastra
Servia
Adriatic Sea
Janina
Aegean Sea
GREECE
Preveza
N
0 ——— 75km
0 ——— 45 miles
Bradt

went to some lengths to help preserve and protect some churches, such as Lešok and Joakim Osogovski, other churches of particular significance, such as Sveti Sofia and Sveti Pantelejmon in Ohrid, were converted into mosques.

In the wake of emigrating Macedonians, the Turks themselves moved into fertile Macedonia in droves to build new villages and towns. This influx built up ethnic tensions and, despite the superficial improvement in trade and town life, Macedonians rose up repeatedly against their new masters. Macedonian bandits did all they could to oust the Turks and many were outlawed and hunted down by Ottoman *janissaries* (the military elite, see the box on the opposite page) and their arnauts (special forces largely recruited from Albanian communities).

The Ottoman rulers adhered to the Sunni school of Islam, and therein to the Hanafi legal code. They also, however, tolerated and legitimised the Sufi side of Islam, which hailed from the more folklorish beliefs of Islam and emphasised the mystic communion of its disciples with Allah. Many Macedonians converted to Islam during the Ottoman period, either as Sunnis or to a Sufi order. The Sufi orders, being less strict and more tolerant of individual expression, were more open to converts from other faiths. This was particularly true of the Bektaši order who were appointed the priests of the janissaries.

Towards the end of the heyday of Ottoman power, the British landscape artist and travel writer Edward Lear, better known today for his nonsense poetry and limericks, travelled through the Balkans in 1848 and 1849. He spent one week painting and writing in Monastir (Bitola) and Akhrida (Ohrid – at that time a part of Albania) in September 1848. His travelogue reveals a Macedonia demographically very different from today's, in which Lear had to appeal for a guard from the local bey to protect him while he drew. (Because the sultan had banned life-drawing – only patterns were allowed – the local peasantry considered his paintings to be the devil's work, and threw stones at him for it.)

The treaties of San Stefano and Berlin By the second half of the 19th century, the Ottomans' iron grip over their empire was beginning to loosen. The Habsburg Empire had won back Serbia and Bosnia, and Greece was also independent again.

KING OF KUMANOVO

In 1689, Austrian emperor Leopold I of the Habsburg Empire sent General Piccolomini towards Macedonia to beat off the Ottoman army which had been encroaching upon Habsburg lands. Karpoš, chief of a band of outlaws based in the mining village of Kratovo, was quick to respond to the general's call for war and decided to rebel against the Ottoman overlords. The outlaws first rose up against the Ottoman stronghold of Kriva Palanka, and this started what came to be known as the Karpoš Uprising. More bandits joined Karpoš and the rebellion next took Kumanovo, then spread east towards Kustendil (now in Bulgaria) and west towards Skopje.

When Leopold heard that Karpoš had taken Kumanovo, the emperor promoted him and named him King of Kumanovo. But Leopold's further assistance to the new king, after Piccolomini had to beat a hasty retreat later that year, came too late. Six weeks after taking Kriva Palanka, Karpoš and 200 of his men were brutally killed and then impaled on the Stone Bridge in Skopje. Leopold's letter of encouragement to the Macedonian people a year later in 1690 fell on deaf ears.

THE DEVŠIRME TAX AND THE JANISSARIES

When the Ottomans expanded into the Balkans, they started to run out of the manpower needed to manage their expanding empire, keep order and conquer new lands. As a result they implemented a tax system in the 1380s that was levied on non-Muslim families within the new territories. This tax, called *devširme*, required between 2.5% and 10% of boys aged 7–14 (not usually the firstborn) to be taken for education and training to run the Ottoman Empire. The boys were encouraged to convert to the Islamic faith and could be enrolled in either a civilian or a military capacity. For many non-Muslim families this tax was understandably extremely unpopular, and certainly did not help to ingratiate the new rulers with their new subjects, no matter what other 'freedoms', donations and perks may have been given in return. But as time went on, non-Muslim families found that the devširme was also a means of advancement within the Ottoman system, and soon selection criteria were attached to the devširme in order to keep down the number of applicants.

On the military side, these boys went into the elite troops of the janissary (literally 'new troops', from the Turkish *yeni čeri*). Their training was harsh; once in the janissary it was forever; and they were forbidden to marry. But these elite troops soon realised their own importance and in 1449 they rebelled, demanding higher pay, pensions and other rights. It took another century before, in 1566, they won the right to marry. By the middle of the 17th century the demand to enter the janissary, particularly from Albanian, Bosnian and Bulgarian families, was so high that the devširme could be abolished.

Although these troops were formed, supposedly as a more loyal section of the army, in order to serve as the sultan's personal household troops and bodyguards, they proved in the end to be no more loyal than the rest of the Ottoman army, which was also made up of conscripted soldiers and tribal warriors. By the 18th century the janissary practically held the sultan hostage against his own imperial affairs and even his daily household. The Bektaši order of dervishes, the appointed priests of the janissary, supported them in their efforts.

The empire was already beginning to shrink due to the ineffectiveness of combat troops and many of the janissary weren't even serving soldiers. By 1826 the janissaries were so out of control that Sultan Mahmoud II finally abolished them, after several years of wresting back power from them and creating a totally new army. Their end, in a bloody revolt of the old 'new troops' against the new 'new army', was a sign of things to come over the next century: the demise of the Ottoman Empire.

The newly freed states in turn wanted their share of Macedonia. This played itself out first of all in the sphere of the Church. In 1870, Russia ordained the independence of the Bulgarian Orthodox Church, with rights of influence over Macedonia. The Greek Orthodox Church took umbrage with this turn of events, and pushed Turkey into taking the issue up with Russia. Among many other issues, this prompted war between the two nations.

The Treaty of San Stefano was the result of Turkey's defeat by Russia in the Russo–Turkish war ending in March 1878. The treaty allowed Romania, Montenegro and Serbia to extend their borders to include much of the land that they now have. Bulgaria, however, was made an autonomous new state, whose new borders extended as far as Niš and Vranje in present-day Serbia, Mount Korab and Ohrid in today's Macedonia, and to the far side of Prespa and Mount Gramos in Greece.

The great European powers of Austro-Hungary, France and Great Britain were dissatisfied with Russia's new extended spheres of influence through Bulgaria, and they convinced Russia to redraw the map. The new treaty, put together in Berlin in June and July 1878, essentially returned Macedonia to the Ottoman Empire, but on the condition, under Article 23, that new statutes of governance be drawn up for all the provinces of European Turkey. Each statute was to be drawn up by a majority of local members and then submitted to the Sublime Porte (as the Ottoman government was known) to be enacted, but only after receiving the opinion (and implied approval) of a European commission on the issue. Such arrangements are not dissimilar to the process that new countries today still need to go through to gain international recognition. Bulgaria was duly annoyed at its loss and saw this as an affront to its long-standing kinship with Macedonia.

The seeds of Macedonian nationalism Some see the Berlin Treaty as the seed for a sovereign Macedonian state. A statute for the *sanjaks* (districts) of European Turkey, however, was never implemented, not least because the Great Powers could not agree on how to use the powers they had accorded themselves. The region languished in ever greater misrule and some started to feel that the only way out was full independence. Macedonian nationalism grew and there were repeated protests and armed clashes by Macedonians throughout the three Macedonian *vilayets* (administrative regions) of Skopje (now lacking Kosovo and Metohia, which had gone to Serbia), Bitola and Thessaloniki. At the same time, Bulgarian forces worked to annex Macedonia to Bulgaria. It was during this time that Pasha Kemal Atatürk attended military school in Bitola (page 237), and the revolutionary mood of the time must have had an influence on him.

The various uprisings against the Ottoman rulers led eventually to the formation of a group of intellectuals under the name of the Internal Macedonian Revolutionary Organisation (VMRO). The founding members, Dame Gruev, Petar Pop Arsov, Anton Dimitrov, Ivan Haži Nikolov, Hristo Tatarčev and Hristo Batanžiev, founded the organisation on 23 October 1893 in Thessaloniki, with the goal of creating an independent Macedonia according to its historical and geographical boundaries. Other Macedonian heroes joined up, such as Pitu Guli and Goce Delčev.

It took another ten years of internal and external dispute for VMRO to engineer the uprising that would hopefully secure Macedonia's independence. It was during this effort that Jane Sandanski engineered the first international hostage crisis of our modern era by kidnapping an American missionary in Macedonia, Miss Ellen Stone, in return for US$63,000 (see box, page 310). Finally, at the Congress of Smilevo (20km northwest of Bitola), the Bitola Revolutionary District set the ball rolling for an uprising in their district. This was later expanded to a general uprising throughout all of Macedonia set for the auspicious date of Sv Elijas Day (literally *Ilija den* or Ilinden in Macedonian), 2 August 1903.

In the end it was the Kruševo Revolutionary District, led by Nikola Karev, that gained the upper hand over the ruling Ottomans, and on 3 August they announced the formation of the Republic of Kruševo. Unfortunately, it was only to last ten days before a detachment of the Ottoman army, outnumbering the 1,200 rebels 16 to one, surrounded Kruševo and brought it to heel. Pitu Guli among many others died in the fighting. Goce Delčev had already been killed three months earlier.

The terror wrought on the local population thereafter was without precedent and much of it was recorded in the photography of the Manaki brothers (see box, page 240).

But this repression only succeeded in indelibly marking in the minds of the Macedonian consciousness that freedom and independence from foreign rule was the only way out.

TWENTIETH-CENTURY MACEDONIA

The first and second Balkan wars By the 20th century, weakened at last by economic fraud, political infighting and a costly war with the Italians in 1911, the Ottoman Empire fell prey to the territorial ambitions of its remaining Balkan neighbours. Serbia, Montenegro, Bulgaria and Greece declared war on Turkey on 18 October 1912, and signed up the help of the Macedonian people by declaring that their anti-Ottoman league was for the liberation of the Macedonians. No such thing was to transpire, but instead the four nations divided Macedonia among themselves as soon as the defeated Ottoman armies finally retreated to Turkey.

Bulgaria, with rekindled memories of a Greater Bulgaria, took the lion's share of Macedonia, to the annoyance of the remaining nations of the anti-Ottoman league. Macedonian expatriate communities appealed to the Great Powers in London, and the Macedonian refugees in St Petersburg, Russia, even sent ahead a map made by Dimitrija Čupovski proposing the ethnic and geographical boundaries of an independent Macedonia in order to bolster their case. The neighbouring Balkan states, however, would have none of it. Serbia was vying for an outlet to the Aegean Sea, and Greece wanted control of Thessaloniki. Thus they decided the following year to challenge Bulgaria militarily for the land.

Unlike the First Balkan War of 1912, which had the strategic goal of ousting the Ottomans in order to divide the land up later, the Second Balkan War of 1913, ending with the Treaty of Bucharest, was all about gaining land back from Bulgaria's spoils in the 1912 Balkan War. Macedonian villages were razed and their inhabitants massacred in an effort to eliminate insurgents. It was during this time that the founder of Save the Children, Eglantyne Jebb, made her journey to Macedonia for the Macedonian Relief Fund to deliver relief from the UK to war-torn Macedonians (see box, page 26). The land exchanged may have passed to a new government, but Macedonia's new masters (Greece and Serbia) continued to suppress any hint of independence by the Macedonian people.

The Great War In 1914 war broke out following the assassination of the Austrian archduke Ferdinand in Sarajevo. The Central Powers of Germany and Austro-Hungary sided with Bulgaria against Serbia and Greece over the division of Macedonia. Macedonia, for the most part, chose the lesser of two evils by siding with only one of its former oppressors (Bulgaria) against Serbia (backed by France) and Greece. In reality, Macedonians were drafted into all three armies to fight against each other. But Germany also enlisted the help of VMRO by financing the formation of a 'Macedonian' army, which fought alongside the Bulgarians on the condition of independence for Macedonia.

But the Central Powers lost the war, and the 1919 Paris Peace Conference set to negotiating the 'Macedonian Question', already an institution and a headache since the Berlin Treaty 40 years earlier. Of the three proposals put forward by Great Britain, France and Italy, it was the French proposal in favour of the Serbs that won out. The British proposal that Macedonia become a protectorate of the newly formed League of Nations, and the Italian proposal for autonomy were rejected as too risky. Thus Macedonia was returned to the 1913 borders of the Treaty of Bucharest. Vardar Macedonia belonged once again initially to the Kingdom of

Abridged text from The Woman Who Saved the Children: A Biography of Eglantyne Jebb, *by Clare Mulley*

Eglantyne Jebb was born in 1876 to a family of social reformers in Shropshire, England. Her brother-in-law Charlie Buxton, a Liberal Member of Parliament, had founded the Balkan Committee in 1902 to campaign against the repressive policies of the Ottoman government in Macedonia. The committee's independent relief arm, the Macedonian Relief Fund (MRF), was set up a year later.

In February 1913, between the two Balkan wars, Eglantyne travelled to Macedonia and Kosovo to deliver aid to the tens of thousands of mostly Muslim refugees displaced as the Balkan League (of Serbia, Bulgaria, Greece and Montenegro) advanced south to oust the Ottoman administration. This Orthodox Christian League resented Muslims for supporting Turkey, and resented Catholics for supporting Austria, a country with its own designs on Macedonia. Thousands of Muslims and Catholic Albanians were massacred by the victorious Serbian army and, in a systematic programme of what would now be called ethnic cleansing, villages and crops were also destroyed.

Eglantyne delivered funding and provided assistance to the MRF agents in Üsküb (Skopje), Prizren and Monastir (Bitola). Over half of the refugees in Monastir were on the verge of starvation. Some 5,000 were being fed by the MRF, through the distribution of 100,000 loaves of bread between January and April 1913, and the provision of a soup kitchen for 200 children daily for a month between February and March. Monastir was at that time a city of 50,000 inhabitants, and would have to absorb 30,000 refugees before the end of the conflict. But funds were never enough, despite the fact that, as the British Consul told her, just two pence a day could keep a man alive.

'Practically all the babies died', Eglantyne wrote in her reports. Among the misery of starvation and disease, her most powerful recollection was that of 30 Turkish boys who had been abandoned at a boarding school when their teachers went to fight. When their food ran out the boys had simply gone to bed to die.

Narrowly escaping her own death from influenza on her return to England, Eglantyne did not venture back to the Balkans. She saw her role very much in policy development rather than in service delivery, and immediately urged the MRF to organise repatriation and resettlement of refugees in addition to relief work. From now on international security, sustainable development and citizenship became a fundamental part of her vision, without which relief, however essential, could only be a palliative measure.

Frustrated by the short-term effect of relief work, and spurred by the further agony wrought on German and Austrian orphans of the Great War, Eglantyne co-founded Save the Children in 1919 with her sister Dorothy. In 1923 she authored the five principles of the Declaration of the Rights of the Child, which was adopted by the League of Nations (the precursor to the UN) a year later.

Serbs and then later to the merged Kingdom of Serbs, Croats and Slovenes (later Royal Yugoslavia). A colonisation of Macedonia by the Serbs began.

The VMRO, however, would not be silenced and continued to fight for freedom. This led in 1934 to the assassination of the Yugoslav king Aleksandar Karagjorgjevic

I by the Macedonian-born Vlada Georgiev. The fighting continued and when in early 1941 Yugoslavia refused to side with the Germans, Germany declared war on Yugoslavia, bringing Vardar Macedonia into the fray.

The communist struggle for Vardar Macedonia Inviting its allies to redivide Macedonia yet again, the Germans, Italians and Bulgarians surrounded and then moved into Vardar Macedonia in April 1941. A secret British military organisation (see box, page 193), established to bring down the Axis forces through sabotage and subversion, was parachuted into Macedonia in order to help fight the fascist forces. Working initially with VMRO, they later switched to the partisan forces of the Communist Party of Macedonia (CPM), set up in October 1941, when it became clear that the communist forces were the more coherent and successful.

Promising national liberty, the CPM managed to recruit many Macedonians to swell their ranks, despite the fact that it was formerly a subgroup of the Communist Party of Yugoslavia under Tito. Most Macedonians feared returning to a rule under anything relating to Royalist Yugoslavia and fought with the CPM, therefore, for the liberation of their nation rather than for any communist ideology. Under the auspices of the CPM, the Macedonians even set up their own government, the Anti-fascist Assembly of the National Liberation of Macedonia (ASNOM), on 2 August 1944, exactly 41 years after the Ilinden uprising of 1903. The government was headed by the pro-independence politician Metodija Andonov, more commonly known as Čento.

One month later, in September, the Bulgarians withdrew from Vardar Macedonia, suffering heavy losses to partisan forces. The Germans followed in their wake, beating a hasty retreat towards Greece, and ordering the deaths of hundreds of Macedonians after the failed attempt to bring a puppet government into Macedonia through the right-wing faction of VMRO. As it turned out, fewer than 300 Macedonians were actually killed under the German captain Egbert's orders, as many German soldiers let the Macedonians escape.

With the end of World War II the CPM, with a decidedly pro-Yugoslav leadership, reneged on its promises of independence for Macedonia. The new borders around Vardar Macedonia enclosed the new People's Republic of Macedonia (later the Socialist Republic of Macedonia – SRM) firmly within communist Yugoslavia. Čento and his supporters were removed from office and replaced by the pro-Yugoslav Lazar Koliševski, who remained in power until the fall of Yugoslavia 55 years later.

As the capital of the SRM, Skopje, formerly a political backwater, was firmly orientated towards Serbia for leadership, and its pro-Serb partisan leaders were not well versed in government. Meanwhile, Bitola, traditionally the powerhouse of the region, languished in the shadows. Cut off from its usual orientation towards the southern regions of geographical Macedonia, Bitola's previous political and intellectual capacity was lost on the partisan government of the SRM. Any hint of dissension by Macedonia's pro-independence intellectuals was firmly put down.

Under Tito's communist Yugoslavia (1945–80), although the SRM was nominally given the status of a federal republic, thereby giving it the right to decentralised government of its own people, this was not the case in reality. Limited autonomy was a move by Tito to divide up Serbian ambitions to take over Yugoslavia as a whole. Interdependence was brought to the federation, however, by dividing up its economic capabilities among the republics. The SRM became a popular tourist destination as part of the Yugoslavia package. Mining and tobacco production were encouraged, and Tito even started a tobacco museum in Prilep in 1973 to celebrate 100 years of the tobacco industry there (page 265).

For the first time in the region's history, ethnic Macedonian arts and literature were encouraged, for which a distinct Macedonian language was recognised and strengthened. The man most known for this was Blaže Koneski (1921–93, confusingly also known under the names Blagoje Konjevic when studying in Belgrade, and Blagoy Konev when studying in Bulgaria), who became the head of the Macedonian Academy of Arts and Sciences (MANU). Some have criticised him for deliberately 'Serbifying' the Macedonian language in order to further differentiate it from Bulgarian influences. Others herald him as one of the greatest Macedonian poets and writers in living history.

Despite efforts to revitalise the SRM's economy, Macedonia remained the poorhouse of Yugoslavia. This was not helped by the isolation of the SRM by three of its neighbours: Albania became deeply introverted, Bulgaria shunned the pro-Serb authorities, and civil war raged in northern Greece until 1949. At the end of the civil war, the border with Greece was closed as Greek authorities tried to stamp out any further spread of communism or secessionist claims by Aegean Macedonians for an independent Aegean Macedonia.

Life in communist Macedonia followed a similar path to that of many other communist countries, although to much lesser extremes. The 1950s saw experimentation with collective production farms and state ownership of land and property. Many officials used these measures to line their own pockets, and although collective production had to be abandoned and a limited private business model was reintroduced in 1965, corruption in state-owned industries remained endemic.

Yugoslavia's break from Soviet tutelage allowed Macedonia to benefit from Yugoslavia's greater freedom of movement and other civil liberties. Nevertheless, one-party rule remained and any talk of an independent Macedonia or a reunification with the other parts of Macedonia was not entertained.

From Tito's death in 1980 and the decline of the Yugoslav economy throughout the rest of the decade, the Yugoslav republics and their many nationalities started to vie for greater degrees of autonomy and power in the federation or even out of it. As Serbia's president, Slobodan Milošević, became more belligerent at the end of the 1980s, the end of Yugoslavia became increasingly inevitable. Despite Lazar Koliševski's attempts to keep the federation together, the decision to move to a multi-party democracy in 1990 essentially spelt the end of one-party communist ideals in Macedonia.

In January 1991, Kiro Gligorov was appointed president of the SRM by the new multi-party parliament of Macedonia, and on 8 September 1991 the people of Macedonia voted in a referendum for the independence of the Republic of Macedonia and bloodlessly left the Federation of Yugoslavia. The Yugoslav army, taken elsewhere in dying Yugoslavia to fight Croatians and Bosnians, left Macedonia in April the next year.

Turnout for the referendum was 74%, of which 95% voted for independence. The Albanian community claims that most of the remaining 26% of the non-voting citizenry was ethnic Albanians who did not want to live under the alternatives being offered, ie: as a minority within an independent Macedonia, or as a minority within Yugoslavia. It was later to turn out significant that this hefty percentage of Macedonia's citizens felt disenfranchised from the political developments of the country.

THE FORMER YUGOSLAV REPUBLIC OF MACEDONIA
Troubled beginnings With the additional difficulties of a disenfranchised Albanian community, the infant years of the Republic of Macedonia were fraught with the usual transitional problems of high corruption and overcentralisation in what was essentially a 'nanny state'. In Macedonia's case this was compounded by its

formerly strong dependence on Belgrade. In the first multi-party elections of 1991, voters were faced with a bewildering plethora of parties and candidates, who were divided along political as well as ethnic lines.

The election produced neither a clear winner, nor a clear opposition, so a governing coalition of three parties was formed: the Social Democratic Party of Macedonia (SDSM) and the Liberal Democratic Party (LDP), both from the old communist leaders, along with the leading Albanian party, the Party for Democratic Prosperity (PDP). The nationalist centre-right Internal Macedonian Revolutionary Organisation-Democratic Party of Macedonian National Unity (VMRO-DPMNE) took up parliamentary seats in opposition along with several other parties. As head of the leading party in the coalition, Branko Crvenkovski, at the young age of 27, became prime minister.

Two and a half years of political infighting ensued until October 1994 when new elections were held. But the bickering continued over the cast of the votes and it was not long before the main party in opposition, VMRO-DPMNE, and others withdrew from the election altogether. As a result, the existing governing parties, presenting themselves for one vote together, won three-quarters of the vote. Forming a government in coalition with the Albanian majority vote, the new government took 112 of the 120 seats in parliament, leaving any form of opposition essentially untenable.

The Albanian community had long been unhappy with their representation in the new Macedonia, for which many had not voted in the first place. In November 1993, Macedonia's police force, strongly linked to the SDSM, arrested 12 people in Tetovo, allegedly for attempting to form an Albanian paramilitary force. The police claimed to find hideouts, weapons caches and other incriminating evidence. Nine of the 12 were jailed for conspiracy and other related charges.

This did not deter the Albanian community, however, who continued to demand greater representation and started to set up their own university in Tetovo in 1995. Considering this a breach of the constitution, in which Macedonian was the only officially recognised language of the new republic, the authorities declared the university illegal and tried to close it down. In the ensuing public demonstrations, three Albanians were killed and ten policemen injured. Shortly thereafter an assassination attempt on President Kiro Gligorov was carried out. He lost one eye in the incident and his driver was killed outright. The unknown assassin has still not been apprehended, even after the government offered US$530,000 in 1999 for information leading to his arrest.

Despite the Liberal Party leaving the governing coalition in early 1996 in order to join the non-parliamentary opposition of VMRO-DPMNE, and the attempt by the opposition to call for new parliamentary elections, the governing coalition continued to hold on to power. But international observers were at last allowed to monitor the local elections held that year, which resulted in an even greater division between the ruling coalition in parliament and the opposition, who had won most of the main local elections. Tensions increased and in 1997 the mayors of Tetovo and Gostivar were jailed for raising the double-headed eagle flag of Albania over government buildings in their respective towns.

During the course of 1998, the National Liberation Army (NLA), a newly formed rebel group fighting for the liberation of Albanians, made its first public announcement by claiming responsibility for the bombings of several police stations and judicial courts in the lead-up to the internationally observed parliamentary elections of autumn 1998. Their tactics did not succeed in bringing greater autonomy to the Albanian community, but the ineffectiveness of the

FORMER YUGOSLAV REPUBLIC OF MACEDONIA This has been the international name for Macedonia as recognised by the UN and all major international organisations since the 1995 interim agreement on the name between Macedonia and Greece. A documentary film on the name dispute between the two countries, titled *A Name is a Name* (w anameisaname.net), highlights, and for many continues, the controversy. Part documentary, part film, it views the issue through the eyes of a visitor to Macedonia travelling through this young nation. The evocative music is provided by some of the best musicians from Macedonia.

FORMER YUGOSLAV SOCIALIST REPUBLIC OF MACEDONIA The Socialist Republic of Macedonia (SRM) was one of the republics making up the Socialist Federal Republic of Yugoslavia (SFRY). Formed from the remains of the pre-war Kingdom of Yugoslavia in 1943, Yugoslavia was proclaimed the Democratic Federal Yugoslavia. In 1946, it became the Federal People's Republic of Yugoslavia and in 1963 the Socialist Federal Republic of Yugoslavia, of which the SRM was a part. SFRY disintegrated in the Yugoslav wars of the 1990s and in reference to the period from 1991 until the recognition of all the former Federal Yugoslav republics as independent the area is collectively referred to as the Former Republic of Yugoslavia or FRY. The many abbreviations are confusing.

REPUBLIC OF NORTHERN MACEDONIA? With the return of SDSM to power in 2017, the careful renegotiation of the name of Macedonia was revived by the Minister of Foreign Affairs, Nikola Dimitrov, who was the previous negotiator to settle the name when SDSM was last in power in 2002–08. In June 2018, the prime ministers of Greece and Macedonia agreed to the official name of Republic of Northern Macedonia. The name change was adopted by Parliament, against the wishes of the opposition, and the name was subject to a non-binding referendum on 30 September 2018 and thereafter to a constitutional vote requiring two-thirds majority. The settlement of the name now opens the doors for Macedonian entry into the EU and NATO, with the country signing accession papers for the latter in February 2019.

ruling coalition to alleviate tensions between ethnic communities and to curb the economic difficulties of the transition to a post-communist system brought the electorate to vote in a new government. The winners, VMRO-DPMNE and the DPA (Democratic Party of Albanians), were both right-wing nationalist parties. Ljubčo Georgievski, aged 32 and leader of VMRO-DPMNE, became prime minister.

The new government was not given an easy start. A crisis was raging in neighbouring Kosovo. In spring 1999, some 360,000 Kosovar Albanians fled into northwestern Macedonia before the NATO bombing of Serbia later that year brought an end to Milošević's offensive in Kosovo. Although most refugees eventually returned to Kosovo or went on to other countries, the Macedonian authorities still feared a rise in the number of Albanians claiming citizenship in Macedonia and forcibly bussed tens of thousands of refugees into neighbouring Albania in April of that year. This fear was aggravated by several factors: first, the Albanian community claim that they comprised up to 40% of the population in Macedonia (as opposed to 19% in the 1994 census); secondly, the unclear status of ethnic Albanians who had failed to change their Yugoslav passport to a Macedonian one in the allotted time frame of the early 1990s, but who were still claiming citizenship; thirdly, widespread electoral fraud in northwestern Macedonia in the local elections of 2000.

Throughout 2000, attacks on the police continued until, on 26 February 2001, the Macedonian authorities retaliated against suspected armed rebels in the village of Tanuševci, north of Skopje on the border with Kosovo, for an attack by the NLA on the police station there. Armed conflict between the authorities and the NLA raged for the next six months, both sides taking casualties and alleging war crimes for the deaths of civilians and the desecration of churches and mosques.

A peace deal and amnesty After President Trajkovski (elected after Gligorov stepped down in 1999) requested help from NATO on 20 June 2001, the international community brokered a ceasefire and a peace agreement. The Ohrid Framework Agreement (OFA) was signed on 13 August 2001 by a new unity government, comprising VMRO-DPMNE, the SDSM, DPA and PDP. It gave the Albanian community much greater representation in state institutions as well as recognition of their language and culture (see box, page 33).

At the end of August, Operation Essential Harvest was launched by NATO troops upon invitation by the government to collect arms from rebel forces. Almost 3,500 weapons were collected in the month-long operation, which was half the number that the government had claimed were out there, but twice what the rebels had claimed they had. Another 7,571 were handed in to authorities in another weapons amnesty in 2003.

In addition to the Ohrid Framework Agreement, the government agreed an amnesty for all former rebel fighters except for those who had committed war crimes. The Albanians read this, as was clear in their negotiations with NATO, to mean an amnesty on all crimes except those cases taken up by the International Criminal Tribunal of Yugoslavia (ICTY) in The Hague. The Macedonian authorities interpreted the amnesty clause to mean that they could prosecute those cases not taken up by ICTY. Of the 100+ alleged cases, most were thrown out of court for lack of evidence.

Only five war crimes allegations were considered serious enough to be taken up by ICTY. These included the massacre at Ljuboten, north of Skopje, where at least six men of Albanian ethnicity were found shot in suspicious circumstances; and the mass grave found in Ne프rošteno containing four Macedonian bodies. After UN Security Council Resolution 1534(5) requested the ICTY consider only the most senior and most responsible leaders in all Yugoslav wars for further indictments, only one indictment was made from the 2001 conflict. This was against the former Minister of Interior, Ljube Boškovski, for his involvement in the massacre at Ljuboten. His command responsibility over the crime could not be established by the ICTY, however, and so he was acquitted in 2008. The remaining four allegations were returned to national jurisdiction in late 2007, despite vocal disagreement by the Albanian community. In the 2011 parliamentary elections, VMRO-DPMNE was returned to government only through coalition with the Democratic Union of Integration, the political party who emerged from the NLA. In return VMRO-DPMNE agreed to give amnesty to the remaining four alleged war crimes.

In comparison, over 40 indictments for war crimes committed in Bosnia during the early 1990s were prosecuted at the ICTY. These include that of the massacre at Srebrenica, where almost 8,000 Bosnian men and boys are alleged to be buried. Many hundreds of bodies have been found, but up to 20,000 remain missing from the war. Twenty-two people went missing in the Macedonian conflict, of which six are ethnic Albanians and one a Bulgarian national. The case against the eight ethnic Albanians accused of the crime was annulled in 2011, though families of the missing 22 are calling on parliament to reopen the case. Eight bodies have been found to date.

Accession years Parliamentary elections were held in September 2002. The electorate, disillusioned by the nationalist rhetoric of the VMRO-DPMNE coalition with the DPA and by the ineffectiveness of the unity government to move forward the Ohrid Framework Agreement, brought back the SDSM government of Branko Crvenkovski. Together with a new party, the Democratic Union for Integration (DUI), led by the former rebel leader Ali Ahmeti representing the majority of votes from the Albanian community, the new government made significant inroads in achieving the Ohrid agenda.

The country's situation did improve, although economic growth didn't catch up with pre-conflict figures, and many would say that standards of living have still not achieved these standards today. In August 2004, the country succeeded in passing a controversial law to reduce the then 123 municipalities to a more manageable 84. Since local elections in March 2005, successive governments have struggled with decentralising and balancing power between the mayors, councils, central government, and the legal coherence required for effective checks and balances.

Macedonia received EU candidacy status on 15 December 2005, but progress was blocked by Greece in 2008 as a result of the continued name dispute and intransigences of the VMRO-DPMNE-led government, who came to power in 2006 (page 35). The name dispute also led to Macedonia's accession path to NATO being blocked by Greece at the April 2008 Bucharest NATO summit, as a result of which Macedonia fell behind the other Adriatic Partnership countries (Albania and Croatia) who joined NATO in 2009. The agreement for the name change of the country has put the accession agendas for EU and NATO back on the table.

The transition from one-party rule to multi-party democracy has brought its usual share of troubles to Macedonia, compounded by inter-ethnic problems and a lack of support from neighbouring countries. Some of the hurdles to progress faced by Macedonia are a lack of a fully participating civil society, the lack of independence of state institutions and with that the lack of public faith in those institutions, the problems of transition from state to private ownership and an antiquated education system. Finally, the lack of an independent civil service able to keep the country running effectively while parties argue out their differences deprives the country of the continuity needed to keep policy agendas on track.

Under the VMRO-DPMNE-led government, Skopje 2014, the enormous – and enormously controversial, not to mention extremely expensive – makeover of the Macedonian capital, has indeed spruced up the city (see box, page 137). Some dispute the value for money of the endeavour considering the state of Macedonia's budget and also the location of Skopje on a tectonic fault-line.

NOT TO BE CONFUSED WITH GREECE Greece and Macedonia have had strained relations since time immemorial. Most Hellenic city-states viewed Macedonians as drunken barbarians from the north. (The word 'Greek', incidentally, was not used until the Romans used this name of a single Hellenic tribe and the closest geographically to Rome to refer to all of the Greek-speaking tribes on the Balkan Peninsula.) Philip II brought Paeonia (the upper Vardar region), Pelagonia (the Prilep area) and Lyncestis (the Bitola area) into his expanding empire and united

In the relative calm and cool of the breezes off Lake Ohrid the international community brought the government and rebel leaders together to thrash out their differences around a table and a piece of paper. The result brought greater rights for the Albanian community and hopes of guaranteed peace for all Macedonians. Although adoption of all the legal provisions envisaged in the agreement was completed with the Law on Flags and Symbols in July 2005, there is still a long way to go on full implementation of these laws in the spirit of the agreement.

CONSTITUTIONAL CHANGES The preamble of the new constitution of November 2002 deleted references to Macedonia as the 'national state of the Macedonian people' whereby Albanians and other minorities were singled out as only having rights as equal citizens, without being acknowledged as actual Macedonian people. The new constitution refers to all Macedonia's population as 'citizens of the Republic of Macedonia', equal before the law.

DEVOLUTION OF AUTHORITY In line with the wishes of the Albanian community for more say over their own affairs and also in line with European Union requirements for increased local self-government, limited powers of authority are being decentralised to the local administrative level throughout the country.

BADINTER MECHANISM Laws directly affecting culture, language, education and issues of local self-government are required to go through the Badinter mechanism in parliament. Named after Robert Badinter, born in 1928 and an experienced leading legal expert on minority rights, the mechanism requires a double majority to pass these laws: an outright majority, as well as a majority of those claiming to belong to the communities not of the majority population of the country.

EQUITABLE REPRESENTATION Equitable representation is now sought throughout all state institutions, and especially in the judiciary and the police. With a lack of sufficiently qualified minority citizens due to previous educational biases, it is proving difficult to increase minority participation in state institutions. It has been even more difficult with the need to downsize bloated institutions, effectively resulting in jobs for Albanians and job losses for ethnic Macedonians. Nevertheless, advances in ethnically mixed policing, for instance, are returning citizens' confidence to institutions of law enforcement.

THE RIGHT TO MINORITY EDUCATION AND LANGUAGE USE Non-majority ethnicities of at least 20% of the population have the right to use their language in state institutions alongside Macedonian (but not in foreign affairs). Although the Albanians are not singled out in the Ohrid Framework Agreement document, this provision has essentially brought the right for the use of Albanian in parliament among other institutions, in bilingual identity papers and other official documents, and has eventually legitimised the long-disputed Albanian University of Tetovo.

Background Information   HISTORY

1

33

the constantly warring Greek city-states in the League of Corinth in 338BC to fight the Persians. Upon Philip's assassination, Aleksandar III of Macedon (see box, page 17) completed his father's dream in the name of a new pan-Hellenic era, and the Greeks have since claimed him as Alexander the Great. While most Greek historians would not dispute Aleksandar's lineage from the royal house of Macedon, they see Aleksandar's Macedon firmly as part of Greek heritage and not as part of the geographical entity that is now the Republic of Macedonia.

Maps from Roman, Byzantine, Ottoman and Yugoslavian times have included the geographical area of the Republic of Macedonia firmly under the label 'Macedonia'. Greek nationalist history, however, does not include the geographical area of the Republic of Macedonia in its view of Macedonia.

History aside, what is most in dispute is the use of the word 'Macedonia' in naming the country. When Yugoslavia named Vardar Macedonia the 'Socialist Republic of Macedonia' after World War II, the Hellenic Republic protested and asked Tito to rename the republic 'Vardar Macedonia' or 'Skopje Macedonia'. This was not accepted and Greece had enough to do fighting its own civil war and keeping out communism to worry too much about the name of its neighbour. But, internally, Greece continued its policy, followed since the end of World War I, of moving ethnic Greeks and Greek-speakers into Aegean Macedonia and moving Macedonians out while suppressing the use of their language and traditions. In this way Greece could at least control from its side any irredentist tendencies that Aegean Macedonia might have towards the SRM.

However, when the Republic of Macedonia claimed itself as the independent 'nation state of the Macedonian people' writ large in its new constitution of 1991, this was too much for the Greeks. Some Macedonian politicians started to call for reunification with Aegean Macedonia, and Athens feared an uprising in Aegean Macedonia and a desire by the two sides to rekindle long-lost dreams of the ancient royal dynasty of the Macedons. Newly independent Macedonia did not help matters by adopting the star of Vergina, formerly the flag of the ancient Macedonian kingdom, as its flag and stamping the star on its coins. Greece slammed a unilateral economic boycott on the fledgling state.

Fearing more troubles in the Balkans the international community worked hard for a solution. The interim title 'Former Yugoslav Republic of Macedonia', or 'FYROM' for short, has been agreed for international official use while diplomats worked harder for something less contentious. Especially since the final demise of the Federal Republic of Yugoslavia in 2003, the name 'FYROM' was as unsuitable as giving the Hellenic Republic the name of 'Former Ottoman Protectorate of Greece', or 'FOPOG' for short.

In a spirit of compromise in 1995, the flag was changed to its present amended form and the coins were reissued without the star of Vergina. The boycott was lifted and relations between the two states have slowly started to improve. An interim accord was brokered that allowed Macedonia to use its constitutional name in bilateral relations with other countries, but use Former Yugoslav Republic of Macedonia in international organisations until another name was agreed on by both countries. In addition, the interim accord agreed that Greece would not block Macedonia's entry to any international organisation on account of the name dispute. As of 2003 and for the first time since World War II, Greece began to issue visas to Macedonians who had previously lived or had family on the Greek side of the border. The dispute over the name gave way to Greece becoming one of the top three investors in the country, despite the fact that some Greeks still refer to the state as simply Skopje. Although the late VMRO-DPMNE government in

Macedonia had dropped its original irredentist claims towards Aegean Macedonia, VMRO-DPMNE did not help matters by naming the country's international airport Alexander the Great (confusing the matter even further with Greece's Macedonia Airport at Thessaloniki), and announcing that Macedonia would seek compensation for Macedonians who were forced out of Greece and thus lost land after World War II and the Greek civil war. The government's lavish spree on historical statues, particularly in the centre of Skopje (see box, page 137), further aggravated animosity between the two countries.

International patience with the dispute grew thin, especially since the EU revealed late in 2004 that Greece had been underreporting its economic figures in order to get into the eurozone in 2000, and by 2011 was subject to a €109bn EU bailout of its national debt, which stood at 180% of its GDP. Greece's blockade of Macedonia into NATO and into the EU in 2008 broke the 1995 interim accord between both countries. As a result Macedonia took Greece to the International Court of Justice in The Hague, which in 2011 ruled in Macedonia's favour.

Both countries were at a disadvantage as a result of the dispute. So when the change of government in Macedonia in 2017 meant that there was a renewed opportunity to revise the Macedonian constitution to accommodate a name change, Greece moved quickly to make the most of a compromise solution. The June 2018 agreement between both countries for Republic of North Macedonia has put NATO and EU accession for Macedonia back on track. Agreements have also been made on how to share ancient heritage such as Aleksandar of Macedon/the Great as part of a shared past. At the time of writing, both the Greek and Macedonian parliaments had voted to ratify the name change, opening up prospects for more cooperation between the two countries as well as accession to EU and NATO for Macedonia.

GOVERNMENT AND POLITICS

The governing system in Macedonia is a parliamentary democracy. As a remnant from communist times, government institutions are not particularly transparent, and engender little public faith. Macedonia's fledgling civil society has a long way to go to achieve full participation in local and national governance, aggravated by low levels of dialogue between government and civil society.

In addition, political parties, electoral practices and the parliamentary system are in a fairly regular state of flux. Wide-reaching changes to the electoral system have been successful in ensuring fairer and more transparent elections. The last few years of VMRO-DPMNE power were quite turbulent, with investigations in wire-tapping of government officials, street protests (Macedonia's own Colourful Revolution), and significant antics in the parliamentary chamber. Parliamentary elections held in 2016 brought the SDSM back into power in a coalition with the DUI, but only after considerable blockage by the VMRO-DPMNE-aligned President of Macedonia.

HEAD OF STATE The current head of state, President Gjorge Ivanov, was elected for a second term in April 2014, having succeeded Branko Crvenkovski in 2009 (Crvenkovski having been elected after the previous president, Boris Trajkovski, died tragically in a plane crash in February 2004). As Macedonia is a parliamentary democracy, the president holds little real power and the post is largely ceremonial. In Macedonia's volatile ethnic environment, however, the president can, and does, play an important role in inter-ethnic and interparty relations. The next presidential election is due in 2019.

LEGISLATURE Parliament is a unicameral Assembly (*sobranje* in Macedonian), which consists of 123 seats. Parliamentary elections are held every four years based on six-district party-list proportional representation. There is no election threshold. Registered parties or coalitions put forward closed candidate lists in one round of votes. The six districts resulted from the Ohrid Framework Agreement in an attempt to more fairly represent minority communities. Professionalisation of the electoral boards (previously run by mixed party appointees) has also helped to eliminate intimidation and collusion in fraud. Since 2011 three additional parliament seats have been allocated to diaspora representation in each of Australasia, Eurafrica and the Americas.

EXECUTIVE The head of government is currently Prime Minister Zoran Zaev, elected in May 2017. The Prime Minister is elected by majority vote by the Assembly, as is his cabinet, the Council of Ministers. Of the 21 cabinet posts, six are held by Albanians: education and science, environment and physical planning, culture and local self-government, and two without portfolio (in charge of diaspora and foreign investments, respectively); additionally, one minister is ethnic Turk and one is ethnic Roma (in charge of strategy for improvement of the situation of Roma in Macedonia). PM Zaev is aided via five Deputy Prime Minister posts of which two are held by ethnic Albanians (DPM in charge of implementing the framework agreement and the political system and DPM in charge of European integration).

JUDICIARY Macedonia's judicial system features a Supreme Court and a Constitutional Court, four Appellate Courts, and 25 Basic Courts of general jurisdiction. The Constitutional and Supreme Court judges are appointed by the Assembly, the former serving nine-year terms with no possibility of reappointment. The president of those courts is elected by his or her peers on the respective benches.

Appellate and Basic court judges, as well as those in administrative and specialised courts, are selected by a judicial council, a feature intended to depoliticise the courts and increase their independence. The judicial council and similar council for public prosecutors manages vetting of candidates, appointments, and dismissals of judges and prosecutors, among other duties.

In 2013, the law on criminal procedure was amended to remove the responsibility for criminal investigation from investigative judges (a normal feature in the civil law system) to having the public prosecutor as leading criminal investigations (more akin to the common law/adversarial system). A new 'judicial reform strategy' was put in place for the 2017–22 period as the court system, together with the justice ministry, works to bring its courts into line with European standards and practices.

ECONOMY

Macedonia's economy was traditionally the poorhouse of Yugoslavia, and deteriorated even further in the early 1990s through the sanctions imposed on Serbia, a unilateral economic boycott levied against Macedonia by Greece, inimical relations with Bulgaria and minuscule trade relations with even poorer Albania, and then the conflict of 2001. However, Macedonia's economy has improved since then as the country focuses more on services, and less on industry and agriculture, but it continues to experience the brain drain so familiar when the country's young and educated, needed to revitalise the economy, leave for more lucrative jobs abroad.

Macedonia exports a number of raw materials such as iron and zinc, and for the building industry it also has abundant granite, gypsum, lignite, siliceous and quartz sands, as well as marble for which there is a large quarry and factory near Prilep. Tobacco has been one of Macedonia's main exports, and during the summer harvests you can see it drying almost everywhere, but especially in Prilep where Macedonia's main tobacco factory is located.

Grapes, too, are on the rise as Macedonia's wines and liqueurs become more popular. The wine industry is poised to take off, and so now is a good time to get in if you want to try Macedonian wines while they are still inexpensive and unadulterated. For more information on Macedonia's wines, including wine tours, see the box on page 282.

PEOPLE

Macedonia is arguably the most ethnically diverse country in the Balkans, if not in the whole of Europe, and a quick look at Macedonia's history will show you why. Aside from various settlers in the Neolithic, Bronze and Iron ages, Macedonia has been invaded, starting with the Romans, by over a dozen tribes, races and empires. And those are the ones that didn't stay. Then there are those who made a home in Macedonia. Interestingly, when French was the language of diplomacy in Macedonia, the French adopted the word *macedoine* to mean anything mixed up, such as a mixed salad or a mixed-fruit dessert.

The country's diverse heritage has largely to do with the fact that Macedonia lies on two important trading routes across Europe. The Via Egnatia linked the sea port of Durres in Albania with Constantinople in Byzantium and brought Romans, Albanians, Gauls, crusaders, Byzantines, Turks, Bulgarians, Roma and Greek tribes. The Diagonal Way linked northern Europe with Greece and brought Vlachs, numerous Slav tribes, Goths, Huns, Avars, more Serbs and more Greeks.

The disputed question of Macedonian identity is one that numerous academics have written about, and there are many books on the subject. If you want a lively discussion in Macedonia, then enquire of a person's origins, and you'll find that your interlocutor will furnish you with a complicated family tree as long as your arm, and each person's background will be different.

If Macedonians and their overlapping neighbours cannot agree on who Macedonians are then I could not possibly hope to write an accurate account of such a topic. Nevertheless, from a lay perspective, which is often at least simple, I shall give an overview of some of the aspects which have contributed to Macedonian identity, and some of the arguments which are out there at the beginning of the 21st century, some 7,000 years after humankind is believed to have first settled in Macedonia.

Neolithic settlers came into Macedonia from 5000 to 2500BC and are believed to have spoken a Proto-Indo-European language. According to Herodotus, the Dorian tribe moved up into southwest Macedonia sometime before the Trojan War, around 1200BC. There they became known as Makedoni, which is derived from the ancient Greek word *makedonos* meaning 'tall', probably at the time referring to highlanders. Some in Macedonia think the word Makedonci might be derived from *majka* in reference to the matriarchal society of the Neolithic settlers (page 15).

The royal house of Macedon, which ruled in the millennium before Christ, has legendary origins from the Greek god of thunder, Zeus. In reality, they are likely to have been a tribe who migrated up from beyond the Greek islands. In the 7th century BC the Makedoni started to mix with the non-Greek-speaking tribes of Paeonia and Pelagonia. Descriptions of these people from the classics of Thucydides, Herodotus and Tacitus show that the Paeons were mostly mountain people, strong and quick, who also influenced the language spoken by the Macedonians. As

Professor Nicholas Hammond, the leading authority on ancient Macedonia, says, ancient Macedonian 'contained words of early Greek origin but was not intelligible to contemporary Greeks. The Macedonians in general did not consider themselves Greeks, nor were they considered Greeks by their neighbours.' The royal house on the other hand 'being of foreign extraction and divine descent' (Hammond) were confirmed as Greek in the 5th century BC when they were allowed to compete in the Olympics.

When the Romans invaded in the 2nd century BC, they most certainly left their seed in Macedonia. The invaders from the north, however – Goths, Huns and Avars – seem to have left nothing behind, not even a village or a crop, but razed everything in their way.

The next most influential invasion was by the Slavic tribes from beyond the Carpathian Mountains. There are many of these tribes, tall and hardy, but those thought to have settled in northern Macedonia were the Mijaks in the Debar and Galičnik region west of the Vardar, and the Brysaks to the east of the Vardar. They came as pagans and were gradually Christianised by the indigenous folk of Macedonia. They were allegedly also quite different Slavs from the Slavic tribes of Serbia and those of Bulgaria, although they all spoke a commonly rooted language.

The creation in AD862 by the monks Cyril and Methodius of a script for the Slavic language (Glagolitic, which was later superseded by Cyrillic) helped them to convert many Slavs to Christianity, and helped to formalise the language of numerous Slav tribes. Bulgarian and Macedonian tribes spoke a very similar language due to the influence of the Bulgarian Empire over Macedonia.

Slav origins remain the base of the Macedonians today, despite Ottoman rule over Macedonia from 1392 to 1912. Although many Slavs converted to Islam they continued to speak Macedonian (now known as the Torbeši – see page 41). It wasn't until the Serb annexation of northern Macedonia to the Kingdom of Serbs, Croats and Slovenes at the end of the second Balkan War of 1913 that the Serb people and language started to gain a serious foothold in northern Macedonia. This was continued during communist Yugoslavia with the Serbification of the Macedonian language under Blaže Koneski, and the prominent influx of pro-Serb Yugoslav partisans into positions of power in the government.

A growing number of Macedonians prefer to see themselves and their country as a heterogeneous mix of the rich tapestry that makes up this crossroads in the Balkans. As a result some prefer not to be called 'Slav' Macedonian as they are no longer purely Slav. Foreigners have always travelled through the land, some bringing products and prosperity, others bringing domination and destruction. New Macedonia wants peace, prosperity and freedom from persecution in a civic-based society rather than to get hung up on ethnic terminology.

MACEDONIAN MINORITIES NEXT DOOR The Hellenisation of Aegean Macedonia, the Serbification of Vardar Macedonia and the Bulgarisation of Pirin Macedonia are topics of continued dispute. Macedonians are not officially recognised as an ethnicity in either Bulgaria or Greece. Both countries recognise Macedonians as Bulgarians. This goes back to the historical quest for influence over, and division of, Macedonia between these two countries and, later, Serbia.

In Bulgaria, some Macedonians had tried to be recognised as an ethnicity and to gain greater autonomy for their culture and self-government. The Bulgarian court judgment banning the formation in Bulgaria of a Macedonian association under the name OMO Ilinden (w omoilindenpirin.org/about.asp) states that 'there is no Macedonian minority in Bulgaria. There are no historical, religious, linguistic or ethnical grounds for such an assertion.' This judgment banning the formation of OMO Ilinden has been deemed contrary to the right of association under the European Convention of Human Rights, and Bulgaria was ordered (again) in 2006 to repeal the judgment. The EU is applying plenty of pressure on Bulgaria to have the party recognised but, at the time of writing, OMO Ilinden is still waiting to be allowed to register – despite having been accepted as a member of the European Free Alliance since 2007.

In Greece, slavophone Macedonians who were exiled and lost property in the civil war just after the end of World War II are also trying to seek recognition from the Republic of Greece, including a return of their property. The plight of slavophone Macedonians in Greece is well described in Anastasia Karakasidou's 1997 book *Fields of Wheat, Hills of Blood* (page 354). In 1994, slavophone Macedonians in Greece formed the political party Rainbow (w florina.org) to campaign for recognition of their culture and language as a minority ethnicity in Greece. The official Greek position is still that there is no Bulgarian or Macedonian minority in Greece. In 1999, the Greek office of Helsinki Monitor estimated that there are some 10,000–30,000 slavophone Macedonians in Greece. If you travel in Aegean Macedonia (northern Greece) you can still find people in their 70s and older who speak Macedonian.

In 2004, the Union of Serbia and Montenegro agreed with Macedonia to recognise each other's ethnicities as a minority in their respective countries. This was generally not a bone of contention. However, there are pockets of Macedonian-speaking Muslims in southern Kosovo and adjoining areas of Albania who are known as Gorani. In Kosovo, the Gorani have claimed that they were persecuted by the Kosovo Liberation Army after the Yugoslav army retreated under NATO bombing in 1999, and that they have since been marginalised further by the redrawing of municipal boundaries in Kosovo.

Macedonians have been recognised as an ethnicity in Albania since World War II, but figures are disputed and range from 5,000 to 350,000. The disagreement over figures, recognition and rights to land is largely a mutual recognition issue as well as a fear of the break-up of sovereignty and territorial integrity. These issues are typical of the Balkans and, while they are progressing towards stability, they are some way from being settled.

MINORITIES IN MACEDONIA TODAY Ethnic minorities in Macedonia are numerous. Their numbers have varied over the years and in Yugoslavia they often claimed different nationalities in order to avoid persecution. So the number of Turks, Albanians or any other ethnic or religious group fell or rose according to who was most in or out of favour with the authorities in the year of the census. Sadly this phenomenon has continued in the years since the independence of Macedonia. Current numbers are particularly vague since the 2011 census was cancelled due to allegations of irregularities.

Albanians Albanians have bordered on the northwest of Macedonia for millennia. Whether they are descendants of Illyrian tribes is disputed, but they have a unique language which, although it has adopted many words over the centuries from Greek, Latin, Turkish and Italian, remains for the most part grammatically distinct and one of the oldest branches of the Indo-European linguistic tree.

Albanians started to make serious inroads into northwest Macedonia and Kosovo, however, only in the 17th century when Ottoman persecution of the native Slav population emptied these areas of their inhabitants. After the fall of the empire of Gjergj Skenderbeg (see box, page 192), the Albanians were largely loyal to the Ottoman beys (chieftains, lords). Most converted to Islam and were rewarded with new lands bordering Albania. Many also learnt the Ottoman elite language and were schooled in Anatolia, later becoming beys in their own right.

However, when the Turkish nationalism of the Young Turks emerged at the beginning of the 20th century, Albanians in Macedonia, fearing repression from the encroaching Serbs, rallied for their own cause. In 1912, at the end of the first Balkan War, Albania became an independent state and with it went a small slice of Macedonia that lay south and north of Debar.

Much of Macedonia's 'Albanian question' is linked with the rise of nationalism in neighbouring Kosovo in the face of Serbian persecution, rather than with any significant desire to join Albania. Communist Macedonia did not help this perception and Albanians were almost as badly persecuted in Macedonia as they were in Kosovo. Fortunately, Serbian/Yugoslav persecution of ethnic Albanians in Macedonia does not go back the centuries that it does in Kosovo, and so there is hope yet that a civic-based state (incorporating EU-preferred rules of subsidiarity or local self-government) might work out for the Albanians in Macedonia.

Unfortunately, however, new Macedonia has inherited the discriminatory leftovers of the Socialist Republic of Macedonia (SRM), which have been compounded by the sudden curb on movement instigated by the erection of borders between the formerly borderless communist republics. So whereas ethnic Albanians used to be able to go to university in Priština in Kosovo to receive teaching in Albanian, suddenly they had no access to teaching in their own language. The

OTTOMAN TURKISH VERSUS TURKISH

It is important to note that the ruling elite of the Ottoman Empire were not necessarily all 'Turkish', in the modern sense. They were made up first and foremost of Muslims, descendants of the Turkic clan which founded the Ottoman dynasty; and secondly of those who spoke Ottoman Turkish. As a result, Albanians such as Skenderbeg (see box, page 192), and the Christian boys taken by the dervish orders of Islam under the devširme tax (see box, page 23) would become a part of the Ottoman elite who ruled the empire on learning Ottoman Turkish and converting to Islam.

Turks on the other hand were considered by the elite to be the uneducated masses of peasant Anatolia. It is from these masses that Atatürk rose up against the Ottoman sultans and pashas to bring about modern Turkey. The masses spoke a different Turkish from that of the Ottomans of the Osmanli elite, which acted as a class barrier in everyday life.

Ottoman Turkish, however, was a language of convoluted court phrases, with words and grammar borrowed from Persian and Arabic for which the Arabic script was used. Arabic words stress the order of consonants as their distinguishing framework, with short vowels only indicated by a series of optional diacritical markings. This does not suit other languages very well, such as the Turkish of the masses, Macedonian or Albanian. As a result, towns such as Debar could be transliterated back out of Arabic script as any variety of spellings such as Diber, Dibrah or Debar, so long as d, b and r were in the same order. The Arabic script seen today above many mosque doorways and windows is therefore the script of Ottoman Turkish, and not related to the modern Latin-script-based Turkish.

number of schools where children could receive instruction in Albanian was also heavily reduced. Less than 5% of the police force was Albanian in a country where Albanians claimed they made up more than a third of the population, yet over 80% of prison inmates were from the Albanian community. Moreover, the 1991 constitution stressed the nationality of the Macedonians, with Albanians as equals, rather than that the new Macedonia was a home for a mix of ethnicities as it had been for many centuries.

Furthermore, disenfranchised from the emerging political process in the new pluralist republic, ethnic Albanians refused to take part in the referendum on independence. They also refused the census of 1991 that would have established their numbers, fearing that the manipulation of the figures by the government would be used against them. Instead the Albanian community carried out their own census of their population in 1992, and it is starting from this time that other Muslim groups in Macedonia, such as the Turks and the Torbeši (see below), have alleged that the Albanian community has pressured them to count themselves among the Albanian community in order to swell the numbers for their census.

The Ohrid Framework Agreement of August 2001 (see box, page 33) established significant civic rights for the Albanian community, and the ensuing census of 2002, which numbered the Albanian community at 25%, settled previous disagreements about population numbers. The tangible lure of EU membership in the years to come is a further stabilising factor.

Turks After the demise of the Ottoman Empire and the withdrawal of the Ottoman elite, many Turks fled back to Turkey in the wake of widespread retaliation by the Serbs who replaced the Ottoman leaders. This policy of encouraging what can only be described as 'cleansing' was continued under communist Yugoslavia in the 1950s and 1960s, through handshake deals with Turkey whereby anywhere between 80,000 and 150,000 'Turks' left Yugoslavia via Macedonia and Bulgaria for Turkey. Many were not in fact Turks at all, nor did they speak Turkish, but were Albanians or Macedonian Muslims (Torbeši – see below) who took advantage of the offer to escape further persecution in Yugoslavia. At the last census of 2002 (the 2011 census was postponed), less than 4% of Macedonians declared themselves to be of Turkish descent. This 4% are spread throughout the municipalities of Čair, Vrapčište, Gostivar, Plasnica, Radoviš and Centar Župa.

The true ethnic Turks of Macedonia are the Yoruks (see box, page 42). Yoruk villages are found in the Radoviš area, Vrapčište and Gostivar.

Torbeši Some of the 'Turks' mentioned above, such as the majority of the population of Plasnica, are in fact ethnically Macedonian Muslims. They cast themselves as Turks in the census because they do not speak Albanian, are not Orthodox Macedonian, but by religion are closer to the Turkish community.

These Muslim Macedonians are sometimes called Torbeši, although this is often seen as a derogatory term, and applies to Muslim Macedonians in Macedonia as well as those in Albania. The Albanians sometimes refer to Muslim Macedonians as Pomaks even though Macedonians might argue that this is a term reserved for Muslim Bulgarians who come from the Rhodope mountain region. Albanians have historically seen the Bulgarians and Macedonians as one and the same.

Roma The Roma, along with their Sinti cousins, total almost 14 million throughout Europe. They migrated from northwestern India between the 11th and 14th centuries as travelling labourers and, although most have settled, many still live transient lives.

Sadly, the 20th century brought considerable misfortune to the Roma, and the wars throughout the former Yugoslavia in the 1990s caused the most significant Roma population movements since the end of World War II. Poorly portrayed in the Western mass media, the Roma have arguably been the most severely affected in the long term by the harsh consequences of war. This is in large part because of their lack of representation in modern-day governing institutions and interest groups: no politician, soldier, businessperson or cleric has come forward to defend them locally.

The Roma's origins in northwestern India are very obvious from their facial features and elaborate traditional dress. They are mostly dark skinned, speak their

YORUKS – AN ETHNIC TURKISH COMMUNITY IN MACEDONIA

Abridged, with permission, from Yoruks *by Elizabeta Koneska, Museum of Macedonia, 2004*

In the eastern part of Macedonia lives the Turkish Yoruk ethnic population, concentrated mostly in the mountainous areas of the Dojran-Valandovo and Radoviš-Štip region. In the historic sources the Yoruks are referred to as nomadic tribes of Turkmen origin who had emigrated from the steppes of central Asia to Anatolia, and from there settled in the eastern part of the Balkans from the 14th to the 16th century.

The migration of the Yoruks was probably the most successful colonising strategy of the Ottoman authorities in the Balkans compared with their attempts at colonising other central Asian tribes. The reasons for their settling in the Balkans were of a socio-economic and military-strategic character. Some researchers suggest that the favourable climate and rich grazing pastures of Macedonia were the crucial motive for the Yoruk migration. In favour of this, some researchers argue that they settled in the areas of rich pastures abandoned by Vlach farmers.

The Yoruk population was tribally well organised and as such fitted easily into the Ottoman army, which led to organising special units for different military, semi-military and other duties (dragging cannons, transporting materials, working in mines, maintaining and securing fortresses, etc). The Yoruks had a privileged status and in order to be motivated for their duties they were exempted from certain state taxes. They were thus treated as 'children of the conquerors'.

In order to get some benefits, substantial parts of the Islamised population joined the Yoruks. The census records from the early 16th century registered the phenomenon of some Islamised Christians joining the Yoruks in the Prilep region, Ovčepole and Tikveš, after the Yoruks crossed from the left to the right bank of the River Vardar. One of the mitigating circumstances for adopting Islam through the Yoruks was the fact that they were organised in *tarikats* – dervish orders that were religiously more tolerant. In this regard, bear in mind that the religious rituals of both populations included numerous pre-Christian and pre-Islamic pagan shaman elements, which brought them closer together.

The Yoruk community transformed from a nomadic to a stationary way of life in the 15th and 16th centuries. As a result, the state passed laws ordering those who hadn't changed their abode for more than ten years to be deprived of the right of Yoruk status, which meant they had to fulfil their duties of paying taxes to the state.

As an individual Turkish ethnic group in Macedonia the Yoruks are distinguished by their language, customs and folkloric particularities and, considering contemporary times, their rather closed social community. The Yoruks of the

own language originating from Sanskrit, and have distinctive customs and traditions. The main ethnic division of Roma can be further subdivided into Arli, Kovaci/ Burgudji, Djambazi, Baruci, Juzari, Pristevaci, Gilanli and Topanli. All subdivisions speak a dialect of the Roma language (for more on the Romani language, see the box on page 152). In addition to sub-ethnic divisions, in Macedonia Romani identity is largely split into those of Muslim faith (Xoraxane Roma) or Christian faith (Dasikane Roma). Faith as a means of identity has changed over time and, as ever, is fickle.

According to the last national census of 2002 (based on official citizenship), the number of Roma in Macedonia was 53,879, or 2.66% of the total population. Field

Radoviš-Štip region who live in the foothills of the Plačkovica Mountain, however, differ with their own particularities, not only from the other Turkish populations, but also from Turks living in the lowland villages in the same region. That's why the villages of Alikoč, Kodjalija, Kaluzlija, Supurge and Prnalija from the Radoviš district are particularly interesting.

The contradiction between the traditional and the contemporary way of life is reflected in the contrast between male and female Yoruks. The women wear their colourful and archaic traditional gowns, and their means of communication is limited, mostly due to the language barrier (the female population, almost without exception, speaks only Turkish). The men, meanwhile, have already adopted modern behaviour, dress and mobile phones.

The unfavourable conditions and living standards in the Yoruk villages in the past decades gave rise to emigration, mainly to Turkey and to some western European countries. The Yoruks from Macedonia were not involved in the great migrations of the Turkish population typical for the period after the fall of the Ottoman Empire. The first massive emigration of the Yoruks from these villages occurred in the 1950s, together with the emigration of a considerable part of the Turkish population from Macedonia. The second wave of emigration took place at the beginning of the 1990s, following the dissolution of Yugoslavia, and was motivated by economic conditions as well as actual political events. Since the end of the 1990s emigration has slowed.

The present language of the Yoruks is a conserved, archaic, specific Turkish dialect that has endured thanks to the considerable isolation of this population and the minimal external influences. The folkloric particularities of the Yoruks are most impressively reflected through the colourful traditional gowns worn by the female population of all ages. The Yoruk women make all the parts of the gowns, through weaving to sewing and embroidering. From the period of adolescence to marriage, girls are constantly preparing their dowry. For everyday use women and girls usually wear colourful dresses of ready-made fabric.

According to the old tradition, on Bajram or for weddings the Yoruks organise wrestling (*pehlivan*) contests, stone-throwing (*tašitmak*) contests and horse or donkey races. The wedding customs are certainly the most impressive. Marriages between blood relatives are avoided, but it often happens that two brothers marry two sisters (a kind of 'exchange' of a sister and a brother for another brother and a sister, which saves money).

Elizabeta Koneska is Macedonia's leading ethnologist on the Yoruk community and works at the Museum of Macedonia.

research indicates, however, that actual numbers are much closer to 150,000. In the biggest built-up settlement of Roma in the world, some 13,300 people have their home in Šuto Orizari, north of Skopje (page 147). They mix very little with the remainder of the Macedonian community and inter-ethnic marriages are extremely rare. Part of the reason that they have not mixed with their host communities has traditionally been because of their transient lifestyles.

In Macedonia in recent decades, however, many Roma have settled permanently all over the country. Now, it is discrimination and a significant difference in lifestyle and outlook that keep the Roma from acceptance by, and even wanting to integrate fully into, their place of settlement. Traditionally, the Roma have been skilled labourers in carpentry, copper and blacksmithing, leather upholstery, basket-weaving, repairs and more. They are also renowned as skilled musicians and dancers. Their tendency towards a life on the move has not led them to put much emphasis on formal education, and so as the 20th century moved away from a product-based economy towards a service- and technology-based economy, the Roma and their skills were somewhat left behind. The move towards a throwaway society has not helped either, and so the Roma are largely left to manual labour and menial jobs; many have taken to begging.

In Skopje, especially in the municipality of Šuto Orizari, there is quite a significant class difference among the Roma. Some have gone abroad, earned good money visible by their small, well-kept houses, and have qualified in recognised trade skills. Within Macedonia, from a mere handful in tertiary education in the early 1990s there are now some 200 Roma studying at university level. Most of them are pursuing careers in human and social sciences and are actively taking part in various academic training modules. It is hoped that these students will be the driving forces behind reorganising and modernising their communities.

THE MIJAKS OF WESTERN MACEDONIA   *Mimoza Gligorovska*

The Mijaks have lived in western Macedonia for at least five centuries. The Mijak region, Mijachija or the Reka region, is named after the Radika River and its tributary the Mala River. Broadly speaking the area is bound by the Šar Planina to the north; the Korab, Dešat and Krčin mountains to the west; Bistra and Stogovo to the east; and the Debar Valley to the south. Within this area, the Mijaks are pocketed into four smaller regions. The Gorna (Upper) Reka region, from the village Brodec to the village Volkovija, is mostly abandoned today but, in the past, was inhabited by Albanian-speaking Macedonians, called Shkreti. The Dolna (Lower) Reka, from the village Žirovnica to the village Skudrinje, and the Golema (Big) Reka, from the confluence of Mala Reka into the Radika to the confluence of the Radika into Lake Debar, are barely much more populated. Only the Mala (Small) Reka from the village of Galičnik to the village of Gari is seeing a small revival of seasonal tourism.

Over the course of time, the Mijaks have become a mix of Orthodox and Islamic religions. Their Islamisation started in the 16th century but was not widespread, rather individual, and lasted for a long period of time. Some authors note cases where half of the family was Orthodox and the other half Muslim. The conversion to Islam divided the Mijaks into Mijaks (Orthodox Macedonians) and Torbeši (Muslim Macedonians).

Their main occupation was and still is cattle breeding, and some records from before World War II note that they also used to herd more than 2.5 million sheep and 150,000 horses. They are known as the best woodcarvers and icon painters in Macedonia. Petar Filipovski-Garka, his brother Marko Filipovski and Makarije

At the other end of the spectrum, there are those who live in slums, such as on the outskirts of Bitola or Prilep, or the 1,700-plus remaining refugees from the conflict in Kosovo who mostly beg or wash windscreens at the traffic lights in Skopje. You will also see many of the Roma hawking clothes, hats and alarm clocks on the Stone Bridge, or plying the street with their boxes of cigarettes, tissues and chewing gum. Often you can also see a matriarchal figure order children to beg from potential clients as they come along the street. Although these children are forced to beg, they can still appear happy, laughing and playing as children do even if they have been on their feet all day. Occasionally, if they receive no alms they will get angry, not exactly a good sales technique, but understandable when they are likely to receive a clip around the ear from mum or dad for not returning with cash. Then they will return to playing a game of tag or jumping in the water fountain. It is questionable how much of the money they receive from begging ends up in their pockets or is taxed from a cartel that 'runs' the area.

The spiral of poverty in which the Roma have found themselves has led to international efforts to try to stop discrimination against them and to bring them back up above the breadline. The OSCE's Office for Democratic Institutions and Human Rights, based in Warsaw, does significant work in this regard throughout Europe, and a number of non-governmental international Roma networks have started up as the Roma try to lift themselves out of poverty. Macedonia signed up to the Roma Decade of Inclusion 2005–15, in which the government pledged to tackle improvements for Roma in basic services, health, education, housing and employment. Improvements are not easy: the Roma themselves are not keen to adopt the trappings of conventional Western lifestyles, while developing (and especially former socialist) economies struggle to harness the potential of entrepreneurship for self-employment and small businesses.

Frčkovski, all from the village of Gari, are the sculptors of the iconostasis in the Sv Spas Church in Skopje, the Sv Gavril Lesnovski Church near Kratovo and the Sv Jovan Bigorski Monastery near Debar. Another famous artist, icon and fresco painter, Dimitrie Krstev (1819–72), known as Dičo Zograf, came from the village of Tresonče. He painted more than 1,500 artefacts all over the Balkans, and his work is still exhibited today as an example of a then very unique style of combining harsh post-Byzantine symbolism with Baroque ornamentation.

The Mijaks speak the Mijak dialect, part of the western Macedonian dialects. Some of the main differences from standard Macedonian are the use of the consonant group 'šč' instead of 'št' – *ščo* and not *što* (meaning 'what'); the replacement of consonant 'a' with 'o' in many words – *zobi* instead of *zabi* (teeth), *kode* instead of *kade* (where), *roka* instead of *raka* (arm); and the transformation of 'lj' into the palatal 'l'.

Finally, the Mijaks have a most intriguing flag, one of the oldest in Macedonia. It is white with a red-and-yellow border and a yellow cross inside a red-and-yellow circle. The yellow segments of the circle represent the rays of the sun and, of course, is not unlike the symbolism of Macedonia's star of Vergina. The cross divides the letters ИС ХР (IS HR standing for Jesus Christ) and НИ КА (NI KA meaning 'victory'). Four symbols standing in each corner of the flag are the ancient Macedonian lion, the Byzantine double-headed eagle, the Bogomil star and prostrate half-moon, and a Celtic dragon.

For more on the Roma in Skopje, see page 147. A good website on the human rights and legal struggles of the Roma is that of the European Roma Rights Centre (w errc.org). In Macedonia there are several charities – for more information see page 104. Donating to a charity that has long-term goals for the community as a whole has proved to be far more effective in reducing long-term poverty than putting money directly into a bottomless pit. Unfortunately, like most of those living on the breadline or below, many Roma see little use for training in computers and sewing when this may not get them jobs in the current climate and their immediate needs are for food and housing. Trying, therefore, to get past the initial stumbling block of 'teaching a man to fish rather than giving him the fish' is still proving difficult.

Aromanians/Vlachs The Aromanians (known as Vlachs in Macedonian) arrived in Macedonia in Roman times from the 2nd century BC onwards. They are not related to the Romanians of Romania in language or ethnicity, although many did emigrate there over time. They have always spoken a Latin-based language and refer to themselves as Armčnji. There are a number of names for them, however: the word *vlach* comes from the Greek and, along with other derivatives, has a mostly derogatory meaning centred around 'idiot' or 'bleat'. The Greeks in fact call them Koutzovlachs (*koutzos* meaning 'lame') – connected to a story that the Aromanians refused to participate in the Greek wars by claiming to be lame in one leg! They are called Ulah in Turkish, Tschobani in Albanian and Cincari by the Serbs. *Cincari* denotes 'stingy' and is often confused with the Aromanian and Romanian word for 'five'.

The Vlachs have always been in the business of trade. Many did well out of sheep farming, and it is not difficult to suppose that they may have followed the Roman legions who needed supplies. Certainly the main Vlach settlements in Macedonia are along the Via Egnatia, and their traditional villages, such as Malovište, show a once wealthy standard of living. Although the Vlachs today are well integrated into Macedonian society, and now mostly live in the towns rather than in their old villages, many can still be found to the fore of prosperous local businesses and hotels. They remain well educated, often speaking a number of languages, and have a knack for figuring out good market niches.

Due to their relatively recent assimilation into Macedonian life it is difficult to assess the exact numbers of Vlachs, not least because many Vlach descendants may no longer consider themselves Vlach, but prefer in these times of possible ethnic segregation to call themselves simply 'Macedonian'. The 2002 census numbered Vlachs at less than 0.5% of the population.

Other minorities There are lots of other very small ethnic groups in Macedonia. The next most significant group are the Serbs who were encouraged to settle in Macedonia when Vardar Macedonia became a part of the Kingdom of Serbs, Croats and Slovenes after World War I. Serbs made up 1.8% of the population in the 2002 census, but they do not form a particularly homogeneous group as they are scattered throughout the country and are completely assimilated into Macedonian life. Nevertheless, the Serbs have their own political party, as do most of the ethnicities in the country, reflecting a politics divided along ethnic lines rather than along any real differentiation in political platform. There are also significant groups of Croats and Montenegrins from Yugoslav days; Greeks from the 19th century when the Orthodox Church was governed from Athens; Armenians who immigrated during the Middle Ages; and Ashkali Egyptians who immigrated along with the

Indian Roma. The Ashkali Egyptians, and many of the poor Turks who were left in Macedonia after the demise of the Ottoman Empire (eg: parts of Strumica), are often discriminated against as Roma.

The Mijak (see box, page 44) are the next most well-known minority. They were not officially counted in the census and so their numbers are unknown.

LANGUAGE

There are two official languages in Macedonia: the Slavic-rooted Macedonian spoken by most of the population; and Albanian, which has equal status alongside Macedonian in municipal and government affairs where Albanian speakers make up 20% or more of the citizens in a particular municipality. For basic phrases in both Macedonian and Albanian see *Appendix 1*.

The **Macedonian** language is firmly based in the Slavic family of languages. Traditionally written in Cyrillic, it is occasionally found in Latin script, especially in advertising. In past centuries it was closely related to Bulgarian and remains very similar in certain aspects of grammar and some vocabulary. Macedonians and Bulgarians can usually understand each other even if they can't speak the other's language. During both world wars Bulgaria's short rule over Macedonia saw an attempt to sway the Macedonian language back towards Bulgarian. When communist Yugoslavia won Macedonia, it set about reversing this and Serbifying the language. Today, the Macedonian alphabet is more similar to Serbian but has 31 letters instead of Serbian's 30, and four differing letters. Macedonian grammar, however, remains closely linked to Bulgarian. Serbia is also now increasingly using the Latin script rather than Cyrillic.

The Macedonian brother-saints Kiril and Metodi (Cyril and Methodius), followed by saints Kliment and Naum, invented and spread Cyrillic throughout Slavic-speaking countries (see box, page 221) from the 9th century onwards. Old Church Slavonic is still the language and script used in sermon books today in Macedonia.

Albanian belongs to the Indo-European family of languages, but its roots, going back to the ancient language of the Illyrians, are some of the oldest, and as a result its basic grammar and vocabulary resemble no other in the same family. Since its evolution in Albania, however, it has come under the influence particularly of Greek, Latin and Italian, therefore you will find a lot of words which are similar to these neighbouring languages. There are also some Slav and Turkish words.

There are two main dialects in the Albanian language: Gheg, spoken in the north of Albania, Kosovo and northwestern Macedonia, and Tosk, spoken in southern Albania. Up to the 19th century, Albanian could still be written in five different alphabets. This made communication and learning difficult, and in 1908 at the Conference of Monastir (Bitola) the decision was made to try to unify the language under one alphabet and literary standard. The Latin alphabet was chosen to provide 36 letters.

It was not until the 1960s and 1970s that a standard literary form of Albanian was finally formalised. This standard form, which is taught throughout the Albanian-speaking world, consists mostly of the Tosk dialect and grammar, with some Gheg additions. The Albanian given here is the standard literary form.

Most Macedonians below the age of 50 will speak at least a smattering of English and some are fluent. Among older Macedonians, and especially in the Albanian communities, German is more likely to be the second language of choice. On the odd occasion when you will find explanatory literature at a historic site or church, it will probably be in French rather than English.

1

Today, most of Macedonia is either Orthodox Christian or Sunni Muslim. There are some Roman Catholics, Bektaši and Methodists, as well as a good smattering of agnostics and atheists. Despite Yugoslavia's efforts to keep the states secular and to discourage religious life, the downfall of communism has brought about a revival in religion that is now proving to be both a unifier within a community, and a separator of those communities within the state.

Many Macedonians have rallied around the Orthodox Church as a means of expressing their hard-won national identity, a trend that was inadvertently encouraged through the Ottoman millet system (see box, opposite). The rise of the Orthodox Church is most obvious by the increasing number of huge metal crosses lit up across the country, and the number of new churches being built despite the terrible state of the economy (a lot of this money comes from the Macedonian diaspora). Monasticism has also been injected with a new lease of life as of 1995, with the revival and refurbishment of a great many monasteries in Macedonia.

Muslim Albanians have expressed their distress at the use of the Orthodox Church as a symbol of the Macedonian nation, and while this has fuelled the conflict between the Albanian community and the Macedonian authorities, Muslim Albanians have also retaliated with the construction of many new mosques. This has not helped matters, especially as non-Albanian Muslim numbers have been used to justify the need for new mosques, yet services are often only held in Albanian.

Both sides in the conflict of 2001 desecrated churches and mosques, which is a war crime under the Geneva Convention, and sadly reflects a history of such practices in the region. Many churches were destroyed or built over by the Ottomans during their time in Macedonia. Of note was Sv Sofia in Ohrid (page 212) – photographs of it as a mosque can still be found. Even more mosques were destroyed by the Macedonians when the Ottomans finally left in 1912.

HISTORY OF THE ORTHODOX CHURCH IN MACEDONIA Jesus's disciple Paul was called upon by the vision of the 'man of Macedonia' to spread the word of God along the River Vardar. His journey in the middle of the 1st century is detailed in Acts 16:10–17:15, and many believe he made it as far as northern Macedonia. Timothy and Silas stayed on in Macedonia after Paul left, and they may have made greater inroads into the wilds of the upper Vardar. But by the 4th century, Macedonia had an established Christian Church under the Metropolitan of Skopje. Aside from written records elsewhere, early evidence of Christianity in northern Macedonia can be seen by the remains of numerous Christian basilica across the country.

When the Slav tribes came in the 7th century, they too were converted to Christianity. These newcomers brought with them the problem of how to teach the Scriptures through a foreign language such as Greek or Latin. To alleviate this problem the Byzantine emperor Michael III summoned the monks Cyril and Methodius (Kiril and Metodi in Macedonian), who were natives of Macedonia, to go forth and teach the Scriptures to the many Slav speakers in their native language. This they did in the year 862, travelling along the River Bregalnica, and to do so they created the Glagolitic and Cyrillic scripts, variations of which we are familiar with today.

Thus Byzantium increased its influence over the region by using what is now known as 'Old Slavonic' to win over the local slavophone population. Shortly afterwards, as Byzantium began to fall and Bulgaria was first made a state, Bulgaria continued this practice of exerting influence through the Church by establishing the

Bulgarian Patriarchate, with its sphere of influence away from the Greek Orthodox Church and the influence of Byzantium.

The Bulgarian prince Boris ordained Kliment in 893 as the first Macedonian Slav Bishop of the Bishopric of Velika (believed to be around the River Treška). Kliment had been a disciple of Kiril and Metodi during their travels in Macedonia, and so had much influence in the land. His seat was at Ohrid, and he brought his fellow disciple from those travelling days, Father Naum, with him to Ohrid. There they set up the first Slavic monastery and school.

Later in 976, Tsar Samoil (see box, page 20), who had rebelled against Bulgarian authority and founded his own empire, also founded his own church, the autocephalous Ohrid Archdiocese, in order to bolster his own empire. But with the fall of Samoil in 1014, the Byzantine emperor Basilius reduced the new archdiocese to a mere archbishopric.

Thus the Archbishopric of Ohrid remained for seven and a half centuries until in 1767 the Turkish sultan Mustapha III gave in to Greek pressure and allowed the Archbishopric of Ohrid to be dissolved, and even the eparchy of Ohrid was reshuffled to have its seat at Durres in present-day Albania, thereafter known as the Eparchy of Albania. Along with the reshuffle, Greece bargained the right to administer the Orthodox Christian faith in upper Macedonia. New churches built in Macedonia during this period of the late 18th century and the 19th show a lot of Greek influence and engravings, as do older churches that were renovated or

THE MILLET SYSTEM OF GOVERNANCE AND ITS AFTERMATH

The Ottoman millet system, whereby people were classed according to religion rather than race, allowed Christianity to live effectively alongside Islam. For the Ottomans an elite ruling class was important, and so the Church's influence over its subjects was just as much an integral part of their rule over the empire as the Islamic faith was over its respective followers. Within each millet system (the word millet comes from the Arabic word *millah* and literally means 'nation'), the Ottomans were just as likely to inflict havoc on the lower echelons of the Christian millet as they were on the Muslim millet or the Jewish millet. The corollary of this millet system was that several religion-based 'nation states' grew up alongside each other. In addition, political infighting within each millet system caused even further rivalry in the power vacuum left by the Ottomans following their demise, as played out in the desire of various factions of the Orthodox Church and their national leaders to 'rule' over Macedonia in the Balkan wars of 1912 and 1913.

Whereas the Jews were deported en masse during World War II to concentration camps and gas chambers such as those in Treblinka in Poland, many Muslims remained, and some believe even today that they should still be allowed free rein over their followers as in the millet days. The Orthodox Church, already disunited by national factions, more easily made the transition to the Westphalian nation-state system, which upholds sovereignty and non-interference in internal affairs as the key pillars of government and international relations. Unfortunately, the Westphalian nation-state system does not sit alongside the millet system so well, as a nation state must have complete jurisdiction over a geographical area, whereas the millet system allows for several separate jurisdictions to apply to different people within the same geographical area.

refurbished during this time, and many of them were refurbished purely in order to illustrate the authority of the Greek Church.

During the Russo–Turkish wars of the late 19th and early 20th centuries, Russia granted Bulgaria its wish for orthodox influence over northern Macedonia. Bulgaria then lost out to the Serbs at the end of the second Balkan War of 1913 and northern Macedonia fell under the influence of the Serbian Orthodox Church, long since separate from the Greek Orthodox Church.

It was not until March 1945 that the Archdiocese of Ohrid put forward a resolution to create an autonomous Macedonian Orthodox Church. The Serbian Orthodox Church, of course, refused. Thirteen more years of discussions ensued until finally, in 1958, the Serbian Orthodox Church gave in and, in the following year, the Macedonian Orthodox Church gained its autonomy, although still under the patriarch and canonical unity of the Serbian Orthodox Church.

The Macedonian Church was still not happy, however, and after more heated debate, the Holy Synod of the Macedonian Orthodox Church proclaimed itself autocephalous and completely independent of the Serbian Orthodox Church on 19 July 1967, exactly two centuries after the Archbishopric of Ohrid had been dissolved by the Ottomans. The legality of this move under the respective constitutions of both the Macedonian and Serbian Orthodox churches is still a bone of contention between the two churches, and the Serbian Orthodox Church still doesn't recognise the independence of the Macedonian Orthodox Church.

Whether you are a believer or not, the churches, mosques and monasteries in Macedonia are amazing treasures which deserve to be kept for posterity. Although monastic life and the Church have received a new boost since the independence of Macedonia, many of the churches and monasteries do not receive much funding. It is obvious which ones receive fewer donations by the state of disrepair that the churches and inns are in. The more remote and less well-known monasteries are particularly badly off. Well-wishers usually leave 10 or 50MKD at the church altars, and you might want to consider giving more generously to some. If you would like to make a larger donation by banker's draft or international money order, the residing father or sister will be able to furnish you with suitable details.

THE ISLAMIC RELIGIOUS COMMUNITY IN MACEDONIA Of the two main Islamic groups of believers, Sunni and Shi'a, most Muslims (about one-third of the population) in Macedonia are **Sunnis**. Not all of these are Albanian or Turkish, but many are ethnic Macedonian Muslims (Torbeši, see page 41), Roma or other ethnicities.

In addition, there are also a small number of **dervish** believers of different tarikat (subdivisions or orders of the dervish Muslim faith) such as the Halveti, Bektaši, Nakšhi-Bandi, Kadiri, Melami, Rufa'i or Sinani. Officially, there are no Shi'a followers in Macedonia, but some of the orders, especially Bektaši, contain some Shi'a doctrinal elements. The connection stops there, however, and there is no contemporary hierarchical connection with the Shi'a in Iran.

During Ottoman rule over Macedonia, there was no separation of 'Church' and state, and the millet system (see box, page 49) was used by the Ottoman sultans to rule over the different religious communities. At that time, the sultan was the highest Muslim religious authority. From 1918 to 1927, the Islamic community in Macedonia came under the authority of the Great Mufti of Belgrade, after which the Islamic believers of all Yugoslavia were unified under the Great Mufti of Sarajevo.

When Yugoslavia was formed in 1944, the Islamic Religious Community (IRC) in Macedonia registered in its own right with the Socialist Yugoslav Republic of Macedonia as the sole representative of the Muslim faith. The IRC is built on the doctrinal foundations of Sunni Islam, and has about 450 registered mosques and some 500 clerics.

There is only one Islamic school in Macedonia, the Isa Bej Medrese in Kondovo. Originally established in the 15th century, and revived in the 1930s as a rival private school to the Royal Yugoslav state-run Big Medrese of King Aleksandar set up in Skopje, the Isa Bej Medrese was reopened in 1979 in Kondovo after a period of closure during early communist times. By then many believers had gone abroad (and still do) to receive their religious education before taking up religious leadership positions at home. Due, of course, to the strong influence of the Ottoman period and continued links with Turkey, most receive their religious education in Turkey. The Turkish school of Islam teaches a modern secular version of the Muslim faith and these teachings continue to dominate in Macedonia. As in many other countries in the region, however, reactionary leanings in the Islamic community have led some to seek more traditional schooling in Egypt, while others have gone to Syria and Saudi Arabia, which offered scholarships to students from abroad. Some students returning from Saudi Arabia have brought back the experience and preaching of Wahabi and Salafi Islam, both of which teach relatively radical views and practices. Wahabi and Salafi preaching in Macedonia is weak although Wahabi- and Salafi-linked NGOs continue to try to further their influence through their work in poor communities and in building new mosques. Most mosques, especially in major towns, such as the Motley Mosque in Tetovo, are of the Turkish school, and open and friendly to (appropriately clad) visitors, including women.

The only other Islamic organisation in Macedonia that has tried to register itself separately from the IRC is the Bektaši dervish community. Macedonia's law on religion, however, stipulates that only one representative of each major faith is allowed to register. While this arbitrary provision has allowed for Orthodox, Catholic and various Protestant branches of Christianity to register, only one organisation is allowed to represent the Muslim faith. This serves the IRC (and the Macedonian Orthodox Church) well as this way it has better control of the influence of various sects of Islam (and the considerable funding that can go with them). It clashes, however, with the European Convention on Human Rights and will probably have to change in due course if Macedonia wants to get into the EU (although Greece still has an equally restrictive law on religion).

The head of the IRC in Macedonia today is the Reis-ul-Ulema (president). He governs the Riyaset, which is an executive body responsible for religious and spiritual activities and which is answerable to the Meshihat (the Assembly of the Islamic Community, consisting of 51 members). Below the Riyaset and Meshihat, mosque communities are divided into 13 religious committees, each of which is headed by a mufti.

EDUCATION

The Macedonian Constitution mandates free and compulsory primary and secondary education. Children begin schooling at the age of six, enrolling in primary school, which lasts nine years. Primary school enrolment in 2012 was 89%. The dropout figures are highest for Roma and Muslim girls in both primary and secondary school.

Secondary school lasts a further three or four years, depending on the type of school, which only became compulsory in 2006. In addition to teaching in Macedonian, teaching is also available in Albanian, Turkish and Serbian in some schools. In the past few years, certain public high schools have also begun teaching classes in English or French.

Skopje has two international schools, the American school NOVA (w nova.edu.
mk), and QSI International (w qsi.org/macedonia/mcn/), both of which offer pre-
kindergarten through to high school. In addition, the British Children's Academy
(w tbcacademy.com) offers nursery care from six months to six years old. Post-
secondary education can be obtained at one of the five state universities, located in
Skopje (w ukim.edu.mk), Bitola (w uklo.edu.mk), Tetovo (w unite.edu.mk), Štip
(w ugd.edu.mk) and Ohrid (w uist.edu.mk).

Macedonia's education system suffers from low salaries, poor facilities and old-
style teaching based on rote learning rather than developing analytical skills. There
is an excess of law and economics graduates and a dearth from technical sciences.
Professors rarely keep to exam timetables or office hours and students feel that they
should pay bribes in order to pass an exam and get their diploma. A study conducted
in 2011 by the UN Office on Drugs and Crime (UNODC) placed Macedonia highest
in the region for bribery, with doctors, police and teachers most subject to it.

However, over the past few years the government, supported by international
organisations, has slowly started reforming the education system. Free books
for elementary and high schools as well as a number of scholarships for the best
university students have been introduced. Schools are being renovated all over
the country, and computers installed for every pupil. The government project to
translate a thousand prominent technical textbooks is near completion.

The literacy rate in Macedonia averages at 97.8%.

CULTURE

Macedonia's potentially most important and unique contribution to world art is
its little-known and unverified claim that 12th-century Renaissance art originated
in its secluded monasteries (see box, page 150). Religious art is certainly making a
comeback in Macedonia. On other fronts, while there are no big, famous museums,
art galleries or world-renowned festivals, there are always plenty of smaller events
going on, in Skopje year-round and all over the country during the summer festival
season. Venues and playlists are usually announced only a few days before the event,
so you need to keep your eyes peeled for the information. Festivals and saints' days
also have a big following in Macedonia. A list with approximate dates is covered on
page 88. Skopje, and some of the other larger towns in Macedonia, have a small but
thriving classical arts scene in music, ballet, opera and drama, as well as modern
drama in Macedonian and minority languages. In 2013, the Feast of the Holy Forty
Martyrs in Štip (page 305) was inscribed on the UNESCO list of Intangible Cultural
Heritage – the first element from Macedonia to join the list. The Kopachkata, a social
dance from the village of Dramče, was inscribed on the list in November 2014.

HANDICRAFTS Macedonia has a long tradition of indigenous handicrafts mostly
developed around religious art (see below). In addition, there are manmade
Ohrid pearls (page 215), silver filigree jewellery, iron- and copper-work, carpets,
embroidery, and local musical instruments (see box, page 54) to be found here. See
page 133 for where to purchase most of these items.

RELIGIOUS ART The arts in Macedonia, like its nationhood and politics, are
fractured. During Ottoman times, still life was banished and so depictions of such
retreated to Macedonia's many monasteries. These took the form of frescoes, icons
and woodcarvings, of which there are a great many in Macedonia that are literally
priceless and uninsurable.

Makarije Frčkovski and the Mijak brothers Marko and Petar Filipovski from Gari were famous in the early 19th century for their iconostasis carvings. In total they carved four iconostases during their lifetime. Three can still be admired at Sv Spas Church in Skopje, the Monastery of Sv Jovan Bigorski near Debar, and Sv Gavril Lesnovski near Kratovo. A fourth in Sv Nikola Church in Kruševo was destroyed when the church was razed during the Ilinden Uprising in 1903. In 1999, a tourist is alleged to have offered the head priest at Sv Jovan Bigorski a blank cheque for the church's iconostasis. Aside from the fact that dedications to God cannot be bought at any price, the piece is irreplaceable and so it remains there today and hopefully forever.

Icons up until the 10th century were made of terracotta, such as those found in Vinica (page 307), and many are now on view at the National Museum of Macedonia in Skopje. Thereafter they were generally paintings inlaid with silver and sometimes gold from the gold mine outside Radoviš. Most of these are still in their original churches, but some of the more important icons and frescoes, rescued from centuries of neglect during the Ottoman Empire, have been put on display in Skopje's and Ohrid's galleries.

The influence of Macedonian Byzantine church frescoes on the Renaissance is described in the box on page 150. The best three examples of these are at Sv Pantelejmon near Skopje (page 149), Sv Sofia in Ohrid (page 212) and Sv Gjorgi near Kurbinovo (page 145). A good website with more information on many of the monasteries is w preminportal.com.mk, which has a specific section on monastery tourism and on religious art in some of the monasteries.

MODERN ART Modern art has taken hold of Macedonian artists in a big way, as if trying to catch up with centuries of artistic deprivation. The Museum of Contemporary Art, which was set up in 1964 after the disastrous earthquake in Skopje the year before, houses a permanent collection of modern art as well as frequent travelling exhibitions. Many pieces were donated to the museum as a result of the earthquake, including a piece by Van Gogh, which is usually stored down in the basement but can be viewed on request.

The Museum of the City of Skopje (the old railway station) and the national galleries of Čifte Amam and Daud Pasha Amam, both former Turkish baths, also hold travelling exhibitions. Those living in Skopje will not have failed to notice the amount of modern art, alongside the compulsory icon or two, that adorns the walls of modern Skopje apartments. Today, the works of Macedonians such as Iskra Dimitrova, Omer Kaleši and Ibrahim Bedi are beginning to travel the world. The Skopje 2014 regeneration project included the renovation of a number of museums, and the unveiling of plenty of new sculptural monuments (see box, page 137).

Since Yugoslav times, and especially since independence, Macedonia has encouraged artist colonies to grow and flourish. Ohrid is home to many Macedonian artists and you will frequently see budding artists trying their hand at representations of city life. The monasteries have also encouraged art, where the tranquillity of monastic life is often conducive to artistic development. Several art colonies take place in Macedonia during the month of August, including those at the Monastery of Sv Joakim Osogovski near Kriva Palanka, the Mijak village of Galičnik, the Monastery of Sv Petka in Velgošti near Ohrid, and the village of Kneževo near Kratovo.

FILM AND PHOTOGRAPHY Photography and photojournalism have strong pioneering roots in Macedonia going back to the early 19th-century days of the

Manaki brothers (see box, page 240). Today, exhibitions of the works of Alexander Kondev or Samir Ljuma can be found around Macedonia, and the works of Rumen Kamilov and Marko Georgievski can be seen in numerous magazines and articles about Macedonia.

The Manaki brothers also experimented with film back in the early 1900s, and Macedonia had a vibrant film-making industry during Yugoslav times. This has continued since independence with Milčo Mančevski's outstanding 1994 release *Before the Rain*. Others have followed, such as *Dust* (Mančevski, 2001), *The Great Water* (Ivo Trajkov, 2004, based on the book of the same title by Živko Cingo), *Soul Hunter* (Oliver Romevski, 2004), *Secret Book* (Vlado Cvetanovski, 2004), *How I Killed a Saint* (Teona Mitevska, 2004), *Bal-Can-Can* (Darko Mitrevski, 2005), *Shadows* (Mančevski, 2007), *Mothers* (Mančevski, 2009), *Punk's Not Dead* (Darko Popov, 2011), *The Third Half* (Mitrevski, 2012), *To the Hilt* (Stole Popov, 2013), *Lazar* (Ristovski, 2014) and *Secret Ingredient* (Stavrevski, 2017).

For an interesting and thought-provoking insight into the undercurrents of the 2001 conflict (especially as it was made seven years before the conflict broke out), *Before the Rain* is an excellent introduction. *Dust* gives a view of early 20th-century Macedonia under the Ottoman Empire, while *Bal-Can-Can* portrays through black

MACEDONIA'S TRADITIONAL MUSICAL INSTRUMENTS

Like its people, Macedonia's musical instruments have a mixed origin. Many were brought to this land with the various invaders passing through over the centuries, while others are home grown. Playing traditional instruments is seeing a small revival in fusion music and in the revival of ethnic festivities. It is a rare wedding, holiday or religious event that doesn't bring out one of these traditional instruments – or perhaps an entire band of them. To give you an idea of what they are and how they sound, below is a snapshot of the most common ones.

Kaval Traditionally a shepherd's instrument, the *kaval* resembles a flute. It is made of one piece of wood about 70cm long, usually ash, open at both ends and ornately decorated throughout. It produces a lovely warm sound, almost melancholic. You can hear the kaval frequently played in pairs, with the first leading a melody and the second one droning along in a slightly lower key.

Gajda Macedonia's version of the bagpipe – its origins are in Macedonia's mountain villages. *Gajdas* have four main parts: the chanter (*gajdarka*), a wooden tube with seven finger-holes in front and a thumb-hole at the back; the drone (*brchalo*) producing the constant sound; the *duvalo*, a wooden pipe attached to the bag where the musician blows air in; and of course the bag itself (*mev*), made of tanned sheep or goat skin. The gajda is usually accompanied by a kaval or two, a *tambura*, and perhaps a percussion instrument like the *tapanče*, *daire* or *tarabuka*.

Zurla Typically played at weddings, social occasions and Turkish wrestling matches (*pelivan*), the *zurla* has a distinct piercing sound that is usually heard well above the drum (*tapan*) that accompanies it. It is a wooden (walnut or plum), two-part wind instrument, the body of which is a conical pipe. A beak (*slavec*) is inserted into the upper, narrow part. Zurlas originated in the Middle East and were brought to Macedonia either by the Turks or the Roma, the latter of whom most often play it today. The larger (male) zurla is usually found in Skopje, Tetovo,

comedy the continued mêlée of relations in the Balkans a century later. *Punk's Not Dead* is a very up-to-date road-movie-style depiction of ever-present tensions in the Balkans and a thorough indictment of nationalist trends emerging in Macedonia. Fortunately for English-speakers visiting Macedonia, foreign films are usually given Macedonian subtitles rather than dubbed, so going to the cinema needn't be hard work if you don't speak Macedonian, and it is one of the reasons why so many young Macedonians speak such good English.

MUSIC The soundtrack for these films has also injected life into Macedonian musical compositions by bands that combine traditional music with modern sounds such as Anastasia (*Before the Rain*) and Olivier Samouillan and Project Zlust (*How I Killed a Saint*). Other popular artists on the scene are Kiril Dzajkovski (*Dust, The Great Water*); Trifun Kostovski (Macedonian soul); Toše Proeski (modern pop and fusion – sadly, Proeski was killed in a car accident in Croatia in 2007); Kaliope (a long-time favourite of the Macedonians); Synthesis, who use traditional Macedonian instruments and vocal tones (see box, below); Tung Tung, an Albanian ethno jazz group (albums include *Red Grapes*, 2003, and *Gold Coin*, 2005); and Adrian Gadja (modern Albanian).

Veles, Prilep, Bitola and Kratovo, while the smaller (female) zurla is played around Gostivar and Kumanovo.

Supelka A shepherd's instrument that looks and sounds like a recorder.

Duduk A blocked-end flute that can be found in two lengths: 70cm like the kaval, and 25cm.

Tambura Brought to Macedonia in the 14th and 15th centuries via the Turks from the Middle East, the tambura is a long-necked string instrument with a pear-shaped body, made of walnut. It produces a metallic, tingling sound, and is played both solo and as part of an ensemble.

Tapan This is a good-sized drum. What sets it apart is that the musicians of Macedonia play it with two specially designed drumsticks – known as a *kukuda* and a *pračka*. The kukuda is a narrow pipe made of wood, while the pračka is more like a thin switch. Each one strikes a different side of the drum and the difference in sound is remarkable; together they produce an impression that something big is about to happen. The *tapan* is the traditional accompaniment for most folk bands playing at special occasions. You'll find it at the Galičnik wedding, for instance (see box, page 184).

Daire Essentially a tambourine.

Tarabuka An hourglass-shaped drum, medium size, made of wood and animal skin. Its origins are uncertain, but it has been variously connected with Greece, the Middle East and India. It is quite often used as accompaniment to the tambura.

Kemane An instrument similar to the violin or viola.

1

One of the easiest introductions to the Macedonian modern/traditional music mix is the album *Treta Majka* (Third Mother) by the famous and phenomenally talented Serbian Leb I Sol lead guitarist Vlatko Stefanovski, the Macedonian guitarist Miroslav Tadic and the Bulgarian *kaval* player Theodosii Spasov. Equally good is the album *The Path in the Sun* by the Dragan Dautovski Quartet. *Music from Macedonia* (available as 2 CDs, World Caprice Records, 2004) provides another good introduction.

Unless you look out for these new sounds, however, you will find an overwhelming amount of traditional Macedonian music played in restaurants and at family gatherings all over Macedonia. This is an acquired taste and a must for traditional ceremonies where Macedonia's national dance, the *oro* (*kola* in Serbian), is compulsory for all participants. The *oro*, a circle of dancers holding hands, proceeds in an anticlockwise circle getting gradually faster. There are a number of different versions of the steps to the dance, the most basic being a three steps forward, one step backward arrangement. The *oro* generally comes across as quite a serious affair, although allegedly they are having fun.

Even more serious is chalgia music from the 18th and 19th centuries. Chalgia mixes secular Byzantine music with classical Turkish music from earlier centuries. It comes across as generally sober and its lyrics frequently tell of loss and yearning. Chalgia was played on traditional Macedonian musical instruments such as the canoon, kemane, oud, tambourine and tarabuka (see box, page 54). A six-CD anthology was brought out in 2006, and can be bought from Jugoton in Skopje. If you don't fancy the six-CD set, there is an interesting, more modern rendition of chalgia in the album *Kaldrma* (referring to an old type of road construction from the Ottoman period) by the pop/modern jazz Macedonian group String Forces and the traditional Macedonian Pece Atanasovski Ensemble.

Many of the bands hired for traditional functions and festivities are Roma bands, and one of the songs almost invariably played is 'Mjesečina', meaning 'moonlight', by Goran Bregovič, made famous in the Yugoslav film *Underground* (Emir Kusturica, 1995). The Roma have a strong history of music-making, immortalised in the songs of Esma Redžepova, the queen of Roma music – *Legends of Gypsy Music from Macedonia* (2014) is available in the UK and provides a decent introduction to her voice, along with Roma saxophonist King Ferus Mustafov.

LITERATURE Macedonian literary history is also split into two sections. The spread of the Cyrillic and Slavic languages is very much connected to the saints Kiril, Metodi, Kliment and Naum (page 47) and the development of the Archbishopric of Ohrid. Ohrid's Museum of Slavonic Literacy is dedicated to the historiography of its development.

While much of Europe underwent a great literary phase during the Renaissance, Macedonia was firmly under Ottoman and Greek influence, which did not encourage indigenous writings. The 19th-century Miladinov brothers (see box, page 228) went a long way to cast off this dark period in Macedonian song, poetry, literature and literacy. A whole slew of authors and poets have appeared since then, most recently Živko Cingo, Radovan Pavlovski and Petre M. Andreevski. The works of Božin Pavlovski, now living in Australia, are also available in English (see *Appendix 3* for titles).

ARCHITECTURE Macedonian architecture goes back a long way, the earliest discoveries dating to the Bronze and Iron ages. The ancient Paeons built fortresses out of huge limestone blocks, using a technique called Cyclopean masonry. No mortar was used, but the precise joints of the rocks and their huge size kept these constructions together for thousands of years. Very little of this architecture is visible today, although some remains can be found at Prosek above Demir Kapija, Mariovo and Vajtos (page 287).

Thereafter, Macedonian architecture is centred largely round the development of the Church, until the arrival of the Ottomans at the end of the 14th century when Turkish inns, baths, mosques and clock towers influenced the skylines of towns such as Skopje and Bitola. During the 18th century the development of what has become known as the 'old style of Ohrid, with extended eaves, spacious and splendid, with two entrances' (Pavlovski, *The Red Hypocrite*) became common among the rich and influential, such as the Ottoman lords, monastery inns and wealthy traders. One of the finest examples of this type of house is the Robev residence, now the National Museum of Ohrid, but they can be seen all over Macedonia in various states of disrepair, desperate for renovation. Some excellent architectural drawings of this type of architecture are on display at the Museum of Bitola.

Sadly, the renovation of traditional houses is costly, and therefore largely left undone. In addition, many of the beautiful 19th-century buildings of the grand European style, which used to adorn most of central Skopje, collapsed during the earthquake of 1963. In the aftermath, the money donated by hundreds of international donors to rebuild Skopje was used to bring in the latest competitive craze in concrete creations, both communist and international, which is still to be seen today. A fine example of this is the main post office in Skopje next to the Stone Bridge.

In 2010, the government revealed its plans, named Skopje 2014, to transform the centre of the capital. Some of the old buildings that had been destroyed by the 1963 earthquake have been rebuilt, such as the National Theatre, the Officers House and the Museum of the Macedonian Struggle (if in a slightly different location). They are joined by endless statues, a mini Arc de Triomphe, a prominent Archaeological Museum sporting Corinthian columns, a new Ministry of Foreign Affairs and headquarters of the Financial Police, and a new bridge. The makeover is spectacular, and Skopje is a sightseeing occasion in itself. The cost, however, has been prohibitive, and contributes to the image of the lavish former Prime Minister, Nikola Gruevski, who now faces corruption charges.

1

2

Practical Information

... for one does not come to Macedonia every day, and time and opportunity are not to be thrown away.

Journals of a Landscape Painter in Greece and Albania, Edward Lear, 1851

WHEN TO VISIT

Located so far south in Europe, Macedonia is great to visit most of the year round. It is particularly welcoming during spring and autumn, outside the high tourist seasons and when the weather is at its most pleasant. It can be warm and sunny during the day from as early as March until as late as November, while skiing is usually available from December through to early April. July and August can be very hot, sometimes getting up to 40°C during the day in Skopje and along the Vardar Valley. This can be particularly unpleasant if taking lengthy journeys by public transport where there is no air conditioning and the local population fears getting ill from a breeze from an open window. The mountains remain pleasantly cool, however, and even Ohrid is relatively quiet midweek in the summer.

HIGHLIGHTS AND SUGGESTED ITINERARIES

SCENIC OUTDOORS The lake and town of Ohrid (page 199) are seen as the jewel of Macedonia's crown, and it is not without reason that Ohrid's medieval architecture and pristine natural setting are preserved by UNESCO as a place of historic, cultural and scenic significance. Outside the height of the summer season it remains a wonderful little getaway spot, and should not be missed on any trip to Macedonia. The back route from Skopje through Debar to Struga and on to Ohrid is worth the extra time.

All three of Macedonia's **national parks** – Pelister, Mavrovo and Galičica – offer many marked hiking trails, and beautiful scenic drives on improving roads. The one hike not to miss is the 10km route from Mount Vodno just outside Skopje down to Lake Matka (page 153), which also offers rock climbing, caving, camping, kayaking and yet more scenic hikes to local monasteries and beyond. There are also many attractive hikes to waterfalls, glacial lakes and other scenic spots and along the Via Egnatia (see box, page 6). If you'd like to tandem paraglide or learn for yourself, this is one of the cheapest places in Europe. Mountain biking, horseriding or a hot-air balloon are also great ways to experience Macedonia (page 91).

WINE AND *RAKIJA* TASTING Macedonia has a very old history of winemaking going back to Philip II, and there are some indigenous grapes in the country that make a very quaffable vino. It's difficult to find Macedonian wines outside the Balkans so make the most of trying them here (see the box on page 282 for more on Macedonia's wine varieties). Macedonia's *eau de vie* is *rakija*. For most, rakija is rakija is rakija, but Alchemist is leading the way in producing rakija differentiated by grape, such as their very smooth Black Muscat (for more on rakija, see the box on page 274).

In Skopje visit Skovin wine cellars (see box, page 275), or the rakija bars, wine bar and Old Town Brewery Temov in Čaršija. If you get the chance though, go to Tikveš Wine Cellars (see box, page 282) in Kavadarci, the home of Macedonian wine, or take the opportunity to stay at Popova Kula vineyard (page 287). Two wine festivals not to miss are Sv Trifun Day on 14 February (page 89) and the harvest festival in September, both in Negotino.

ARCHITECTURE AND ARCHAEOLOGY Don't miss out on the 16th-century villages of the Macedonian minorities. **Galičnik** of the Mijaks hangs on the edge of a deep ravine and every July holds the biggest wedding party you'll ever go to (see box, page 184). Malovište (page 253), located in Pelister National Park, is an old Vlach village, formerly housing rich traders, which is now being renovated to preserve its heritage and is a beautiful example of the rich variety of Macedonian culture. There are hundreds of other fine old villages off the beaten track that have yet to be fully discovered and you'll find that taking a trip away from your main route will always reap a reward.

Macedonia's Turkish history is well worth looking into, and is best preserved in Skopje's old town, **Čaršija** (page 140). There are some fine Ottoman mosques in **Bitola**, too (page 246).

Macedonia is literally buried in **archaeological ruins**, which are becoming more accessible every year: Neolithic villages can be found on Lake Ohrid and in Skopje; Cyclopean fortresses at Prosek and Mariovo; Roman towns at Heraklea and Stobi; and World War I battlefields at Dojran and outside Bitola. It's also possible to take part in archaeological digs through the Balkan Heritage Field School (see box, page 13).

SPIRITUAL INNS
Orthodox A trip to Macedonia would be incomplete without visiting at least one monastery. They are renowned for their intricate woodwork and delicate architecture and for some of their remote but beautiful locations. The country boasted over a thousand churches and monasteries at the zenith of Orthodox ministry in the region during the 14th to 16th centuries, during which time Ohrid was the centre of the Orthodox Church and still has over 200 churches and monasteries overlooking its shores. Some of the most spectacular working monasteries to visit are Sv Joakim Osogovski (page 328) near Kriva Palanki; Sv Jovan Bigorski (page 183) near Debar; the World Monuments Fund-listed Treskavec Monastery (page 266) near Prilep; Sv Gavril Lesnovski (page 335) near Kratovo; Kališta Monastery (page 229) for its nearby cave churches looking over Lake Ohrid; and Monastery of Zrze (page 268) set high on a cliff.

For those who want to make churches and monasteries the theme of their visit, further suggestions include: the Monastery of Sv Naum (page 222) on Lake Ohrid; the women's Monastery of Jankovec (page 258) near Resen; the Monastery of Sv Leonthius (page 317) near Vodoča village; the women's Monastery of Eleusa (page 318) in Veljusa village; the Monastery of Sv Archangel Michael (page 265) in Varoš, Prilep; the women's Monastery of Sv Gjorgi (page 290) in Debar; the Church of Sv Spas (page 142) in Skopje; the Church of Sv Gjorgi (page 259) in Kurbinovo for examples of 12th-century Renaissance art; the cave Church of Archangel Michael (page 229) in Radožda on Lake Ohrid; the Christian basilicas in Heraklea Linkestis (page 249); Plaošnik (page 213) for its early Christian mosaics; and of course all the churches listed in the chapter on Ohrid (page 212).

Muslim/dervish True to the religious variety of Macedonia, there are also some beautiful mosques and dervish *teke* worth seeing. Marvel at the Motley Mosque in Tetovo (page 169), beautifully painted like a house of cards outside and like a tea tray inside, or admire the blue artwork of the Mustafa Pasha Mosque in Skopje (page 143). Also in Tetovo is the best-preserved dervish Arabati Baba Bektaši Teke (page 169), and in Struga the best-preserved Halveti teke (page 227).

A DOZEN MORE HIGHLIGHTS
* Ascend to the Towers of King Marko in **Prilep** for a 360° view of the Pelagonia plains or visit Prilep Tobacco Museum; catch the Prilep Beer Festival in July (page 264)
* Visit the town of **Kratovo**, situated around an old volcanic crater, for its rock art and volcanic droplets (page 330)
* See where Atatürk went to school in **Bitola** (page 236)
* Visit **Kruševo** (page 269), the capital of the ten-day Republic of Kruševo in 1903 where one of the most successful Macedonian revolutions against the Ottoman Empire took place, to see some of the best-preserved architecture from the 18th and 19th centuries, and a re-enactment of events on 2 August
* Bathe in the renovated local **hot springs** at Katlanovska Banja (page 158), communist style at Banjište (page 194) and visit the progressing renovation of the Roman baths in Bansko (page 318)
* **Ski** at Popova Šapka, Mavrovo, Kožuf, Kruševo or Pelister, and relax afterwards with a massage and a choice of local grills
* Ride the cable car to the top of **Mount Vodno** outside Skopje (page 149)
* Learn of Macedonia's tragic Jewish history at Skopje's **Holocaust Memorial Centre** (page 140)
* Watch the solstice on the Palaeolithic throne of **Cocev Kamen** sacrificial and megalithic ancient observatory (page 334)
* Safari in **Mavrovo National Park** to try to catch a rare sighting of the Balkan lynx or endangered vultures (page 178)
* Scuba dive in **Lake Ohrid** (see box, page 218)
* See the procession of the Feast of the Holy Forty Martyrs in **Štip** (page 305)

SUGGESTED ITINERARIES
One week More than likely you will land in Skopje, so take two days to visit the capital (page 109) before hiring a car to take the back road to Ohrid, or take the early bus there direct. Spend two days in Ohrid, one to see the town, the second to hike in Galičica National Park, tandem paraglide or take the boat to Sv Naum, swim and sunbathe. Finally drive over to Galičica National Park to hike up to Two Lake viewpoint, and down to Lake Prespa. Stop in Bitola for a late lunch on the fashionable Širok Sokok, then journey on to Prilep to visit Treskavec Monastery (page 266), or take the bus there direct. Treat yourself to a night at Popova Kula winery and hotel (page 287) to sample their wines before returning back to Skopje the next day.

Two weeks After three days in Skopje, including one when you visit nearby Lake Matka (page 153) and Katlanovska Banja (page 158), travel to Ohrid via Tetovo to see the Motley Mosque, Arabati Baba Bektaši Teke and the Tetovo Kale (page 170). After two days in Ohrid, make your way to Bitola to spend a full day visiting the Roman ruins of Heraklea (page 249), Atatürk's former military school and museum (page 246), and the best ethno museum in Macedonia at Kurklino (page 249). Take a day to visit Prilep (page 259) and pop over to Kruševo (page 269), home of the Ilinden Uprising and pop star Toše Proeski. Overnight in Popova Kula winery and hotel before hiking up to Prosek (page 287) to visit the tiny Demir Kapija Museum. Move on to Strumica and then overnight in Berovo, where you should take a day to

2

hike in the area and breathe in the pristine air. Then make your way to Kratovo to visit the stone towers, see the nearby Stone Dolls, and hike up to Gorni Kratovo to see volcanic bombs (page 334). Return to Skopje via the Devil's Wall near Sv Nikole (page 281).

TOUR OPERATORS

Operators outside Macedonia who can book your ticket and hotel and make up an itinerary for you are relatively few, but increasing:

AUSTRALIA

Tucan Travel 📞02 9326 6633, 0800 804 8435; e adventures@tucantravel.com; w tucantravel. com. Offers 12- to 60-day tours through the Balkans with 1 or 2 days in Ohrid. They have extended phone hours & call centres in other countries (including the US & UK) so it is worth looking at the contact page on their website to see if they have a telephone number for your country.

UK

Andante Travel 📞01722 569429; e tours@ andantetravels.co.uk; w andantetravels.co.uk. Specialising in archaeology & the ancient world, Andante has espied the potential in Macedonia by offering a tour focusing on the Via Egnatia in Albania, Macedonia & Greece.

Cox & Kings 📞020 3883 6880; e info@ coxandkings.co.uk; w coxandkings.co.uk. Group

---

VISITING CHURCHES AND MONASTERIES
Sally Broughton Micova

Macedonia is full of amazing churches and monasteries. Although many of them date back to Byzantine times, they are most often still working churches or inhabited monasteries. Therefore it is good to know a bit about their decorum in order to avoid feeling uncomfortable and to understand some of what is going on.

There is a difference between parish churches and monasteries. It is important to remember that when entering a monastery complex you are entering the place where the sisters or brothers of that community live. Most monasteries have members of their community dedicated to dealing with visitors, and will often have signs out front explaining what is expected, such as respecting the dress code, not making too much noise, and not going nosing around the living quarters unaccompanied.

In both parish churches and monasteries, men and women should wear tops that cover their shoulders and are not too revealing. Men should wear trousers that come below the knee at least and women should have skirts below the knee. Often a box of skirts for covering legs and shawls for shoulders can be found at the entrance of the monastery. However, women regularly visit churches and attend services in trousers, so there will be no box of skirts at the entrance of a church. Unlike in many other Orthodox countries, it is not necessary for women to cover their heads when entering churches in Macedonia.

Most of the time you will be entering the monastery to see the church inside, but there will often be members of the community at the entrance or inside the church welcoming visitors, so feel free to ask about the residences, called *konaci*, as some might also have areas open to the public. Some of the larger monasteries even take in overnight guests. They do not charge officially, but it is customary to leave a few hundred denars as a donation and/or a packet of coffee or box of cookies. Monastic communities do not eat meat and live simply, but they often have guests who they provide with coffee and cookies so such gifts are always appreciated.

tours of Macedonia & Albania focusing on art & cultural heritage, & bespoke itineraries.

Exodus ✆020 3811 6120; e sales@exodus. co.uk; w exodus.co.uk. Offers a handful of tours to Macedonia & the Balkans, including an 8-day cycle tour through Macedonia & northern Albania.

Explore! ✆01252 883 959; e sales@explore. co.uk; w explore.co.uk. Runs several interesting tours through Bulgaria, Macedonia & Greece, focusing on ancient Macedonia & Europe's last frontier.

Intrepid ✆0808 274 5111; e ask@intrepidtravel. com; w intrepidtravel.com. Several Balkan itineraries including Macedonia.

Newex ✆01824 710 320; e contact@newex. co.uk; w newex.co.uk. The 1st tour operator outside Macedonia to provide walking holidays exclusively in Macedonia. Their self-guided 1-week hotel-to-hotel trek includes the Shar, Mavrovo &

Galičica Mountains, with your baggage shuttled ahead to the next hotel for you.

Reality & Beyond ✆01285 750 358/888; e lucy@ realityandbeyond.co.uk; w realityandbeyond.co.uk. Historian & art historians Lucy Abel Smith & Harriet Landseer provide high-quality individually tailored tours, providing exclusive insight into architecture, culture & history.

Regent Holidays ✆020 3131 4144; e regent@ regent-holidays.co.uk; w regent-holidays.co.uk. The 1st UK tour operator to branch out into the region, Regent Holidays offer several tours of Macedonia, can book you accommodation, or provide you with a tailored package.

Undiscovered Destinations ✆0191 296 2974; e travel@undiscovered-destinations.com; w undiscovered-destinations.com. Adventure travel specialists that offer a 16-day 'Hidden Europe' tour through Macedonia, Albania & Kosovo.

Monasteries in Macedonia often close their doors in the evening, but churches are always open unless they are in remote areas, in which case you may have to look around for a key tucked somewhere outside or find someone in a nearby village who has the key.

People come in and out of Macedonian churches all the time, just to light a candle or leave an offering or spend a bit of time reflecting. There is usually a small window where someone sells candles, small icons, prayer bracelets, etc. In village churches or remote locations often there is just a pile of candles on a table or window ledge and people leave money, usually 5–10MKD per candle. There may be special stands for candles or boxes with sand. People light candles in the upper parts of the stand for the living and in the under part of the stand for the dead. Smaller churches might have a separate box placed lower or to the side.

Most churches, except for very small ones, will have an icon placed on a stand in the middle. This will be either the patron saint of the church or the saint relevant to the day in the calendar. People will usually cross themselves at the entrance and then go to that icon, cross themselves and kiss the icon. They usually leave small change, banknotes or other offerings on the central icons and on other icons around the church. However, this is actually discouraged by the church and it is more appropriate to place any offerings in the slots or boxes next to the icons.

You will notice that there are no pews or rows of chairs in Macedonian churches. There may be a few around for those who need to sit, but the congregation stands for the service. It is not uncommon for people to come and go during the service, especially those with small children, so don't feel like you have to stay outside if you happen upon a service when visiting a Macedonian church. Feel free to enter and spend a bit of time listening to the choir and watching the service. Just be careful not to make too much noise or be disruptive.

If you specifically want to attend a service, they usually start at 07.30 or 08.30 on Sundays, though in monasteries they may start earlier.

USA

Kutrubes Travel ✆800 878 8566, 617 426 5668; e adventures@kutrubestravel.com; w kutrubestravel.com. Provides tours including Macedonia, & individually tailored packages (including birdwatching tours), as well as just accommodation bookings.

Serious Traveler ✆800 762 4216; e info@ serioustraveler.com; w serioustraveler.com. Offers a 13-day extension 'Wild Europe' tour through Serbia, Kosovo, Albania & Macedonia, including visits to Ohrid & Tetovo's Motley Mosque.

LOCAL TOUR OPERATORS

Macedonia's National Tourism Portal (w exploringmacedonia.com) offers thousands of ideas, links & contacts for visiting the country, including local tour operators specialising in Macedonia.

In addition to those listed below, the **Association of Tourist Guides** (Dame Gruev, Block. 3, Skopje; ✆023 118 498; e ztvmk.official@ gmail.com) can also help with guides. To arrange outdoor sports activities, see more specific details listed on page 91.

Cycle Macedonia e info@cyclemacedonia.com; w cyclemacedonia.com. Offers 8-day road cycling tours around Macedonia, covering 35–60km per day. Includes bike rental, food, accommodation & full vehicle support. Self-guided tours also available. Proving very popular.

Go Macedonia Ankarska 29A, Skopje; ✆023 104 520; w gomacedonia.com. Go Macedonia caters almost exclusively for foreign tourists. They offer themed tours – wine & countryside, adventure & recreation, history & archaeology, etc. They can also arrange group tours, make individual arrangements, & are the original Macedonian specialists in family holidays. Bike tours also available.

Macedonia Experience [119 E3] Ul Nikola Kljusev 3, Skopje; m 075 243 944; e info@macedoniaexperience.com; w macedoniaexperience.com. High-quality, personalised travel operator offering adventure sports, culinary & wine tasting tours & cultural trips.

Macedonia Holidays w macedonia-holidays. com; see ad, inside front cover. As well as tours & trips within Macedonia (& one of the few to offer tours of religious Macedonia's amazing churches, monasteries, frescoes, ikons & iconostases), Macedonia Holidays also offers combined trips to other neighbouring Balkan destinations.

Macedonia Travel [114 C4] Orce Nikolov 109/3, Skopje; ✆023 112 408; m 078 337 335/6; e info@ macedoniatravel.com; w macedoniatravel.com; see ad, page 106. Conveniently located, this company specialises in travel within Macedonia, & particularly hiking & adventure in the northwest & centre of the country, as well as food & wine itineraries. Also offers car rental & hotel bookings.

Plus Travel Skopje Angel Vinički 5a, Skopje; m 071 237 447; e info@plus-travel.mk; w plus-travel.mk; see ad, 2nd colour section. Focuses mainly on daily tours, including horseriding, kayaking & wine.

Ride MK [115 H6] Angel Dinev 3B, Skopje; ✆023 098 314; m 075 341 131; e contact@ride. mk; w ride.mk. Offers regular 8-day scheduled mountain-bike tours across Macedonia & a variety of other 8- to 10-day itineraries, or flexible non-scheduled tours if your dates don't coincide with the scheduled tours. Family bike tours available, as well as hike & bike tours, hiking-only tours visiting national parks & rural villages, & 'high octane' bike tours over 2,000m for the superfit. Full vehicle support & hotels. An awesome way to see Macedonia.

Simonium Travel [123 B3] Podgrage 76, Čaršija, Skopje; m 070 319 301; e contact@ simoniumtravel.com.mk; w simoniumtravel.com. mk. Specialises in discreet travel for the discerning within Macedonia, especially Byzantine art tours. Located in the heart of Čaršija, it is also a good little souvenir shop.

Skopje Daily Tours [123 B3] Salih Asim, Čaršija, Skopje; m 070 319 301; e info@skopjedailytours. com; w skopjedailytours.com. Full-day city tours of Skopje and trips further afield to the likes of Mount Vodno, Matka Canyon & Ohrid. Well priced. Online booking available.

Turist Bitola Krali Marko 16, 7000 Bitola; ✆047 202 777; e turist@turist.com.mk; w turist.com. mk. Has extensive experience working with foreign tour groups & agents & can organise accommodation throughout Macedonia as well as arrange trips.

Visit Macedonia [114 A5] 3b Angel Dinev 2, Skopje; ✆023 098 314; w visitmacedonia.com.mk. Good website with useful links page to help plan what you want to do in Macedonia.

VISAS Nationals from neighbouring countries, Australia, Canada, the EU, Iceland, Israel, New Zealand, Norway, Switzerland and the US, among others, do not need visas at present for stays of less than 90 days within a six-month period starting from the day you first enter the country. Nationals of Japan, Montenegro and Turkey can enter visa-free for up to 60 days in a six-month period. For those who do require visas, these can be obtained through any Macedonian embassy abroad, a full list of which is maintained at w mfa.gov.mk. For an up-to-date check on which nationals do require visas, visit w macedonia.visahq.co.uk. Visa requirements tend to change with a change of government, so keep this in mind. Your passport will need to be valid for at least six months beyond the end of your visa. If you wish to change your status in the country from one of short business trip or holiday to one of temporary residence, this can only be done back in your home country through your country's Macedonian embassy. The US Embassy in Macedonia has a good webpage on the requirements of foreign stay in Macedonia (page 74).

POLICE REGISTRATION The Law on Foreigners (at the time of writing, available in English at w refworld.org/pdfid/44b2668a4.pdf and on UNHCR's website) governs the stay of foreigners in the country. It is essentially based on the old Yugoslav law and is similar in all the former Yugoslav republics. Under Article 139 (amended in 2010 to double the time allowed to register) a foreigner staying in private accommodation must be registered with the police by their host at the latest within 48 hours of arriving in Macedonia, and within 24 hours if changing temporary address within Macedonia. If your host is unavailable for any reason, then you will need a letter of invitation to stay at their house, accompanied by a copy of their identification papers and, if they are not Macedonian, a copy of their legal basis for residency in the country (work or residency permit, diplomatic status, etc).

If you are staying in a hotel or other licensed accommodation, then the hotelier will do this for you and must register you within 12 hours of your arrival at the hotel. The hotel will fill out the necessary *potvrda* (certificate) for you and you need do nothing except provide your passport for your identification details. You are entitled to keep your section of the potvrda (normally returned with your passport at the end of your stay) and it is advisable to make sure you do keep it, because if you can't prove your official registration for any part of your stay in Macedonia then you could be subject to deportation.

While police checks are not stringently enforced, if you are not registered, the police have every right to deport you, and your host will be fined.

CUSTOMS You can bring in as much personal luggage as you like, although expensive items such as laptops, cameras, musical instruments, sporting equipment, radios and jewellery should be declared on entry if you want to leave with them without any hassles. You must declare if you bring in over €10,000 in cash (or travellers' cheques). You will need to ask for a customs declaration form to fill out, as they are not automatically given out as they are in the USA.

You may leave with more than you entered, providing you can prove that it was bought with legally exchanged money, so make sure you keep any bank or ATM receipts. Antiques and icons require a certificate of approval from the Ministry of the Interior before they can be exported.

Duty-free allowances are 1 litre of spirits; 200 cigarettes or 50 cigars or 250g of tobacco; perfume for personal use.

Practical Information RED TAPE

2

Low-cost airlines serve Skopje throughout the year, though the volume of flights increases in summer. Most regional public transport users travel by the frequent and cheap buses to Macedonia as the train is slow and decrepit. Aside from the car option, and if you are thinking of walking in, make sure you enter at a designated border crossing.

BY AIR For daily flight times in and out of Macedonia see w airports.com.mk. At the time of writing, Wizz Air is the only airline offering direct flights to Skopje International Airport from the UK (London Luton), which can cost as little as £20 one-way (though the return portion is often significantly higher and, as with all so-called budget airlines, checked-in luggage brings the price of a ticket up steeply).

In the summer a few airlines also fly direct to Ohrid's St Paul the Apostle Airport (page 202), including from London Luton, Vienna and Zurich.

Various other airlines that also operate flights to the UK fly direct to Skopje from continental Europe (for example Croatia Airlines from London via Zagreb, Swiss from London via Zurich, Alitalia via Rome) For more details about arrival at Skopje International Airport, see page 120.

The alternative to expensive flights into Skopje is to look at neighbouring airports such as Priština, Sofia or Thessaloniki for cheap deals and then take the bus.

BY RAIL (͏ 022 449 212, 023 248 701; e mztransportad@t-home.mk; w mzi.mk) There are only three international trains to Macedonia. The daily overnight service from and to Belgrade takes 9 hours, which is ludicrously slow and you would be much better taking the 4-hour bus service. The daily service from Priština leaves Skopje mid-afternoon and departs Priština early in the morning, and the 2½-hour journey spends 40 minutes at the border changing engines. The train is well used on the Kosovo side, but few use it on the 35-minute Macedonian passage. If you get stuck at Blace border on the way to Skopje, then it is only a 20-minute walk to the road crossing where you can pick up a taxi to Skopje for 900MKD. There's also a daily service to Thessaloniki (Solun), which takes 4–5 hours from Skopje.

Online train bookings are not possible at the time of writing.

BY BUS Due to the lack of cheap flights and frequent comfortable trains, Macedonia is well served by international-standard coaches, especially to and from Germany and Switzerland. See w balkanviator.com or w sas.com.mk for more-or-less complete bus listings. Destinations to and from Skopje (one-way ticket) include:

🚌 **Belgrade** 14 a day (7hrs; 1,300–1,420MKD)
🚌 **Istanbul** 3 a day (14hrs; 2,460–2,570MKD)
🚌 **Ljubljana** 5 a day (14–17hrs; 3,200MKD)
🚌 **Priština** at least 20 a day (2hrs; 340MKD)
🚌 **Sofia** 5–6 a day (5–6hrs; 980–1,040MKD)

🚌 **Thessaloniki (Solun)** 2 a day (departing Skopje at 06.00 & 17.00; 5hrs; 1,280MKD)
🚌 **Tirana** Once a day (departing Skopje at 06.00; 7hrs; 1,280MKD)
🚌 **Zagreb** 4 a day (12–14hrs; 3,200MKD)

International coaches also serve other locations in Macedonia, especially between Germany and the northwestern towns of Gostivar and Tetovo. For bus station details in Macedonia see individual chapters. Timetables and price information from some countries to Macedonia are available at w balkanviator.com. There is a left luggage service at Skopje Bus Station.

BY CAR The easiest and most convenient way to get around Macedonia is still by car (a 4x4 if you plan to go anywhere off the beaten track). But driving to Macedonia from the further reaches of Europe, especially places such as Britain and Finland, is an extremely long journey – at least three days.

If you do intend to drive from Britain, for instance, a recommended route would be to cross at Calais for a cheap, short ferry journey, drive along the roads of France, which are usually fairly empty although there are road tolls to pay (German roads are toll-free, but packed, and speed restrictions are becoming more widespread), cross the Alps at the Simplon Pass and head for Venice. From here take the overnight car ferry to Durres in Albania, or Igoumenitsa in Greece. Either journey from these ports to Skopje is arduous mountain driving (6 hours from Durres via Ohrid, or 10 hours via Bitola from Igoumenitsa), but the scenery is fantastic. The drive down through Italy, while making the ferry journey shorter, is packed with other drivers, often resulting in traffic jams in motorway scenery. For times and prices of ferries between Italy and the Balkans see **w** cemar.it.

If you're hitchhiking around the Balkans, a good place to find lifts is **w** gorivo. com.

MAPS AND TOURIST INFORMATION

TOURIST INFORMATION Tourist information centres are only found in major towns in Macedonia (Skopje, Ohrid, Bitola), although there are a number of privately run 'information centres' that are more of an outlet for local souvenirs rather than useful maps and information. In some cases you might be much better off going to a travel agency for information, especially in towns outside Skopje.

MAPS Maps of Macedonia are in a variety of formats from most bookshops and big supermarkets, such as Vero, Ramstore or Tinex. Town maps of Tetovo, Struga, Skopje, Prilep, Ohrid, Makedonski Brod, Kruševo, Dojran, Demir Kapija and Berovo are made by Trimaks (**w** 3maks.com) and available throughout Macedonia. Maps to more towns are becoming available and many can also be bought for download from Trimaks. Locally made maps of Bitola, Kratovo and Strumica are available in those places only.

Street names in Macedonia can make your stay a bit like playing hide and seek. Many streets don't have a name, but simply a number. In addition, some street names have changed at least twice since independence and the name given on the map may not correspond to the name actually signposted and used by the locals. Maršal Tito Street in Skopje, the main pedestrian street, is a case in point. On some maps of the city it is named Makedonija – and that is still what people call it on the ground.

This guide follows Macedonian common usage as much as possible and street names are in their Macedonian spelling followed by the house number. If it is a numbered street then it is given as, for example, *Ulica 000*, followed by the house number (*broj*) *br0*. Many streets are named after dates in history, so house number 60 on the street of First of May is written here as '1st Maj 60'. As if all this is not confusing enough, some buildings, especially large factories or institutions, do not have numbers at all, in which case the street name is followed by *bb*, indicating *bez broj* meaning 'without number'.

Note that some streets have been renumbered several times due to new building work; as a result several buildings have the same number or have their old number still showing!

2

Since topographical mapping was declassified, new 1:25,000 **hiking maps** of Macedonia have become available for 250MKD each. Note that these maps do not use the WGS84 military grid referencing system (MGRS), but the old Yugoslav Croatian-based referencing using the Gaus-Krüger (Krigerova) ellipsoid. The grid co-ordinates used in this guidebook are based on the old Yugoslav Croatian-based grid referencing system currently used by the new Macedonian maps. Eventually the maps will be available with WGS84 MGRS.

HEALTH *with Dr Felicity Nicholson*

IMPORTANT PHONE NUMBERS
Emergency (fire, police or ambulance) ☏112   **Police** ☏192
Ambulance ☏194   **Road help** ☏196
Fire service ☏193

BEFORE YOU GO Make sure you get **health insurance** that is valid for Macedonia before arrival, unless you are prepared to pay for any mishaps yourself. Macedonian doctors and hospitals expect to be paid in cash on the spot by foreigners seeking treatment and, once furnished with your receipt, appropriately translated, you can reclaim your money back from your insurer. Most travel agents abroad will be able to sort you out with the appropriate health insurance, and some give a good deal, combining health and travel insurance with insurance against theft. Make sure that your insurance covers you for the activities you intend to do and always declare any health issues you may have.

It is usually a good idea to take any medication you need with you rather than trying to obtain it once you arrive. Compared with some countries, **medical treatment** is cheaper in Macedonia than in, say, the US, and standards can be as good as at home. Most doctors speak English.

Common illnesses can be treated in Macedonia by the pharmacists in any local pharmacy (*apteka*). Many have English-speaking staff, and they can also advise you of the nearest family practitioner if you are in need of a doctor. If you need hospitalisation, this is best left till you get home, unless it is an emergency, in which case either call ☏194, or it may be quicker to get a taxi to take you to the nearest hospital (*bolnica*).

Vaccinations There are no vaccinations that are legally required for entry into Macedonia, but health-care practitioners will advise the following to be on the safe side: tetanus, diphtheria and polio (this comes as an all-in-one injection – Revaxis – and lasts for ten years), and hepatitis A. It is wise to visit your doctor or a travel health clinic about four to six weeks before travel. If you are going to be in the country for a long time (four weeks or more), are dealing with refugees or children or are working in a medical setting, then immunisation against hepatitis B is worth having. For hepatitis B ideally three doses of vaccine should be taken before travel. These can be given at 0, 1 and 6 months; 0, 1 and 2 months; or if time is short at 0, 7 and 21–28 days if you are 16 or over. Only Engerix B is currently licensed for the last schedule. Rabies vaccine would also be recommended as Macedonia is classified as a high-risk country. This means that potentially all mammals can carry the disease. Treatment is not always available if you have not had the pre-exposure course of three doses of the vaccine over a minimum of seven days, although a longer is preferred and requires fewer boosters.

Rabies Rabies can be carried by all warm-blooded mammals. It is not commonly reported, but Macedonia is classified as a high-risk country. It can be passed on to humans through a bite, scratch or a lick over an open wound and also through saliva getting into the eyes, nose or mouth. You must always assume any animal is rabid and seek medical help as soon as possible. It is not possible to look at an animal and know whether it has rabies as they often look quite well. Scrub the wound with soap and under a running tap or pouring water from a jug for at least 10–15 minutes. Find a reasonably clear-looking source of water but at this stage the quality of the water is not important; then pour on a strong iodine or alcohol solution or gin, whisky or rum. This helps stop the rabies virus entering the body and will guard against wound infections, including tetanus.

Pre-exposure vaccinations for rabies are ideally advised for everyone, but are particularly important if you intend to have contact with animals and/or are likely to be more than 24 hours away from medical help. Ideally three doses should be taken over four weeks, though three weeks will do if time is short. Contrary to popular belief these vaccinations are relatively painless.

If you are bitten, scratched or licked over an open wound by a sick animal, then post-exposure prophylaxis should be given as soon as possible, though it is never too late to seek help, as the incubation period for rabies can be very long. Those who have not been immunised will need a full course of injections. The vast majority of travel health advisers, including WHO, recommend rabies immunoglobulin (RIG), but this product is expensive (around US$800) and is often hard to come by – another reason why pre-exposure vaccination should be encouraged, as if you have had all three pre-exposure doses then most people will no longer need RIG, but just two further doses of modern cell-derived vaccine three days apart.

Tell the doctor if you have had pre-exposure vaccine, as this will change the treatment you receive. And remember that, if you do contract rabies, mortality is 100% and death from rabies is probably one of the worst ways to go.

Travel clinics and health information A full list of current travel clinic websites worldwide is available on w istm.org. For other journey preparation information, consult w travelhealthpro.org.uk (UK) or w wwwnc.cdc.gov/travel (US). Information about various medications may be found on w netdoctor.co.uk/travel. All advice found online should be used in conjunction with expert advice received prior to or during travel.

First-aid kit As with any travels away from your medicine cabinet at home, it is a good idea to have a small first aid pack with you. You can buy these ready-made from any good pharmacy at home, such as Boots in the UK, or Walgreens in the US, or you can just make up a small kit yourself from the following items:

- plasters/Band-Aids
- painkillers such as aspirin, paracetamol or Tylenol
- lipsalve
- sunscreen
- antiseptic cream (diluted tea-tree oil works well)
- mosquito bite cream (this should ideally contain DEET or a natural-based insect repellent containing citronella or eucalyptus)
- spare contact lenses if you are a contact lens wearer

COMMON PROBLEMS To state the absolutely obvious, it is a good idea to be fit and healthy before going on holiday! Many of us, though, have usually just raced through a work or college deadline before leaving and the time to unwind and relax is just when the common cold or stomach flu takes hold. Food hygiene standards and tap drinking water in Macedonia are safe for the average traveller. If you have never allowed your stomach to harden to foreign bacteria, then drink the ubiquitous bottled water, and avoid drinking from mountain streams and water fountains. Water fountains in towns are usually from the same source as tap water and therefore safe.

Diarrhoea Unless you are a seasoned world traveller and have a stomach like cast iron, you may get a small bout of the trots on coming into contact with new foods, water and cooking. In Macedonia this is unlikely to turn into full-blown diarrhoea requiring antibiotics to clear it up. If it does, the pharmacy can sort you out, or, if you are prone to a bit of Delhi belly, bring some suitable medication with you from home. There is good evidence that two doses of ciprofloxacin given 12 hours apart (assuming that it is not contraindicated for you) and a couple of stopping agents such as Imodium will stop about 80% of travellers' diarrhoea very quickly. Another and better option for treating travellers' diarrhoea is rifaximin. This antibiotic is not absorbed so is unlikely to give side effects. Also it does not contribute to global resistance to antibiotics, unlike ciprofloxacin. This medication is taken three times a day for three days. That aside, the most important thing is to rehydrate and replace any lost salts. This can be done by either using oral rehydrating salts or by drinking full-fat cola with a pinch of salt.

If you are particularly susceptible to travellers' diarrhoea you should always ensure that you drink bottled, boiled or filtered water and clean your teeth with the same to minimise upset stomachs. It is also wise to stay away from dairy products as they may not be pasteurised and therefore can put you at risk of TB. If you do get travellers' diarrhoea then it is important to replace not only the fluids that you have lost but also the salts.

Mosquitoes These are not prevalent in most of Macedonia as the country is so mountainous, but in the low-lying areas around Skopje and south along the Vardar, you might find one or two. You'll find many more to the north and south of Macedonia in Serbia and Greece. Malaria in Macedonia was last seen in World War I, so it is no longer necessary to take anti-malarial tablets.

Ticks While Macedonia does not report any cases of the potentially fatal viral infection tick-borne encephalitis, there will be ticks present which are best avoided. There has been an increase in Crimean Congo Haemorrhagic fever cases in Europe, outbreaks of which have caused case fatality rates of 5–40%. There is no vaccine against this disease so the best way to avoid it is by observing the following.

Always wear long-sleeved clothing, trousers tucked into boots and a hat. Ticks can drop from overhanging branches on to your head and this is particularly a problem with children. Ticks should ideally be removed as soon as possible, as leaving ticks on the body increases the chance of infection. They should be removed with special tick tweezers that can be bought in good travel shops. Failing that you can use your fingernails by grasping the tick as close to your body as possible and pulling steadily and firmly away at right angles to your skin. The tick will then come away complete as long as you do not jerk or twist. If possible douse the wound with alcohol (any spirit will do) or iodine – though not before the tick has been removed, otherwise it is likely to regurgitate into your body. Irritants (eg: Olbas oil) or lit cigarettes are to be discouraged since they can cause the ticks to regurgitate and therefore increase the risk of disease. It is best to get a travelling companion to check you for ticks, and if you are travelling with small children remember to check their heads, and particularly behind the ears. Spreading redness around the bite and/or fever and/or aching joints after a tick bite imply that you have an infection that requires antibiotic treatment, so seek medical advice.

HEALTH AND SAFETY IN THE MOUNTAINS In the mountains, health and safety go hand in hand. Although Macedonia's mountains are not very big, they are sufficiently remote, and trails sufficiently obscure, that without a good hiking map (preferably 1:25,000, 1cm = 0.25km) it's very easy to get lost. Make sure you are a proficient hiker before venturing for long hikes into the mountains here, otherwise a 2-hour walk in the park could turn into an 8-hour mountaineering ordeal. Alternatively, and preferably, go with a guide (see the box on page 96 for details).

Know the potential dangers of mountaineering and how to deal with them before you venture out on a hike, and preferably be first-aid proficient. If you've no idea what you are getting into and have come to Macedonia for the mountains, then there are safer playing grounds than these for an introduction to mountaineering, but the list of health and safety considerations below will give you an idea of what you are up against. If you get into trouble, call ☏ 192 for the police, who will be able to get the mountain rescue service out.

Your medical pack for any extended hiking trip (more than 2 hours) should contain at least the following:

- large plasters/Band-Aids and surgical gauze
- antiseptic cream and wipes
- painkillers
- crêpe bandages x 2
- surgical tape and zinc-oxide tape
- Compeed for blisters
- chlorine dioxide water purification tablets (available from any good mountaineering shop, but hard to find in Macedonia) or better still a water filtration bottle such as Aquapure which does not rely on any chemicals
- emergency blanket and inflatable splint if you are going on a long trip

Dehydration In these untamed mountainous regions, the going can get tough and, like all mountains, water can sometimes be hard to find when you need it. Bring plenty of water with you, at least a litre per hour of uphill in the summer, and especially if you don't know where your next water source will be. It is very arid here and the lack of overhead cover can cause excess sweating. Dehydration will make you tired and prone to injury, and makes some people's vision blur. If you find yourself short of water, try to conserve what you have left, and take small sips every now and again. Don't overexert yourself, and breathe through your nose rather than your mouth to stop excess moisture escaping. Keep covered to prevent excess moisture being lost in sweat.

Injury Injuries are usually caused when you are tired and/or hiking beyond your limit. It is, therefore, important to know what your limits are, and those of your travelling partners, and to recognise when it is time for a rest. Come properly equipped for the task at hand, with good hiking boots and an appropriate overcoat as a minimum. Many Macedonians wander around in flimsy, inappropriate shoes. This may suffice for a hike to a popular monument, but will get you into trouble further afield. If you do sustain an injury that would normally require stitching, then bind the wound with a large plaster or surgical tape and then secure it laterally with zinc-oxide tape.

Sunburn Do wear a hat, sunglasses and plenty of sunscreen. Use a sunscreen with an SPF of at least 15 or more and a UVA of 4 or more stars. The sun here is stronger than in northern Europe and it is easy to forget that point until it is too late. If you do get badly burnt, apply an after-sun cream or calamine lotion, cover up and don't go back out in the sun without a total sunblock. A cold wet teabag also works well for sunburn.

Sunstroke After the onset of dehydration and sunburn you are heading for heat exhaustion and then sun/heatstroke. While heatstroke can be fatal, if you recognise the early stage symptoms soon enough you should never get that far. It is usually more difficult to tell in oneself than in others, so watch your hiking partner carefully. The easiest signs to look for are muscle cramps or numbness, dimmed or blurred vision, weakness, irritability, dizziness and confusion. If any of your hiking partners are talking utter drivel (more than normal anyway), are not able to have a logical conversation with you, and particularly if they say they don't need water or to get out of the sun, then sit them down in the shade immediately, loosen any tight clothing, sprinkle water on them and fan them to cool them down. They should take regular sips of water, but not drink a pint down flat. If your hiking partner shows the above signs, and feels sick, and particularly if their skin feels hot and dry, then the body has gone into shut-down mode. They may soon fall unconscious and medical attention is required quickly. Phone ⟋194 for help.

Altitude sickness You are unlikely to suffer from altitude sickness in Macedonia, as it is difficult to gain enough height to do so. Nevertheless, altitude sickness does not discriminate, and should you decide to climb Mount Korab or Titov Vrv in one day from Skopje, no matter how young you are or how much mountaineering you have done sometime in the past, it may still hit you. The best way to avoid altitude sickness is to acclimatise. If you don't have that option open to you, and you start to feel dizzy, sick and overly short of breath, then the next best thing to do is to stop and rest. If this doesn't help then descend slowly to a lower level (500m is usually enough), and consider doing something else for the day.

Hypothermia Hypothermia occurs when the body loses heat quicker than it can make it. This is most likely to happen when the body is wet and cold, inactive, hungry and tired. Uncontrollable shivering, drowsiness and confusion are telltale first signs. If the person has stopped shivering, is physically stiff, and indifferent to their surroundings, then the body is already in shut-down mode. The person's body temperature must be raised immediately with plenty of warm, dry clothing, shelter and warm sweet drinks to increase the blood sugar level. Exercise will not help. At severe levels, skin contact with another warm body, preferably in a sleeping bag, might be required. At this point the medical services should be brought in. Do not heat the person with anything hotter than body temperature or immerse the person in hot water as this might simply cook outer extremities. Do not rub or massage the person, but warm the core of the body first.

WILD AND DEADLY NASTIES Some poisonous snakes and spiders do exist in Macedonia, such as black and brown widow spiders, and some adders and vipers. However, they do not seek out humans, so you are extremely unlikely to come across any.

You are less likely to get bitten if you wear stout shoes and long trousers when in the bush. Most snakes are harmless and even venomous species will dispense venom in only about half of their bites. If bitten, then, you are unlikely to have received venom; keeping this fact in mind may help you to stay calm. Many so-called first-aid techniques do more harm than good: cutting into the wound is harmful; tourniquets are dangerous; suction and electrical inactivation devices do not work. The only treatment is antivenom. In case of a bite that you fear may have been from a venomous snake:

- Try to keep calm – it is likely that no venom has been dispensed
- Prevent movement of the bitten limb by applying a splint
- Keep the bitten limb BELOW heart height to slow the spread of any venom
- If you have a crêpe bandage, wrap it around the whole limb (eg: all the way from the toes to the thigh), as tight as you would for a sprained ankle or a muscle pull

And remember:

- NEVER give aspirin; you may take paracetamol, which is safe
- NEVER cut or suck the wound
- DO NOT apply ice packs
- DO NOT apply potassium permanganate

If the offending snake can be captured without risk of someone else being bitten, take this to show the doctor – but beware since even a decapitated head is able to bite.

DENTAL TOURISM Dental work in Macedonia is of a very high standard and often less than half the price of private dental treatment at home. Most dentists speak English and have trained in Europe or the US. With the advent of low-cost flights to Macedonia, some dental practices are working together with tour operators to provide you not only with excellent affordable dental care but a fantastic and unique holiday experience with it. While information available in English is still limited, more is coming online. Try the following website: **w** dentaltourismmacedonia.com.

SECURITY AND SAFETY

The security situation in Macedonia has calmed down significantly since the end of the hostilities of 2001 (page 117) and foreigners have never been a target. In fact, you are likely to be safer in Macedonia than you are in most major Western cities, from both theft and terrorism.

To be on the safe side, avoid areas known to be unsafe and large public demonstrations which may get heated. The website of your embassy in Macedonia will usually carry the most up-to-date information on the security situation, and the US embassy site also has comprehensive security and safety advice on their Consular Information Sheets at w travel.state.gov. Many embassies advise their citizens to register at the embassy if they intend to stay in the country for any length of time, and to phone for the latest security advice on a particular area if they are going off the beaten track.

INTERNATIONAL TRAFFICKING OF WEAPONS, DRUGS AND PEOPLE While national crime levels are relatively low (see below), international trafficking of humans more than makes up for the deficit. The porous, forested mountain borders of Macedonia are easy trafficking routes and have long been a route for heroin and opium from Afghanistan to Europe.

Illegal wood-cutting is also a problem (and a threat to animal habitat) especially when Kosovo continues to have an abysmal supply of electricity. If you are hiking up in the border areas, the chances of you stumbling across illegal trade are very slim. Always bring ID with you, however, just in case, and looking very obviously like a hiker will ensure that any smugglers will keep out of your way.

Illegal trade in weapons is much less of a problem here than trafficking in people. The government's efforts to combat trafficking have varied over the years, and in 2018 Macedonia remained on a Tier 2 grading by the US government in its annual Trafficking in Persons (TIP) report (w state.gov/g/tip). Such a grading highlights continued poor prosecution of perpetrators, and decreased support for victims, showing an overall decreased effort to combat trafficking. Macedonia is both a transit country and an end user of trafficked people. Most are women who come from countries even poorer than Macedonia and, tempted by the lure of easy money abroad waitressing or as a domestic help, they are often beaten, raped and forced into prostitution and modern slavery. Victims include minors who believe they are going for better schooling, and the 2018 TIP report for Macedonia acknowledges that Roma children continue to be forced into begging. While numbers of foreign women trafficked to or through Macedonia seem to have decreased, numbers of Macedonian women who are trafficked internally within Macedonia are on the increase. According to the Global Slavery Index, some 18,000 people in Macedonia (just less than 1% of the population) live in slavery.

Due to the difficulty in policing this issue, foreign visitors who bring their children with them are advised to bring the appropriate documents proving the legal relationship of parent and child. A passport may suffice, but if you have separate passports with different names then you may want to bring additional proof. Although traffickers don't usually take children so blatantly over an established border crossing, border police may suspect the worst. The same goes for young couples entering Macedonia. If you would like to help with the anti-trafficking effort here in Macedonia see the *Travelling positively* section at the end of this chapter, page 104.

PERSONAL SAFETY In many respects crime is lower in Macedonia than in many countries in western Europe or in America. Nevertheless, you should take the usual precautions: this is not a country where you can leave your house unlocked when you are out, and you should keep your valuables close if you are going through a crowded place or travelling by public transport.

If you come to live in Macedonia as part of the international community then, as with a move into any new property, you may want to make sure the locks are changed in case former tenants have a key that falls into the wrong hands. Car theft is generally not a problem in Macedonia.

If you get stopped or detained by the police, for any reason whatsoever, remember to stay calm and polite. In any nation, smart-alec wisecracks, sarcasm, anger and lack of co-operation are seen as suspicious behaviour. You do have the right to ask why you have been stopped or detained, however, and, of course, the right to legal representation once you have been charged. You can be detained for up to 24 hours without being charged, by which time your embassy or consulate should have been informed of your detention. You also have the right to be spoken to in a language that you understand, so you might be better off waiting for an interpreter or a policeman who speaks your language rather than digging yourself into a bigger hole. The interpreter may take a while getting to you!

DRIVING AND ROAD SAFETY Speed restrictions are enforced here. Speed limits are posted and are generally 50km/h in built-up areas, 80km/h outside built-up areas, 100km/h on dual carriageways and 120km/h on motorways. Seat belts must be worn in the front and back seats of a car if fitted. Children under the age of 12 are not allowed in the front of cars, but there is no requirement for child seats in the back. The blood alcohol limit is 0.05% (0% for newly licensed drivers, who may not drive between 23.00 and 05.00 unless accompanied by a driver older than 25). Visibly drunk people may not travel in the front of a vehicle. Dipped headlights during the day are compulsory. Crash helmets are compulsory for motorcyclists. For more on Macedonian driving regulations and conditions, visit w theaa.com and search for Macedonia.

Macedonian lane discipline and driving etiquette has improved over its poor record a decade ago. Nonetheless, you would do well to be wary. Don't be surprised to find vehicles without headlights at night, extremely little use of indicators, lorries backing down the road when they have missed their exit, parking on the pavement and two cars stopped in the middle of the road for a chat. As a pedestrian, you'll also have to keep your wits about you when crossing the road, as drivers pay scant attention to zebra crossings.

If you get into an accident or breakdown, the AutoMobile Association of Macedonia (℄196; w amsm.com.mk) can assist, while AMSM Services (℄02 15 555; w amsmspi.mk) also gives good information on roadworks and traffic congestion, including at the border crossings.

If you are fined by the police, remember to make sure you are given a ticket/receipt for your fine so that you can be certain the money is going into the government coffers not the policeman's pocket. Fines can be paid at a post office or bank and are reduced by 50% if paid within eight days.

PERSONAL HARASSMENT Don't expect to always be left alone as you wander around Macedonia looking at antique treasures and antiquated institutions. You'll likely encounter harassment from begging Roma (page 41) who may follow you around for up to 15 minutes quietly begging for money, and may even get angry, though rarely physically violent, if you don't give them money. Macedonians get this treatment too, and the best thing to do is not to give them any (giving money tends to encourage more begging); you can try what most Macedonians do, which is to say sternly '*begaj, odmah*', meaning 'scram, immediately'. If this does not succeed then dive into a café where the waiter will encourage anyone begging to move on.

DOGS There are a lot of stray dogs in Macedonia, and while they don't tend to be savage, or even a nuisance, some of them do carry disease and infections, so don't approach them, or take them in. Rabies is not common here, although Macedonia is classed as a high-risk country so pre-exposure vaccinations for rabies are advised (page 69). Leishmaniasis is more prevalent, transferred by sandflies from host to new prey, and can be deadly if left untreated. Dogs with a mangy appearance and losing clumps of hair could have the disease.

WOMEN TRAVELLERS Sexual harassment is not usually a problem in Macedonia, and women here dress as skimpily as in the West. Macedonians think it is a bit strange, however, to travel on your own, especially as a woman; and keeping in mind the high level of trafficking in women which has gone on in Macedonia in the past (page 74), you'd better have your wits about you if you travel alone as a woman in out-of-the-way places after dark. There are no obvious red-light districts in Macedonia, as prostitution is illegal, but there are bars and hotels and parts of towns that service this trade.

As with anywhere in the rest of the world, if you are a single female driver and an unmarked police car indicates that you should pull over, you should turn on your hazard lights and drive slowly to a public area such as a petrol station before stopping. You could also phone the police on ☏192 to check if the police car is genuine.

GAY TRAVELLERS The gay and lesbian scene is very limited in Macedonia and it would be considered most strange, if not offensive, for same-sex couples to walk hand in hand down the street, never mind kiss in public. Booking into a hotel would not be considered so strange unless you insisted on a '*francuski krevet*' (double bed), as double rooms normally come with twin beds.

When being gay was decriminalised in 1996, the gay community in Macedonia cautiously took steps to promote greater acceptance. That trend has ground to a halt over more recent years, however, and LGBT United Macedonia (w lgbtunited.org) is currently one of the only organisations in Skopje working on gay and lesbian issues. There are currently no venues openly welcoming gays and lesbians in Macedonia, although private parties in some public venues do take place.

TRAVELLING WITH A DISABILITY Disabled travel in Macedonia is very challenging. Pavements are uneven and often completely blocked by parked cars. Wheelchair accessibility is poor even in Skopje. Most big shopping malls, museums and many government buildings have wheelchair ramps. Some buses in Skopje operate wheelchair lifts, but at the time of writing it's not known whether such buses will be available in other towns around the country. Local municipalities are working hard, however, to catch up to ensure better access for wheelchair users. The Holiday Inn and Aleksandar Palace in Skopje, and the Ramada Plaza outside Gevgelija, offer rooms equipped for wheelchair accessibility.

For the visually impaired, most of the traffic lights are accompanied by a fast beep for red and slower beep for green. Don't be afraid to ask for help – many Macedonians, at least in Skopje, speak English. The staff in some SP (СП) food stores are trained in sign language but, of course, this won't be helpful if you're not familiar with Macedonian sign language.

The UK's **gov.uk** website (w gov.uk/guidance/foreign-travel-for-disabled-people) provides general advice and practical information for travellers with disabilities preparing for overseas travel. **Accessible Journeys** (w disabilitytravel.com) is a comprehensive US site written by wheelchair users who have been researching wheelchair-accessible travel full-time since 1985. There are many tips and useful contacts (including lists of travel agents on request) for slow walkers, wheelchair travellers and their families, plus informative articles, including pieces on disabled travelling worldwide. The company also organises group tours. **Global Access News** (w globalaccessnews.com/index.htm) provides general travel information, reviews and tips for travelling with a disability. The **Society for Accessible Travel and Hospitality** (w sath.org) also provides some general information.

Specialist UK-based tour operator **Disabled Holidays** (w disabledholidays.com) offers trips to and advice for Macedonia.

TRAVELLING WITH CHILDREN *Gerard and Sonja McGurk*

Visitors to Macedonia will quickly realise that the country is very accommodating towards children. Macedonian attitudes towards children are tolerant and relaxed and Macedonians themselves are exceptionally welcoming to families with children. Safety standards will not be up to US litigious culture, but costs are low, making a family holiday less of a shock to your wallet.

Eating out Most restaurants and cafés are happy for children to run around unsupervised. Some restaurants with larger space have dedicated play areas for children outside, and some inside, especially in family-run hotel restaurants. Cafés located along Skopje's riverside quay (*kejot* in Macedonian) have small play areas for children, allowing parents and guardians a relaxing respite.

Breastfeeding There is traditionally a positive attitude in Macedonia towards breastfeeding. While it's not too common in public, it is not discouraged or frowned upon. You may prefer, therefore, to be discreet, and cover up with a light scarf.

Baby changing facilities Skopje has an increasing number of locations that cater for children of young ages. Public toilets with baby changing facilities are non-existent and should generally be avoided for their lack of hygiene. It is perfectly acceptable, *in extremis*, to make use of nearby restaurants or cafés, which in larger towns will have clean toilet facilities. The further you go from Skopje, the less likely you will be to find bespoke child changing facilities. Check on arrival if you need to make use of such facilities.

Supplies Most of the larger, more well-known supermarkets (Vero, Ramstore, Reptil or Tinex) and pharmacies across Macedonia will have well-stocked supplies of kid-friendly products, milk formula, creams, wipes, nappies (including pull-ups) and medicines for young children. Some of the products' names may not be the same as at home.

Getting about Transporting children around Macedonia can still be a challenge. Access ramps for buggies are rare. The arrival of new, modern buses in Skopje makes it easier for families travelling with buggies to move around the capital city. Taxi drivers can be found in most towns and cities and will usually help with putting buggies in the car – as ever it depends on their general mood at the time.

Hotels Many of the smaller family-run hotels listed in this guide have three- or four-bed rooms, so ask at the time of booking whether an extra bed can be added for the duration of your stay. Some hotels will make every effort to help out by putting a small camp bed into a room if given some notice, while larger hotels usually have suites with pull-out sofas. Children under five can often stay free if using your bed, and under 12s might be half price. It's worth checking the hotel website for these offers or to ask in advance.

2

Recommended sites and activities *Groteka* (children's play area) are common across the country and they're available for private party bookings or to simply take your younger children to run off their excess energies. For details of children's activities in Skopje, see page 136, while other family-friendly sites include: Aquapark at Probištip (page 334); Etno Selo Timčevski in Kumanovo (page 324); Park Ginovci near Kriva Palanka (page 328); Ohrid Luna Park (page 215); Berovo for easy hiking and outdoor activities (page 308).

WHAT TO TAKE

CLOTHING Unless you know you are staying only in Skopje and Ohrid in the summer, then bring an overcoat or jacket, and it is cold enough for a fleece in the mountains no matter what time of year. Casual dress is the norm on the streets. Businessmen tend to wear short-sleeved shirts in the summer, and you may wish to pack such a shirt or polo shirt if you intend to go to one of the nicer restaurants in Skopje. Nightclubs here don't have a dress code, but some churches and mosques do (see box, page 62). In spring and autumn it may be very warm during the day, but in the evening it can also get quite cold, and some state-run hotels may have not yet turned on or already turned off the central heating, so bring warm enough clothes.

PLUGS, ADAPTORS AND CONVERTERS Macedonia's electricity is 220 volts and uses two types of plug, both with the same two round pins commonly used in northern Europe. Plug casings come in the round-case variant as well as the six-sided flat-case variant.

There are a number of great travel adaptors available now that take a multiple choice of plugs and give multiple options in pins. If you are coming from North America and wish to bring American electrical appliances with you, then you can also purchase a power voltage converter which will convert the 220 volts of European electricity into 110 volts for your appliance.

Bring a universal sink plug, especially if staying in lower-end accommodation.

TOILETRIES AND MEDICINES You can buy all the basics in Macedonia, although if you are coming here to live for a while you may wish to bring your favourite face cream or aftershave lotion. Contact lens solutions are expensive here, and contact lenses can take a while to order, so bring plenty with you. Always bring spare glasses if you wear them; it is a nightmare anywhere in the world if you break your only pair.

Bring clothes washing powder (unless you want to buy a large tub in the supermarket here) as launderettes are almost impossible to find, although there are dry cleaners. The Western four- and five-star hotels have a laundry service. A basic first-aid pack (page 69) is also useful.

DOCUMENTS Obviously a passport, with visa if required, ticket and money (page 79) are essential. If you are travelling with children then some sort of proof that you are their legal guardian is advisable to stop a potentially harrowing ordeal at the border when police might think you are trafficking children. If you are bringing your own car, then make sure you have the right insurance. The international blue or green card insurance, which does not have Macedonia (MK) or any other countries you want to visit or travel through struck off, is valid here. A photo ID driving licence is required here, for both hiring and driving a car.

GIFTS It is always a good idea to bring family photographs and postcards of your home town with you on holiday. They make good talking points and you can give the postcards out as a small gift. If you are invited into a Macedonian home, you may be given sweet syruped preserved fruits as a welcome. It is also a good idea to give something in return, and sweets from your home country are an ideal gift. Note that Macedonians can get all the German chocolates and many others besides, and anyway chocolate is not a good thing to bring in the summer as it will melt. More permanent small souvenirs are ideal.

For an idea of gifts to bring back from Macedonia see page 52.

SPORTS GEAR Light sports shoes or open-toed hiking sandals are fine for sightseeing or a short hike to a popular monument, but anything more arduous requires suitable hiking boots. A long pair of hiking trousers is useful, as the paths here are often overgrown and prickly, thorny or full of nettles. Dock leaves can be a remedy for nettle stings but unlike in the UK they rarely grow next to nettles here. A hiking pole (or a stick picked up at the beginning of your hike) is a useful nettle and bramble whacker and helps to scare away snakes and dogs. Hiking without a stick is bound to elicit the comment from locals who meet you on your hike that you should have one. It is easier to get sports and hiking gear here than it used to be (but it will be more expensive than the outlets at home). It does get very hot in the summer, so bring enough changes of clothing so that you can swap out of your sweaty T-shirt when you get to the top of your hike. This helps to prevent you from getting a chill, which can easily happen when you reach the colder climes of the summit.

Bring a good daypack and your favourite water container: wide-mouthed Nalgene bottles are far easier to fill from a mountain stream than re-used plastic water bottles. The Camelbak (w international.camelbak.com) is very useful in this arid climate, as are Platypus (w platy.com) collapsible 'bladder'-style bottles. You'll need to bring your own climbing boots if you intend to do any rock climbing, but the rest you can hire here from one of the clubs. Ski hire, including carving skis, is reasonable, but telemark skis, *skis de randonnée* or cross-country skis are seldom available to hire.

CAMPING There are no dedicated base-camp stores here, so you'll need to bring outdoor accessories with you. There is only one type of bottled stove fuel here, and it is not the butane/propane self-sealing screw-on Coleman type, so you'll either need to bring plenty of canisters (and most airlines won't let you bring them any more) or buy one of the local stoves, which you can find in any outdoor market. Alternatively, bring an all-purpose fuel stove and buy petrol.

MONEY AND BUDGETING

The Macedonian denar (MKD) has been pegged to the euro since 1998, and is therefore very stable.

It comes in 10, 50, 100, 500, 1,000, 2,000 and 5,000 notes, although you'll often find the 1,000 and 2,000 denar note hard to change, and the 5,000MKD note usually stays firmly on the cashier's side of the bank counter. Macedonian shops never seem to have much change, so hoard your small notes, and change large notes whenever you can. Coins come in one, two, five, ten and 50 denar.

There are no money changers on the street here, so money is either changed in banks or in the many legal money-changing booths in the main towns. Assuming you have a widely recognised debit card or credit card (ideally Visa or MasterCard)

2

then you'll find lots of cash machines available all over Macedonia, although not all accept international credit cards, so look out for the Visa/MasterCard and other labels indicating that they can do international transactions. You can change money at the airport both before you exit the arrivals lounge and in the departure hall. Remember to phone your bank to let them know where you are travelling and when, so that they don't block your bank card the first time you use it abroad!

Euros are the foreign currency of choice here. All the main hotels, restaurants and even a lot of the bed and breakfasts, especially in Skopje and Ohrid, will accept euros, although they may not always be able to give you all the right change in euros.

BUDGETING On the most meagre of budgets, staying in local rooms, at monasteries, mountain huts and campsites, buying from the market or *kebapči* stalls, and using public transport, you could manage on around €15 a day, excluding your ticket to Macedonia. Trains are cheaper than buses, but there are few trains. Most museums in Skopje and a lot of the churches in Ohrid charge a 100MKD entrance fee, but many things are also free. Hiking in Macedonia's beautiful mountains and national parks doesn't yet require an entrance fee, but wild camping is forbidden.

Some €25 a day would just about bring you into the bed and breakfast bracket and it is hard to pay more than €10 for a meal, except in Skopje. At the other end of the scale you would be hard pressed to spend €350 a day here even if you were staying at the Aleksandar Palace Hotel in Skopje for your entire trip and hiring a 4x4 vehicle. Macedonia's local gifts (woodcarvings, Ohrid pearls, filigree, embroidered linen) are not all that cheap by comparison, and buying these items could deprive you of several hundred more euros.

At the time of writing these are shop prices for:

1½ litres water	25–40MKD
½ litre beer	35–40MKD
loaf of bread	30MKD
street snack	45–60MKD
1 litre milk	50MKD
postcard	50MKD
T-shirt	250MKD
1 litre petrol	72MKD

GETTING AROUND

BY BUS Buses cover all main routes and are the preferred mode of transport for Macedonians because they're frequent and cheap, despite the fact that they are not air conditioned and do sometimes break down. Few of them have on-board toilet facilities either, so you may have to wait for the toilet break along the road. For more on bus times and prices, see individual towns in the following chapters, or check the following searchable links: w mktransport.mk/en and w sas.com.mk/en/VozenRed.aspx.

BY RAIL There are fairly limited options available for travel by train and the number of services has decreased in recent years as most people prefer to use buses, which are faster and leave more regularly. The most important lines run from Skopje to Kičevo via Tetovo and Gostivar (but not Mavrovo and Debar), from Skopje to Bitola via a scenic route through Veles and Prilep, from Skopje to Kumanovo, and from Skopje to Gevgelija via Veles and Demir Kapija. Details of current services are included under the relevant sections in the regional guide, and up-to-date timetables can usually be obtained at w mzt.mk. Fares are very cheap; the maximum one could pay for a train ride anywhere in Macedonia would still be under 500MKD for a Skopje–Bitola single ticket.

BY CAR Macedonia's roads are currently undergoing a facelift and driving around the country is now a joy, and in fact highly recommended. If you love driving and yearn for the open road with uncluttered vistas and little in your way except for the odd turtle/tortoise or a few goats, then Macedonia is the place to drive. See the section on page 75 for tips on driving in Macedonia, especially if you are not used to driving on the right-hand side of the road.

There are many places to hire clean, reliable, modern cars in Skopje and other big cities, as well as at the airport. **Setkom** (📞 023 298 392; e 1990@t-home.mk; w setkom-rent.com.mk) in the Hotel Continental in Skopje rent out a Kia Rio for as little as €27 per day for a two-week period, making them the cheapest place in Macedonia for car hire; 4x4 vehicles are also available. For road distances, see the box on page 82. You'll pay about 72MKD per litre for unleaded petrol in Macedonia, and about 62MKD per litre for diesel.

Car-hire agencies
Avis 📞 023 222 046; w avis.com.mk
Budget w budget.mk
Europcar 📞 023 091 141; w europcar.com.mk

Hertz 📞 023 134 391; w hertz.mk
Setkom 📞 023 298 392; w setkom-rent.com.mk
Sixt 📞 023 06 4666; m 075 448 902; w sixt.com

Road tolls (Peage, Патарина) Tolls operate on the highways, of which there are currently only two in Macedonia: north–south between Blace and Gevgelija (minus the single-lane carriageway through Demir Kapija); and east–west between Kumanovo and Tetovo. Prices are posted at the entrance to the toll, and range from between 30MKD (eg: from the airport to Skopje) up to 120MKD (for the longest section of road) for a car without a trailer. Payment is accepted only in cash, in denar, and it's rare for a toll both to be able to change 1,000MKD, so make sure you have plenty of small change on you.

BY TAXI All taxis now have a minimum fare of 40MKD (50MKD in Ohrid) with a 30MKD/km and 5MKD/minute tariff (40MKD/km and 5MKD/minute in Skopje). It is difficult to take even a short taxi ride in Skopje now for less than 100MKD. Outside Skopje, taxis are still a quick and cheap way to get around town and to places further afield. All official taxis should be metered and carry a taxi sign on the roof of the car. When phoning for a taxi from a mobile phone always add the local prefix before the four- or five-digit taxi number (eg: 📞 02 15157 to call Lotus Transport in Skopje).

Most of the longer journeys outside of the main towns have a fixed price and drivers will often refer to a printed list provided by their company. Make sure you agree the price before taking a longer journey so that you run less risk of being overcharged. For instance, the posted price for a trip from Skopje Airport to the centre of town is 1,220MKD, but most drivers charge 1,500MKD. If you book with a taxi firm in advance they can send a taxi to the airport to bring you into the centre for only 900MKD. They will usually run the meter, then stop the car at the 900MKD point to turn off the meter and continue the journey unmetered.

If you are going to a remote part of town, there's quite a high chance that the taxi driver taking you there will not know where it is, so you may wish to ask a

```
Blace
 70 Tabanovce
187 166 Delčevo
188 183 142 Dojran
179 174 150  38 Bogorodica
208 204 259 198 189 Medzitilija
202 237 330 268 259 111 Kafasan
178 155  44  98 106 248 318 Berovo
183 181 239 177 168  16  92 227 Bitola
156 177 243 181 170  91  99 226  78 M.Brod
175 171 146  34   4 185 258 102 166 166 Gevgelija
 86 117 246 248 229 138 119 240 124  75 225 Gostivar
150 183 312 291 282 150  65 300 134 115 278  68 Debar
178 155  11 131 239 248 319  35 228 232 137 230 297 Delčevo
122 118 161  94  79 110 183 138  90  86  75 167 202 150 Kavadarci
131 162 263 209 191  91  73 255  78  25 187  46  89 252 111 Kičevo
132 102  64 146 149 196 278  52 178 178 145 180 245  53  90 222 Kočani
121  70 162 205 212 262 286 151 241 227 208 166 234 151 172 211  99
115  63 118 168 174 212 280 107 196 197 170 160 224 107 137 205  55
178 173 230 174 165  65 166 218  52  55 161 140 154 219  81  62 174
 62  10 156 176 170 189 227 139 176 162 166 107 172 145 113 152  92
111 107 143  82  68 121 195 127 100  98  64 156 214 132  10 201  80
193 224 305 249 194  79  28 293  56  86 190 107  66 294 155  61 250
142 140 199 143 128  61 134 187  41  37 125 108 153 188  49  62 141
142 112 124  80  94 166 244  82 147 147  90 177 253 113  49 232  66
218 213 267 214 232  44  63 255  30 108 228 142 102 256 120  96 215
102  54 118 138 147 162 267 107 149 149 143 147 210 107  82 192  49
 22  49 179 171 162 182 187 163 176 137 160  67 134 168 105 112 115
193 224 317 264 249  92  13 305  79  86 245 106  52 306 170  60 265
171 141  95  51  55 188 268  54 175 173  51 216 281  85  82 261  98
 61  92 221 223 204 162 145 217 149  99 200  24  94 210 147  70 157
 70  65 120 124 110 133 203 111 120 116 106 110 184 109  52 155  63
108  75  94 109 122 163 243  83 150 155 118 157 219  83  63 181  32
```

few drivers until you get one who knows, or make him (there are extremely few female taxi drivers) phone into his radio centre so that they can give him directions. Otherwise they may drive around for a while and charge you the extra time and fuel.

A good, clean and reliable taxi firm, based in Skopje, who can drive you or transport personal items (including pets) on your behalf anywhere in Macedonia is **Lotus Transport** (15157 for taxis in Skopje or 023 109 116 for other services). If a taxi number becomes defunct, check w infotaxi.org for the most up-to-date information.

BY BICYCLE Biking tours are a great way to get around Macedonia, but you do need to be fit as it is a hilly little country. For some web accounts of unguided cycle tours through Macedonia see page 64.

K.Palanka															
44	**Kratovo**														
220	190	**Kruševo**													
60	53	162	**Kumanovo**												
157	103	93	97	**Negotino**											
273	266	138	214	167	**Ohrid**										
195	160	32	130	61	106	**Prilep**									
132	88	141	102	37	211	110	**Radoviš**								
256	231	103	206	132	35	71	181	**Resen**							
103	57	144	44	73	213	112	58	183	**Sv.Nikola**						
99	93	159	39	95	174	131	125	198	80	**Skopje**					
273	267	153	214	182	15	121	231	50	254	174	**Struga**				
156	117	166	131	75	237	134	29	205	87	149	255	**Strumica**			
141	135	164	82	136	132	132	167	184	122	44	132	196	**Tetovo**		
116	86	111	55	41	180	79	77	145	33	50	190	113	85	**Veles**	
90	52	151	66	51	215	119	37	180	25	86	230	66	128	40	**Štip**

To hire a bike, or to join or arrange a bike tour in Macedonia, see page 64, and the biking section on page 91.

ACCOMMODATION

Accommodation in Macedonia is generally inexpensive, but the standard you receive for the price you pay is a bit of a lottery.

HOTELS Many state-run hotels are now being privatised and with that will hopefully come some improvements. Between late spring and early autumn (15 April to 15 October), state-run hotels may get a bit cold as the heating is turned off during this period.

Family-run or boutique hotels are excellent value for money and are increasing in number. Many petrol stations have small motels on the side and as most of them have been built fairly recently they are usually clean and tidy if basic, but reasonably priced. Hotel prices usually include breakfast, although only the top-notch hotels will manage to serve a buffet breakfast or provide room service.

In this guide, unless otherwise stated, all rooms come with an en-suite bathroom, free Wi-Fi and breakfast, and all prices are per room per night. If you ask for a room for two people you will usually get a twin room with two single beds. To get a room with a double bed in, you must ask for '*soba co eden krevet za dvojica*' (a room with one bed for two people), sometimes called a '*francuski krevet*' meaning 'French bed'. Even if you ask for this, don't be surprised in cheaper and older accommodation if you end up with a twin room in which the hotel staff expect you to simply push the beds together. Or they may give you the *apartman*, which is the Macedonian equivalent of the honeymoon suite and usually much more expensive. Rooms with three single beds are also quite common.

Top 10 The following is a list of recommended 'boutique-type' hotels, chosen in part for their strategic locations around the country so that you can visit all of Macedonia in comfortable value-for-money accommodation, but also in part for their peculiarities. Anticlockwise around the country starting in the capital, they are:

🏠 **Rose Diplomatique** Skopje. Small, beautiful, near the centre of town. Page 125.

🏠 **Bistra** Mavrovo. A fireside over the lake, by the ski resort. Page 180.

🏠 **Kalin Hotel** Lazaropole. Beautifully refurbished, beautiful setting. Page 182.

🏠 **Kutmičevica** Vevčani. Small & quaint in the Republic of Vevčani. Page 232.

🏠 **Villa Jovan** Ohrid. A genuine Ohrid-style house. Page 206.

🏠 **Hotel Teatar** Bitola. Page 241.

🏠 **Podgorski An** Kolešino (near Strumica). Out of the way but worth it. Page 320.

🏠 **Popova Kula Winery** Demir Kapija. Fine wine & dining overlooking the vineyards. Page 287.

🏠 **Etno Selo Timčevski** Kumanovo. Traditional yet modern. Page 324.

🏠 **Ethno House Shancheva** Kratovo. Family-run old house in a historic town. Page 330.

BED AND BREAKFASTS The collapse of the Yugoslav economy and the 2001 conflict in Macedonia all but killed off the thriving bed and breakfast scene in Macedonia, but it has made a real comeback in recent years, especially but not exclusively in Ohrid. Many of the best choices are listed in this book, but you could also browse online booking sites such as Airbnb and booking.com for more and newer options. The nascent tourist industry in Macedonia is also trying to encourage this sector. Sometimes the bed comes without breakfast, so make sure you ask what your options are. Bed and breakfast usually starts at about €10–15 per night.

SELF-CATERING ACCOMMODATION There is actually quite a lot of this in Macedonia as it is popular with locals, but the properties are not well advertised in English. Some private accommodation (ie: self-catering) is listed at w hotels.exploringmacedonia. com and local tour operators listed in this book will also have some contacts.

MONASTERIES Monasteries are excellent value for money, even if you are not on a shoestring budget. As most of them were revived fairly recently, accommodation in their new inns is generally better than in most state-run hotels and half the price. Prices range from about 300MKD for a bed in the old quarters with shared bathroom, to 800MKD for a bed in an en-suite room in the new quarters. The

Based on a double room per night.

Exclusive	$$$$$	€136+; 8,500MKD+
Upmarket	$$$$	€76–135; 4,500–8,500MKD
Mid-range	$$$	€38–75; 2,500–4,500MKD
Budget	$$	€18–37; 1,200–2,500MKD
Shoestring	$	<€18; <1,200MKD

monasteries don't usually have a restaurant attached but, as they are remote, they usually have cooking facilities available to guests.

The catch with staying in the monasteries is that they are not always very convenient to book into and, as they are popular with Macedonians, they are often booked up quite early. Very few of the staff/monks/nuns in them speak any English so you may need to get a Macedonian friend to help you, or a tour operator. If you want to try turning up without a booking, then aim to get there before 17.00 otherwise the inn staff may have gone home already, as they usually only stay around until all the pre-booked guests have arrived. Finally, soon after you arrive, you will need to get a registration card from the inn staff and go and register yourself at the local police station. Unlike in hotels, the inn staff will not do this for you. Some monasteries also expect you to attend a church service if you are staying the night.

CAMPING Yugoslav-style camping is not always public transport friendly as people usually come in their car, hence why they are called *autocamps*. Such campsites are often large, full of old caravans, and not always scrupulously clean. Facilities and amenities, such as showering blocks and shops, are also not good or nearby. They are cheap, however, and 500MKD will usually get you a tent space for four plus your car. Tourism tax is an additional 40MKD per person.

Strictly speaking, wild camping is illegal but many Macedonians do it, especially at a local festival or event. If you are going to camp wild, then please take away all your rubbish and leave the place in a good condition.

MOUNTAIN HUTS Most of the 30 mountain huts in Macedonia are covered on page 92. They cost about 300MKD for a bed with bedding. It is best to phone ahead (Macedonian usually required) as most of the huts are not permanently staffed, or go with one of the many hiking and mountaineering clubs. The huts rarely provide food, so you will need to bring all your provisions, but there is always plenty of water.

BACKPACKER HOSTELS A number of friendly, efficient and affordable private hostels are available in Skopje, and there are also a few in Ohrid, and one each in Bitola and Mavrovo National Park. Details are included in the regional listings elsewhere in this guide. Most can be booked directly or through w hostelworld. com/hostels/Macedonia.

EATING AND DRINKING

FOOD Macedonian cuisine combines simple, healthy, Mediterranean cooking with centuries of spicy Ottoman influence. It is a celebration of fresh, organic, small-scale produce, and its wine is traditionally made with no sulphites. Summer markets teem with good local fruit and vegetables, while the winter holds crisp pickles (*turšija*) and jars of tasty red pepper spreads. Restaurants are getting better at offering some of the delicious *domašni* (home-style) dishes, but outside the main towns simple restaurants might only serve grilled chicken breast or pork chops and a few basic side dishes. Like most of continental Europe, Macedonians have a tradition of going out to eat, and with their children, so you'll find many places (fewer in Skopje) are very child friendly.

Macedonian **meze** (from the Turkish, and ultimately Persian *maze*; also known as *ordever*, literally 'hors d'oeuvre') are the best-kept secret of Macedonian cuisine. Usually served at the start of a banquet, meze are so tasty and varied that they can make a whole meal on their own. The Macedonian meze are a variety of cold 'creamed' vegetable spreads, initially cooked till soft and then hand blended with herbs and spices, onions and garlic, and doused with not too much oil. The most common are *ajvar* (see below), *pindžur* (roasted aubergine and peppers), *tarator* (yoghurt, cucumber, walnuts and garlic), *kajmak* (a type of clotted cream, often mixed with hot chillies and potatoes), egg and mushroom, and sweet grilled red peppers doused in garlic and oil (the latter usually only available in late summer). Eaten with pitta bread, *sarma* (stuffed vine leaves), local cured ham, Parmesan and a strong local drink such as *mastika* or *rakija*, they are a real treat.

The most famous of these meze is **ajvar**, made every autumn when red peppers are at their most abundant. The best, of course, is homemade (*domašni*). To be invited into a Macedonian home to make ajvar is quite a privilege (some say it is like being offered the possibility of citizenship), and will give you an idea of the meticulous preparation that must go into this Macedonian speciality. Without giving away the secret recipe, in essence the peppers must be softened to remove their skins and then simmered for hours, while stirred constantly, so that the peppers plus other added ingredients become a rough paste. The prepared ajvar is then sealed in jars for use throughout the coming year till the next pepper harvest. Macedonians will make ajvar by the vat load, and family members will often come home from distant lands in order to partake in the occasion.

The main fare of any Macedonian meal is either meat or freshwater fish. **Lamb** is the most expensive and therefore not often served in cheaper restaurants. It comes roasted either in the oven or on a spit, and served in a big chunk on your plate, usually without rosemary, never mind mint. Otherwise the staple meat dish for most Macedonians is **skara**: plain grilled pork or chicken, usually salted and basted. Skara is so popular that you can buy it from street stalls by the kilo! Veal (*teleško meso*), beef, eel (*jagula*), stroganoff, thinly sliced garlic liver (*džigr*), schnitzel, fresh pork ribs (*svježe rebra*), pork chops (*kremenadle*) and skewered kebabs (*ražnič*) are also prolific. *Kebapči* are an extremely popular form of skara, a Balkan speciality of small sausage-shaped burger meat, well seasoned and very tasty with a beer and some good bread. Other popular traditional meat dishes are stuffed peppers, pork knee-joint and *selsko meso* (village meat), which is a stew of different meats and sausages in an earthenware pot. *Makedonsko meso* is a variation of this with Macedonia's famous capsicum peppers.

Freshwater fish, either trout or carp (*krap* in Macedonian), is abundant in Macedonia. Ohrid is most famous for its *letnica* and *belvica* trout, and Dojran for its native carp. These particular fish varieties are peculiar to the lakes and cannot be found outside Macedonia, and for this reason (among others) Ohrid is protected under UNESCO. Sadly, Ohrid trout, which has been caught in the past at over 20kg in weight, has been overfished and this is not helped on the Albanian side of the

Based on the average price of a main course.

Expensive	$$$$$	€15+; 1,000+MKD
Above average	$$$$	€8–15; 500–1,000MKD
Mid-range	$$$	€4–8; 250–500MKD
Cheap & cheerful	$$	€2–4; 120–250MKD
Rock bottom	$	<€2; <£1.75; <US$2.75; <120MKD

border by lakeside boys selling trout by the bucketful. You may, therefore, want to think twice before partaking too often of this famous and increasingly rare Ohrid dish. It is now illegal to fish for Ohrid trout (page 10).

Fresh **salads** in Macedonia, especially outside Skopje, are not very inventive. Your four main choices are a green salad (lettuce); a mixed salad (cucumber, tomato, grated cabbage and carrot); a Šopska salad (cucumber, tomato and grated white goat's cheese); and Greek salad (cucumber, tomato, cubes of feta cheese and maybe some olives). Vinaigrettes and salad dressings are almost unheard of, so don't expect a choice of thousand island dressing, blue cheese or ranch, or even salad cream. There is usually olive oil and vinegar served alongside and balsamic vinegar available in Skopje.

Other Macedonian specialities include *tavče gravče*, butter beans stewed in an earthenware pot; *pastrmajlija*, a famous bread dough, pork and egg dish from Strumica that seems to be the Macedonian equivalent of pizza; *turlitava*, a vegetarian baked mix of local vegetables; and *piti*, usually translated as 'pies', but not in the English sense with a shortcrust top and bottom and fruit or stewed meat in the middle, but a *burek*-type affair consisting of layers of filo flaky pastry or pancake interlaced with egg and cheese, or sometimes meat and the odd spring onion.

There are also plenty of other Macedonian dishes that are usually cooked at home rather than served in restaurants, as they are more labour intensive. These include *juvki*, a semolina-based pancake which is allowed to dry crisp before being broken and recooked with milk and water for breakfast or lunch; *sirden*, which is the Macedonian equivalent of haggis; *pača* (brawn), made from the boiled meat of a pig's head or knuckles, fried with onions and herbs, and served cold in slices; *mantiji*, a seasoned meat pasty; and *mezelek*, offal stew.

Macedonian **desserts** – if you still have room by the time you have eaten your meze, hearty soup (*čorba*), skara by the kilo served with fried chips and several glasses of Macedonian wine – are few and mostly borrowed from other cultures, such as pancakes, baklava, *sutljaš* (rice pudding cake), fresh fruit and ice cream. *Ravanija* and *gurabii* are two types of syrupy cake, which you may be served in a Macedonian home, but rarely in a restaurant. Mouth-wateringly delicious, dark red forest honey (*šumski med*) can be bought at roadside stalls on the way to the Ohrid region – some of the best are at the stalls south of Kičevo.

The art of **breakfast** is slowly coming to Macedonia, and traditionally consists of a strong coffee before work possibly with bread and cheese or jam, and at the weekends *juvki* or *tarama* (a cereal-based baked dish), then a break at around ten for a *gevrek* or *kifla* (sesame bread ring) and plain drinking yoghurt or *ajran* before settling down for a long lunch around 14.00. In Skopje, bakeries serving delicious pastries are becoming common, but outside the capital it is wise to make sure you have breakfast included in your hotel bill, or buy something in, as you'll find few

Practical Information EATING AND DRINKING

2

places on the streets that will serve you anything to eat. In Ohrid you can get sweet and savoury muffins, including *proja* (corn muffin with spinach) at Dva Biseri café from 08.00 in the morning.

If you're a **vegetarian**, travelling in Macedonia need not be too difficult although you'll probably have had enough of meze, turlitava, tavče gravče and *pohovani kromid* (breaded onions) by the end of your stay. If you're a coeliac, then your time might be more difficult as rice dishes and chips are usually served everywhere. You might want to make sure you ask for everything *bez leb* in order to avoid the waste of ubiquitous bread.

DRINK The preferred drink in Macedonia is **coffee**, either the strong Turkish variety that is a challenge to drink without sugar, served in espresso-size cups, or the usual cappuccinos, macchiatos and espressos. Turkish **tea**, served in small glasses, is popular in Albanian areas, and you'll sometimes see servers on bicycles or rollerblades carrying trays of them through the streets to customers. Fruit tea is usually considered a drink for the sick, but don't be deterred! Macedonia has lots of fruit teas (*ovošen čaj*) and mint tea (*čaj od nane*), and their mountain tea (*planinski čaj*) is a refreshing drink served in all the mountain huts and many restaurants. *Majčina dušica* (mother's little soul) is also a very popular tea of wild thyme. And beware the hot chocolate – it is often a filling warm chocolate mousse served in a cup!

Salep, a drink made of ground wild orchid root and hot milk, is of Turkish origin and usually served with a sprinkling of ground cinnamon. You won't find it everywhere, but it's very tasty and warming on a cold winter's day. Another Turkish drink plentiful in B vitamins and carbohydrates is *boza*, a thick tart drink made from slightly fermented wheat (4% alcohol content) whose origins go back to Mesopotamia; it came to Macedonia with the Ottoman Empire. Available in ice cream parlours and sweet shops, it is also good mixed with blueberry juice (*borovnica*).

If you are ever invited into a family home it is likely you will be offered syruped and candied fruits and a glass of homemade **liker** or **rakija** (see box, page 274) made from grapes. Macedonia's particular speciality is *žolta* (meaning literally 'yellow'), which is rakija yellowed by the addition of extra wheat at a secondary fermenting stage. It is usually very strong, but often sipped rather than thrown back in one as rakija is in many other Balkan countries. *Mastika* is another Macedonian speciality liqueur, which is remarkably similar to ouzo. For more on Macedonian **wines**, see the box on page 282.

PUBLIC HOLIDAYS AND FESTIVALS

Macedonian national holidays with fixed dates are as follows. Other national holidays set on movable days are Good Friday, Easter Sunday and Easter Monday (usually but not always in April) and the Muslim Eid-al-Fitr.

1 January	New Year's Day
7 January	Orthodox Christmas
1–2 May	Labour 'Day', when everybody goes picnicking
24 May	Sv Kiril and Metodi's Day
2 August	Republic Day (also known as Ilinden)
8 September	Independence Day (also known as Referendum Day)
11 October	Revolution Day (also referred to as National Day)
23 October	Day of the Macedonian Revolution
8 December	Sv Kliment Ohridski's Day

Other important national days not taken as public holidays are:

13 August   Ohrid Framework Agreement
22 November   Albanian flag day

SAINTS' DAYS Every saint has his or her festival day and these are celebrated by the locals at the church dedicated to the named saint. Usually, the villagers gather at the church or monastery with pot luck food dishes, drink and music, and make merry. Some of the bigger monasteries such as Sv Joakim Osogovski attract thousands of visitors on these days, and donations to the church funds are usually generous.

As the Macedonian Orthodox Church runs on the amended Gregorian calendar first adopted by the Eastern Orthodox Church in 1923, some of the saints' and holy days that western Europeans might know are celebrated in Macedonia 13 days later. Some have a completely different celebration day. Below are a few of the Orthodox saints' days with their western Gregorian dates, followed in brackets by the page number reference to the church where you can see the celebrations in action. For the full Macedonian Orthodox calendar see **w** mpc.org.mk. The Macedonian for Saint is Sveti/a (Sv).

28 January	Sv Gavril Lesnovski (page 335)
14 February	Sv Trifun (page 285)
22 March	Sv Leonti (Leonthius) (page 317)
6 April	Sv Metodi
6 May	Sv Gjorgi (George, Gjurgjovden) (pages 145 and 227)
14–15 June	Sv Erasmus of Ohrid (page 219)
2–3 July	Sv Naum of Ohrid (page 221)
2 August	Sv Ilija
7–8 August	Sv Petka (Peter, or Paraškjevija in Vlach) (page 234)
9 August	Sv Pantelejmon (pages 149 and 280)
14 August	Sv Stefan (celebrated on 26 December in the UK) (page 216)
28 August	Sv Bogorodica (the Virgin Mary) (pages 159 and 308)
29 August	The 15 martyrs of Tiberiopolis (Strumica) (page 315)
10 September	Sv Jovan Krstitel (John the Baptist) (page 333)
8 November	Sv Dimitri
21 November	Sv Archangel Michael (page 265)
4 December	Sv Bogorodica Prečista (page 197)
19 December	Sv Nikola (known to many of us as Father Christmas)

FESTIVALS There are many festivals throughout the year, but most take place in the summer. The year kicks in with an Orthodox New Year festival, also known as the **Twelfthtide Carnival**, in the village of Vevčani (see box, page 234) on 13 and 14 January. It is a colourful two-day event attracting several thousand visitors who dress up in fancy dress and masks. 19 January is **Epiphany**, when Bishop Naum throws a golden cross into Lake Ohrid in honour of John the Baptist and thereby blesses the lake. The practice is repeated all over Macedonia at local lakes and rivers, where men dive in after the cross purely for the honour of retrieving it.

The increasingly popular **Sv Trifun Day**, for the patron saint of wines, is on 14 February. During the first three days of Orthodox Lent (usually the same time as the Catholic/Protestant Easter) is the **Strumica Carnival** (page 317), followed a few weeks later by **Orthodox Easter**. On the Saturday evening of Easter weekend, people go up to their local churches shortly before midnight with a coloured boiled egg

2

and, when the bells of midnight have struck, a competition ensues to see whose egg survives when cracked against another. Fancy dress is the way to celebrate **1 April**, which, however, has nothing to do with fools.

After Easter is the summer-long season of festivals. Bitola kicks off with its **Monodrama Festival** in early May. On 22–23 May every year is the Pece Atanasovski **Musical Folk Instrument Festival** in Dolneni, near Prilep. For more on what some of Macedonia's native musical instruments are see the box on page 54. Next comes **Makedox** (w makedox.mk), which showcases contemporary documentaries in Kuršumli An. Then it's time for the **Buskerfest** (w buskerfestmakedonija.com), when Skopje's main square and other venues around Skopje are the stage for busker performances.

Throughout July and August, Skopje, Ohrid and Bitola hold their **summer festivals**, when blues concerts, plays, ballet and opera fill historical venues and open-air theatres. In Skopje these finish in early August when the government goes on holiday, but they continue in Ohrid, which also holds a Folklore Festival, the Green Beach music festival and Salsa Dance festival in July, and the International Swimming Marathon, a 30km course from Sveti Naum to the town of Ohrid, in August.

The **Prilep Beer Festival** takes place in early July (page 264), where you can sup Macedonia's local brews with čevapi, peppers and other local as well as more international accompaniments to beer (sausage and mustard). The second weekend in July is the very popular **Galičnik wedding festival** (see box, page 184), which attracts many thousands of visitors and is well worth the visit up to this pretty mountain village. For Macedonians, one of the most important events of the year is **Ilinden** on 2 August (page 24), which celebrates when the people of Macedonia stood up against the Ottoman Empire and brought in the ten-day Kruševo Republic. The **Ilinden Sailing Regatta** is held on the first three days in August on Lake Ohrid.

There are numerous **artists' colonies** throughout the summer including the International Pottery Workshop in Resen in early August, the Traditional Costumes Exhibition on the first weekend after 2 August in Struga, and the Painters' Colony in Kneževo. The Monastery of Sv Joakim Osogovski holds a Young Artists' Convention in the last week of August, which is also when its very popular saint's day falls. At the end of August the **Struga Poetry Evenings** (page 228) take place over the bridge where Lake Ohrid empties into the River Drim in Struga.

In September Bitola holds the **International Film Camera Festival** in honour of the Manaki brothers. Štip holds its popular **Makfest of International Music** in October (page 305), while Bitola holds its classical music festival **Interfest**. Skopje holds its **International Film Festival** in October along with the **Skopje Jazz Festival**, which usually puts on some excellent artists. September and October are also very good months for wine tours (see box, page 283).

December finishes up the year with **Christmas markets** selling local crafts and mulled wine. **New Year's Eve** sees fireworks over the River Vardar in Skopje and equally colourful celebrations in many other towns across Macedonia.

SHOPPING

Local handicrafts are plentiful in Macedonia, but in the past they have been hard to find and generally overpriced. Prices are coming down, but are still not low. Indigenous handicrafts include ceramics, stained glass and terracotta as well as traditional icons, manmade pearls, earthenware, traditional blankets, hand-embroidered linen, leather goods, paintings, silver filigree jewellery, iron- and copper-work, carpets, embroidery, local musical instruments, woodwork and museum reproductions.

The best place to purchase handicrafts is still Ohrid, although a number of hotels are now beginning to offer items. The Christmas handicraft fair at Čifte Amam in Skopje is becoming a popular event for making timely and original Christmas purchases and there are sometimes stands in the Ramstore. Skopje's Roma part of town (page 147) is the best place to order their hand-embroidered costumes, but traditional Macedonian costumes, like you might see at Galičnik or Ilinden, are harder to find.

For those living and working in Skopje, *Chapter 3* covers more of the items that you may be looking for while living away from home. In Skopje, English-language books can be found at Ikone Books and Kavkaz. Skopje is a good place to get handmade suits (page 133), and Štip has a number of clothes and shoe outlets who supply Marks & Spencer and other European shops.

If you get hooked on the Macedonian starter ajvar, a delicious dish consisting of stewed red pepper and herbs, you can buy this in jars in the supermarket. However, the best ajvar is homemade so try to buy it locally in places such as Brajčino, where you can also buy local rakija, liker, jams, wild mushrooms and excellent homemade baklava if you eat in a local home (see box, page 254). The best mastika (aniseed liqueur) is bought at monasteries such as Sv Jovan Bigorski.

ARTS AND ENTERTAINMENT

Skopje is the best place for most arts and entertainment in Macedonia, although Ohrid, Bitola and Štip do have some events that rival, if not better, what is available in the capital. With a population of only 500,000 Skopje cannot offer endless variety, but it does have a few drama theatres, its own philharmonic orchestra and a number of art galleries. For more information on all of these see page 132. For more details on Macedonian arts and culture, see page 52.

Summer festivals are aplenty (page 88) and most towns do something. You won't find the latest blockbusters in the cinemas, but the films won't be dubbed so you will be able to hear them in their original language.

Macedonia's national football team, nicknamed the Red Lions, plays in Skopje throughout the season, and the most popular match is always against England, whenever that occurs.

OUTDOOR PURSUITS

Macedonia is a haven for the outdoor sports enthusiast. Its mountains and waterways and lack of paved roads make it a pleasure to hike and bike in, and offer countless opportunities for paragliding, climbing, caving and kayaking. Most sports are regulated by a federation, where you can get further information, including applicable laws and permit requirements, and find out about local clubs. Contact details for most federations and some clubs are given below. The Macedonian Sport Climbing Federation (MSCF), the Macedonian Mountain Sport Federation (MMSF) and the Macedonian Speleological Foundation (MSF) are all co-located at Boulevard 11 Oktomvri 42a, 1000 Skopje. Respective phone, email and web addresses are listed separately below. Information on how to get to the locations mentioned below is given in the individual chapters in *Part Two* of this guidebook.

BIKING Mountain biking is a popular sport in Macedonia, where there are literally thousands of off-road and dirt tracks. **Energi Cycling Club** (affiliated with Bikestop

2

shop (see below), Bd Ilinden 38a, 1000 Skopje; ☏023 231 772; m 075 475 188; e info@energi-cycling.mk; w energi-cycling.mk) rents out bicycles and organises regional mountain-bike and smaller local tours. As a club they also promote developing biking trails in Macedonia as well as local sustainable tourism to historical and natural sites of interest. Various tour operators such as Cycle Macedonia offer cycling tours of the country (page 64), while for **bike hire** check out sites such as BimbimBikes (w bimbimbikes.com). In Ohrid, CityBikeOhrid (w rentabikeohrid.com) hires out city (€8/day) and mountain bikes (€12/day).

Bikestop (Orce Nikolov 101/6, Skopje; ☏ 023 231 772; w bikestop.com.mk; ⊕ 10.00–19.00 Mon–Fri, 09.00–14.30 Sat) is the place to go for parts, servicing or a new bike.

FISHING Fishing in Macedonia is widely done, but only marginally successful. Despite boasting the first recorded instance of fly fishing (see w fishingmuseum.org.uk), Macedonian rivers today tend to suffer from one of two conditions: being overgrown or overfished. Trees, shrubs and heavy overgrowth crowd riverbanks in many of the valleys, making casting nearly impossible and, even if you do manage, odds are you'll lose your gear on a snag. Overfishing is so rampant in the open areas that 'keepers' are rare indeed. Lax enforcement of regulations and licensing mean that every kind of bait is used, limits aren't respected (or imposed), and few buy a licence. Moves are afoot to make fishing more sustainable in Macedonia, but efforts are slow.

For the avid fisherman, Macedonia has trout, carp, bream and other freshwater species native to its streams, rivers and lakes. The Radika, running from Lake Mavrovo to Debar and beyond, is a classic, albeit overfished trout river. Running between craggy, forested mountains, it's got plenty of water and its deep holes hide some big fish – despite the proximity of the road along its entire length. The Crni Drim, running from Ohrid Lake to Debar, offers a number of choice spots, despite most of the river being inaccessible due to heavy overgrowth. The Treška, from Makedonski Brod north is accessible in several places, and therefore heavily fished. But fishing where it empties into the reservoir, or by boat on the reservoir itself, has brought considerable success. Finally, the Pčinja, starting just east of Kumanovo and emptying into the Vardar near Veles, has several accessible parts, including a glorious valley north from the village of Pčinja itself.

Lake fishing in Macedonia is subject to a prohibition on trout fishing in Lake Ohrid (page 199), but the country has several bountiful lakes that offer decent sport fishing. Among the best are Debar, Dojran, Matka, Prespa and Mavrovo.

For more information contact the **Združenija na Sportski Ribolovci** (Association of Sport Fishermen; Kočo Racin 75, Skopje; ☏ 023 238 445; w zk.mk/vardar-zdruzhenie-na-sportski-ribolovci). There you can get a licence for waters in the Vardar region of Skopje, or a nationwide licence. Licences last for one year and are available to foreigners who can show a passport. Various discounts exist for the young and the elderly, and licences for women are free.

Note that many waterways will have additional fees, ranging from 200 to 400MKD, which are levied in one of two ways: on-site (*na lica mesto*) or by purchasing a sticker at the federation to attach to your licence. On-site fees appear to be paid only if the warden finds you. At the time of writing, catch limits were 3kg of fish of all varieties, with the exception of trout, which carries a limit of two fish only, each of 30cm or longer. A good website on fishing in Macedonia is w ribar.com.mk.

HIKING AND MOUNTAINEERING Macedonia is brimming with beautiful countryside that makes splendid hiking for a range of fitness and experience levels.

There are several multi-day hikes, including two 200km hikes from Ljuboten to Struga along the border with Albania (permit still required) and from the capital Skopje to the beautiful Lake Ohrid. There are also many shorter hikes of an hour or less to waterfalls, caves, glacial lakes, hidden monasteries, or other points of interest.

The **Macedonian Mountaineering Sports Federation** (MMSF; 11 Oktomvri 42a, 1000 Skopje; \ 023 165 540; e contact@fpsm.org.mk; w fpsm.org.mk) is starting to put together hiking booklets and guides in English with the aim of providing western European-standard information on trails and huts. Together with brand-new 1:25,000 hiking maps being published on the whole country by the State Authority for Geodetic Works (page 68), only a fresh coat of paint on some of the old hiking-trail markings and some much neglected trail maintenance is needed to bring hiking up to the recreational standards enjoyed in the US, and in France, Germany or elsewhere in western Europe.

Other guidebooks are available in Macedonian. However, even if you can read Macedonian, information on how to get to the trail head, good route descriptions, a basic route map, water supply locations, etc are somewhat obscure, never mind grid references. Admittedly grid references were difficult to give when maps were once a state secret and only officers were taught how to read them!

This book offers information on 12 hikes of differing grades to whet your appetite (see box, page 94). More routes are available at w summitpost.org (type in the name of a mountain peak or hut), while a downloadable free 200-page book called *Balkan Hiking Adventure* (w balkanhikingadventure.com/uploads/bha_guidebook.pdf) includes detailed route descriptions and maps of several good hikes in Macedonia, Albania and Kosovo. As with mountaineering anywhere in the world, respect the terrain and know your own limits especially if you intend to venture out without a guide (see box, page 96). If you would like a guide and none of the clubs below can help, then **Macedonia Travel** (w macedoniatravel.com) in Skopje or **Dea Tours** (w deatours.com.mk) in Ohrid can arrange multi-day hikes, with prices dependent on the number of hikers, length of tours and type of accommodation.

For more on where and how to buy maps, and the peculiarities of the new Macedonian maps, see page 67.

Hiking clubs There are over 70 hiking clubs in Macedonia, some more active than others. You'll find somebody who speaks English at most of these clubs. A few are listed here, and are mentioned in relevant sections throughout this guidebook. For a complete list of all the clubs contact MMSF (see above).

Ljuboten Planinarski Klub m 075 649 393, 070 321 621; e contact@sharamountainguide. com.mk; sharamountainguide.com.mk. Based in Tetovo, the club's national day hike is along the River Pena to Lešnica Waterfall. Their website highlights a number of hiking options in the Šar Mountains, & their costs include guide.

Makedon Planinarski Klub m 078 310 552; w makedon.mk. This young club meets every Wed at 20.00 at the faculty of mechanical engineering in Skopje (barrack no 5).

Mountain hut system Serving the needs of the clubs and individuals is an extensive system of over 40 mountain huts in Macedonia (called *planinarski dom* in Macedonian). Although most of these rarely require you to book ahead, it is best to phone before arrival as some are only staffed if they know there will be overnight visitors. The huts offer clean sheets in a dormitory bed space, and cost around 300MKD for the night. This does not include food and most huts offer only small snacks and drinks, so bring your own provisions. For a detailed list of huts

We have highlighted 12 of our favourite hikes in grey boxes dotted through the relevant regional chapters. These are as follows:

1 Vodno Cross to Matka Dam (near Skopje; page 154)
2 Mount Kitka (near Skopje; page 158)
3 Popova Šapka to Titov Vrv (Popova Šapka; page 174)
4 Kriva Šija Waterfall (Popova Šapka; page 175)
5 Rostuše and Duf Waterfall (Mavrovo National Park; page 186)
6 Janče to Galičnik (Mavrovo National Park; page 186)
7 Biljana Waterfalls and Dolna Alilica Cave (Mavrovo National Park; page 187)
8 Two Lakes View (Galičica National Park, near Ohrid; page 223)
9 Oktisi to Vajtos and Vevčani (Vevčani, near Ohrid; page 233)
10 Brajčino to Pelister Lakes and Nižepole (Pelister National Park; page 252)
11 Marko's Tower to Treskavec (near Prilep; page 266)
12 Demir Kapija to Iberlija and Korešnica (Demir Kapija; page 289)

see **w** travelmacedonia.info/discover-macedonia/mountain-huts-in-macedonia, but below is a list of some of the more popular huts.

Outside Skopje
🏠 **Dare Džambaz** (25 beds) **m** 078 413 051; **e** pskbistra@gmail.com; 🖪 @PSKBistrapriMVRSkopje; location: 1,066m, peak of Mt Vodno, south of Skopje.
🏠 **Karadžica** (50 beds) **m** 071 511 444; **e** spd_dracevo@hotmail.com; 🖪 Планинарски-дом-Караџица-Mountain-house-Karadzica; location: 1,450m on Karadžica Mountain above the village of Aldinci, south of Dračevo.

Veles area
🏠 **Čeples** (60 beds) **m** 075 644 000; location: at 1,445m near the village of Nežilovo on Jakupica Mountain. Renovated in 2013. Eat at the Nežilovo Trout Farm (**m** 070 303 029) on the way up or down to the hut.
🏠 **Papradište** (30 beds) **m** 075 361 877; 🖪 Планинарскиот-дом-ПапрадиштеMountain-Hut-Papradiste; location: the old school house, 1,000m, in Papradište village.

Strumica area
🏠 **Dedo Kožjo Murtinski** (10 beds) **m** 070 535 688; location: 1,160m on Belasica Mountain near Strumica.
🏠 **Ezero** (20 beds) 📞 034 325 282, 043 343 122; location: on Lake Vodoča near the village of Popčevo, southwest of Strumica.

🏠 **Šarena Češma** (16 beds) 📞 034 345 062; 🖪 @planinarskidomsarenacesma; location: 1,300m near Šarena springs on Belasica Mountain near Strumica.
🏠 **Vrteška** (64 beds) **m** 070 210 063; location: on Plačkovica Mountain.

Popova Šapka
🏠 **SaraSki** (14 beds) **m** 070 533 303; location: next to the church on Popova Šapka.
🏠 **Smreka** (100 beds) 📞 023 221 350; **m** 070 641 998; location: ski resort of Popova Šapka.

Northeast
🏠 **Kozjak** (15 beds) 📞 031 430 990; location: near the village of Malotino, northeast of Kumanovo, towards Prohor Pčinski.
🏠 **Pojak Kalman** (22 beds) 📞 031 430 990, 031 373 216; **m** 075 591 990; location: near the village of Dejlovce, northeast of Kumanovo, south of Mt Peren.
🏠 **Toranica** (15 beds) 📞 same as Pojak Kalman; location: near the village of Kostur, east of Kriva Palanka.

Baba Mountains
🏠 **Golemo Ezero** (50 beds) Lies 600m below Pelister peak at 2,225m. To arrange an overnight stay contact Petar Nolev (**m** 075 458 782; **e** pnolev@gmail.com; 🖪 golemo.ezero). Staffed

at w/ends in summer only. No food available. Water & washing facilities are outside.

🏠 **Kopanki** (110 beds) 1,630m Mount Baba; PSK Pelister, Bitola; m 070 804 130; or contact Petar Nolev, details opposite. Further info from Pelister National Park office (☏ 047 233 464). Serves food & drink (including alcohol); washing facilities are indoors; TV & video available. A very popular outing for Bitolites & locals.

🏠 **Neolica** (48 beds) PD Gjorgji Naumov, Bitola; ☏ 047 242 879; m 078 851 396. Staffed during the w/ends.

Gostivar–Kičevo–Mavrovo

🏠 **Leunovo** (20 beds) m 075 554 595; location: near Mavrovo Lake.

🏠 **Sarski Vodi** (8 beds) ☏ 042 214 505; m 070 298 757; location: near the village of Gorno Jelovce, west of Gostivar.

🏠 **Tajmište** (40 beds) m 072 212 264; 📹 @kitka.planinarskodrustvo; location: near the village of Tajmište, northwest of Zajas, Kičevo.

🏠 **Zelezna reka** (20 beds) m 075 554 595; location: west of Gostivar.

HORSERIDING There are two riding schools outside Skopje (page 136) and numerous stables around the country. Sherpa Horse Riding (m 077 648 679; e hcbistragalicnik@ gmail.com; w horseriding.com.mk) offers single- and multi-day tours on horseback to Vodno, through Mavrovo National Park and elsewhere, with prices from €40. Local tour operators can arrange horserides outside Skopje and guided donkey rides to local sites are becoming increasingly available: see individual chapters for more.

KAYAKING Once a big sport in Macedonia, kayaking appears to be on the decline, perhaps due to the expense of equipment and the upkeep of courses. Nevertheless, Macedonia offers numerous white-water rapids and a number of competition courses including those on the River Vardar in Skopje itself and at Lake Matka just outside Skopje. For more information contact the **Macedonian Canoe Federation** (☏ 023 131 139; e contact@canoe.mk; w canoe.mk).

PARAGLIDING Paragliding is a very popular and awesome experience in Macedonia, which is crammed with great accessible take-off sites, such as Mount Vodno outside Skopje, Popova Šapka above Tetovo, Galičica Mountain above Lake Ohrid, as well as sites in Kruševo, Strumica and Prilep. The interconnectivity of mountains, valleys, ridges and ravines here makes it possible to fly for several hours and up to 30km in one direction. It is also relatively cheap to learn to fly here compared with club rates in western Europe. Good commercial paragliding clubs offering courses and tandem flights include **Paragliding Ohrid** (m 075 281 090; e info@paraglidingohrid.com; w paraglidingohrid.com), **Heli XC** (m 070 333 859; e info@paraglidingmacedonia.com; w paraglidingmacedonia.com) and **Fly Ohrid** (m 070 969 080; e epilotkiko@gmail.com; w flyohrid.com).

ROCK CLIMBING *Kačuvačka*, as it is called in Macedonian, is a fast-growing sport, and there are some excellent climbs to be had at Lake Matka near Skopje (traditional, multi-pitch), Kaneo at Ohrid (bolted), Pilav Tepe (also known as Ploča) near Radoviš, and Demir Kapija (bolted) right off the main road to Greece, among other places. The **MSCF** (Macedonian Sport Climbing Federation; ☏ 023 165 540; e contact@climbing.mk; w climbing.mk) is very active and their website lists a number of affiliated clubs and a guide to climbing routes. For climbs specific to Pilav Tepe, see page 96. Have a look at w climb-macedonia.com/sport-climbing-crags for detailed information including route grading (in English) on climbing areas in Macedonia. For rock-climbing gear, try **Vertikal Sport** (Lazar Lichenoski bb, Skopje; m 078 333 733; w vertikalsport.com.mk) or **Würth** (Industrial Zone Vizbegovo 39, Skopje; ☏ 022 728 080; w wurth.com.mk).

Sanne van den Heuvel

Although Macedonia's natural beauties and countryside have long attracted people's interest and desire to go out in the mountains, organised mountaineering in Macedonia did not start until the 1920s. Before that time, visits were mainly organised around religious holidays, where people gathered at the monasteries often located in remote places. Soon after the first mountaineering club was founded in Prilep in 1924, the same initiative followed in other towns. Today's clubs offer weekend trips and courses for their members in a variety of outdoor disciplines: Alpinism, speleology, mountaineering, climbing and orienteering. All mountain sports organisations in Macedonia are united under the umbrella of the Macedonian Mountaineering Sports Federation (MMSF – see contact details on page 93). Located in Skopje, they are the contact point for all information and details about visiting the Macedonian mountains. The MMSF supports the protection of nature, mountains and hiking trails in close co-operation with local communities. Besides awareness campaigns and maintenance of mountain trails, the MMSF has set up a training centre for professional mountain guides. Members of mountaineering clubs can follow the training for the Mountain Guide A Certificate, through which they receive qualifications to guide organised mountain trips. Because of the remoteness of the Macedonian landscape it is highly recommended to make use of experienced mountain guides. If you wish to contact a mountain guide, contact the MMSF.

If you prefer to travel without a guide, however, there are a couple of ways to find more information. The MMSF publishes two booklets with a concise description of the best-known tracks: *The Mountains and the Mountaineering Huts in the Republic of Macedonia* and *Eastern Macedonian Mountaineering Transversal*. The first covers hikes from all over Macedonia. Unfortunately the booklet lacks good maps and, since most tracks were last marked when Macedonia was still a part of Yugoslavia, only a few of the hikes are described extensively enough to be taken without a mountain guide. The maps in the second booklet are better, although the scale is still fairly large for orientation in an area visited for the first time. The booklet describes the newly marked international hiking trails, which connect with hikes in Bulgaria. In contrast to the more popular mountaineering destinations in western Macedonia, this booklet highlights less trodden trails in the east. A long overdue promotion!

Active clubs include:

Ploča Climbing Club Pilav Tepe, 17km west of Radoviš on the road to Štip & Skopje; m 070 550 058; e alpinistzm@yahoo.com (club president Zoran Majstorski); w plocaclimbing. com. The rock climbing park at Pilav Tepe, known as Ploča (Macedonian for 'slab' or 'tile'), is the most developed & most accessible climbing site in Macedonia. Golem Ploča features 12 bolted multi-pitch routes, while Mala Ploča has bolted & traditional routes. There are also 7 boulders below the big wall featuring bolted routes & bouldering problems. All the different sections are connected by maintained trails with signs & are a mere 10min walk from the Climbing Hut Ploča. The climbing hut, complete with kitchen, bathroom (with hot water for showering) & 2 dorm-style bedrooms with a total of 12 beds, is available for use by all. There are also opportunities for camping, hiking

& mountain biking on marked trails around Lake Mantovo, the village of Brest & the Monastery of Sv Pantelejmon. The restaurant Pilav Tepe is located a stone's throw from the hut, offering traditional Macedonian cuisine & a great view of the rock & its climbers. The club meets every Tue & Thu 19.30–21.00 at the Sportska Sala, Radoviš, where they have an indoor climbing wall.

Other indoor walls can be found at:

OU 'Tošo Arsov' Borko Talev bb, Štip; m 070 527 586
Sport Hall 'Karpoš' Lindenska; m 071 555 185

Sport Hall 'Mladost' Negotino; m 075 615 931
Sport Hall 'Nikola Karev' Negotino; m 070 781 685

SAILING There is only one lake really worth sailing on in Macedonia, and that is of course Lake Ohrid. **AMAC SP-BOFOR Boat Club** (Kaj Maršal Tito bb, 6000 Ohrid; \046 256 386; w amac.com.mk) has been sailing on the lake since 1937 when it was established under the club's original name 'Strmec', a fast regional wind. It offers a variety of small to medium sail boats for hire at around 4,000MKD per day as well as reasonably priced sailing lessons. It also organises the annual Ilinden Sailing Regatta on Lake Ohrid on Macedonia's national day, Ilinden, on 2 August every year. The **Sailing Federation of Macedonia** is also based in Ohrid (Kaj Maršal Tito bb, 6000 Ohrid; \046 262 697; f @macedoniansailing), while another company offering reliable sailing excursions out of Ohrid is **Sailing Macedonia** (Promenade Macedonia; m 078 269 041; e info@sailingmacedonia. com; w sailingmacedonia.com).

SCUBA DIVING If you fancy exploring the tectonic edges of Lake Ohrid then **Amfora Dive Centre** (Lazo Trposki 35, 6000 Ohrid; m 070 700 865; e sekuloski@ yahoo.com; w amfora.com.mk) can take you. Lake Ohrid has a dramatic drop-off at its tectonic shelf, which is worth exploring, and there is also a Neolithic stilt village (Bay of Bones, page 220), which can be accessed with special permission.

SKIING There are three main ski resorts in Macedonia: Mavrovo, Popova Šapka and Kožuf. **Mavrovo** (page 182) is the most popular by far, with a day pass costing 1,100MKD. It is the best equipped in terms of facilities, hotels, restaurants and bars, but it is also the lowest of the three ski resorts, going up to only 1,860m (from a base lift of 1,255m). **Popova Šapka** (page 172) and **Kožuf** (page 292) both offer more exciting terrain, but are also prone to high winds. Popova Šapka, set between 1,708m and 2,510m, has been long in need of funds, and charges €15 for a day pass. Kožuf, having only opened in 2007, is still in the process of being completed. It lies between 1,480m and 2,150m and charges 700/900MKD for a weekday/weekend day ski pass. There is also some skiing on Pelister, Kruševo and Galičica.

SPELUNKING/POTHOLING/CAVING Macedonia is probably most well known outside the country for its speleology or caving. The karst formations of so much of Macedonia's ground structure make it ideal for caves. There are over 500 caves (*peštera* in Macedonian) in the country, only 300 of which have been explored. Only four are protected: Pešna, Ubavica, Mlečnik and Gorna Slatinska. This number does not, however, reflect the amount of spectacular caves. Some of the caves have underground rivers, lakes, multiple caverns and of course stalagmites and stalactites. Many are home to rare underground life forms as well as prehistoric fossils. Most caves have not yet been made tourist-friendly and so most are really accessible only with the correct equipment, experience and preferably a guide. The only cave open daily to tourists (300MKD entrance fee) is Vrela at Lake Matka (see page 153 for more on the caves there).

For clubs and potential expeditions, contact the **MMSF** (page 93) or take a look at the website of Speleo Macedonia (**w** speleo.mk). By area the best-known caves are at:

Gostivar The longest cave in Macedonia, at 1.2km, is Gonovica south of Gostivar, which has an underground river and the highest underground waterfall of 7m. Near here is also Ubavica Cave, almost 1km in length, also with a waterfall.

Karadžica and Sopište The deepest cave in Macedonia is Solunska 4, just below Solunska Glava on Mount Karadžica. It is 450m in depth, with a single shaft of 250m in depth, and contains the only ice cave formations yet known in Macedonia. Spela Bobguni near Patiška Reka is one of the more speleologically difficult and rewarding caves. There are about 50 other caves in the Sopište karst region.

Kavadarci Named the most beautiful cave in Macedonia is the 120m-long Gališka Cave near Tikveš Lake. Its entrance at 10m high is easily accessible and its numerous water cascades and high humidity show off the colours of the various minerals inside. Bela Voda Cave, 955m in length, with a lake at the end is near Demir Kapija.

Kičevo Slatinksi Izvor (meaning 'Slatino Springs') is near the village of Slatino south-southeast of Kičevo. It is over 1km in length and was considered significant enough in caving terms (stalagmites, stalactites, river and lake features) to be submitted to UNESCO in 2004 for consideration as a World Heritage Site.

Makedonski Brod Pešna Cave (page 269) near Makedonski Brod is the most accessible of caves, with a large entrance and the ruins of a medieval fortress. The Slatino caves are also near here, as well as Golubarnik, Momiček and Laprnik caves near the village of Gorna Belica. In Golubarnik (meaning 'pigeon roost') have been found ancient human skulls and the largest (2m) cave pearl in Macedonia.

Other areas There are numerous other caves along Matka Dam, in Galičica National Park and around Lesnovo. Zemjovec Cave near Krapa, Kumanovo, allegedly emits healing waters. The small cave of Alilica near Tresonče marks the start of the Biljana waterfall series along the River Tresončka. Some of the largest caves in the country include Dolna Duka and Krstalna.

WILDLIFE SAFARIS Game hunting is popular in Macedonia and the Jasen Forestry Reserve is still an exclusive wildlife range, once the preserve of the military and the president though the previous president, Branko Crvenkovski, elected in 2004, dropped the annual diplomatic hunt and took up tree-planting instead. Hunting and wildlife safaris can be arranged through local hotels, such as the Bistra in Mavrovo (page 180) and the Hotel Molika on Pelister Mountain (page 253). See page 6 for more on the types of wildlife to look out for on a wildlife safari.

MEDIA AND COMMUNICATIONS

NEWS OUTLETS The centre-right VMRO government under Nikola Gruevski and later Emil Dimitriev hit out hard on the media prior to being voted out of power in 2017. Indeed, Macedonia under the VMRO had probably the highest level of state control over the media in the Balkans, a scenario that attracted criticism from various international organisations, European governments and freedom of speech NGOs. The VMRO was supposedly cracking down on tax evasion but appeared to have targeted only media outlets that were critical of the government. As a result, A1 Television, which had been the most reputable station to give relatively balanced news, had its offices raided in November 2010, and had to shut down in 2011. A1 was raided in connection with alleged money laundering through Plus Produkcija, who own the three most widely read newspapers in the country, *Vreme*, *Špic* and *Koha e Re*, which were also forced to close.

In order to silence other democratic mechanisms that might counter this, the VMRO changed the composition of the Broadcasting Council so that it is effectively run by the government. The changes were rushed through parliament in an emergency procedure in July 2011, thus circumscribing public or stakeholder debate. Then in August 2011 the Macedonian state television, MTV, fired its entire board of governors, contravening the country's broadcasting law, and has fired labour union members who are journalists critical of the government. This has affected the independence of another leading newspaper *Utrinski Vesnik*, and the television station Alsat-M. There has been a reduction in government control of the media since Zoran Zaev and the SDSM took power in July 2017, but it is still too early to predict how significant or enduring this will be. In 2018, Macedonia was ranked 109th out of 179 countries in the Reporters Without Borders Press Freedom Index (up from 116 in 2013). For more on the issue see Reporters Without Borders (w rsf.org/en/republic-macedonia).

What's left? Kanal 5, Alfa, Sitel, Skynet and Telma – and other more local channels. MTV2 broadcasts purely in Albanian, and MTV3 broadcasts all the parliamentary sessions. Macedonian Radio and Channel 77 are the two main news-heavy radio stations broadcasting in the Macedonian language, but there are dozens of local radio stations. Some of the most popular radio stations that a lot of the restaurants tune in to are Antenna 5 (95.5) and City Radio (94.7). BBC World Service is available on 104.7 between 22.00 and 08.00 with on-the-hour news.

Several newspapers have also closed in recent years, the latest casualty being the respected *Utrinski Vesnik*, which ceased publication in 2017. Surviving daily newspapers, all produced in Cyrillic, include the well-established and centrist *Večer* (w vecer.mk, founded 1963), *Nova Makedonija* (w novamakedonija.com.mk; founded 1944), and the newer and more right-wing *Sloboden Pecat* (w slobodenpecat.mk, founded 2013) and *Nezavisen Vesnik* (w nezavisen.mk, founded 2017).

The two main Macedonian-language news agencies are MIA (w mia.mk) and Makfax (w makfax.com.mk), both of which used to have very good news in English that is updated several times a day. MIA still does, but it requires paid registration for expanded news articles, while Makfax no longer seems to have a functioning English site.

On the Albanian side the news agencies include Balkanweb (w balkanweb.com) and Kosova Press (w kosovapress.com). There are also Roma and Turkish media stations and papers produced in-country, as well as most of the major international newspapers and magazines available in Skopje after 19.00 every evening.

POST The post in Macedonia is relatively reliable for low-value items, although not very fast. It usually takes between one and two weeks for letters to be delivered between Europe or America and Macedonia by standard post. Stamps can be bought only at the post office, although there is a philatelic bureau at the Ploštad end of the Trgovski Centar in Skopje if you are looking for commemorative stamps.

Most packages are opened on arrival in the country and items of value may be stolen. As a result, high-value items, and even books, should be sent by FedEx or DHL. FedEx services in Skopje can be found at Boulevard Partizanski Odredi 17 (℡ 023 137 233; e macedonia@fedex.com.mk; w fedex.com/mk) opposite the cathedral; DHL (w dhl.com.mk) has offices in most main towns (see website) and in Skopje can be found at the Holiday Inn and at City Travel on the ground floor of Paloma Bjanka business centre (℡ 023 212 203/4; e city@t-home.mk).

TELEPHONE Phone booths accepting coins, credit cards and prepaid phonecards are available all over the country. Prepaid phonecards can be bought at newsagents and are easily visible by the big phonecard advertising boards in the shape of a telephone.

Mobile phone providers are Telekom (formerly T-Mobile; w telekom.mk) and Vip (which includes the obsolete provider One; w vipmobile.rs). You can purchase a local SIM card with an initial few hundred minutes for as little as 250MKD. The easiest place to do this is at the airport when you land, but there are also outlets in all large towns. Monthly contracts are also available. If you are thinking of using your own mobile phone from home with a local SIM card, make sure that your phone is unlocked and enabled for use abroad with non-service-provider SIM cards.

A useful telephone directory website is w imenik.telekom.mk. The local telephone directory is the local dialling code followed by 188.

INTERNET Wi-Fi is open and free throughout most of Macedonia, and mobile users with local sim cards can also buy inexpensive data bundles. Internet cafés are therefore a dying breed; however, **The Contact Café** on the top floor of the Trgovski Centar in Skopje charges 120MKD per hour.

As with writing to any person in anything other than their mother tongue, Macedonians are unlikely to answer an email that is not in Macedonian. So don't expect a reply too quickly, or at all, unless you have already established contact with them by phone or in person (see below).

BUSINESS *Ray Power, CEO of the British Business Group Macedonia*

Business hours in Macedonia are generally adhered to in Skopje but a little less obviously in some of the smaller towns. Opening times vary from 06.30 (post offices), 07.00 (banks), 08.00 (supermarkets and green markets), 09.00 (some shops) to 10.00 (other shops). Some places shut for lunch, especially in the summer when the day is hot, and some travel agents outside Skopje for instance will close from 11.00 to 17.00 and then open again until 20.00. Closing times also vary from 15.00 (some museums and repair stores, even if their stated closing time is in fact 16.00) to 16.00 (government and media offices) to anything between 17.00 and 22.00. Bars and restaurants are required by law to be closed from midnight on weekdays and from 01.00 at the weekends, although licensed nightclubs can remain open until 04.00 on weekends. If you are trying to get hold of government officials it is best to do so between 10.00 and noon and 14.00 and 15.00. Most shops are closed on Sunday.

If you have not done business in the Balkans before, and especially if you come from a time-driven and impersonal business culture such as the US, UK, Germany or Switzerland, you'll probably find doing business in Macedonia requires a slight change of pace. First, Macedonians value their relationships highly and like to engage on a personal rather than exclusively professional level. This can be a little disconcerting for some Western 'go-getters' where the focus is on getting the job done. It's often taken for granted that deadlines are flexible so, when planning meetings or 'back-to-back' agendas, be prepared for reworking it on the fly. In that sense, Macedonia is very Mediterranean.

Secondly, seeing that Macedonia is a country of only two million, it's not unusual to find that people choose relatives and friends to execute services. While this can be helpful, it does pay to shop around a bit and build your own network of less direct relationships as Macedonia does have a culture where favours are a form of capital. This is not necessarily a bad thing and functions well for those who have a sensitivity and consideration for long-term business relationships.

Thirdly, as with many eastern European countries, there is not necessarily a long tradition of customer service so you will still find some older companies and state-run organisations, such as the post office, leaving you a little frustrated at the rather blunt attitude of staff. That being said, a smile and some consideration for their relatively uncomfortable working environment and typically low wages will win friends and a level of service that no trained staff will ever match. Top tip in Macedonia: the relationship is always the priority.

Finally, as a result of the historically centralised communist economy, entrepreneurialism is a relatively new skill so, while you will meet some brilliant business people, you can still find those people who expect opportunities to be handed to them on a platter. In cases of the latter you will be able to discern them by the excessive lunch and dinner meetings with no follow-up or next steps. If you are in a position where you are stuck with such business associates, the best results are achieved by closely managing the process and insisting on office-based meetings and emphasising deliverables.

With the vast majority of people below 50 speaking English, Macedonia is a business-friendly country that has undergone a tremendous amount of change in the last 20 years. Much of the change in recent years has been focused on creating a better business environment so, for example, setting up a company now takes just a couple of days compared with the six weeks it used to take. Please note, however, that setting up your company is only the first step. There may be a number of industry regulatory procedures which your new company may need to hurdle before it can become operational. This can take considerably longer, so it is worth researching these before going ahead with setting up in Macedonia.

Macedonia is very proud of its wine industry, which has been growing steadily during the last ten years; but it also has a lot to offer in the wider context of agriculture with large amounts of unused arable land. The more recent focus on the IT industry also makes Macedonia a suitable choice for outsourcing and it's fair to say they are very well suited to agile development work. With its free economic zones Macedonia is also attracting major manufacturing companies who require a competitive workforce within Europe.

On the whole, business activities are still very personal and ensuring that introductions and relationships are managed accordingly will minimise delays and maximise productivity. For more on setting up a business in Macedonia, see the websites listed on page 359.

BUYING PROPERTY

Buying property in Macedonia as an individual became possible in 2008. Foreigners can purchase from any estate agent, although few will speak English. Property prices in the capital are high considering where Macedonia is on its path to EU accession. Outside Skopje and Ohrid lakeside, prices are much lower, but attractive properties are in much

2

need of renovation, and prices have increased significantly in recent years. Macedonians claim they are some of the best builders in the world, but that does not mean cheap, and there is little substantial corroboratory evidence. Buying property in Macedonia can be very long-winded (over a year from initial offer to completion) and, if you don't speak Macedonian, you will need to pay out for the translation of key documents, even if you do use a local lawyer who speaks English. Make sure that the title of the property is verified independently in case there is an ownership dispute. Websites listing properties for sale in Macedonia include w realestate.com.mk. For a guide on buying property in Macedonia see w globalpropertyguide.com/Europe/Macedonia.

CULTURAL ETIQUETTE

DRESS For the most part modesty is not an issue in Macedonia. That said, you'll find many Muslim women here of all ages dressed from head to foot in a long overcoat and headscarf no matter what time of day or year, and as a woman you may find it uncomfortable to wander around strongly Muslim areas in a crop top and low-cut shorts. Nudism is unheard of on the lake beaches.

DRUGS As everywhere in the world, there is a drugs scene in Macedonia, although it is small. Drugs are also illegal, even marijuana, so don't use/deal unless you want to risk ending up in a Macedonian jail. Dealing in drugs carries a hefty penalty, doubly so if you are caught taking them over a border crossing. Finally, make sure you keep an eye on your bags at all times while travelling into Macedonia so that no-one can stuff anything illegal in there without you knowing.

RELIGIOUS ETIQUETTE You should certainly be modestly dressed to enter a mosque and its grounds, and while most churches don't seem to mind what you wear, there are a few that require decent dress, such as Treskavec, Lesnovo and Marko's Monastery. Decent dress means covered shoulders, torso and legs. It is forbidden to take photographs inside churches.

Although many Macedonians are atheist as a leftover from communist days, increasing numbers have retaken to the Macedonian Orthodox Church with renewed vigour. Aside from in tourist-frequented Ohrid, Macedonians might find it odd if you don't cross yourself three times before entering the church and light a candle immediately on entering it. Practising Macedonians believe that you will not enter through the gates of heaven if you do not bring oil or wax with which to burn the light of God.

PHOTOGRAPHY It is forbidden to take photographs in churches, restricted military areas, and of military installations. Most people do not mind if you take their photograph, but you should always ask first, and if they say no, do not insist. In the more remote villages, farmers may also not agree to you taking photographs of their animals. They believe that if you take a photograph, even of only one animal, it will take a part of the animal's soul and this will affect the whole flock.

TIPPING Tipping is not a necessity here, where most Macedonians can hardly afford more than a coffee in a bar. However, it is greatly appreciated by waiting staff, and as a foreigner if you can afford it, it's certainly a small boost to the economy, morale and attitudes towards tourists. An extra 10 or 20 denar is suitable on smaller sums of money up to 500MKD, usually rounded up to the nearest 50 or 100, and on larger sums, up to 10% is appropriate.

MACEDONIAN HOSPITALITY Macedonian hospitality is extensive and often overpowering. Especially outside Skopje and Ohrid, where people are not used to contact with foreigners, Macedonians whom you meet will go out of their way to show you a site or monument and then insist on giving you a cup of thick, black, sweet Turkish coffee and a gift from their garden, or some other memento. They will do this, even if you speak no Macedonian at all and they do not speak your language, which can make the conversation somewhat one-sided! They are not looking for a passport to your home country or even any other favour, and if you exchange addresses they will not usually follow up on it unless you do.

Macedonians would simply consider it too rude not to answer a request to the fullest extent and offer you a coffee in their home, and of course they are inquisitive to know who you are, where you come from and how you live in your own country. Trying to say no is extremely difficult without being rude, unless you have some handy pressing excuse, like 'I will turn into a pumpkin at midnight if I don't leave right now' or 'We left my mother in the car and she needs to go to the hospital for brain surgery.' In other words, no excuse will be satisfactory and especially the lame excuse that you do not have enough time, for the one thing that Macedonians do have a lot of is time, and they know that if there's 5 minutes' leeway in the schedule somewhere then you can fit in a half-hour coffee, and if there isn't 5 minutes in the schedule then you wouldn't be visiting their remote village anyway.

My advice is to make the most of this laid-back way of life. It probably won't be around for much longer, as the fast pace and impersonal attitudes of modern-day life catch up with Macedonia. You may have to reschedule your cramped itinerary and knock something else off the list in order to fit in that coffee, but an invitation into the tenth house is still a privilege and will give you a momentary snapshot of how Macedonians live today.

A SMILE As you travel around Macedonia, especially off the beaten track, you may be greeted at first with a cold, hard stare. Some communities are not often visited by outsiders and so the locals will be suspicious and inquisitive, if not bewildered by your intentions to sightsee around their home. Even other Macedonians from a far-away town get this treatment. A smile, a wave and a greeting such as '*Zdravo*', or '*Tungjatjeta*' in Albanian regions, or even just 'Hello' will miraculously make your intentions to the locals clear, and their hostile glare will instantly dissolve into a winning smile and a greeting in reply. Initiate a conversation and the obligatory coffee is bound to follow along with a personal tour of their home and town.

CULTURAL QUIRKS Every society has its little idioms and beliefs – here are a few from Macedonia. *Promaja* is the Macedonian word for 'draught', not as in beer, but as in the wind/breeze that blows in through an open door or window. Many (particularly older) Macedonians, like a lot of people in the Balkans, believe that promaja is the root of all illness, so don't be surprised if you are asked to close a window or door even on a blistering hot day. *Le le* is an exclamation which Macedonians say all the time to add emphasis to a sentence. It's not directly translatable into anything in English, but other languages use similar expressions, like *ahh yoaaaa* in some Chinese dialects. *Ajde* is another frequent exclamation. It means 'let's go' or 'come on' or 'you're kidding'. You'll hear these two exclamations in the Macedonian language all over the place.

2

POLITICS AND HISTORY Macedonians are painfully aware of their history and politics, and are extremely interested in the slightest rumour of political intrigue. Macedonians will happily talk politics and history with you, but beware that you may not get them off the topic once started, no matter how many times you've heard the same tale of oppression and inequality. This phenomenon is particularly Balkan, but in Macedonia it is exaggerated by the fact that Macedonia's national neighbours mostly do not believe (largely for political reasons) that there is such a thing as an ethnic Macedonian, and as a result some question whether Macedonia should even be a sovereign state. As a foreigner, you'll never be right, and whatever you read in the history sections of this book is bound to offend someone, be they Macedonian, Serb, Albanian, Turk, Bulgarian, Greek, Orthodox or Muslim. So take what you hear with a small pinch of salt and debate politics with great caution, even if you were a top scorer in the debating society at college.

There is a Macedonian proverb that goes 'If my cow dies, may my neighbour's cow die too.' This, sadly, does sum up a lot of the attitude of people here. But, as Mahatma Gandhi said, 'An eye for an eye makes the whole world blind.'

TRAVELLING POSITIVELY

The interaction of the outside world with Macedonia can have a variety of effects. Hopefully, your visit to Macedonia will have a positive impact on the tourist industry and, indirectly, on the economy and the people. If you would like to get more personally involved with charities and institutions in the country then here are a few to start you off. For environmental protection organisations, see page 11.

ANTI-TRAFFICKING The trafficking of women through and into Macedonia is a particularly entrenched problem, not helped on the Macedonian side by a weak policing and judicial system, and on the international side by the difficulty that the international community has in classing it as a crime separate from slavery, abduction, rape, torture, theft and prostitution. The whole issue is driven by huge financial profits and made easy for traffickers by the lack of public awareness. For further information, see page 74.

Open Gate (\022 700 107/367; e lastrada@lastrada.org.mk; w lastrada.org.mk) campaigns on anti-trafficking, and their work has helped to set up a safe house and helpline for trafficked women in Macedonia.

CIVIL SOCIETY The role that civil society plays in any country is an important contribution to self-governance and to providing checks and balances on government and people's hard-earned taxes. In Macedonia civil society is weak by European and American standards. International funding is trying to develop the role that parliamentarians should play as the elected representatives of the people, as well as the role that non-governmental organisations can play. Sadly, the NGO scene is still largely supply driven by the amount of donor funding available rather than demand driven by the confidence that citizens can make a difference. What are sorely missing are skills and competent local stakeholders (and a responsive government). If you have the skills, the funding or the time to help with civil society development in Macedonia it will make a difference. **Volunteer Centre Skopje** (Emil Zola 3-2/3, Skopje;\022 772 095; e vcs_contact@yahoo.com; w vcs.org.mk) places volunteers in a variety of projects across the country depending on their skills. US citizens might also want to look into two-year placements with the **Peace Corps** (w peacecorps.gov/macedonia).

ROMA To read more about the Roma, see page 41. There are a number of organisations that are trying to serve their needs and bring the very poor back out of poverty and into education and jobs, including the **National Roma Centrum** (Done Božinov 11/5, 1300 Kumanovo; 031 427 558; w nationalromacentrum.org).

SEND US YOUR SNAPS!

We'd love to follow your adventures using our *North Macedonia* guide – why not tag us in your photos and stories via Twitter (✈ @BradtGuides) and Instagram (📷 @bradtguides)? Alternatively, you can upload your photos directly to the gallery on the North Macedonia destination page via our website (w bradtguides.com/northmacedonia).

Part Two

THE GUIDE

www.unityhostel.mk
unity_hostel@yahoo.com +38975942494
Boulevard Ilinden 1/1 Skopje, Macedonia

3

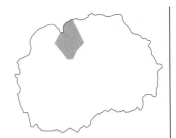

Skopje

Telephone code 02

> The Turkish residue was thick in Skopje. Men in white skullcaps played backgammon
> and drank rose-hip tea from small hour-glass-shaped receptacles … I crossed the
> flagstone bridge over the Vardar River, built on Roman foundations that had withstood
> major earthquakes in AD518, 1535 and 1963 … Ahead of me was 'new' Skopje …
> Robert D Kaplan, *Balkan Ghosts*, 1993

The capital of Macedonia and main port of entry to the country, Skopje is an up-
and-coming city whose population of 550,000 represents more than a quarter of
the national total. It boasts a strategic location on the River Vardar and has been
an important centre of regional trade for several millennia, as evidenced by the
presence within the city limits of archaeological sites dating back to Neolithic,
Roman and Ottoman times. The Vardar divides Skopje into a predominantly
Muslim northern half and predominantly Orthodox Christian southern half. Most
government offices, hotels and shopping malls can be found south of the river,
along with the railway station and main intercity bus station.

A city of many cultures, Skopje is worth at least a couple of days' exploration.
The main attraction is the old Turkish quarter known as Čaršija, which lies to
the north of the river below the imposing Kale Fortress, and houses a large daily
bazaar, several Ottoman architectural landmarks, and a small but buzzing café and
nightlife scene. The city also boasts a varied selection of museums, art galleries and
archaeological sites, ranging from the recently opened Archaeological Museum of
Macedonia and Holocaust Memorial Centre to the Roman-era ruins at Skupi and
reconstructed Neolithic village of Tumba Madžari. Further afield, don't miss out
on the cable car up Mount Vodno, the rare Byzantine frescoes in the 12th-century
Church of Sv Pantelejmon, and the spectacular lake set within the sheer cliffs of the
Matka Canyon.

HISTORY

Nestled in the valley of the Vardar River, Skopje has been a welcome respite from
the surrounding mountains since Neolithic times. It first became a major settlement
around 500BC when it formed part of the outer reaches of the Illyrian nation now
known as Albania. As Rome moved its empire eastward, the settlement became
known as Skupi, and later came under Byzantine rule upon the division of the Roman
Empire. Thereafter Slavs, Greeks, Bulgarians, Austro-Hungarians, Serbs and Turks
all ruled the city. In 1392 began 520 years of Ottoman rule when the city became
known as Üsküb, and it essentially languished as a backwater trade stop compared
with fashionable Monastir (now Bitola). After further swaps among regional powers
during and between both world wars, it was finally incorporated in 1944 into Federal
Yugoslavia and made the capital of the autonomous Republic of Macedonia. It has

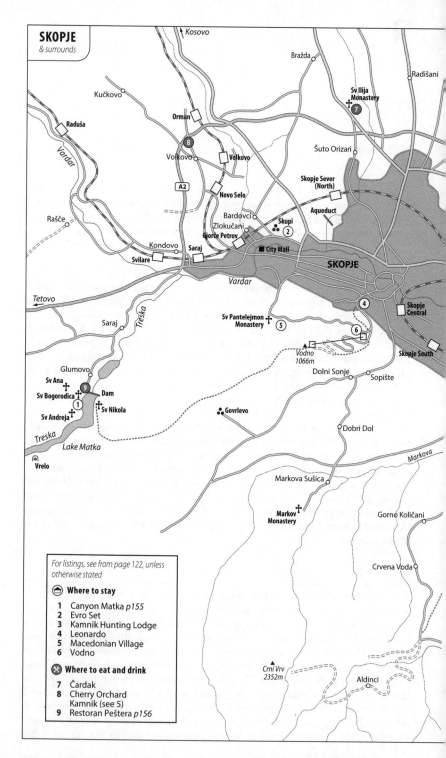

SKOPJE
& surrounds

↑ *Kosovo*

Bražda

Radišani

Kučkovo

Sv Ilija
Monastery ✝ **7**

Raduša

Orman

8

Volkovo **Volkovo**

Šuto Orizari

A2

Novo Selo

Skopje Sever
(North)

Aqueduct

Rašče

Bardovci

Skupi **2**

Zlokučani

Gjorče Petrov

■ City Mall

Kondovo **Saraj**

Svilare

SKOPJE

Vardar

Tetovo

Treska

Saraj

Sv Pantelejmon
Monastery ✝ **5**

4

Skopje
Central

6

Skopje South

*Vodno
1066m*

Dolni Sonje

Sopište

Glumovo

Sv Ana ✝

Sv Bogorodica ✝ **9** **Dam**

1 ✝ **Sv Nikola**

Sv Andreja ✝

Treska

Lake Matka

Govrlevo

Dobri Dol

Markova

⌂ **Vrelo**

Markova Sušica

Markov ✝
Monastery

Gorno Količani

Crvena Voda

*For listings, see from page 122, unless
otherwise stated*

⊕ **Where to stay**

1 Canyon Matka *p155*
2 Evro Set
3 Kamnik Hunting Lodge
4 Leonardo
5 Macedonian Village
6 Vodno

✖ **Where to eat and drink**

7 Čardak
8 Cherry Orchard
  Kamnik (see 5)
9 Restoran Peštera *p156*

▲ *Crni Vrv
2352m*

Aldinci

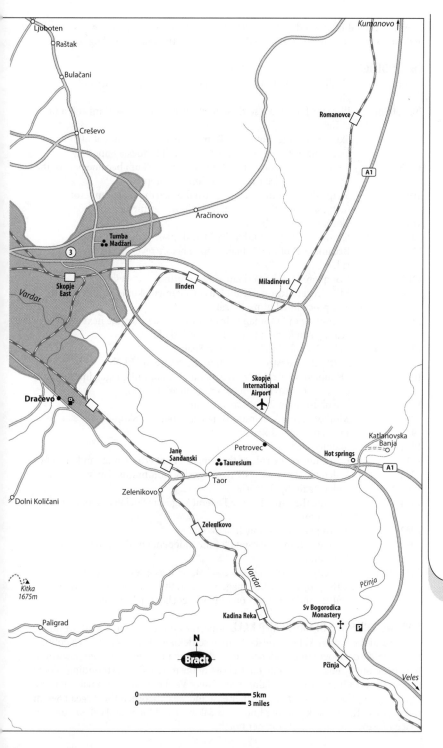

been the capital of the independent Republic of Macedonia since 1991 when the fledgling state broke free from the Federation during the collapse of Yugoslavia.

CHRONOLOGY

6500BC	Neolithic tribes inhabited the Skopje region at Madžari and Govrlevo
700–500BC	Illyrians founded a settlement at present-day Zlokučani and a fort at Kale
148BC	Skupi made the seat of the Roman district government of Dardania as part of the larger province of Moesia Superior
AD395	Under the division of the Roman Empire, Skupi became part of the Byzantine Empire ruled from Constantinople
AD518	Skupi almost completely destroyed by earthquake; Emperor Justinian rebuilt the town a few kilometres further south
AD695	Skupi taken over by Slavs
10th century	Known as Skoplje under the Macedonian-Bulgarian Empire
1189	Became part of the Serbian Empire before reverting to Byzantine rule
1282	Conquered by the Serbian king Milutin II
1346	Milutin's grandson, Stefan Dušan, claimed Skopje as his capital and proclaimed himself Tsar
1392	Beginning of Ottoman rule over the Balkans for the next 520 years; town known to the Turks as Üsküb.
15th century	Many Jews fled to Üsküb from Spain
1555	Earthquake destroyed much of the centre of Üsküb
1689	Occupied by the Austrian general Piccolomini; plague infested the city and, on leaving, Piccolomini burnt it down.
1873	Üsküb to Saloniki railway line built
1910	Mother Teresa – Gondza Bojadziu – born in Skopje
1912–13	First and second Balkan wars
1914	Skopje ruled by Bulgaria
1918	Came under the rule of the Kingdom of Serbs, Croats and Slovenes
1920	Ruled for six months by the Yugoslav Communist Party
1941	Ruled again by Bulgaria
1944	Became the capital of the Federal Yugoslav Socialist Republic of Macedonia
1963	Earthquake razed much of Skopje
1991	Skopje became the capital of the independent Republic of Macedonia
2010–18	The city centre receives a costly facelift as a result of the Skopje 2014 project (see box, page 137) and the erection of dozens of statues and construction of new Neoclassical buildings.

THE ANCIENT SITES OF SKUPI AND KALE Kale, the Ottoman fortress that overlooks Skopje and the Vardar Valley, housed human settlements from as early as Neolithic times c3500BC. Geographic evidence shows that such prehistoric settlements would have been on the edge of a marsh, but the rise of the mountains surrounding Skopje turned the area into the fertile plains of the River Vardar. It became a natural route of passage between greater cities further east and west, between the Aegean Sea in the south at Thessaloniki (earlier known as Saloniki and today still called Solun in Macedonian) and any travels further north.

In the 7th and 6th centuries BC many Greeks, tempted by trade and lands elsewhere, travelled and settled further north. The Illyrians settled in what is now known as Albania, and the outer reaches of their nation covered the source of the River Vardar all the way down to the foothills of the Vodno and the Skopska Crna Gore. They built the first fort at Kale, and others on Gradište above the present-day district of Dolno Nerezi, and later founded the town of Skupi in the area of the present-day Zlokučani village to the northwest of the town centre.

While other ancient cities of today's Macedonia, such as Heraklea near Bitola and Stobi near Gradsko, came under the rule of the Macedonian Empire of Aleksandar III of Macedon, Skupi remained part of the Thracian earldom of Dardania until the 2nd century BC. Roman expansion east brought Skupi under Roman rule in 148BC when it became the seat of local government for the district of Dardania as part of the province of Moesia Superior.

A PART OF THE BYZANTINE EMPIRE When the Roman Empire was divided into eastern and western halves in AD395, Skupi came under Byzantine rule from Constantinople (today's Istanbul) and became an important trading and garrison town for the region. When Skupi was almost completely destroyed by an earthquake in AD518, the Byzantine emperor Justinian (born in Tauresium 20km southeast of present-day Skopje, see page 157) built a new town at the fertile entry point of the River Lepenec into the Vardar. The town was known during his reign as Justiniana Prima.

By the end of the 6th century, Skupi had declined in prestige, although newer settlements were emerging on the northern slopes of Mount Vodno. These were destroyed, however, by invading Slav troops in AD695, who fortified Kale and the northern side of the Vardar.

The region soon came back under Byzantine rule. The town prospered and expanded, while many churches and monasteries were established in the tranquillity and remoteness of the surrounding hills.

MEDIEVAL SKOPLJE By the 10th century, Byzantine rule of Skupi was waning and the town was known as Skoplje under the Macedonian-Bulgarian Empire. In 996 it fell within the breakaway state of Tsar Samoil (see box, page 20). Although Skoplje was not made capital of the new state, the town retained its strategic trading importance until Tsar Samoil's death in 1014, when Skoplje withered again into decline, aided by another earthquake levelling the town at the end of the 11th century.

The Byzantine Empire took advantage of the decline in Skoplje during the 12th century to regain influence in the area, and some fine examples of Byzantine frescoes were painted during this time. Byzantium lost control of Skupi again in 1282 to Serbian king Milutin II. Milutin's grandson, Stefan Dušan, made Skopje his capital, from which he proclaimed himself Tsar in 1346.

FIVE HUNDRED YEARS OF OTTOMAN RULE Rolling back Byzantine rule across much of the Balkans, the Ottoman Turks finally conquered Skopje in 1392 beginning 520 years of Ottoman rule. The Turks named the town Üsküb. At first the Ottomans divided the greater Macedonian region into four vilayets, or districts – Üsküb, Kjustendil, Monastir and Saloniki – and as the northernmost of these, Üsküb was strategically important for further forays into northern Europe. Later Kjustendil was given back to Bulgaria, Janina to Greece and Shkodra went to Albania.

Under Ottoman rule the town moved further towards the entry point of the River Serava into the Vardar. It also became predominantly Muslim and the architecture

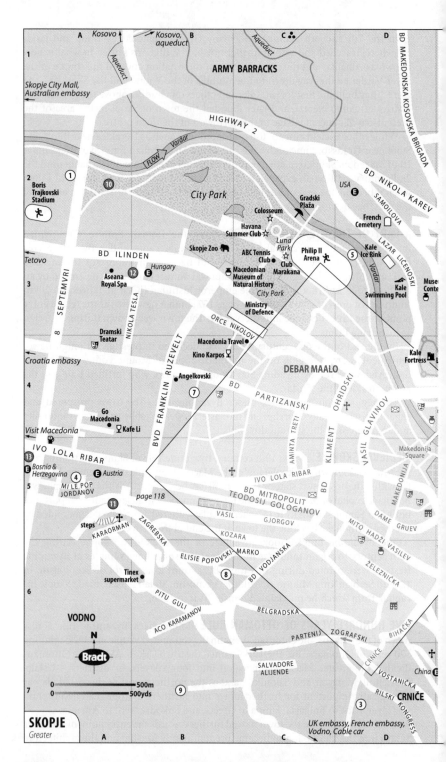

Kosovo ↑   ↖ Kosovo,
                aqueduct   Aqueduct   C ⁂   D

ARMY BARRACKS

Skopje City Mall,   HIGHWAY 2
Australian embassy
←

FLOW Vardar

2 Boris
       Trajkovski   ①
       Stadium   ⑩   *City Park*   USA
       🏃   Gradski   Ⓔ
                                                      Plaža
                                        Colosseum ☆   French
Tetovo   Havana   Cemetery 🏛
←   Summer Club ☆   Luna   Kale
           BD ILINDEN   Skopje Zoo 🐘 Park Philip II ⑤ Ice Rink
                          ⑫ *Hungary*   ABC Tennis   Arena 🏃
3 Aseana   Ⓔ   Club   Club   Kale
       Royal Spa ●   Macedonian Marakana   Swimming Pool Kale
                                            Museum of   Conte
                                            Natural History *City Park*
       Dramski   ORCE NIKOLOV Ministry
       Teatar 🎭   of Defence   Kale
                                       Macedonia Travel ●   Fortress
Croatia embassy ←   Kino Karpos ⛲
                                                                 DEBAR MAALO
                          ● Angelkovski
4   ⑦   BD PARTIZANSKI

       Go
       Macedonia ●
Visit Macedonia ←   ⛲ Kafe Li   IVO LOLA RIBAR   Makedonija
       IVO LOLA RIBAR   Square
⑬
Ⓔ Bosnia &   Ⓔ Austria   BD MITROPOLIT ✉
5 Herzegovina ④   TEODOSIJ GOLOGANOV
       MILE POP   VASIL
       JORDANOV   ⑪   *page 118*   GJORGOV   DAME
                                                                          GRUEV
       steps ✝   ZAGREBSKA KOZARA
                                      ELISIE POPOVSKI-MARKO   BD VODJANSKA   ŽELEZNIČKA
              Tinex ●
6 supermarket   ✉
                          PITU GULI   BELGRADSKA
VODNO   ACO KARAMANOV   BIHAČKA
       N   PARTENIJ ZOGRAFSKI
  Bradt   ✝
                                    SALVADORE   China Ⓔ
       0   500m   ALIJENDE   VOSTANIČKA
7 0   500yds   ⑨   RILSKI KONGRESS **CRNIČE**
                                                          ③
SKOPJE
Greater   UK embassy, French embassy,
                                       Vodno, Cable car
       A   B   C   D

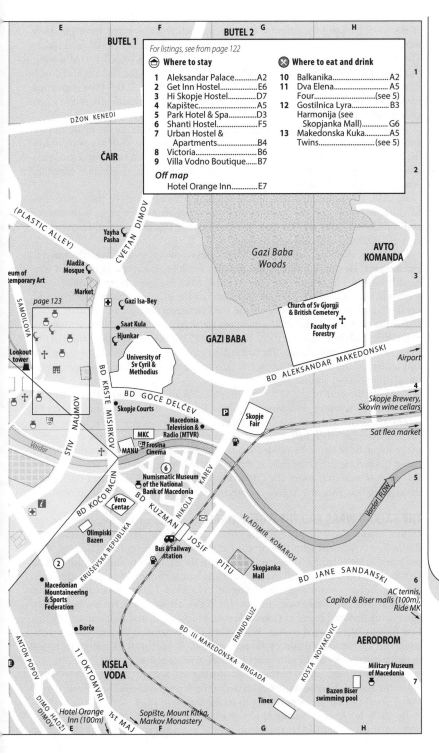

BUTEL 1

BUTEL 2

For listings, see from page 122

Where to stay

1 Aleksandar Palace............A2
2 Get Inn Hostel....................E6
3 Hi Skopje Hostel...............D7
4 Kapištec..............................A5
5 Park Hotel & Spa...............D3
6 Shanti Hostel.....................F5
7 Urban Hostel &
   Apartments.....................B4
8 Victoria..............................B6
9 Villa Vodno Boutique......B7

Off map
   Hotel Orange Inn.............E7

Where to eat and drink

10 Balkanika............................A2
11 Dva Elena...........................A5
    Four...............................(see 5)
12 Gostilnica Lyra..................B3
    Harmonija (see
    Skopjanka Mall)............G6
13 Makedonska Kuka...........A5
    Twins.............................(see 5)

ČAIR

(PLASTIC ALLEY)

DŽON KENEDI

CVETAN DIMOV

Yayha
Pasha

Aladža
Mosque

eum of
temporary Art

Market

page 123

Gazi Isa-Bey

Saat Kula

Hjunkar

Gazi Baba
Woods

AVTO
KOMANDA

Church of Sv Gjorgji
& British Cemetery

Faculty of
Forestry

GAZI BABA

BD ALEKSANDAR MAKEDONSKI

Airport

University of
Sv Cyril &
Methodius

SAMOILOVA

Lookout
tower

BD KRSTE MISIRKOV

STIV NAUMOV

BD GOCE DELČEV

Skopje Courts

Macedonia
Television &
Radio (MTVR)

MKC

MANU   Frosina
        Cinema

Skopje
Fair

Vardar

Skopje Brewery,
Skovin wine cellars

Sat flea market

Numismatic Museum
of the National
Bank of Macedonia

BD KOČO RACIN

Vero
Centar

BD KUZMAN

NIKOLA KAREV

JOSIF PITU

VLADIMIR KOMAROV

Vardar FLOW

Olimpiski
Bazen

Bus & railway
station

KRUŠEVSKA REPUBLIKA

Skopjanka
Mall

BD JANE SANDANSKI

Macedonian
Mountaineering
& Sports
Federation

AC tennis,
Capitol & Biser malls (100m),
Ride MK

Borče

11 OKTOMVRI

KISELA
VODA

ANTON POPOV

1st MAJ

BD III MAKEDONSKA BRIGADA

FRANJO KLUZ

KOSTA NOVAKOVIĆ

AERODROM

Military Museum
of Macedonia

DIMO HADZI
DIMO

Hotel Orange
Inn (100m)

Sopište, Mount Kitka,
Markov Monastery

Tinex

Bazen Biser
swimming pool

of the town changed accordingly. During the 15th century, many travellers' inns were established in the town, such as Kapan An and Suli An, which still exist today. The city's famous Stone Bridge – Kameni Most – was also reconstructed during this period and the famous Daud Pasha baths (the largest in the Balkans and now a modern art gallery) were built at the end of the 15th century. At this time numerous Jews driven out of Spain settled in Üsküb, adding to the cultural mix of the town and enhancing the town's trading reputation.

At the beginning of Ottoman rule, several mosques quickly sprang up in the city and church lands were often seized and given to ex-soldiers, while many churches themselves were converted over time into mosques. The most impressive mosques erected during this early period include the Sultan Murat or Hjunkar Mosque, Aladža Mosque and the Mustafa Pasha Mosque.

In 1555, another earthquake hit the town, destroying much of the centre. The outskirts survived and the town continued, nonetheless, to prosper with traders and travellers. Travel reports from the era number Üsküb's population anywhere between 30,000 and 60,000 inhabitants.

For a very short period in 1689, Üsküb was occupied by the Austrian general Piccolomini. He and his troops did not stay for long, however, as the town was quickly engulfed by the plague. On retreating from the town Piccolomini's troops set fire to Üsküb, perhaps in order to stamp out the plague, although some would say this was done in order to avenge the 1683 Ottoman invasion of Vienna.

For the next two centuries Üsküb's prestige waned, and by the 19th century its population had dwindled to a mere 10,000. In 1873, however, the completion of the Üsküb–Saloniki (now Skopje–Thessaloniki) railway brought many more travellers and traders to the town, so that by the turn of the century Üsküb had regained its former numbers of around 30,000.

Towards the end of the Ottoman Empire, Üsküb, along with other towns in Macedonia – Kruševo and Monastir (now Bitola) – became the main hubs of rebellious movements against Ottoman rule. Üsküb was a key player in the 1903 Ilinden Uprising when native Macedonians of the region declared the emergence of the Republic of Kruševo. While the Kruševo Republic lasted only ten days before being quelled by the Ottomans, it was a sign of the beginning of the end. After 500 years of rule in the area the Ottomans were finally ousted in 1912 during the devastating first Balkan War (see the box on page 26 for an eyewitness account).

THE BALKAN WARS AND THE WORLD WARS As the administrative centre of the region, Üsküb also administered the vilayet of Kosovo under Ottoman rule. This did not go down well with the increasingly Albanian population of Kosovo, who preferred to be ruled by Albanians rather than the ethnic Slav and Turkish mix of Üsküb. Albanians had started to intensify their harassment of Serbs in the area over the past decade, culminating on 12 August 1912 when 15,000 Albanians marched on Üsküb in a bid to take over the city. The Turks, already weak from other battles against the Balkan League of Greece, Serbia, Montenegro and Bulgaria during the first Balkan War, started to flee. When Serb reinforcements arrived some weeks later, the 23 October Battle of Kumanovo (50km northeast of Skopje) proved decisive in driving out the Ottomans from all of Macedonia.

Skopje remained under Serbian rule during the second Balkan War of 1913 when the Balkan League countries started to fight among themselves. Then World War I gave Bulgaria the opportunity to retake Skopje in 1914.

By 1918, however, it belonged to the Kingdom of Serbs, Croats and Slovenes, and remained so until 1941, apart from a brief period of six months in 1920 when

Skopje was controlled by the Yugoslav Communist Party. The interwar period of Royalist Yugoslavia saw significant immigration of ethnic Serbs into the region. An ethnic Serb ruling elite dominated over Turkish, Albanian and Macedonian cultures, continuing the repression wrought by previous Turkish rulers.

During World War II, Skopje came under German fascist occupation and was later taken over by Bulgarian fascist forces. March 1941 saw huge anti-Nazi demonstrations throughout the streets of the town, as Yugoslavia was dragged into the war. But Nazi war crimes were not to be stopped, and on 11 March 1943 Skopje's entire Jewish population of 3,286 was deported to the gas chambers of Treblinka concentration camp in Poland. Another year and a half later, on 13 November 1944, Skopje was liberated by the partisans, who wrested control after a bitter two-day battle.

THE FEDERAL YUGOSLAV SOCIALIST REPUBLIC OF MACEDONIA From 1944 until 1991 Skopje was the capital of the Federal Yugoslav Socialist Republic of Macedonia. The city expanded and the population grew during this period from just over 150,000 in 1945 to almost 600,000 in the early 1990s. Continuing to be prone to natural disasters, the city was flooded by the Vardar in 1962 and then suffered considerable damage from a severe earthquake on 26 July 1963. Over a thousand people were killed as a result of the earthquake, almost 3,000 injured, and over 100,000 were made homeless.

Nearly all of the city's beautiful 18th- and 19th-century buildings were destroyed in the earthquake, including the National Theatre and many government buildings, as well as most of Kale Fortress. Fortunately, though, as with previous earthquakes, much of the old Turkish side of town survived. International financial aid poured into Skopje in order to help rebuild the city. The Japanese architect Kenzo Tange headed the mixed Japanese-Yugoslav team that laid the plans for Skopje's reconstruction, and the result was the many concrete creations of 1960s communism that can still be seen today. Even Mother Teresa's house was razed to make way for a modern shopping centre (the Trgovski Centar).

INDEPENDENCE Skopje made the transition easily from the capital of the Federal Yugoslav Socialist Republic of Macedonia to the capital of today's Republic of Macedonia. The city livened up considerably when Skopje housed the headquarters of the NATO intervention into Kosovo in 1998 and 1999, but saw some rioting of its own during 2001 when internal conflict between the Albanian community and the Macedonian majority erupted over the lack of Albanian representation in government and other social institutions. This effectively killed off business in the old town, Čaršija, which would no longer be frequented by ethnic Macedonians from the south side of the river. It took almost ten years to reverse this trend, and Čaršija is now alive and kicking again, and *the* place to go out at night.

This upturn in business for Čaršija, some say, is just one concession gained by the minorities in the massive and overtly ethnic Macedonian urban renewal programme on the south side of the river that got under way in 2011. Skopje 2014, as it is known, reputedly cost the country as much as €500 million to build new public buildings and over 120 statues which also antagonised the country's relationship with Greece (page 32). The lack of public consultation has also neatly sidestepped any debate on the geological suitability of building so many large public buildings in the centre of Skopje. The 1963 earthquake destroyed most of central Skopje and, in line with geological studies done at the time, it is the reason why Kenzo Tange did not simply rebuild the old centre. The project was officially put on hold in 2018 following a change of government (see box, page 137).

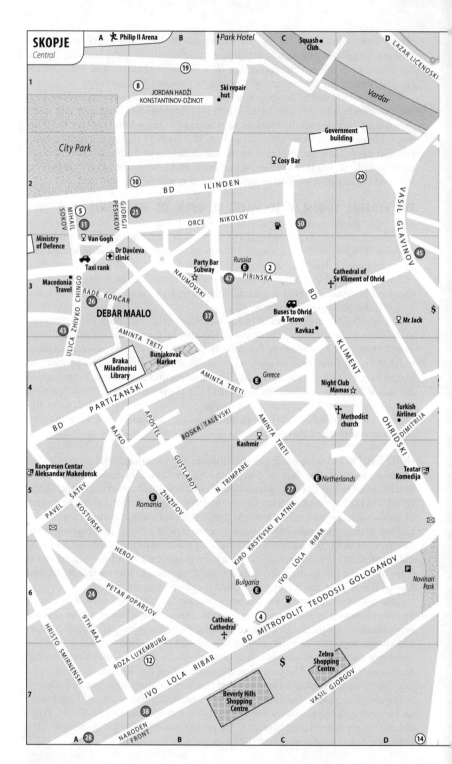

SKOPJE
Central

A 🏃 Philip II Arena   **B**   ↑Park Hotel   **C**   Squash ● Club   **D** LAZAR LIČENOSKI

Vardar

19

8   JORDAN HADŽI KONSTANTINOV-DŽINOT

Ski repair hut ●

Government building

City Park

🍷 Cosy Bar

10   **BD ILINDEN**   20

5   31   🍷 Van Gogh

MIHAIL SOKOV

GJORGJI PEŠKOV

25

ORCE NIKOLOV

50

VASIL GLAVINOV

Ministry of Defence

➕ Dr Davčeva clinic

🚗 Taxi rank

45

Macedonia Travel ●

RADE KONČAR

DEBAR MAALO

NAUMOVSKI

Party Bar Subway ☆

Russia 🇪   2

47   PIRINSKA

BD

Cathedral of ✝ Sv Kliment of Ohrid

26

43

37

🚌 Buses to Ohrid & Tetovo

Kavkaz ●

KLIMENT

$

🍷 Mr Jack

AMINTA TRETI

Braka Miladinovici Library

Bunjakovač Market

AMINTA TRETI

🇪 Greece

Night Club Mamas ☆

PARTIZANSKI

BD

RAJKO

APOSTEL

BOSKA TALEVSKI

AMINTA TRETI

✝ Methodist church

Turkish Airlines ●

OHRIDSKI

DIMITRIJA

Kongresen Centar 🎭 Aleksandar Makedonsk

GUSTLAROT

Kashmir

🇪 Netherlands

Teatar 🎭 Komedija

PAVEL ŠATEV

KOSTURSKI

🇪 Žinzifov

Romania

N TRIMPARE

KIRO KRSTEVSKI PLATNIK

27

✉

HEROJ

IVO LOLA RIBAR

Bulgaria 🇪

P

Novinari Park

24

PETAR POPARSOV

9TH MAJ

BD MITROPOLIT TEODOSIJ GOLOGANOV

4

HRISTO SMIRNENSKI

ROZA LUXEMBURG

12

Catholic Cathedral ✝

$

Zebra Shopping Centre

VASIL GJORGOV

38

IVO LOLA RIBAR

Beverly Hills Shopping Centre

28   NARODEN FRONT   **B**   **C**   **D**   14

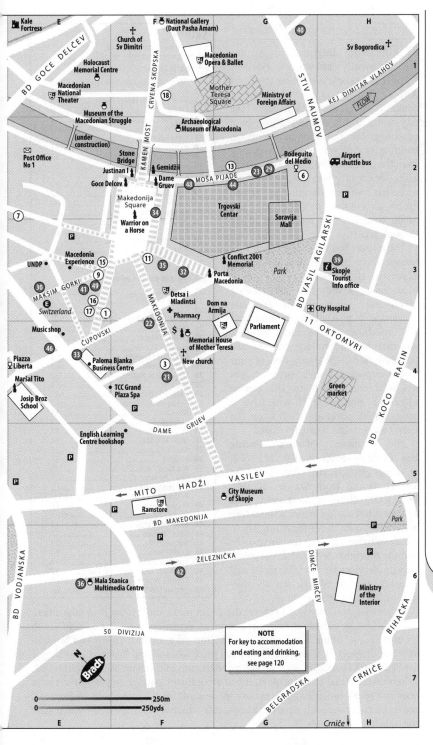

Kale Fortress E
Church of Sv Dimitri
National Gallery (Daut Pasha Amam) F
G
40
H
Sv Bogorodica
Holocaust Memorial Centre
BD GOCE DELČEV
CRVENA SKOPSKA
Macedonian Opera & Ballet
18
Mother Teresa Square
Ministry of Foreign Affairs
STIV NAUMOV
KEJ DIMITAR VLAHOV
FLOW
1
Macedonian National Theater
Museum of the Macedonian Struggle
(under construction)
Archaeological Museum of Macedonia
Post Office No 1
Stone Bridge
Justinan I
Goce Delcev
KAMEN MOST
Gemidžii
Dame Gruev
13
MOŠA PIJADE
48
44
23 29
Bodeguito del Medio
6
Airport shuttle bus
P
2
Makedonija Square
Warrior on a Horse
34
Trgovski Centar
Soravija Mall
7
UNDP
Macedonia Experience
15
11
35
32
Porta Macedonia
Conflict 2001 Memorial
Park
BD VASIL AGILARSKI
39
Skopje Tourist Info office
3
9
MAKSIM GORKI
41 49
16
Switzerland
17 1
Detsa i Mladintsi
Pharmacy
Dom na Armija
City Hospital
30
Music shop
ČUPOVSKI
22
MAKEDONIJA
$
Memorial House of Mother Teresa
New church
Parliament
11 OKTOMVRI
BD KOČO RACIN
46
Piazza Liberta
Maršal Tito
Josip Broz School
33
Paloma Bjanka Business Centre
3
21
TCC Grand Plaza Spa
P
DAME GRUEV
Green market
4
English Learning Centre bookshop
P
P
MITO HADŽI VASILEV
5
P
Ramstore
City Museum of Skopje
BD MAKEDONIJA
Park
BD VODJANSKA
P
ŽELEZNIČKA
DIMČE MIRCEV
P
6
36
Mala Stanica Multimedia Centre
42
Ministry of the Interior
BIHAĆKA
50 DIVIZIJA
N
Bradt
NOTE
For key to accommodation and eating and drinking, see page 120
CRNIČE
7
0   250m
0   250yds
E
F
G
Crniče
H

Skopje HISTORY

3

119

GETTING THERE AND AWAY

BY AIR Skopje International Airport (SKP; formerly known as Petrovec Airport and Skopje Alexander the Great Airport; ✆ 3148 333; w skp.airports.com.mk), stands about 25km east of the city centre and is connected to it by a good highway. The shiny new terminal building is still very small, so getting from the check-in desks to the departure gates doesn't take very long – although when the overseas Macedonians return for holidays in the summer months you might want to allow more time to get through security.

The airport has cafés and snack bars (which you'll probably find shockingly expensive after prices in the rest of Macedonia), a duty-free shop selling Macedonian wines as well as some souvenirs, a post office counter and cash machines. On a multi-leg trip, you may have to collect your onward boarding card at the transit desk of your transit airport as Skopje Airport might not be able to issue these. This can be somewhat harrowing if you have a very short stopover and don't know the transit airport, but it usually works.

The reliable **Manora Shuttle Bus** (✆ 3115 539; m 070 233 882; w manoragroup.com) runs from the airport to and from Skopje (30mins; 180MKD), calling at the Capital Mall and main bus station before terminating at a bay opposite the Holiday Inn. Up to a dozen shuttles run back and forth daily, and the timetable is posted at the above website. Services are not necessarily well timed to meet the Wizzair arrivals (they may be too soon after landing).

SKOPJE Central
For listings, see from page 122

🛏 **Where to stay**
1 Alexandar Square Boutique...............E3
2 Ambassador.....................................C3
3 Best Western Hotel Turist.................F4
4 City 5..C6
5 City Park...A2
6 Holiday Inn.....................................G2
7 Ibis Skopje......................................E2
8 Kanet..B1
9 London B&B....................................E3
10 Lounge Hostel.................................B2
11 Pelister...F3
12 Rose Diplomatique..........................B7
13 Senigallia..G2
14 Seven..D7
15 Skopje Marriott...............................E3
16 Solun Hotel & Spa...........................E3
17 Square...E3
18 Stonebridge....................................F1
19 Tomče Sofka....................................B1
20 Unity Hostel....................................D2

🍴 **Where to eat and drink**
21 Amigos..F4
22 Bistro Skopje...................................F4
23 Carpe Diem......................................G2
   Da Gino (see Trgovski Centar)..........G2
24 Dalma...A6
25 Dneven Prestoj................................B2
26 Frutti di Mare..................................A3
27 Gostilnica Dane...............................C5
28 Gostilnica Dukat..............................A7
29 Irish Pub St Patrick..........................G2
30 Kaj Jole...E3
31 Kamin Čamo....................................A2
32 Kebapcilnica Destan........................F3
33 Kibu..E4
34 Kolektiv Bar.....................................F2
35 La Terrazza......................................F3
36 Mala Stanica....................................E6
37 Mechos..B3
38 Mulino...B7
39 Nacional..H3
40 Old City House.................................G1
41 Peking Garden.................................E3
   Pelister....................................(see 11)
42 Public Room.....................................F6
   Senigallia..................................(see 13)
43 Skopski Merak..................................A3
44 Soul Kitchen....................................G2
45 Squeeze Me......................................D3
46 Star Ocean.......................................E4
47 Sushico..B3
48 Telekom Trend Lounge Bar...............F2
49 Trend Lounge/Bistro London...........E3
50 Vegan 365 Kitchen...........................C2

Otherwise, the only way to travel the 25km into Skopje town is to take a **taxi**. Taxis picked up outside the airport charge an extortionate €25 or 1,500MKD to go into Skopje. Some hotels pick up and drop off guests for free if you book in advance. Airport Taxi also runs to a fixed price list, and will take you into Skopje for 1,220MKD (€20); see w skp.airports.com.mk/default.aspx?ItemID=384. When taking a taxi to the airport, if you are unlucky enough to get a driver who does not speak much English, make sure you ask for the 'aerodrom vo Petrovec', not to be confused with a part of Skopje city which is also called Aerodrom after the old airport!

BY RAIL Skopje railway station [115 F6] (Nikola Karev 20; ✆ 3116 733; w mz. com.mk) is about 15 minutes' walk east of the city centre next to the main bus station. It is probably one of the sorriest main stations you will come across in the Balkans, but it is as safe as anywhere else in Skopje. The information desk staff do not speak much English, but fairly good German. Domestic trains run from Skopje to Kumanovo, to Kičevo via Tetovo and Gostivar, to Bitola via Veles and Prilep, and to Gevgelija via Veles and Demir Kapija. Details of current services are included under the relevant sections in the regional guide. Up-to-date timetables can usually be obtained at w mzt.mk. Fares are cheaper even than buses. There are also international train services to Thessaloniki (Greece) and Priština (Kosovo).

BY BUS The Inter-Town Bus Station [115 F6] (Nikola Karev 20; ✆ 2466 011/313; w sas.com.mk) is located alongside the train station about 1.5km east of the city centre. Plenty of buses run daily from here to all larger towns in Macedonia, as well as to many smaller towns and international destinations. Out-of-the-way places will need a change of bus at the local main town; for instance, buses to Oteševo or Brajčino require a change at Resen. Prices of domestic buses are very low by international standards (although more expensive than the train), ranging from around 100–150MKD one-way to Kumanovo, Veles or Tetovo to 450–550MKD to Ohrid or Strumica. Further details of buses to other towns in Macedonia are included in the relevant regional chapters of this guide, and details of buses to international destinations are on page 66. The information and ticket desk staff speak good English, and timetables and prices are included on the searchable websites w sas. com.mk/en/VozenRed.aspx (international and domestic), w mktransport.mk/en (domestic) and w balkanviator.com/en (international).

GETTING AROUND

BY TAXI Taxis are plentiful and inexpensive. The minimum fare is now 40MKD and 40MKD/km plus 5MKD/minute. Taxis come in a variety of four-door sizes and makes; you might find a few old Skodas and former Yugoslavian Zastavas, but most are now new, clean and air-conditioned models. All are marked with lighted taxi signs on the roof, and you can flag them down almost anywhere on the street. Taxi ranks can be found at the main intersections of town, the central one being around the corner from Alexandar Square Boutique Hotel on Dimitrija Čupovski near the Ploštad [119 E4]. Taxis can also be ordered from any of the following telephone numbers: ✆ 15152 (Naše Taxi – all yellow cabs; ⓕ @NaseTaxi) and ✆ 15177 (English speaking), 15190, 15192, 15193, 15194, 15195. Many taxi drivers also speak good English or German, and those who do will be quick to give you their business card for repeat business. Remember to prefix with 02 if phoning from a mobile.

BY CAR Cars can be hired from the rental companies listed on page 81. You can now pay parking from your mobile phone credit via SMS (w parking.mk). Instructions are indicated at each of the parking zone boards and pay meters. Type in the zone code (eg: A3) then space and your car registration number. Send the SMS to 144144. To end your parking session, simply text the letter S to 144144. You don't need to register online to use this service, but online registration does give you your parking history and other options.

BY BUS These can get very crowded during rush hour, but they are frequent and cover a wide area. The Trimaks Skopje map has a good inset of the city bus routes.

Timetables for local bus routes in and around Skopje can be viewed at **w** jsp. com.mk/VozenRed.aspx. The site is in Macedonian only, but is easy enough to navigate: click on Транспортен успуги then возен ред ('vozen red', meaning 'timetables') if the above link doesn't get you further than the homepage. Choose градски лини (gradski lini) for services within town, or приградски лини (prigradski lini) for local routes outside the city such as the #60 to Matka, then click on the route number you require. The outward schedule (ie: from Skopje, if you're travelling out of town) is shown in the left column; return schedule on the right (in both cases, under Тргнува од). The bus/railway station in Skopje is listed as Транспортен центар (transporten centar). To change the date of travel select Избери датум.

City bus timetables and maps for both the inner city and to outlying villages are available at **w** jsp.com.mk.

TOURIST INFORMATION

The Skopje Tourist Information Office is at Vasil Agilarski bb [119 H3] (next to Restoran Nacional; ☎ 3223 644; ⏰ 08.30–14.30 Mon–Fri). Otherwise, consult **w** exploringmacedonia.com and **w** skopje.gov.mk. Tour operators specialising in Skopje are listed on page 64, and details of local walking tours can be found on page 137. Good maps of Skopje abound, and the Trimaks map includes all the bus routes.

WHERE TO STAY

TOP END

🏠 **Skopje Marriott** [119 E3] (164 rooms) Makedonija Sq; ☎ 5102 520; **w** marriott.com/ hotels/travel/skpmc-skopje-marriott-hotel. Skopje's poshest hotel, the super-central Marriott opened in 2016 & its Neoclassical exterior lends an air of somewhat contrived class to statue-studded Makedonija Square. Public areas have a contemporary feel & are dominated by clean lines. Rooms & suites are spacious, well-equipped, decorated with muted colours offset by modern art on the walls, & come with a private balcony. **$$$$$**

🏠 **Hotel Aleksandar Palace** [114 A2] (135 rooms) Bd 8 Septemvri 15; ☎ 3092 392; **e** info@ aleksandarpalace.com.mk; **w** aleksandarpalace. com.mk. This riverside hotel on the western outskirts of town has comfortable & well-maintained rooms, a well-priced restaurant & good fitness centre with sauna, steam bath & heated indoor pool. **$$$$**

🏠 **Hotel Arka** [123 D3] (26 rooms) Bitpazarska 90/2; ☎ 3230 603; **e** reservation@hotelarka.mk;

w hotelarka.mk. Modern & well-maintained hotel located right on the edge of the Čaršija. There's a small pool & restaurant on the 7th floor. Easier to find on foot than in a car; it's signposted from Bd Krste Misirkov, or turn behind the small fountain on Bitpazarska. **$$$$**

🏠 **Best Western Hotel Turist** [119 F4] (85 rooms) Gjuro Sturgar 11; ☎ 3289 111; **w** bestwestern.com. Central & convenient high-rise aspiring to but not quite attaining international 4-star standards. There's a coffee shop entrance on the pedestrianised Makedonija St. **$$$$**

✳ 🏠 **Bushi Resort & Spa** [123 A3] (48 rooms) Samoilova St; ☎ 3125 130; **e** info@bushiresort. com; **w** bushiresort.com. Opened in 2014, this swish 5-star resort is tucked away in small walled gardens on the west side of the Čaršija below Mustafa Pasha Mosque. Public areas border on the ostentatious, but the carpeted rooms & suites boast an uncluttered modern décor & good amenities including TV, AC & coffee/tea-maker. The spa has an indoor swimming pool, Turkish baths & jacuzzi.

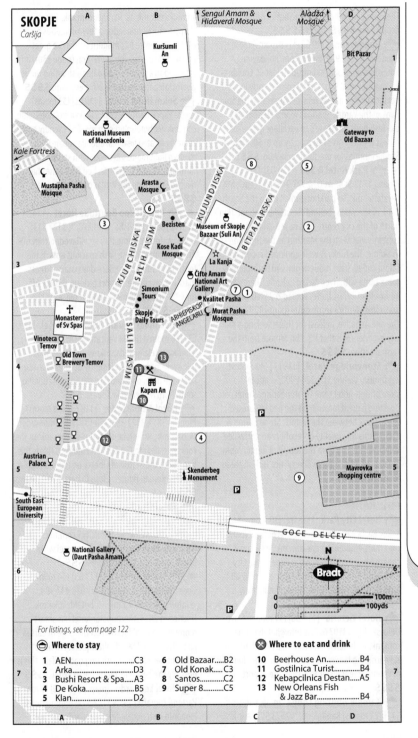

SKOPJE
Čaršija

Kuršumli An

↑ *Sengul Amam & Hidaverdi Mosque*

↑ *Aladža Mosque*

Bit Pazar

National Museum of Macedonia

Kale Fortress →

Mustapha Pasha Mosque

Gateway to Old Bazaar

Arasta Mosque

KJURCHISKA

SALIH ASIM

Bezisten

Kose Kadi Mosque

KUJUNDJISKA

BITPAZARSKA

Museum of Skopje Bazaar (Suli An)

☆ La Kanja

Čifte Amam National Art Gallery

Simonium Tours

Skopje Daily Tours

Kvalitet Pasha

ARHIEPISKOP ANGELARIJ

Murat Pasha Mosque

Monastery of Sv Spas

Vinoteca Temov

Old Town Brewery Temov

Kapan An

Austrian Palace

South East European University

Skenderbeg Monument

GOCE DELČEV

Mavrovka shopping centre

National Gallery (Daut Pasha Amam)

N

Bradt

0 ___ 100m
0 ___ 100yds

For listings, see from page 122

🏠 **Where to stay**

1 AEN..............................C3
2 Arka..............................D3
3 Bushi Resort & Spa......A3
4 De Koka.........................B5
5 Klan..............................D2
6 Old Bazaar.....B2
7 Old Konak.....C3
8 Santos...........C2
9 Super 8...........C5

❌ **Where to eat and drink**

10 Beerhouse An.................B4
11 Gostilnica Turist.............B4
12 Kebapcilnica Destan.....A5
13 New Orleans Fish
     & Jazz Bar.......................B4

There are 2 restaurants & large buffet b/fasts. *Rooms from* **$$$$**; *suites* **$$$$$**

🏠 **Holiday Inn** [119 G2] (178 rooms) Moša Pijade 2; 📞 3292 929; w ihg.com/holidayinn/ hotels/gb/en/skopje/skpmp/hoteldetail. Couldn't-be-more-central 4-star hotel conveniently located next to the row of riverside restaurants on the South Bank of the Vardar. Spacious rooms are slightly old-fashioned but there's an excellent guests-only fitness centre. Prices can drop by up to 50% when Skopje empties for the summer in Aug. **$$$$**

✴ 🏠 **Park Hotel & Spa** [114 D3] (79 rooms) 1732 St 4; m 070 377 948; e reception@ parkhotel.mk; w parkhotel.mk. Set on the South Bank of the Vardar behind the stadium about 1km north of the city centre, this new 6-storey hotel currently vies with the Marriott as the top address in Skopje. The funky & well-equipped rooms are colour coded, have modern glass-in bathrooms & some come with river-facing balcony. There's also an excellent b/fast buffet spread & 2 well-priced waterfront terrace restaurants (pages 129 & 130). The one negative, at least for those seeking a real city experience, is that it's a bit remote from the central action. **$$$$**

🏠 **Stonebridge Hotel** [119 F1] (40 rooms) Kej Dimitar Vlahov 1; 📞 3244 900; e info@ stonebridge-hotel.com; w stonebridge-hotel.com. Boasting a great location on the pedestrianised North Bank between the historic Stone Bridge & Čaršija, this top-quality hotel offers an unrivalled view over the city from the top-floor dining room. Small pool, fitness room & very nice Turkish steam room. **$$$$**

MID-RANGE

🏠 **Hotel City Park** [118 A2] (20 rooms) Mihail Sokov 8a; 📞 3290 860; e contact@hotelcitypark. com.mk; w hotelcitypark.com.mk. Well-run & cheerful business hotel on the edge of the City Park, with bright, spacious modern rooms & all mod cons. Well placed for dining out in lively Debar Maalo. **$$$$**

🏠 **Hotel Victoria** [114 B6] (11 rooms) Slave Delovski 18; 📞 3107 600; e info@hotelvictoria. com.mk; w hotelvictoria.com.mk. Nicely furnished & welcoming family-run hotel in the quiet foothills of Vodno. Free transfer to & from the airport. **$$$$**

🏠 **Kamnik Hunting Lodge** [map, page 111] (21 rooms) Kamnik bb; 📞 2523 522; e info@

kamnik.com.mk; w kamnik.com.mk. This characterful hilltop lodge a few kilometres east of the city centre has modern rooms & a great restaurant specialising in venison (page 130). It is attached to a winery & also has a shooting range downstairs, tennis courts & fitness gym. **$$$$**

🏠 **Solun Hotel & Spa** [119 E3] (53 rooms) Nikola Vapcarov 10; 📞 3232 512; e info@hotelsolun. com.mk; w hotelsolun.com.mk. Eco-friendly hotel centrally located near Makedonija Square with modern light rooms kitted out with stylish Italian furniture. A good spa is attached & an annex has riverside rooms on the Vardar near Kale Fortress. **$$$$**

✴ 🏠 **Villa Vodno Boutique Hotel** [114 B7] (12 rooms) Perisha Savelikj 8; 📞 3177 711; e villavodno@t-home.mk; w villavodno.com.mk. An immaculate house with spacious apts in the foothills of Vodno. Fireplace downstairs, fitness machines available; airport pick-up & drop-off for €15. One of the most popular places to stay in Skopje. **$$$$**

🏠 **Alexandar Square Boutique Hotel** [119 E3] (26 rooms) Nikola Vapcarov 13A; 📞 3111 141; e info@hotelalexandar.mk; w hotelalexandar. mk. Well-managed & elegantly decorated 4-star boutique hotel on a pedestrianised road running south from Makedonija Square. **$$$**

🏠 **Hotel Ambassador** [118 C3] (35 rooms) Pirinska 38; 📞 3121 383; e info@hotelambasador-sk.com.mk; w hotelambasador-sk.com.mk. In the courtyard next to the Russian Embassy. This is the hotel with the Statue of Liberty on top & a couple of other Roman figures. Close to bars & restaurants. **$$$**

🏠 **Hotel City 5** [118 C6] (11 rooms) Mitropolit Teodosij Goloanov 27; 📞 3220 706; e contact@ hotelcity5.com.mk; w hotelcity5.com.mk. Relatively new & modern-feeling hotel with bright, spacious, stylish rooms. **$$$**

✴ 🏠 **Hotel De Koka** [123 B5] (14 rooms) Goce Delčev 5; 📞 3112 200; m 078 447 384; e info@hoteldekoka.mk; w hoteldekoka.mk. Opened in 2014, this popular hotel has smart rooms in a central location on the edge of Čaršija just 500m from Makedonija Square. Friendly, efficient, welcoming & offering good b/fast, this is possibly the best mid-range bet in Skopje. **$$$**

🏠 **Hotel Leonardo** [map, page 110] (9 rooms) Partenij Zografski 19; 📞 3177 517; e info@hotel-leonardo.com.mk; w hotel-leonardo.com.mk.

Small & welcoming hotel with stylish rooms in the quiet foothills of Vodno. Small garden; buffet b/fast. **$$$**

🏠 **Hotel Pelister** [119 F3] (6 rooms) Makedonija Sq; ☎3239 584; e contact@pelisterhotel.com.mk; w pelisterhotel.com.mk. Spacious, well-equipped & brightly furnished rooms & suites in a small central hotel with a great terrace restaurant & prime views towards the *Warrior on a Horse*. **$$$**

🏠 **Hotel Senigallia** [119 G2] (18 rooms) Kej 13 Noemvri; ☎3224 044; e info@senigallia.mk; w senigallia.mk. This one-of-a-kind hotel comprises an imitation wooden galleon docked permanently in the Vardar River off Makedonija Square as part of the Skopje 2014 project. The plush carpeted rooms really feel like they are on a ship, & come with good amenities, but the atmosphere can be a bit dark & contrived. There's a good restaurant/bar on the deck & plenty of other dining & drinking choices on the South Bank opposite. **$$$**

🏠 **Hotel Super 8** [123 C5] (23 rooms) Bd Krste Misirkov 57; ☎3212 225; e contact@hotelsuper8.com.mk; w hotelsuper8.com.mk. Popular new place close to Čaršija & 1.5km from railway/bus stations. **$$$**

🏠 **Hotel Vodno** [map, page 110] (28 rooms) Sredno Vodno; ☎3177 027; e info@hotelvodno.com.mk; w makedonijaturist.com.mk. This timeworn old hotel at the bottom of the cable car to Mount Vodno has a fabulous location, but restaurant & rooms are both mediocre. **$$$**

🏠 **Ibis Skopje** [119 E2] (110 rooms) Orce Nikolov 55; ☎3123 700; e h9672@accor.com; w accor.com. A few paces around the corner from Makedonija Square, this 8-storey international chain hotel has small but well-equipped rooms & often offers fabulous online specials. **$$$**

✳ 🏠 **London B&B** [119 E3] (8 rooms) Maksim Gorki 1; ☎3116 146; e booking@londonbnb.mk; w londonbnb.mk. Well-priced boutique hotel set above the eponymous bistro on Makedonija Square. Stylish rooms & suites have parquet floors, muted contemporary décor, large TV, AC, writing desk & good quality beds. Exceptional value. **$$$**

🏠 **Macedonian Village Hotel** [map, page 110] (49 rooms) Gorno Nerezi; ☎3077 600; m 072 220 600; e info@macedonianvillage.mk; w macedonianvillage.mk. Situated on the slopes of Mount Vodno close to Pantelejmon Monastery,

this themed hotel has rooms spread across a dozen wood-&-stone houses built according to various regional architectural traditions, from Bitola & Prilep to Kratovo & Kumanovo, with matching ethno décor. The complex also includes several traditional restaurants & artisanal shops. **$$$**

✳ 🏠 **Rose Diplomatique** [118 B7] (8 rooms) Roza Luxemburg 13; ☎3135 469; e info@rosediplomatique.com.mk; w rosediplomatique.com.mk. A very nice small hotel with an attractive interior & a good residents-only restaurant & buffet b/fast. Rooms & suites are warmly decorated & have parquet floors & good amenities. Often full so book well in advance. **$$$**

🏠 **Tomče Sofka** [118 B1] (17 rooms) Jordan Hadži Konstantinov-Džinot 14, City Park, near the stadium; ☎3117 250; e tomcesofka@yahoo.com; w tomcesofka.mk. Comfortable hotel set in green gardens on a bustling strip of cafés & restaurants near the river & City Park. **$$$**

BUDGET

✳ 🏠 **AEN Hotel** [123 C3] (22 rooms) Bitpazarska 70; ☎3131 353; m 070 724 242; e nfo@aenhotel.com; w aenhotel.com. This well-run & relatively smart new hotel in Čaršija has a Tardis-like quality of seeming far larger inside than you'd expect from the exterior. Bright, clean & attractively furnished rooms come with TV, AC, fridge, art on the walls & metal-tile bathrooms. Great location & fair prices. **$$$**

🏠 **Hotel Evro Set** [map, page 110] (7 rooms) Skupi bb, 2km northwest of city centre; ☎3095 385; m 070 843 054; e contact@evroset.mk; w evroset.mk. Simply furnished modern rooms with balconies. Tennis courts. **$$$**

🏠 **Hotel Kapištec** [114 A5] (11 rooms) Mile Pop Jordanov 3; ☎3081 424; m 075 242 898; e hotel-kapystec@t-home.mk; w hotel-kapistec.com.mk. Clean & quiet. West of the city centre off Bd Mitropolit Teodosij Gologanov. **$$$**

🏠 **Hotel Old Bazaar** [123 B2] (6 rooms) Kavtandziska 105; ☎3241 176; m 078 336 795; e hotel@old-bazaar.com; w old-bazaar.com. Tucked away on a quiet road behind Arasta Mosque, this affordable guesthouse in Čaršija has clean rooms with AC & TV, & a pleasant terrace restaurant. **$$$**

🏠 **Hotel Orange Inn** [115 E7] (20 rooms) Todor Panica 2; ☎2772 254; e info@orangeinn.com.mk; w orangeinn.com.mk. En suite, AC, Wi-Fi. All rooms have balconies. **$$$**

🏠 **Hotel Seven** [118 D7] (9 rooms) Vodnjanska 28; ☎ 3176 905; e contact@hotel7. com.mk; w hotel7.com.mk. Basic rooms, directly opposite the entrance to the main hospital. Secure parking available. B/fast can be brought up from Žužu bakery downstairs. **$$$**

🏠 **Hotel Santos** [123 C2] (7 rooms) Bitpazarska 125; m 076 421 983; e hotel.santos@ live.com; f @hotel.santos1. Simple but adequate rooms in the heart of Čaršija. Among the cheapest private rooms in the city. **$$**

🏠 **Hotel Square** [119 E3] (10 rooms) Nikola Vapcarov 2, 6th Floor (take the lift to the 5th & walk the final floor); ☎ 3225 090; e hotelsquare@ mt.net.mk; w hotelsquare.com.mk. Nicely furnished small rooms with a good view over the square. **$$**

🏠 **Kanet** [118 A1] (13 rooms) Jordan Hadži Konstantinov-Džinot 20; ☎ 3238 353; e contact@ hotelkanet.com.mk; w hotelkanet.com.mk. This clean basic hotel is on the edge of the City Park near the river, bars & restaurants. **$$**

🏠 **Hotel Klan** [123 D2] (10 rooms) Old Bazaar 75; ☎ 3296 093; m 070 517 035; e hotelklan@ hotmail.com; w hotelklan.com. Comprising a converted old house in Čaršija, this place has large, comfortable & eccentrically decorated rooms whose slightly faded décor befits the old-town location. **$$**

🏠 **Old Konak Hotel** [123 C3] (23 rooms) Bitpazarska bb; ☎ 3257 303; e info@ hoteloldkonak.mk; w hoteloldkonak.mk. Opening out on to the main square in Čaršija, this pleasant hotel has clinically clean white-painted rooms with good amenities. **$$**

HOSTELS
Skopje has a thriving & fast-growing backpacker hostel scene. Any of the excellent places listed below would qualify as an author's pick were it not that all the others do, too!

🏠 **Get Inn Hostel** [115 E6] (2 rooms, 1 4-bed dorm, 1 6-bed female-only dorm, 1 8-bed dorm) 2nd floor, Stiv Naumov 102; ☎ 3136 241; m 077 551 455; e info@getinnskopjehostel.com; w getinnskopjehostel.com. Friendly & colourful hostel conveniently situated halfway between the city centre & the main bus & railway stations. There's a common room, self-catering kitchen & balcony. Dorm beds from €10. **$$**

🏠 **Hi Skopje Hostel** [114 D7] (2 rooms, 2 6-bed dorms, 1 8-bed dorm) Crniche 15; ☎ 6091 242; m 070 333 171; e hiskopjehostel@gmail.com; w hihostelskopje.com. This long-serving & popular owner-managed hostel stands in a converted house in a nice 600m² garden on the slopes of Mount Vodno some 15mins' walk from the city centre. There's AC, kitchen, lounge, washing facilities, lockers in dorms, free Wi-Fi & a nice b/fast. Lounge parties & summer cinema in garden. Affiliated to Vertical Hostel in Mavrovo National Park (page 180) & arranges transfers there. Clean, friendly & efficient. Dorm beds from €8. **$–$$**

🏠 **Lounge Hostel** [118 B2] (1 room, 1 6-bed dorm, 1 8-bed dorm) 1st floor, Naum Naumovski Borce 80; m 076 547 165; e skopje.lounge@ gmail.com; w loungehostel.mk. Situated opposite the City Park, this is a small & brightly decorated hostel with a well-equipped kitchen & plenty of useful tourist info on site. Dorm beds from €8. **$–$$**

🏠 **Shanti Hostel** [115 F5] (1 rooms, 1 4-bed apt, 3 4-bed dorms, 1 8-bed dorm) Rade Jovcevski Korcagin 11; ☎ 6090 807; m 078 708 004; e hostelshanti@gmail.com; w shantihostel.com. This long-serving owner-managed hostel is set in a quiet residential area close to the railway & main bus station, only 10mins' walk from the South Bank & Čaršija. Now spilling across 2 buildings on parallel roads, it's a good choice for those seeking a party atmosphere & also operates its own day tours in and around the city. Dorm beds from €8. **$–$$**

🏠 **Unity Hostel** [118 D2] (1 room, 2 6-bed dorms, 1 8-bed dorm) 1st Floor, Bd Ilinden 1; m 075 942 494; e unity_hostel@yahoo.com; w unityhostel.mk; see ad, page 108. This small & sociable hostel has a large common room with TV, well-equipped kitchen & super-central location only 5mins' walk from Makedonija Square, Kale Fortress & Čaršija. Discounts for stays of more than 3 days. Dorm beds from €9. **$–$$**

✳ 🏠 **Urban Hostel & Apartments** [114 B4] (19 rooms & apts, 3 4-bed dorms, 1 6-bed dorm) Adolf Ciborovski 22; ☎ 6142 785; m 078 432 384; e contact@urbanhostel.com.mk; w urbanhostel. com.mk; see ad, page 160.
The largest & probably the smartest hostel in Skopje, this place has friendly & helpful staff, immaculately maintained & brightly decorated rooms & dorms, a useful location for eating out in lively Debar Maalo, & great amenities including

free use of bicycles, a comfortable common room with large 120-channel TV, laptop, aquarium & piano, & a self-catering kitchen. Dorm beds from €8. **$–$$**

✖ WHERE TO EAT AND DRINK

Traditional food abounds in the city and, slowly, there is some variety moving in too, including Japanese, Chinese and Indian, as well as Italian, Greek and Turkish. Eating out is still quite cheap. A lunch dish is often as little as 150–250MKD, while evening meals might be slightly higher, going up to 1,000MKD or more if you opt to eat on the expensive side. Almost any menu in Skopje will appear in English as well as Macedonian. All restaurants are now non-smoking indoors, and in the summer there is an abundance of outdoor seating. Most restaurants (unless otherwise stated) open at noon daily and stay open until midnight. Some restaurants open at 08.00 for breakfast, especially of the cooked variety.

There are three main concentrations of eating establishments in the city, all quite central. Most varied in terms of cuisine is the plethora of restaurants on and around **Makedonija Square**, which includes the row of attractive terrace eateries that lines the South Bank of the Vardar running east towards the Holiday Inn. Shaded by plane trees and cooled by a river breeze, these riverside restaurants are a most agreeable place to sit and sip a chilled draught beer, cocktail or glass of wine on a balmy summer evening. As might be expected, restaurants in and around Makedonija Square tend to be slightly pricey, but not off-puttingly so.

Rather more down-to-earth is the concentration of restaurants and *kebapcilnicas* (kebab houses) in the old Turkish quarter of **Čaršija**. *Kebapči* at any of these restaurants are very good, especially if accompanied with grilled red peppers and a beer.

Less touristy than either of the above is the lively suburb of **Debar Maalo**, which stands about 1km east of Makedonija Square, and is entrenched among younger fun-loving Skopjites as *the* place to hang and eat out. Several of the suburb's most popular eateries are found on the pair of recently pedestrianised 'Bohemian streets', namely Ulica Zhivko Chingo and Gjorgji Peshkov, but there is plenty of choice elsewhere, especially along and around Aminta III Street.

Pure **vegetarian** restaurants are thin on the ground in Skopje. The only exceptions are the Harmonija and Vegan 365 Kitchen. That said, most Macedonian meze choices will be vegetarian, and many restaurants, such as Pelister, Skopski Melak and Kibo [119 E4] also have good salad bars and vegetarian dishes. Beerhouse An and Squeeze Me offer quite a few vegetarian options, and a lot of Italian places will have non-meat pizzas and pastas. A good place to search for vegetarian options is w happycow.net.

MAKEDONIJA SQUARE AND SURROUNDS

✖ **Amigos** [119 F4] Makedonija 11; ✆3228 699; m 071 230 314; w amigos.com.mk. Decent Mexican cuisine in a popular location. Serves a wide variety of cocktails for a very good price. **$$$**

✖ **Bistro Skopje** [119 F4] Makedonija 41; m 071 352 265; ⨍ @BistroSkopje. Pleasant blues- & jazz-themed bar with appropriate music & monochrome photos on the wall, & a good cigar & wine selection. Cosmopolitan menu includes stir-fries, burgers, pasta, pizza & grilled meat & fish. Varied b/fast selection, too. **$$$**

✖ **Kolektiv Bar** [119 F2] Makedonija Sq; ✆3213 099; w kolektiv.business.site. The liveliest bar on Makedonija Square serves organic craft beers from Temov Brewery at prices slightly (but not prohibitively) pricier than they are *in situ*. A small but tasty selection of light meals & pub grub – salads, sandwiches, grills & some of the best burgers in town – is complemented by an unusually contemporary music selection. **$$$**

✕ **La Terrazza** [119 F3] Italian 11 Oktomvri 2; ☎3113 380; ᶠ @LaTerrazzaSkopje. Boasting a wide shady terracotta-tiled terrace just off Makedonija Square, this stylish restaurant has a laid-back Mediterranean feel & diverse Italian/Macedonian menu including pizza, pasta & grills. Good wine list & dessert selection. A varied selection of inexpensive soups & salads (120–200MKD) makes for an ideal light lunch. $$$

✳ ✕ **Peking Garden** [119 E3] Maksim Gorki 3; ☎3221 173; m 071 381 981; w pekinggarden.mk. Very popular with the local Asian community, this Chinese & sushi restaurant just off Makedonija Square isn't quite a world-beater, but the food is tasty enough, portions are generous, & it makes a refreshing change from typical Macedonian fare. Lunch specials at 200MKD inclusive of soup are a bargain. $$$

✕ **Da Gino** [119 G2] Trgovski Centar, 2nd Floor; m 070 342 191; w restorangino.mk. Established in 1997, this Tuscan owner-managed place offers the city's best pizza, made in true Italian style, as well as an impressive fresh seafood platter, squid ink pasta & very good beef carpaccio. The setting, in a modern mall, is somewhat deficient in ambience. $$

✕ **Kebapcilnica Destan** [119 F3] 11th Oktomvri bb, next to the Triumphal Arch; ⊕ 08.00–23.00 daily. This central outlet of a Čaršija institution founded in 1913 only serves kebapči, which are acclaimed for their adherence to a special family recipe handed down over several generations. $$

✕ **Pelister** [119 F3] Makedonija Sq; ☎3112 482; w pelisterhotel.com.mk. Lots of outside seating from which to observe the square & even in the winter the glass-fronted restaurant offers plenty of sunlit areas as well as upper seating in a cosier atmosphere. Specialises in Macedonian & Mediterranean fare. $$

✕ **Trend Lounge/Bistro London** [119 E3] Makedonija Sq, Nikola Vapcarov 2; ☎3132 425; m 071 368 846; w caffetrend.mk; ⊕ 08.00–04.00 daily. As its name suggests, this is one of the places to be seen, with its bright contemporary décor & walls plastered with prints of Amy Winehouse, The Beatles & the like. Modern menu, 3 b/fast choices & lots of desserts & cocktails. $$

✳ ✕ **Squeeze Me** [118 D3] Vasil Glavinov 14; ☎3222 230; ᶠ @SqueezeMe.sk; ⊕ 07.00–22.00 Mon–Fri, 08.00–22.00 Sat, 08.00–17.00 Sun.

Skopje's healthiest & arguably best favourite b/fast venue, this funkily decorated, sensibly priced & friendly self-service juice bar serves excellent coffee, yoghurt & muesli, & an imaginative selection of fruit & vegetable smoothies, egg-based dishes & sandwiches. Vegetarian-friendly, too. $

VARDAR SOUTH BANK
✳ ✕ **Carpe Diem** [119 G2] Kej 13 Noemvri; ☎3256 456; m 070 355 750; w carpediemrestaurant.mk. The classiest joint on the riverfront specialises in Italian dishes (pizza, pasta, risotto) & seafood, but the globetrotting menu also includes the likes of beef Wellington, Corsican squid, chicken arrabbiata & Thai pork. $$$

✕ **Senigallia** [119 G2] Kej 13 Noemvri; ☎3224 044; w senigallia.mk. Difficult to beat in terms of location & ambience, the open-air restaurant on the deck of Skopje's most shipshape hotel (page 125) serves a decent selection of local & international dishes with the Vardar lapping the sides. $$$

✕ **Soul Kitchen** [119 G2] Kej 13 Noemvri; m 078 887 733; w soulkitchen.mk. Possibly the most extensive pan-Balkan menu in town, as well as a good wine list & chilled draught beer. $$$

✕ **Irish Pub St Patrick** [119 G2] Kej 13 Noemvri; ☎3256 337; m 070 260 366; w irishpub.com.mk. Aside from Guinness, Skopje's oldest Irish pub – established back in 2000 – has a large menu of non-Balkan dishes, including stir-fries & curries. $$

✕ **Telekom Trend Lounge Bar** [119 F2] Kej 13 Noemvri; m 070 277 137; w caffetrend.mk. Brightly decorated waterfront snack bar serving good burgers, pizzas & sandwiches. $$

ČARŠIJA
✳ ✕ **Beerhouse An** [123 B4] Kapan An, off Bitpazarska; ☎3212 111; ⊕ 10.00–midnight Mon–Sat, noon–23.00 Sun. Also signposted as Pivnica An, this has an atmospheric setting in the inner courtyard of an old Turkish inn & specialises in traditional Macedonian fare, with a few decent vegetarian options. $$$

✕ **New Orleans Fish & Jazz Bar** [123 B4] Off Bitpazarska; ☎3224 560. Better at jazz than fish, the jazz being live every Fri–Sun evening. There's not just fish on the menu, & it's certainly a welcome & varied offer in the old town. Great setting with a cosy upstairs for the winter. $$$

✗ Kebapcilnica Destan [123 A5] Salih Asim; 🕿 3224 063; ⊕ 08.00–23.00 daily. This Čaršija institution was founded in 1913 & serves some of the best-value grills in the old town. $$

✗ Gostilnica Turist [123 B4] Arhiepiskop Angelarij bb; m 070 700 720. Inexpensive traditional restaurant, shaded by a plane tree & umbrellas at the north entrance to Kapan. Here, the bread is always grilled with lashings of kebapči dripping & plenty of *vegeta* seasoning. $

DEBAR MAALO

✗ Frutti di Mare [118 A3] Cnr Zhivko Chingo & Rade Končar; 🕿 3132 145; m 075 360 636; w fruttidimare.mk; ⊕ Mon–Sat. Award-winning restaurant specialising in Dalmatian & Mediterranean seafood dishes, with wood & exposed brickwork interior, as well as some garden seating. $$$$

✳ ✗ Sushico [118 B3] Aminta III 29; 🕿 3217 874; m 072 303 303; w sushico.mk. This modish restaurant hemmed in by a bamboo hedge has a lengthy menu of Chinese, Japanese & Thai dishes. The sushi is good & vegetarians are well catered for. Pricey but tasty & a refreshing change from the usual Balkan fare. $$$$

✗ Dneven Prestoj [118 B2] Gjorgji Peshkov 5; 🕿 3100 605. Super but unpretentious local eatery with plenty of pavement seating on the shorter of the city's 2 'Bohemian streets'. The Macedonian food is tasty, the wine is affordable & street musicians wander in & out. Good value. $$$

✗ Gostilnica Dane [118 C5] Kiro Krstevski Platnik 2; 🕿 3140 666. Dane serves very good *pleckavica* (hamburger patties) & *meso vo salamura* (pork preserved in salt vats). $$

✳ ✗ Skopski Merak [118 A3] Cnr Zhivko Chingo & Debarca 51; 🕿 3212 215; m 078 343 630; w skopskimerak.mk; ⊕ 09.00–midnight Sun–Thu, 09.00–01.00 Fri–Sat. One of the city's longest-serving restaurants, this place specialises in traditional dishes including oven-baked specialities from the wood-fired oven, from roast lamb or pork to baked carp, & a delightful summer stew with tomatoes & eggs. Delicious salads & various other dishes. A lovely restaurant, & enormously popular. $$

✗ Kamin Čamo [118 A2] Mihail Sokov 6a; 🕿 3161 130; m 070 265 657; ✦ @camokamin. Situated down a small garden path just past the City Park Hotel, this unassuming but long-serving local eatery is so popular you may need a reservation during peak lunchtimes. Try their *sarma*, braised tongue & *pavlaka* (sour cream cheese). $

✳ ✗ Vegan 365 Kitchen [118 C2] Kliment Ohridski Bd; m 077 616 446; ⊕ 09.00–17.00 Mon–Fri. Skopje's only vegan restaurant serves falafel & veggie burgers, a varied selection of salads, freshly squeezed juices, sugar-free cakes & sweets, & other healthy fare using fresh & mostly local &/or organic ingredients. $

REST OF SKOPJE

✗ Dalma [118 A6] Petar Poparsov 22/3; 🕿 6136 700; m 078 305 234; w dalma.com.mk; ⊕ 10.00–midnight Mon–Sat, 13.00–midnight Sun. Very good Dalmatian dishes in a small exclusive atmosphere. Superb fresh octopus (best eaten with truffle oil), lamb chops & salt-baked fish. $$$$

✗ Four Restaurant [114 B3] 1732 St 4; m 070 377 948; w parkhotel.mk. The excellent fine-dining restaurant in the Park Hotel (page 124) is simply but stylishly decorated & the terrace offers a rare view right on to the Vardar River. The international cuisine places a strong emphasis on Italian ($$$) as well as seafood & grilled steak ($$$$).

✗ Mulino [118 B7] Bd Mitropolit Teodosij Gologanov 69; 🕿 3232 877; w vodenicamulino. com.mk. Known as Vodenica in Macedonian, this restaurant sports a decorative waterwheel & fishpond & is very popular with government & ambassadors. If you want to eat during the popular hrs after 20.00, you may need to phone in advance to reserve a table. $$$$

✗ Old City House [119 G1] Phillip II of Macedonia 14; 🕿 3131 376; m 071 263 181; ✦ @StaraKuka. Also known by its Macedonian name Stara Kuka, this beautifully renovated house from 1836 is atmospheric, complete with intricate wooden ceiling & traditional food. $$$$

✗ Balkanika [114 A2] Bd 8 Septemvri; 🕿 3073 712. Nice outdoor seating. Best pastrmajlija in town. $$$

✗ Dva Elena [114 A5] Zagrebska 31; 🕿 3060 900; m 070 545 158. An excellent steakhouse whose name literally means 'Two Deers' & whose décor comes replete with a stuffed bear. $$$

✗ Gostilnica Dukat [118 A7] Bd Mitropolit Teodosij Gologanov 79; 🕿 3211 011; m 072 306 198. Specialises in local fish & traditional dishes. $$$

✗ Gostilnica Lyra [114 B3] Nikola Tesla 11; ✆ 3083 020; **f** @gostilnicalyra. Excellent traditional live music every night, & a nice fireplace & patio. Try the lamb in a cream sauce. **$$$**

✗ Harmonija [115 G6] Skopjanka Mall 37; ✆ 2460 985; ⏰ Mon–Sat. Strictly vegetarian restaurant offering a feast of macrobiotic meals. The owner & cook earned her degree in macrobiotic cuisine in the US & is able to give you a dietary consultation on appointment. **$$$**

✗ Kamnik [map, page 110] Kamnik bb; ✆ 2523 522; **w** kamnik.com.mk. Hidden in Avtokomanda district; turn immediately before the Lukoil petrol station on the way from the airport into town. Lots of stuffed animal trophies deck the walls. Serves wild boar sausages, Macedonian venison, rabbit béchamel stew & more. Try their cold cut sausages, salamis & hams for a range of game choices. Also has a wide choice of Macedonian & foreign wines. **$$$**

✗ Makedonska Kuka [114 A5] Bd Mitropolit Teodosij Gologanov, opposite the Alumina factory; ✆ 3296 415; **m** 070 208 519; ⏰ 08.00–midnight daily. Traditional Macedonian décor & food; live music in the evenings. **$$$**

✗ Star Ocean [119 E4] Lermontov 19; ✆ 3222 723; **m** 075 287 345; **w** starocean.mk; ⏰ 10.00–midnight Mon–Sat, noon–midnight Sun. Authentic Chinese food, very reasonably priced & fairly popular. **$$$**

✗ Kaj Jole [119 E3] Maksim Gorki 18; ✆ 3220 099. This is the hang-out of the Macedonian Writers' Association. Its basic décor & unassuming signage ('Jole' is written in Cyrillic above the entrance at the street, then take the 2nd door on the left down the corridor) belie its good, traditional food. **$$**

✗ Mala Stanica [119 E6] Moskovska 26; ✆ 3061 024; **w** malastanica.com. Run by the chefs of Macedonia's 1st president, this place offers up exceptionally good food, especially for the price. Richard Gere ate here when filming for *Hunting Party*, & his photo is on the wall as you enter. Try *tikvica meze* (courgette spread) to start, & *sutljaš* (rice pudding cake) for dessert. **$$**

✗ Nacional [119 H3] Bd Filip Vtori Makedonski bb, opposite the park by the Trgovski Centar; ✆ 3214 200. Has excellent pizza bread served as a big domed spaceship accompanied by live elevator music. Lovely outdoor patio. **$$**

✗ Public Room [119 F6] 50 Divizija St 22; **m** 078 250 554; **w** publicroom.org. Trendy wine

bar, bistro & café with shady terrace seating & large warehouse-style interior decorated with photos of historic presidential meetings & processions. The Mediterranean menu includes Turkish meatballs, falafel, moussaka, escargot, wraps, pasta, salads & wholegrain sandwiches. Good selection of healthy b/fasts. Well priced. **$$**

✗ Twins [114 B3] 1732 St 4; **m** 070 377 948; **w** parkhotel.mk. Situated in the Park Hotel, this downmarket counterpart to the Four (page 124) overlooks the Vardar & serves a varied menu of well-priced burgers, pizzas & salads as well as the likes of chicken tikka & fish & chips. **$$**

OUT OF TOWN *Map, page 110*

Outside Skopje are several great traditional restaurants serving good quality food. Although they can be difficult to find & certainly quicker & more convenient to get to by car/taxi than by public transport, they are all set in beautiful scenery, where a hike in the local hills & woods is rewarding & helps to work up an appetite.

✗ Čardak Sv Ilija Monastery, 5km north of Skopje; **m** 070 410 919; ⏰ 10.00–midnight daily. A good place to eat if you have been out walking in the Skopska Crnagore. In the grounds are a small fishpond, a 300-year-old aspen tree & a kids' play area. In summer, seating is outside under the trees, & in winter in the large balconied *čardak* (traditional inn). To get here take the road through Butel & turn left before Radišani village & head towards Mirkovci. The restaurant & monastery are signposted (just keep your eyes peeled). To get here by bus, the 61 (towards Pobožje), 71 (towards Banjani) & 81 (towards Blace) all go past the turn-off to Čardak. Ask the driver to let you off at Restoran Čardak Sveti Ilija. **$$**

✗ Cherry Orchard Volkovo; ✆ 2055 195; **m** 070 225 642; ⏰ 09.00–21.00 Tue–Sun. In the grounds of the El Kabon riding stables, which have a well-manicured terrace & lawns overlooking the exercise paddocks & a delightful children's play area. The restaurant building itself was used in the Macedonian movie *Dust* by Milčo Mančevski, & was reconstructed as the stables (whose horses were used in the movie) at the end of filming. The well-groomed interior offers fireside seating in winter, but is sadly not well frequented, not least because it is complicated to get here by car. If you want to try, follow the ring-road signs towards Priština then take the (1st exit) turn-off for Orman, driving under the bridge following signs for Volkovo. Follow the newly laid tarmac road & take the 1st right after the bus station, following signs for the stables. Alternatively, bus 22 from anywhere on Partizanski ends its journey 700m from the restaurant where it is signposted for the stables. $$

ENTERTAINMENT AND NIGHTLIFE

BARS Skopje's most popular place for a drink is now Čaršija old town, which surpasses the still popular strip from the old railway station and current Museum of Skopje along Makedonski pedestrian area to the café-bars on the riverside ground floor of the Trgovski Centar. The cafés along the pedestrian area often sport large comfortable armchairs outside under big shady umbrellas to help you while away a summer afternoon. Most of these are open 08.00–midnight or 01.00.

♀ **Austrian Palace** [123 A5] Bd Mitropolit Teodosij Gologanov 3; m 070 435 272. Chic new 2-storey bar with a wide terrace set at the southern end of Čaršija. Has a good cocktail menu & attracts a student-dominated crowd.
♀ **Bodeguito del Medio** [119 G2] Kej 13 Noemvri; 3122 309; ⊕ 10.00–01.00. Popular Cuban-themed bar-restaurant, with plenty of cocktails & Latin music.
♀ **Cosy Bar** [118 C2] Bd Kliment Ohridski; m 070 364 224. This beer-lover's paradise offers a selection of more than 50 unusual home-grown & imported brews from Belgium, Germany & the like. Good snack menu.
♀ **Kafe Li** [114 A4] Ankarska 23; ⊕ 08.00– 01.00. Café-bar that sometimes has exhibitions.
♀ **Kashmir** [118 C4] Cnr of Nicola Trimpare & Aminta III. A Bohemian-themed bar with intimate seating cubicles facing a small fountain in the centre.
♀ **Kino Karpos** [114 B4] Blagoj Davkov 2/1; 3213 515; w kinokarpos.mk. Lively cinema-themed bar with a good whisky & cocktail menu & occasional live music & DJ sets.
♀ **Mr Jack** [118 D3] Partizanska Odredi 3; 3231 999; @Mr.Jack.Sk. A true Irish bar, as even the Irish in Skopje would claim, but hard to find back off the main road at the bottom of a high-rise complex. Pleasant, relaxing & welcoming.
♀ **Old Town Brewery Temov** [123 A4] Off Samoilova; m 076 462 372, 075 235 781;

w oldtown-brewerytemov.com. Macedonia's only craft brewery serves a selection of delicious & well-priced draughts free of preservatives & artificial colouring & flavourants. There's an atmospheric interior, a shaded terrace next to Sv Spas, & a great menu of well-priced Macedonian food.
♀ **Piazza Liberta** [119 E4] Dimitrija Čupovski 24; 3224 807; w piazzaliberta.mk; ⊕ 08.00– midnight daily. This is also known as Kikiriki, meaning 'peanut', due to the free peanuts served with your drinks, the shells of which are simply thrown on the floor. It has an old reading-room atmosphere with shelves filled with books & big upstairs windows that look out on to the street, & is named after the square that used to be here before the 1963 earthquake.
♀ **Van Gogh** [118 A3] Mihail Sokov 74; ⊕ 09.00–midnight Sun–Thu, 09.00–01.00 Fri– Sat. Established in 1986, this ever-popular bar has a quiet setting spilling out on to the cobblestone road & attracts a cosmopolitan arty crowd with regular live music, DJ nights & salsa dancing.
♀ **Vinoteka Temov** [123 A4] Gradište 1a, Stara Čaršija; 3212 779; w vinotekatemov.com; ⊕ 11.00–01.00 daily. Quaint wine bar in the old town, situated next to the Old Town Brewery Temov, & serving a wide variety of Macedonia's own finest wines as well as an extensive range of wines from abroad. Live music is played most evenings, including traditional chalgia on Thu.

CLUBS AND LIVE MUSIC Clubs are generally open 22.30–04.00 daily, and some of the bigger ones listed here move outdoors to the City Park [114 C2] in the summer. For a list of some of the bands touring during your trip see w password.mk, and for tickets to tour concerts go to w mktickets.mk. For more information on Skopje's lively club scene see w likealocalguide.com/skopje/nightlife.

☆ **Club Marakana** [114 C3] City Park; ⏲ 21.00–04.00 daily; restaurant downstairs ⏲ 08.00–midnight daily. Laid-back club playing an eclectic mix of rock, jazz & blues. Live music most nights. Can get very busy but attracts an older & relatively sedate crowd.

☆ **Havana Summer Club** [114 C3] City Park; m 078 591 500; ⏲ 20.00–03.00 daily. Very popular in the summer, with large outdoor area.

☆ **La Kanja** [123 C3] 50 Divizija 33; m 075 223 340; ⏲ 21.00–02.00 daily. Underground gay-friendly bar in Čaršija holding live gigs most nights.

☆ **Night Club Mamas** [118 D4] Kliment Ohridski 60; ☎ 3239 120; ⏲ 10.00–midnight Sun–Thu, 10.00–01.00 Fri–Sat. Wonderful blues & jazz bar with comfortable seating & live piano or jazz trios providing an atmosphere in which you can still (just about) talk to accompanying friends.

☆ **Party Bar Subway** [118 B3] Pirinska 45; m 077 663 810; w partybarsubway.com. Sophisticated cocktail & lounge bar with DJs playing loud contemporary dance sets over the w/end.

OTHER ENTERTAINMENT Despite its small size, but being the capital, Skopje has a choice of theatre, dance, concerts and cinema venues. The Skopje Tourist Information booklet, available free every month from many travel agencies and hotels, lists a full calendar of events in the city, as well as many useful addresses and telephone numbers.

Theatres and concert halls

🎭 **Dramski Teatar** [114 A4] Šekspirova 15; ☎ 3063 453; w dramskiteatar.com.mk

🎭 **Kongresen Centar Aleksandar Makedonsk** [118 A5] Partizanski Odredi bb; ☎ 3245 615; w kongresencentaraleksandarmakedonski.mk. The former Univerzalna Sala holds concerts 2 or 3 times a week, both classical & modern jazz/rock. Skopje's jazz festival is held here for a week every Oct.

🎭 **Macedonian National Theatre** [119 E1] 11 March 3; ☎ 3230 304; e contact@mnt.com.mk; w mnt.com.mk. Hosts modern drama & plays. Opposite the Holocaust Memorial Centre.

🎭 **Macedonian Opera and Ballet** [119 F1] Quay Dimitar Vlahov; ☎ 3118 451; m 078 426 536; w mob.com.mk. Stages opera & ballet.

🎭 **Teatar Komedija (Comedy Theatre)** [118 D5] Kliment Ohridski bb 15; ☎ 3119 990; 🟦 @TeatarKomedija

🎭 **Teatar za Detsa i Mladintsi** [119 F3] Dimitrija Čupovski 4; ☎ 3222 619; w puppet.com. mk. Children's & youth theatre.

Cinemas

As well as those listed below, there's also a Cineplexx at City Mall (w cineplexx.mk).

🎬 **Frosina Cinema** [115 F5] Youth Culture Centre, Quay Dimitar Vlahov; ☎ 3115 225; w mkc. mk. Often shows art or foreign movies, usually a different one every evening at 20.00.

🎬 **Milenium** [119 G2] Kej 13 Noemvri, Trgovski Centar, 1st Floor; ☎ 3120 389; w kinomilenium. mk. The biggest & best cinema in Skopje.

SHOPPING

FOOD The **Vero supermarket** chain, found at the huge Vero Centar shopping mall [115 F5] and Ramstore [119 F5], has the widest range of food available in Skopje, including ginger, basil, fresh limes, mint and horseradish sauce, fresh seafood (from Greece) and Jamie Oliver sauces. Another supermarket chain is **Tinex** [115 G7] (w tinex.com.mk) which, along with Vero, takes all major credit cards. Local fresh produce is best bought from the big fresh markets either at the Bit Pazar (see opposite), the **Green market** [119 H4] on the western corner of Kočo Racin and 11 Oktomvri, or **Bunjakovač Market** [118 B4] on Partizanski just after Aminta Treti.

The **Bit Pazar** [123 D1] is the biggest outdoor market in Skopje. Not only does it have fresh vegetables, fruit, meat products, fish, spices, pulses and tea, it also has a large ironmongery section and, in fact, you can buy almost anything here. Now open every day, it used to be held on Tuesdays and Fridays only, following a 600-year-old tradition, being first held by the monks of the Monastery of Sv Gjorgi Gorga. The monastery no longer exists but the market is still on the same spot and has expanded over the former grounds of the monastery.

There are several **health food** stores in Skopje, including Biona (with shops at Gradski Zid and in Beverly Hills Shopping Centre [118 C7]), Vitalia (various locations including Skopje City Mall; w vitalia.com.mk), Biocosmos (shops at Skopje green market & elsewhere; w biocosmos.mk) and Anni Di Vita (16 Makedonska Brigada 2/2; ☎3175 539).

SOUVENIRS AND LOCAL CRAFTWARE
Conveniently, many souvenirs are now sold in a number of shops around the town, although these are still sometimes a little obscure. Čaršija is the best place to get genuine locally made handicrafts such as leather slippers, hand-embroidered cloths, musical instruments and ethnic-style clothing. Šutka (page 147) is the place to order lavish Roma costumes. Ramstore has two souvenir stores, Ikone and Vivaldi.

Balkan Corner Ul 106 no 42 (Podgrage 28). Handmade filigree & jewellery shop.
Džambaz Ul 106 no 34. Traditional shoes & souvenirs from wood, copper & terracotta.
Dzelo Stara Čaršija 39 (Gold St). Handmade filigree & silver jewellery.
Hemboj Debarska 3; ☎3226 236; m 071 518 369; 🖬 @Hemboj. Wool & cotton carpets & traditional clothes.
Ikone [119 F5] Ramstore Mall. Icons & traditional souvenirs.

Kvalitet Pasha [123 B3] Gradište 19, opposite Murat Pasha Mosque. *Opinci* (traditional shoes).
Lisec Ul 106 no 2. Also sells opinci.
Macedonian Corner Podgrage 76; ☎3222 702; m 070 319 929; w macedoniancorner.mk. Traditional & handmade souvenirs, T-shirts, books on Macedonia & Macedonian films & music.

CLOTHES
Skopje is awash with shoe shops and there are also plenty of clothes shops, although most of products they sell are mass-produced in China and imported. Local **tailors** in the old town are still cheap, especially for repairs and copying, although the choice of materials from which to make clothes is not the best. For a top-class men's tailor used by the diplomatic community, **Borče** [115 E6] (11 Oktomvri; ☎3133 065; m 075 230 061; w borce.mk) offers prompt service and a wide choice of materials, and women's suits are also available. **Angelkovski** [114 B4] (Bd Partizanski 57; ☎3211 069), used by the first president of Macedonia, pays good attention to detail and is slightly more expensive, although his choice of materials is not as wide as Borče's.

For a more international selection of clothes, try one of the shopping malls, all of which offer the likes of Benetton, Wolfords, Hugo Boss and Mango:

Capitol Mall [115 H6] Jane Sandanski 71; w capitolmall.mk
Ramstore [119 F5] Mito Hadži Vasile bb; w ramstore.com.mk
Skopje City Mall [114 A1] Ljubljanska 4; w skopjecitymall.mk

Soravia Filip II Makedonski II; w soravia.at/en/project/soravia-center-skopje
Trgovski Centar [119 G2] Moša Pijade; w tc.mk
Vero Centar [115 F5] Also has an enormous Jumbo Land full of kids' stuff.

BOOKS The largest bookshop chain in Macedonia is **Ikona Books** (w ikona.mk) with stores in Skopje at City Mall and on the ground floor of the Ramstore [119 F5]. They carry an extensive range of English books, as well as Bradt and other travel guides. **Kavkaz** [118 C3] (Gjuro Gjakovic 16; ⨍ @KAVKAZ.Knizarnica) is another place to go for English books.

OTHER PRACTICALITIES

TELEPHONE AND INTERNET The telephone centre located in the main post office, Post Office No 1 [119 E2] (Orce Nikolov bb; ✆3105 105; w posta.com.mk; ⊕ 07.00–17.30 Mon–Sat, 07.00–14.30 Sun), is open 24 hours. Calls at the post office or at telephone kiosks on the street need to be made either with tokens or using a prepaid phonecard, both of which can be purchased from post offices and newspaper stands. Mobile SIM cards and phonecards can be bought at Telekom and Vip outlets at the airport or in the Ramstore and other malls.

Internet cafés are a dying breed, but Wi-Fi is available in almost all hotels, hostels, restaurants and cafés.

FOREIGN EMBASSIES AND CONSULATES Most countries in the EU and the Balkans, and many elsewhere, have an embassy or consulate in Skopje. Those most likely to be of interest to Bradt readers are listed below, but a full list can be found at the regularly updated website w embassypages.com/macedonia.

ⓔ Australia [114 A1] Londonska 11b; ✆3061 834; e austcon@mt.net.mk
ⓔ Belgium Kočo Racin 14/4–3 9; ✆3136 209; e skopje@diplobel.fed.be
ⓔ Canada Praska; ✆3225 630; e honcon@unet.com.mk
ⓔ Germany Lerinska 59; ✆3093 900; e info@skopje.diplo.de; w skopje.diplo.de
ⓔ Netherlands [118 C5] Aminta III

69–71; ✆3109 250; e SKO@minbuza.nl; w netherlandsandyou.nl/your-country-and-the-netherlands/macedonia
ⓔ UK [114 C7] Todor Aleksandrov 165; ✆3299 299; e britishembassyskopje@fco.gov.uk; w ukinmacedonia.fco.gov.uk
ⓔ USA [114 D2] Samoilova 21; ✆3102 000; w mk.usembassy.gov

MEDICAL City Hospital [119 G3] (Gradska Bolnica), the red-brick building on 11 Oktomvri opposite the parliament, deals with all emergencies requiring anaesthesia. The emergency outpatients' entrance is around the back. There are several 24-hour pharmacies in the city.

ACTIVITIES

Skopje offers a host of sports facilities and outdoor pursuits. For more on more adventurous activities such as biking, tandem paragliding, hot-air ballooning and rock climbing, see page 95.

SPORTS HALLS

Boris Trajkovski Stadium [114 A2] Bd 8 Septemvri 13. Named after the late president who died in a plane crash in 2004, this stadium opened in 2008 & is home to the Macedonian national basketball, handball and volleyball teams, holding up to 10,000 spectators. It has an ice hockey rink, bowling hall, carting circuit (⊕ 09.00–midnight), fitness gym, table tennis & aerobics. There are also 4 restaurants, sports clothing outlets & a large sports bar. The Olympic-size pool is in the building next door on the east side (⊕ 10.00–17.00 & 22.00–midnight Mon–Sat, 10.00–midnight Sun; entry 200MKD).

The southern bank of the Vardar to the west of the Stone Bridge is paved all the way to the Aleksandar Palace Hotel and another 3km beyond. With views on to the surrounding mountains, this 6km stretch makes a wonderful walking, rollerblading, cycling or running route, and is a great place to see the locals taking a stroll, too. It is lit at night most of the way. A paved riverside walk also extends several kilometres along the opposite southeastern half of the river. Two sand beaches with café-bars at Gradski Plaža are found near the City Park and at Kamen Most Plaža (⊕ 09.00–22.00), at the northern end of which is a large sanded volleyball and handball court that is available to use for free with prior booking in person at the court.

Kale Sports Complex [114 D3] Lazar Ličenoski 316; ☎3118 711; ⊕ 09.00–22.00 Mon–Thu, 09.00–midnight Fri–Sun. Another big sports complex (& sometimes a venue for large concerts), with an outdoor swimming pool & an ice-skating rink in the winter.

Philip II Arena [114 C3] City Park. This is the home of the Macedonian national football team, who are most often seen practising & playing here. Tickets for matches can be purchased at the stadium box office or from the **Football Association of Macedonia** (8th Udarna Brigada 31a; ☎3235 448, 3229 042). For more on Macedonian football see w macedonianfootball.com.

SWIMMING
There are 2 other pools in addition to those mentioned above.

Bazen Biser [115 H7] Just off Kosta Novakovič in the Aerodrom part of town; m 077 903 834; ⊕ 10.00–18.00 & 21.30–01.00 daily; entry 100MKD. This 25m outdoor pool has a grass area & a smaller children's pool. Serves drinks & snacks. It's packed after midday so go early or in the evening.

Olimpiski Bazen [115 E5] Kočo Racin; ☎3162 958; w olimpiskibazen.com.mk; ⊕ 20.00–23.00 Tue–Fri, 10.00–17.00 & 20.00–23.00 Sat–Sun; entry 1,600MKD 10 visits, 2,250MKD 15 visits. Also has a fitness centre open 09.00–23.00 daily. More pleasant to work out in is the fitness centre at the Aleksandar Palace Hotel (page 122), although its layout is not the best for privacy.

TENNIS
Clubs are plentiful in Skopje, & private lessons cost 700–1,000MKD per hour. Courts are an additional 300–450MKD per hour, with lighting adding another 100MKD. Try one of the following:

ABC [114 C3] Ilindenska; ☎3063 622. Also has a popular café & drinks bar.

AC [115 H4] Bd Avnoj, Aerodrom; ☎2403 114. A big fitness complex with 10 courts.

Evro Set [114 A1] Skupi bb; ☎3095 385; w evroset.mk. Nice viewing area & café looking down on the courts. Part of the hotel of the same name (page 125).

Jug [114 C2] City Park; ☎3118 530

Kamnik [map, page 110] Kamnik bb; ☎2523 522; w kamnik.com.mk. Part of the hotel of the same name (page 124), which also has an excellent restaurant.

SQUASH
Squash Club [118 C1] Lazar Ličenoski 31; ☎3227 077. Nice café with a view on to the courts.

SPAS
After a day of sports or hiking, opportunities to relax and pamper yourself, especially if you can't get as far as Katlanovska hot springs (page 158) include:

Aseana Royal Spa [114 A3] Orce Nikolov 190; m 070 371 842; w aseanaroyalspa.eu.mk; ⊕ noon–22.00 Tue–Sun. Treatments include Balinese body massage, facials, body toning & pedicures. Prices range from 550MKD for a 30min head massage to 4,200MKD for an exotic flower bath.

TCC Grand Plaza Spa [119 E4] Vasil Glavinov 12; ☎3080 850; m 070 312 459; w tccgrandplaza. com/spa-centra. This is a membership-only spa, but has an excellent-value monthly half-day membership. Inc hot stone loungers, massage, a gym & a very nice bijou pool.

CHILDREN'S ACTIVITIES

For more ideas on child-friendly activities in Skopje see page 77.

Habyland [114 A2] Boris Trajkovski Centre, see page 134; ☏ 3120 275; m 070 388 963; e habyland@yahoo.com; w habyland.mk; ⏰ 10.00–22.00 daily; entry before 13.00 100MKD, after 13.00 150MKD Mon–Fri, 200MKD Sat. For children up to the age of 12, this centre is the best value for money in Skopje by far. Has a massive indoor jungle gym, a ball pit, games area, outdoor jungle gym & a child-friendly carting rink. The indoor has limited AC due to the doors opening out on to the patio café. The café, overlooking the outdoor activities (which are not in the shade), serves snacks, small pizzas, ice cream & the usual range of drinks. Caters for parties with advance booking.

Skopje Zoo [114 B3] Ilinden 88; ☏ 3220 578; w zooskopje.com.mk; ⏰ 09.00–18.00 daily; entry

50MKD. Founded in 1926, this small zoo has seen a resurgence of popular interest in the last few years, with significant investments being made to the infrastructure & services. Well-kept animals include lions, tigers, cheetahs, monkeys, zebras, dromedaries, ostriches, deer & alligators. There's a jungle gym & horseriding for younger children, & a welcome outdoor café in the shade.

HORSERIDING

Horseriding is becoming increasingly popular around Skopje. Try:

El Kabon Stables [map, page 110] Cherry Orchard in Volkovo district; ☏ 2055 195; m 070 225 642; w cherryorchardskopje.com. To get to El Kabon see the details for the Cherry Orchard restaurant, page 130. A great place for kids to have riding lessons while you enjoy a meal.

Sherpa Horse Riding See page 183. This club based in Galičnik can bring their horses up to Skopje for rides up to Vodno by prior arrangement (all year).

WHAT TO SEE AND DO

Most of Skopje's major museums and historic buildings are clustered in a compact and largely pedestrianised central district bisected by the Vardar River as it flows eastwards below the elevated stone walls of the hilltop Kale Fortress. Extending over roughly 1km², this central district can be divided into three broad sectors, each covered under a separate heading: the bustling new city centre focused on Makedonija Square as it extends southwards from the Vardar River; the corresponding section of the North Bank, and the labyrinthine Čaršija – also known as the Old Turkish Town or Old Bazaar – immediately to the north of that. By far the most interesting sector is Čaršija, which can easily be explored in half a day, combined with the adjacent Kale Fortress. One full day should be sufficient if you also want to take a good look around the new city centre and investigate the museums on the North Bank.

Looking further afield, an unquestionable highlight of the greater Skopje area is the spectacular Matka Canyon, which offers some great canoeing and walking only 15km southwest of the city centre by road, and also hosts some impressive caves and monasteries. Also highly recommended is the cable car to the summit of Mount Vodno and Millennium Cross, an excursion that can be combined with a visit to the venerable Monastery of Sv Pantelejmon, which lies on the mountain's northern footslopes and houses some of the country's oldest and finest ecclesiastic artworks. For keen walkers, it is also possible to stroll up the mountain (allow roughly 3 hours in either direction from the city centre) or more ambitiously to hike from the summit to Matka Canyon, a very scenic route that takes about 4 hours.

For those with more time to explore, other worthwhile sites of interest include the two Roman sites north of the city centre, namely the ruined city of Skupi and old stone aqueduct, the reconstructed Neolithic village at Tumba Madžari, the Roma district of Šuto Orizari, and the hot springs resort at Katlanovska Banja.

A great introduction to Skopje is provided by a couple of small operators that run daily fixed-departure walking tours led by licensed and registered English-speaking guides. There is no charge for these tours, but a fair tip is expected. A 3-hour walking and sightseeing tour with Skopje Walks (w skopjewalks.com) departs from in front of the Memorial House of Mother Teresa [119 F4] at 10.00 daily; no reservation is required and the guide will wear a blue ID badge around their neck. Free Skopje Walking Tours (m 071 385 939; w freeskopjewalkingtours. com) runs tours at 10.00 and 17.00 daily, leaving from in front of the Pelister Hotel on Makedonija Square [119 F3]; no reservation is required for the morning tour but the afternoon one is by advance arrangement only.

An excellent little guide to exploring Skopje on foot is *Skopje City Walk* (2014), available from w walkingmacedonia.com in English or Dutch, either as a printed booklet or a PDF download.

NEW CITY CENTRE AND SOUTH BANK
Makedonija Square [119 F2] Extending across 1.5ha south of the ancient Stone Bridge that spans the River Vardar, the Ploštad Makedonija is the city's main square. It is lined with restaurants and hotels, most notably the Neoclassical Marriott Hotel that opened on its southwest corner in 2016, and studded with statues associated with the Skopje 2014 project. Most controversial among the latter is the 24m-high *Warrior on a Horse* statue that was unveiled on 8 September 2011 to commemorate

SKOPJE 2014

The overall look of central Skopje has changed radically in recent years as a result of the Skopje 2014 project, an ambitious and controversial urban renewal programme instigated by the centre-right government in 2010. Skopje 2014 was ostensibly an attempt to beautify a city centre whose most attractive Neoclassical landmarks had been destroyed in the 1963 earthquake, only to be replaced by plain Soviet-style modernist constructions such as the riverfront post office [119 E2], designed to resemble a stylised lotus flower, and the Macedonian Opera and Ballet [119 F1] on the North Bank.

A conspicuous product of Skopje 2014 is the rash of imposing Neoclassical buildings that now lines both banks of the Vardar as it flows through the city centre. Another is the trio of statue-studded pedestrian bridges (one still incomplete at the time of writing) that connect the North and South banks near Makedonija Square. Skopje 2014 also aimed to bolster the ethnic Macedonian side of the country's history by erecting dozens of monuments commemorating the likes of Alexander the Great, his father Philip II, and various Christian saints.

However, the project has been criticised not only for its political agenda and bizarre transformation of parts of the city centre into a something approaching a kitschy Neoclassical theme park, but also for its profligacy (the cost is estimated at more than €500 million) in a country where unemployment and poverty are rife. Having overrun its original completion deadline by four years, the project was halted by the new government in February 2018, and a commission was established to look into the possibility of removing some of the more controversial monuments and statues associated with it.

3

the 20th anniversary of the referendum that gained Macedonia its independence from Yugoslavia. The square's most prominent feature, the statue stands in a fountain decorated with bronze reliefs depicting the life of the warrior, and bathed in lurid coloured lights. Despite its official name, it is clear that the warrior is Alexander the Great on his horse, Bucephalus. Its obscure title is in deference to the ongoing dispute with Greece over Macedonian history.

Other monuments unveiled as part of the Skopje 2014 project include Tsar Samoil and the Roman Emperor Justinian, both on Makedonija Square; and the so-called Porta Macedonia [119 F3], a 21m-high triumphal arch 150m to the south of the square. The Justinian and Tsar Samoil monuments were made in Florence at a cost of some €3.5 million and €1 million respectively.

Memorial House of Mother Teresa [119 F4] (Makedonija 9; ☎ 3290 674; e info@memorialhouseofmotherteresa.com; w memorialhouseofmotherteresa.com; ⏱ 09.00–20.00 Mon–Fri, 09.00–14.00 Sat–Sun; entry free) On 27 August 1910, Gonxha Bojaxhiu, of Albanian descent, was born in Skopje. A devout Catholic, she went on to be known to the world as Mother Teresa. Her memorial house in Skopje was opened in 2009; it is not a replica of her actual house, which was just in front of today's Trgovski Centar and is marked with a small plaque at the western entrance, but it is designed to give an idea of how she might have lived in a similar house (although considerably enlarged for visitors). The museum also has a glass chapel at the top and a conference hall in the basement. The memorial house was deliberately built on the site of what used to be the old Catholic church where she was baptised, received communion and sang in the church choir, and the exhibition here on her life is first class. Outside is a larger-than-life statue of her. There's a free guiding service in several languages including English, French and Italian.

City Museum of Skopje [119 G5] (Mito Hadži Vasilev Jasmin; ☎ 3114 742; w mgs.org.mk; ⏱ 09.30–17.00 Mon–Sat, 09.30–13.00 Sun; entry free) Housed in the old railway station on the southern end of Makedonija, this museum is once where the original Skopje–Thessaloniki railway started in 1873, but the present building was built in 1940–41. The earthquake of 26 July 1963 destroyed a large portion of the building and station, leaving the station clock fixed at 05.17 when the earthquake hit. The clock hands have remained at this time ever since and the building became the city museum soon after, with exhibits illustrating the history of the city through the centuries (although the 20th-century section has been closed for years) as well as temporary exhibitions of local artists, architects and designers.

VARDAR RIVER AND NORTH BANK The North Bank of the Vardar is connected to the 700m stretch of the South Bank flanking Makedonija Square by the historic Stone Bridge, as well as a trio of modern pedestrian bridges (one still incomplete) whose sides are adorned with statues of historic Macedonian figures. The riverfront is lined with Neoclassical buildings associated with Skopje 2014, most notably the superb new Archaeological Museum of Macedonia and handsome National Theatre. Behind this stands a 1.5ha open square that effectively forms a northeastern extension of the Ploštad Makedonija, and is also lined by museums and historic buildings. As with the main square, it is dotted with statues built for Skopje 2014, most prominently the massive *Man without Horse* (resembling Phillip II of Macedonia), a fountain adorned with several pregnant female figures (which may or may not represent Olympias, the fourth wife of Philip II and mother of Alexander the Great), and more modestly proportioned representations of Sv Kliment of Ohrid and Sv Cyril and Methodius.

Kamen Most [119 F2] The 214m Stone Bridge, which joins the old Turkish town to what has now become the centre of the city south of the river, was first built in the late 15th century under the orders of Sultan Mehmet II the Conqueror. By then the population of the city was increasing so rapidly due to the draw of merchants to this important trading town that people were already living beyond the original town walls. The only bridge across the river was many miles away further west, so a new bridge here, close to the main hub of the town, helped with the problem of overcrowding on the north side of the river as well as easing the arduous trading route into the town from the south.

The original stonework of 13 arches of travertine stone still stands, although the top of the bridge has been changed a number of times since it was built. Originally at a width of 6.33m, it was widened to 9.8m in 1909, and then returned to its original width in 1992. During the conflict of 2001 the bridge was badly damaged and, due to the bad relations between the communities, it took almost ten years to add the final piece to a replica of the old lookout post.

The bridge was originally built with stone pillar railings, used by the Ottoman rulers of Skopje to spike the heads of traitors and criminals. The bridge became a public execution place and, among many others, the Ottomans sentenced Karpoš, the 'King of Kumanovo', to death by impalement on the bridge in 1689.

Archaeological Museum of Macedonia [119 F2] (Kej Dimitar Vlahov bb; ☏3233 999; w amm.org.mk; ⊕ 10.00–18.00 Tue–Sun; entry 300MKD; photography permitted but flash & video forbidden) This superb museum opened in 2015 in the same imposing building, replete with Corinthian columns, that forms the new seat of the Supreme Court and home of the National Archives. Extending over two floors, it comprises a series of halls that are arranged in broad chronological order, from the Neolithic era to Byzantine times via the Hellenistic, Roman and Ottoman periods. The single most astonishing item on display, in our estimation, is an 8,000-year-old clay altar of a point-breasted fertility god dubbed the Golemata Majka (Great Mother) found at Madžari, a mere 5km to the east, back in 1981. It also displays a wealth of Iron Age artefacts, strange terracotta figures from the Hellenistic period, haunting Roman tomb reliefs depicting the deceased, and Byzantine icons and church paintings. Probably the most important and broad-ranging museum in Macedonia, it is worth at least an hour of your time, considerably longer if you've a strong interest in its subject matter.

Museum Complex of the Macedonia Struggle [119 E1] (11 Mart; ☏3256 667; w mmb.org.mk; ⊕ 10.00–18.00 Tue–Sun; entry 100MKD) Opened on Independence Day, 8 September 2011, this was constructed as part of the Skopje 2014 urban renewal programme and the move by the government to hallow and materialise Macedonian ethnicity and culture. Its original title of VMRO Museum and the Museum of the Victims of Communism really does signify the perspective of the exhibition, and there has been criticism that the museum doesn't fairly represent some of the positive benefits that also came with communism and socialism, and fails to give an entirely balanced picture of the activities of the VMRO itself. For more on the formation and struggles of VMRO and on the communist years, see page 27.

This museum literally is history in the making and is intended to show a different perspective from that of the Museum of the Macedonian Struggle in Thessaloniki, which looks at the issue from a Greek perspective. For your entry fee you'll get a 90-minute guided tour of the museum in one of several languages, including English. The museum's huge artistic depictions are mostly by Russian or Ukrainian painters, as Macedonia does not have a strong heritage in still-life painting. Be warned: the many life-size wax figures in the museum will fool the innocent, and as such the exhibition is not recommended for children under the age of ten or those who might be sensitive to seeing depictions of torture, death and the execution by hanging of a wax figure.

Holocaust Memorial Centre [119 E1] (11 Mart; ↘3122 697; ☉ 08.00–16.00 Tue–Fri; entry free) Opened in 2011 in what was formerly the Jewish Quarter of Skopje, this memorial centre was made possible from funds received when Macedonia's denationalisation law took effect in 2000. This law returned property that had been nationalised during the communist era back to its original owners. In the case of the 7,148 Macedonian Jews documented as victims of the Holocaust during World War II, their property was sold and the money received was put into the Holocaust Fund for the museum. It is a vivid and sobering memorial, and a very worthwhile visit.

Church of Sv Dimitri [119 F1] Standing in handsome isolation in the centre of the North Bank square, this rather plain church was originally built in the 14th century, and served as a cathedral in the 18th century and the seat of Metropolitan of Skopje in the 19th century. The present structure was built in 1896 and incorporates several frescoes dating from that time. In typical Macedonian fashion, the belltower is separate from the main building.

Daud Pasha Amam Gallery/National Gallery of Macedonia [119 F1] (Kruševska 1a Jordan Mijalkov 18; ↘ 3133 102, 3124 219; w nationalgallery. mk; ☉ Oct–March 10.00–18.00 Tue–Sun, Apr–Sep 10.00–21.00 Tue–Sun; entry 50MKD) This is the obvious copper cupola building to your right as you enter the old town from the North Bank, and is well worth a visit just for the building itself. Constructed in the 15th century as a bathhouse while Skopje was under Turkish rule, it was then one of the most magnificent of its kind, boasting 13 different-sized copper cupolas and varying degrees of hot steam rooms and cold baths separated for men and women. Nowadays only the beautiful roof and ceiling architecture remain. The gallery houses mostly contemporary art, although there are a few older pieces, including one dating back to the 13th century. The art is an added bonus to the building if you like modern art, although a good working Turkish steam bath in Skopje is sorely missed.

ČARŠIJA (OLD BAZAAR) A mercantile centre since the 12th century, the old Turkish quarter of Čaršija took its present-day shape in the early Ottoman era and is studded with venerable Turkish trading inns, baths and mosques, many dating to the 15th century or thereabouts (though many have been restored or reconstructed in the wake of one or other tragedy; for instance the earthquakes of 1555 and 1963, or the fire started by the Austrian general Piccolomini in order to rid the town of a rampaging plague in of 1689). In their mid-17th-century prime, Čaršija and the neighbouring Čair district boasted a full 120 mosques, according to the contemporary Turkish travel writer Evlija Čelebi. The area still houses more than 30 such structures today, as well the historic Monastery of Sv Spas.

Also known as the Old Bazaar, Čaršija today is the most compelling part of Skopje, a maze of cobbled pedestrianised streets and alleys whose organic layout and lived-in feel is typical of Islamic quarters of its vintage. Čaršija is also the most obviously touristy part of Skopje, partly for its wealth of museums and architectural gems, but also for the countless craft shops, jewellers, clothes boutiques and hole-in-the-wall bakeries, confectionaries and gelaterias selling fresh pastries, handmade sweets and a rainbow of ice creams. If nothing else, Čaršija is undoubtedly the best part of Skopje for cheap eats – every other building seems to be a terrace café or kebapcilnica serving freshly grilled kebabs, Macedonian burgers and salads, and other traditional fare. Unexpectedly, perhaps, given the old town's strong Islamic flavour, beer and wine is served freely at most such establishments – indeed, Macedonia's only craft brewery (page 131) serves a great selection of cheap and tasty draught beers on the edge of Čaršija, next to Sv Spas.

Skenderbeg Monument [123 B5] After considerable controversy, a statue of Skenderbeg (see the box on page 192 for more about him) was erected on 28 November 2006 (Albanian Flag Day) in front of Ilinden shopping centre at the southeast entrance to Čaršija. An Albanian national hero, Skenderbeg was a Catholic who stood up in the mid 15th century against the Ottoman colonisation of the area, and the erection of his statue was controversial for three reasons. For many ethnic Macedonians, admitting the statue of an Albanian hero into Skopje touches upon a sore point regarding ethnic Albanian encroachment on ethnic Macedonian land, rights and nationhood. For the Turkish community (who once built the old town) Skenderbeg is seen as the enemy, while for the Islamic community, Skenderbeg's reconversion back to Catholicism is seen as treachery. On the purely aesthetic side, though, the statue does a lot to enhance this modern concrete edge of the old town.

Kapan An [123 B4] Shortly after you enter Čaršija from the North Bank, a large plane tree to the right shades several terrace kebapcilnicas while obscuring the entrance to the well-hidden Kapan An, one of several old Turkish trading inns that dot the old town, which usually have one or two entrances but no windows on the outside. The entrances lead into a large courtyard, which is surrounded on all four sides on the first floor by wooden-balconied guest rooms looking out on to the courtyard. Underneath these, on the ground floor, are what were formerly the stabling and storage quarters. There was often a well in the centre of the courtyard where guests would usually gather to while away the evening. Kapan An now houses Pivnica (Beerhouse) An (page 128), a renowned purveyor of traditional Macedonian fare. Several other restaurants can be found inside and outside its walls.

Museum of Skopje Bazaar [123 C3] (☏3114 742; ⊕ 10.00–14.00 Tue–Fri; entry free) A recommended first stop for anybody wanting to familiarise themselves with the history of Čaršija, the Museum of the Skopje Bazaar is housed in a 15th-century trading inn called Suli An and holds an interesting exhibition on trading life in Skopje during the Ottoman Empire. Note, though, that the museum and exhibits are in need of repair and all the text is in Macedonian. The museum itself is upstairs, while downstairs is the university's Department of Applied Arts. You can walk around the courtyard to see the students working in the downstairs rooms and the department's entrance hall has several modern art paintings. Exhibitions and public lectures are advertised in Macedonian on the front door. Suli An lies in the centre of the old bazaar area and the front entrance to the inn often looks closed, but it is usually in fact open.

Čifte Amam National Art Gallery [123 B3] (Bitpazarska bb; ☎ 3126 856; w nationalgallery.mk; ⊕ 08.00–18.00 Tue–Fri, same hrs at w/ends of special exhibitions only; entry 50MKD) Situated immediately south of Suli An, this former Turkish bathhouse, the second largest in Skopje, was built at the beginning of the 16th century under the orders of Isa Bey, the son of Isak Bey. It ceased functioning in its original capacity in 1917, and now houses various travelling exhibitions.

Murat Pasha Mosque [123 C3] (Opposite Čifte Amam) This modern square-roofed mosque was built in 1802. The original 15th-century structure was burnt down when General Piccolomini set Skopje alight in 1689.

Bezisten [123 B3] The covered marketplace of the old bazaar area is a courtyard-type building with more stores built inside the courtyard itself. It is located behind Čifte Amam to the northwest. Originally built in the 15th century for trading cloth and material, the store soon spilt outside the original structure, forming narrow little cobbled lanes between the one- and two-storey shops, which leaned on to each other. The old bazaar quickly became 18 different trading houses – goldsmiths, cobblers, ironmongers, corn exchange, etc – and the remnants of these can still be seen today. The Bezisten of today is a 19th-century structure, housing some non-governmental organisations, and occasionally a café-bar.

Kose Kadi Mosque [123 B3] (Bezisten) At the western end of Bezisten (the covered market) above a passageway of shops, this 17th-century mosque was last renovated in 1993.

Monastery of Sveti Spas (Holy Salvation) [123 A3] (Makarije Frčkovski 8; ☎ 3163 812, 3109 401; ⊕ 09.00–16.00; entry to courtyard free, 120MKD to enter church) This is the only remaining monastery in the centre of Skopje and houses one of its most beautiful churches. Some of the foundations of the monastery date back to the 14th century, before Ottoman times, but under Ottoman rule it became illegal for a church to be taller than a mosque, and so the church was mostly rebuilt from below ground in order to accommodate the height of the original church belltower.

The present three-naved church dates from rebuilding in the 18th and 19th centuries. Three of the most famous woodcarvers of the time, Makarije Frčkovski of Galičnik and the brothers Marko and Petar Filipovski from the Mijak village of Gari, worked for five years from 1819 to 1824 to create the 10m wide, 6m high **iconostasis** (the intricate woodwork divider between the nave and the main part of the church). It is cut from the wood of walnut trees, and is made up of two rows of partly gold-inlaid icons depicting scenes from the Old and the New Testament. Many of the scenes have been carved to reflect Macedonian traditions and folklore, such as the figure of Salome, who is dressed in traditional Macedonian garb. Among their more famous works, Frčkovski and the Filipovski brothers carved even more stunning iconostases for the Monastery of Sv Jovan Bigorski in Mavrovo National Park (page 183) and the Monastery of Sv Gavril in Lesnovo (page 335).

In the monastery courtyard is the marble sarcophagus of the revolutionary **Goce Delčev**, leader of the Independence for Macedonia Revolutionary Organisation (IMRO – to which the present-day government VMRO-DPMNE traces its roots), until he was shot in 1903 by Ottoman soldiers at Banica (Karié in Greece). His remains were exhumed during the Bulgarian occupation of Banica during

World War I and moved to Sofia, when Tsar Ferdinand I of Bulgaria awarded his father a life pension in recognition of the price three of his sons paid with their lives to further the freedom of Macedonia. When Bulgaria occupied Banica again during World War II, his grave was restored (but not his remains). As part of a policy to recognise Macedonian consciousness, Delčev's remains were finally moved to Skopje in 1946 and interred at Sv Spas. His ethnicity remains a bone of contention between Macedonians and Bulgarians, many of whom say he is Bulgarian (and that there is no such ethnicity as Macedonian). A small exhibition on his life is inside the inns of the monastery, and his statue is on the south side of the Stone Bridge.

National Museum of Macedonia [123 A2] (Čurčiska bb; ☎ 3116 044, 3129 323; ⏰ 09.00–17.00 Tue–Sat, 09.00–13.00 Sun; entry 100MKD) Situated between Mustafa Pasha Mosque and Kuršumli An, this museum is not marked up as the 'Museum of Macedonia' from the outside and the entrance is merely a break in the red railings on the southernmost side of the complex. If you haven't got much time to visit ancient sites in Macedonia, then the museum is a good way to get an overview of all the civilisations that have passed along the River Vardar. Many of the best iconostases in the country are also housed here, and there are some excellent exhibits of the world wars, including weaponry and ammunition. Many of the exhibits are being revised and the number of texts in English is increasing.

Mustafa Pasha Mosque [123 A2] (Samoilova, opposite the main entrance to Kale) The largest and most decorated of all the mosques in Skopje was built in 1492 at the order of Mustafa Pasha while he was Vizier of Skopje under Sultan Selim I. The entrance to the mosque is through a four-column porch, which is crowned with three cupolas, and a 124-step white minaret rises from its western end. Inside, the pulpit and prayer recess are made from intricately worked marble and the walls are of a beautiful blue pattern work. The five windows in each wall are staggered, rising up the walls of the mosque to create a pyramid effect. Despite having stood the test of time well, the mosque did have to undergo major restoration after the earthquake of 1963 and was refurbished again through Turkish funding over a five-year period ending in 2011. In the grounds of the mosque are Mustafa Pasha's mausoleum and his daughter Umi's sarcophagus.

Kuršumli An [123 B1] Probably the most impressive trading inn in Čaršija, the 16th-century Kuršumli An (meaning 'Bullet Inn' or 'Lead Inn') was built by a community of merchants from Ragusa (a defunct empire centred on the Croatian port of Dubrovnik). Situated at the northwest end of the old town, it was designed to stable up to a hundred horses, and it also had space to house their traders and owners. Some of the rooms even had their own fireplace, which was deemed quite a luxury in those times. In 1878 the building became the town prison. More recently, it housed some archaeological exhibitions associated with the National Museum of Macedonia, and was used as a concert venue. You can walk past the impressive outer walls, but the building has been closed for renovation for some years now, and shows no sign of reopening in the foreseeable future.

Šengul Amam [123 B1] This disused bathhouse, also known as Gurciler Amam, stands next to Kuršumli Han. It was badly damaged in the 1963 earthquake, and has not been repaired.

3

Hidaverdi Mosque [123 B1] (Between Kuršumli An & the Theatre for Minorities) This looks more like a half-renovated shopfront than a 16th-century mosque, despite having been restored in 1995. It lacks the usual distinguishing minaret.

BORDERING ČARŠIJA

Hjunkar Mosque [115 F4] (Bd Krste Misirkov) Also known as the Sultan Murat Mosque, Hjunkar predates the Mustafa Pasha Mosque by some 50 years. Situated a couple of hundred metres east of Čaršija, it was built next to the Monastery of Sv Georgi Gorga near the present-day university of Sv Cyril and Methodius. At the time, it was one of the most important monastic centres in the Balkans, but when Isak Bey, then commander of the Turkish army, built the Aladža Mosque [115 E3], the Pasha Bey Mausoleum (still visible in the grounds of the Aladža Mosque) and a *madrasa* (school for teaching the Koran) on the actual grounds of the monastery, he effectively destroyed life at the monastery. The madrasa no longer exists, nor the monastery, but both mosques remain on either side of Boulevard Krste Misirkov. The mausoleums of Sultan Beyhan and Ali Pasha of Dagestan also lie in the grounds.

Saat Kula [115 F4] The dark red-brick clock tower near Hjunkar Mosque is the last remaining portion of the old city walls. Erected in the mid 16th century, the top half of the clock tower was originally made of wood and housed a clock brought over from Hungary. In 1904 the wooden structure was replaced with stone and a new clock was procured, but this was then destroyed in the earthquake of 1963 and has not been replaced since.

Gazi Isa Bey Mosque [115 F3] (Čairska) Situated about 200m north of Hjunkar Mosque, this was one of the first libraries in Skopje. A 560-year-old plane tree (*Platinus orientalis*) stands in the mosque grounds.

Yayha Pasha Mosque [115 F3] (Bd Krste Misirkov) Another 300m to the north on Boulevard Krste Misirkov, this mosque was built in 1504 for Yayha Pasha, the son-in-law of Sultan Bayazit II. Notable for its modern four-sided roof, this imposing mosque is visible as you come off the highway from the airport into the centre of town. Originally, the prayer area was roofed with one large and five small domes, but these were destroyed in the last earthquake of 1963.

Kale Fortress [119 E1] (Free entry, but charges may apply as and when restoration is complete) This site has seen some sort of occupation since 4000BC and has been a working fortress since the 6th century AD. It served as a barracks to the Turkish army during Ottoman rule, and then to the JNA (Jugoslav National Army) until the 1963 earthquake razed most of the fortress. Much of it is only now being restored. Continuing excavations have revealed artefacts dating back to the Thracian era of 200BC when the Dardanians fought from Kale to defend the surrounding area from the invading Romans. In May 2010, archaeologists discovered the largest find of coins from the Byzantine era ever unearthed in Macedonia. Some of the current visible structure dates from the 10th-century enlargement of the fort under Tsar Samoil. The ramp was partly built of stones from the ancient town of Skupi, which was destroyed in AD518.

In 2011 Kale was closed because of demonstrations, which erupted there over the attempt to rebuild a church in the grounds, but it has now reopened. The main gateway of Kale can be approached just after the flyover entering Čaršija, or a more scenic route is to follow the cobbled street up Gradište past all the bars, then up the steps to the forecourt of the Monastery of Sv Spas. The main entrance is opposite the old post office. The fortress has been a bit of a building site for some years, and parts were still closed off for restoration in 2018, but it is still worth a visit, and the views from the walls are wonderful.

Museum of Contemporary Art [114 D3] (Muzej na Sovrjeme Uumetnost, Samoilova bb; ☎3117 734; w msu.mk; ⊕ 09.00–17.00 Tue–Sat, 09.00–13.00 Sun; entry free) The museum lies to the west of Kale on top of the hill. A large, airy building, it holds 4,360 prominent international as well as national exhibits, many of which were donated to Macedonia after the 1963 earthquake when the 1963 New York convention of the International Association of the Plastic Arts called upon the artists of the world to support the city's reconstruction through associated artwork. The custom-built museum opened in 1970 with a remarkable collection of international donations created especially for it. Such pieces include a canvas named *Head of a Woman* (1963) by Picasso, which is usually stored in the basement, but can be viewed upon request. The piece was stolen from the museum in 1995 but intercepted at the border and returned.

AROUND SKOPJE

WEST-CENTRAL SKOPJE
Cathedral of Sv Kliment of Ohrid [118 C3] (Cnr Partizanski & Ohridski) Consecrated in August 1990 to commemorate the 1,150th anniversary of the birth of the namesake saint, Macedonia's largest cathedral is an interesting modern building shaped in the form of a dome with a smaller dome at each corner, making it easily mistaken for a mosque at a quick glance.

Macedonian Museum of Natural History [114 B3] (Ilinden 86; ☎3117 669; ⊕ 09.00–16.00 Tue–Sun; entry 60MKD) There is not much to see in this museum bordering Skopje Zoo, and all the text is in Macedonian, but there are some impressive remains of prehistoric animals found in Negotino and other areas of Macedonia, and lots of stuffed eagles and vultures, as well as other animals of the region. Make sure you have small change as the ticket attendant might not.

EAST-CENTRAL SKOPJE
Numismatic Museum of the National Bank of Macedonia [115 F5] (Bd Kuzman Josifovski Pitu 1; ☎3108 108; w nbrm.mk/muzej-en.nspx; ⊕ 09.00–15.00 Tue–Thu; entry free) A truly amazing collection which will take you through the history of coinage right from Paeonian times. Literature available in English – you can download a detailed guide to the collection as a PDF from w nbrm.mk/WBStorage/Files/Trezor_Trezor_Macedonia_coins_and_history_opt.pdf. Bring ID in order to get through the main bank entrance.

Military Museum of Macedonia [115 H7] (Military Academy in Aerodrom; ☎3283 624; ⊕ 09.00–15.00 Mon–Fri; entry free) This museum covers Macedonian military history in the broadest sense of the term, starting with the campaigns of Alexander the Great up until World War II.

Church of Sv Gjorgi and British Cemetery [115 H3] (1st left off 16 Makedonska Brigada) This cemetery houses over a hundred graves of British servicemen who died during the two world wars. A service is held by the British Embassy here each November.

Tumba Madžari [map, page 110] (Kej Dimitar Vlahov bb; ☏3233 999; e contact@ amm.org.mk; w tumbamadzari.mk; ☉ 08.00–14.00 Wed–Fri, 10.30–17.30 Sat–Sun; entry free) One of the most important Neolithic sites in Macedonia, Tumba Madžari lies in the eastern suburbs about 5km from the city centre. Nine houses dating back to the 6th millennium BC have been excavated at the site, which archaeologists first identified in 1980 and now regard to be a kind of proto-Skopje. Archaeological evidence suggests Tumba Madžari supported a society of some sophistication, with dwellings built of mud brick and/or wood. Its inhabitants venerated the earth as the sustainer and ultimate repository of all human life, a belief represented by the Golemata Majka (Great Mother), a 'Venus'-like figurine that was found here in 1981 and served as an altar. (The Golemata Majka is now on display at the central Archaeological Museum of Macedonia, along with dozens of earthenware pots and other prehistoric clay artefacts unearthed at the site.) But it is worth visiting Tumba Madžari itself to see a reconstruction of the original village, complete with life-size models of its inhabitants doing their Neolithic thing. For those without transport, the site is accessible by bus; take number 65 and ask to get off at Tumba Madžari.

NORTH OF THE CITY CENTRE

French Cemetery [114 D2] (Samoilova bb, after the Museum of Contemporary Arts) The cemetery houses the graves of almost 1,500 French servicemen who died in World War I. A tiny museum at the entrance displays documents and photographs of the period.

Skupi Archaeological Site [map, page 110] (off Skupi Rd) Emanating from the North Bank of the Vardar less than 5km northwest of the modern city centre, Skupi became the administrative, cultural, economic and religious centre of the entire region following the Roman victory over Perseus in the third Macedonian war of 168BC and the foundation of the Roman province of Dardania. In the year AD313, following the Edict of Milan, it became the seat of the episcopate. Skupi was razed by the earthquake in AD518, during the reign of Emperor Justinian (page 157), but did witness low-level squatter reoccupation.

The extent of the Roman colony of Skupi is largely unknown even after significant archaeological excavation, the most recent being in 2008 when a church was discovered. The buildings visible within the excavations are a hall reputed to be the civil basilica, the centre of civil administration of the town, with its mosaic floors; a small Roman bath; a north–south aligned street (or *cardo*), possibly the Cardo Maximus; a theatre; remnants of part of the city wall; and the ground plan of a church or basilica.

Recent excavations by the Museum of Skopje have uncovered part of the city wall and have identified that the limit of the urban area (though still unknown) was greater than suspected. A basilica was also discovered along with a complete and rather beautiful statue of Venus Pudica associated with a possible bath building. The statue is 1.7m high, white marble and has a dolphin tattooed on the left leg. It is the only complete sculpture to be found on Macedonian soil yet and dates to the 3rd century.

By far the most remarkable discovery relating to Skupi, by dint of its preservation, is the standing Roman gravestones or stele some 150m further up the road towards Bardovci. What makes these gravestones unique is that they were found *in situ*, preserved by being buried under a later mound. This level of preservation of Roman monuments is unparalleled in the Roman world.

The archaeological site is next to the road to the village of Bardovci and has an obvious access, though opening hours are erratic and unpublicised. A newly constructed path leads the visitor around the excavations; a number of noticeboards along the path explain a little of what you are looking at. To get here from the city centre, follow Ilinden Boulevard west for about 2.2km, passing the zoo to your right, then turn right on to Boulevard 8-mi Septemvri. After another 800m, having passed the Alexandar Palace Hotel to your left and crossed a bridge over the Vardar, turn left at the traffic lights on to Skupi Road. After another 1km, take the second right turn, and you'll see the ruins on the right after 100m.

Skopje Aqueduct

Skopje Aqueduct [114 C1] (off Bd Slovenia) Standing isolated and neglected in a field only 3km north of the city centre and 2km northeast of Skupi, this 55-arch, 385m-long stone aqueduct is a hidden gem. Its provenance is unclear. Some sources say the aqueduct dates back to 1st century AD when it brought water 9km from Lavovec to the Roman city of Skupi. Others say it was built by Justinian I (page 113) when he rebuilt Skupi after the earthquake of AD518. Still others say the Ottoman lord Isa Bey built it in the 16th century to supply the many hammams (Turkish baths) dotted around what is now the Old Bazaar district of Čaršija.

The stone aqueduct remained in active use into the 18th century, and when the English traveller Dr Edward Brown wrote about it on a 1673 visit, he counted around 200 arches. It is now in disrepair and completely unprotected, though all the surviving arches are intact and attempts have been made to keep it from falling down completely. Despite this, it is one of the three largest and best-preserved relics of its type in the former Yugoslavia (the other two being Diocletian's aqueduct on the outskirts of Split in Croatia, and the Bar aqueduct in Montenegro).

It can be visited in isolation or in conjunction with the nearby Skupi Archaeological Site. Coming from the city centre, directions are the same as for Skupi (see opposite), except that after crossing the bridge over the Vardar you need to curve rightwards at the traffic lights, than after another 300m turn left at the T-junction with the E65 highway north to Kosovo. About 1km after joining the E65, there's another traffic light where you need to turn right on to Slovenia Road. After 250m, turn right again on to a small side road, then after another 50m turn left, passing through a small Roma settlement before you emerge at the aqueduct after 500m. The aqueduct stands close to a military barracks and you may not be allowed to take photographs with this in the background, so position yourself with it behind you to take your shots.

Šuto Orizari

Šuto Orizari Also known as Šutka, Šuto Orizari, the home of Skopje's sizeable Roma minority (page 41), is little visited by tourists, and most Macedonians would think you were a bit crazy to want to go there. Nonetheless, the daily market is super-cheap (and filled with a lot of junk) and it's where you can get some of the hand-sewn and embroidered Roma clothing and shoes.

More interesting than a wander through the market (where even the Roma will tell you to keep a tight hold on your wallet) is a walk around some of the side streets off the northern end of Vietnamska. This area of their settlement will give you a feel of how the Roma live and love a carefree and artistic life. The closely packed one- or two-storey houses are usually immaculately whitewashed with a decorative fence of moulded concrete or ironwork, topped with whitewashed lions and Pekinese dogs pawing a ball. Wooden caravan wheels, harking back to the nomadic days of the Roma, adorn the walls and fences. Many of these lovely homes are not built from money earned here in Macedonia, but are the result of years away working in Germany and Austria.

The atmosphere and surroundings are not unlike a Chinese or Indian neighbourhood in Malaysia or some other southeast Asian country. Children laugh and play in the streets and this is a world away from the Roma who have

3

been trafficked to beg on the streets with their children. But behind the laughter of children, the concerns of adults are not difficult to find.

In a community where education is not always highly valued, it is difficult enough to get the really poor of the Roma community to attend school. It is even more difficult when the main school in Šutka, Brakja Ramiz i Hamid, is filled three times over capacity and has few facilities and insufficient teaching staff. The school gymnasium has no heating in winter and most of the windows are broken. Water runs down the walls of the changing rooms and many of the corridors.

On the bright side, the Roma are outstandingly talented in music and dance. The school has a few musical instruments of its own, but most of the children bring their parents' instruments into school, the very instruments that their parents earn their living from by playing in bands for hire at parties and festivals. In recent years, despite the poor teaching conditions and the other overwhelming concerns of poverty, Brakja Ramiz i Hamid has repeatedly won the first prize in the annual Skopje school choir and school orchestra competitions.

To get to Šuto Orizari, take the 19 or 20 bus heading north from Dame Gruev outside the main post office, and ask to be dropped off at the main street Šutka Pazar. Alternatively, the 10-minute taxi ride should cost less than 350MKD.

Bražda [map, page 110] Some 10km north of Skopje, at the foot of the Skopska Crna Gora Mountain, lies the village of Bražda. The picturesque surroundings of this village host the Iron Age or proto-historic and early antique (800–300BC) antecedent to Skopje, which is on the top of a small hill covering some 4.5ha and is reputed to be the capital of the Agriani tribe. Details of the settlement morphology are rather poor and little is visible, but one monumental building, probably the tomb of a noble or a king, is extant. The Agriani, an ethnic community that lived in the northeastern part of modern-day Macedonia around Skopje, are frequently mentioned in inscriptions from the 4th century BC. Renowned for their fighting prowess, they were one of the elite units in the Macedonian army of Alexander the Great. Čardak restaurant near here is listed on page 130.

To get here, take bus 61 (towards Pobožje), 71 (towards Banjani) or 81 (towards Blace), all of which go through Bražda along the bumpy cobbled road.

MOUNT VODNO AND SURROUNDS Topped by the 66m-tall Millennium Cross, Mount Vodno is the prominent 1,066m summit that dominates Skopje's southern horizon. The panorama from the summit – embracing Skopje and Skopska Crna Gore to the north and Mount Kitka to the south – is spectacular and all the main sites of the city can be viewed easily. In late autumn, vistas of vivid red-and-yellow foliage laced with clouds and evergreens are particularly striking. Wild mushrooms are also plentiful at this time. Wooden benches, tables and a children's wooden play area can be found at the summit, but so too can an untidy miscellany of incomplete and ruinous concrete structures that rather undermine the area's natural beauty.

The construction of the yellow steel Millennium Cross on the summit of Vodno provoked a lot of controversy among Albanians when it was first started in 2002, just after the 2001 conflict. Some ethnic Albanians, most of whom live on the opposite side of the valley, see the cross – which is brightly illuminated at night, visible from afar – as a symbol of their domination by the ethnic Macedonian majority. The cross is also a convenient orientation marker denoting the south of the city if ever you are lost at night in the streets of Skopje.

Most people visiting Mount Vodno do so as a half-day trip from Skopje using the cable car, a spectacular ride that is arguably a great deal more compelling than the summit itself. You can also walk from the city centre to the summit, and hike on from there to Matka Canyon (see box, page 154). It is also possible to stay overnight at the 50-bed mountain hut Dare Džambaz (📞 3234 365, 3143 236; **$**), which stands on the summit and offers beds, basic food, a collegial atmosphere and welcome shelter if the weather has turned foul. The hut is well worth visiting for the numerous photos of Macedonians who have climbed mountains around the world to proudly fly their flag, and also for a cheap cup of the hot sweet mountain tea (*planinski čaj*).

Mount Vodno cable car (📞 0800 15115; w zicnica.jsp.com.mk; ⏱ Apr–Sep 09.00–19.30 Tue–Thu, 09.00–20.00 Fri–Sun, last car back 19.45 Tue–Thu, 20.45 Fri–Sun; Oct–Mar 09.00–16.30; entry 100MKD rtn, over 64s free with ID, children under 6 free)

The 1,600m *žičnica* leaves from Hotel Vodno, halfway up the mountain, but is due to be extended to the bottom of the mountain in due course. It is a short but spectacular ride, terminating almost next to the Millennium Cross. A special bus (number 25) to Hotel Vodno leaves approximately once an hour from the central bus station in Skopje. The first bus is at 08.00, and further buses run at 09.00 and 09.40, then every hour at 20 minutes past the hour from 10.20 to 18.20. Buses back from Hotel Vodno leave at 40 minutes past the hour from 10.40 to 18.40, with a last bus at 20.00. The bus picks up and drops off at the Macedonian National Bank, Jugdrvo, City Hospital, Ploštad and the State Hospital. The full timetable is posted at the tourist information office on Boulevard Vasil Agilarski.

Hiking up Vodno
It takes almost 3 hours to walk up from the town centre, a popular walk with Macedonians on a sunny weekend. The easiest and most popular route to the summit is from the entrance to Vodno National Park on Ulica Salvador Aljende. The westernmost road opposite the turn-off to the Hotel Panorama takes you over a couple of small bridges, up past a modern apartment block to your left, and then past some lovely old farmhouses. This quickly leads up into the woods above the town, and the main path is easy to follow. There are numerous diversions off the main path, and almost all diversions heading upwards will pop out at the summit eventually. The main path is marked with red and white stripes painted on trees, and joins the road again just before the entrance to Hotel Vodno and the turn-off to Sv Pantelejmon Monastery. It's also possible to take the bus as far as here.

From Hotel Vodno many people simply walk along the tarmac road and there are numerous tracks from the road where sweet chestnuts can be harvested in abundance on an early morning walk, provided you're prepared to compete with the many locals with the same idea. The dedicated hiking path through the woods, however, actually starts to the left of the restaurant and mountain hut Skopje 63 above the barrier on the tarmac road. It is marked with yellow and green stripes painted on the trees. The path joins the road again about 1,200m from the road's end at the mountain hut and cross.

Sv Pantelejmon Monastery
By far the most interesting church in the immediate vicinity of Skopje stands in the small forest-fringed village of Gorni Nezeri, halfway up Mount Vodno. Dedicated to Sv Pantelejmon, the patron saint of physicians, it was built in 1164 by Aleksij (Angelus) Komnen, the grandson of Byzantine Emperor Alexios Komenos I, on what had formerly been a Roman cult site. The frescoes inside the church are some of the few surviving Macedonian relicts of the body of Byzantine art believed to have influenced and ushered in the Renaissance (see box, above).

The fresco of the *Lamentation of Christ* unusually shows Mary cradling Jesus between her legs, again in keeping with the increasing realism of the artistic style of the time. The church is often closed in the evening, so go early if you intend to stay on to eat at the restaurant here. It is always closed on Mondays.

The church is serviced by a simple but expensive inn called the Hotel Pantelejmon (12 rooms; ✆ 3081 255; $$$). The nearby Klet Restaurant (✆ 3081 255/250; ⊕ 08.00–midnight daily; $$$) offers traditional Macedonian fare as well as other regional delicacies such as Istrian *pršut* (dry cured ham) and *Paški sir* (cheese from the island of Pag) from Croatia. The long outdoor patio offers excellent views of the Vardar Valley, and is a pleasant place to be at sunset on a summer evening.

There are two routes to Pantelejmon Monastery from central Skopje. The easiest option is to take the road just below Hotel Vodno around the mountain for 4.5km until you reach the monastery. The shorter route is to take Kožle Street all the way

from classical antiquity itself. Increasing emphasis was placed on the individual and their faith. Artists strove to portray emotion such as in the Church of Sv Pantelejmon in Nerezi, where the late Roman 'damp fold', which conveyed three-dimensionality, was used to great effect in the *Lamentation of Christ* in the naos. Experimenting with light and shade, a few years later, created the monumental classical figures of Studenica, in Serbia. These developments are paralleled in frescoes, sculpture, metalwork, ivories and enamels in Germany, Italy, France and England. This new approach to the human figure transformed the fear-inducing God and Judge of the early Romanesque period to the forgiving Christ with Mary, his Mother, as intercessor for mankind.

When it comes to the next Renaissance, the better-known Italian Renaissance, there is no doubt that Byzantium held the key both in the range of storytelling and the sense of placing a credible human form in credible space. The backgrounds of gold or blue are infinite but the architecture and landscape within them experiment with perspective. Many of the painterly techniques, iconography and forms of the precursors of the early Renaissance in Italy, such as Cimabue or Cavalini, were those of the artists of Byzantium. The two seminal masters of the early Renaissance, Giotto and Duccio, took liberally from the tradition. Although 1453 was a disaster for Constantinople, the style and quality from this period can still be enjoyed in many of the churches of Macedonia.

Meanwhile the Italian Renaissance returned once more to the exploring and experimenting classical antiquity and broke free from its links with Byzantium. These ideas developed into the High Renaissance and the arts of Bramante, Raphael, Michelangelo and Leonardo. The Orthodox Church, meanwhile, chose to retain its traditional forms and techniques, veering little from the ideas laid down under the Comenian dynasty (1081–1185).

This subject is complex with much cross-fertilisation, but as Ernst Kitzinger pointed out in his *Art of Byzantium and the Medieval West*:

It is a fascinating field encompassing as it does the whole problem of the Greek and the Western world in their estrangement as well as in their kinship ... [My purpose] will have been accomplished if I have been able to show that during a crucial period of its artistic development the West received from Byzantium vital help in finding itself.

to the end past the long blue factory on the right, then at the end of the factory complex take a left turn marked Gorni Nezeri. Half a dozen buses (number 28) run here and back from the central bus station daily from Tuesday to Friday, and there are ten buses daily on Saturday and Sunday. The full timetable is posted at the tourist information office on Boulevard Vasil Agilarski. Alternatively, a taxi should take 20 minutes and cost around 700MKD.

Macedonian Village (3077 600; m 072 220 600; w macedonianvillage. mk; ⊕ 08.00–midnight daily; entry 100MKD) Situated in Gorni Nezeri a few hundred metres from Sv Pantelejmon Monastery, this themed hotel (page 125) attempts to recreate a dozen different types of regional architecture, and it also incorporates weaving, pottery and silversmith workshops, a small ethnographic museum, a specialist Macedonian wine store, and a trio of traditional restaurants. It feels a bit contrived but nevertheless provides an enjoyable introduction to

The Romani language belongs to the North Indo-Aryan (Indic) languages and is close to Hindi, Punjabi and the Dardic languages. There are numerous Romani dialects, influenced by the Roma's place of settlement. For example, Romani words of Iranian origin include *baxt* (luck, fortune), *ambrol* (pear), *khangeri* (church), *angustri* (ring), *ruv* (wolf) and *vurdon* (wagon). Romani words of Greek origin include *drom* (path, road), *isviri* (hammer), *karfin* (nail), *klidi* (key), *kokalo* (bone), *papin* (goose), *petalos* (horseshoe), *tsox* (skirt), *amoni* (anvil) and *zumi* (soup).

In return Romani has also contributed a significant number of slang words to the languages of the countries where Roma people have settled. The following English slang words (standard meaning in brackets) have come from Romani:

Bamboozle (cheat)	Dad (father)
Bosh (nonsense)	Lolly (money)
Bungalow (one-storey house)	Nark (informant)
Busk (play music)	Pal (friend)
Char (clean)	Posh (classy)
Chav (youth)	Rogue (rascal)
Corker (tell a lie)	Rum (strange)
Cushty (good)	

A good website on the Romani language is www.rroma.org.

Here are a few phrases in the Macedonian Romani language:

Lacho dive	Good day/Hello
Sar san?/So keres?	How are you?/What are you doing?
Ov sasto (m)/Ov sasci (f)	Thank you
Naj pala soste!	You're welcome!
Katar aves?	Where are you from?
Sar si to anav?/Mo anav si …	What's your name?/My name is …
Va/Na	Yes/No
Tjiri familija si vi tusa?	Is your family with you?
Kaj djas?	Where are you going?
Na haljovava tut	I don't understand you
Haljoveja man?	Do you understand me?
Av mansa (sing)/*Aven mansa* (pl)	Come with me
Ava kari	Come here
Roma	People
Achov devlesar	God be with you/Farewell

Famous Roma people or famous people of Roma origin are mostly musicians, dancers and actors. These include Elvis Presley, Django Reinhardt, Yul Brynner, Michael Caine, Charlie Chaplin and Bob Hoskins. Others include the former footballer Eric Cantona. The new Roma Ambassador to the EU is the world-famous Spanish flamenco dancer Joaquín Cortés.

traditional Macedonian culture and is also a nice spot for lunch after a visit to Sv Pantelejmon Monastery.

Govrlevo This Neolithic archaeological site below the southern footslopes of Vodno is of a similar vintage to its counterpart at Tumba Madžari (page 146), but it is more remote and thus far undeveloped for tourism. It is renowned for the discovery of a partial clay figure depicting an inhaling male torso with details of the spine, ribs, navel and penis. Dubbed the Adam of Macedonia, it dates from the early 6th millennium BC, making it the oldest artefact of its type yet discovered in Macedonia, and some archaeologists consider it to be one of the ten most important archaeological discoveries in the world.

Markov Monastery Tucked in the foothills of the Jakupica Mountains, south of Mount Vodno, is the village of Markova Sušica, at the southwestern end of which is King Marko's Monastery. The monastery church dedicated to Sv Dimitri was started by Marko's father, King Volkašin, in the mid 14th century, and then finished by Marko after his father's death in 1371. This may have been as close as Marko's kingdom got to Skopje, and from here the border probably went through his brother's Monastery of Sv Andreja at Matka and on to the Šar Mountains.

The monastery has frescoes of the king himself, as well as an interesting fresco of the Three Wise Men visiting baby Jesus, and one of Sv Kliment, the first archbishop of Ohrid. Although Ohrid was never a part of Marko's kingdom, the archbishopric was always behind the fledgling kingdom, and the absence of Serbian saints and church figureheads in Marko's monastery is seen as a good indicator that Marko adhered to the Church of Ohrid rather than the new Church of Serbia.

Bus 80 connects Skopje to the village of Markova Sušica. To drive or bike yourself, take Ulica 11th Oktomvri southeast out of town and keep on this road as it becomes Ulica Sava Kovačevik and leads on to the village of Sopište. Take care to keep going straight on in Sava Kovačevik and do not follow the main road around to the left when it turns into 1st Maj Street. After Sopište bear left towards Dobri Dol and Markova Sušica (signposted). At the crossroads just before the village, go straight on over the bridge and into the village until you reach the monastery on the other side. You will require shoulder and leg coverings to enter the church itself.

The small stream running below the monastery is a popular picnic site.

MATKA CANYON AND LAKE A beloved getaway retreat of Skopjites, the spectacular Matka Canyon, its base submerged by a manmade lake, also forms a highly rewarding excursion for tourists visiting the capital. Activities on offer include hiking, canoeing, motorised boat excursions, cliff-climbing, and visits to caves and monasteries, and the canyon entrance is also home to a characterful old hotel and at least half a dozen restaurants. In 1938, a hydro-electric dam was built at the canyon entrance, transforming the River Treška (a tributary of the Vardar) into a brilliant aquamarine serpentine lake hemmed in by an awesome steep-sided ravine that's particularly beautiful in late afternoon light. Before the canyon was dammed, the Lake Matka Hotel – then an unassuming mountain hut – and adjacent church of Sv Andreja stood 20m above the water, but today they are practically lapped by it, and form the base for canoeing and motorboat excursions deeper into the canyon.

Getting there and away It is a mere half-hour drive from the city. Bus 60 from the main bus/railway station does the return trip around a dozen times every day of the week. The first and last buses from Skopje leave at 07.00 and 23.30, while those

Distance	10.5km (18km from the centre of Skopje)
Altitude	Skopje 245m, Hotel Vodno 600m, Vodno Cross 1,066m, Matka 310m
Rating	Moderate: ridge walk followed by steep downhill section
Timing	4hrs (+2hrs from Hotel Vodno to Vodno Cross)
In reverse	Possible, better light for taking photographs of the lake if starting from Matka, but more dramatic to end at Matka and then eat a late lunch afterwards
Trail head	Taxi, bus or hike to Hotel Vodno, then take a cable car or hike to the Millennium Cross
Map	1:25,000 SAGW Map Sheets Matka 731-2-1 and Skopje 731-2-2, January 2007

Route description For a description of the route from Skopje to the Hotel Vodno, and on to the summit of Mount Vodno, see page 149. Starting at the upper cable-way terminus and Millennium Cross, the route is west-southwest along Vodno ridge and mostly gently downhill for about the first 7km. The last 3.5km is a steep descent, which ends with terrific views of the lake and a small boat crossing to reach the Canyon Matka Hotel and Sv Andreja Monastery. The route is well marked until the last 4km when the trail veers off into the woods and is lost in overgrown fields and poor markings. For good orienteers with GPS, there is a detailed route card below. Bring plenty of water for this hike as there is none along the way once you leave Vodno Cross until you reach the spring at Leg 10, some 7km into the hike and halfway down the other side. Hikers have been known to suffer from heat exhaustion hiking this route in the summer. If the Dare Džambaz Hut is (unusually) shut, there is signage for a tap pointing around the back of the cross. In fact it is for a spring that is very difficult to find unless somebody shows it to you. The Canyon Matka Hotel and the Restoran Peštera (page 156) and other restaurants at Matka Dam serve good traditional food.

GPS DIRECTIONS
Start point: Dare Džambaz Hut at Vodno Cross 1,066m

Leg	From Grid	Distance/Time	To Grid	Height
1	332 468	approx 3km/40mins	3045 4658	907m

Starting at Dare Džambaz Hut at Vodno Cross – tank hideouts to left, right track goes to Krušopek. Continue straight on.

returning from Matka are at 05.50 and 23.20. The full timetable is posted at the tourist information office on Boulevard Vasil Agilarski. Alternatively, a taxi from the centre of Skopje should cost around 600MKD, or you can take bus 12 or 22 as far as Saraj, and pick up a taxi for around or 200MKD. Once at Matka bus stop and car park it is a 10-minute walk along the River Treška from the parking area and bus stop to the foot of the dam, and then another 10 minutes up past the dam where

Leg	From Grid	Distance/Time	To Grid	Height
2	3045 4658	approx 2.8km/40mins	2812 4588	898m

To this point is easy, frequently marked with fresh red-and-white paint along an easy trail. This point is the first key turn in the entire route, and turns SSW off main track into woods between burnt and cut-down trees. At the turning point there is a faded red-and-white mark on a pine tree. From here on the path is marked but infrequently, with faded paint and the path is often not visible for several metres ahead.

Leg	From Grid	Distance/Time	To Grid	Height
3	2812 4588	250m	2780 4567	908m

Top of small wooded hill

Leg	From Grid	Distance/Time	To Grid	Height
4	2780 4567	250m	2756 4563	874m

Bottom of hill, no trees, bear left along wide track for 50m then turn right up hill along small track

Leg	From Grid	Distance/Time	To Grid	Height
5	2756 4563	800m	2710 4547	880m

Alpine field

Leg	From Grid	Distance/Time	To Grid	Height
6	2710 4547	100m	2695 4545	889m

Follow ridge line SW

Leg	From Grid	Distance/Time	To Grid	Height
7	2695 4545	150m	2678 4524	888m

Turn W down gully

Leg	From Grid	Distance/Time	To Grid	Height
8	2678 4524	400m	2653 4532	836m

Turn NW down track (to right)

Leg	From Grid	Distance/Time	To Grid	Height
9	2653 4532	900m	2618 4590	732m

Turn W off the track

Leg	From Grid	Distance/Time	To Grid	Height
10	2618 4590	500m	2605 4587	700m

Spring running into a concrete container

Leg	From Grid	Distance/Time	To Grid	Height
11	2605 4587	400m	2586 4542	488m

Fork in the track; up to Sv Nikola Church (recommended), or down to the bottom of Matka Dam

Leg	From Grid	Distance/Time	To Grid	Height
12	2586 4542	200m	2564 4538	598m

Sv Nikola Church. From here descend to the lake and sound the gong for a boatman from the hut to fetch you across the lake.

Leg	From Grid	Distance/Time	To Grid	Height
13	2564 4538	900m	2525 4520	310m

End Destination: Canyon Matka Hotel (☎ 205 5655) and Sv Andrea Church

the path opens up to the grounds of the Canyon Matka Hotel and Restaurant and the Church of Sv Andreja.

🏠 Where to stay and eat   *Map, page 110*

🏠 **Canyon Matka Hotel & Restaurant** (10 rooms) Matka; ☎ 2052 655; m 078 503 000; e info@canyonmatka.mk; w canyonmatka.mk. Water's-edge hotel with simply furnished rooms

& pretty terrace restaurant. All rooms are en suite with Wi-Fi, large flat-screen TVs, & all mod cons. Beautiful location & excellent value for money. Free airport pick-up and drop-off. **$$**

✕ Restoran Peštera Just before the dam; ☏2052 512. Also known as the Bear Cave, this is the pick of several restaurants that run along the river below the dam. It has a nice outdoor patio & a small indoor restaurant set into the rock walls, making it pleasantly cool in summer. The food is traditional Macedonian including good house stew. **$$$**

What to see and do Small **boats** from outside the hotel will take you down the lake for €10 a boat.

There are several impressive **caves** around Matka. The main ones are Ubava, Vrelo, Podvrelo and Krstalna. Vrelo, accessible by boat only, is open to the public for 300MKD (per person, including a 30-minute boat trip, and 30 minutes back). A small landing dock between the entrance information centre and the hotel runs the boats for the lake, and a boat leaves once five or more people are queued up. Podvrelo is almost completely underwater: with a depth of well over 500m, it may be the deepest known underwater cave in the world, and so is for the accomplished cave diver only. Ubava (meaning 'beautiful') has the most stalagmites and stalactites, waterfalls and colours, and archaeological findings in the cave indicate that it may have been used as a shelter during Palaeolithic (Old Stone Age) times almost 10,000 years ago. For more about the caves see Canyon Matka's website (**w** canyonmatka.mk).

There is a lot of **hiking** in the surrounding hills, which are home to over 50 species of protected butterflies and moths. Various paths lead to over a dozen churches and monasteries, some long abandoned, some in full working order.

Next door to the Canyon Matka is **Sv Andreja Church**, built in the 14th century by another Andreja (not the saint), the brother of King Marko (see box, page 264).

Near Restoran Peštera the bridge over the river takes you to a path leading up to the **Church of Sv Nikola**, which has an excellent view on to the hotel and café. Above the Restoran Peštera is the **Monastery of Sveta Bogorodica**. It is a working monastery with inns, which are not open to the public, and a small church. Above the entrance to the church is an inscription reading:

> By the will of the Father, the Son and the Holy Ghost and the divine temple of the Mother of God came Lady Milica. She found this church unroofed, built a roof for it, painted its frescoes and built a wall around it. Mention, Lord, that this took place in 1497.

To the left of the entrance to the monastery is a path marked red which leads up to the churches of Sv Spas (80 minutes) and Sv Trojica (85 minutes) and the ruined Monastery of Sv Nedela (95 minutes). The walk to these churches is beautiful, although the trail is steep and badly marked so patience is required to get there. **Sv Spas** was built in the 14th century on the foundations of an earlier church, and renovated in 1968. To the right of the church as you approach it (ie: to the northeast) are the large and overgrown limestone blocks of an ancient fortress. The site continued to be populated into Ottoman times when it was known as Markov Grad (Marko's Town). It was also a hideout for Macedonian revolutionaries, until it was discovered by the Ottomans and ransacked.

An alternative rendition to the end of this fortress comes in the form of a love story. Allegedly, an Ottoman *bey* fell in love with the beautiful Bojana from Marko's Town and, when she refused his overtures, the bey decided to take her against her will. The citizens of the fortress helped her and killed almost a hundred Turk soldiers before Bojana realised her fate was sealed and threw herself to her death from the steep cliffs of the canyon into the River Treška. The soldiers took revenge by razing the fortress to the ground. The only building still left standing (just about) is the **Church of Sv Nedela** (Sv Sunday) with its ruined archway and old fresco of the saint. Take care going up to this church, as it stands on precariously steep ground.

There are two paths from here back down to the lake at Sv Andreja. The longer path marked yellow goes via Matkin Dol. It is very steep and should be walked with care. The name Matkin Dol means Torture Valley, which might give you an idea of how difficult it is. There are a few small caves along this path where monks retreated in order to find union with God.

To the left of the Canyon Matka are several boards showing the walks, animals and sites in the area, as well as a guide board with the climbing routes on the large rock face on the opposite side of the lake. For those wishing to do some serious climbing or extended hiking and mountaineering in Matka, or anywhere else in Macedonia or Bulgaria, Matka Climbing Club offers experienced guides as well as rock-climbing lessons.

The path along the river continues after the monastery, past a huge memorial of a karabiner hung on a piton stuck into the rock. The memorial was put up to commemorate the lives of climbers lost in a climbing accident at that spot in the early 1990s. The rest of the path along the lake is mostly good, but in some places it is crumbling and requires a bit of careful footwork. Again, it's not a walk for those with severe vertigo.

Eventually, the hike comes to the end of the lake and continues up the River Treška. Parts of the river cliffs are quarried for rock, so you may not be able to walk more than the first 3km, as the cliffs become unsafe. The middle reaches of the Treška between Makedonski Brod and Lake Matka are meant to be good fishing, and these can be reached more quickly by driving around via Sopište.

SOUTHEAST OF SKOPJE

Tauresium On the northeast side of the village of Taor are the excavations for the town of Tauresium. The oldest section of the excavation has revealed the foundations of a four-towered castle, which was known as Tetrpirgia, built in the 4th century AD. The Ostrogoth Theodahad was born here around AD480. After he arrested Queen Amalaswintha, he went on to become king of the Ostrogoths for a short period from AD534 to 536. He ruled the Kingdom of Italy, which was formed by the Ostrogoths after the collapse of the Western Roman Empire, and which was in turn defeated in the Gothic Wars of AD535–54 by another man born in Tauresium. That man was the Byzantine emperor Justinian I. He was born in AD483 and ruled Byzantium from AD527 to 565. Justinian rebuilt Skupi in its current location after the Roman town was destroyed in the earthquake of AD518.

The site was first excavated by the famous British archaeologist Sir Arthur Evans. He wrote about his discoveries in the 1880s in his book *Ancient Illyria: An Archaeological Exploration*, which covers extensive observations on the wider Illyria region. For more on the excavation site see w www.tauresium.info.

The village of Taor is 25km southeast of Skopje, on the River Vardar. To get here, you can either drive the old road via Dračevo and cross the river at Orešani, or go to Katlanovo and head for Orešani and Zelenikovo. By public transport you can take the train to Zelenikovo and then cross the Vardar at the bridge behind the station (don't head into Zelenikovo village) and take the 3km track north over the hills or along the river to Taor. The track over the hills leads you past an old cross at the 454m trig point and then past the excavation site itself. From here it is another 7km to Katlanovska Banja hot springs (page 158), where you can take bus 53 back.

Katlanovska Banja Situated 30km outside Skopje near the airport, this *banja* (Macedonian for 'thermal bath') is mentioned in ancient Roman writings and is now serviced by Katlanovska Spa (✆2581 002; e katlanovskaspa@katlanovskaspa. com; w katlanovskaspa.com; ⊕ 07.00–21.00 Tue–Sun, 07.00–17.00 Mon; entry: main pool €4/hr; private pool for 2 €15/hr). This is Macedonia's only Western-standard spa, and the only hot spring complex in the country open to both sexes at the same time. Some excellent spa packages are available, including the full range of massage, body mud-packs and facials, as well as monthly special offers. The spa has

HIKING MOUNT KITKA

Distance	10km round trip
Altitude	Motel Kitka trail head 903m, Kitka mountain hut 1,320m, Kitka peak 1,675m
Rating	Easy
Timing	4–5 hours
Alternative	14km round trip from Gorno Količani
Trail head	Bus 74 to Gorno Količani or car/taxi to Motel Kitka trail head (*grid 3935 3140*)
Map	1:25,000 SAGW Map Sheet Umovo 731-2-4, January 2010

Route description Mount Kitka is the beginning of the next mountain range behind Vodno, south of Skopje. At 1,675m the peak has a mountain hut and lots of adventurous hiking trails in the beautiful forests of the Jakupica mountain range. Bus 74 from Skopje only goes as far as Gorno Količani (from where there is a faint and unmarked 5km mountain trail up to the Kitka peak, but this is not recommended without a guide).

To get to the Motel Kitka trail head by car from Skopje, take 11th Oktomvri heading southeast out of town until it becomes Sava Kovačevik and follow the road around to the left as it becomes Ulica 1st Maj (Sava Kovačevik continues straight on to Markova Sušica). Ulica 1st Maj will take you to the village of Dračevo where you should turn right (south) opposite the village petrol station to get to Kitka Mountain. The turning is signposted in Cyrillic for Kitka and the Količani villages, and the road will take you past the Dračevo village graveyard and the red-and-white radio mast. Just before the village of Dolni Količani are many old marble Muslim gravestones. Keep right when you get to the village itself in order to continue on to Kitka.

The trail from Motel Kitka starts (grid 3935 3140) 200m before the prominent Motel Kitka crossroads after the village of Crvena Voda. Motel Kitka itself has long been abandoned, so no hopes of relaxing on a café terrace there. The path winds along the northeast side of the mountain for 3km to Kitka mountain hut. From the hut it is another 1.5km along a winding path to the summit.

Beyond the Motel Kitka crossroads, the left-hand fork heading east follows the steep Kadina ravine to the Torbeši (Macedonian Muslim) village of Paligrad. Here the asphalt road runs out and a 4x4 is required to continue. Back at the crossroads there is a dirt track turn-off on the right that is signposted for Karadžica mountain hut, and the road ahead, signposted for Solunska Glava, becomes a dirt track going to the village of Aldinci and beyond.

a restaurant, and a little shop for snacks and small supplies. A couple of old picnic gazebos still stand in the grounds.

There are two approaches to Katlanovska by car, one from the north side when coming from Kumanovo, and one from the south. To get to the south side, go east out of Skopje, past the airport as if going to Greece, and then take the Katlanovska Banja exit on the right. Keep following the signs and, when you run out of signs, follow the river. If you get disoriented or lose the river on your right, just open the window and follow the faint sulphur smell. Katlanovska and its spa are connected to Skopje by bus 53, which covers the route at least a dozen times daily in either direction. An up-to-date timetable is also available on the spa website.

Monastery of Sv Bogorodica near Kozle
On the drive to Veles from Skopje, the road south follows the River Pčinja from Katlanovska Banja until it joins the Vardar. The road winds around the sides of a steep gorge making interesting driving and offering fantastic scenery. Fortunately, at this section there are (or at least should be) no oncoming cars as the road north takes a completely separate route further east. On this southerly road, a couple of kilometres before the River Pčinja joins the Vardar, there is a spacious stopping place on the right-hand side of the road with a couple of holy roadside shrines and a water fountain. This place also marks the stop for the Monastery of Sv Bogorodica, which can be seen across the river from the roadside.

The 500m hike starts through a metal entrance to the left of the fountain, goes across a small wooden bridge crossing the river, and ends up in the courtyard of the monastery. It is no longer a working monastery, but is kept by two wardens who live here. They might join you at this juncture to explain the place.

The site was originally just a shrine in the rocks and, like many rock shrines in Macedonia, it eventually became a cave church. This one was built using old train rails from 1918 to help support the roof, but by the 1930s it was completely abandoned. It took another 40 years for the church to be rebuilt in 1976, thereby saving some of the original roof frescoes and replacing the old iconostasis.

If you spy the monastery on the way down south, but don't manage to stop, remember you won't be able to see it on the way back north as the north road does not pass this way.

UPDATES WEBSITE

You can post your comments and recommendations, and read feedback and updates from other readers online at w bradtupdates.com/northmacedonia.

4

Polog and Mavrovo

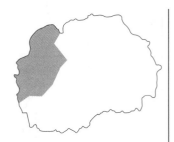

> ... every inch of the [Šarena] mosque inside was painted with fripperies in this amusing and self-consciously amused style. There was a frieze of tiny little views, of palaces on the Bosporus with ships neatly placed around the sound, of walled gardens with playing fountains ... it was like being inside a building made of a lot of enormous tea-trays ...
>
> Rebecca West, *Black Lamb and Grey Falcon*, 1941

The northwest of Macedonia along the upper reaches of the Vardar is known as Polog, edged by the Šar Mountains bordering Kosovo, while further south the Korab and Dešat mountains border Albania. The main towns of Tetovo, Gostivar and Debar are predominantly Albanian, with significant pockets of Turks in Vrapčište, Centar Župa, Plasnica and Vraneštica. If you don't speak any Albanian, you'll be more warmly welcomed among most of the Albanian community if you speak German as it is more widely spoken here than English as a second language.

Mavrovo National Park and Jasen Nature Reserve are home to some stunning mountain scenery, waterfalls and wildlife. Skiing is available at Popova Šapka near Tetovo, and at Mavrovo, and in the summer the wedding festival of Galičnik takes place every July. The back road to Ohrid from Gostivar goes past Mavrovo Lake and down the Radika River into the manmade dammed valley of Debar Lake. From there it follows the Crni Drim River past the dammed Globočica Valley on to Struga on the north shore of Lake Ohrid. In the autumn it is probably one of the prettiest routes in Macedonia, when the densely wooded mountainside becomes a riot of red, orange and yellow. This is the area of Macedonia that could earn itself the name of 'Little Switzerland'.

TETOVO *Telephone code 044*

Bisected by the Pena River some 40km west of Skopje, Tetovo is a substantial and lively university town with an estimated population of 70,000. The atmospheric old town, flanking the Pena, is lined with jewellery shops, old-fashioned tailors and boutiques selling modern and traditional clothes, and it also houses a museum and art gallery, and a number of historic mosques and churches, most famously the colourful 15th-century mosque known as Šarena Džamija. Other worthwhile historical sites in Tetovo include the well-tended complex of early 19th-century Islamic buildings known as Arabati Baba Bektaši Teke, and an impressive hilltop fort.

Tetovo is also the gateway to the Šar Mountains and to the popular Popova Šapka ski resort. Towering above the town, covered in snow until July and as early as September, is Macedonia's second highest mountain, Titov Vrv (Tito's Summit, 2,748m). This is in fact the highest mountain that lies completely in Macedonia; the higher peak of Mount Korab (2,764m) lies further to the south above Lake Mavrovo on the border with Albania.

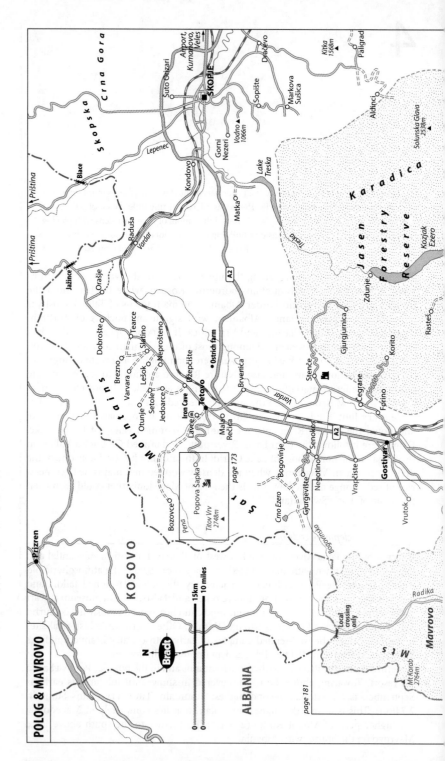

POLOG & MAVROVO

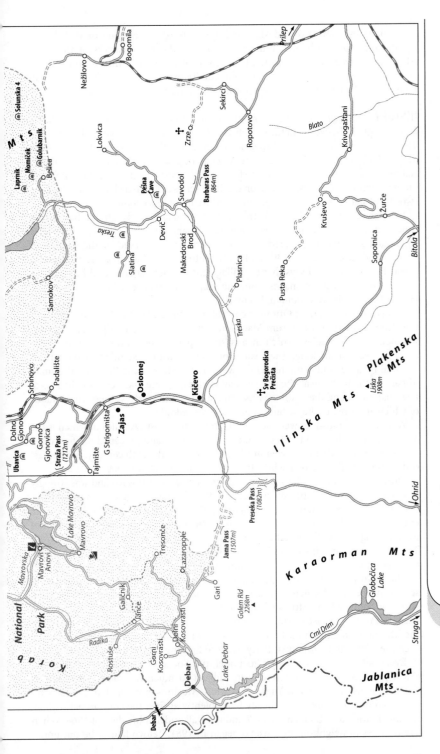

Nestled close to Kosovo and Albania, Tetovo is the de facto capital of Macedonia's significantly sized Albanian minority. It is also the headquarters of the main Albanian-centred political parties, the Democratic Union of Integration and the Democratic Party of Albanians. Just outside Tetovo is the South East European University, Macedonia's third-largest university after Skopje and Bitola.

HISTORY Although Tetovo is a relatively new town by Macedonian standards, archaeological discoveries in the vicinity date back to the Bronze Age (2200–1200BC). The country's oldest artefact, a Mycenaean sword from this period, was found outside Tetovo. So too was the 6th-century BC Maenad of Tetovo, a small (9cm tall) bronze statuette of a dancing girl regarded to be of such importance that it features not only on the town's coat of arms, but also on the 1996 series 5,000MKD banknote. Both the sword and statue are now displayed in the Museum of Macedonia in Skopje.

Copper and gold in the local streams first attracted Greek settlers, but during Roman and early Slav times there were few inhabitants here. The first signs of a significant settlement appeared as a small rural village served by the Church of Sv Bogorodica during the 13th and 14th centuries. At that time the village was called Htetovo. Legend says that the village got its name after a local hero, Hteto, succeeded in banishing snakes from the village. Thereafter it became known as Hteto's Place or, in Macedonian, Htetovo.

Tetovo remained under Ottoman control from the end of the 14th century until the Ottomans were ousted from Macedonia in 1912. During that period the town was named Kalkandelen, which means 'shield penetrator', in honour of the local smithies' weapon-making. Their superior craftsmanship extended to the advent of small firearms and cannons, which were traded all over the Balkans. The small hill above the town, near the present-day village of Lavce, has been fortified since Paeonian times and the Ottomans also built a substantial fortress there, the remains of which are some of the better preserved in Macedonia.

A number of mosques were built in the town, the most beautiful of which is the Šarena Mosque, built in the 16th century, which fortunately escaped the fire of the mid 17th century that destroyed most of the town. In the 16th century, the Bektaši order also settled in Tetovo, where they remain at the Bektaši teke.

During Turkish times Tetovo came under the vilayet of Kosovo and was strongly orientated towards its Albanian brothers and the Albanian struggle for independence from Ottoman rule. But the Serb victory in the Balkan wars of 1912 and 1913 left the entire vilayet of Kosovo, including Tetovo, Gostivar and Debar, under the control of Royalist Yugoslavia. The resulting crackdown on Islam forced many Muslims from Tetovo to emigrate to the US and Canada, while thousands of Serbs were encouraged to move into the town to develop the mining and hydro-electric industries.

The town prospered: orthodox churches were built, skiing and pony trekking started in the Šar Mountains, and White Russian settlers arrived. The 1930s were good for the new Slav settlers of Tetovo; and then came World War II and Tetovo became a part of fascist Albania. In resistance, some of the new Serb settlers set up the Macedonian Communist Party, founded on 19 March 1943 in Tetovo, but by then the Albanian Communist Party was also fighting for the town.

Eventually, the town fell to Tito under the Socialist Republic of Macedonia (SRM), and Albanians in Tetovo were subject to much the same repression as the Albanians of Kosovo in Yugoslavia. More Muslims emigrated and those who remained demonstrated periodically but violently against the communist regime, notably in the Yucel Incident of 1957 and the Kalkandelen Incident of 1968. When the troubles in neighbouring Kosovo began in 1981, Tetovo had to be put under the control of paramilitary police due to the rioting and show of sympathy with the Kosovar Albanians. The same happened again in 1989.

When it became obvious in 1990 that Yugoslavia was about to fall, over 2,000 ethnic Albanians marched through Tetovo demanding secession from the Socialist Republic of Macedonia and unity with Albania. Self-determination of an ethnic minority within a state was not a right under the SRM constitution and, protesting their lack of representation under the constitution of a new Republic of Macedonia (RM), the Albanians of Macedonia boycotted the referendum on independence from Yugoslavia and were thus excluded from almost any representation in the new government. Tetovo became the headquarters of the new Albanian political parties, which were regarded as unconstitutional by the new RM. Tensions worsened, and were fuelled by increasing lawlessness in neighbouring Kosovo. Prior to the NATO bombing of Serb forces in Kosovo, Tetovo became the rear supply base for the Kosovo Liberation Army, and then later home to thousands of Kosovo refugees.

In 1997, Ajladin Demiri, the mayor of Tetovo, was jailed for raising the double-headed eagle flag of Albania from Tetovo Town Hall, and by 2000 the outbreak of hostilities in Tanuševci, north of Skopje on the border with Kosovo, had spilled into the towns of Tetovo and Gostivar. Even after hostilities had ceased and a peace deal had been brokered by the international community, there was still inter-ethnic tension in the area. The old Tetovo–Gostivar–Debar highway (now the back road through Bogovinje and Vrapčište), linking these predominantly Albanian towns, was the scene of many armed blockades in 2001–02.

Today, although some tensions remain, they are either intergang disputes, which are not aimed at the innocent tourist, or are purely of a political nature. Since the recent formation of two universities in the town (see box, below), Tetovo has become a young and vibrant place that is welcoming and interesting.

LEARNING IN ONE'S OWN LANGUAGE

In the early 1990s, the Albanian community tried to start the first university in the country to offer courses in Albanian. The government disapproved, repeating that Macedonian was the only official language allowed under the then constitution (the writing of which the Albanians had not participated in), and with that the struggle for the right to learn in one's own mother tongue ensued. Eventually, after intense mediation from the OSCE's High Commissioner for National Minorities, Max van der Stoel, both sides agreed on a compromise in the form of the South East European University (SEEU, also known as the Van der Stoel University; w seeu.edu.mk) offering courses taught in Albanian, Macedonian and English.

In many ways the SEEU was set up to be independent of the government by being a fee-paying establishment built with international money. In the academic year of 2004/05, it enrolled 3,886 students, of whom 78% spoke Albanian as their first language. The SEEU has the potential to be a role model for education among mixed ethnicities around the world, and could make for a valuable exchange year for students of Balkan history and language.

With the rights enshrined in the Ohrid Framework Agreement, the Albanian community finally won their struggle for state funding for Albanian-language tertiary education with the legal recognition of Tetovo University in 2003. The following year, 1,550 students enrolled. For more on education in Macedonia, see page 51.

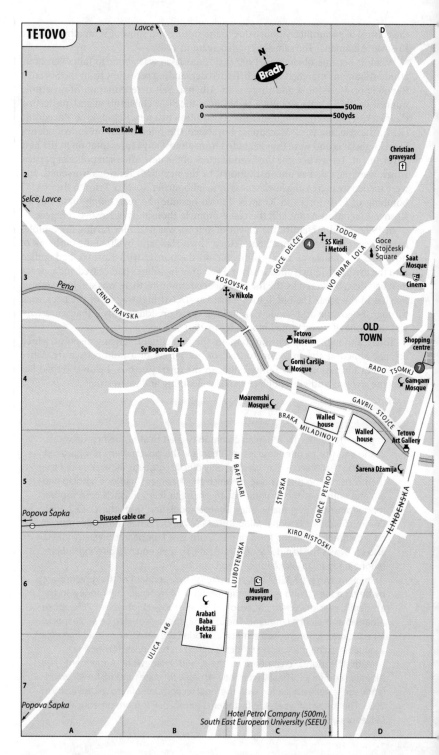

TETOVO

Lavce

N

Bradt

0 — 500m
0 — 500yds

Tetovo Kale

Selce, Lavce

Christian graveyard

TODOR

GOCE DELČEV

SS Kiril i Metodi ④

IVO RIBAR LOLA

Goce Stojčeski Square

Saat Mosque

Cinema

Pena

CRNO TRAVSKA

KOSOVSKA

Sv Nikola

Tetovo Museum

OLD TOWN

Shopping centre

Sv Bogorodica

Gorni Čaršija Mosque

RADO TSOMKJ ⑦

Gamgam Mosque

Moaremshi Mosque

GAVRIL STOJČE

BRAKA MILADINOVI

Walled house

Walled house

Tetovo Art Gallery

Šarena Džamija

Popova Šapka

Disused cable car

M BAFTIJARI

ŠTIPSKA

GORČE PETROV

HINĐENSKA

KIRO RISTOSKI

LUJBOTENSKA

Muslim graveyard

ULICA 146

Arabati Baba Bektaši Teke

Popova Šapka

Hotel Petrol Company (500m),
South East European University (SEEU)

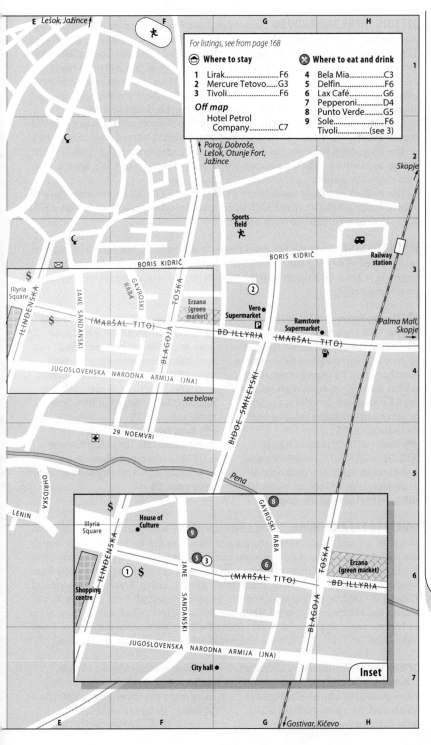

For listings, see from page 168

Where to stay

1 Lirak............................F6
2 Mercure Tetovo......G3
3 Tivoli...........................F6

Off map
   Hotel Petrol
   Company.................C7

Where to eat and drink

4 Bela Mia.................C3
5 Delfin......................F6
6 Lax Café................G6
7 Pepperoni..............D4
8 Punto Verde.........G5
9 Sole.........................F6
   Tivoli................(see 3)

Lešok, Jažince

Poroj, Dobroše,
Lešok, Otunje Fort,
Jažince

Skopje

Sports
field

BORIS KIDRIČ

BORIS KIDRIČ

Railway
station

Illyria
Square

JANE SANDANSKI

GAVROSKI RABA

TOSKA

Erzana
(green
market)

Vero
Supermarket

Ramstore
Supermarket

Palma Mall,
Skopje

(MARŠAL TITO)

BD ILLYRIA

(MARŠAL TITO)

BLAGOJA

BD-DE SMILEVSKI

JUGOSLOVENSKA NARODNA ARMIJA (JNA)

see below

29 NOEMVRI

OHRIDSKA

LENIN

Pena

House of
Culture

Illyria
Square

HINDENSKA

JANE SANDANSKI

GAVROSKI RABA

TOSKA

Erzana
(green market)

BLAGOJA

(MARŠAL TITO)

BD ILLYRIA

Shopping
centre

JUGOSLOVENSKA NARODNA ARMIJA (JNA)

City hall

Inset

Gostivar, Kičevo

Polog and Mavrovo   TETOVO

4

GETTING THERE AND AROUND Tetovo lies about 45km west of Skopje, a 40-minute drive on the E65 toll highway (Motorway 2). Tetovo **bus** station [167 H3] (✆336 331, 339 130) is on Ulica Boris Kidrič, almost 1km to the east of the town centre, although most buses also stop and pick up in the centre of the town. More than 30 buses run daily to/from Skopje, leaving between 04.30 and 21.30, and there are around 50 daily to/from Gostivar, departing between 05.10 and 22.45. There are also several direct buses daily to Kičevo and Ohrid, or you could do it in hops via Gostivar.

Local area buses to villages on the old road north to Vratnica and south along the old road to Debreše leave every 15 minutes from Potok in the centre of town 05.50–20.00.

The once-daily **train** service between Skopje and Kičevo (page 196) stops at Tetovo and Gostivar. The train station [167 H3] (✆336 660) is on Ulica Boris Kidrič, next to the bus station.

Tetovo itself is a fairly small town. Taxis run for a combined minimum fare of 50MKD, plus 30MKD/km and 5MKD/minute. Taxi numbers include ✆1560, 1575, 1577, 1590 (prefix with 046 from a mobile).

WHERE TO STAY There are few good places to stay in town, but Tetovo can also be easily visited as day trip from Skopje, which is only around an hour away. Another option is to head directly up into the mountains and stay at the Popova Šapka ski resort (page 172).

Mercure Tetovo [167 G3] (101 rooms) Bd Illyria; ✆511 276; e ha356-re@accor.com; ☐ @MercureTetovo. Opened in 2018, this 12-storey 5-star representative of the international Accor chain is easily the largest & smartest hotel in Tetovo. Modern & well-equipped non-smoking rooms & suites are complemented by a quality restaurant & amazing rooftop terrace bar facing the Šar Mountains. **$$$**

Tivoli [167 F6] (30 rooms) Bd Illyria 19; ✆352 370; m 071 389 213; e tivoli@tivoli.com.mk; w tivoli.com.mk. Run by one of the most popular restaurants in the town. All mod cons; friendly, helpful staff; buffet b/fast & oranges at reception. **$$$**

Hotel Lirak [167 F6] (39 rooms) Bd Illyria 10; ✆338 578; m 070 209 030; e hotel.lirak@ gmail.com; w lirakhotel.mk. Tetovo's oldest hotel, still sometimes referred to by its original name of Makedonija, is usefully located on central Illyria Square, & the rooms are comfortable, well-maintained & attractively priced. Street-facing rooms can be noisy. **$$**

Hotel Petrol Company [166 C7] (14 rooms) Studena Voda, 3km south of the centre; ✆378 120; e info@petrolcompany.com.mk; w petrolcompany.com.mk. Clean rooms above the petrol station. **$$**

WHERE TO EAT AND DRINK The main thoroughfare, Boulevard Illyria, is lined with places to eat and drink, as are the parallel streets to the north and south, which are slightly less busy and have a more relaxed atmosphere. Contrary to what you might think, Tetovo offers a great variety of places for entertainment, especially from Thursdays to Sundays. Tetovo's main green market, called Erzana, on Boulevard Illyria [167 H6], is packed with fresh local produce and all sorts of other knick-knacks and cheap clothing items. There are also some nice restaurants on the way up to Popova Šapka and some at the ski resort itself. On the eastern outskirts of town, **Palma Mall** [167 H4] (Bd Illyria; w palmamall.mk) has shops, cafés and bowling.

Bela Mia [166 C3] Goce Delčev 108 (just west of Kiril i Metodi Church); ✆331 332; w belamia. mk; ⊕ 09.00–23.00 daily. Serves traditional Macedonian fare in a pretty, traditional setting in the old town with a nice *čardak* (patio) in the summer. Good *tava* & *pindžur*. It's poorly signposted but you can't miss the old wooden wagon draped with flowers in the car park. **$$**

Delfin [167 F6] Bd Illyria 18; ✆339 125; m 075 432 495; ☐ @delfintetove; ⊕ 10.00–

midnight Sun–Thu, 10.00–01.00 Fri–Sat. Much less trendy than Tivoli next door; popular with the literati. Pizza, etc. $$

✗ **Pepperoni** [166 D4] Rado Tsomkj; m 071 881 832. Situated on the edge of the old town, this brightly painted bistro has an attractive tree-shaded terrace & well-priced menu of pizzas, burgers, sandwiches & salads. $$

✗ **Sole** [167 F6] Jane Sandanski 98 (opposite the House of Culture); ☏ 333 238; ⏰ noon–midnight Sun–Thu, noon–01.00 Fri–Sat. Popular with businessmen, artists & local politicians. Delicious pasta & seafood. The focaccia with garlic is especially tasty but do not leave without trying the homemade crème caramel. $$

✗ **Tivoli** [167 F6] Bd Illyria 19; ☏ 352 370; m 071 389 213; w tivoli.com.mk; ⏰ 08.00–midnight Sun–Thu, 08.00–01.00 Fri–Sat. A very popular place on the main boulevard, owned by the hotel of the same name. Serves a range of good salads, risottos & excellent b/fast omelettes. Pleasant atmosphere & fine service. $$

✗ **Punto Verde** [167 G5] Boris Kidrič; ☏ 337 498; w puntoverde.mk. A pizzeria & popular bar with a huge terrace, normally packed on summer afternoons. $

☕ **Lax Café** [167 G6] Bd Illyria; ⨍ @laxcafe. Coffees, cocktails & juices.

WHAT TO SEE AND DO
Around town

Šarena Džamija [166 D5] The most celebrated landmark in Tetovo, situated in the town centre just south of the river, the Šarena Džamija (literally 'coloured' or 'painted mosque') is known locally as Pasha Djamija (Prince's Mosque) and often called the Motley Mosque by English-speakers. Its colourful exterior makes the building look like it is clad in a deck of playing cards, and over 30,000 eggs were used to manufacture the paint and glaze. The site used to include an inn as well as the bathhouse that has now been restored as an art gallery on the opposite side of the river. The mosque stands in landscaped green grounds that contain an octagonal *turbe* (grave) of Hurshida and Mensure, the two women who paid to have the mosque built in the mid 15th century. The original structure burned down in the 16th century and has undergone several restorations since then, the most extensive of which occurred in the 1820s under Pasha Abdulrahman, who added the colourful veneer for which the mosque is now famed.

Tetovo Art Gallery [166 D5] (71 Ilindenska; ☏ 340 811; ⏰ Oct–Mar 10.00–18.00 Tue–Sun, Apr–Sep 10.00–21.00 Tue–Sun; free admission) Opened in 2015 following extensive restoration work, this small art gallery occupies a domed 15th-century stone hammam (Turkish bath) that stands on the north bank of the river opposite the Šarena Džamija. The spacious interior houses an interesting selection of contemporary artworks, both paintings and photographs.

Tetovo Museum [166 C4] (92 Radovan Conikj; ☏ 338 912; ⏰ 10.00–15.00 Tue–Sun; free admission) Founded in 1950, this small local history museum, signposted in Macedonian, stands in a distinctive Ottoman-style wooden-doored two-storey building in the old town. It houses some interesting ethnographic and historical displays about the Polog region, and occasional special exhibitions.

Arabati Baba Bektaši Teke [166 B6] One of the prettiest sites in the town, the Arabati Baba Bektaši Teke is a complex of old-style inns and meditation platforms set in a well-kept walled garden about 800m south of the Pena. A teke is the Sufi (a branch of Islam) or dervish equivalent of a monastery belonging to one of the 12 orders of dervishes (Muslim mystics).

This teke was built at the end of the 18th century and remained the seat of the Bektaši until 1912 when the Ottomans were driven out of Macedonia; no longer welcome, most of the dervishes fled to neighbouring Albania or elsewhere. Although the teke saw a small revival between 1941 and 1945, the lands were taken as state property during Yugoslav times and made into a hotel and museum. In recent years, however, the Bektaši order has regained access to the teke and the site is being slowly refurbished. Although in considerable disrepair, it is still the largest and best-preserved teke in the western Balkans.

The prayer room and library are open to visitors if accompanied by the *baba* (priest), who will welcome any library donations of Islamic books to replace the many burnt in 1948 when partisan forces set the library alight. Next to the baba's courtyard is the *meydan*, which used to be the main place of worship for the Bektaši. Now it has been converted into a Sunni mosque (much to the annoyance of the dervishes who would like to see their teke completely returned to the Sufi order).

Other religious buildings Three important mosques stand in the old town: the **Saat Mosque** [166 D3], which as its name implies used to have a clock in its minaret; the **Gorni Čaršija Mosque** [166 C4], so called for its proximity to the upper bazaar area; and the **Gamgam Mosque** [166 D4]. Historic churches include the 14th-century **Church of Sv Bogorodica** [166 B4] on the south bank of the river, the **Church of Sv Nikola** [166 C3] on a low hill overlooking the north bank on the way to Lavce and the fortress remains, and the **Church of Kiril i Metodi** [166 C3] in the heart of the old town.

Tetovo Kale [166 B2]About 2km north of the town centre as the crow flies (but twice as far on foot or by car), just above the small village of Lavce, stands the hilltop fortress known as Tetovo Kale. Essentially an Ottoman construction, the citadel was built by Pasha Abdulrahman in the 1820s, but it stands on the foundations of an older medieval fort and incorporates remains dating to Roman times. Kale and its accompanying mosque were destroyed in the 1912 and 1913 Balkan wars. Although no longer the glorious fortress it once was, it remains one of the better-preserved remnants after Tsar Samoil's Fortress in Ohrid and the Kale in Skopje. It has also been undergoing considerable excavation and renovation work in recent years.

In its heyday it was quite the construction with a series of tunnels from all the main Ottoman houses in the town leading to the fortress. The thinking behind the tunnel system was to enable the defenders of the fortress to escape behind enemy lines if the fortress was besieged, allowing the besiegers themselves to be encircled. The last tunnel collapsed in the 1960s and, since excavation started, two of the tunnels, to Selce and Lavce, have been found.

While the Kale can't be seen from Tetovo, floodlights at night can be, and the views of Tetovo and the River Vardar from the Kale are magnificent. The site remains strategically important and was used in the last conflict of 2001, as was the Pena Valley behind, for shoring up troops and supplies. In World War II the Pena Valley was bombed repeatedly by the Germans.

Further afield
Pena Valley The paths up the River Pena lead to a number of mountain villages and past the Iron Cave, a large underground system popular with cavers and pot-holers. There are also attractive villages along the Tetovo road to Prizren in Kosovo.

ALI SERSEM BABA AND THE ARABATI BABA BEKTAŠI TEKE

Ali Baba (not Ali Baba of the *Arabian Nights*) was the brother-in-law of Sultan Suleijman the Magnificent, and had been a high-ranking *baba* in the important Dimotika Teke (now in Greece) when his sister (who was one of the sultan's wives) fell into disfavour with her husband. As a result, Ali Baba was banished to Tetovo at the outer fringes of the Ottoman Empire, where he started his own teke.

Another version of the story goes that Ali Baba was an official of the Ottoman Empire who gave up his position in order to live the simple life of a Bektaši monk. The sultan, angered by the departure of one of his favourite officials, yelled after Ali as he departed Constantinople, 'If you will be a fool, then go.' *Sersem*, the old Turkish for 'fool', became Ali Baba's nickname thereafter.

Whichever is the true story (the Turks favour the first one), Sersem travelled the vast empire of Turkey until he came upon the River Pena in the tranquil mountains of Tetovo. There he settled until his death in 1538, quietly practising the 'way' of the Bektaši order. After his death, his only pupil to survive him, Arabati Baba, founded a monastery in Tetovo to commemorate Sersem's life.

The present-day buildings were built at the end of the 18th century by Rexhep Pasha, also a dervish, whose tomb lies next to Sersem's in the teke mausoleum. Not all the buildings are still standing today: in the courtyard can be seen the foundations of what might formerly have been the teke stables; a fountain, meditation platform and a watchtower are also original. Some say that the blue-painted tower next to the baba's private courtyard was originally built to house the sick daughter of Abdulrahman Pasha. The reception inn is still in disrepair, although the library is being refurbished. One of the buildings has been turned into a Sunni mosque, but the inns around the Bektaši graveyard have been preserved for the baba.

Many Sufi/dervish orders include a ceremony or dance ritual called *zikr*. This involves swaying movements in time to music and/or the repetition of Islamic texts by the lead dervish or *zakir*. The ceremony requires a lot of control and concentration in order to empty the mind of all but God, and can appear to result in an almost trance-like state. The zikr is performed on a meditation platform like the one at the Bektaši Arabati Baba Teke. (For the Rufa'i dervish order, renowned for their feats of walking on hot coals and swallowing swords, the zikr often appears quite frantic and it is from this order of zikr that the phrase 'whirling dervish' comes.)

At the Arabati Baba Bektaši Teke another ceremony takes place once a year in recognition of the martyrdom of the Shia Imam Hussein family, who were stabbed to death in Kerbela, Iraq, for their religious beliefs. As in other Shi'a communities, worshippers beat themselves to relive the martyrdom of the Imam and his family.

Orašje, close to the Kosovo border, has the remains of another once strategic castle guarding the Pena Valley. In villages such as **Brezno** and **Varvara**, you can still see good examples of traditional village architecture – wattle-and-daub houses with stone roofs. Some villages, such as **Jedoarce**, **Setole** and **Otunje**, are former weekend house retreats that were damaged during the conflict and are now slowly being rebuilt. While you are unlikely to come across many people, there are wonderful views over the Polog (Vardar) Valley, as well as several mountain walks through mature beech and sweet chestnut forests on to the top of the Šar range.

Lešok Monastery Situated in the village of the same name 8km to the northeast of Tetovo, Lešok Monastery houses two 14th-century churches: Sv Bogorodica (the Holy Virgin Mary, built in 1326) and Sv Atanas (mid 14th century). The Church of the Holy Virgin contains frescoes from three different dates: the time of construction, the 17th century and lastly 1879. The original iconostasis and several marble columns from the original church are now on show in the city museum. The monastery was one of several in the area favoured by the 19th-century Pasha Abdulrahman, who donated money to their upkeep. Later, he attempted an uprising against the sultan and failed (it wasn't just the locals who were unhappy with the Ottoman elite) and was packed off to fight in the Crimea, where he died. Unfortunately, during the conflict of 2001, the Church of Sv Atanas was severely damaged by a bomb. It is now being reconstructed with international financing and work on new frescoes started in 2004. In the yard of the Monastery of Lešok is the tomb of the educator Kiril Pejchinovik, who was born in 1770. In his honour, the monastery hosts an International Meeting of Literary Translators every year. There is a fish farm and restaurant **Trofta** (m 071 357 346) as you approach the monastery.

POPOVA ŠAPKA SKI RESORT AND MOUNTAIN RANGE

Popova Šapka lies to the west of Tetovo, 1,000m above the town. In days gone by it was the most successful ski resort in Macedonia, but it suffered during the conflict years for being in the heart of the predominantly Albanian region of the country and local economic renewal has been sporadic at best. The continued closure of the cable car from Tetovo town centre to Popova Šapka illustrates the problems at the local government level, while the arrival of cat-ski opportunities for off-piste skiers does at least show room for entrepreneurship. Overall, facilities are improving and it remains cheap.

GETTING THERE AND AWAY The 17km road to Popova Šapka is well paved, if long and zigzaggy, and the snow at the top and the views of Kopilica Mountain on the way up are well worth the drive, although parking is at a premium. During the winter there is a minibus that goes up at 08.00 and comes down at 15.00, although it's hard to pin down as it picks up from various differing places depending on clients, so ask through your hotel. Alternatively, a taxi ride from Tetovo to Popova Šapka is 900MKD. For the journey back down, ask a restaurant or café on the slopes to send up a taxi for you.

WHERE TO STAY *Map, opposite*

Noli's Konak (16 rooms) 521 055; m 075 330 830; e info@noliskonak.com; w noliskonak. com. The first privately owned hotel at the ski centre, opened in 1982 by a Swiss couple. Has its own restaurant. **$$$$**

Casa Leone (5 apts) 361 002; m 072 515 240; e casaleone.mk@gmail.com; w casaleone. mk. Nice new private apts above the restaurant of the same name, all with balcony; 1 with kitchen. Wi-Fi. **$$**

Popova Šapka (53 rooms) At the end of the tarmac road & parking; 361 108; w popova-sapka.mk. This state-run monstrosity has the advantage of always having rooms available. Ski rental available in the lobby. **$$**

Konak Šara Ski Planinski Dom (1 mountain hut, 5 rooms totalling 18 beds) Blagoja Toska 37-1/6; m 070 329 898. Bijou & basic, with shared bathroom & kitchen, but based right on the slopes at the popular little café next to the new church. **$**

Smreka Planinski Dom (1 mountain hut, 100 beds) m 070 278 418; f @PlaninarskiDomSmreka. Pink building at the west end of the village. **$**

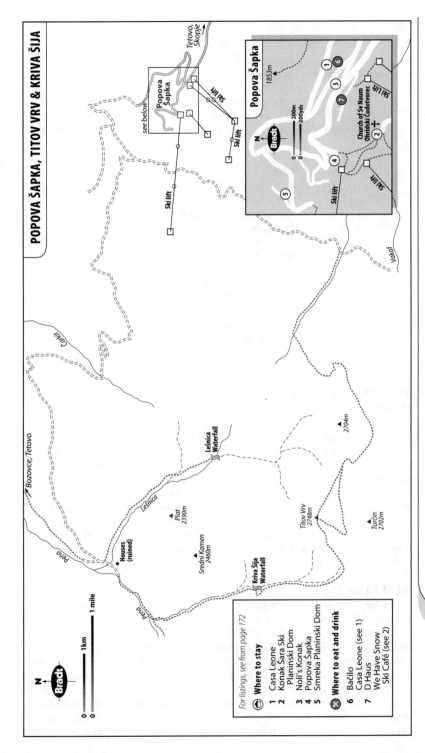

POPOVA ŠAPKA, TITOV VRV & KRIVA ŠIJA

Popova Šapka

1853m

Church of Sv Naum
Ohridski Čudotvorec

For listings, see from page 172

Where to stay
1 Casa Leone
2 Konak Šara Ski
  Planinski Dom
3 Noli's Konak
4 Popova Šapka
5 Smreka Planinski Dom

Where to eat and drink
6 Bačilo
  Casa Leone (see 1)
7 D Haus
  We Have Snow
  Ski Café (see 2)

4

The most popular summertime hike out of Popova Šapka leads to the 2,748m summit of Titov Vrv, the highest mountain situated completely within Macedonia. It is a relatively long hike at 14km in either direction, with an altitude gain (and loss) of almost 1,000m. Rather less demanding is the 19km round hike to Kriva Šija Waterfall, which stands at an altitude of 1,865m. Very fit hikers could combine the two hikes over a long day as a 37km round trip, but most prefer to keep the hikes separate.

POPOVA ŠAPKA TO TITOV VRV

Distance	14km one-way (28km round trip)
Altitude	Popova Šapka 1,782m; Titov Vrv 2,748m
Rating	Moderate: lengthy, steep ascent to the summit
Timing	5 hours one-way
Map	1:25,000 SAGW Map Sheets Bešala 680-4-3, Tetovo 680-4-4 and Titov Vrv 730-2-1, January 2010

Route description Starting from Smreka Planinski Dom, head towards the top of the ski lifts until you cross the 4x4 track heading southeast. Follow this road just below the 2,000m contour for almost 5km until you reach a ravine. Follow the left/north bank of the ravine along a marked mountaineering path (red and white) in a northeasterly direction. The path crosses the ravine after 2km and heads southwest, continuing to rise steeply for another 1.5km. The path then levels out

✕ WHERE TO EAT AND DRINK   *Map, page 173*

✕ **Bačilo** Once you're in the village, take the first right & follow the road about a third of the way up; m 070 222 706; ☐ @BaciloPopovaShapka; ⊕ 10.00–23.00 daily. A very popular local restaurant with good views over the ski slope. Book a table in advance if you want to be guaranteed a place on a busy w/end. **$$**

✕ **Casa Leone** Two-thirds of the way up the same road as Bačilo; ☎ 361 002; m 072 515 240; w casaleone.mk; ⊕ noon–23.00 daily. A delightful pizzeria with a sunny dining room & narrow balcony offering even better views of the slopes. Also does a very tasty *džigr al Venezia* (liver in red wine) & offers rooms (page 172). **$$**

✕ **D Haus** Popular café next to the Teteks Hotel at the bottom of the ski runs; ⊕ 09.00–23.00 daily. Accessible from the slopes, it is the perfect place to enjoy a hot chocolate or mulled wine while viewing the skiers below. Rooms available. **$**

✕ **We Have Snow Ski Café** At the Konak Šara Ski mountain hut, by the church; m 070 329 898; ☐ @wehavesnow; ⊕ until 1hr after the closure of the ski lifts. One of the few ski-in ski-out cafés offering basic but hearty snacks. Extremely popular. **$**

WHAT TO SEE AND DO Even if you don't ski or snowshoe, the views of the Vardar Valley from the drive up to Popova Šapka are outstanding. At the top is the new Church of Sv Naum Ohridski Čudotvorec.

For **skiing**, the resort (☐ @popovasapka) offers 20km of groomed ski runs and over 35km² of terrain for off-piste skiers. A three-day ski pass including accommodation for two nights and half board costs around €90 per person, while a day ski pass costs €15 (€6.50 for kids). Carving skis and snowboards are available for rent for as little as €7 including boots and poles (bring ID to leave at the ski rental hut) at either the orange 'cone'-shaped hut just before Hotel Popova Šapka, or from the shop in Hotel Popova Šapka's lobby. For the off-piste skier, Eskimo Freeride (m 071 951 287; e info@eskimo-freeride.com; w eskimo-freeride.com)

and follows the 2,450m contour line for another 2km and rises on to the saddle southeast of Titov Vrv. From here there is a less trodden path directly to the summit or the well-trodden path heading west around the southern base of Titov Vrv to the shorter ascent to the summit. It's a 28km return hike on this route. A steep drop to the west of Titov Vrv will take you almost 4km to the beautiful Kriva Šija Waterfall (see below).

POPOVA ŠAPKA TO KRIVA ŠIJA WATERFALL

Distance	19km round trip
Altitude	Popova Šapka 1,782m, Kriva Šija Waterfall 1,865m
Rating	Moderate: lengthy, steep ascent to the summit
Timing	7+ hours
Map	As above for Titov Vrv

Route description The hike from Popova Šapka can be shortened considerably if you can take a 4x4 to the end of the northern dirt track where the Lešnica River enters the Pena (the disused homes here were burned down in the 2001 conflict). From here it is a half-hour steep hike along the right/north bank of the Lešnica River to the **Lešnica Waterfall**, or a 1½–2-hour hike to Kriva Šija Waterfall. The path along the Pena requires you to jump or ford the river several times. Once across the river of the Kriva Šija ravine, the path follows the left/west bank until it plateaus out after almost 3km. The waterfall can be seen across the other side of the alp.

offer day packages on their snowcats (including accommodation) for less than €200. Ski lessons are available from Zemri Beluli at Ski School Profi (m 070 981 395; e atomic_180@hotmail.com). Snowshoeing and winter mountaineering guides are available through Ljuboten Planinarski Klub (w pkljuboten.org.mk; see page 93).

In the summer, the Šar Mountains offer a host of **hiking** trails, which have all recently been re-marked, maintained and signed. An excellent trail map is available in English from Ljuboten Planinarski Klub (page 93), as well as mountain guides ranging from €15 per hour to €125 for the weekend. Sadly, 1:25,000 hiking maps need to be ordered in advance from the Katastar in Skopje (page 68). The area has **49 glacial lakes**, including Golemo Ezero, Belo Ezero, Bogovinsko Ezero and Crno Ezero; several waterfalls at Lešnica and Kriva Šija (see box, above); and there are also rock-climbing sections at Crnen Kamen, Kopilica and below Mount Plat. For most, though, the attraction is to reach the top of **Titov Vrv** at 2,748m (see box, above). For those seeking a greater challenge there is the 80km ridge hike all the way from Ljuboten peak to Mount Korab near Debar.

GOSTIVAR *Telephone code 042*

Today, Gostivar municipality has over 81,000 inhabitants. The town itself, while offering few renowned tourist sites, is pleasant, multi-cultural, a frequent location for seminars and conferences, and a convenient stopping point on the way south. With the source of the River Vardar being at Vrutok, less than 10km from Gostivar, the river is clean and rapid as it courses through the town. For these reasons and more, Gostivar is slowly becoming more popular.

HISTORY Habitation of the Gostivar area and the Polog Valley goes back to the 7th century BC. In 170BC, the town of Draudak was built near Gostivar. The Roman historian Livy mentions that the last Macedon king, Perseus (ruled 179–168BC), attacked Draudak with 10,000 men. Later, Turkic settlers started coming to the region with the Hun settlement in the area dating to AD378, while Avar, Bulgar, Kuman, Oğuz, Pećenek and Vardar Turks settled here throughout the next millennium. Later, Slav tribes came to the region and the town's current name Gostivar comes from the Slavic word *gosti* meaning 'guests' and the Turkish word *dvar* meaning 'castle' or 'fort'. In the first half of the 14th century, Gostivar is mentioned in the 1313 Bath Declaration of Serbian king Milutin, as well as by Tsar Dušan at the opening ceremony of the Hagia Maria Monastery in Kalkandelen (Tetovo).

The first Ottoman attack on Gostivar was in 1336, but it wasn't until the invasion of Yildirim Bayezid in the 1390s that the Ottomans took effective rule of Gostivar and the Polog Valley. Many Turkish families moved here from Turkey during the favourable emigration policies promoted by Sultan Murat II and Sultan Mehmet the Conqueror, and so the town grew. Over the years, Gostivar flourished as a cultural centre and by the late 19th century the town boasted seven inns, five mosques, three schools, two libraries, two dervish teke, a bathhouse and a clock tower. Of all of these, only the clock tower built in 1566 and the Bey Mahala Mosque built in 1688 remain today.

After Ottoman rule ended in Macedonia in 1912, many Turks migrated to Turkey, especially after the world wars as suppression of Turkish culture and persecution of Turks themselves became more common. The push of the Prizren Union's Megalo Idea for a Greater Albania into the Tetovo, Gostivar and Debar regions only made life more difficult for the Turks left in Macedonia. The Yucel Incident of 1947 saw a backlash from the Turkish community and more Turks emigrated to Turkey when Yugoslavia signed an agreement with Turkey in 1950 to encourage the emigration. The agreement came about when government relations with the Soviet Union were cut in 1950 and Yugoslavia looked elsewhere for international friends. It was at this time that Turkish primary schools reopened after many years of no education in the Turkish language.

After the 1996 municipal election of an ethnic Albanian mayor in Gostivar, Turkish was forbidden as an official communication language. The following year the mayor was arrested for flying the Albanian flag over the municipal building, which resulted in a shoot-out with government security forces. When the mayor tried to take the government to the European Court of Human Rights for infringement of freedom of speech, his case was struck down, in part because the mayor's use of guns to defend 'free' speech was seen to justify the state's use of force.

Successive mayors since then have done a lot to clean up Gostivar. Its central area is a pleasant place to while away some time, and many of the town's different ethnic communities do just that.

GETTING THERE AND AWAY Gostivar lies about 65km (1 hour) southwest of Skopje via Tetovo. It is served by dozens of **buses** daily along the main road connecting Skopje to Struga/Ohrid route via Tetovo and Kičevo, as well as offering good connections to and from Debar. The once-daily **train** service between Skopje and Kičevo (page 196) via Tetovo also stops at Gostivar. The bus (✎217 344) and train stations are co-located in the town centre.

 WHERE TO STAY *Map, opposite*

Barok (12 rooms) Goce Delčev 461; ✎214 472; m 070 215 115; e barok_sera@yahoo.com. Above the furniture store of the same name. Rooms have wooden floors & modern décor. The 5th-floor restaurant keeps long hours. **$$**

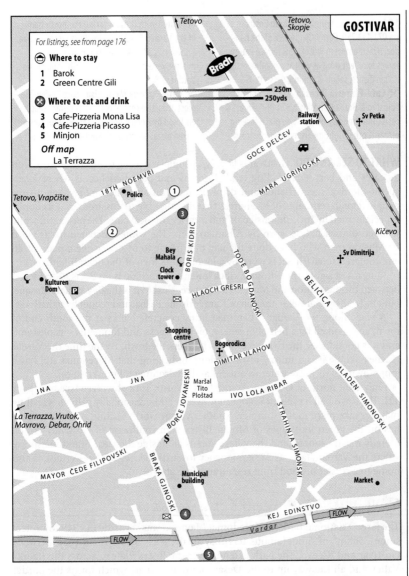

For listings, see from page 176

Where to stay

1 Barok
2 Green Centre Gili

Where to eat and drink

3 Cafe-Pizzeria Mona Lisa
4 Cafe-Pizzeria Picasso
5 Minjon

Off map
    La Terrazza

Green Centre Gili (13 rooms) Goce Delčev 14; 222 600; e contact@gcgili.com; w gcgili.com. This central hotel, also known as the Hilton, has smart & very well-priced rooms with contemporary décor & modern facilities. The 4th-floor terrace restaurant is on the pricey side but offers views to the clock tower & old mosque. Advance booking recommended. **$$**

WHERE TO EAT AND DRINK *Map, above*

The town centre has several pizzerias, kebapči diners and cafés, while a smaller choice of smarter restaurants lines the Vardar River as it runs through the south end of town. There are many more restaurants on the main street from the highway. The hillside village of Vrutok, 9km southwest of Gostivar, is not only the source of the Vardar but also the site of several highly rated restaurants specialising in fresh trout.

La Terrazza Vrutok, 9km from Gostivar; m 071 433 259. Currently the pick of the half-dozen restaurants in Vrutok, this terrace eatery serves excellent trout as well as a good selection of Italian dishes, salads & yummy desserts. $$$$

Cafe-Pizzeria Picasso Cnr Kej Bratstvo Edinstvo & Braka Gjinoski; 371 064. Smart & cosy contemporary bistro-style place serving pizzas & other light meals in a conservatory

decorated with flowers facing the north bank of the Vardar. $$ Minjon Restaurant Braka Gjinoski; 273 049. Smart Italian eatery set in a converted house on the south bank of the Vardar. $$

Cafe-Pizzeria Mona Lisa Goce Delčev. The most attractive central eatery has terrace seating enclosed by a green hedge & serves proper oven-baked pizzas as well as the usual local grills. $

WHAT TO SEE AND DO Gostivar is largely a people-watching town. The centre, with its cafés and bars surrounding tended greens and park benches, is where locals spend the day, meet friends and drink coffee. You are much more likely to see people here in remnants of local dress than in other big towns around Macedonia, especially men in Turkish waistcoats and a variety of local hats. The *plis*, a stiff white woollen domed hat, is worn by Albanian men. The white crocheted hat is worn by Muslim men who have done the hajj pilgrimage to Mecca, while a plain or an embroidered squarish hat is worn by a lot of Roma men of the Bektaši faith.

In terms of sights, the Ottoman **clock tower** built in 1566 is on Boris Kidrič street between the bus station and Marsal Tito Square. Next to it is the **Bey Mahala Mosque**, built in 1688 by Ebu Bekir, the son of Kara Mustafa Pasha, and rebuilt by Ismail Aga.

A walk along the Vardar – hemmed in by concrete banks at the south end of town, and flanked by a belt of greenery, bicycle tracks and footpaths – is pleasant, and it is good to see the river so clean as it enters the town. By the time the Vardar reaches Skopje it is a murky brown colour, indicating that Macedonia still has a long way to go in waste water treatment and environmental preservation.

Only 6km north of Gostivar, **Vrapčište** is a Yoruk Turkish village (see box, page 42). The town hall has an ethnological museum and occasionally *pelivan* wrestling matches take place in the summer. Another village worth visiting is **Vrutok**, which lies on the green footslopes of Mount Bistra 9km southwest of Gostivar. Vrutok literally means 'source', and the village stands alongside the clear limestone spring where the Vardar starts its 388km journey towards the Aegean Sea. Vrutok is also home to a cluster of good trout restaurants (see above).

MAVROVO NATIONAL PARK *Telephone code 042*

The largest national park in Macedonia, Mavrovo was set aside in 1949 to protect some 730km² of mountainous territory to the west of the main road between Gostivar and Kičevo. The park extends over the Bistra Plateau across the Radika Valley and all the way up to the Dešat mountain range, which forms the border with Albania. It incorporates more than 80 peaks that top the 2,000m mark, most notably the 2,764m Golem Korab, which lies on the Albanian border close the country's tallest waterfall.

Set entirely within the watershed of the Radika River, the park is centred on the artificial Lake Mavrovo, which is named after the small town at its southernmost tip. It protects large swathes of highland forest that includes more than 140 tree species, among them Macedonian pine (*Pinus peuce*), Balkan maple (*Acer heldreichii*), Crimean juniper (*Juniperus excelsa*) and European yew (*Taxus baccata*). Of the 84 mammal species recorded in Macedonia, 50 are present in Mavrovo, most famously a well-monitored population of Balkan lynx estimated to number 60 individuals. Other large mammals include brown bear, grey wolf and Balkan chamois. Though none of these are likely to be seen by casual visitors, many of the park's 130 recorded bird species are conspicuous, especially in summer. Key species include grey hawk, imperial eagle, golden eagle, pallid harrier, steppe harrier and the country's only population of the gorgeous Guldenstadt's redstart.

One of the most rewarding but underestimated travel destinations in the Balkans, Mavrovo National Park is easily visited as an overnight or multi-day trip from Skopje or Ohrid, and the main road through it also forms an alternative route between these two cities. Simply driving through the national park is a scenic delight, as the road follows babbling streams lined by verdant forests and hemmed in by majestic mountains. Traversed by hundreds of kilometres of footpaths, Mavrovo is a great hiking, rambling and horseriding destination in summer, but it operates primarily as a ski resort in winter. Aside from being an important preservation area for the montane flora and wildlife of the Balkans, the park also hosts several culturally unique and isolated Mijak villages (see box, page 44), most famously Galičnik, the county's highest settlement, and it is also home to the historic Monastery of Sv Jovan Bigorski. Note that visitors to the area must pay a tourist tax of 30MKD, payable at the tourist office (see below).

GETTING THERE AND AWAY The small town of Mavrovo, in the heart of the park, lies about 100km southwest of Skopje via Tetovo, Gostivar and the small junction village of Mavrovo Anovi. Much of the route is on multi-lane toll roads, but self-drivers should allow up to 2 hours, depending on how quickly they get out of the city. Heading south, it is 115km from Mavrovo to Ohrid via Debar, a fabulously scenic drive from start to finish, and one that should take around 2½ hours without stops, but it is worth allocating most of a day to it in order to stop at Sv Jovan Bigorski and divert to some of the Mijak villages in the far south.

Using public transport, a few direct buses run back and forth daily between Skopje and the junction village of Mavrovo Anovi during the summer, and some go all the way to Mavrovo during the ski season. If you can't get further than Mavrovo Anovi, a taxi will take you over the dam for the 7km ride to Mavrovo itself for somewhere around 400–500MKD. Heading south, buses from Skopje to Debar can pick up passengers at Mavrovo Anovi, and there are several buses daily from Debar that go on to Ohrid. Alternatively, catch a Skopje-bound bus as far as Gostivar and change vehicles there.

Travellers heading to Vertical Hostel might take note that the management can arrange direct transfers to/from Skopje or Ohrid at €40 one-way for up to four people, or to/from Mavrovo Anovi for €5.

TOURIST INFORMATION A well-organised tourist office (\489 425; m 078 495 592; infopoint@npmavrovo.org.mk; w npmavrovo.org.mk; ⊕ 08.00–18.00 daily) stands on the west side of the Debar road at the south end of Mavrovo Anovi some 300m northeast of the junction for Mavrovo village. It stocks a good selection of brochures and maps, and can also offer useful advice about hiking and other activities. Hikers can also pay the nominal tourist tax of 30MKD here.

🏠 **WHERE TO STAY** *Map, page 181*
The village of Mavrovo, at the southern tip of the eponymous lake, is home to the park's main cluster of accommodation facilities, and it makes a good base for hiking, skiing and watersports, or simply as a quiet getaway. A handful of other lodgings can be found around the lake, notably the recently opened Vertical Hostel, which caters specifically to independent travellers. A scattering of other lodges can be found in the southern half of the national park.

Mavrovo town

⌂ **Alpina** (23 rooms) At the entrance to the village; ☎ 388 024; m 071 265 667; e hotel_alpina@ yahoo.com; w hotelalpinamavrovo.net. This large white 4-star hotel has its own restaurant, & is just a few hundred metres from the chair-lifts. Spacious rooms & suites come with all mod cons. **$$$$**

☀ ⌂ **Bistra** (42 rooms) At the end of town; ☎ 489 027/219; e bistra@bistra.com; w bistra. com. This is a true ski-resort hotel, with spacious lounges & reception areas, welcoming open-hearth fire, good restaurant & bar, fitness centre, pool & conference facilities. All the rooms are en suite with AC & TV. They also have overflow accommodation in Hotel Lodge (located right next to the ski lift) & the more central Hotel Sport, but these annexes are not nearly as luxurious, even though you get to use all the facilities of the main hotel. **$$$$**

⌂ **Srna** (30 rooms) At the entrance to the village; ☎ 388 083. All mod cons. **$$$**

⌂ **Apartments Kristijan** (2 rooms) m 078 423 330. Attractively located on the lakeshore, this owner-managed annex to the eponymous restaurant has comfortable & well-priced rooms that sleep up to 4. **$$**

Elsewhere on Lake Mavrovo

⌂ **Radika Hotel & Resort** (62 rooms) ☎ 223 300; m 075 325 306; e info@radika.com.mk; w radika.com.mk. The park's smartest & most dazzling resort, this 5-star property has an indoor & outdoor pool, spa, restaurant & fireside bar. It has an isolated location near the village of Leunovo on the eastern lakeshore 11km northeast of Mavrovo town. **$$$$**

☀ ⌂ **Vertical Hostel** (3 rooms sleeping up to 4 & a 10-bed dorm); m 078 915 757; e hostelverticalmavrovo@gmail.com; w hostelverticalmavrovo.com; ▮ HostelVertical. The only backpacker-oriented accommodation in any of the country's national parks, this 2-storey building stands in the village of Nikiforovo a few hundred metres from the eastern lakeshore & 7km northeast of Mavrovo. Private rooms & a dorm (split into 5 semi-private cubicles, each with 1 2-berth bunk-bed) all offer access to gender-separated showers & toilets & a common kitchen/dining/ lounge area with sat TV & an impressive vinyl collection. The management can arrange sensibly priced transfers to/from Skopje, Ohrid or Mavrovo Anovi, as well as a range of day trips & hikes to the

likes of Galičnik, Sv Jovan Bigorski, Duf Waterfall & the summit of Golem Korab. Note that meals & drinks are by prior arrangement only; otherwise it is best to buy all you need at Mavrovo Anovi. **$$**

Galičnik

⌂ **Vila Neda** (25 rooms) 18km southeast of Mavrovo; m 070 772 688, 075 420 128; ⊕ 1 Jul–1 Oct. Rooms are basic with no TV or AC, & aside from 4 rooms that are en suite, bathroom facilities are in the corridor. **$**

Along the Debar Road (north to south)

⌂ **Hotel Tutto** (7 rooms) Janče, Mavrovo National Park; ☎ 470 999; m 072 204 014; e info@ tutto.com.mk; w tutto.com.mk. Built into the hillside overlooking Janče, this small hotel is constructed to high ecological standards, & the food at the restaurant is part of the Bitola Slow Food movement. Child-friendly with lots of play areas & small tables. Old mountain footpath to Sv Bigorski Monastery goes out of the back of the hotel & takes only 25min. **$$–$$$**

⌂ **Complex Koleb Trnica** (10 rooms) m 076 361 953; e hotelkorabtrnica@gmail.com, info@ korabtrnica.mk; w korabtrnica.mk/en. Set on a forest-fringed roadside farm that's been renowned for its cheese since it was founded in the 1940s, this new lodge has well-equipped modern rooms & apts, a great restaurant specialising in traditional regional food, & a deli-like store selling produce made on-site. Good value. **$$**

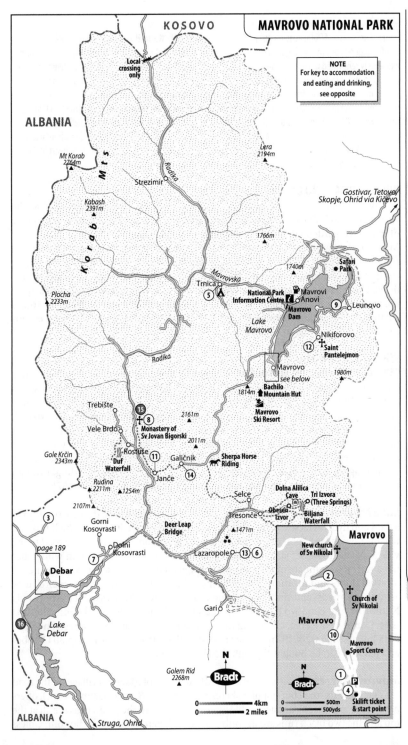

MAVROVO NATIONAL PARK

KOSOVO

ALBANIA

NOTE
For key to accommodation
and eating and drinking,
see opposite

Local crossing only

Mt Korab
2764m

Korab Mts

Strezimir

Radika

Kabash
2391m

Lera
2194m

*Gostivar, Tetovo,
Skopje, Ohrid via Kičevo*

1766m

Plocha
2233m

1740m

Safari
Park

Mavrovska

Trnica
⑤

National Park
Information Centre

Mavrovi
Anovi

⑨ Leunovo

Mavrovo
Dam

*Lake
Mavrovo*

Nikiforovo

⑫ Saint
Pantelejmon

1980m

Radika

Mavrovo
see below

1814m

Bachilo
Mountain Hut

Trebište

⑮
⑧
Monastery of
Sv Jovan Bigorski

Mavrovo
Ski Resort

2161m

Vele Brdo

2011m

Gole Krčin
2343m

Rostuše ⑪

Duf
Waterfall

Galičnik

Sherpa Horse
Riding

Janče

⑭

Rudina
2211m

1254m

Selce

Dolna Alilica
Cave

Tri Izvora
(Three Springs)

2107m

Gorni
Kosovrasti

Deer Leap
Bridge

Tresonče

Obešen
Izvor

Biljana
Waterfall

③

page 189

⑦

Dolni
Kosovrasti

1471m

Debar

Lazaropole ⑬ ⑥

Gari

⑯

*Lake
Debar*

Golem Rid
2268m

N

Bradt

0 ———— 4km
0 ———— 2 miles

ALBANIA

Struga, Ohrid

Mavrovo

New church
of Sv Nikolai

②

Church of
Sv Nikolai

Mavrovo

⑩

Mavrovo
Sport Centre

N

Bradt

①
④

Skilift ticket
& start point

0 ——— 500m
0 ——— 500yds

🏠 **Monastir Sveti Jovan Bigorski** (35 beds) 17km north of Dolni Kosovrasti; ☎ 333 399; e info@bigorski.org.mk; w bigorski.org.mk. The exquisitely renovated inn at this historic monastery (see opposite) is by far the most beautiful place to stay in Macedonia, provided you are OK with being inside the monastery gates by 21.00 & up for prayers at 06.00. Bring your own food for use in the communal kitchen, or eat at the House of Mijaks restaurant 500m away at the junction with the main road. **$**

Lazaropole
✳ 🏠 **Kalin Hotel** (16 rooms) ☎ 846 222; e info@kalinhotel.com.mk; w kalinhotel.com.mk. This beautifully refurbished & attractively located hotel is well worth staying at, and has its own restaurant. **$$$**

🏠 **Vila Katerina-Irena** (3 rooms) m 078 647 817; e vilakaterinairena@gmail.com; 🇫 @vilakaterinairena. Picturesque, affordable & friendly owner-managed villa in the heart of the village. **$$**

✕ WHERE TO EAT AND DRINK *Map, page 181*

A few tavernas are dotted around Mavrovo town, the most alluring being the **Kristijan** (m 078 423 330; **$$**), which has a friendly vibe, a pretty location, the choice of indoor or garden lakefront seating, and a varied menu of grills, soups and other Macedonian standards. In Mavrovo Anovi, a surprisingly varied cluster of cafés and restaurants catering to passing traffic line the main road; those on the left (coming from Skopje) have the bonus of a lake view. Otherwise, almost all the places to stay listed above have a restaurant, the one main exception being the Vertical Hostel. At the junction for the monastery of Sv Jovan Bigorski, the church-run **House of Mijaks** (m 070 378 333; w kukjanamijacite.mk; ⊕ 08.00–22.00 daily; **$$**) is a popular ethnorestaurant specialising in Mijak and other Macedonian cuisine.

WHAT TO SEE AND DO
Mavrovo village and surrounds Lapped by the southern tip of the eponymous lake, Mavrovo is a scenic resort village that caters primarily to domestic skiers during winter, but also attracts hikers and watersport enthusiasts in summer. Architecturally, its most striking and photogenic feature is the **church of Sv Nikolai**, which was constructed in 1850 but partially submerged – and replaced by a newer namesake on higher ground – when the lake was dammed a century later. The park's ski resort is less than 10km south of the village, while summertime visitors can arrange a variety of **activities**, including kayaking, cycling and riding, through the prominent lakeside Mavrovo Sport Centre (☎ 489 027; m 071 252 467).

Lake Mavrovo This 13km² lake was created in 1953 following the construction of a dam and hydro-electric plant on the eponymous river, a tributary of the Radika, at what is now the junction of the main road to Debar and the 6km feeder road to the village of Mavrovo. Set at an altitude of 1,200m, it often freezes over in winter, but has a refreshing climate in summer, one complemented by its scenic location below forested slopes and the more distant peaks of Mount Korab. The lake is encircled by all-weather roads, and the one running to its east from Mavrovo village north via Nikiforovo and Leunovo (respectively the site of Vertical Hostel and Radika Resort) is very quiet and scenic, traversing through some lovely patches of forest, and ideal for a long, gentle walk. Fishing season on the lake is from 1 February to 30 October and permits can be bought through the Hotel Bistra.

Mavrovo ski resort Situated less than 10km south of Mavrovo village off the road to Galičnik, this small but popular ski resort (☎ 489 065/6; w skimavrovo.com), offers black, blue and green runs accessible by chair-lift. Oddly, the green runs are all at the top and the two black runs are the only way to ski/board down to the bottom. Unless

above   The country's second-largest city, Bitola is home to some very pretty 18th- and 19th-century architecture (PB) page 236

right   Mavrovo is one of North Macedonia's most popular mountain villages, attracting skiers in winter and hikers in summer (SS) page 182

below   Boasting a ruined medieval fortress and a well-preserved Turkish quarter, the town of Prilep is so symbolic of Macedonian culture that it has been used twice as a film setting (PB) page 259

above The Stone Doll natural rock formations near the village of Kuklica — legend says the figures are the result of a petrified wedding (PV/S) page 336

left After a period of instability, Popova Šapka is once again becoming Macedonia's most popular ski resort (NP/D) page 172

below Offering an abundance of water-based activities, the spectacular Matka Canyon and Lake is an enjoyable day trip from Skopje (m/S) page 153

above left   Galičica National Park offers miles of hikes through lush countryside, boasting verdant plateaus that open out on to beautiful wide valleys (PB) page 222

above right   Towering to 1,013m above sea level, the megalithic observatory at Kokino dominates the surrounding area (j/S) page 327

below   The highest peak in the Balkans, Mount Korab straddles the border with Albania (LS/S) page 188

above   The remains of the early 10th-century church are buried beneath the Monastery of Sv Naum, which lies on Lake Ohrid (VE/S) page 222

left   Known as Motley Mosque by English speakers, Tetovo's Šarena Džamija (literally 'coloured' or 'painted' mosque) is as impressive on the inside as it is on the outside (SS) page 169

below   Remote Treskavec Monastery is built on the ancient town of Kolobaise, 8km north of Prilep (SS) page 266

above   The fully working monastery of Sv Jovan Bigorski is famous for its architecture, ornate iconostases and relics (SS) page 183

right   The current church at the Monastery of Sv Gavril Lesnovski stands on the foundations of an earlier 11th-century church (ZK/S) page 335

below   Sv Joakim Osogovski is probably the most-visited monastery in North Macedonia (PB) page 328

above   The eastern part of North Macedonia is home to the Turkish Yoruk ethnic population, who are distinguished by their language, customs and bright traditional dress (FOT/A) page 42

left   The Twelfthtide Carnival is held every January in Vevčani (M/D) page 234

below   Traditional dishes, including *kebapči* and *skara* are prepared on the grill (VE/S) page 86

right   *Ajvar* is the most famous of Macedonia's meze dishes, made during the autumn when red peppers are abundant (JJ/S) page 86

below   Traditional Macedonian folk dancing is performed at festivals up and down the country, such as here at Velestovo (JC)

bottom   The Sv Ahil choir sings at the Macedonian Orthodox Church in Resen (NS/D)

there has been an exceptionally snowy winter, the blacks are quickly iced up and sporting bare patches that you might prefer to leave for your best rock skis. For those who would rather not risk the narrow and icy descent, the midway station picks up skiers. Many day trippers go up just to plod around at the top, admire the view and snack at the little restaurants. A day ticket to ski in the park is 1,100MKD (850MKD for a half-day pass), 2,100MKD for two days, 3,000MKD for three days, a week ticket is 6,000MKD and a season ticket is 20,000MKD. Prices drop slightly in low season.

Galičnik Undoubtedly the most famous Mijak village in the national park, Galičnik is nestled on a remote cliffside at the end of a rough 17km cul-de-sac running south from Mavrovo village over the Bistra Plateau. Reputed to be more than a thousand years old, it was a major trading centre in the 19th century, with thousands of inhabitants, and it was also the birthplace of Georgi Pulevski (1817–93), a pioneering Macedonian nationalist, military leader and writer who authored the first dictionary and grammar book of the Macedonian language. Galičnik is today the highest village in Macedonia, with an upper town set at around 1,500m, and it is notable for its well-preserved two- and three-storey square houses and other traditional architecture. Another attraction are the excursions led by Sherpa Horse Riding (m 077 648 679; e hcbistragalicnik@gmail.com; w horseriding.com.mk; ☉ summer only), an excellent family-run stable just 1km from Galičnik back along the road to Mavrovo village. Well worth a visit at any time of year, the village peaks in popularity during the nationally acclaimed annual wedding festival that takes place here every July (see box, page 184). There is no public transport here, but those without a vehicle could either arrange a day trip in a rented car with Vertical Hostel or their hotel, or else hike here from Janče (see box, page 186), a 2-hour walk that offers spectacular views of Mount Korab and the Radika Valley.

Along the Debar road
The sites described below all lie alongside or within a kilometre or two of the 35km stretch of the main Skopje–Debar road that runs west then south from Mavrovo Lake to the southern park boundary.

Trnica Site of a farm and affiliated hotel, restaurant, stable and fresh produce store 7km west of Mavrovo Lake, the tiny village of Trnica has an attractive location below conifer-swathed slopes rising from the Mavrovo River just before it merges with the Radika. It is a nice spot to stop for a snack or ramble, and those determined to try something really local should try the sour cheese and ground corn, reputedly the best in the region.

Monastery of Sv Jovan Bigorski (☎ 478 675; e info@bigorski.org.mk; w bigorski.org.mk) This fully working monastery stands a few hundred metres uphill of the Debar road some 25km southwest of Mavrovo Anovi. It was first established in 1020 when the miraculous icon of John the Baptist, after which the church is named, first appeared at the spot where it now stands. The present-day structures of the church and the surrounding monastery were built, however, in the 18th and 19th centuries. The church closely resembles those of Mount Athos in Greece, characterised by two octagonal domes, the smaller of the two near the main entrance, and the larger residing over the area of worship.

In its day, this church's influence stretched over a large part of the region and into present-day Albania as far as Elbasan. Today the church is renowned for containing the final one of only four iconostases carved by the famous Makarije Frčkovski from Galičnik and the Filipovski brothers from Gari (two are in the monastery at

Lesnovo (see page 335) and the Church of the Holy Saviour in Skopje; the third in a church in Kruševo that was burnt down after the Ilinden Uprising of 1903). The iconostasis has over 500 humans and more than 200 animals carved into it depicting scenes from the Old and New Testaments, and also includes a representation of the woodcarvers themselves. Many of the people depicted in the iconostasis are wearing the traditional 19th-century Macedonian costumes despite the fact that the scenes depict an era many centuries earlier. The bishop's and prior's chairs are also carved by the Filipovski brothers and Frčkovski.

The chest of relics in the church contains a fragment of bone allegedly from the right humerus of St John, as well as bone fragments of the bodies of other saints. They are apparently preserved by their holy nature. The remainder of St John's arm lies in the Cetinje Monastery in Montenegro.

The beautiful old inns, where the 1958 movie *Mis Ston* was filmed, were tragically burnt down in an electrical circuiting fire in 2010. The church was untouched and much of the original stonework has also survived, but the dark cherry wood façades and balconies and the priceless monastery library are irrecoverable. The old inns are now undergoing reconstruction, and more of the new inns and a clock tower have been completed. To stay at the monastery, see page 182.

Church services take place at 06.00, 16.00 and 19.00 every day. The brotherhood of Jovan Bigorski pride themselves on their revival of old Eastern Orthodox ecclesiastical liturgy, which is sung according to the Byzantine tradition as opposed to the Serbian tradition brought in after the fall of the Ottoman Empire. It involves no instruments and is very melodic. The liturgy is sung by the priests

GALIČNIK WEDDING FESTIVAL

Tradition going back hundreds of years saw the travelling traders of the Mijak village of Galičnik returning once a year in July in order to marry their sweethearts. Up to 40 weddings would take place on St Peter's Day (Petrovden), entailing a massive guest list and followed by a huge party. Village residents of Galičnik have dwindled since those giddy days, and so from 1999 onwards couples from elsewhere in Macedonia have been allowed to apply to be the privileged bride and groom for the mid-July *Galičnika svadba* (wedding). Thousands of visitors flock every year to see the rituals, costumes, folk dances, traditional music and, of course, the Orthodox wedding ceremony itself.

Preparations for the wedding start days in advance. People from surrounding villages gather for a sheep-milking competition. One of the few of its kind in the Balkans, it is spectacular to see the milkmen and maids at their work. The milk is then used in a variety of local culinary specialities, including various cheeses, kajmak (sour clotted cream) and *sutljaš* (rice pudding cake).

With the gathering in the past of such a posse of men, the stag night equivalent was and continues to be a day of pelivan wrestling. In each round two men, smothered in sunflower oil and wearing only leather breeches, compete to tussle the other to the ground. The winner is he who beats all others in his weight class by keeping his opponent's back pinned to the floor for a count of three. Traditionally viewed by men only, it is increasingly drawing a female crowd.

On Saturday morning, the day before the wedding ceremony itself, the future son-in-law adorns the wedding hall with flowers and garlands. He then fires three shots to warn off any usurpers and to signal to the guests to make their way to the village. As guests arrive, the future mother-in-law welcomes them

at 07.00 (after an hour of prayer) and at 19.00 to start the church service, and is well worth attending. Alternatively, a double CD set of the liturgy can be bought for 600MKD at the monastery shop after the services (also available in Jugoton in the Trgovski Centar in Skopje). Monastery mastika (Macedonian ouzo), icons and other religious items can also be bought here.

The short but steep feeder road to the monastery stands on the east side of the Debar road alongside the conspicuous car park for the House of Mijaks restaurant (page 182). Accommodation is available at the monastery, too (page 182).

Rostuše and Duf Waterfall Not quite 2km south of the Monastery of Sv Jovan Bigorski, just after crossing a bridge over the Radika River, a 1km feeder road winds uphill into the small Mijak village of Rostuše. The main attraction here is the out-of-town Duf Waterfall (in fact a sequence of six falls of which the tallest and best-known is 28m high), the goal of the lovely short hike described in the box on page 186.

Janče Among the prettiest and most accessible of the many ancient Mijak villages set on the slopes of Mavrovo, Janče comprises a small collection of traditional multistorey stone-and-wood houses typical of this rural part of Macedonia. It stands on the east bank of the Radika and can be reached by following the main Debar road south for 2km past the junction for Rostuše, then turning left on to a 500m feeder road that crosses a bridge over the river. As the home of the Hotel Tutto (page 180), it makes a great base for exploring the

with bread and water and hosts a dance in traditional dress with the closest relatives. Today, professional dancers are brought in for a colourful show of costumes and synchronisation. With the pressure mounting, the groom is then shaved in public at the village spring as a sign of the impending end of his bachelor days.

On the wedding day itself on Sunday, the day starts with the stormy arrival of the wedding party on galloping horseback to visit the bride. Reduced often to a slow trot through throngs of onlookers, the party brings a young boy with them, whom the godfather-to-be (*kum*) places with the bride's party, as a good luck charm to bring the couple a son. A bridle is then placed symbolically on the bride's head as a gesture of her devotion, faithfulness and obedience to her husband. While the requirement for a son and unconditional love is no longer paramount, the tradition lingers on. The kum then delivers a finely adorned banner to the bride's house while she serves the guests local wine and rakija.

Afterwards at the village spring, mirroring the groom's ritual the day before, the bride fills jugs with water for her last time as an unwed maid. Another dance ensues at the village square, where the men dance the *teškoto*, a virile representation of the hardships of migrant workers.

Finally, clad in her finest, a Galičnik folk dress of silk and gold braid weighing almost 40kg, the bride is escorted to the central Church of Sv Petar i Pavle where, in the eyes of the honoured few who can fit in the church, the wedding ceremony itself takes place in the late afternoon. Traditionally, the groom stayed until Mitrovden (8 November), but these days the groom leaves with the guests after the wedding and Galičnik returns to its sleepy self by Monday afternoon.

surrounding vicinity on foot, with the Monastery of Sv Jovan Bigorski and Duf Waterfall both about an hour away, and only 2 hours from Galičnik following the scenic hike described in the box below.

Traditional villages in the southeast A trio of interesting traditional Mijak villages called Gari, Lazaropole and Tresonče stand on the southeastern slopes of Mavrovo, and can be reached along a feeder road that branches east from the main drag to Debar as it exits the park 35km southwest of Mavrovo Anovi. All three villages are quite easily reached in a private vehicle, but the closest you'll get using

---

THREE MAVROVO HIKES

HIKE 1: ROSTUŠE AND DUF WATERFALL

Distance	5km round trip
Altitude	River Radika bridge to Rostuše 700m, Duf Waterfall 840m
Rating	Easy, but narrow parts with steep drops
Timing	3 hours
Trail head	River Radika bridge stop for Rostuše
Map	1:25,000 SAGW Map Sheet Debar 730-3-3, January 2010; Prilep 782-1-3, January 2007

Route description From the bus stop and junction on the main Debar road 1.8km south of the Monastery of Sv Jovan Bigorski, drive or hike 1km to the village of Rostuše. At the entrance is a small fountain on the left next to the cemetery. At the back of the cemetery a path leads along an irrigation channel to the waterfall. The more conventional route is to take the route above the church. If taking this route, take care to descend rather than take the high road, which becomes very steep and turns into mountain goat tracks. The path along the irrigation ditch is well maintained and scenic. There are bridges at crossing points over the river and benches along the way. The path leads to Rostuše Waterfall 2, which is the most spectacular of all six waterfalls along the Duf ravine. It is not safe to try to access the higher waterfalls from number 2; better to attempt to do so by taking the higher path from before Vele Brdo village. The steep sides of the Duf ravine make it difficult to take good photos of the waterfall unless you arrive around midday. Return along the same route.

HIKE 2: JANČE TO GALIČNIK (WEDDING FESTIVAL)

Distance	4.5km
Altitude	Janče bus stop 660m, Galičnik 1,415m
Rating	Easy
Timing	2 hours
In reverse	Possible
Trail head	Janče
Map	1:25,000 SAGW Map Sheet Lazaropole 730-3-4, January 2010

Route description An alternative route to see the annual summer wedding festival in mid-July, avoiding the hordes taking the tarmac road from Mavrovo.

The hike takes almost 2 hours and gives spectacular views of Mount Korab and the Radika Valley. Once the asphalt road ends in the village, head left along

public transport is on a bus heading between Skopje and Debar that can drop you at the junction on the national park boundary.

Deer Leap Bridge Known locally as Mostot Elenski Skok, this tall arched stone bridge stands on the left-hand side of the road towards Gari, Lazaropole and Tresonče about 1.7km past the junction with the Debar road. Legend has it that it was built more than 600 years ago by the local bey (Ottoman lord) during the 14th century to commemorate the gallant death of a deer that he and his army had been hunting. Badly wounded, nevertheless the deer continued to elude the bey and his

the 4x4 track that curves around the mountain. After about 45 minutes by foot, the 4x4 track turns right and is blocked off, while the footpath heads left. After another 5 minutes there is a water fountain. The path is mostly shaded and levels out at Markovi Nogi, a small stone site with a foot-size depression in the stone, from where King Marko is said to have flown to the other side of the valley in the late 14th century. Views of the village can be seen just around the corner.

Note that Galičnik is accessible by public transport only in the summer. You can order a taxi at Hotel Neda to take you back down to Mavrovo or it is a beautiful 15km hike along the Mavrovo Plateau and down to the lake. Alternatively, take the ski lifts down (even in the summer) if they are working (usually at the weekends).

HIKE 3: BILJANA WATERFALLS AND DOLNA ALILICA CAVE

Distance	8km round trip
Altitude	Tresonče 1,005m, Alilica Cave 1,268m, Biljana Waterfall 2 1,296m
Rating	Easy: last 200m to the waterfall is impassable after rain
Timing	3–4 hours
Trail head	Tresonče, 12km from the Debar road
Map	1:25,000 SAGW Map Sheets Lazaropole 730-3-4 and Bistra 730-4-3, January 2010

Route description From the village church in Tresonče, head along the valley and the 4x4 route through the meadows along the river. After about 1.5km the road becomes steeper, narrower and more damaged, making it difficult even for a 4x4 to pass. There is a spring at this point. Another 1.5km takes you to Obesen Izvor, a small waterfall-like spring on the right-hand north bank of the Tresončka River. There is also a small hut here for wood cutters and water service tools. A single-track path continues another 500m along sometimes slippery rocks to Dolna Alilica Cave, again on the north bank. Some large branches across the now narrow river will aid you across it. Hiking poles are useful at this stage. If you don't have a torch there are usually church candles on either side of the entrance, but you will need your own lighter. While the entryway is small and requires a bit of crouching, it is possible to stand up towards the rear. Back outside, it is only 200m or so to Biljana Waterfall 2, but this is difficult to negotiate unless it is the end of the summer and the water level is low. To reach the remaining ten waterfalls a higher path needs to be taken from Tresonče village. Access to the higher waterfalls is difficult.

4

army, until it reached the Garska River, over which it leapt but died on the other side. To commemorate the deer's bravery, the bey ordered a bridge to be built in the likeness of the deer's last leap. A shaded footpath on the far side of the river makes for a pleasant hike along the Mala River.

Gari Set at an altitude of 1,100m roughly 10km from the junction, this pretty traditional village was once home to the famous iconostasis woodcarver Petre Filipovski, who carved the iconostases of the Sv Jovan Bigorski, Sv Spas and Sv Gavril Lesnovski churches.

Lazaropole Situated some 9km north of Gari along a switchback road that ascends to an altitude of 1,350m, this former hunting village vies with Galičnik as the country's oldest and largest Mijak village. Home to the popular Kalin Hotel (page 182), it is now a tourist centre thanks to its clean air, traditional architecture, hiking trails (detailed on boards in the village centre) and small ski lift.

Tresonče Less than 5km north of Lazaropole as the crow flies but almost 20km by road, Tresonče is the gateway village for hikes to Biljana Slap and Dolna Alilica Cave (see box, page 187). It lies just 12km by road from the junction with the Debar road, a very beautiful ride along the pretty Mala Reka.

DEBAR

The road past Mavrovo Lake through the Mavrovo National Park snakes its way along the River Radika to the small town of Debar (Diber in Albanian, and also seen in older writings on the town as Dibri or Dibra), which serves a municipality of 20,000 inhabitants. Although it lies in Macedonia and is only 137km from Skopje and 67km from Ohrid, its traditional cultural and economic orientation has been towards towns further afield in Albania, and as a result of

GOLEM KORAB PEAK

Perched on the border with Albania, the 2,764m Golem Korab is not only the highest peak on Mount Korab, but also the loftiest point in Macedonia. A secondary peak called Mal Korab (2,683m), and beneath it the country's longest waterfall, can be seen from the hike up here. Although permission is no longer required from the Ministry of the Interior Border Police to hike in the border area, it is a good idea to notify the border police hut at the start of the climb, in case of an accident. Affordable guided climbs can be arranged with Vertical Hostel (page 180), which has plenty of experience in the area.

Once a year Korab Mountaineering Club arrange their annual climb on the weekend closest to Independence Day (8 September). It is a big event attracting over a thousand hikers from all over the Balkans and further afield. It is usually a long and arduous walk of 25km in 9 hours or more, and many enthusiasts go for the day out even if they don't make it to the top. Police escorts, guides and medical staff attend on the day. For further details see w psdkorab.wordpress.com.

SAGW map sheet 730-1-3 (*Korab Sever, 1:25,000, January 2009*) covers the hike. Type in 'Korab' at w summitpost.org for a good route description, photographs and a map.

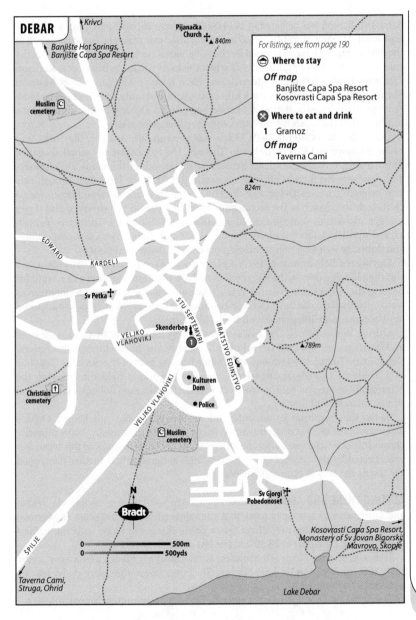

DEBAR

↑ Krivci

Pijanačka
Church † 840m

↗ Banjište Hot Springs,
Banjište Capa Spa Resort

For listings, see from page 190

⊜ **Where to stay**

Off map
    Banjište Capa Spa Resort
    Kosovrasti Capa Spa Resort

✖ **Where to eat and drink**

1   Gramoz

Off map
    Taverna Cami

Muslim Ⓒ
cemetery

▲ 824m

EDWARD

KARDELJ

Sv Petka †

Skenderbeg
1

STU SEPTEMVRI

VELJKO
VLAHOVIKJ

BRATSTVO EDINSTVO

▲789m

VELJKO VLAHOVIKJ

● Kulturen
Dom

Christian †
cemetery

● Police

Ⓒ Muslim
cemetery

N

Bradt

Sv Gjorgi †
Pobedonoset

0 ————— 500m
0 ————— 500yds

*Kosovrasti Capa Spa Resort,
Monastery of Sv Jovan Bigorski,
Mavrovo, Skopje*

ŠPILJE

*Taverna Cami,
Struga, Ohrid*

Lake Debar

today's more open borders with the country, life in Debar is reviving again, but the town is still in need of significant repair and rejuvenation. There is not much of note in the town itself, but it has a rich strategic history and lies in magnificent countryside, so this is an area well worth exploring for the intrepid and is sure to be developed over time.

HISTORY The earliest recording of Debar is under the name 'Deborus' on a map drawn by the Greek astronomer and cartographer Ptolemy in the 2nd century.

After Tsar Samoil was defeated in 1014 (see box, page 20) by the Byzantine emperor Basilius II, Debar was administered under the Bishopric of Bitola. In the latter half of the 14th century Debar was ruled by the Albanian Kastrioti clan, but fell under the rule of the Ottoman Empire in 1423 when the local Albanian ruler Gjon Kastrioti died shortly after his four children were taken hostage. His son, Gjergj Kastrioti Skenderbeg, survived to take back his father's land and unite all of Albania in 1444. A larger-than-life-size statue of Skenderbeg adorns Debar's centre, showing the fondness that the locals have for his cause (see box, page 192).

Only a few years later in 1449, Debar was overrun once again by the Turks, and became known as Dibri or Debra in Turkish. The city constantly rebelled against Turkish rule, however, not least because of the wealth of the many Turkish beys and agas who lived there off local taxes and the fat of the land. But Turkish rule also brought trade to Debar and the city centre grew and became known for its crafts industry. Much of the architecture from that period still survives, and if you can get a look into some of the older houses you will find the distinctive Turkish carved wooden *dolapi* (wardrobes), *minderliki* (built-in benches), intricate ceilings and doors, as well as *cardaci* (enclosed porches on the second floor).

During the Balkan wars of 1912–13 Debar was taken back by the Albanians, but was then handed over to the Kingdom of Serbs, Croats and Slovenes as a reward for helping the Allies during World War I. Thereafter many Serbs and Montenegrins were encouraged to settle in Debar, a common tactic to ensure that newly acquired land became more integrated with the motherland.

During World War II, Debar was again fiercely fought over by various partisan and fascist groups and their Great Power backers, but in the end the Socialist Federal Republic of Yugoslavia won out and Debar became part of the Socialist Republic of Macedonia in Federal Yugoslavia. Socialist Yugoslavia helped to develop the economy of the region with hydro-electric dams (Debar and Globočica lakes), local mines, quarries and tourism.

Sadly, the transition to an independent Macedonia has not helped Debar's economy in the same way the transition to communism did initially. Many minority communities left the town after the independence of Macedonia, and this trend was exacerbated by the conflict of 2001. Such high emigration has further dampened the town's chances of economic revival.

GETTING THERE AND AROUND Debar lies 135km southwest of Skopje via Tetovo and Gostivar, a 2–3-hour journey that runs through the scenic heart of Mavrovo National Park. Around ten direct buses cover this route daily, with the earliest departure out of Skopje at 08.30 and the last at 19.00.

Debar is around 70km (90 minutes) from Ohrid via Struga and a very scenic road that runs alongside Lake Debar. Six buses cover the route daily, leaving between 07.45 and 16.40.

Debar is small enough to walk around. Taxis cost a minimum fare of 30MKD.

 WHERE TO STAY *Map, page 189*
There is no longer any accommodation in Debar itself, but there's a hotel at each of the two out-of-town spa resorts described below. Hotels listed for the southern part of Mavrovo National Park (page 179) also lie within easy distance of Debar.

Kosovrasti Capa Spa Resort (75 rooms) Kosovrasti, 7km northeast of Debar; 046 842 095; e info@bdcapa.com; w bdcapa.com. This recently privatised & renovated spa resort has an attractive riverside location in the Radika Canyon & good en-suite rooms with TV. It caters to the

ST GEORGE THE VICTORIOUS

Sv Gjorgj Pobedonoset, or St George the Victorious in English, is indeed the same patron saint of England who slayed the dragon from his gallant white horse in order to save the princess. St George is a legend in many countries and it is astounding that his benevolence should reach as far as the Russian, Greek and Macedonian Orthodox churches as well as the Church of England and many other churches around the world.

George was born in AD280 in Cappadocia, now in modern-day Turkey. He joined the Roman cavalry at the age of 17 and rose to become a great swordsman and favourite of the then Roman emperor, Diocletian. George had converted to Christianity, while Diocletian was a firm believer in the pagan traditions. Eventually this rift in their beliefs brought George to his death. After doing his best to save Christians who had been sentenced to death by Diocletian, George was cast in prison to be tortured until he renounced his belief in Christ. Despite extreme forms of torture he did not renounce his faith and finally he was beheaded on 23 April 303 in Nicomedia near Lydda, Palestine.

He became the patron saint of the little church in Debar because that church contains the only replica of St George's original icon that stands in the Zograf Monastery at Mount Athos in Greece. When the original icon appeared miraculously in the Zograf Monastery shortly after it was built, the local monks claimed that it had been sent from Lydda by St George himself. The local bishop did not believe in the veracity of this story and so touched the icon to check for telltale signs of fresh paint. As soon as he touched the nose of the icon his finger stuck fast and eventually it had to be chopped off when all other efforts at removal failed. It is claimed that the finger remains stuck to the original icon and a bloody digit represents this on the replica icon at St George's Church in Debar.

The church frescoes reveal the life and times of St George, including his many miracles. Depictions of the terrible Emperor Diocletian show him wearing a Turkish turban, indicating the locals' views of the Turks at the time.

Many of the nuns speak English and will be able to tell you much more of the history of the church and the frescoes if you have time.

4

domestic market more than international visitors, but FB rates are good value. **$$$**

🏠 **Banjište Capa Spa Resort** (75 rooms) Banjište, 6km north of Debar; ☏ 046 832 680;

e info@bdcapa.com; **w** bdcapa.com. Owned by the same people as Kosovrasti, this resort feels like a slightly more downmarket variation on the same theme. FB rates are good value. **$$**

🍴 WHERE TO EAT AND DRINK

🍴 **Gramoz Restaurant** [map, page 189] Velko Vlahovikj; **m** 070 241 533; **f** restaurantgramoz; ⏰ 08.00–23.00 daily. Founded in 1994, this stalwart at the southern end of town is the pick of the central eateries. It specialises in grills & other Macedonian dishes, but it is also good for salads & b/fast. **$$**

🍴 **Taverna Cami** [map, page 181] 3km southwest of town after the dam; **m** 070 391 355; **f** @TavernaCami; ⏰ 11.00–23.00 daily. Offering a wonderful view of Debar Lake, this serves a varied menu of fish, pasta & Macedonian dishes, but the main attraction is the lovely location & pleasant atmosphere. **$$**

WHAT TO SEE AND DO Debar is sorely missing a small museum that could tell the rich history of this strategically important town and its various rulers. But there are

GJERGJ KASTRIOTI (SKENDERBEG)

Gjergj Kastrioti is known as the greatest hero of the Albanians for freeing and uniting all Albanians against the Turks in 1444.

Gjergj was born in Kruja, Arberia (today's Albania), to the Lord of Middle Arberia, Gjon Kastrioti, and Voisava, a princess from the Tribalda family of the Polog (Upper Vardar) Valley. Gjon had four sons, all of whom were kept hostage by the Turks in return for loyalty from the Albanian lord. When Gjon died, the Turks poisoned the four sons, but Gjergj managed to survive. He went on to convert to Islam and attend military school. He so excelled in swordsmanship and other military skills that he earned himself the title of Iskander Bey, meaning 'Lord Alexander'. He then successfully led several Ottoman campaigns in Europe and Asia Minor, and was appointed general and then governor general of several provinces in Middle Albania.

But Gjergj missed his homeland, and in 1443, after being defeated by the Hungarians at Nišin Serbia, he deserted the Ottoman army and went back to recapture his home town of Kruja. On raising the Albanian flag – red with a double-headed black eagle, the flag that remains – Gjergj claimed, 'I have not brought you freedom, I have found it here among you.' Less than a year later, having reconverted to Christianity, he united the Albanian princes against the Turks at the Assembly of Alesio (Lezha in Albanian) with an army of a mere 20,000. He won 25 out of his 28 battles against the Turks and was supported by the Italian princes and popes across the Adriatic for staving off the Turkish assault from western Europe for 25 years.

In 1468 Gjergj died of fever, but his army kept the Turks out of Albania for another 12 years. He is the national hero of Albania and all Albanians, and his valour has been the inspiration of many national and foreign poets and writers.

two orthodox churches, whose priests can tell you a lot about the town, if you want to take the time. As you come to the centre of town from the Skopje road you will be faced by the statue of **Skenderbeg** (see box, above), also written as Skenderbeu or Skenderbey, and not to be confused with the Skenderbeg fascist troops of World War II. This is the town's main street and continues on to Banjište, skirting the edge of the old town of Upper Debar.

Just before you exit Debar on the Skopje road is the **Nunnery of Sv Gjorgi Pobedonoset** (see box, page 191), completed in 2001 and dedicated to the church of the same name. Its grounds are small but very well kept, and hang on the edge of the cliffs of Lake Debar. If the main vehicle gate is closed, enter through the house door a little further down the nunnery outer wall. The effect of entering the door on a sunny evening accompanied by the ding-a-ling-ling of the doorbell is like being transported to another world or a secret garden. The church itself is one of the best preserved in Macedonia, with all its 19th-century frescoes intact, giving it a much richer feeling than many other Macedonian churches which are obviously in great need of repair. Although this church dates back to only 1835, it is built on the foundations of a 16th-century church which was destroyed by the Arnaut invasion. The 16th-century church had in turn been built on the grounds of the 11th-century castle of St George. The nuns sell a variety of handicrafts and are renowned throughout the churches of Greece and Macedonia for their excellence in making the ornate Orthodox bishops' hats.

Lake Debar, spread out magnificently below the town of Debar, is a 22km artificial lake built in 1964 as a means of producing hydro-electricity, and at its

BRITISH OPERATIVES IN DEBAR

By 1943 the Axis advance into the Balkans threatened Macedonia. Albania was already held by the fascist Italian powers and the Allies were concerned that, without help from special forces, the Macedonian region would also fall into fascist hands. As a result the British Special Operations Executive (SOE), a secret military branch set up by the British government in the 1940s to help defeat the enemy through sabotage and subversion, parachuted operatives into the Debar region. Their mission was to liaise with anti-Axis elements of the local resistance and the Allied forces in order to advise and see how best to help the resistance.

Major Richard Riddell, Captain Anthony Simcox, Flight Lieutenant Andy Hands and Lieutenant Reginald Hibbert were four such British SOE officers. They had been given only a few weeks' notice of their impending insertion into Debar and barely received enough language training or in-depth political background briefings, not least because their mission was to aid the resistance and not report on political developments.

The political situation there was complicated. Albania had divided into two main political factions, the pro-fascists of the puppet government under King Zog (who was living in London at the time) and the republicans, and the anti-fascist resistance of the National Liberation Movement (LNC) headed by Enver Hoxha. To complicate this otherwise clear division, there were various tribal chieftains in the hills around the Debar region who were prepared to go with either party depending on who would give them the most autonomy. And then there was the Communist Party of Albania (CPA), an offshoot of the Communist Party of Yugoslavia (CPY), which had joint control with the LNC over the Albanian National Liberation Army (ANLA), otherwise known as the Partisans. In addition, having lost the Debar, Gostivar and Tetovo regions to Royalist Yugoslavia after the Great War, many Albanians were wary of the ANLA and their political masters the CPA and LNC for their close links to the CPY. It was difficult to know in the end who would help whom.

By early 1944 Debar was firmly in the hands of the Germans and it was impossible to drop supplies into Albanian territory to help any potential pockets of resistance. Nevertheless in July 1944, Mehmet Shehu, commander of the 1st Brigade of the ANLA, now holed up north of Peshkopia in the foothills of Mount Korab, decided to march the 1st Brigade into Macedonia in order to try to regain Debar from the east. The British SOE officers went with him. In four days the brigade marched over Mount Korab, down to the Gostivar–Dibra road, then up to the Bistra Plateau above Mavrovo and back down to the Dibra–Kičevo road, possibly close by Tresonče, Lazaropole and Gari. Finally, marching up again towards Struga and Ohrid, the British officers heard of a supply-drop base for the Macedonia partisans only 4 hours' march away from their position. They convinced HQ Balkan air force to drop 'Albanian' supplies into Macedonia from where they could reinforce the ANLA with ammunition, arms and equipment. With additional help from the Royal Air Force, Debar was finally brought back into the hands of the Allies on 30 August 1944.

For a lengthier account of this operation read Sir Reginald Hibbert's piece in *The New Macedonian Question* (2001), edited by James Pettifer (page 354).

deepest point it is just less than 100m deep. It's a popular lake for fishing and swimming although it is little visited from outside the local area. At the southern end of the lake is the Globočica power station, which also serves Globočica Lake further upstream towards Struga. At the northern end of the lake, where the Radika River enters, is Kosovrasti spa. This is also a favourite fishing spot for the locals, as the lake fish come up to the mouth of the Radika to feed. Lake Debar was until recently the largest artificial lake in Macedonia (of which there are ten) – but Lake Kozjak, behind the enormous Kozjak Dam on the River Treška, is now officially the country's largest, at 32km long and 130m deep.

AROUND DEBAR

SPA CAPA DOLNI KOSOVRASTI (⏰ 08.00–21.00 daily; 1hr; entry 50MKD) These hot springs, like all the others in Macedonia, are indoors. There are separate baths for men and for women (no mixed bathing) and each bath is about 3m by 4m. Sunday evenings tend to be pretty busy. The 72-room hotel here has been completely renovated but the Banjište location of Spa Capa (see below) is a better experience.

To get here turn off the Debar–Gostivar road at the northern end of Lake Debar, and cross the bridge back over the Radika River. Follow the dirt track on the left and over the small hill for 200m back towards the lake. Over the hill are the hot springs, now inside a concrete one-storey building. Next to it is a ramshackle old Turkish house that used to cater for the hot springs, but has long since fallen into disrepair. There is a small outdoor pool available occasionally.

GORNI KOSOVRASTI VILLAGE If you follow the tarmac road straight up the side of the mountain for 20 minutes (2 hours by foot), you'll come to the ethnic Albanian village of Gorni Kosovrasti. There's not much here except excellent views of the valley floor, the terraced fields on the way up and some fascinating wooden houses and barns. You'll get a real taste of mountain village life here, with cattle and goats wandering around in and out of houses and stables, and the local herdsmen riding mules and donkeys. There is a small mosque in the village.

SPA CAPA BANJIŠTE (⏰ 07.00–21.00 daily; entry 50MKD) In the foothills of the Gole Krčin Mountain (2,341m), 6km north of Debar, close to the Albanian border, lies this little haven of hot springs. Still more of a medical facility than a modern spa, recent renovations have rid it of the old Ottoman/communist experience. There are three springs (Nova Kaptaža, Goren and Dolen), and the baths themselves (separated for men and women) are nicely sunlit. The small lawn area outside the entrance to the baths is a pleasant place to sip a coffee and take in the magnificent view of the surrounding mountains. Until 15.00 every day the baths are reserved for medicinal bathing and relaxing, but after 15.00 the spring is open to the public. As you approach the village you can see the run-off from the hot springs tumbling down the ditch on the side of the road, and where it burbles over the hill the water minerals have formed deposits of calcium, lime and sulphur. The smell of sulphur is strong.

KIČEVO   *Telephone code 045*

Known in ancient times as Uskana, Kičevo was mentioned by the Roman historian Livy when he recorded that the last Macedon king, Perseus, took Uskana with an army of 10,000 men during the third Macedonian War against the Romans. Kičevo

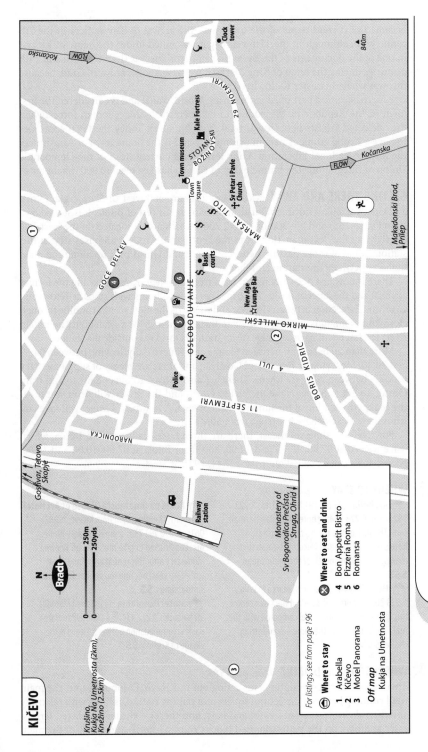

KIČEVO

N
Bradt

0 ——— 250m
0 ——— 250yds

Goshvar, Tetovo, Skopje
Krušino, Kukja Na Umetnosta (2km), Knežino (2.5km)

Kočanska
FLOW

Kočanska
FLOW

840m

Clock tower

Kale Fortress

Town museum

STOJAN BOZINOVSKI

29 NOEMVRI

Town square

✝ Sv Petar i Pavle Church

MARŠAL TITO

GOCE DELČEV

Basic courts

OSLOBODUVANJE

☆ New Age Lounge Bar

MIRKO MILESKI

BORIS KIDRIČ

4 JULI

Police

11 SEPTEMVRI

NARODNICKA

Railway station

Monastery of Sv Bogorodica Prečista, Struga, Ohrid

Makedonski Brod, Prilep

✝

✈

For listings, see from page 196

Where to stay
1 Arabella
2 Kičevo
3 Motel Panorama

Off map
Kukja na Umetnosta

😊 **Where to eat and drink**
4 Bon Appetit Bistro
5 Pizzeria Roma
6 Romansa

became the current name of the town with the arrival of Slav settlers in the 7th century AD, although in the 11th century it was noted under the name of Kicavis in one of the documents of the Byzantine emperor Basilius II. In the 13th and 14th centuries during the reign of King Marko it was also known as Katin Grad, because this was where his sister Katina lived.

Kičevo became a part of Albania during World War II and is considered the first town in the Republic of Macedonia to be liberated by Macedonian forces when they defeated fascists here (it was retaken again later). Today the town continues to have a strong ethnic Albanian community and is the home town of Ali Ahmeti, the former National Liberation Army leader and current head of the Democratic Union of Integration. The municipality of Kičevo has just over 30,000 inhabitants.

GETTING THERE AND AWAY Kičevo lies 110km southwest of Skopje via Tetovo and Gostivar, 60km north of Ohrid, and 80km northwest of Bitola. It is served by a train (☎225 168) and bus station (☎272 206), which are co-located on the west side of Highway E65 less than 1km from the centre of town. Not all buses stop at this station; some of those passing between Skopje and Ohrid pick up along the main highway between the station and the town.

There is now just one daily return **train** from Skopje to Kičevo, leaving the former at 16.50 and the latter at 05.30. The trip takes about 2 hours with stops at Tetovo and Gostivar. The section between Gostivar and Kičevo is the most scenic, running through close-knit mountains, numerous small tunnels, and alongside a clean pretty mountain river. The last 60cm narrow-gauge steam train to Ohrid sits outside the station.

More than 20 **buses** run between Skopje and Kičevo daily, leaving between 04.30 and 20.30. Most stop at Tetovo and Gostivar, and there are plenty of supplementary services between all these towns. There are also at least 15 buses daily to and from Ohrid. To get to Struga, take the bus to Ohrid and the driver will drop you off at the Makpetrol station at the junction near Struga. A minibus (*kombe*) will take you from there to anywhere in Struga from 50MKD.

For those heading southeast, there are three buses daily to/from Bitola, which leave Kičevo at 07.00, 13.00 and 14.00, and from Bitola at 07.00, 10.00 and 16.00. Kičevo taxis can be called on ☎(045) 1544, 1991 or 1594.

WHERE TO STAY *Map, page 195*

Arabella (25 rooms) Maršal Tito; ☎222 552; m 070 223 104; e hotelarabella@hotmail.com. The pick of the town's more central hotels offers a friendly welcome & clean new rooms about 500m north of the main square. **$$$**

Hotel Kičevo (27 rooms) Marko Mileski; ☎223 362. A short walk south of the town centre, this feels rather down-at-heel compared with the Arabella, but rates are the same – a 2nd string choice! **$$$**

Kukja na Umetnosta (House of Art Hotel) (20 rooms) Knežino, 6km from Kičevo; ☎262 061; m 070 793 739; e umetnosta@t-home.mk. Constructed to take the strain off Knežino Monastery after the annual art colony there (Jul every year) became too secular. Beautiful surroundings. **$$**

Motel Panorama (11 rooms) Metodija Stefanovski; ☎222 434; f @MotelPanorama. Basic accommodation between Kičevo & the village of Krušino. **$$**

WHERE TO EAT AND DRINK *Map, page 195*

There is no shortage of options for eating out in Kičevo. Osloboduvanje, the main road running between the central square and railway station, is lined with relatively smart sit-down restaurants, cafés and bars, and there's a cluster of relaxed terrace cafés and bars on the pedestrianised blocks running north and south of the main square. Several cheap grills and čevapi stores line the stretch of Maršal Tito running north towards the market, and there's a row of fast-food stalls at the junction of Marko Mileski and Osloboduvanje.

✗ **Bon Appetit Bistro** Ulica Janko Mihajloski 58; ☎221 986; ⓕ @bonappetitbistro; ⊕ 08.00–midnight daily. Inexpensive bistro serving pasta, grills, salads, sandwiches & excellent b/fasts & Julius Meinl coffee. $

✗ **Pizzeria Roma** Osloboduvanje; ☎221 232; ⓕ @PizzeriaRomaa. Pizzas straight from a clay oven are the speciality here, but they also serve a good selection of Italian & Macedonian dishes. Pleasant atmosphere. $

☕ **Romansa** Osloboduvanje. A relaxed café offering sweet pastries & ice creams as well as the usual drinks.

☆ **New Age Lounge Bar** Marko Mileski. Stylish & modern cocktail bar with indoor & terrace seating 200m south of the main drag.

WHAT TO SEE AND DO

Around town Kičevo appears uneventful, although it has seen refurbishment around the tiny town square. The **clock tower** and **Kale Fortress** (Stojan Božinovski 1; ☎222 949; ⊕ 11.00–16.00 Tue–Sun; entry free) are all that remain of note from the Ottoman period, the latter of which is a short hike up the hill behind the **town museum** on the town square. The building itself was used by the Partisan Army in World War II after it liberated the town, and the museum exhibition is mostly dedicated to that story. If the museum is shut when it says it should be open, try asking at the town hall, one block further north on Maršal Tito.

Monastery of Sv Bogorodica Prečista

Set high in the mountains a 10km drive southeast of Kičevo, this monastery dedicated to the Holy Immaculate Mother of God has tall majestic walls that can be seen imposing over the landscape for some distance. Although the monastery originally dates back to the 14th century, it has been burnt down (on the orders of Sultan Selim in 1515) or destroyed by fire (1558 and 1843) several times. The current construction of stone is from 1848. The monastery is most renowned for Blagovestie Day on 17 April 1924, when Bishop Dositej entered the brotherhood. In 1963, Dositej became the first archbishop of the revived Ohrid Archbishopric, now known as the Macedonian Orthodox Church. A few years later in 1967, Archbishop Dositej proclaimed the autocephaly (independence) of the Macedonian Orthodox Church from the Serbian Orthodox Church. This was without the consent of any of the other orthodox churches and has been a point of dispute ever since.

A legend of a flying icon accompanies the monastery: an icon of Mary has been taken three times to Knežino Monastery, northwest of Kičevo, and each time it has returned the same night via a ray of light. The icon is still on display in the church today. The church's saint's day is 21 September, the birthday of the Virgin Mary.

To reach this monastery, head south out of Kičevo towards Ohrid and take the turn-off for Bitola. About 1.5km after the turn-off is a sign for the left-hand turn to Prečista. The last 3.5km to the car park is steep and traverses several hairpin bends.

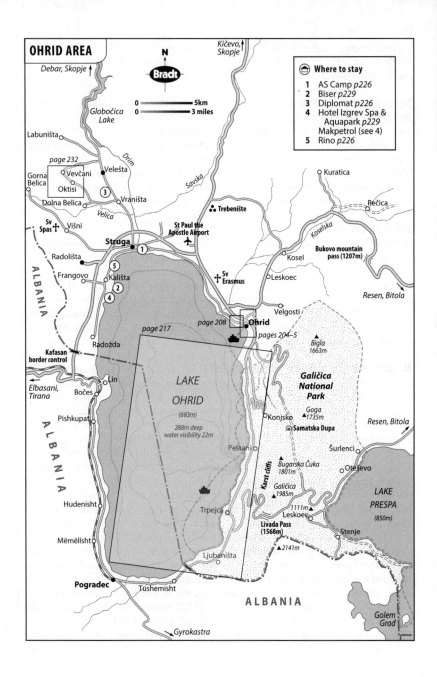

OHRID AREA

Debar, Skopje

Kičevo, Skopje

page 232

page 208

page 217

pages 204–5

N

Bradt

0 — 5km
0 — 3 miles

Globočica
Lake

Labuništa

Gorna
Belica
Dolna Belica

Vevčani

Oktisi

Velešta

Vraništa

Kuratica

Rečica

Drim

Savska

Koselska

Velica

Sv
Spas

Višni

Trebenište

Struga

St Paul the
Apostle Airport

Kosel

Bukovo mountain
pass (1207m)

Radolišta

Frangovo

Kališta

Sv
Erasmus

Leskoec

Resen, Bitola

A L B A N I A

Radožda

Velgosti

Ohrid

Bigla
1663m

Kafasan
border control

LAKE
OHRID

(693m)

288m deep
water visibility 22m

Galičica
National
Park

Elbasani,
Tirana

Boçes

Lin

Konjsko

Goga
1735m

Resen, Bitola

Samatska Dupa

Pishkupat

Peštani

Šurlenci

Bugarska Čuka
1801m

Oteševo

A L B A N I A

Hudenisht

Galičica
1985m

Karst cliffs

1111m

LAKE
PRESPA

(850m)

Trpejca

Leskoec

Mëmëllsht

Livada Pass
(1568m)

2141m

Stenje

Ljubaništa

Pogradec

Tushemisht

A L B A N I A

Golem
Grad

Gyrokastra

Where to stay

1 AS Camp *p226*
2 Biser *p229*
3 Diplomat *p226*
4 Hotel Izgrev Spa &
  Aquapark *p229*
  Makpetrol (see 4)
5 Rino *p226*

5

Lake Ohrid and Galičica National Park

Telephone code 046

> The waters, limpid as the crystal of the rock, from which property the lake perhaps acquired its Greek name (for lychnis signified transparent), discover a bottom of clear sand, at even a depth of from nine to fourteen English fathoms.
>
> F C H L Pouqueville, *Travels in Epirus, Albania, Macedonia and Thessaly*, 1820

Ohrid is the jewel of the Macedonian crown. Both the lake and town of that name form part of the country's only UNESCO World Heritage Site, which was inscribed as a mixed natural and cultural property in 1997 in recognition of its rare environmental and historical significance. And not without reason. The oldest continuously existing lake in Europe, Ohrid formed in a geotectonic depression around five million years ago, placing it in the same ranks of antiquity as lakes Baikal (Russia), Tanganyika (East Africa) and Titicaca (Peru/Bolivia). Extending over 358km², it is the deepest lake in the Balkans, with a maximum depth of 288m, and some scientists regard it as the world's most biodiverse water body of comparable size, hosting more than 200 endemic species, most famously the heavily fished Ohrid trout (*Salmo letnica*).

The lake's principal port town, also called Ohrid, sprawls picturesquely across the hilly northeastern shore. One of the oldest continuously occupied towns in Europe, with roots going back to Neolithic times, it's renowned for the old churches and traditional architecture that characterise its atmospheric old town. The most important tourist focus on the lake, the town is serviced by a large and varied selection of hotels, restaurants and other amenities catering to domestic and foreign visitors alike. And although it can get very busy during July and August and over long weekends, the old town is much quieter and cheaper on weekdays and out of season.

Enclosed on all sides by pretty green mountains whose peaks are brushed white with snow in winter, Lake Ohrid is noted for its beaches and transparent clean blue water, which offer ideal swimming conditions in the warm Balkan summer, as well as some great diving and sailing opportunities. Points of interest include the little-visited but quaint port town of Struga on the northern shore, the historic Monastery of Sv Naum and associated lake springs near the Albanian border, the tiny cave churches at Kališta and Radožda, and tranquil lakeshore villages such as Trpejca, Peštani and Lagadin. Lake Ohrid is also the obvious base from which to make day trips by jeep, donkey or foot to the characterful old mountain villages of Oktisi and Vevčani, or to go caving, hiking and paragliding in the scenic Galičica National Park.

OHRID TOWN

Boasting a memorable setting on a hilly peninsula lapped by a calm aquamarine bay and a historical pedigree that stretches back 2,500 years, Ohrid has few rivals when it comes to the accolade of Macedonia's prettiest town. The labyrinthine old town, overlooked by a formidable walls of Tsar Samoil's Fortress, is a veritable architectural treasure where handsome 18th- and 19th-century town houses rub shoulders with medieval churches adorned with Byzantine frescoes and Roman-era relicts such as a theatre dating back to 200BC and some early Christian mosaics. Historical sites aside, Macedonians love Ohrid because it is their seaside: the crystal-clear waters beckon in the long hot days of summer, followed by a cocktail at any of the dozens of laid-back waterfront cafés. Then there is the Ohrid Festival, which attracts world-renowned artists to perform in the old Roman theatre and various lakeside venues. And once you've exhausted the town itself, you are ideally placed for exploring the many other sites covered in this chapter – the most popular goals for day trips being the tranquil lakeshore Monastery of Sv Naum and mountainous Galičica National Park – or driving further afield to the western shore of Lake Prespa.

HISTORY The shores of Lake Ohrid have been inhabited since prehistoric times. The earliest signs of humankind in the area have been found in Dolno Trnovo, to the north of the main town, and at the Bay of Bones at Gradište, dating from the late Bronze Age (around 12000–7000BC). Although there is nothing of the graves left to see at Dolno Trnovo, the Bay of Bones stilt village has been reconstructed, and some of the related artefacts are on display in the Ohrid Museum.

Later, tribes known as the Brigians, Ohrygians and Enhelians settled in the area. These tribes neighboured the Illyrians, who at that time had moved through Ohrid into areas further west (now Albania). They were displaced by the Desaretes (also of Illyrian descent), and it is as the capital of Desaretia that the present-day town of Ohrid, then known as Lychnidos, is first mentioned.

Lychnidos was founded and named by Cadmus the Phoenician (from Canaanite lands in today's Middle East). Legend has it that after he founded Thebes in the 14th century BC, he abdicated in favour of his grandson and travelled further north to fight for the Enhelians. There are two possible meanings to Lychnidos. In ancient Greek the name means 'town of lamps' (*lychnis* = lamp, *dos* = town). In Phoenician, however, *lihnis* means 'water reeds'. Lake Ohrid has gone through periods of partial desiccation when the water level has varied. When Cadmus founded Lychnidos, the lake may have been much smaller with significant reeds along its edges, just as parts of Lake Prespa are today.

By the 4th century BC, the town was conquered by the Macedonians of Philip II, and then the Romans in the late 2nd century BC. The town was developed further during Roman times by traders travelling along the Via Egnatia (see box, page 6), which passed through Radožda and Lychnidos. A Roman fort also existed further around the lake at Gradište (the first 0.5m of the outer wall of which has now been rebuilt for visitors to view). With these travellers came preachers of Christianity.

By the 5th century AD, the first early basilicas were being built in Lychnidos. Twelve are believed to have been built in total, although only six have been found so far. The largest and most significant of these is at the site of today's Monastery of Sv Kliment at Plaošnik. The large size of the basilica indicates the importance of this church and of the bishops who resided here, whose work grew with the arrival of pagan Slav tribes in the 6th century. Other basilicas found around Lake Ohrid are at Sv Sophia, Sv Erasmus and another in the hills above Biljana Springs.

By AD879, the town was no longer called Lychnidos but was referred to by the Slavs as Ohrid, possibly from the Slav words *vo hrid*, meaning 'on a hill' as the ancient town of Lychnidos was at the top of Ohrid Hill.

A few years later, the missionaries Kliment and Naum came to Ohrid and set up the first monasteries that taught in Slavic. This strengthened the already strong religious tradition in the town, and a century later, when Tsar Samoil (see box, page 20) moved the capital of his empire to Ohrid, he also made Ohrid the head of its own autocephalous patriarchate.

Tsar Samoil's fortress city at Ohrid is still visible today, although parts of it were destroyed when Samoil was defeated by the Byzantine emperor Basilius II in 1014. Ohrid then became a part of the Byzantine Empire again and the patriarchate of Ohrid was reduced to an archbishopric. But it remained an influential archbishopric nonetheless, whose reach extended from the Adriatic in the west as far as Thessaloniki to the south and all along the River Danube in the north to the Black Sea, and the Archbishop of Ohrid was always a powerful political appointee.

The Archbishopric of Ohrid, although nominally under the patriarch of Constantinople, went from strength to strength as well as growing in geographical influence even under the Ottoman Empire (see box, page 23). By the end of the 16th century the jurisdiction of the Archbishopric of Ohrid went as far as the Orthodox communities in Dalmati and Venice in mainland Italy, as well as to Malta and Sicily.

Ohrid's privileged position within the Ottoman Empire through its seat as the archbishopric was rarely challenged, although in 1466 this was jeopardised when the citizens of Ohrid sided with the Albanian Lord Skenderbeg (see box, page 192) against their Ottoman rulers. Several high-ranking church officials and the archbishop were jailed as a result and died in prison, and the Church of St Sophia, which was the seat of the Ohrid archbishopric, was converted into a mosque.

When the Archbishopric of Ohrid was abolished in 1767 at the behest of the Greek patriarchate, Greek influence on Ohrid's religious life became pronounced, much to the dislike of the locals. It took just over a century for the locals to then

THE GOLDEN MASKS OF MACEDONIA

North of Ohrid Airport, outside the village of Trebenište, are some of the most important and richest archaeological discoveries ever to be made in Macedonia. The unearthing of ten burial chambers in 1918 revealed the lavish ceremonies of the ancient Paeons and Macedonians of the 1st millennium BC. Four almost complete golden masks were found in the graves as well as jewellery, pottery, ceremonial clothing, shoes and part of a fifth mask. The burial chambers belonged to rich princes of the region who were cremated at death, so only the burial riches remain. Two of the masks were taken to Belgrade and are on display at the National Museum of Serbia. The other two were taken to Sofia, where they are displayed at the Archaeological Museum. Each mask is worth in the region of €18 million. Part of a sixth mask has been found at the Petilep tomb in Beranci, near Bitola, and more tombs, long since ransacked, exist all over Macedonia.

Sensationally in 2002, Paško Kuzman made his name as Macedonia's leading archaeologist when he discovered a fifth complete golden mask during excavations at Tsar Samoil's Fortress in Ohrid. Little but age-old scars in the ground exist at the Trebenište tomb now, and Ohrid Fortress is still under excavation, but replicas of the golden masks are now on display in a Golden Room at the new Museum of Archaeology in Skopje.

5

convince the Ottomans to shut down Greek teaching in Ohrid in 1869. Thereafter, Ohrid's history follows a very similar pattern to the rest of northern Macedonia. VMRO's branch in Ohrid rose up on Ilinden in 1903 like the rest of the land, and was brutally put down again afterwards. Under Yugoslavia, Ohrid saw development in tourism, and Tito even had a summer residence on the lake, now reserved for Macedonia's government.

Tourism is picking up again now in Ohrid, so many of the socialist-style hotels are being completely renovated and many smaller family-run hotels and new apartments are springing up along the lake. The Macedonian parliament enacted zoning laws in 2010, and so most of the old town is protected in keeping with its status as a UNESCO heritage town. Enforcing the law is another matter, and you will still see a few new builds. Jet skis are now banned from the lake between 08.00 and 19.00 in July and August, but legislation has yet to catch up with speedboat use and the mix of raucous bars in the predominantly residential old town.

GETTING THERE AND AWAY

By air Macedonia's only international airport outside Skopje, Ohrid's St Paul the Apostle Airport (w ohd.airports.com.mk) lies 14km north of town, closer to Struga than to Ohrid itself. There are only a few flights a day, mostly in the summer, during which time Wizzair offers direct services from London Luton, Vienna and Basel.

By car If you are driving to Ohrid from Skopje, the most direct route is the 170km A2 and E65 via Tetovo, Gostivar and Kičevo, which should take around 2½ hours. It is also worth considering the dramatic 200km back road through Mavrovo National Park via Debar, which winds past four dams (Mavrovo, Debar, Golema and Mala Globočica) and close to the border with Albania. This route is especially worthwhile in the autumn when the trees turn colour. Allow 3½ hours for the direct drive, but it is worth making a day of it and stopping at a few sites of interest en route. A third option is the 240km easterly route through Veles, Prilep and Bitola, but this is probably only worth considering if you plan on stopping overnight along the way. Coming from the east, a lovely alternative to the direct 70km road between Bitola and Ohrid is the more southerly 100km route via the western shore of Lake Prespa, Galičica National Park and the eastern shore of Lake Ohrid.

By bus Long-haul buses all arrive and leave at the main inter-town bus station (✆260 339), which lies about 1.5km north of the city centre at the junction of Pitu Guli and Sedmi Noemvri. More than 20 buses run back and forth daily between Skopje and Ohrid, leaving between 04.30 and 21.30. There are also frequent buses to/from Kičevo, Bitola, Prilep and Kočani. International services include at least one bus daily to Belgrade (Serbia) and Sofia (Bulgaria), and two weekly to Frankfurt and Dortmund (Germany), leaving at 05.30 on Wednesday and Saturday. A taxi ride from the centre of town to the bus station should cost around 100MKD.

For more local destinations, you are best picking up a bus along the central Turistička Boulevard. Heading south along the eastern lakeshore, a couple of dozen buses run back and forth daily to Peštani via Lagadin, leaving between 05.50 and 21.30, and a few continue to Sv Naum via Trpejca. The best place to pick these up is the bus stop on the southwest side of the roundabout with Jane Sandanski. Buses also leave for Struga every 15 minutes from 05.30 and 22.30, and can be picked up on the north side of the roundabout with Abas Emin [205 G1]. In both cases, buses are supplemented by an informal network of shared taxis.

By rail The railway line to Ohrid closed down in 1966 when the decision was taken not to upgrade the 60cm gauge line to the current 143.5cm gauge. Although trains and lines are to be upgraded in Macedonia, the Kičevo to Ohrid line is unlikely to receive funding. For details of the old 17-hour steam journey, check out w penmorfa. com/JZ/ohrid.html.

GETTING AROUND

By taxi The old town is small enough to walk around (but hilly) and driving is restricted. Taxis have a minimum fare of 50MKD plus a per kilometre charge of 30MKD. Taxi ranks can be found at either end of Makedonski Prosvetiteli street, or call one of the following numbers (prefixed 046 from a mobile phone): ☎1580, 1583, 1585, 1588, 1591, 1592, 1595, 1599.

By boat A good way to get around the lake is by boat. During June to September a daily boat service runs from the main boat quay in Ohrid [205 G6] to Sv Naum and returns in the late afternoon (page 216).There are also lots of boat taxis that will take one or a whole boatload of passengers for a ride for a minimum of €10. An extended tour around the harbour will cost you €20; €30 will take you to Struga, Kališta or Radožda, where the view of the cave church from the water is quite striking (at least 1 hour's boat journey); and €45 will take you on the 2-hour journey to Sv Naum. Trips can be arranged directly with a boat captain at the harbour or through any tour agency. For longer trips, a full-day cruise on a 30-passenger boat, for instance, including lunch on board with drinks, works out at about €50 per person.

It's worth mentioning that a boat that was carrying too many passengers sank on the lake in 2009, resulting in 15 fatalities.

During the summer months (Jun–Sep), there may be a ferry service connecting Ohrid with Podgradec on the Albanian shore, a journey time of around 2 hours.

Town maps Free town maps are available in some of the big hotels. A 1:6,000 map of Ohrid can be bought in most supermarkets and bookstalls, both in Skopje and in Ohrid itself. The Trimaks map also includes a 1:65,000 map of the lake on the back of the city map, as well as some useful information on sites, telephone numbers and street names.

The creators of *Skopje City Walk* (page 357) have now published *Ohrid City Walk*, a useful guide with maps downloadable in English or Dutch from w walkingmacedonia.com.

TOUR OPERATORS/TOURIST INFORMATION For help with bookings, tours and further information once in Ohrid, check out w visit-ohrid.com or contact one of the agencies listed below.

Cultura 365 [204 C2] Tsar Samoil 34; m 070 507 424; e itvo@t-home.mk, yuzmeski@t-home.mk; ◻ @cultura365. This small art gallery in the old town arranges bespoke guided tours in & around Ohrid.
Dea Tours [208 B5] Kej Maršal Tito 40; ☎265 251; m 077 733 733; e info@deatours.com. mk; w deatours.com.mk; ◷ 09.00–20.00 daily. Friendly multilingual staff with a wealth of knowledge about the region. They can arrange

various tours including ethno-tourism, donkey rides, adventure tours, mountaineering & other possibilities. Can also help with finding accommodation in all price ranges.
Free Pass Ohrid [204 A2] Kosta Abraš 74; m 071 906 616, 070 488 231; e freepassohrid@gmail. com; w freepassohrid.mk. Based in the old town, this dynamic agency run by 2 sisters offers a variety of boat trips, village visits & winery tours, as well as hikes in Galičica & Mavrovo national parks, &

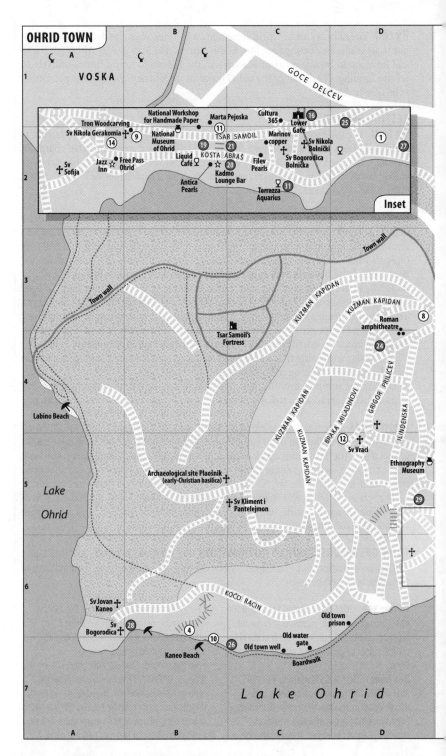

OHRID TOWN

VOSKA

GOCE DELČEV

Inset

Tron Woodcarving
Sv Nikola Gerakomia
National Workshop for Handmade Paper
Marta Pejoska
Cultura 365
Lower Gate
TSAR SAMOIL
National Museum of Ohrid
Marinov copper
Sv Nikola Bolnički
Sv Sofija
Jazz Inn
Free Pass Ohrid
Liquid Café
KOSTA ABRAŠ
Kadmo Lounge Bar
Filev Pearls
Sv Bogorodica Bolnička
Antica Pearls
Terrazza Aquarius

Town wall

Town wall

KUZMAN KAPIDAN

KUZMAN KAPIDAN

Tsar Samoil's Fortress

Roman amphitheatre

KUZMAN KAPIDAN

KUZMAN KAPIDAN

GRIGOR PRLIČEV

BRAKA MILADINOVI

ILINDENSKA

Labino Beach

Sv Vraci

Ethnography Museum

Archaeological site Plaošnik (early-Christian basilica)

Lake Ohrid

Sv Kliment i Pantelejmon

Sv Jovan Kaneo

KOČO RACIN

Sv Bogorodica

Old town prison

Kaneo Beach

Old water gate

Old town well

Boardwalk

Lake Ohrid

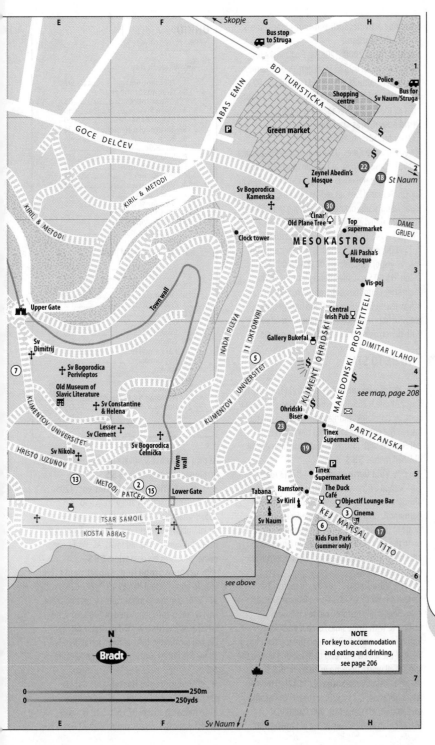

Skopje
Bus stop
to Struga

BD TURISTIČKA

Police
Bus for
Sv Naum/Struga

ABAS EMIN

Shopping
centre

P

GOCE DELČEV

Green market

$

$

$

22

18   St Naum

KIRIL & METODI

Zeynel Abedin's
Mosque

2

DAME
GRUEV

KIRIL & METODI

Sv Bogorodica
Kamenska

30

Top
supermarket

'Činar'
Old Plane Tree

Clock tower

MESOKASTRO

Ali Pasha's
Mosque

3

Vis-poj

Town wall

Upper Gate

Central
Irish Pub

Sv
Dimitrij

Gallery Bukefal

$

DIMITAR VLAHOV

7

Sv Bogorodica
Perivleptos

5

$

see map, page 208

Old Museum of
Slavic Literature

Sv Constantine
& Helena

Ohridski
Biser

$

KLIMENTOV UNIVERSITET

Lesser
Sv Clement

23

PARTIZANSKA

Sv Nikola

Sv Bogorodica
Celnička

Tinex
Supermarket

HRISTO UŽUNOV

19

Tinex
Supermarket

13

METODI PATČEV

2   15   Lower Gate

Town wall

P

Tabana   Ramstore

The Duck
Café

Sv Kiril

Objectif Lounge Bar

3   Cinema

Sv Naum

6

17

KOSTA ABRAS

TSAR SAMOIL

Kids Fun Park
(summer only)

6

see above

N

Bradt

NOTE
For key to accommodation
and eating and drinking,
see page 206

0   250m
0   250yds

E   F   Sv Naum   G   H

adventure activities such as diving, paragliding & horseback excursions.

General Turist 2000 [208 A4] Partizanska 6; 260 423; m 070 232 235; e gen2000@t-home. mk; w generalturist2000-ohrid.com.mk; ⏱ 09.00–20.00 daily. Aside from tours in the region they also offer all the usual travel agency services.

Ohrid Adventures m 078 931 533; e ohridadventures@gmail.com; ⓕ @ohridadventures. Based out of the ever-popular Robinson Sunset House in Lagadin (page 220), this hands-on operator offers hiking to remote villages in Galičica National Park, as well as canoeing, kayaking, paragliding, scuba diving & snorkelling from a boat. Prices are aimed at budget travellers.

Vis-poj [205 H3] Makedonski Prosvetiteli 7; 255 600; m 072 255 600; e info@vispoj.com. mk; w vispoj.com.mk; ⏱ 08.00–20.00 Mon–Fri, 09.00–15.00 Sat. Conveniently located on the main street into the centre of town, with a larger office also at Turistička 50. Good link on their website to private accommodation. Private tour with driver/guide from 150MKD for 4 people.

🏠 **WHERE TO STAY**
Old town

🏠 **Hotel Aleksandrija** [204 D2] (15 rooms) Kosta Abraš; 258 860; e info@hotelaleksandrija. com; w hotelaleksandrija.com. Overlooking the lake at the entrance to the old town, offers 2 deluxe apts with jacuzzi, & the remainder are all dbl-bed rooms. **$$$**

✻ 🏠 **Villa Germanoff** [204 B2] (3 rooms) Tsar Samoil 57; m 070 261 301; e germanoff. ohrid@gmail.com; w visitohrid.org/room/villa-germanoff. Great owner-managed villa in the heart of the old town. The Piano Room with a view on to the lake is one of the nicest in Ohrid. Say in advance if you want b/fast inc. Electric kettle in each room. **$$$**

✻ 🏠 **Villa Jovan** [204 B2] (9 rooms) Tsar Samoil 44; m 075 377 644; e vilajovan@gmail. com. Beautifully restored old town house, complete with stone sinks, even if en-suite bathrooms are small. Deluxe on the top floor has a view of the lake & a jacuzzi bath looking out on the stars. Well worth booking in advance. **$$$**

✻ 🏠 **Villa Sveta Sofija** [204 A2] (5 rooms) Kosta Abraš 64; 254 370; e contact@vilasofija. com.mk; w vilasofija.com.mk. Traditional Macedonian architecture in the old town, with

its own restaurant & private bar. Exquisite service accompanies every room. **$$$**

🏠 **Villa & Winery Mal Sv Kliment** [205 F5] (8 rooms) Metodi Patčev 10; 250 655; e vilamalsvetikliment@t-home.mk; w vilamalsvetikliment.com. Beautiful rooms & beautiful views in the old town. AC, Wi-Fi. The owner produces his own wine. **$$$**

🏠 **Grebnos Stone House Apartments** [205 F5] (6 apts) Metodi Patčev 19; 272 625; m 070 331 706; e info@grebnos.com; w grebnos.com. Lovely stone apts, renovated in 2008. En suites, terrace with nice view, Wi-Fi, garden, kitchen. Central location in the old town immediately above the Robev House Museum; good value. **$$**

✻ 🏠 **Sunny Lake Hostel** [205 G4] (3 dbl rooms, 3 4-bed dorms, 2 8-bed dorms) 11 Oktomvri St 15; m 075 629 571; e info@ sunnylakehostel.mk; w sunnylakehostel.mk. The oldest backpackers in Macedonia, celebrating its 10th anniversary in 2018, this popular owner-managed set-up has bright little rooms & dorms, a sociable vibe, a great location in the old town & good amenities including a common room with TV, book swap & regular evening BBQs. All rates include b/fast. Bicycle hire €3 per day. Dorm beds from €10. **$$**

✳ 🏠 **Vila Kale** [205 E4] (8 rooms) Klimentov Universitet; ☎ 262 208; e vilakale@gmail.com. Bright & colourful rooms that let in plenty of light, friendly & helpful owner-manager & a useful location near the Roman theatre & northern city gate. Great value. **$$**

🏠 **Villa Forum** [204 D3] (4 rooms) Kuzman Kapidan 1; ☎ 251 340; m 070 819 713; e ljupcomalezan@yahoo.com. At the top of the old town overlooking the Roman theatre & lake. 1 twin, 2 dbls & 1 suite, all with an extra fold-out armchair-bed. **$$**

🏠 **Villa Kaneo** [204 B7] (4 rooms, 2 apts) Kočo Racin 21; m 070 353 999, 078 609 698; 🅵 @villakaneo. Nice tasteful rooms in 2 houses, 1 in Kaneo overlooking the lake & another in the centre of town, Villa Dudan. Private bathroom but not en suite. **$$**

🏠 **Villa Ohrid** [204 D5] (5 rooms) Braka Miladinovi 11; m 078 484 190; e villaohrid@ gmail.com. Super little owner-managed villa with 3 small dbl rooms that share a kitchen & 2 well-equipped self-catering apts whose balconies offer as fine a view over town & lake as you could hope for. **$$**

🏠 **Villa Rustica** [205 E5] (5 apts) Hristo Uzunov 1; ☎ 265 511; m 070 212 114; e villaoh@ yahoo.com. Fantastic 270° view of the lake from the top suite & a beautiful garden, below a massive kiwi tree, for b/fast in the morning or a nightcap. **$$**

🏠 **Stefan Kanevče** [204 B6] (9 rooms in various houses) Kaneo; ☎ 260 350, 234 813; m 070 212 352; e stefan.kanevce@gmail.com. See box, page 211. **$–$$**

Along the quay

🏠 **Hotel Garden** [208 C6] (28 rooms) Kej Maršal Tito 114; ☎ 260 261; e info@hotelgarden. com.mk; w hotelgarden.com.mk. Set at the quiet southern end of the quay overlooking the lakefront part & only 100m from Cuba Libre Beach, this is a well-priced hotel offering a couple of smaller

cheaper rooms at the back or nicer & larger rooms with veranda & lake view. Nice terrace restaurant/bar. Decent value. **$$$**

🏠 **Hotel Lebed** [208 C6] (28 rooms) Kej Maršal Tito 112; ☎ 250 004. Situated alongside the Hotel Garden, this renovated hotel offers private parking with 24hr surveillance. Prices vary according to whether rooms have a lake view. **$$$**

🏠 **Hotel Nova Riviera** [205 H5] (39 rooms) Kej Maršal Tito; ☎ 209 900; e hotelnovariviera@ gmail.com; w novariviera.mk. This recently refurbished stalwart has a restaurant with patio seating, a piano bar & mini-shop. Good location. Buffet b/fast. **$$$**

🏠 **Hotel Tino** [205 H6] (18 rooms) Kej Maršal Tito 55; ☎ 230 450; e hoteltino@t-home.mk; w hoteltino.com.mk. Standard clean rooms with AC & bathroom. **$$$**

🏠 **Hotel Villa Jordan** [208 C6] (24 rooms) Kej Maršal Tito 100; ☎ 200 122; e villa_jordan_ohrid@ yahoo.com; w villa-jordan-mk.book.direct. This smart & popular multistorey hotel 100m from the beach has bright airy rooms, some with a lake & mountain view, & good amenities including a swimming pool & restaurant, both for the exclusive use of guests. **$$$**

🏠 **Millenium Palace** [208 C6] (25 rooms) Kej Maršal Tito 110; ☎ 263 361; e millenium_ palace@t.mk, ohrid@milleniumpalace.com.mk; w milleniumpalace.com.mk. Standard smart hotel. Also has its own sauna, fitness centre & restaurant. A great buffet b/fast is well priced for non-residents. **$$$**

🏠 **Apartments Tomic** [208 B5] (4 rooms) Off Kej Maršal Tito; m 070 856 759, 070 987 161; e aleksandazohrid@hotmail.com. Friendly & accommodating owner-managed lodge on a quiet alley just 100m from the beachfront. Neat & spacious rooms have AC, TV & private terrace. Rates include a transfer from the airport or bus station by prior arrangement. **$$**

🏠 **Villa Biljana** [208 C4] (3 rooms) Kej Maršal Tito 111; m 070 320 444; e btanasoska@yahoo. com; w apartmani-ohrid.com/villa-biljana. Sandwiched between the Millenium & the Lebed, these pleasant apts offer the view & location of the other hotels but without the extra trimmings. **$$**

🏠 **Villa Dea** [208 B5] (10 rooms) Kej Maršal Tito 40; ☎ 265 251; m 077 733 733; e info@ deatours.com.mk; w deatours.com.mk. Excellent

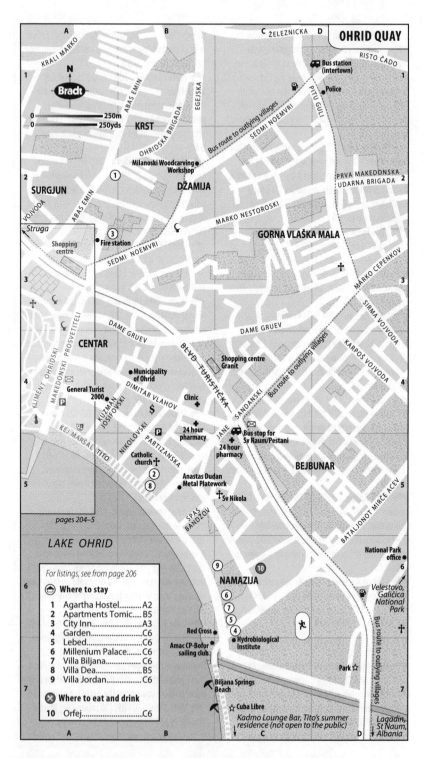

OHRID QUAY

A

KRALI MARKO

N

Bradt

0   250m
0   250yds

KRST

ABAS EMIN

SURGJUN

VOJVODA

ABAS EMIN

B

EGEJSKA

OHRIDSKA BRIGADA

Milanoski Woodcarving ●
Workshop

DŽAMIJA

Ç

MARKO NESTOROSKI

SEDMI NOEMVRI

● Fire station

C ŽELEZNICKA   **D**

RISTO ČADO

🚌 Bus station
(intertown)

PITU GULI

Bus route to outlying villages

SEDMI NOEMVRI

🚓 Police

PRVA MAKEDONSKA
UDARNA BRIGADA

GORNA VLAŠKA MALA

†

MARKO CEPENKOV

Struga

Shopping
centre

†

Ç

Ç

KLIMENT OHRIDSKI

MAKEDONSKI PROSVETITELI

CENTAR

P

KEJ MARSAL TITO

DAME GRUEV

● Municipality
of Ohrid

General Turist
2000 ●

DIMITAR VLAHOV

KUZMAN JOSIFOVSKI

$

NIKOLOVSKI

P

DAME GRUEV

BLVD TURISTIČKA

Shopping centre
Granit

Clinic
✚

24 hour
pharmacy

JANE SANDANSKI

Bus route to outlying villages

SIRMA VOJVODA

KARPOŠ VOJVODA

✉ Bus stop for
Sv Naum/Pestani

PARTIZANSKA

Catholic
church †

②

⑧

24 hour
pharmacy
✚

Anastas Dudan
Metal Platework

† Sv Nikola

BEJBUNAR

BATALJONOT MIRČE ACEV

LAKE OHRID

SPAS
BANDZOV

pages 204–5

For listings, see from page 206

⬢ **Where to stay**

1   Agartha Hostel............A2
2   Apartments Tomic.....B5
3   City Inn.....................A3
4   Garden.....................C6
5   Lebed.......................C6
6   Millenium Palace........C6
7   Villa Biljana................C6
8   Villa Dea...................B5
9   Villa Jordan...............C6

❌ **Where to eat and drink**

10   Orfej.......................C6

⑨

⑥

⑦

⑤

④

NAMAZIJA

⑩

Red Cross

Amac CP-Bofor
sailing club

● Hydrobiological
Institute

🧍

National Park
office ●

Velestovo,
Galičica
National
Park

†

Bus route to outlying villages

Park ☆

Biljana Springs
Beach

☆ Cuba Libre

Kadmo Lounge Bar, Tito's summer
residence (not open to the public)

Lagadin,
St Naum,
↓ Albania

A   **B**   **C**   **D**

value & location for the price. Rooms have balcony & view over the lake. B/fast available at Hotel Royal next door. Run by the tour operator of the same name (page 203). **$$**

North of Bd Turistička
🏠 **Agartha Hostel** [208 A2] (2 rooms, 3 4- to 10-person dorms) Bekir Ali Riza 39; m 078 261 231; e hostelagarthaohrid@hotmail.com; w hostelagarthaohrid.wordpress.com. Comprising a 3-storey house on a quiet road about 10mins' walk north of the old town, this is a very well-run &

welcoming small hostel with a common room, self-catering kitchen & small garden where you can chill out. Good value with dorm beds from €8. **$$**

🏠 **City Inn** [208 A3] (5 twin rooms, 14 3- to 8-bed dorms) Makedonski Prosvetiteli 22; ☎ 262 626; m 078 208 407; e cityinnohrid@gmail.com; w cityinnohrid.com. Large owner-managed hostel sprawling across the upper floors of a multistorey building 200m north of the old town. Rooms & dorms are spotless & well priced, & there's a common kitchen & lounge, but it is slightly lacking in atmosphere. Dorm beds from €11. **$$**

✖ **WHERE TO EAT AND DRINK** Ohrid has a host of little pizzerias and fish restaurants along Tsar Samoil and Kosta Abraš, and fast-food joints and cafés galore along Kliment Ohridski. They can quickly become much of a muchness, and Ohrid is begging for some cuisine alternatives and a really good breakfast café in the centre. Despite the fact that Ohrid trout is endangered and illegal to fish, restaurants here still occasionally serve it.

✳ ✖ **Kaneo Restaurant** [204 B7] Kočo Racin 43, Kaneo; m 070 776 837; e kaneorestaurant@ gmail.com; ⊕ 08.00–midnight Sun–Thu, 08.00–01.00 Fri–Sat. Probably the top fine-dining venue in Ohrid, this restaurant also has a great setting with a stilted deck right above the lake in Kaneo. The small menu, curated by a world-class chef, includes rabbit & 4 types of lake fish, & places a strong emphasis on fresh locally sourced ingredients. **$$$$**

✖ **Antiko** [204 C1] Tsar Samoil 30; ☎ 265 523; m 075 397 908; ⊕ noon–midnight daily. An upmarket place to eat, with a wooden interior. Traditional Macedonian dishes take 3hrs to prepare so order ahead. **$$$**

✖ **Belvedere** [205 H6] Kej Četkarot, Kej Maršal Tito 3; ☎ 231 520; ⊕ 08.30–midnight daily. Notable for its old wooden wagons on the lawn outside, this place serves traditional food in a national-style setting, including cooked b/fasts. The spoof street name Kej Četkarot was coined by the owner, Klime, in reference to his father, who used to make brooms (*četke*). **$$$**

✖ **Dalga** [204 C2] Kosta Abraš 3; ☎ 255 999; ⊕ 10.00–midnight Sun–Thu, 10.00–01.00 Fri–Sat. Ohrid's original lakeside fish restaurant, sporting photos of all the rich & famous who have ever eaten here. **$$$**

✖ **Gladiator Restaurant** [204 D4] Braka Miladinovi 14; m 078 261 482. Overlooking the old Roman theatre, this characterful little

restaurant has limited pavement seating offering a stunning view of the lake & surrounding mountains, & the menu includes a varied selection of soups, salads, grills & Macedonian casseroles. **$$$**

✳ ✖ **Kaj Kanevche (aka Summer Terrace)** [204 B7] Kočo Racin 43, Kaneo; m 070 776 837; ⊕ 08.00–midnight Sun–Thu, 08.00–01.00 Fri–Sat. Fish & other dishes in a relaxed lakeside setting. **$$$**

✳ ✖ **Potpes Beach Restaurant** [204 C7] Kaneo; m 071 231 022; w plazapotpes.mk. Situated alongside the wooden walkway between the old town & Sv Jovan Kaneo, this cheerful eatery is popular with a young crowd thanks to its attractive swimming & sunbathing beach. The speciality is pizza but they also serve a good selection of seafood & other grills. **$$$**

✖ **Restaurant Cun** [204 D2] Kosta Abraš 3; ☎ 307 117; e likocundoo@yahoo.com; ⊕ 13.00– 22.00 Mon, 08.00–01.00 Tue–Sun. Attractive harbour-front restaurant with a rustic stone-dominated interior & plenty of terrace seating right on the water. Traditional Macedonian stews & grills, with a strong emphasis on fish. **$$$**

✖ **Restoran Sv Sofija** [204 D5] Tsar Samoil 88; ☎ 267 403; m 070 261 573; w restoransvsofija. mk; ⊕ 08.00–midnight daily. On the uphill side of Sv Sofija Church, this has a wonderful outdoor patio overlooking the church, & good food. Try their excellent fried squid. **$$$**

5

✖ **Taverna MoMir** [204 C2] Kosta Abraš 3; ✆262 117; w momir.com.mk/taverna.html; ⏱ 08.00– midnight Sun–Thu, 08.00–01.00 Fri–Sat. Nice lakeside seating with more Macedonian food. Same ownership as the out-of-town Eco Resort MoMir. **$$$**

✖ **Da Gino** [205 G5] Main square; ✆121 109; ⏱ 08.00–midnight Sun–Thu, 08.00–01.00 Fri– Sat. Branch of the Skopje pizzeria. Excellent pizzas with fresh mushrooms rather than tinned. **$$**

✖ **Damar** [204 C2] Kosta Abraš, near Robev House Museum; m 075 277 543; ⏱ 08.00–midnight Sun–Thu, 08.00–01.00 Fri–Sat. Popular place with traditional Macedonian fare including several fish dishes. Live music at w/ends (& reservation advised). **$$**

✴ ✖ **Kaj Tanja** [204 D1] Tsar Samoil 23; ✆205 303. Named after its beaming owner-manager, this refreshingly untouristy taverna is set in a ramshackle wooden building in the heart of the old town. Serves a good selection of inexpensive Macedonian-style grills & stews & while it lacks the grand wine list of its posher neighbours, there's affordable jug wine, beer & spirits. **$$**

✖ **Orfej Restaurant** [208 C6] Partizanski; m 075 463 445. Untouristy & sensibly priced traditional Macedonian restaurant with a peaceful garden setting a block back from the southern quay. The terrace seating on wooden benches &

good drinks selection makes it popular with locals. **$$**

✖ **Restoran Sv Jovan Kaneo** [204 B6] Kaneo; ⏱ summer only 09.00–01.00 daily. Right on the water, with some comfy seats & serving basic dishes as well as cocktails. Lots of sunloungers. **$$**

✖ **Bistro Corner** [205 H2] Makedonski Prosvetiteli Bd; m 070 537 901; f @CornerBistroOhrid; ⏱ 08.00–01.00 daily. This modern café off the main roundabout on Turistička Bd has industrial-style décor, indoor & terrace seating, energetic staff & a great selection of sandwiches, salads & other light meals. Good smoothies & coffee, too. **$**

✖ **Dr Falafel** [205 H2] 7-Mi Noemvri 8; m 077 897 167. Wallet- & vegetarian-friendly take-away (with some outside seating) serving an excellent hummus & falafel plate with pita bread, tahini & salad. **$**

✖ **Fruit Box** [205 G5] Kliment Ohridski; m 078 237 659. Vegetarian-friendly take-away serving great fruit & veggie smoothies, muesli, homemade cakes & sweets. **$**

✖ **Star Činar** [205 H2] 7 Noemvri 1; ⏱ noon–midnight daily. Local food at local prices overlooking the old plane tree. Serves great *tavche gravche* (beans & spicy sausage in a pot) & extremely strong green rakija (*zelena rakija*). **$**

ENTERTAINMENT AND NIGHTLIFE Bars and cafés stretch all the way down Kaneo Beach to Cuba Libra at Biljana Springs, although it is mostly hotel fronts along the quay. Nightclubs are abundant in Ohrid. A few are listed below.

Bars and cafés

♀ **Central Irish Pub** [205 H3] Bd Makedonski Prosvetiteli; ⏱ 10.00–01.00 daily. Just like you would expect an Irish pub abroad to be; serves draught beer but not Guinness.

♀ **The Duck Café** [205 H6] Kej Maršal Tito 1; ⏱ 09.00–02.00 daily. Plays classic blues & jazz, with a live band every night in the summer.

♀ **Liquid Café** [204 B2] Kosta Abraš 19; ⏱ 10.00–01.00 daily. Ultra-trendy nightspot on the lakefront featuring contemporary DJ sets at w/ends.

♀ **Objectif Lounge Bar** [205 H5] Maršal Tito 12; ⏱ 10.00–01.00 daily. Trendy cocktail bar with occasional live music & DJs.

♀ **Tabana** [205 G5] Hotel Tabana, Tsar Samoil 11; ⏱ 10.00–01.00 daily. Has a fantastic rooftop pub overlooking the lake.

♀ **Terrazza Aquarius** [204 C2] Kosta Abraš 30; w aquarius-oh.mk; ⏱ 10.00–02.00 daily. Established in 1991, this popular shaded terrace bar is right on the lake & hosts occasional live music.

Nightclubs

☆ **Cuba Libre** [208 C7] Biljana Springs Beach; w cubalibreohrid.com; ⏱ 11.00–04.00. The hottest nightspot in town, & right on the water if you need a dip. A café-bar during the day, live bands every night.

☆ **Jazz Inn** [204 A2] Kosta Abraš 74; ⏱ 22.30– 02.00. Good, live music Thu–Sat. Very popular.

☆ **Kadmo Lounge Bar** [204 B2] Kosta Abraš 9; ⏱ 09.00–01.00 (till 02.00 Fri–Sat). Named after the Phoenician Cadmus (page 200), this is a lakeside restaurant during the day & nightclub in the evening; also has a beach location at Biljana Springs [208 C7].

FIVE HUNDRED YEARS OF THE KANEVČE FAMILY AT KANEO

The Kanevče family came to Kaneo from Kičevo over 500 years ago in the late 1400s. They settled in the sheltered nook of the rocks of Kaneo still protected within the town walls, and quickly became wealthy lake fishermen after they bought the fishing rights for the northern half of the lake from Peštani to Kališta from the Ottomans. The family soon outgrew the small settlement at Kaneo and expanded into Ohrid itself where some of the early 19th-century houses still belong to the family, such as the one below Sv Sofija Church and their older houses on Kaneo Beach. Ohrid's abundant fishing and its position on a major trading route kept the Kanevče family busy up until the beginning of the 20th century.

Then with the Balkan wars, the division of Macedonia, the closed-door policies of early communism, and the negative effects of a bloated and over-centralised socialism, the luck of the Kanevče family went downhill. Stefan Kanevče, who remembers those days of good fishing with his grandfather, is still a keen fisherman and will happily take you out fishing on the lake if you want. He's also a mine of knowledge on many things in Ohrid and Macedonia. But the fishing trade isn't what it used to be, and he and his family have little money now to renovate the beautiful but crumbling houses at Kaneo. His family, however, has the few rooms in Macedonia where you can actually stay in an original 19th-century house, complete with intricate wooden ceiling, closets and wardrobes. No heating and no television, only the sound of the waves of the lake to lull you to sleep at night.

WHAT TO SEE AND DO A first-time trip to Ohrid would be incomplete (and almost impossible) without seeing at least one church (even if only from the outside) and taking a walk along the lakeside boardwalk.

Beaches Most people come to Ohrid to go swimming in the pristine waters. In addition to the following popular places to take a dip around town, there are also some good beaches on the lakeshore south of Ohrid (page 216).

Biljana Springs [208 B7] Dedicated beach with lifeguards, children's play area & sand. Changing facilities available. Close to Cuba Libre café.
Kaneo [204 B7] Next to the Church of Sv Bogorodica. No dedicated changing facilities aside from the restaurant toilets outside. Sunloungers for those ordering from the café.
Labino [204 A4] Accessed via a walk through the forest or by boat. Still relatively quiet & out of the way at the time of writing. No facilities.

Historical sites
Tsar Samoil's Fortress [204 C3] (⊕ 09.00–19.00 daily; entry 30MKD) The fortress dates only from the end of the 10th century, but records from Livy and other ancient historians tell that a fortress has stood on the top of Ohrid Hill since at least the 3rd century BC and other findings go back even further. In 2002, a golden mask and glove similar to those found in Trebenište (see box, page 201) from the Paeonian period were found behind the fortress walls. Today much of the 3km fortified wall which enclosed the fortress can still be seen, although the inside of the fortress itself was mostly destroyed and is still awaiting restoration. Up until the Ottomans arrived in Ohrid in 1395, the town was completely enclosed within these great city walls, and only two gates, the Upper Gate [205 G3] and the Lower

Gate [204 C1], existed by which to enter the town. With the arrival of the Ottoman Turks the town expanded beyond its walls, with the Christian population within the town walls, and the Ottoman Turkish population outside it.

Mesokastro [205 G3] The Turks meanwhile built up what came to be known as the Lower Town of the Mesokastro area. There you will find two working mosques, the Zeynel Abedin Mosque and Ali Pasha's Mosque, astride the **900-year-old plane tree** (*Platanus orientalis*) known locally as Činar in the middle of Kruševska Republika Square. Allegedly, this tree's hollow trunk used to house a barber's shop at sometime in its history and later a very small café. As the old Turkish town winds around the back of the town wall you can still see a few old Turkish shops which are no longer in use, but their dust-covered artefacts and tools are still on display. These may not be around for much longer as new buildings encroach.

Roman theatre [204 D3] The Roman theatre near the Upper Gate is just over 2,000 years old, but had been buried for centuries until, in the early 20th century, trial excavations confirmed its location. The next few decades of turmoil put the full excavation on hold, until in the 1960s the excavations finally got going again. By the 1990s the amphitheatre was fully uncovered and is now once again being used in the summer as in days of old for outdoor concerts and performances. If you manage to attend a concert here, take a close look at your seat to see if you can decipher the name of the season ticket holder who owned that seat thousands of years ago.

Museums and galleries
National Museum of Ohrid [204 B1] (Tsar Samoil; \267 173; ☉ 10.00–14.00 & 18.00–21.00 Tue–Sun) The museum was first established in 1516 in Sv Kliment's Church of Bogorodica Perivleptos as a museum to the Archbishopric of Ohrid. This must make it one of the oldest museums in the world. Now the collection is divided into the archaeological display housed in the Robev residence and the ethnographic display housed in the Urania residence. The Robevi house on Tsar Samoil is the renovated wooden three-storey house, which is a museum piece in itself, and one of the finest examples of 19th-century Macedonian architecture in the land; well worth a visit.

Icon Gallery [205 E4] (\ 251 395, 262 498; ☉ 09.00–17.00 Tue–Sun; entry 100MKD) Within the grounds of Sv Bogorodica Perivleptos Church, this gallery displays some of the most valuable – and beautiful – icons of the 11th to 19th centuries saved from churches all over Macedonia.

Churches and monasteries According to legend recorded by the Turkish chronicler Evlija Čelebi in the 17th century, there were once 365 churches within the city boundaries. While that is not so now, if ever it was, there are a lot of churches still within the old walls. Here are six of the most important within the town to start you off, Sv Sofija being by far the most significant. Details of many more of the lesser churches can be found in various booklets available in most of the church shops and bookshops in Ohrid. Many of the churches require an entry fee of around 100MKD per person. In those few that do not charge an entry fee it is customary to leave some money at the altar or icons anyway.

Sv Sofija [204 A2] The church was built in the early 11th century as a cathedral church for Archbishop Leo of the Archbishopric of Ohrid. It was also built on the remains of a former basilica. It still contains a few fragments of rare 11th- and 12th-century Byzantine frescoes (see box, page 150). Much of the original fresco work was destroyed when the church became a mosque in 1466 (page 201). During the Bulgarian occupation of Ohrid in the second Balkan War of 1913, the mosque was used as a warehouse, then reconverted to a church at the end of that war.

As a mosque the inside of the cathedral had been completely whitewashed and so it took extensive work during the second half of the 20th century to retrieve the 11th-century frescoes that lay underneath. Most of these are now on display again, as well as some of those from later renovations of the church in the 12th and 14th centuries. Sv Sofija is one of only two churches in the world to display such a high number of well-preserved 11th-century frescoes. The other is Sv Sophia in Kiev.

Sv Kliment at Plaošnik [204 C5] Dedicated to saints Kliment (Clement) and Pantelejmon, this was completed in 2002. It stands beside the original site of Kliment's very own monastery school, started in AD893. Kliment had built the original church on the ruins of the early 5th-century basilica at Plaošnik, and had even built his own tomb into the church, in which he was buried upon his death in AD916. Almost 150 graves were recently found and suggest that the church was also a hospital during Kliment's time.

The church was renovated and enlarged three times in the 12th, 13th and 14th centuries, but during the time of Ottoman rule it was transformed into the Imater Mosque. Sv Kliment's relics were then hastily moved to the 10th-century Church of Sveta Bogorodica Perivleptos. The mosque did not survive the end of the Ottoman Empire and after its destruction only the legend remained that Sv Kliment's monastery and his tomb used to stand at Plaošnik.

Excavations started in 1943, and it was not long before the foundations of the church, the basilica and the tomb were found. Frescoes from the renovation and enlargement periods have also been found, but none from the original 9th-century church. The foundations of the 5th-century basilica have been preserved and are on display in front of the new church. Excavations continue, and there is discussion in the town about restarting a theology university at the site.

Sv Bogorodica Perivleptos (Sv Kliment's Church of the Holy Mother of God Most Glorious) [205 E4] Built in 1294–95, this church is an identical replica of the Panagia Bellas Church in Boulgareli, Epirus, almost 200km to the south in Greece. It took on the Sv Kliment prefix only when Sv Kliment's relics were transferred here during the Ottoman Empire. At the same time the church became the cathedral of the archbishop when the original cathedral at Sv Sofija was converted into a mosque. By the end of the 15th century the cathedral had started to become a collection point for historical records and artefacts saved from other churches around Ohrid. In 1516 the cathedral's collection and its library became the archbishopric museum, which is now the National Museum of Ohrid housed in the Robev residence (see opposite).

In the 1950s, centuries of smoke and soot from candles and incense were carefully cleaned from the frescoes to reveal some interesting examples of late medieval painting. Look out for the fresco of the Last Supper, which is being eaten outside rather than inside, and note the use of perspective from Byzantine renaissance painting of the late 12th century as opposed to the older style still employed in many of the more traditional churches. In the grounds of the church is the Icon Gallery, and the late 19th-century town house now housing the Office of the Protection of Ohrid (despite the fact that it itself looks run-down and inactive).

Sv Jovan Kaneo [204 A6] This is the most frequently visited church in Ohrid because of its beautiful location on the cliffs directly above the lake. It was built at the end of the 13th century by an unknown benefactor, but shows signs of both Byzantine and Armenian influence. Inside, a group fresco of the 3rd-century Sv Erasmus, believed to be one of the first missionaries to the area, together with the 9th-century Sv Kliment and the early 14th-century Archbishop Constantine Kavacila of Ohrid, betrays the eclectic nature of the church. Despite being built around the same time as Sv Kliment's Church of Sv Bogorodica Perivleptos, it was painted in the older style of pre-Byzantine renaissance frescoes.

This church features visibly in Mančevski's *Before the Rain*, a must-see film about Macedonia (page 360). Behind the church, a small path leads up to Sv Kliment's Church at Plaošnik. Tucked away in the rock below the entrance to the church grounds is also the very small cave Church of Sv Bogorodica.

Sv Bogorodica Bolnička and Sv Nikola Bolnički [204 C2] These are to be found on either side of a small lane leading from the Lower Gate of the town wall to the lake. Both were built in the 14th century and were originally hospital churches (*bolnica* in Macedonian), separated into the women's hospital of the Virgin Mary and the men's hospital of Sv Nikola. The men's hospital is some 70 years older than the women's and is an interesting construction of an older church inside a newer one. Both back on to the town wall, parts of which can still be found in the church grounds. Sv Nikola is usually closed, but well worth a look – ask Slavica next door at the women's hospital to open the heavy walnut doors for you.

Local artisan arts and crafts Ohrid is home to many painters, sculptors, woodcarvers and other artisans hidden away in narrow streets. For **silver filigree**, check out local jewellery maker Marta Pejoska (daughter of a prominent local artist, the late Živko Pejoski) at Tsar Samoil 52 [204 B2] (m 070 691 251; e martapejoska@ gmail.com) or sixth-generation craftsman Vangel Dereban at Sv Kliment Ohridski 40. The Marinov family have a century-long tradition of making **copper** products in Ohrid [204 C2] (Kosta Abraš 44; m 078 375 760; w marinovohrid.com). **Paintings and artwork** can be found in many galleries in the old town (keep an eye out for work by local artist Vangel Naumovski, 1924–2006). **Ohrid pearls** made from the scales of local fish are sold in many shops along Kliment Ohridski. More information on the traditional crafts of Ohrid can be found at w ohrid.com.mk/ information/ohrid/handicrafts.

Artisans
Anastas Dudan Metal Platework [208 B5]
Jane Sandanski 14; ☎ 264 804; m 070 501 573;
e dudan1@t.mk; w anastasdudan.com.mk;
⊕ 09.00–20.00 daily. Anastas is a skilled & unique craftsman in producing art on metal sheets, be they copper, silver, gold or plated. His small shop offers a variety of icons, pictures, mirrors & plated books, but he can also produce work to order in 2–3 days, if you provide him with a picture of the image you want him to produce. His work has been presented to the famous & beatified, including several popes.
National Workshop for Handmade Paper
[204 B1] Tsar Samoil 60; ☎ 223 231; m 078

266 789; e contact@ohridhandmadepaper.mk;
w ohridhandmadepaper.mk; ⊕ 08.30–21.00 daily. Fascinating little shop with 1 of only 2 replicas of the Gothenburg press. Paper is handmade, hand-printed in the press & sold in the shop.

Galleries
Gallery Bukefal [205 G4] Sv Kliment Ohridski 54; ☎ 264 052; m 070 232 459; e contact@ bukefal.com.mk; w bukefal.com.mk. Longstanding gallery showing work by local artists. There are also Bukefal galleries in Struga & Skopje.

Ohrid pearls

Filevi Pearls [204 C2] Kosta Abraš 13;
m 070 590 822; e mihajlo_filev@yahoo.com;
w ohridpearl.com. With a tradition stretching back
to 1928, & clients include Queen Silvia of Sweden.
In addition to the original shop there are now
branches at Tsar Samoil 20 & Ilindenska 40.
Ohridski Biser [205 G4] (Talev family jewellers)
Kliment Ohridski 64; m 070 261 216, 071 261 216;
w ohridskibiser.com.mk. The Talev family have
been making Ohrid pearls for 80 years, including
work for Queen Elizabeth II.

Woodcarving

The workshops below specialise in traditional
walnut wood, floral & other motifs, similar to those
in many churches, but mainly for home decoration.
You can see the woodcarvers at work.

Milanoski Woodcarving Workshop [208 B2]
7-mi Noemvri 157; m 075 931 362
Tron Woodcarving [204 B2] Tsar Samoil (near
Villa Germanoff); m 075 362 581/3

Walking along the lakeside

Heading south out of Ohrid along Kej Maršal Tito is particularly pleasant in the evening when the sun is setting on the lake. Sometimes there are buskers and street performers on the quayside, and in the summer there is also a Luna Park with rides, trampolines, and a bouncy castle for children. At the end of the quay (1.3km from the centre's main street, Makedonski Prosvetiteli) is the yacht club AMAC SP-BOFOR and the Biljana Springs estuary [208 B7], renowned for its refreshing drinking water, which is bottled and sold throughout Macedonia. For more information on the yacht club's membership, docking fees and yacht hire, see page 97.

On the far side of the small bridge over the Biljana Springs estuary is the Army Water Training Centre, which has a beautiful little beach with a view on to Ohrid town, Tsar Samoil's Fortress and the Church of Sv Jovan Kaneo. Cuba Libre and Kadmo café-bars and nightclubs are also here. The next 1.7km along the lake goes through partially wooded grounds away from the main road to the Hotel Park. Cyclists and rollerbladers frequent the path and there are several little entry points to the lake. At Hotel Park, the path skirts around Tito's summer residence, which sits atop the promontory that marks the south end of Ohrid Bay. It is now used by the government of Macedonia for officials visiting the country and so is not open to visitors.

Heading north out of Ohrid old town, past the Church of Sv Jovan Kaneo, is a pleasant walk for about 500m to the back of the town. There is plenty of exploring to be done among the old wall and fortress, with splendid lake views.

Festivals and events in Ohrid

Summer is the big festival season for Ohrid, and the programme for most of the events can be seen on the events calendar at w ohrid.com.mk. The season kicks off in the first weekend in July with the **Balkan Festival of Folk Song and Dance**, which was founded in 1962 and is part of the UNESCO-associated International Council of Organisations of Folklore Festivals and Folk Art. Despite its name, this festival includes song and dance from around the world. The **Ohrid International Swimming Marathon** comes to town in August, in which select international swimmers are invited to test their strength against a 30km course from Sv Naum to Ohrid.

From mid-July to mid-August is the **Ohrid Summer Festival**, which will be 60 years old in 2021. Classical concerts and plays are held in historical and outdoor locations around the town, such as in the amphitheatre, basilicas, churches and Tsar Samoil's Fortress. The **Ohrid Folklore Festival** (w iffom.com) also takes place over mid-July to mid-August, while the five-day **Ohrid Choir Festival** (w ohridchoirfestival.com) is in early August. The **Ilinden Sailing Regatta** is held on Ilinden (2 August).

The 30km stretch of Lake Ohrid's eastern lakeshore that runs south from Ohrid town to the Albanian border is well worth exploring. Its most popular and worthwhile attraction is the medieval monastery of Sv Naum, which practically lies on the border with Albania, but there are also good beaches at the villages of Lagadin, Peštani and Trpejca, while cultural attractions include the Museum of the Lake at the Bay of Bones, and the Monastery and cave church of Sv Stefan. The lakeshore road to Sv Naum also provides access to the main road cutting across the hiker-friendly heights of Galičica National Park to the western shore of Lake Prespa. All the sites described in this section are easily visited as a day trip out of Ohrid town, but plenty of lakeside accommodation is available to those who prefer to base themselves out of town

GETTING AROUND

By road The 30km road from Ohrid to Sv Naum via the eastern lakeshore is quite narrow and sometimes gets busy, so allow 45 minutes for the drive. It is covered by regular buses that are best picked up on the southwest side of the roundabout at the junction of Turistička Boulevard and Jane Sandanski. Buses from Ohrid to Peštani via Sv Stefan and Lagadin leave every 30 minutes or so between 05.50 and 21.30. At least five buses daily continue on Sv Naum via Trpejca, leaving Ohrid at 05.00, 06.00, 12.15, 15.30 and 18.30, and starting the trip back north at 07.15, 08.00, 13.15, 16.30 and 17.15. There are usually more buses in summer, and these are often supplemented by shared taxi. Private taxis can all be chartered and are not prohibitively expensive.

By boat In summer, usually from June to September, a daily return boat service runs from the main quay in Ohrid to Sv Naum. It usually leaves Ohrid at 10.00, and arrives in Sv Naum 45 minutes later, stopping en route at the Park, Granit, Metropol and Desaret hotels. It starts the return trip at 16.30, but check this with the captain when you arrive. Most hotels also post the boat times. There are also many private boats that take groups to and from Sv Naum.

SV STEFAN AND SURROUNDS Just 5km outside Ohrid, the village of Sv Stefan has a pretty setting backed by Galičica National Park and is flanked by some of the most attractive upmarket beach hotels on the lakeshore. Sv Stefan is best known, however, as the site of the eponymous monastery and cave church, which are hidden away above the lake 500m from the lake road.

 Where to stay

 Hotel Inex Gorica [217 D1] (125 rooms) Naum Ohridski St, 2km north of Sv Stefan; ☎277 520; e marketing@hotelinexgorica.com.mk; w hotelinexgorica.com.mk. Pleasant & high quality. Access to 3 small beaches & a café pavilion on the water. **$$$$**

LAKESHORE SOUTH OF OHRID
For listings, see from page 216, unless otherwise stated

🛏 **Where to stay**

1	Dva Bisera *p219*	A3
2	Camp Gradiste	D4
3	Elesec Campsite *p220*	A4
4	Granit	A2
5	Inex Gorica	D1
6	Lagadin *p219*	A3
7	Ljubaništa Camp	C7
8	Metropol Lake Resort	A2
9	Ohrid Apartment & Studio *p220*	A3
10	Robinson Sunset House *p220*	A3
11	Sv Naum	A5
12	Sv Stefan Guesthouse	A3
13	Tino Sv Stefan	A1
14	Vila Katerina *p220*	A3
15	Villa Aleksandar	D1
16	Villa Sandra *p220*	A3

✖ **Where to eat and drink**

	Dva Bisera	(see 1)
17	Gostilnica Kaj Mece	A2
18	Ostrovo	A5
19	Skapa Grill *p220*	A3
20	Vila Dionis *p220*	A3

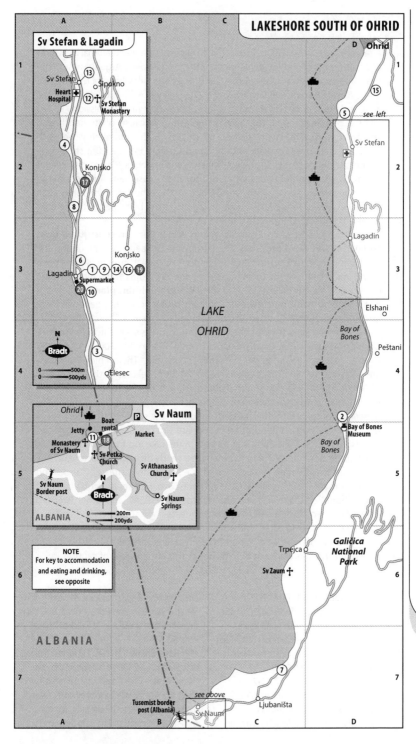

Sv Stefan & Lagadin

Ohrid

D

1

Sv Stefan
Heart Hospital
Sipokno
13
12
Sv Stefan Monastery

15

5
see left

4

Konjsko
17

Sv Stefan

2

8

Konjsko
6
Lagadin
Supermarket
1 9 14 16 19
20 10

3

Lagadin

Elshani

LAKE
OHRID

Bay of Bones

Peštani

N
Bradt
0   500m
0   500yds

3

Elesec

Bay of Bones

Sv Naum

Ohrid
Boat rental
P
Jetty
11
18
Market
Monastery of Sv Naum
Sv Petka Church
Sv Athanasius Church

Bay of Bones Museum
2

Bay of Bones

Sv Naum Border post
Sv Naum Springs
N
Bradt
0   200m
0   200yds

ALBANIA

Galičica National Park

Trpejca

Sv Zaum

6

NOTE
For key to accommodation
and eating and drinking,
see opposite

ALBANIA

7

7

Tusemist border post (Albania)
see above
Sv Naum
Ljubaništa

A   B   C   D

A tectonic lake almost 300m in depth with endemic plant and animal life, Ohrid offers a number of underwater attractions to the scuba diver. Arguably one of the most interesting sites is the submerged Bronze Age stilt village of Michovgrad in the **Bay of Bones** near Peštani (page 220). The site is a nationally protected area, and experienced divers may explore underwater with permission.

As a geological area, the lake is interesting because of its depth and steep drop-offs. The steepest drop-off closest to the shoreline is beneath the karst cliffs over Gradište and Sv Zaum Church. Here, a 20m sheer wall shelters endemic plants, freshwater mussels and sponges. *Plašica*, *belvica* and gudgeon are plentiful to see when diving, and occasionally it is possible to see some *mrenka* and crayfish. Ohrid trout, on the other hand, are rarely seen as they live deep in the lake. Night diving offers the best chance to see eels, as well as chub and larger fish coming up to feed.

Just south of Struga is a sunken **World War II German coastguard boat** and two **World War I tugboats**. The latter were deliberately sunk during the war to stop them getting into enemy hands. An Ottoman Empire rifle has been found in the lake (see the town museum, page 212), and on the Albanian side of the water there is believed to be a small **World War II aeroplane**. A project is ongoing to try to find part of the Via Egnatia, which is believed to lie somewhere underwater between Struga and Ohrid around Sv Erasmus Church.

All of these sites (except the aeroplane) can be seen through **Amfora Dive Centre**, based at Gradište (Lazo Trposki 35a; m 070 700 865, 071 359 810; e sekuloski@yahoo.com; w amfora.com.mk). Their chief instructor and divemaster, English-speaking Miko (Milutin Sekuloski, the discoverer of Michovgrad), has done over 5,000 dives in Lake Ohrid, and is also the Macedonian army's special forces diving instructor. As with diving anywhere, take care not to disturb the lake bed: not only is the sandy bottom very easily disturbed, causing a deterioration in visibility, but the lake's endemic species are also vulnerable. Visibility is at its best in the lake (up to 22m) during May and September. You will need to purchase a yearly dive licence before diving. Thereafter the dive fee to Michovgrad is €30; all other sites €20, including all equipment. Tank refill is €10. Amfora Dive Centre is Scuba Schools International certified and will also accept PADI, BSAC and other licensed divers. Diving courses are available on request.

Check you are satisfied with the equipment provided before diving. A diving buddy of mine who is a British army diving instructor noticed on our dive that the tanks were out of date, hence this added word of caution.

Metropol Lake Resort [217 A2] (370 rooms) Konjsko, 2km south of Sv Stefan; ✆ 203 001; e info@metropol-ohrid.com.mk; w metropol-ohrid.com.mk. Sprawling lakeside resort comprising 3 hotels (Metropol, Bellevue & Turist), complete with casino, nightclub, etc. **$$$$**

✳ **Villa Aleksandar** [217 D1] (12 apts) Naselba Rača; ✆ 261 644; m 070 391 125; e reception@aleksandarvilla.com.mk; w aleksandarvilla.com.mk. Colonial in style, this

luxurious hotel & spa complex is 2km north of Sv Stefan & 3km from the centre of Ohrid. Only 100m from the water, it backs on to Galičica National Park. **$$$$**

Hotel Granit [217 A2] (233 rooms) 1km south of Sv Stefan; ✆ 207 100; w hotelgranit.com.mk. Despite its name, this is a pleasant, large hotel with direct access to the lake & a jetty for boats. Lakeside rooms are subjected to the café music & evening conferences or events spilling on to the lawn. Paddle boats on the beach are 200MKD per hr. Suites are better value for money for 2 ppl sharing. $$$

🏠 **Hotel Tino Sv Stefan** [217 A1] (52 rooms) Sv Stefan, at the junction for the monastery; 📞 209 340; e tino_svstefan@t-home.mk; w hoteltino-svstefan. com. Sister hotel to its namesake on Ohrid Quay, this occupies a rather cramped compound but the setting is lovely, the rooms are well equipped & good value & there's a pleasant swimming pool area. $$$

✳ 🏠 **Sv Stefan Guesthouse** [217 A1] Sv Stefan Monastery; m 070 227 237, 076 440 435; e hotelmonastery@gmail.com. Attached to the monastery, this has a peaceful setting overlooking the lake through the treetops & pleasant clean rooms with AC, TV, fridge, Wi-Fi & semi-private balcony. Good value. B/fast not inc but only €2.50pp extra. $$

✗ Where to eat and drink
All the hotels listed above serve food but the local standout is:

✗ **Gostilnica Kaj Mece** [217 A2] Konjsko; m 078 350 955. Situated opposite the Metropol, this unpretentious small restaurant serves an

interesting selection of Macedonian specialities & has terrace & garden seating. Good value & highly recommended. $$

What to see and do
The original cave **church of Sv Stefan** [217 A1] (entry 60MKD) was built out from a crack in the rock face in the 9th century, at the time of Sv Kliment. Villagers from the surrounding settlements of Šipokno, Gorica and Konjsko up the hill have since built the present walls. The tiny but atmospheric church interior is adorned with 15th-century frescoes, many of which are still clearly discernible but quite faded.

The monastery is clearly signposted from alongside the Hotel Tino Sv Stefan, 4.5km from the petrol station on the eastern edge of Ohrid. A winding road now leads to a car park immediately below the monastery, but there is also a shorter and steeper footpath.

At the gateway into the monastery the path continues up above to the villages of Šipokno in the north and Konjsko in the south, and further hiking into Galičica National Park. Beware the Šarplaninec sheepdogs in the old and dying settlement of Šipokno, and note that the villagers don't like strangers wandering around on their own. Guided hikes to both villages can be arranged through Ohrid Adventures (page 206), which is based at Robinson Sunset House in nearby Lagadin.

There are two more cave churches on the eastern side of the lake: one at Sv Erasmus and Sv Ekaterina between Ohrid and Struga, and one on Gradište II beach at Gradište campsite near Peštani halfway to Sv Naum. There are good views of Lake Ohrid from these churches.

LAGADIN
This pretty village 9km south of Ohrid has a cracking setting sandwiched between a long stretch of pebble beach and the steep and well-wooded footslopes of the Galičica Mountains. There's lots of reasonably priced accommodation here, as well as restaurants and cafés, yet it still feels very low-key and untouristy in comparison to Ohrid. A variety of aquatic activities and hikes can be arranged through Robinson Sunset House, the home of Ohrid Adventures (page 206).

🏠 Where to stay
🏠 **Hotel Lagadin** [217 A3] (10 rooms) 📞 285 227; m 070 261 448; e dance@hotellagadin. com.mk; w hotellagadin.com.mk. Comfortable & attractively furnished rooms above a restaurant. $$$

🏠 **Hotel Dva Bisera** [217 A3] (7 rooms, 4 apts) 📞 285 920; m 076 280 900; e hoteldvabisera@yahoo.com; w hoteldvabisera. com.mk. Spacious modern lakeside rooms & apts set above a great terrace restaurant. $$

🏠 **Ohrid Apartment & Studio** [217 A3] (2-bedroom house, 1 apt) Lagadin 14; m 075 303 084, 070 278 566; w ohridforever.com. Up on the hill behind the main bustle of little Lagadin, the pleasant garden & seating area offers a view of the lake. **$$**

✳ 🏠 **Robinson Sunset House** [217 A3] (12 rooms, 2 dorms) Lagadin; m 075 727 252, 078 931 533; e andon_mise@yahoo.com, mise_ohrid@yahoo.com; w robinsonsunset. com. Situated in the forested hills above Lagadin (a steep 5min walk from the village), this family-run gem is an oasis of calm with its big garden, panoramic views & home-cooked food. You can arrange for them to pick you up from the bus station in Ohrid for 200MKD, or jump on a bus. The hands-on owner-managers can arrange a wide variety of hikes & aquatic activities. Chilled out

& sociable vibe. Dorm beds cost €12 & are very popular with backpackers looking to stay outside the city. **$$**

🏠 **Vila Katerina** [217 A3] (8 apts) Lagadin; m 070 273 926; e info@villakaterina.mk; w villakaterina.mk. Supremely stylish apts with balconies & kitchenettes. **$$**

🏠 **Villa Sandra** [217 A3] (6 apts) ☎285 624; m 070 200 356; w visitohrid.org/booking/villa-sandra. Spacious apts, dbl & trpl rooms. View & sounds of the lake from the balcony. Lagadin Beach, a shop & restaurants are a few mins away. **$$**

🏕 **Elesec Campsite** [217 A4] (70 tent spaces) 1km south of Lagadin; ☎285 926. Pleasant lakeshore campsite. Around 500MKD per tent space plus 50MKD tourism tax pp. **$**

✖ Where to eat and drink

✖ **Dva Bisera** [217 A3] ☎285 920; m 076 280 900. Attached to the eponymous hotel, this is arguably the best restaurant in Lagadin, with a lovely terrace perfectly positioned to catch the sunset over the lake. It's renowned for its fish stew & other Macedonian village fare (**$$$**) but also serves a varied selection of cheaper grills (**$$**).

✖ **Vila Dionis** [217 A3] m 077 732 414. Pleasantly leafy garden restaurant set around a small swimming pool. Specialises in traditional Macedonian stews & grills. **$$**

✖ **Skapa Grill** [217 A3] Lagadin's most attractively situated eatery stands on a stony beach shaded by tall cypresses. Aimed mainly at a local market, it serves inexpensive burgers & grills as well as coffee & beer. **$**

PEŠTANI AND THE BAY OF BONES The most substantial village of the east shore south of Ohrid, Peštani lies just 3km south of Lagadin. It has an attractive long promenade, several apartment complexes and restaurants, and is also where most buses heading south from Ohrid terminate. Two well-known local landmarks, nestled together about 2km to its south, are the perennially popular Campsite Gradište and the so-called Bay of Bones, a submerged archaeological site that now houses a fascinating open-air museum.

🏠 Where to stay

🏕 **Camp Gradište** [217 D4] (100 tent spaces, 20 c/vans, 8 bungalows) ☎285 945; e campgradiste@ gmail.com; w hoteldvabisera.com.mk. Located 2km south of Peštani & immediately north of the Bay of Bones, this large campsite stands on a long

& scenic stretch of beach with several ball courts. It tends to be crowded in peak season & closes during the winter. 500MKD per tent space plus 50MKD tourism tax pp. **$**

What to see and do Also known as the Museum of the Lake, the **Bay of Bones Museum** [217 D5] (🕘 09.00–19.00 daily; entry 100MKD) is a recreation of a submerged 3,200-year-old Bronze Age stilt village that was discovered in 1997 and named Michovgrad after the diver who found it. Set on a stilted wooden platform, the museum comprises a dozen or so mud-and-thatch huts built in the original style, and houses broken amphora and other items uncovered below the water. A popular and worthwhile stop en route between Ohrid and Sv Naum.

Kliment (Clement, AD840–916) and Naum (AD835–910), like the brothers Kiril and Metodi, were native Macedonians. Both had been disciples of the brothers and travelled with them on their pioneering journey to Moravia in Hungary, to teach the Slavs in their own language, which brought about the invention of the Glagolitic and Cyrillic scripts. The diaries of both men have been passed on through the ages, the best-known of which are the Extensive Hagiography and the Short Hagiography of Sv Kliment.

Kliment would have been 22 when he accompanied Kiril and Metodi to Moravia, and 46 by the time he came to the Ohrid region to teach the Scriptures here. In 893 at the age of 53 he was appointed Bishop of Velika, a large swathe of land reaching up to the River Treška around Kičevo, by Tsar Simeon of the new Bulgarian state recently freed from Byzantium. As a result of his new duties he had to move from his original monastery up in the wilds, north of Ohrid, into Ohrid itself where he founded a new monastery, the Monastery of Sv Kliment, and asked for his former fellow disciple, Naum, to join him in order to help teach the Scriptures to their ever-increasing congregation. They mostly taught in the Glagolitic script, which only fully died out to be replaced by the dominant Cyrillic script in the 12th century.

The diaries record that over 3,500 pupils attended the Monastery of Sv Kliment, and numbers became so demanding that Naum set up the Monastery of Sv Naum in 900 at the other end of the lake. When he died in 910, he was buried in the vaults of the church, and it is believed that if you stand over his crypt and put your ear to the wall, you will hear Naum's heart beating even today.

TRPEJCA Set in a pretty sheltered bay that slopes downhill from the main Ohrid–Naum road 7km south of Peštani, the tiny lakeshore hamlet of Trpejca is known for its small but very pretty pebble beach. There's a mooring deck from which to dive into the lake, and boat trips to other small nearby beaches, as well as to the **church of Sv Zaum** [217 C6], can be arranged for around 100MKD. The village is popular as a lunch stop after a morning visit to Sv Naum thanks to its lakeside restaurants, the best-known of which is the legendary Ribar Trpejca (m 070 249 472; $$$), which – as suggested by its name (literally 'fish') – specialises in whole grilled fish, ideally accompanied by local white wine.

SV NAUM Situated 30km south of Ohrid at the south end of the lake near the border with Albania, the medieval Monastery of Sv Naum is a beautiful and popular site, and well worth visiting, whether you do so as a day trip from Ohrid or elsewhere on the lake, or stay overnight at its attractive inn. In addition to housing a handsome 16th-century church adorned with ancient frescoes, the well-kept grounds are home to a flock of peacocks, and incorporate the springs that form the main source of Lake Ohrid.

Where to stay

Hotel Sv Naum [217 A5] (28 rooms) 283 080; e info@hotel-stnaum.com.mk; w hotel-stnaum.com.mk. Your chance to stay in the holy grounds where Sv Naum himself taught & preached. Situated at the south end of the lake, the monastery is tranquil at night but can be just as busy as Ohrid during the day with visitors. The peacocks crow loudly early in the morning. $$$

⚠ Ljubaništa Camp [217 C7] (65 tent spaces)
☎ 283 240. This attractive beach campsite lies about
3km from Sv Naum in the village of Ljubaništa. **$**

✕ Where to eat and drink
✕ Restaurant Ostrovo [217 A5] ☎ 283 091;
📱 072 210 906; e ostrovo-svetinaum@hotmail.
com; w restoranostrovo.com.mk. Set in the shady
forest that lines Sv Naum Springs, this delightful
restaurant is the pick of a few places that line the
footpath between the car park & the monastery.
It serves a good selection of affordable grills (**$$**)
along with a few pricier specials (**$$$**).

What to see and do
Monastery of Sv Naum [217 A5] The actual early 10th-century Church of the
Holy Archangels built by Sv Naum is, in fact, buried beneath the present 16th-
century church, which stands in the middle of the monastery courtyards. The
church had been destroyed during Ottoman rule and its remains were rediscovered
only in 1955 when excavations beneath the present church floor were carried out.
The original church was a typical trefoil or clover-leaf design and contained the
tomb and relics of Sv Naum himself. These have been preserved and reinterred
beneath the new floor of the present church, which is now marked with black and
white marble to show the floor plan of the original 10th-century church.

The present church was enlarged in the 17th and 18th centuries, and in 1799 the
tiny chapel over Sv Naum's underground tomb was built. It has a cupola roof and the
interior is decorated with some well-preserved old paintings. When you enter the
chapel, which is to the right as you enter the narthex, and listen very carefully above
the tomb, you are said to be able to hear Sv Naum's heart still beating. Touching the
stone above the tomb is also meant to make a wish come true.

Sv Naum Springs [217 B5] Adjacent to the monastery but protected within
Galičica National Park is a field of 45 subterranean cold springs that bubble up into
a beautiful crystal-clear stream that flows into Lake Ohrid. The springs mostly bring
water from Lake Prespa, which stands 157m higher in altitude than Lake Ohrid, on
the other side of Galičica National Park, so the water is effectively siphoned through
the lower strata of the Galičica Mountains before emerging at Sv Naum. A boat trip
down the lushly vegetated river to the springs is available from Sv Naum. Trips and
boat numbers are limited by the Galičica National Park authorities as the springs
are a rare natural phenomenon and therefore it is important not to disturb the
ecological balance in the waters. This doesn't stop unlicensed boatmen from trying
to take surplus visitors in the busy summer months, so make sure you take a legal
ride. Expect to pay around 200MKD for the half-hour trip.

GALIČICA NATIONAL PARK
Founded in 1958, the 225km² Galičica National Park extends from Ohrid Lake
shore immediately west of Velestovo, through Velestevo village, around the peak of
Bigla at 1,663m and then down to the shores of Lake Prespa just east of the village
of Šurlenci. It includes all the land south of this line to the border of Albania. The
park also includes Lake Prespa's island of Golem Grad (page 258).

The park offers endless hikes in pristine countryside, although few of them are well
marked so be confident of your orienteering skills before you go into the park, or take
a guide. The top of the range plateaus out to a beautiful wide valley with a dirt vehicle
track running through it. Some old ski lifts go up to some of the peaks. The highest

TWO LAKES VIEW

Distance	3km north to Galičica 1,985m; 3.5km south to Albanian border ridgeline 2,100m, a further 3km along the ridge
Altitude	Livada Pass: 1,568m to highest point on Galičica range in Macedonia 2,275m
Rating	Easy to moderate: initially steep
Timing	To the viewpoint: north 1½ hours; south 2–3 hours
Alternative	2 hours to Bugarska Čuka from the plateau road
Trail head	Bus to Trpejca, taxi to Livada Pass
Map	1:25,000 SAGW Map Sheets Ohrid 780-4-3, Gorno Dupeni 780-4-4, Ljubaništa 830-2-1, Oteševo 830-2-2, January 2007

ROUTE DESCRIPTION The route north is a steep climb to reach the Galičica peak (✣ 8629 3648), and is the shortest way to gain the view of both Lake Ohrid and Lake Prespa. From Galičica peak, there is a good ridge walk all the way to Bugarska Čuka (5km, ✣ 8751 4018) that maintains the view of both lakes. The easier but slightly longer climb is to the south. This route is also to the highest point on the Galičica range inside Macedonia. The route is obvious at the bottom and peters out towards the top, but head towards the summit where you can see both lakes and then along the ridge.

peak completely in the park, Bugarska Čuka (meaning 'Bulgarian peak'), so named because it was held by the Bulgarian army during World War I, lies midway through the park, and from this peak there's a panoramic view of both Lake Ohrid and Lake Prespa. A new rangers' hut (✣ 8914 4265) has been built along the plateau road, some 2.5km from which is the small cave of Samatska Dupa. A mere 235m long, but high enough to walk through for the most part, it is one of the few caves in Macedonia that has electric lighting. The entrance to the cave is locked. To visit the cave with the lights turned on, arrange a tour with one of the tour agencies on page 203.

Almost 3km south of Trpejca village is the turn-off to the southern mountain pass of Livada at 1,568m. The winding asphalt road gives spectacular views of Lake Ohrid on one side and Lake Prespa on the other. From the pass, a 2-hour hike south on a marked path leads to the peak of the range on the border with Albania. Both Prespa and Ohrid lakes can also be seen from this point. On the Prespa side the road continues past the dishevelled holiday resort of Oteševo and on to Carev Dvor and Resen.

STRUGA

The town of Struga stands on the northern shore of Lake Ohrid some 15km northwest of Ohrid town. Also boasting human settlements going back to Neolithic times (3000BC), the old name of Struga is Enchelon, the ancient Greek word for eel, which is still a popular food in the area (page 230). The new name Struga comes from the old Slavic *straga* meaning 'cross', but some say it also comes from the word *struže* meaning 'blowing wind'. With just over 16,000 inhabitants in the town and 35,000 people in the municipality, Struga is less than half as populous as nearby Ohrid. Dwarfed in size and popularity by its neighbour, Struga is nevertheless an up-and-coming town and a delightful getaway from busy Ohrid in the height of the summer season, though it

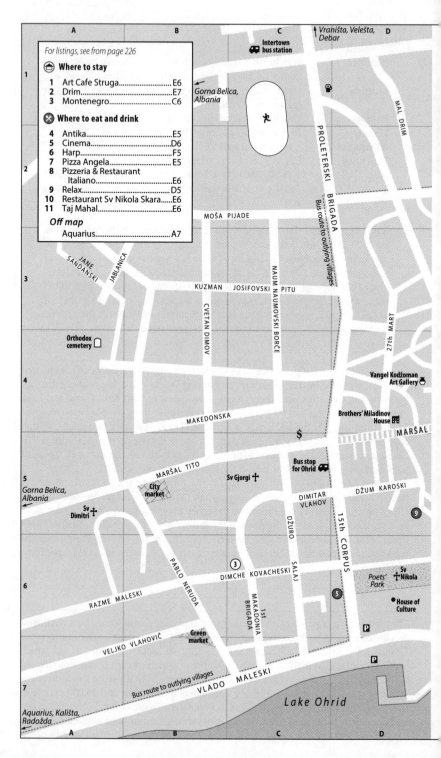

For listings, see from page 226

Where to stay

1 Art Cafe Struga...........................E6
2 Drim...E7
3 Montenegro..............................C6

Where to eat and drink

4 Antika.......................................E5
5 Cinema.....................................D6
6 Harp...F5
7 Pizza Angela.............................E5
8 Pizzeria & Restaurant
   Italiano..................................E6
9 Relax..D5
10 Restaurant Sv Nikola Skara......E6
11 Taj Mahal.................................E6

Off map
   Aquarius..................................A7

Vraništa, Velešta, Debar

Intertown bus station

Gorna Belica, Albania

MAL DRIM

PROLETERSKI BRIGADA

Bus route to outlying villages

MOŠA PIJADE

JANE SANDANSKI

JABLANICA

KUZMAN JOSIFOVSKI PITU

CVETAN DIMOV

NAUM NAUMOVSKI BORČE

27th MART

Orthodox cemetery

Vangel Kodžoman Art Gallery

MAKEDONSKA

Brothers' Miladinov House

MARŠAL

MARŠAL TITO

Bus stop for Ohrid

Gorna Belica, Albania

Sv Dimitri

City market

Sv Gjorgi

DIMITAR VLAHOV

DŽUM KAROSKI

9

DŽURO

15th CORPUS

Poets' Park

Sv Nikola

3

PABLO NERUDA

DIMCHE KOVACHESKI

SALAJ

5

House of Culture

RAZME MALESKI

MAKADONIA BRIGADA

1st

P

Green market

VELJKO VLAHOVIČ

P

Bus route to outlying villages

VLADO MALESKI

Lake Ohrid

Aquarius, Kališta, Radožda

224

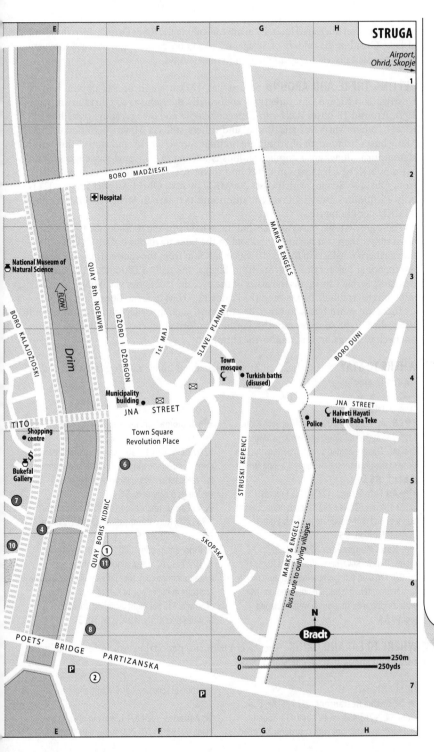

STRUGA

Airport,
Ohrid, Skopje

BORO MADŽIESKI

✚ Hospital

National Museum of
Natural Science

QUAY 8th NOEMVRI

FLOW

MARKS & ENGELS

BORO DUNI

Drim

BORO KALADŽIOSKI

DŽORD I DŽORGON

1st MAJ

SLAVEJ PLANINA

Town
mosque
☾   ● Turkish baths
           (disused)

Municipality
building
●   ⊠
⊠
JNA   STREET

JNA STREET
☾ Halveti Hayati
  Hasan Baba Teke
● Police

TITO

Shopping
● centre
$

Bukefal
Gallery

Town Square
Revolution Place

STRUSKI KEPENCI

⑦

⑥

④

QUAY BORIS KIDRIČ

⑩

①
⑪

SKOPSKA

MARKS & ENGELS

Bus route to outlying villages

N

⑧

POETS'   BRIDGE
            PARTIZANSKA

Bradt

0 ————————— 250m
0 ————————— 250yds

P

②

P

may suffer from uncleared litter. Its many cafés along the River Drim, which flows out of Lake Ohrid in the middle of Struga, make a good day or night out and there are some pleasant places to stay and to visit in the vicinity.

GETTING THERE AND AROUND Struga lies 172km south of Skopje via Tetovo, Gostivar and Kičevo, and directions are broadly the same as to Ohrid town (page 199). Around 18 buses daily run between Skopje and Struga, some travelling via Kičevo, others via Veles and Bitola, and others still via Mavrovo National Park. Many **buses** from north of Struga are on their way to Ohrid, and stop at the petrol station turn-off, where a kombe minibus is waiting to transport passengers for an extra 50MKD each the 15 minutes into town. It is less than half an hour's drive from Ohrid to Struga, which costs 300MKD by **taxi**; Ohrid Airport (page 202) is only 15 minutes away by taxi. The minimum taxi fare in Struga is 40MKD plus 30MKD per kilometre.

There are no town buses as such, but buses to Ohrid and to Radožda do pick up in town rather than you having to trek out to the inter-town bus station (780 770) at the northern outskirts of the town, which is 1.5km from the centre. There are several international bus services leaving from Struga: the daily 12.30 and 17.30 buses to Belgrade, Serbia (the first is the faster of the two; the latter goes via Skopje); the daily noon bus to Istanbul, Turkey; and the Friday 18.30 bus to Sofia, Bulgaria.

There are more buses to other destinations, such as Prilep, Štip, Strumica and Veles, during the summer months. For more information enquire at the bus station or check w struga.org/eng/authorities.htm.

WHERE TO STAY Struga has a number of lakefront hotels ranging from ten to 250 rooms in size.

In Struga

Drim [225 E7] (200 rooms) Kej Boris Kidrič 51; 785 800; e hdrim@t-home.mk; w drim. com.mk. Massive domed Soviet-style construction close to the town centre, the quay & a long stretch of beach. $$$

Art Cafe Struga [225 E6] (23 rooms) 783 109; m 070 442 192. Unpretentious central budget hotel with adequate rooms & a great riverside location. $$

Hotel Montenegro [224 C6] (20 rooms) Dimche Kovacheski 20; 780 330; m 078 370 074; e info@hotelmontenegro.mk; w hotelmontenegro.mk. Friendly medium-rise with comfortable, spacious & well-equipped rooms. $$

Around Struga

Diplomat [map, page 198] (43 rooms) Velešta village, 4km north of Struga; 793 022/720; m 070 212 507; e info@diplomatstruga. com; w diplomatstruga.com. Clean new rooms in a pleasant setting, but can be popular with weddings & banquets. $$

AS Camp [map, page 198] (500 tent spaces) 785 800. Huge lakeshore camping & c/van site 2km east of Struga. $

Rino [map, page 198] (15 tent spaces) m 072 743 260; e campingrino@gmail.com; w campingrino.com. Nice little family-run lakeside campsite in the village of Kališta, 4km southwest of Struga. €12 per night including use of all facilities (electricity, shower, Wi-Fi). $

WHERE TO EAT AND DRINK The River Drim and pedestrian zone offer lots of little pizza and snack places, cafés and bars.

Restaurants

Antika Restaurant [225 E5] Kej Boris Kidrič 34; 783 468; m 071 249 432. Superb Macedonian restaurant with cosy décor & a good

selection of soups, salads & traditional stews. $$$

Aquarius [224 A7] 1.5km out of town on Vlado Maleski; 780 273; w restaurantaquarius.

com; ◷ 08.00–01.00 daily. Bar-club-pizzeria rolled into one with a glitzy atmosphere overlooking the lake. Lots of blue lighting & an enviable boardwalk into the lake. $$$

✱ ✘ **Pizza Angela** [225 E5] Dimitar Vlahov 2; m 070 603 705; ◷ 11.00–23.00 daily. A small restaurant/pizzeria with modern blues music & rough-hewn wooden tables & chairs. Serves local dishes including *furnagiska* (a pastrmajlija or pitta bread base with pork or chicken, egg & cheese) & Turkish coffee. $$

✘ **Pizzeria & Restaurant Italiano** [225 E6] Kej Boris Kidrič; m 070 552 144. Well-priced pizza & pasta place with a pretty riverside location & pavement seating. $$

✘ **Restaurant Sv Nikola Skara** [225 E6] Goce Delčev 88; m 070 362 720; ◷ 11.00–01.00 daily.

A tiny grill joint on the river blessed with good food & friendly staff. $$

✘ **Taj Mahal** [225 E6] Kej Boris Kidrič 31, east bank; m 071 220 366; ◷ 11.00–01.00 daily. Not a curry in sight, but traditional Albanian food. $$

Cafés and bars

▽ **Cinema** [224 D6] 15th Corpus 41; ◷ 11.00–02.00 daily. Busy café-bar prior to going over to Glamour nightclub.

▽ **Harp** [225 F5] Kej Boris Kidrič, east bank; ◷ 11.00–01.00 daily. Some 8 years ago there was only 1 Irish pub in Macedonia, in Skopje; now they are in almost every town. This one offers the best margaritas in town, as well as a Guinness.

▽ **Relax** [224 D5] 15th Corpus 41; ◷ 08.00–01.00 daily. Popular waterfront bar.

WHAT TO SEE AND DO Struga offers a long pebble beach right in the centre of town, a lovely riverside walk from the lake through town along the River Drim, and a small, compact, pedestrian old town area. Aside from wandering around the narrow streets, here are a few noteworthy sites.

National Museum of Natural Science [225 E3] (Boro Kalajdžioski; ☎786 664; m 070 786 644, 070 782 487; e info@museumstruga.mk; w museumstruga.mk; ◷ 09.00–17.00 daily; entry free) The legacy of the late Dr Nikola Nezlobinski, this museum has over 10,000 examples of flora and fauna, local history, archaeology and ethnology from around Ohrid and Prespa. Mostly from his own collection and displayed in his original house, the collection is the best available on the region. Dr Nezlobinski, a Russian doctor who immigrated here in 1924 during Royalist Yugoslavia when Serbia encouraged many Russians to move to Macedonia, first put his collection on display in 1928. It is best to phone ahead to make sure or arrange for the museum to be open as it is often closed despite its alleged opening hours.

Vangel Kodžoman Art Gallery [224 D4] (Boro Kalajdžioski; m 070 786 644, 070 782 487; ◷ 09.00–17.00 daily; entry free) An annexe to the Natural Science museum (see above), this gallery houses Kodžoman's paintings of old Struga. He was one of the founders of the Society of Macedonia Artists and his work has been recognised with several awards.

Brothers Miladinov House [224 D4] (Maršal Tito; ☎786 270; e struga@svp.org. mk; open by prior appointment only) This beautifully restored old town house hosts the Struga Poetry Evenings Collection (page 228).

Church of Sv Gjorgi [224 C5] On the western edge of the old town, this was built in 1835 in the grounds of an older, 16th-century church, which contains a number of icons dating back to the 13th century, including one of Sv Gjorgi from 1267.

Halveti Hayati Hasan Baba Teke [225 H4] (Turistička, next to the police station) This small dervish inn and mosque was built in the first half of the 18th century at the request of Hasan Baba of the Halveti order of dervishes. The Halveti

sect (originating from their founder Omer Halveti from 14th-century Iran and Afghanistan) are renowned for cultivating a quiet and more introverted following than some of the other dervish sects.

Town mosque and disused Turkish baths [225 G4] (Next to the post office on JNA St) Badly in need of renovation before it is lost forever, but if other renovations in the town are anything to go by, then this could be due soon, and will most likely end up as an art gallery. Worth noting on the way to the teke.

Festivals and events The **Struga Poetry Evenings** (w svp.org.mk) is an international festival held every year in mid to late August in the beautifully restored

MILADINOV'S 'LONGING FOR THE SOUTH'

The Miladinov brothers, Dimitrija (1810–62), Naum (1817–95) and Konstantin (1830–62), were pioneers in re-establishing the supremacy of the Macedonian language in Macedonia during a time when Greek had been brought into Macedonian schools and sermons. Dimitrija was a prominent Macedonian-language teacher and struggled daily for the Ottoman authorities to recognise the Macedonian language. His brother Naum was a distinguished musician, and his youngest brother Konstantin became one of Macedonia's most famous poets with his poem 'Longing for the South' ('T'ga za Jug', in Macedonian), written while studying in Russia. T'ga za Jug is now the name of a popular Macedonian wine and of numerous restaurants throughout Macedonia. Dimitrija and Konstantin both died in prison in 1862 for their efforts to bring the Macedonian language officially back to Macedonia. Their efforts were not wasted, however, and seven years later, in 1869, the Greek schools in the Ohrid region were finally shut down.

Longing for the South

If I had an eagle's wings
I would rise and fly with them
To our own shores, to our own climes,
To see Stamboul, to see Kukuš,
And to watch the sunrise: is it
Dismal there, as it is here?
If the sun still rises dimly,
If it meets me there as here,
I'll prepare for further travels,
I shall flee to other shores
Where the sunrise greets me brightly
And the sky is strewn with stars.
It is dark here, dark surrounds me,
Dark fog covers all the earth;
Here are frosts and snows and ashes,
Blizzards and harsh winds abound.
Fog everywhere, the earth is ice,

And in the breast are cold, dark thoughts.
No, I cannot stay here, no,
I cannot look upon these frosts.
Give me wings and I will don them;
I will fly to our own shores,
Go once more to our own places,
Go to Ohrid and to Struga.
There the sunrise warms the soul,
The sunset glows on wooded heights;
There are gifts in great profusion
Richly spread by nature's power.
Watch the clear lake stretching white
Or bluely darkened by the wind,
Look upon the plains or mountains:
Beauty's everywhere divine.
To pipe there to my heart's content!
Ah! Let the sun set, let me die.

Konstantin Miladinov (1830–62). Translated by Graham W Reid.

Brothers Miladinov House (page 227). Always opened with Konstantin Miladinov's famous *Longing for the South*, the poetry evenings were started in 1962, exactly 100 years after the death of two of the brothers. Recitals take place throughout the town on the bridges over the Crni Drim. At the beginning of August is the festival of **Kengo jeho** (meaning 'Songs' Echo') celebrating Albanian songs and dances from Macedonia and the regions. **Lake Day** is celebrated on 21 June with kayak races, music and food stalls. A festival of Byzantine music, the **Struga Autumn of Music**, takes place in the second half of autumn.

OTHER SHORT TRIPS FROM OHRID AND STRUGA

KALIŠTA AND RADOŽDA The picturesque lakeside villages of Kališta and Radožda are respectively situated 5km and 10km southwest of Struga on the Ohrid's western shore. Both villages are the site of interesting cave churches and Radožda is also renowned for its row of lakeside restaurants. Both can both be reached by car from the turn-off at Frangovo on the E850, or by taking the coastal road from Struga. By far the most attractive way to get here though is by boat taxi from Ohrid town, as it is quite impressive to see the cliffs and church loom up over the village. A boat taxi from Ohrid will cost you €30 for the round trip whether there is one passenger or six, but the boat will wait for you and your party to finish your half-day around Radožda before taking you back to Ohrid. Buses to the villages leave from Struga at 06.15, 09.00, 13.00, 15.00 and 19.00.

Kališta The small settlement and monastery complex of Kališta is located right on the shores of the lake 5km from Struga, next to the Hotel Biser. The monastery is the summer residence of Archbishop Naum, the highest church official in the Holy Synod of the Macedonian Orthodox Church. Within the monastery complex is the **cave Church of Sv Bogorodica** (entry 120MKD), where frescoes date back as far as the 15th century. Access to the church is often closed, so ask for the key at the monastery.

A 500m walk south of the monastery along the shore is the tiny **cave Church of Sv Atanas** set high in the cliffs. The steps up to the church are not for those who suffer from severe vertigo, and one would be hard pushed to deliver a service inside the church to a congregation of more than half a dozen people.

Where to stay and eat *Map page 198*

🛏 **Hotel Biser** (79 rooms, 5 suites) On the lakefront; ☎ 785 700; e info@hotelbiser.com. mk; w hotelbiser.com.mk. Built as a traditional Macedonian house, but much bigger. Open all year & recently refurbished, it is a tranquil place with a wide beachfront, a restaurant set into the rock wall, & a small pizzeria near the beach. Nice views from the balconies, though some mixed reviews for the rooms. **$$$**

🛏 **Hotel Izgrev Spa & Aquapark** (210 rooms) 5km southwest from Struga; ☎ 552 590; e reservations@hotelizgrev.com; w hotelizgrev. com. The newest place in town, with 500m of private beach. **$$$**

🛏 **Makpetrol** (49 rooms) Elen Kamen, 4km southwest of Struga; ☎ 797 466; m 071 267 760; w hotels.makpetrol.com.mk. Lakeside hotel with nice views. **$$$**

Radožda The last village before Albania on the western side of Lake Ohrid, sleepy Radožda, located right on the shore, comes alive in the summer; its many restaurants are renowned for offering the very best fish from the lake. The village **cave church** high on the cliffs is dedicated to the Archangel Michael; to ascend the many steep steps is a small pilgrimage in itself and will certainly help you work up a good appetite. Among

5

the frescoes on the cave rocks is one of the archangel at the Miracle of Chonae, while some of the frescoes inside the church date back to the 13th century. The door to the cave itself is usually kept locked, so ask for the key in the Dva Bisera Restaurant at the bottom of the steps before you find the door locked at the top.

Less well known is that sections of the Roman **Via Egnatia**, which followed the much older Candavian Way, can still be seen at the back of the village. As they are mostly built of blocks some 3m wide and perfectly jointed, it is easy for the visitor to appreciate what a feat of civil engineering the Via Egnatia was. This section of the road, however, is made of smaller blocks. It lies around 2km or a half-hour walk from the centre of the village. After the Dva Bisera Restaurant, at the first village shop, turn right up the hill to a small church where the tarmac runs out. A pleasant hike along a stone-walled road through the woods goes past a section of stone road and a small church dedicated to Sv Bogorodica. Until here the path follows a contour around the mountain and then rises for another 10 minutes to the flagstones of the Via Egnatia. The exact lie of the road beyond this section has still not been uncovered, but part of it is now believed to be underwater below Sv Erasmus between Struga and Ohrid. To get to see the road ask for the *kaldrma* (meaning 'flagstone'). For more on the Via Egnatia see w viaegnatiafoundation.eu. For details of the new hiking route following this section of the Via Egnatia, see the box on page 233.

Where to stay and eat There are a number of small guesthouses and restaurants along the Radožda shore road. Rooms here are uniformly quite basic and cost around €8–10 per person, making it a great lakeside budget getaway. Listed from north to south:

Dva Bisera ☎787 118; m 070 261 585; ⏱ 11.00–23.00 Sun–Thu, 08.00–01.00 Fri–Sat. Primarily known for its restaurant, whose cooks hold the secrets of their fresh-cooked lake trout close to their heart. It really is the most divine trout you'll ever taste, as good as if you had caught it yourself & whisked it straight on to the BBQ. The friendly service & lovely stilted deck only add to its charms. Rooms also available. **$$**

Vila Marij Blaž (7 rooms) ☎787 056; m 071 616 627; e j.jovanoska@yahoo.com; w vila-marij-blaz.hellomacedonia.com. This small hotel offers b/fast outside right on the shorefront. The menu offers a wide variety of the lake's fish, including Struga's famous baked eel. There is also a small swimming deck & a pontoon inviting you for a dip before your meal. **$$**

✖ Ezerski Raj (Paradise Lake) ☎787 193; ⏱ 11.00–midnight Sun–Thu, 11.00–01.00 Fri–Sat. The last restaurant before the entrance to the campsite & the footpath to Albania has a beautiful wooden deck overlooking the lake as well as views on to the Albanian peninsula of Lin village. Serves the local specialities of *gjomlezec* & *vitkalnici*. **$$**

OKTISI, VEVČANI AND GORNA BELICA Clustered close together less than half an hour north of Struga, the historic villages of Vevčani, Oktisi and Gorna Belica stand in mountainous surrounds overlooking the lake. All three villages are worth visiting, whether individually or collectively, with the most interesting being Vevčani, which is renowned for its lushly vegetated springs and scattering of handsome old houses. For more active travellers, the relatively undemanding 7km return hike between Oktisi and Vevčani is highly recommended.

Getting around Oktisi and Vevčani respectively lie about 10km and 12km northwest of Struga. To get here, follow the Debar road north out of town for about 4km, then just after you pass through the village of Vraništa, take the conspicuous turn to the left, which passes through Oktisi after 6km and reaches Vevčani 2km further. It's another 7km from Vevčani to Gorna Belica along a road that leads

A good half-day trip in the area if you have a car and car insurance to cover you in Albania (most hire cars from Macedonia aren't covered for Albania) is to drive around the lake. It is not uncommon for many countries to become 'blurred' at the edges, a little neglected by central administration and adopting some of the characteristics of the country next door.

The border crossing itself is straightforward. Once on the other side the full effect of former communist Albania's paranoia about foreign influence and invasion comes into plain view. The countryside is strewn with concrete dome lookouts and troop defences, which appear like giant molehills strewn across the landscape. These defensive positions, complete with rifle lookouts, do not cease until you are back in Macedonia on the other side of the lake. Most have now fallen into disrepair, and some have even fallen into the lake.

Along the lake in summer, boys will hold up strings of fresh trout caught from the lake, and a number of nice-looking lakeside restaurants on the way around will serve freshly caught fish and local vegetables.

At the southern end of the lake is Podgradec, which has a few shops and buffet bars along its main street and a lot of money changers who will buy your euros and dollars from you. A passenger ferry route across the lake from Podgradec to Ohrid began in 2014. On your way out of Podgradec back to Macedonia, make sure you head towards the lakeside road shortly after the centre of town before you go veering off on the main road into the wilds of central Albania. There are a couple of nice restaurants set in a park just before you get to the Sv Naum border.

It doesn't matter which way round you go, although the anticlockwise direction can appear more of an eye-opener than the other way around.

Alternatively, for the fit and keen, a bike ride around the lake is 90km, including some serious hills. One day for the superfit; two or three days for a more leisurely ride. Bikes can be hired along the quay in Ohrid or ask at Cycle Macedonia, Sunny Land Tourism or Vis-poj.

---

uphill close to the entrance to the springs. From Gorna Belica a more direct 16km road leads back to Struga via Višni.

Buses from Struga go to Vevčani via Oktisi every hour from 05.00 until 20.00.

Oktisi This pretty old village lies along a tributary of the Crni Drim and has a number of old watermills hidden along its banks. On the outskirts of the village is a 5th-century Christian basilica with some excellent examples of late Roman mosaics. Above the village in the hills is the overgrown **Vajtos Kale** site where a castle is alleged to have stood from Paeonian times. Some say that Vajtos is the eighth stopping place on the Via Egnatia, and the last stop before Ohrid, but it is much more likely that this was a stop on the Crni Drim road to northern Albania. The rock outcrop shows little sign of having been a castle, but the vantage point is pretty and it is easy to imagine that the wide road up to Vajtos might have been the Via Egnatia. For a circular route description to Vajtos and Vevčani, see the box on page 233.

Vevčani Situated less than 2km north of Oktisi, Vevčani is a truly beautiful village of old-style houses, many dating to the 18th or 19th century, run through by babbling brooks. Here there are a number of old babas and tatkos in traditional

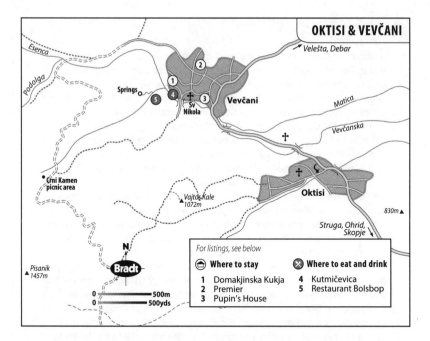

Velešta, Debar

Esenca

Podolga

Springs

Matica

Vevčani

Sv Nikola

Vevčanska

Crni Kamen picnic area

Vajtos Kale 1072m

Oktisi

830m ▲

Struga, Ohrid, Skopje

N

Pisanik 1457m

0 ————— 500m
0 ————— 500yds

For listings, see below

🛏 **Where to stay**
1 Domakjinska Kukja
2 Premier
3 Pupin's House

❌ **Where to eat and drink**
4 Kutmičevica
5 Restaurant Bolsbop

dress who will be happy to have their photograph taken. The main attraction is the Vevčani Spring (entry 20MKD), which erupts from the rocks in the lush forest at the back of the village, and is maintained as a park with a small bridge, walkways and benches for all to enjoy. Allegedly, the proud villagers of Vevčani held their own referendum during the break-up of Yugoslavia for their very own republic. Although they didn't manage to gain independence, they nevertheless created their own coat of arms, passports and even printed specimen currency, replicas of which can be bought in the local shops (but not to be used as legal tender).

🛏 **Where to stay and eat** *Map, above*

🛏 **Premier** (10 rooms) ☎ 790 620; m 071 380 295; e hotelpremiermk@yahoo.com; w hotelpremier.com.mk. Modern rooms, bar & b/fast room. Wi-Fi, all mod cons. **$$$**

🛏 **Domakjinska Kukja** (4 rooms) ☎ 790 505, 798 435; m 070 366 855; e gliso_kompani@t-home.mk; w hoteldomacinskakuca.com.mk. The 1st traditional inn to be revived in the village, its restaurant has a fireside atmosphere, beer-barrel tables upstairs & good food. **$$**

❋ 🛏 **Pupin's House** (3 rooms) ☎ 700 002; m 070 212 560. Built in 1690 & restored in the early 20th century as the house of the Armenian-born physicist Mihajlo Idvorski Pupin, this offers some of the best-value & most characterful accommodation in the Ohrid area. All rooms are dominated by wood & are en suite but the pick, if

it's available, is the one with balcony – excellent value at €10pp. The ground floor is maintained as a museum to its former owner & also houses a pleasant restaurant. **$$**

❋ ❌ **Kutmičevica** (2 rooms) Nr Sv Nikola Church; ☎ 798 399; m 070 249 197; e kutmicevica@yahoo.com; w kutmicevica.com.mk. Predominantly a traditional restaurant with indoor & outside seating, & 2 small rooms with fireplaces. **$$**

❌ **Restaurant Bolsbop** ☎ 798 527; m 071 241 427. Situated alongside a babbling stream right outside the springs complex, this has a great wooden terrace, traditional architecture, friendly staff, & a long menu of Macedonian stews & grills at decent prices. **$$**

Distance	7km round trip
Altitude	Oktisi 780m, Varoš 1,072m, Crni Kamen Park 1,195m, Vevčani Springs 910m
Rating	Easy to moderate
Timing	3–4 hours
In reverse	Possible
Map	1:25,000 SAGW Map Sheet Vevčani 780-3-1, January 2007

ROUTE DESCRIPTION A pretty and gentle hike taking in a mixed ethnic village, the alleged eighth stopping point of the Via Egnatia, and the Republic of Vevčani Springs. Starting in the centre of Oktisi, head to the top of the village and ask for Vajtos Kale. You will head up an eroding sheep herd track for about 1km towards the obvious hilltop appearing on your left to the west. At a dip in the hillside, skirt round the valley and upwards on to a difficult-to-find wide leafy avenue that could be imagined as once part of the Via Egnatia Roman network of roads. At the top of the avenue, a turn-off leads to the site of Vajtos Kale (✪ 6600 6525). Once a Paeonian fortress, perhaps, there is little left to see here now except some very large rocks and a lot of digging, probably from site robbers with a metal detector.

Back on the leafy avenue, continue for another kilometre until you come out to some meadows, pass a crossroads in the path and on to a 4x4 dirt track. This road winds its way for 1.5km north-northwest along the 1,220m contour offering good views of both Vevčani and Oktisi. After the road appears to head west away from the direction of Vevčani for some 350m, it turns to head northeast and downhill into the park area called Jankov Kamen (but confusingly signposted Crni Kamen, the name of a nearby mountain). Here there are a number of park benches and tables, places to hold barbecues and a couple of huts. The road continues over a small stream at the bottom of the park and slightly uphill for a 3km gentle trek back down into Vevčani. A shortcut by foot is to follow a narrow path before the stream, heading down the right-hand bank of the stream following the electricity pylons into Vevčani. After almost 2km the path crosses a small bridge into the back of the village.

Head left of the bridge to get to the Vevčani Springs, eat at the quaint Domakjinska Kukja or Kutmičevica, and visit Sv Nikola Church. Head right to get to the main road through Vevčani and follow it downhill alongside the stream for 1.4km to get back to Oktisi. A number of old watermill houses adorn the road that criss-crosses the stream.

Other hikes in the area go up to Gorna Belica village, Labuništa village and its glacial lakes and the fabled Church of Perumba on the border with Albania.

Gorna Belica Another good day trip away from the lake is up to the village of Gorna Belica, 16km northwest of Struga. The village is now mostly the weekend residence of Strugites, but it has a fine Vlach church, a high view on to Lake Ohrid, proximity to the Via Egnatia and good hiking up to a glacial lake and a cave church. The village first became a settlement in 1769, when the Aromanians (Vlachs) of Moskopole, southern Albania, were driven out of that town by the destruction wrought by the local Ottoman bey, and moved up here with all their

Vevčani has held a Twelfthtide Carnival on 13 and 14 January every year since the middle of the 6th century. The 12 days after Christmas, which in the Orthodox calendar is on 7 January, are meant to be a time when evil spirits are at their most active with regards to wreaking havoc on the coming year. On New Year's Eve (13 January in the Orthodox calendar), the villagers start a two-day event designed to banish evil spirits from entering into the New Year. People dress up in costumes and masks representing all things evil and unlucky in the hope that if evil is faced with its own reality this will scare it away. The costumes and disguises are a testament to what Macedonians find evil or unlucky. Typical costumes include policemen, soldiers, pregnant brides, an old groom, a funeral procession as well as ghoulish monsters of all varieties. Local politicians and international organisations are ridiculed, and the Ottoman times are also caricatured. A procession of floats starts at midday on the 14th when all sorts of ingenious horror story are depicted and include tables of human heads, bird flu inspectors (including live chickens) and giant condoms. The procession ends in the village square in the late afternoon with a lot of parading around a fire in which all the costumes are ritually burned.

Concentrating on the banishment of evil as a serious business rather than on the celebration of the end of fasting, this festival has some sinister overtones when mixed with alcohol. A fight or two usually breaks out between inhabitants of the upper village and the lower village and it is allegedly the time to punish dogs! Nevertheless, the carnival has started to become a popular national event, attracting over 2,000 visitors every year. When you arrive in the village on the carnival days, you will be stopped by masked men in camouflage uniforms who will ask to see your passport before letting you into the village. The correct passport to show is, of course, that of the Republic of Vevčani, which can be purchased from the masked 'police' for 200MKD. Grill and drink stands provide revellers with sustenance through the small hours, and if you have not managed to book yourself (well in advance) a room in the village, then try the Hotel Diplomat outside Struga (page 226).

animals, belongings and families. They chose this spot along the River Belica, where villagers believe that the old crumbling **Church of Sv Kliment** is no less than his actual 9th-century summer monastery from before he moved to Ohrid permanently as bishop.

The Aromanians built their own church, **Sv Petka**, or Paraškjevija in Vlach, up above Sv Kliment's Church, and it is a fine example of an early 19th-century Vlach church. By that time, 1829, the Greek influence on the old Ohrid archbishopric was all-pervasive and so all the original inscriptions on the church are in Greek. The church is cared for by the Dunoskis and if they are around they will be happy to tell you more about it. Look out for the **wooden hawk** above the central lantern in front of the iconostasis. The original pulley system still flaps the wings of the hawk as the lantern is pulled up and down, making a loud clapping noise.

The village celebrates two festivals in honour of both patron saints, Sv Petka on 8 August and Sv Kliment on 9 August. This double whammy fills the village up with visitors on those two days and it is well worth a visit if you can make it. Other patron saint festivals exist for neighbouring churches and holy sites, one of the most interesting being the dedication to the **Church of the Perumba**.

The tiny cave church was built in 1998 in honour of a local legend about a girl who, several centuries ago, was being chased by the local Ottoman thugs. The girl ran up against the steep cliff rocks where the church is now and fell to the ground exhausted, knowing that there was nowhere for her to escape. She prayed to God for deliverance and, just as the thugs were catching up with her, they saw her fragile body fly up into the air as a pure white dove (*perumba*). The dove flew away and locals have honoured the place as a holy site ever since.

The locals walk up to the site once a year on the first weekend in June. Due to the proximity of the site to the Albanian border, the hike takes place only with the accompaniment of local Macedonian soldiers. For more information on how to join the hike, ask in Gorna Belica. Any other hikes west of Gorna Belica and up to the glacial lake in the north are also best accompanied by a professional guide or other Macedonian who knows the area. The tracks are not well marked and encounters at the border could become difficult.

REČICA More as an aside on the way between Ohrid and Resen, if you want to see some natural, 100% ecologically sound washing machines, go to the tiny hamlet of Rečica. Called *valavica* or *valajca* for short in Macedonian, they are also sometimes referred to as *virovčanka* (whirlpools). Essentially a local stream is siphoned off via a small wooden canal and allowed to drop a few metres into a huge wooden, lined bowl set in the ground. The rush of water swirls around in the bowl into which the blankets, rugs and some modern-day washing liquid are added. After the time taken to have a small picnic with rakija and a good chat, the rugs and blankets are hung up to dry on wooden poles in a nearby field and collected in a few days when the items are dry. This was once a centre for traditional blanket and rug-making, and local people still come here to have their old rugs and blankets washed. Sadly, traditionally made rugs and blankets are not for sale here, although local honey is.

Getting there and away To get to Rečica, take the road towards Resen. After 15km take the turning left towards Kuratica, and after 1km take the turning right through the working quarry. Less than 3km along this dirt track will take you to the valavica area just before the village. The village itself has a small church and several old watermills further upstream.

6

Pelagonia, Prespa and Pelister

This is the story of Kruševo:
Just after midnight on the morning of August 2, 1903 (this was the day that the general uprising was proclaimed), a rattle of rifles and a prolonged hurrahing broke the quiet of the peaceful mountain town. Some three hundred insurgents under 'Peto-the-Vlach' and four other leaders had taken the town by surprise.

Frederick Moore, *The Balkan Trail*, 1906

This southeastern corner of Macedonia, known as Pelagonia in ancient times, is rich in history both natural and manmade. The **Via Egnatia**, a monumentally long Roman road linking the Adriatic crossing at Durres with Constantinople (now Istanbul in Turkey), traverses Pelagonia, which has traditionally been rich in trading towns. **Pelister National Park**, on the Baba mountain range, is the oldest national park in Macedonia. It conserves some rare glacial lakes, the Pelister Eyes, and is a haven of hiking and hidden Vlach villages. From up in its hills you can see both major and minor **Prespa lakes** (the latter lies in Greece and Albania), as well as the mountain range of Galičica National Park on the other side of the lake. When Ohrid is heaving with tourists in the summer, genteel Lake Prespa beckons with its deserted sandy beaches at Stenje, Konsko and Nakolec.

If you visit nowhere else in this region, spend at least a couple of days in Prilep to see the ruined **Towers of King Marko** and the remote **Treskavec Monastery**. The scenery at these two sites is magnificent and is the setting of the films *Before the Rain* and *Dust* by Macedonia's most famous film director, Milčo Mančevski. Prilep's Beer Festival in mid-July is also quickly becoming the most popular festival in Macedonia.

BITOLA *Telephone code 047*

The main town of the region and once a major trading centre, Bitola is currently the second-largest city in Macedonia with over 80,000 people, and is the seat of the country's second university. It has managed to maintain its pretty 18th- and 19th-century architecture in the centre of town, and these buildings tell of the former glory of Bitola when every major European country had a consulate here due to the amount of trading and business conducted in the town. The River Dragor divides the old Turkish town from the 18th-century town and conjures up a beautiful tree-lined canal effect, drawing in the cool air of the Baba Mountains. Despite being further south than Skopje, Bitola is usually cooler year round, sometimes by up to 12–15°C – lovely in the summer when Skopje can get up to the high 30°Cs, but bring an extra sweater in the winter. Major attractions include the impressive Roman archaeological site of Heraklea Linkestis on the town's southern outskirts, and the mountainous Pelister National Park 15km to the west.

HISTORY It is believed that a tribe known by the name of Linkestris was the first to inhabit the area south of Bitola around 4500BC. Just over 4,000 years later the first major town to be established in the rich Pelagonia Valley was the ancient Macedonian town of Heraklea Lyncestis. It was founded by Philip II of Macedon (the father of Aleksandar III of Macedon) in the middle of the 4th century and named in honour of Hercules, with whom the Macedonian royal dynasty of the Argeads identified. The additional name 'Lyncestis' in turn honours the ancient tribe of Linkestris. Although Philip lived there for some time, his son was eventually born in Pella over the present-day border in Greece.

With the fall of the ancient kingdom of Macedonia, Heraklea came under Roman rule in the 2nd century BC and continued to grow as an important trading town. By this time the Via Egnatia passed through Heraklea where it crossed the Diagonal Way, another major north–south road joining Heraklea with Stobi, Štip and then Kustendil (now in Bulgaria).

Julius Caesar used Heraklea as a supply depot during his campaigns and many of his veterans settled there. Later, during the time of early Christianity in the 4th century, Heraklea developed as the seat of the regional bishopric. By the 5th century, Roman rule was in decline and Heraklea was ransacked several times by marauding Avars, Goths and Huns from the north. When a large earthquake struck in AD518, the inhabitants of Heraklea abandoned the city.

Later, in the 7th century the Dragovites, a Slavic tribe pushed down from the north by the Avars, settled in the valley and gave the river its present name of Dragor. Eventually a new town was established immediately north of Heraklea, mentioned under the name Obitel in one of the charters of Tsar Samoil, showing that even then the town was closely associated with churches and monasteries (*obitel* means family chamber of a monastery). The town continued to prosper from trading and eventually became the third-largest city in the Balkans after Constantinople and Thessaloniki. The surrounding area also thrived as a centre of Christian worship, so that by the time the Ottomans came at the end of the 14th century they named the town Monastir due to the number of monasteries in the surrounding hills, which served the monks of the 500 churches in the region.

Soon, Monastir became so important that the French set up a consulate there. Eleven other countries followed suit. The influx of 18th- and 19th-century architecture can still be seen in Bitola today, despite artillery fire and bombing during the world wars. Mixed with the influence of Ottoman architecture in the form of mosques, covered markets and bathhouses, Bitola has a very cosmopolitan feel to it even today, and its inhabitants still pride themselves on their international heritage.

At the beginning of the 19th century, Monastir was at the zenith of its trading history and the railway even came to town, linking southern Macedonia with Skopje, Belgrade and beyond. French was widely spoken in the town, which included a number of foreign and international schools as well as a military academy that was attended by Turkey's pro-reform leader, Kemal Atatürk. The town boasted 2,000 households, and every second one owned a piano, on which many a song about Bitola was composed. Allegedly there are over 200 songs about Bitola.

The Manaki brothers (see box, page 240), famous for their pioneering work with the camera, opened their studio of art photography in Bitola in 1905. In honour of their work in photography and later cinematography, Bitola started the first international Manaki Film Camera Festival in the world in 1979, which continues every September.

6

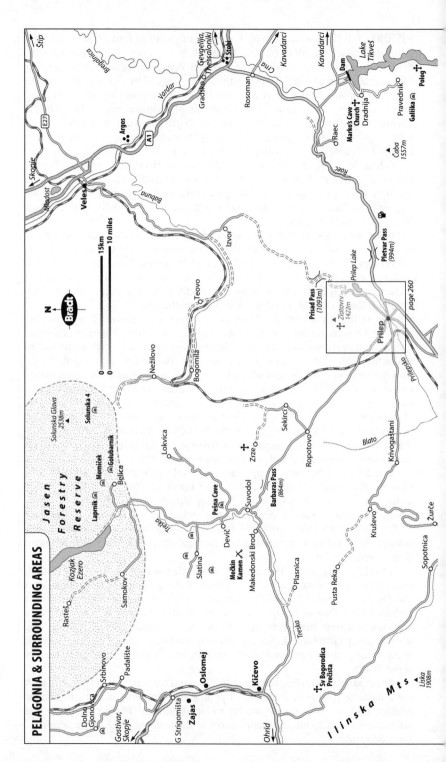

PELAGONIA & SURROUNDING AREAS

Jasen Forestry Reserve

Solunska Glava 2538m
Solunska 4 ▲

Golubarnik
Laprnik ⋒   Momiček ⋒
Belica

Kozjak Ezero

Rasteš
Samokov

Dolne Gjonovica
Gostivar, Skopje
G Strigomišta

Zajas●
Oslomej ●
Kičevo ●

Srbinovo
Padalište

Ohrid →

Sv Bogorodica Prečista ✝

Illinska Mts

Liska 1908m

Nežilovo
Bogomila

Lokvica
Zrze ✝
Pešna Cave ⋒
Suvodol
Devič ⋒
Slatina ⋒
Makedonski Brod
Mečkin Kamen ✗

Barbaras Pass (864m)
Plasnica

Treska
Treska

Pusta Reka
Kruševo

Sekirci
Ropotovo
Blato
Krivogaštani

Sopotnica
Žurče

Teovo

Izvor

Babuna

N
Bradt

0 10 miles
0 15km

Mladost
Veles ●
Skopje →

Argos ●

A1
E27

Štip →

Bregalnica

Vardar

Gradsko
Gevgelija, Thessaloniki
Stobi ✝

Rosoman
Crna

Kavadarci
Kavadarci →

Lake Tikveš
Dam

Marko's Cave Church ✝
Dradnija ✝
Raec

Pravednik
Gališka ⋒
Polog ✝

Čaba 1557m

Raec

Pletvar Pass (994m)
Prilep Lake

Prisad Pass (1093m)
Zlatovrv 1422m ▲
✝
Prilep ●

Prilepsko

page 260

238

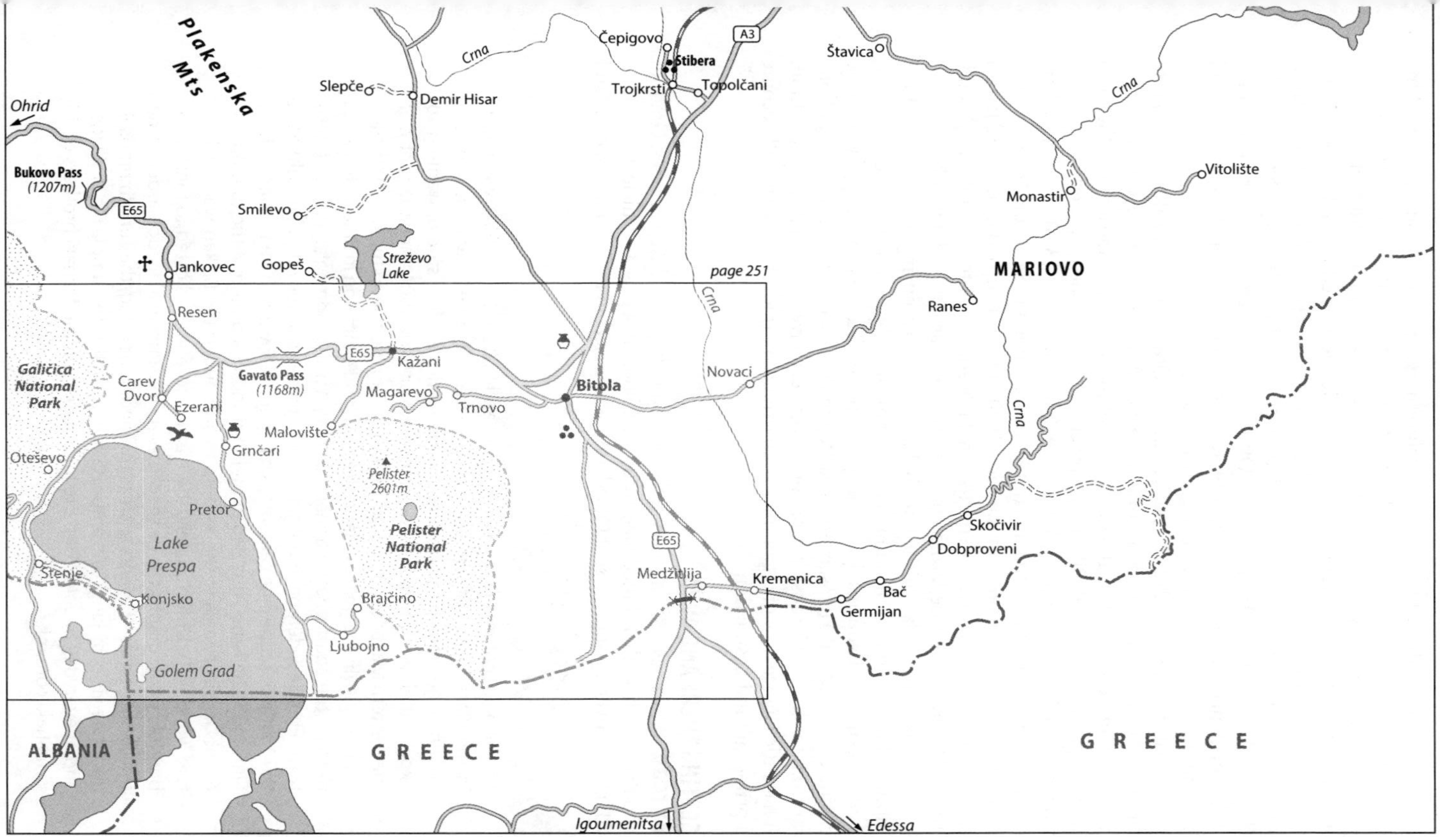

GREECE

GREECE

ALBANIA

MARIOVO

Plakenska
Mts

Pelister
National
Park

Galičica
National
Park

Lake
Prespa

Streževo
Lake

Vitolište

Monastir

Ranes

Štavica

Čepigovo
Stibera
Topolčani
Trojkrsti

Skočivir
Dobroveni

Bač
Germijan

Kremenica

Medžitlija

Novaci

Bitola

Trnovo

Magarevo
Kažani

Demir Hisar

Slepče

Smilevo

Gopeš

Jankovec
Resen

Carev
Dvor
Ezerani

Grnčari
Malovište

Pelister
2601m

Brajčino

Ljubojno

Pretor

Konjsko

Stenje

Oteševo

Golem Grad

Bukovo Pass
(1207m)

Gavato Pass
(1168m)

Ohrid

Edessa

Igoumenitsa

Crna

Crna

Crna

Crna

A3

E65

E65

E65

E65

page 251

239

At the end of the 19th century, revolution against the Ottomans was taking hold all over Macedonia, and Bitola was no exception. The Internal Macedonian Revolutionary Organisation (IMRO) was very active in Bitola and there are those who say that some of the guerrilla warfare tactics developed in Bitola during those years were even exported to other nations rising up against foreign rule, such as Ireland. The Ilinden Festival every 2 August (a national holiday) celebrates the Ilinden Uprising of 1903 against the Ottomans. The Republic of Kruševo which was proclaimed the next day in nearby Kruševo lasted only ten days before it and all other regions of dissent were sharply put down.

The Balkan wars of 1912–13 put an end to Ottoman rule in Bitola and all of Macedonia, but many more years of foreign rule still followed. Reprisals against the Turkish community were high and over 40 of the 60 Turkish mosques in the town were destroyed. Beautiful Bitola was practically demolished by German shelling from Pelister Mountain during World War I, in which over 13,000 French soldiers died, almost as many Germans, and unrecorded numbers of Serbs and Macedonians. In addition, Nazi occupation in the early 1940s annihilated Bitola's thriving Jewish scene when 3,011 Jews were deported on 11 March 1943 to Treblinka in Poland. Today, Macedonia's entire Jewish community is only around a thousand.

While Bitola has languished in Balkan obscurity during the 20th century, modern lines of communication and transport have bypassed the once important trading centre. To add insult to injury, the provincial town of Skopje was made capital of the Federal Yugoslav Socialist Republic of Macedonia. Since then, Bitola, far from the heart of Yugoslavia, has only ever been given secondary consideration. It has little chance now of regaining its importance in trade, but it may still become a prime cultural destination.

GETTING THERE AND AWAY

By road Bitola lies 170km south of Skopje using the A1 and A3 via Veles, Gradsko and Prilep, a drive that should take around 2½ hours in a private vehicle. It is around 70km (just over an hour) east of Ohrid, unless you elect to use the more scenic (and

THE MANAKI BROTHERS

The Manaki brothers Yanaki (1878–1960) and Milton (1882–1964), were born in the Vlach village of Avdela, near Grevena in present-day Greece, where they first got into photography and opened their first studio. Wanting to expand their work, however, they moved to Bitola in 1904, then the centre of the western Macedonian region. After opening their new studio in 1905 they went on to win the gold medal in the Big World exhibition in Sinaia, Romania, became the court photographers for King Karol of Romania, and started to travel Europe widely on photographic assignments. In 1907 they brought back the 300th Bioscope cine camera from London, allowing them to start making films in the Balkans. Thus began their historical recording of the tumultuous events in Macedonia in the lead-up to and during the Balkan wars and the two world wars. Unfortunately, there is no museum dedicated to their work, but their photographs can be seen in every museum in Macedonia, depicting the life and times of events such as the Ilinden Uprising, the Turkish reprisals and state visits by kings and ambassadors, as well as the simple life in villages and of everyday people. For more information on the Manaki brothers go to w manaki.com.mk.

highly recommended) 100km route via Galičica National Park and Lake Prespa, in which case allow at least 2 hours without stops.

The main **bus** station [243 D7] (✎231 420; w transkop.mk) is on Ulica Nikola Tesla about 1km south of the city centre, but all buses heading northeast to Prilep, Veles and Skopje also stop at the more central old bus station [242 E2] opposite the Čaršija (old bazaar). Four direct buses run daily in either direction between Skopje and Bitola, and if the times don't suite, it is also quite straightforward to hop using more regular services to Veles and/or Prilep. In addition, at least ten buses run back and forth daily between Ohrid and Bitola, and there are also several buses daily to Kičevo, Gostivar and Tetovo. Note that if you are heading between Bitola and Kruševo, it is best to change buses at Prilep. There is no public transport between Bitola and Florina, the closest town on the other side of the Greek border at Niki; you'll need a private taxi, which can be arranged through the helpful people at Goldy Hostel for €28 per car.

By rail The train station [243 D7] (✎237 110) stands opposite the bus station on Ulica Nikola Tesla. Four trains run daily in either direction between Skopje and Bitola via Veles and Prilep. These leave from Skopje at 06.42, 14.30, 17.10 and 20.10, and from Bitola at 03.10, 05.20, 12.50 and 18.30. The train is slow (average train journey time 3½ hours) but the journey is scenic, at least between Skopje and Prilep. A railway line has connected Bitola to the Greek city of Thessaloniki since the 1890s, but the Macedonian section has long been disused.

GETTING AROUND Most places of interest in Bitola lie within easy **walking** distance of each other, but if necessary **taxis** are abundant. The minimum fare is 40MKD, plus 30MKD per kilometre, with set prices for destinations further outside the town. A taxi to Kurklino or Dihovo is 150MKD, while a taxi to Magarevo, Trnovo or Nižepole is 200MKD. Operators include those on ✎1577, 1591, 1592 (prefix with 047 if calling from a mobile phone).

There are also four city buses in Bitola: 1, 4, 5 and 6. Two buses serve surrounding villages: 11 and 12.

TOUR OPERATORS

Balojani Tourist Services [242 A3] 111d Solunska (difficult to find); ✎220 204; e reserve@balojani.com.mk; w balojani.com.mk. Exceptional service, especially for hiking in all 3 national parks & visiting the eco-villages, as well as for wider-ranging tours combining neighbouring countries in the region. Very well connected in the local area.

WHERE TO STAY There are several more hotels and villas less than 10km away in the villages of Dihovo, Magarevo and Trnovo in Pelister National Park (page 250).

Bela Kuka [243 G8] (12 rooms, 4 apts) Boris Kidrič 20; ✎225 225; m 075 220 667; e bela.kuka2012@yahoo.com; w belakuka.mk. Smart place in a nice old building opened in 2012, near Širok Sokok. Own restaurant. AC, TV, Wi-Fi. **$$$**

Hotel Epinal [243 F8] (175 rooms) On the cross of the pedestrian zone Maršal Tito & Goce Delčev; ✎224 777; e reservation@hotelepinal.com; w hotelepinal.com. Popular with tour groups of Greek visitors, this slightly timeworn monolith offers full comfort, including gym, pool, sauna, jacuzzi & casino. Sometimes has some very good deals as low as €20pp. **$$$**

Hotel Premier Centar [242 B3] (20 rooms) Stiv Naumov 12; ✎202 070; m 077 914 888; f @ PremierCentar. Simply furnished rooms in central location. **$$$**

✳ **Hotel Teatar** [242 A3] (10 rooms) Stiv Naumov 35; ✎610 188; m 075 383 283; e hotelteatar@gmail.com; w hotelteatar.com.

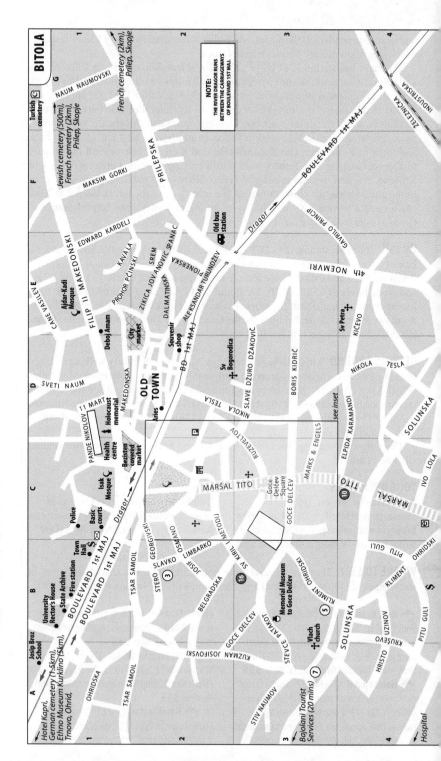

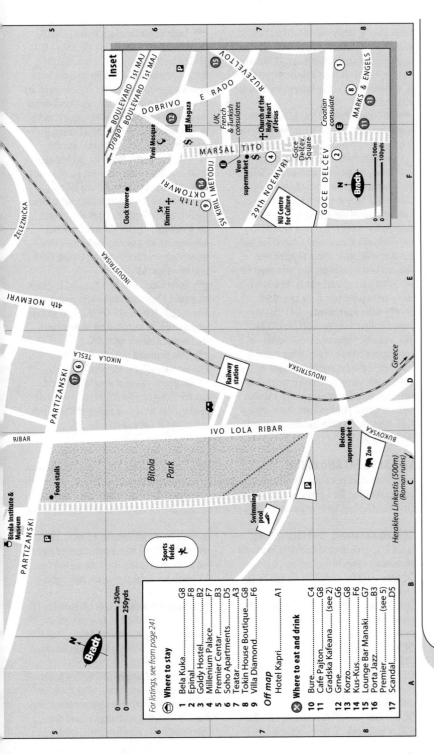

For listings, see from page 241

Where to stay

1	Bela Kuka	G8
2	Epinal	F8
3	Goldy Hostel	B2
4	Millenium Palace	F7
5	Premier Centar	B3
6	Soho Apartments	D5
7	Teatar	A3
8	Tokin House Boutique	G8
9	Villa Diamond	F6

Off map

| | Hotel Kapri | A1 |

Where to eat and drink

10	Bure	C4
11	Cafe Pajton	G8
	Gradska Kafeana	(see 2)
12	Grne	G6
13	Korzo	G8
14	Kus-Kus	F6
15	Lounge Bar Manaki	G7
16	Porta Jazz	B3
	Premier	(see 5)
17	Scandal	D5

Small, friendly, family-owned hotel with central location & stylish rooms, purpose built in the style of a traditional Macedonian house. All rooms with en suite, AC & Wi-Fi. It has a pleasant courtyard bar &, as the name implies, an independent theatre is attached. **$$$**

🏠 **Millenium Palace** [243 F7] (26 rooms) Maršal Tito 48; 📞 241 001; e h.milenium@t-home. mk; w milleniumpalace.com.mk/en/bitola. Accessed from the front through an indiscernible door among the throng of cafés on Širok Sokok, you'll step through the narrow Balkan-style dbl doors as if into another world of nostalgic calm when travel was a privilege & a pleasure. Beautifully restored to its former 19th-century glory (but with all mod cons), cabinets line the corridors with artefacts from a bygone year. You can't beat the location. Also has a beautiful restaurant & bar upstairs with buffet b/fast, & its own pizzeria downstairs at the back. **$$$**

✳ 🏠 **Soho Apartments** [243 D5] (10 rooms) Partizanski 3; 📞 610 043; m 075 414 185; e sohobitola@gmail.com; w sohobitola. com. Located between the main bus station & town centre, this dynamically managed modern complex offers accommodation in tastefully & cohesively decorated open-plan apts & studios with self-catering kitchen, comfortable seating & AC. It lies directly above the excellent Scandal Restaurant. **$$$**

🏠 **Tokin House Boutique Hotel** [243 G8] (10 rooms) Marks & Engels 7; 📞 232 309; m 074 334 366; w tokin-house.com. A beautiful 1915 Austrian exterior, with an additional sunny b/fast room & grapevine-shaded yard. En-suite rooms are well-equipped but the décor is more fuddy-duddy than the 'boutique hotel' moniker suggests. **$$$**

✳ 🏠 **Goldy Hostel** [242 B2] (2 rooms, 1 4-bed dorm, 1 2-bed dorm) Slavko Limbarko 15; 📞 552 034; m 075 555 911; e goldyhostel@ gmail.com. This friendly hostel has a useful central location & is the best place in Bitola to hook up with other travellers & arrange transport to Greece. The helpful & well-informed staff also arrange day & overnight trips to Pelister National Park. Amenities include a spotless shared bathroom/ shower & communal self-catering kitchen. Dorm beds from €9pp. **$$**

🏠 **Hotel Kapri** [242 A1] (20 rooms) Dovledzik bb, around 3.5km from Bitola on the road to Trnovo; 📞 256 500; m 076 479 382; e hotelkapri@ kapri.com.mk; w kapri.com.mk. Modern hotel/ restaurant just outside town. **$$**

🏠 **Villa Diamond** [243 F6] (10 rooms) 11th Oktomvri 4; 📞 251 632; m 070 536 922; e villadajmond@yahoo.com; w villadiamond. com.mk. This central hotel is set in a restored old building close to the main square, offering plenty of character as well as good value. **$$**

🍴 **WHERE TO EAT AND DRINK** The main pedestrian area, **Maršal Tito**, hosts numerous café-bars and restaurants. There is a small **Vero supermarket** [243 F7] at the north end of Maršal Tito if you want to buy provisions for a day out or simply a snack and drinks. The big Vero superstore is on Partizanski, 2km west of the centre. Try also:

🍴 **Gradska Kafeana** [243 F8] Maršal Tito; 📞 224 777; ⏰ 08.00–midnight daily. Traditional Macedonian dishes; in the Hotel Epinal. **$$**

🍴 **Grne** [243 G6] Maršal Tito 37; 📞 237 800; m 075 468 161; w .grne.mk; ⏰ 11.00–midnight Sun–Thu, noon–01.00 Fri–Sat. Overlooking the statue of Philip II, this is a classic-style national restaurant. **$$**

🍴 **Korzo** [243 G8] Maršal Tito 95; 📞 612 602; m 070 332 678, w restaurantkorzo.com; ⏰ 08.00–midnight Mon–Thu, 08.00–01.00 Fri–Sat, 08.00–23.00 Sun. Traditional Macedonian dishes & pizza; covered terrace. **$$**

🍴 **Kus-Kus** [243 F6] Kiril i Metodij 2a; 📞 222 603; w kuskus.mk; ⏰ noon–midnight Sun–Thu,

noon–01.00 Fri–Sat. Primarily a pizzeria, this cosy restaurant spills out on to a pedestrianised alley just off the main square. The pizzas are very good & it boasts a wide range of salads, stews, grills & pasta dishes. **$$**

🍴 **Lounge Bar Manaki** [243 G7] Ruzveltov 17; 📞 212 121; ⏰ 08.00–01.00 daily. Very popular, serving traditional Macedonian dishes, pizzas & salads, & drinks. Covered terrace & slick interior. **$$**

🍴 **Premier Restaurant** [242 B3] Stiv Naumov 12. Attached to the eponymous hotel, this has an attractive interior with retro décor, terracotta tiling & split-level seating separating a relaxed diner-style eatery from a more formal restaurant. There's also an elevated terrace. It serves a massive variety of international & Macedonian dishes, all very tasty & well priced. $$

✕ Scandal [243 D5] Partizanski 3; ☎ 610 614; m 075 453 917; w scandal.mk. Situated on the ground floor of the affiliated Soho Apartments, this stylish bar & restaurant has a large modern warehouse-like interior as well as terrace seating in the front & courtyard seating in a garden at the back. It claims to serve fusion cuisine, which amounts to a fairly predictable selection of pizzas, burgers & pasta dishes supplemented by the likes of chicken teriyaki/cordon bleu & a variety of salads. Still, the modern vibe, good food, sensible prices & extensive wine list add up to an attractive package. $$

✕ Bure [242 C4] Maršal Tito 82–88; ☎ 225 522; w bure.com.mk; ⊕ 11.00–midnight Sun–Thu, 11.00–01.00 Fri–Sat. Quaint décor & very good pizzas. $

☆ Cafe Pajton [243 G8] Maršal Tito 85. Boasting a handsome old interior decorated in classic Ottoman style, as well as terrace seating on a wide pavement, this is a great spot to enjoy a central beer or coffee as Bitola goes by.

☆ Porta Jazz [242 B3] Sv Kiril i Metodij 12; ☎ 208 033; ◻ @portajazz.bitola. Bitola's most appealing nightspot is set in an old churchlike building with Byzantine-style walls, & has a large garden courtyard with ample seating. Essentially a drinking hole, it has a large eclectic CD collection & there's often live music at w/ends. No food served.

OTHER PRACTICALITIES The main **post office** [242 C1] is at Boulevard 1st Maj – the actual service counter is outside. Stationery can be bought at the *knigoteka* on the other side of the boulevard where you see the Фотокопир sign. Free **Wi-Fi** is available along the whole of Širok Sokok. **Together** (part of the Together and Tobacco chain of newsagents), on Maršal Tito 37, sells phone top-ups.

For medical emergencies, the **Clinical Hospital Bitola** [242 A4] is on Partizanski (☎ 251 211; w kbb.org.mk) and there's a **24-hour health centre** at Pande Nikolov [242 C1] (☎ 194). **Feniks Apoteka** is a 24/7 pharmacy (☎ 242 575) in the same building. **ATMs and money exchanges** are abundant, especially along Maršal Tito.

WHAT TO SEE AND DO Bitola is a pretty town to walk around. Its centrepiece is the large and well-wooded **central square** [242 C1] that stands on the south bank of the River Dragor at the junction of Boulevard 1st Maj and Maršal Tito Street, where it is flanked by the old Ottoman bazaar and several other important landmarks (see below). Running west out of town past the square, the tree-lined **Boulevard 1st Maj** is bisected by the river and fringed with a number of old consular residences.

Running for almost 2km south from the old Ottoman bazaar and central square, Maršal Tito Street, known locally as **Širok Sokok** (Turkish for 'wide alley'), is reputedly the longest pedestrianised road in the Balkans. At its northern end, the terrace cafés and restaurants that spill out on to the pavement are a lovely spot to watch the world go by, but this stretch is also lined with some impressive 18th- and 19th-century protected buildings, so don't forget to look up at the architecture as you wander along. Maršal Tito then continues southward past the House of Culture and now disused Dom na Armija officers' club to the Bitola Institute and Museum, which stands on the junction with Partizanski Street. After crossing Partizanski, the pedestrianised street continues south for about 800m through Bitola Park, which has some children's fun rides, small food stalls and lots of busts of famous Bitolans lining its leafy avenues, before finally terminating at a T-junction less than 1km north of the old Roman city Heraklea Linkestis.

Ottoman bazaar and old town This was once the centre of trade with over 900 shops grouped according to craft. You'll still see a few of the old storefronts at the cobblers and the furriers but the intense trading of old has moved to out-of-town shopping centres such as Vero. West of the old bazaar is the covered **Bezisten** [242 C1], which still houses one of Bitola's markets and whose gates are still locked at night, while on the northern side are the old Turkish baths, **Deboj Amam** [242 E1], which now serve as the large kitchen of a bakery.

Surrounding the old town are several **mosques**, of which the most prominent is the **Isak Mosque** [242 C1] (Mosque of Isaac Celebi Ibn Isa), built in 1506 with its 50m-high minaret. It was once part of a much larger complex including a madrasa and shops, with revenue coming in from surrounding vineyards and some 20 watermills. The domed **Ajdar-Kadi Mosque** [242 E1], just north of the city market, was built in 1562 by Mimar Sinan, the greatest Ottoman architect (whose better-known work includes the Süleymaniye and Rüstem Pasha mosques in Istanbul). The exterior has been under scaffolding for some years, and the interior is closed to the public.

Situated on the central square, the so-called **Yeni Mosque** [243 F6] (meaning 'new'), also known as the Khadi Mehmed Effendi Mosque, was built in the late 1550s over three older churches dating from as early as the 11th century, as revealed by archaeological excavation in 2010–11. The interior, which has some attractive Ottoman tile-work, served for some years as an art gallery, but is currently closed due to ongoing excavations.

Opposite the Yeni Mosque is the **clock tower** [243 F6] built in the 1830s, whose bells and musical mechanisms have been renewed several times, most notably in 1936 by the then German government as a gift of gratitude for the cemetery for German soldiers killed in World War I (see opposite). Erected on the central square in the frenzy of beautifying Macedonia that accompanied 'Skopje 2014' (see box, page 137) is a new statue of Philip II seated on a rearing horse in front of a fountain surrounded by Macedonian shields.

Finally, to the south of the old town is the **Magaza** [243 F6] (⊕ 10.00–20.00), which used to operate like a corn exchange (it is the Turkish word for 'shop'), where all sorts of goods, not just corn, were bartered and traded in the large hall. Today, it hosts a gallery for travelling exhibitions from all over the world. Further south, opposite the Hotel Epinal, is the **NU Centre for Culture** [243 F7] (formerly Dom na Kultura; Širok Sokok 66; ☏ 233 419; w centarzakultura.com), a modern concrete and glass structure that houses the National Theatre Bitola (☏ 552 244) and the American Corner, which has a wide range of books by American authors available to borrow. Beyond this is the **Memorial Museum to Goce Delčev** [242 B3] (Stevce Patakot 11), the Macedonian revolutionary who stayed at this house on a visit to Bitola in 1901.

Bitola Institute and Museum

[243 B5] (Kliment Ohridski bb; ☏ 233 187; e info@muzejbitola.mk; w muzejbitola.mk; ⊕ Apr–Sep 09.00–18.00 Tue–Sun, Oct–Mar 09.00–6.00 Tue–Sun; entry 120MKD, plus 500MKD to take photos, 1,000MKD to take video) The museum building itself was once one of two buildings housing a local Ottoman military academy – the one that Atatürk attended from 1896 to 1899 prior to him going on to become commander-in-chief of the Turkish military and then the first president of Turkey. One wing of the museum is dedicated to an excellent exhibition in English, Macedonian and Turkish about Atatürk, rivalling even the one at Gallipoli. Most interestingly, don't miss the love letter from Atatürk's only true love, the Bitola-born Vlach girl Eleni Karinte, which is translated on to a big poster in the entrance of the exhibition. Of the two buildings, known as the Red Building and the White Building, only the latter still exists; the Red Building was destroyed in World War I.

The other wing of the museum has an equally excellent exhibition dedicated to the history of Bitola and artefacts found in its surroundings. Some enormous mammoth teeth are on display, as well as further historical finds through to World War II. One notable find is the 'Bitola inscription' stone of Jovan Vladislav (Ioan the Autocrator), which marks the building of a fortress in Bitola by him in 1015. The inscription reads that Jovan was Bulgarian by birth and related to Tsar Samoil, whose army was defeated by the Byzantine tsar Vaslius II in 1014; such a statement contradicts the Macedonian theory that Samoil was Macedonian rather than Bulgarian. Some say, on the other hand, that the stone is a fake. The exhibition also includes displays focusing on local architecture, Bitola's partisan movement, and the status of Bitola as the fashion centre of the region in the 19th century, when anybody who wanted to be dressed in the latest European fashion would come to a renowned Bitola tailor for *à la fanga* fashion.

There are also some good temporary exhibits, which in recent years have included traditional Macedonian embroidery, and comparisons of old paintings and photographs with modern images to see how the city has changed.

The Bitola Museum is responsible for several other properties in Bitola, including the archaeological site of Heraklea Linkestis (page 249), the Memorial Museum to Goce Delčev (see opposite), the art gallery in the Yeni Mosque (see opposite) and the Old Barracks.

Jewish memorials Little remains of Jewish life in Bitola, which had the second-largest Jewish population in the region after Thessaloniki in the 19th century. Only the **Jewish cemetery** [242 G1] on Ilindenska (behind the Makpetrol station at the entrance to Bitola from Skopje) still exists, with a display room in the memorial house there showing photos, letters and other documents. A room at the Ethno Museum Kurklino (page 249) is also dedicated to Jewish life and artefacts from the 19th century, and the Bitola Museum has a new dedication to the 3,011 Jews of Bitola who were gassed at Treblinka in Poland, including a list of those deported and an urn of ashes. A **memorial** to the victims stands in front of the health centre on Pande Nikolov [242 D1]. For more on the Jewish history of Bitola visit w cassorla.net/Monastir.

Cemeteries In addition to the Jewish one mentioned above, Bitola has several other noteworthy cemeteries. The **French memorial cemetery** [242 G1] to the fallen of World War I is sandwiched between the corner of Dolni Orizari and Novački Pat, 2km east from the centre of town. It holds the graves of 6,230 named French soldiers of Christian and Muslim faith, as well as a monument dedicated to a further 7,000 unknown French soldiers. The main entrance is on Novački Pat, and another entrance on Dolni Orizari is by the side of the memorial house, which holds the list of those interred at the cemetery, a small photographic exhibition and the guest books (*livre d'or, zlatna kniga*) for signing. The groundsman, who can open the **memorial** house for you, took over tending the graves from his father. He speaks some French (but no English).

The **German memorial cemetery** [242 A1] to the fallen of World War I is 1.5km west from the town centre. After crossing the last bridge north over the River Dragor, follow the main street called Deveani uphill for almost 1km. Although it does not contain the thousands of graves that the French cemetery has, it is home to an impressive and solemn monument and offers excellent views of the valley. (The **British memorial cemetery** is in Greece behind the village of Dojran, further to the east.)

The **Turkish cemetery** [242 G1] is on Ilindenska, behind the Makpetrol fuel station, next to the Jewish cemetery. Sadly, it has not been maintained and is an eerie reminder of the Ottoman period when the Turkish community was a majority.

6

Abridged from text by Eric Allart, history teacher, former professional archaeologist. Translation by M Marc (w albindenis.free.fr/Site_escadrille/departement33.htm)

On 5 April 1918, Brigadier (Corporal) Pilot Léopold Michel Montoya was reported missing in action when his plane – a Nieuport 24 – was shot down by the German ace Gerhard Fieseler behind the Bulgarian lines, south of Caniste. (Fieseler, who later became an aerobatics champion, aircraft designer and manufacturer, was awarded the Golden Military Merit Cross and the Iron Cross, first and second class, for 19 aerial victories he won over Macedonia during World War I.) On 21 April 1920, the French court of Bordeaux officially declared Brigadier Montoya killed in action, and his family were informed by the German Red Cross. Although Montoya's wife died in childbirth, her daughter, Audette, survived her and was brought up by her grandparents. In between the two world wars, the family attempted in vain to have Léopold's burial place located.

In 2005, while off duty, Captain Fief, of the French gendarmerie, came across Montoya's identity disc at an antique dealer's shop in Skopje. On enquiring around the battlefield site where the disc had come from, a shepherd from Kruševica confirmed to him that his father had been requisitioned to bury 'both pilots' killed on the ground by Bulgarians in 1918. Another shepherd on the plateau south of Caniste was able to point out a bush commonly known as the location of the pilot's burial place. The topography of the site hardly allows an emergency landing and the plane is likely to have been seriously damaged before Montoya was killed on the ground by Bulgarian troops.

Back in France, Captain Fief found the pilot's grand-nephew, Christophe Montoya, who confirmed that Léopold's daughter was still alive. With the help of a war veterans' society, the Montoya family contacted the French Ministry of Defence and the French Embassy in Skopje to ask for the location and repatriation of Léopold's body. The family have been trying to uncover, positively identify and repatriate Brigadier Montoya's body since 2009, but seeking funding and battling through government red tape is hindering progress. Ongoing archaeological and regressive mapping work with the aid of photos of the area taken in 1918 by an anonymous pilot of the 504th Squadron based in Bac, northeast of Bitola, which was Montoya's squadron, will help to solve much of the contradictory data surrounding the circumstances of the death of Brigadier Léopold Michel Montoya, killed in action, *'mort pour la France'*.

Churches There are a number of churches in Bitola, the most significant being that of **Sv Dimitri** [243 F6], renowned as one of the biggest churches in the Balkans. Built in 1830 during Ottoman times when churches were not allowed to be ornate or ostentatious on the outside, its interiors are decidedly lavish and have been well preserved to this day. The opulence of the church is captured in the opening scenes of *The Peacemaker* (1997) starring George Clooney, which were filmed here. Elsewhere, the Catholic **Church of the Holy Heart of Jesus** [243 F7] on Širok Sokok was first founded in Easter 1857, although the current neo-Gothic-style structure dates from 1909 after the earlier Baroque-style church caught fire and was destroyed.

Heraklea Linkestis [243 C8] (Entry 100MKD) Founded by Philip II in the 4th century BC and an active centre of trade for another eight centuries afterwards, this once-significant town on what is now the southern outskirts of Bitola rivals Stobi as the most worthwhile Roman-era archaeological site in Macedonia. Only a small part of the old town has been uncovered and excavated, so visits in future years should prove ever more fruitful, especially as historical records show that there are still a number of houses and tombs of the rich and famous at the time to be found. Several important relics and buildings have already been uncovered including the amphitheatre, baths, basilicas and some impressive mosaics, only some of which are on show in the summer. There is a small museum, a snack and drink shop, and a souvenir shop with books on the site in English available for sale. Most of the more important statues are on display in the town museum or in the National Museum in Skopje.

The site lies about 2.5km south of the town centre, a 25–30-minute walk depending on where you start. To get here, follow the pedestrianised Maršal Tito Street south across Partizanski and through Bitola Park until you reach a T-junction in front of a car park. Turn left here, then continue for 100m to another T-junction where you need to turn right on to Ivo Lola Ribar Street. Shortly after this, immediately past the Belcom supermarket [243 D8], turn right on to the (indistinctly signposted) 500m feeder road that leads to the archaeological site. If you don't feel like the walk, a taxi shouldn't cost more than 100MKD.

Considerable archaeological work continues here every year, and for those who wish to take part, the Balkan Heritage School (w bhfieldschool.org) has organised volunteer workshops here in recent years.

Ethno Museum Kurklino (Antique Museum 'Filip')
[242 A1] (📞 286 666; m 070 312 146; e info@muzejkrklino.mk; w muzejkrklino.mk; ⊕ by appointment (or chance – the family live next door); entry 100MKD) At the back of the village of Kurklino, 5km northeast of Bitola, is by far the best ethno museum in all of Macedonia: the private collection of the Tanevski family. Boris has dedicated an entire two-storey building to housing a rich collection of motorbikes, cars, household goods and clothing from over the last century. The collection has motorbikes from World War II, a 'Wanted' poster for Tito, old gramophones and some of the very few Jewish household items from Bitola not destroyed by the Bulgarians, among many other things. Boris also sells homemade wine and rakija. A taxi from Bitola costs 150MKD.

Festivals Several festivals take place in Bitola every year, of which the largest is **Bit Fest** (w bitfest.mk). Comprising a variety of events ranging from musical to theatre to comedy in several venues across the town, it takes place between the last week in June and the third week in August. Other festivals include **Small Montmartre of Bitola** (w smallmontmartreofbitola.com), a festival of children's art which has been running for over 30 years, that takes place in May, and **Bitola Open City** (w mkcbt.org.mk), an international youth art festival held at the end of August. **Heraklea Evenings** are a series of outdoor theatre and musical events held over the summer in places such as the amphitheatre in Heraklea as well as other outdoor venues. Other summer events include the **International Graphics Triennial**, the **Contemporary Arts Festival**, and the **'Ilinden Days' Song and Dance Festival** with plenty of colourful folk costumes from local folklore groups. In September, the **Manaki Brothers International Cinematographers' Film Festival** (w manaki.com.mk) offers a programme of contemporary European and World Cinema, as well as coveted awards for best cinematography, while **Interfest** (w interfest.com.mk), an international celebration of classical music, is held in October.

PELISTER NATIONAL PARK *Telephone code 047*

Established in 1948, Pelister is Macedonia's smallest but oldest national park, extending for 171.5km² along the southwest border with Greece. Doubling as a ski destination in winter and hikers' paradise in summer, Pelister is famous for its rich flora and fauna, which includes ancient stands of the localised Macedonian pine (*Pinus peuce*; known locally as *molika*), as well as the rare Balkan lynx, the magnificent bearded vulture, and a variety of flowering gentians. Bears are quite often seen in winter but tend to be more secretive in summer. Mount Pelister, at 2,601m, is the summit of the Baba Mountains, which are in fact a part of the Rhodope range in Bulgaria.

There are three main access points to the park. The most popular and best developed of these, situated on the northeast park boundary, comprises the village of Nižepole and nearby Hotel Molika, which respectively lie around 10km and 15km from Bitola along a road that splits at the junction village of Dihovo. Rather more obscure are the isolated Vlach villages of Malovište and Gopeš, the first of which stands on the northern boundary some 22km from Bitola by road. Finally, on the southwestern border 50km from Bitola, the lovely village of Brajčino is now also a well-organised ecotourism centre.

NIŽEPOLE, HOTEL MOLIKA AND SURROUNDS The most accessible and busiest gateways to the park, Nižepole and the Hotel Molika lie just 3km apart as the crow flies, and are the sites of the only two ski lifts to the upper slopes. The surrounding area is well equipped with hotels and other tourist amenities, and forms the hub of all winter skiing activity. The winding 7km walk from Trnovo village to Hotel Molika provides a lovely introduction to the lower slopes, taking you along part of the Via Egnatia with cobbles laid down by French troops during World War I. In summer, Hotel Molika is a popular starting point for day hikes deeper into the park, further details of which can be obtained at the helpful hotel reception, or at the Info Centre Pelister (✆ 237 010; e infocentarpelister@yahoo.com; w park-pelister.com; ☉ 09.00–15.00 Tue–Sun) on the right-hand side of the road 1.5km back towards Bitola.

Getting there and away Coming from central Bitola, follow the road east out of town towards Ohrid for 3km, then turn left on to the side road to Pelister National Park. After another 3km, you'll reach the junction village of Dihovo, where a fork right leads to the Hotel Molika after 9km, passing through the villages of Trnovo and Magarevo en route. A nominal park entrance fee of 50MKD is levied at a toll on the way up, and you'll pass the Info Centre Pelister about 1.5km before the hotel. If heading to Nižepole, then you need to branch left at Dihovo, and keep going for another 4km. There is no public transport along these roads, but a taxi from Bitola to Hotel Molika should cost around 350–400MKD. The hotel can also call a taxi when you are ready to return to Bitola.

🏠 **Where to stay and eat** *Map, opposite*
In addition to the accommodation listed here, **mountain huts** on the Baba Mountains are listed on page 94.

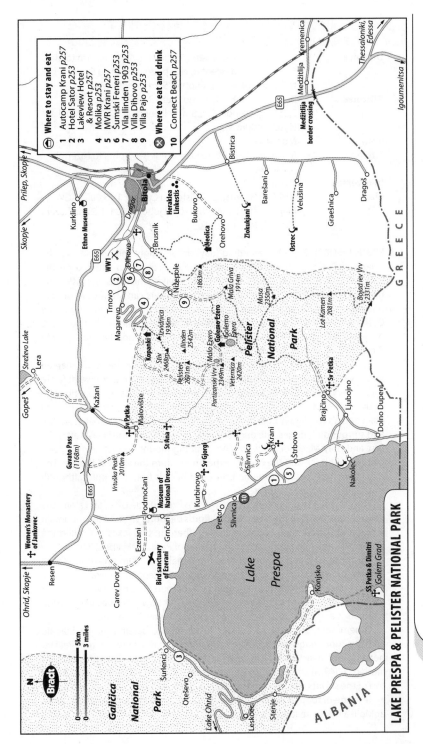

LAKE PRESPA & PELISTER NATIONAL PARK

Where to stay and eat

1 Autocamp Krani *p257*
2 Hotel Sator *p253*
3 Lakeview Hotel
   & Resort *p257*
4 Molika *p253*
5 MVR Krani *p257*
6 Šumski Feneri *p253*
7 Vila Ilinden 1903 *p253*
8 Vila Dihovo *p253*
9 Villa Pajo *p253*

Where to eat and drink

10 Connect Beach *p257*

HIKING FROM BRAJČINO TO PELISTER LAKES AND NIŽEPOLE

Distance	12km Brajčino to Golemo Ezero Hut. Another 3km to Malo Ezero or 6km descent to Nižepole. From Malo Ezero, 3km to Pelister peak, and another 5km to Hotel Molika.
Altitude	Brajčino 1,020m, Golemo Ezero 2,235m, Malo Ezero 2,250m, Nižepole 1,028m, Pelister peak 2,601m, Molika Hotel 1,400m
Rating	Moderate
Timing	5–7 hours to Golemo Ezero, plus 5–6 hours to Nižepole or Molika
In reverse	Possible
Map	1:50,000 Geomap of Pelister (in Cyrillic); 1:25,000 SAGW Map Sheets Nakolec 831-1-1, Ljubojno 831-1-2 and Kažani 781-3-4, January 2007

ROUTE DESCRIPTION This rewarding day or overnight hike connects the village of Brajčino, a well-organised centre of ecotourism situated on the park's southwestern boundary, to the Hotel Molika, which lies just inside the northern boundary only 15km from Bitola. Fit hikers can attempt to do it in one day, but it can also be broken into two sections by overnighting at the Golemo Ezero mountain hut. To get to and from the trail heads, two buses daily run along the 50km road between Bitola and Brajčino, and a taxi back to Bitola can be ordered at the Hotel Molika.

The section from Brajčino to Golemo Ezero (Big Lake) has been well marked and several information boards about the surrounding area and wildlife are set at intervals on the way. Golemo Ezero mountain hut sits right on the edge of the waters of this glacial lake and is arguably the most picturesque of all Macedonia's mountain huts. It lies in the shelter of Veternica Peak (2,420m) and surrounding ridges. The original name of the hut is Dime Ilievski after the first and only Macedonian who died climbing Mount Everest, in 1989, and pictures of his life and the Everest expedition adorn the walls of the hut. The most common route to Golemo Ezero and back is from Nižepole, although this route is also the steepest.

The ridge hike from Golemo Ezero to Malo Ezero (Little Lake) and along the Pelister Peak is above the treeline and affords beautiful vistas of the mountain range and surrounding countryside. Together the two lakes are called the Eyes of Pelister. Malo Ezero sits in the shelter of Partizanski Vrv (2,349m).

For those who can no longer face the remaining 400m ascent to Mount Pelister, or want a more gentle (and longer) descent to Molika, there is a 4x4 dirt track from Malo Ezero heading west around the next peak of Široko Stapalo (2,435m) and to the west of Pelister. The track heads down through the woods and ends up at the tarmac road just below the hotel.

Otherwise the ascent to Pelister heads north, passing Široko Stapalo and two more ridge peaks before summiting. The return route from Pelister heading northeast to Molika takes in two more panoramic viewpoints at Ilinden (2,542m) and Stiv (2,468m) and then descends into the woods. At the top of the ski lifts, 1km before Hotel Molika, is Kopanki mountain hut. Quite a wide range of food to eat and take away is for sale at Kopanki. The restaurant at Molika is also inviting after a long hike.

🏠 **Villa Pajo** (2 rooms) Nižepole; m +31 (0)64 483 0526; 🏠 @www.villapajonizepoleMacedonie. Dutch-run property comprising 2 beautifully kept villas, one sleeping up to 6, the other up to 14, just a 10min drive from Bitola. Huge garden, a play area for kids, BBQ area & Finnish sauna. Min 2-night stay; from €110/villa per night. **$$$–$$$$**

🏠 **Hotel Sator** (13 rooms) Trnovo; ☎ 293 409; e info@hotelsator.com.mk; w hotelsator.com.mk. Smart, modern rooms & a nice terrace. Restaurant. **$$$**

🏠 **Šumski Feneri** (17 rooms) Trnovo; ☎ 293 030; e sfeneri@t.mk; w sumskifeneri.com. Set around a cosy foyer & landings laden with well-kept plants & flowers, this stalwart has been in the same Vlach family since it was founded in 1988 & is now managed by the original owners' English-speaking daughter, Ljubica, a former guide & enthusiastic source of local travel information. The hotel can arrange skiing outings & other winter sports. It also has conference facilities for 40 & restaurant seating for 140. **$$$**

✳ 🏠 **Hotel Molika** (56 rooms) ☎ 229 406; m 075 495 725; e hmolika@t-home.mk; w hotelmolika.com.mk. Perched at an altitude of 1,420m at the top of the mountain road next to the car park for the Ski Centre Kopanki, this architecturally quirky hotel is almost ski-in ski-out in winter, & it makes a fine base for hiking in summer. All rooms are en suite with TV, central heating & balconies offering commanding views. It offers particularly good value out of the ski season, when rooms cost little more than dorm bed in a backpacker hostel. **$$**

🏠 **Vila Ilinden 1903** (2 rooms) Dihovo, 5km outside Bitola; m 076 697 909; e Bozidar_v@ hotmail.com. Small, attractive family-run B&B with home-cooked food & a nice garden. Rooms with wooden furniture & open stonework. Shared bathroom. **$$**

🏠 **Villa Dihovo** (6 rooms) Dihovo, 5km outside Bitola; ☎ 293 040; m 070 544 744; e contact@ villadihovo.com; w villadihovo.com; see ad, page 273. A beautifully renovated traditional house in the village of Dihovo in the foothills of Pelister with very pleasant lawns, fruit trees & excellent food. Part of the Slow Food Movement, they serve home-cooked meals using locally sourced ingredients. Interestingly, the property does not have a set price for rooms & food, but asks you to pay what you think your stay is worth. Alcohol, however, does have a set price, & their homemade wines (tastings from €6), beers & rakija are well worth trying in their tasting room. Bee-keeper visits, honey tastings, cooking lessons & hiking & biking trails also available. **$$** – at your discretion.

MALOVIŠTE AND GOPEŠ

A Vlach settlement perched at an altitude of 1,165m on the northern slopes of the mountains, **Malovište** is a real museum piece and well worth a visit. It was once a rich trading village, and it is not difficult to see that some of the houses were very stylish in their time. Most are now in various states of decay. The Church of Sv Petka is seldom open, so you will need to ask around to locate the key. Unusually for most churches in Macedonia, its exonarthex is on the left of the entrance rather than on the right. Behind the church is a graveyard containing some gravestones as old as the church itself. Forty minutes' hike from Malovište is the Monastery of Sv Ana, keys for which must be obtained in the village before you head up. Malovište is also the trail head for a steep but scenic 6km hike to the 2,010m Vrtuška Peak, from where you can either turn back the way you came, or descend along another 6km trail to the Gavato Pass.

About 15km north of Malovište, **Gopeš** is another formerly rich Vlach village, and although it hasn't had as much funding as Malovište, it is also a good potential museum town showing a glimpse of life back in the wealthier days.

Getting there and away

To get to Malovište from Bitola take the highway towards Ohrid for 18km, then take the exit to the right marked Kažani. After 200m, turn left at the crossroads, then after another 100m, at the village shop, turn left again on to a one-lane road that leads under a bridge across the main Ohrid road. Follow this for 4km until you enter Malovište.

To get to Gopeš from Kažani, head north along a road that follows the River Šemnica for roughly 5km to Streževo Lake. Then turn left at the lakeside village of Lera, and left again at Sviništa, to follow a dirt track uphill to Gopeš.

BRAJČINO The traditional village of Brajčino, perched on the edge of Pelister National Park less than 5km from the border with Greece, can claim to be the first ecotourism initiative in Macedonia. Pristine and picturesque, it has an idyllic location away from the hustle and bustle of city life, and is protected by the Baba

EATING AT HOME

Brajčino offers the chance to eat with the locals. Some friends and I ordered a day ahead for the special set menu to be served at 19.00 upon our arrival in the village. There is no à la carte menu, but vegetarian food or other dietary requests can be included, if the order is placed in advance.

We arrived in good time and walked up the narrow winding roads of the village to Jadranka's little farm at house number 144 (the village is so small that there are no street names). The family were waiting for us and ushered us into their tiny Sunday room, the one reserved for guests and special occasions.

Sitting at the neatly laid table we were offered a shot of rakija or liker as an aperitif to welcome us to their home. I chose the liker made of a rakija base redistilled with blueberries and sugar. Fortunately, the Macedonians take their time over their liqueurs, and this one was well worth savouring; accompanied by salad fresh from their garden, I could have drunk two or three glasses, but saved myself for the homemade wine which was to come with the main course.

We moved on to a country veal soup, so delicious that I asked the origin of the calf. 'Yes, it is our calf,' Jadranka replied. Feeling slightly guilty that I was eating from their larder, I continued the conversation enquiring if the calf had had a name. 'Rusa,' came the reply. 'Ah yes, well Rusa is indeed most delicious,' I added in my best Macedonian. Everyone burst out laughing at this point, probably at my attempt to speak Macedonian.

The next course included more of Rusa's melt-in-the-mouth offerings, accompanied by sweet roasted peppers and sautéed potatoes. Their homemade wine was fruity and mild, quaffable by the jugful, although we restrained ourselves to fit in some of their homemade peach juice, while we chatted away with the family about each other's lives. Formerly the area had lived well from sheep farming, but now Macedonia's depressed economy could not support the high price of sheep. With so little work in the locality, Jadranka and Jonce were glad to receive the extra income that ecotourism might bring their way. Jonce can be hired as a mountain guide by the day or half-day (1,500/800MKD) and, in addition to set meals, Jadranka sells dried boletus mushroom, liker, rakija and other homemade products such as jam, juice and wine.

We finished the meal with some homemade marble cake, cherries from their garden and a cup of coffee or mountain tea. Fully satiated, we then meandered back down the hill to our beds for an exquisite night's sleep.

The next evening we ate at Milka's house (now Vila and Restoran Raskrsnica). We were greeted with the Macedonian tradition of candied fruits (locally grown and produced, of course) and shots of mint or cherry liker. More homemade courses followed, ending with a delicious baklava made of walnuts and poppy seed.

massif, with a view on to Lake Prespa. It offers good access to the glacial lakes atop the range and from there to Pelister summit and the mountain huts. It is easily accessible by car, or by bus from Bitola (two daily) or Resen (several daily). It is also the starting point for the longer day or overnight hike to Hotel Molika via Pelister National Park, as described in the box on page 252.

Formerly a rich trading village, Brajčino still has a small population of mixed ages despite the emigration of many of the villagers in the middle of the 20th century to Canada and Scandinavia due to a lack of employment, or in order to escape communist persecution. However, the departure of most of the business know-how from the village has left it in hard times, even more so since the break-up of Yugoslavia which has taken its toll on the village's formerly prosperous apple trade. Previously, apples from the area would be sold as far away as Zagreb and Ljubljana, whereas new borders and taxes have all but eliminated the apple export. Today, the villagers, through the help of Swiss funding and the local non-governmental organisations of DEM (Ecological Movement of Macedonia) and BSPM (Bird Society Protection of Macedonia), are reviving the local economy by offering visitors access to their pristine lifestyle in return for keeping it so. Some 10% of the income of the guides, accommodation and the village shop is reinvested into preserving the local area.

About 3km before the road arrives at Brajčino, it weaves through **Ljubojno**, a larger village comprising a similar style of traditional stone houses, together with a few 19th- and 20th-century town houses on the central square. Clearly seen above the village are the two churches of **Sv Petka** and **Sv Pavle**, which vigilantly watch over Ljubojno.

Where to stay and eat There is a small café just off the main square that also offers information on the village guides and tours. A village lunch or evening meal can be arranged in one of the local houses, giving you that extra-special local experience, eating almost entirely locally grown and produced food (see box, opposite). You can order three types of menu: a basic menu for around 350MKD (three courses), a standard menu for 450MKD (four courses) and a special menu for 550MKD (for special occasions). Children aged between five and 12 years pay half price, younger than five years free. Wine with your meal is not included in this cost. See contact details below for Manastir Sv Petka, or Balojani Tourist Services (page 241) can organise everything for you.

Vila Raskrsnica (2 rooms) Brajčino; ☎482 322; m 075 796 796; e vila.raskrsnica@gmail. com; ⓕ @VilaRaskrsnicaBrajcinoPrespa. Likeable local guesthouse with the only full-time restaurant in Brajčino, offering very tasty local food in a rustic setting. **$$**

Vila Stara Cešma (5 rooms) Ljubojno; m 070 822 642, 072 629 021; e lisa.ljubojno@ yahoo.com. This charming homestay-like set-up stands alongside the main road to Brajčino as you exit Ljubojno. Only 2 rooms are en suite but the setting is pretty & the local home cooking excellent. **$$**

Manastir Sv Petka (24 dormitory beds) Brajčino; ☎482 444; m 070 497 751. Manastir

Sv Petka is no longer a working monastery, but was renovated by the villagers in 2003 under the ecotourism project in order to accommodate visitors. It is set in a meadow above the village & offers utter tranquillity, a view on to Pelister & a fantastic night sky. The accommodation price at the monastery includes bedding & use of the bathrooms, but you will have to pay 30MKD extra for a towel if you need one, & another 60MKD for use of the kitchen. There is so far no heating, so once the weather turns cold you may prefer to seek accommodation elsewhere. B/fast is not provided. A bed in the dorm is 350MKD. **$**

What to see and do The village has done a lot of work to tidy up local hiking trails and to keep them well marked and signposted. Hiking guides can be arranged for 800–1,200MKD for a half-day or 1,500–3,600MKD for a full day (depending on the number of people) to take you on less well-trodden trails and to give you an insight into local flora, fauna and history. It's a 5–6-hour hike to the mountain hut of Golemo Ezero at one of the 'Eyes of Pelister', and then another 3-hour hike from there to the summit of Pelister.

Brajčino village itself is pretty to walk around and an ideal setting for walks with children. There are many animals to be seen in the village farmyards and a number of buildings are marked with information plates on the usage, architecture and previous owners of the building. Much of this information is from the book *Brajčino Stories* by Meto Jovanovski from Brajčino, a former chairperson of the Macedonian Pen Club. The **bey's house** (Begot Kukja), the house of the last Ottoman commander for the area from the end of the 19th century, can be viewed inside if you ask for the key in the neighbouring houses or at the village shop.

There are six **churches** near the village dating from medieval times through to the beginning of the 20th century. The medieval churches are those dedicated to Sv Petka, Sv Bogorodica and Sv Atanas. It's not known exactly when these churches were built or even in what order, but all contain frescoes of the same era and, like so many churches in Macedonia, are in various stages of disrepair. The **Church of Sv Petka** lies in the grounds of the old monastery 15 minutes' walk outside the village. Sv Petka's holy day is 8 August, when up to 600 of the local villagers gather in the monastery with food and drink to celebrate. The small **Church of Sv Bogorodica** leans against a cliff above the village. The cliff can be seen from the village and, although the church itself is obscured by trees, the rock face is marked out with a cross at the top of the cliff. Set into the cliff are a number of 'cells' where local monks used to stay overnight in days of old. The medieval church 15 minutes' walk to the south of the village is dedicated to **Sv Atanas**. It is mostly in ruins but the grounds still house some graves. The church closest to the village and still used by its inhabitants is the **Church of Sv Nikola**. Built in 1871, it is in a pretty location with a good view on to Lake Prespa. The main nave of the church is usually locked, although you may be able to access the glass-fronted exonarthex. Ask in the village for the key. The belltower is a recent addition, made of a simple metal frame but in the traditional Macedonian style of being separate from the church itself. The churches of **Sv Ilija** (1915) and **Sv Archangel** (1919) are located outside the village and are very simple and rarely used.

LAKE PRESPA *Telephone code 047*

Lake Prespa, on the other side of the Galičica Mountains from Lake Ohrid, offers a peaceful, cooler and cheaper alternative to its better-known neighbour, and is well worth a visit in July and August when even Ohrid can get blisteringly hot and the festivities can be too much. Combined with Pelister Mountain, which is exactly 800m higher than the Galičica Mountains, the area offers a lot for those who love the outdoors. Most people access Lake Prespa via Bitola, but if you're coming from Ohrid by car, then a trip over the southern end of the Galičica range offers fantastic views and the opportunity to hike up to the Two Lakes Viewpoint (see box, page 223).

The lake is 850m above sea level, and the surroundings are refreshingly cooled by the mountain air. Due to the relatively shallow depth of Prespa, only just over 50m, the lake itself can get quite warm, up to 25°C in the summer. A shallow sandy shoreline allows children to play and swim safely where their feet can still touch the bottom.

Sharing its borders with Greece and Albania, the lake lies close on the Greek side to a smaller lake of the same name. The two lakes are separated by only a narrow strip of land in Greece, and in centuries gone by the two lakes used to be one. During that time, the name Prespa, meaning 'blizzard', came about because of the illusion created of an almighty blizzard when the lakes would freeze over; covered in snow, they would resemble a white-out to anyone looking in their direction. Other legends abound as to how the lake came into existence (see box, page 259).

WHERE TO STAY AND EAT *Map, page 251*

There is limited choice on the lake itself, in part because it is not as good for swimming as Ohrid. Most Macedonians tend to stay in Pelister National Park (page 250) or in little villages such as Brajčino (page 255). Ezerani bird sanctuary also offers basic accommodation (page 258).

☀ ⌂ Lakeview Hotel & Resort (23 rooms) Oteševo; ☎551 195; m 072 706 549; e contact@ lakeviewotesevo.com; w lakeviewotesevo.com. Far & away the most appealing overnight option on Lake Prespa, this attractive resort stands in large green grounds only 4km north of the junction with the scenic road that crosses from Lake Ohrid via Galičica National Park. The modern rooms are set in a 2-storey block & all have lake-facing balconies. Activities include swimming, fishing, birdwatching & kayaking. The pleasant terrace restaurant forms an ideal lunch stop for day visitors coming from Ohrid. Good value. **$$$**

⌂ Hotel MVR Krani (56 rooms) Krani; ☎483 247; e 629@gmail.com; ◆ Hotel MVR Krani. This is arguably the safest hotel in Macedonia as it belongs to the Ministry of the Interior & is reserved primarily for use by the police. It is rarely anywhere near full, however, & it has a good location on the lake. With a small exclusive beach for hotel customers, it's good value. Rooms are basic in that very 'socialist' style, all en suite but no TV or AC (it rarely gets that hot here anyway). The hotel

has a restaurant that seats over 100 guests & is sometimes booked up for weddings, but usually you will have the terrace to yourself. It also has about 20 hook-ups for c/vans & camping, with block showers & toilets. **$$**

⌂ Autocamp Krani (50 bungalows) Krani; m 071 256 500. Situated almost right next to the Hotel MVR, this peaceful lakeshore resort offers accommodation in slightly run-down bungalows, each with 2 dbl rooms, & it also has a campsite. It's not as nice as the hotel but it is a little cheaper & would be a useful fall-back when its neighbour is full. **$$**

✗ Connect Beach Restaurant m 077 994 635, 075 460 858; w connect.net.mk. Set on the east shore a few kilometres north of Krani, this vast resort-like restaurant has hundreds of deckchairs lined up on its reasonably sandy beach & serves a varied menu of grills, salads & fish dishes, as well as cocktails & other drinks. It can feel a bit moribund during the week but gets busy at w/ends. **$$**

WHAT TO SEE AND DO

Beaches There are a number of access points to the shores of Lake Prespa where there are small beaches and resorts. The largest of these is at **Oteševo** on the northwestern side of the lake, which also houses the national centre for respiratory illnesses, due to the superb quality of the air at Lake Prespa. On the western side of the lake near the border with Albania, **Konjsko** has a lovely little public beach, which is quite secluded, and the village itself is the site of an ancient settlement that is largely intact and now protected as part of Macedonia's cultural heritage. A small cave church dedicated to Sv Elias can also be found near the village. The asphalt road does not go all the way, so be prepared for a hike or take a 4x4. **Krani** has a lovely small private beach available to those staying at the Hotel MVR (see above), whereas the beach at **Dolno Dupeni**, right on the border with Greece (the border crossing here was still closed at the time of writing) is larger and public, and has a small food and drinks hut.

The beach at **Nakolec** has the added attraction of being next to this small mixed ethnicity village, one of the few in the area along with Krani, Grnčari and Arvati. The **Church of Sv Atanas** on the shore of Nakolec used to stand practically in the water, but now lies some way off due to the water loss from the lake. The receding shoreline has allowed for some excavation, however, which has revealed the foundations of buildings further into the lake. As measures are now being taken to refill the lake, these excavations will undoubtedly be covered over once again but hopefully not before the research on them has been finished. Nakolec also used to have a number of wooden houses on stilts, but these are no longer standing. The old Bektaši teke in the village is being rebuilt.

Golem Grad
Aside from swimming in the lake and enjoying the cooler temperatures of Pelister Mountain, the must-do thing at Lake Prespa is to visit the uninhabited island of Golem Grad, sometimes known as Snake Island for all the water snakes that live around its shores. Part of the nature reserve of Galičica National Park, it contains endemic flora and fauna protected by the island's lack of contact with the rest of the world, so if you do get the chance to go, be sure to leave no trace. Previously inhabited over the centuries going back to Neolithic times, the island is said to be where Tsar Samoil was crowned tsar in AD976, and the remains of two 14th-century churches, dedicated to Sv Petka and to Sv Dimitri, are built on the foundations of 6th-century early Christian basilicas. Other ruins of an old village can also be found here.

If you can't find a local to take you out to the island, then boat trips can be arranged with Go Macedonia or Macedonia Travel in Skopje (page 64), during which you will see a variety of birdlife. You'll probably spot the (perfectly harmless) water snakes, too, which may gather around your boat but disappear as soon as you step into the water or move the boat. Make sure you visit the island in the morning and return very soon after an early lunch at the latest, as the winds on the lake can pick up in the early afternoon. In 2011, two tourists had to be rescued by helicopter from the island in the afternoon when a storm brewed up, despite the fact that there had not been a cloud in the sky on the morning when they left.

Other sights
If you are approaching the lake from Ohrid via the E65 then it is worth a look into the **women's Monastery of Jankovec**, a few kilometres before the town of Resen. This was the first women's monastery to be brought back to life after several decades of neglect during communist times. Sister Kirana, who heads the best group of fresco painters alive today in Macedonia, brought the nuns to the run-down 16th-century monastery in 1998. They have done a lot of work to it since then and their skills as fresco artists are in high demand throughout Macedonia. They also weave, and sometimes you can purchase their handicrafts at the monastery.

At the northern end of the lake, the village of Podmočani has a **small museum** of national dress and artefacts in a little house on the main road. Still the private collection of a local farmer, Jone Eftimoski, it is open to public viewing for a small entry fee. There are over 140 costumes from all over Macedonia along with jewellery, weapons and coins. Just as you get to the start of the cobbled part of the road there is a small green sign marked 'museum' pointing to the house on the right of the main road. It may not look open, but there is usually someone around in the front garden who will let you in and give you a guided tour.

Further along the lakeside road is the **bird sanctuary of Ezerani**. As with any birdwatching it is best to go early in the morning or in the evening, otherwise you

Legend has it that a town once stood in place of the great Lake Prespa. While walking through the local woods one day, the son of the king of the town chanced upon a wood nymph whose beauty surpassed that of any girl he had hitherto laid eyes upon. On asking her name, she replied in an enchanting voice 'Nereida'. The king's son fell immediately in love with the nymph and came to the woods many times to woo her and take her hand in marriage, offering her all the riches of his father's land and a place by his side as the queen of the kingdom. But the nymph turned down his generous offer, saying that she could not marry a mortal without sinister consequences befalling the groom and his homeland. Unable to imagine a deed so awful and unable to suppress his love for the nymph, he chose one night to have her kidnapped and kept her in confinement until she accepted his offer of marriage. Upon their pronouncement as husband and wife, however, the heavens opened and a downpour of rain ensued. The rain did not stop until the whole town was underwater and every citizen had drowned. The result is the present-day Lake Prespa. The moral of the story is that when a woman says 'no' she really does mean it.

may find only a herd of cows among the rushes, eating discarded apples. Part of the University of Skopje and internationally protected by EURONATUR, the sanctuary is home to over 115 different species of bird, including wild geese, pelicans and local moorhens. University members can stay at the sanctuary for a discounted price (€15 per night for bed and breakfast for non-members), although the rooms and facilities are in great need of attention.

The next turn-off on the left leads to the village of **Kurbinovo**. This is a typical working local village along a pot-holed tarmac road crowded with meandering sheep, goats and cows. At the second house on the left, a two-storey white building with a railed front lawn, ask for the key to the **Church of Sv Gjorgi** (*kluč za Sveti Gjorgi*), and continue on up the road. At the crest of the hill in the village turn right through a narrow row of houses and continue another couple of kilometres until you turn into a large tarmacked parking area, obviously out of keeping with the surroundings, above which is the 12th-century church. There are a number of medieval frescoes inside dating from when the church was first built in 1191, and some in Macedonia believe that the style of these was the seed of the Renaissance arts in Italy (see box, page 150). Unfortunately, of the many frescoes depicting the life of St George, few can be seen now.

PRILEP *Telephone code 048*

If you are venturing beyond Skopje and Ohrid and are wondering where to go next, and/or want a compact representation of Macedonian life through the ages, then go to Prilep. Situated under the Towers of Marko, a ruined medieval fortress, the town has two worthwhile monasteries in the vicinity, as well as a well-preserved, if small, old Turkish town and a pedestrian area where it is simply nice to drink coffee and relax. The area is so symbolic of Macedonian culture that it has been used twice as a film setting by Macedonian director Milčo Mančevski. The name of the city itself derives from the ancient tribe of the Pelazgi. Macedonia's fledgling beer festival takes over in mid-July and attracts over 300,000 people.

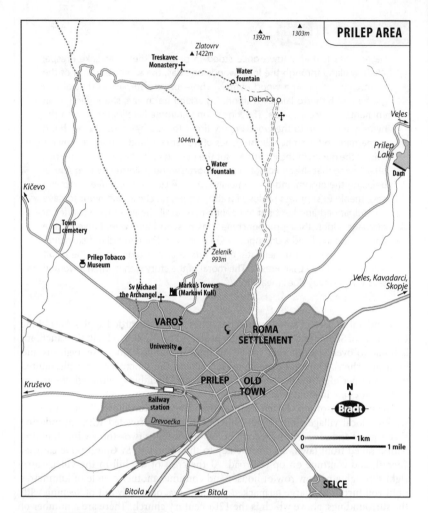

PRILEP AREA

1392m

1303m

Zlatovrv
▲ 1422m

Treskavec
Monastery ✝

Water
fountain

Dabnica

Veles

Prilep
Lake

Dam

1044m ▲

Water
fountain

Kičevo

Town
cemetery

Prilep Tobacco
Museum

Zelenik
993m

Veles, Kavadarci,
Skopje

Sv Michael
the Archangel ✝

Marko's Towers
(Markovi Kuli)

VAROŠ

ROMA
SETTLEMENT

University ●

PRILEP

OLD
TOWN

N

Kruševo

Railway
station

Bradt

Drevoećka

0   1km
0   1 mile

Bitola

Bitola

SELCE

GETTING THERE AND AROUND

By road Prilep lies 130km south of Skopje along the A3 via Veles and Gradsko, a trip that shouldn't take more than 2 hours in a private vehicle or by bus. A slightly shorter but slower and more scenic back road also connects Veles to Prilep (page 281); if you use it to get from Prilep to Veles, take the lake road out of town and, at the marble statue of a cannon above the lake, take the right-hand fork on to a dirt track.

Prilep lies 110km from Ohrid via Bitola, another straightforward drive of up to 2 hours. Coming from the southeast, the drive to Prilep between the Babuna and Dren mountains is also very pretty, although the road is often only one lane wide and blocked with tractors, lorries or expansion work. The pass at Pletvar lies at 994m above sea level.

Frequent **buses** connect Prilep to most main cities. This includes around ten buses daily in either direction to/from Skopje via Veles, ten daily to/from Ohrid, 15 to/from Bitola, four daily to/from Štip (where you can change coming to or from Strumica), seven to Kičevo and one to Gevgelija. All leave from the new bus station

(↖425 555), which lies on the north side of Goce Delčev Street, about 1km west of the junction with Kuzman Josifovski.

By rail Prilep train station (↖412 660) is about 100m west of the bus station. Four trains daily travel through in either direction en route between Skopje/Veles and Bitola. If you don't manage any other train journey in Macedonia, the section from Veles to Prilep is the one to do, as it takes you through some great mountain scenery, some parts of which are not even accessible by road. A highlight, midway between the towns of Sogle and Bogomila, is the fantastic view of the Solunska Glava Mountain with its 800m drop from the summit. Trains bound for Veles and Skopje pass through Prilep at 03.45, 05.50, 13.30 and 15.10 daily, while those heading to Bitola pass through at 09.32, 17.08, 19.20 and 22.58.

GETTING AROUND Once in Prilep, the best form of transport if you get tired of walking through the small town is one of the numerous taxis. Contact Prilep Taxi Service (↖15188). The minimum fare is 50MKD, plus 30MKD/km thereafter.

TOUR OPERATORS Info Tours (Kuzman Josifovski 11; ↖419 418; m 075 259 000; e contact@infotours.mk; w infotours.mk; ⊕ 08.30–13.30 & 17.00–19.30 Mon, Tue, Thu & Fri, 08.30–15.00 Wed & Sat, Sun closed) is conveniently located near the old bus station. For more information on the town, visit w prilepinfo.mk/en.

⌂ WHERE TO STAY *Map, page 262*

⌂ **Atlas City Centre Hotel** (70 Rooms) Goce Delčev St; ↖550 700; e frontdesk@ atlasinvest.com.mk; w atlas-city-center-hotel. business.site. Centrally located multistorey hotel with comfortable modern rooms & a 4th-floor restaurant offering views over the clock tower & roofs of the old bazaar. **$$$**

⌂ **Hotel Breza** (10 rooms) Moša Pijade 24a; ↖423 683; m 071 214 071; e contact@breza.com. mk; w breza.com.mk. Rooms in a large house with a nice small b/fast area. Half price for children aged 5–11. **$$$**

⌂ **Hotel Salida** (33 rooms) Ivo Lola Ribar; ↖400 333; e contact@hotelsalida.com.mk; w hotelsalida. com.mk. Modern hotel with simply furnished rooms in the south of the town. A 2nd branch is located on Orde Čopela, in the western part of town. **$$$**

⌂ **Hotel Sonce** (52 beds) Aleksandar Makedonski 4/3a; ↖401 800; e contact@soncega.com. Pleasant rooms. Large fitness centre & outdoor pool. **$$$**

⌂ **Kristal Palas** (22 rooms) Lenin 184; ↖418 000; m 076 444 081; e info@kp.mk; w kp.mk. Situated to the west of the town centre, near the bus & railway station, this modern hotel is arguably the best place to stay in Prilep, thanks partly to the small but lovely rooftop indoor heated swimming pool offering a 270° panorama of the town. Popular with wedding receptions, which can get a bit noisy in the evening. **$$$**

✳ ⌂ **Kostoski Inn** (2 rooms) Aleksandar Makedonski 520; m 077 630 458, 079 246 194; e metodijakostoski@gmail.com; ❋ @kotoskiinn. Run by a very friendly & helpful couple who live on-site, this budget guesthouse has spacious, spotless rooms with kitchenette. Great value. **$$**

✗ WHERE TO EAT AND DRINK *Map, page 262*

The pedestrian area and the old town offer a lot of places to eat. Recommended options are:

✗ **Del Posto** Ilinden St; ↖435 000; w delposto. mk. Situated on the same pedestrianised alley as Cafe Stara Charshija, this top-notch Italian restaurant has a smart interior, plenty of shaded terrace seating & an imaginative selection of cocktails & salads. **$$$**

✗ **Makedonska Kuka** Joska Jordanovski 4; ↖433 419; m 070 208 519; e contact@ makedonskakuka.com; ⊕ noon–midnight Sun–Thu, noon–01.00 Fri–Sat. The sister of its namesake in Skopje, this justifiably popular

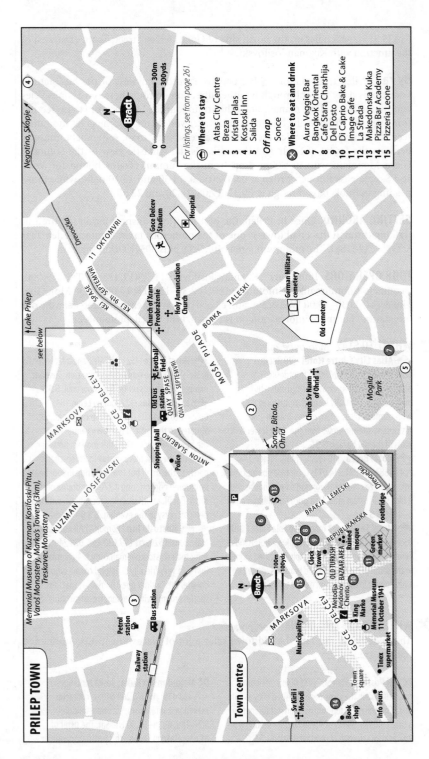

PRILEP TOWN

Negotino, Skopje

Lake Prilep

Memorial Museum of Kuzman Kosifoski-Pitu,
Varoš Monastery, Marko's Towers (3km),
Treskavec Monastery

see below

DEVOEŠKO

11 OKTOMVRI

KEJ 9th SEPTEMVRI

KEJ SPASE

MARKSOVA

GOCE DELČEV

KUZMAN JOSIFOVSKI

Goce Delčev
Stadium

Hospital

Church of Kram
Preobraženie

Holy Annunciation
Church

MOŠA PIJADE

BORKA TALESKI

German Military
cemetery

Old cemetery

Shopping Mall

Old bus
station

Football
field

QUAY SPASE 9th SEPTEMVRI

Police

ANTON SLABEJKO

Church Sv Naum
of Ohrid

Sonce, Bitola,
Ohrid

Mogila
Park

Bradt

N

0   300m
0   300yds

For listings, see from page 261

Where to stay
1 Atlas City Centre
2 Breza
3 Kristal Palas
4 Kostoski Inn
5 Salida

Off map
   Sonce

Where to eat and drink
6 Aura Veggie Bar
7 Bangkok Oriental
8 Cafe Stara Charshija
9 Del Posto
10 Di Caprio Bake & Cake
11 Image Cafe
12 La Strada
13 Makedonska Kuka
14 Pizza Bar Academy
15 Pizzeria Leone

Town centre

Railway
station

Petrol
station

Bus station

Devoeško

Footbridge

BRAKJA LEMESKI

REPUBLIKANSKA

Ruined
mosque

Green
market

Clock
tower

OLD TURKISH
BAZAAR AREA

Metodij
Andonov
Chento

DEL ČEV

GOCE

King
Marko

Memorial Museum
11 October 1941

Tinex
supermarket

MARKSOVA

Municipality

Sv Kiril i
Metodi

Book
shop

Town
square

Info Tours

Bradt

N

0   100m
0   100yds

262

restaurant offers traditional food & ambience, with the option of eating in the traditionally decorated interior or large courtyard. Live Macedonian music & folk dancing most evenings. $$$

* **✕ Bangkok Oriental** Ivo Lola Ribar; ✆ 425 027; ✕ @BangkokPrilep; ⏰ 10.30–midnight Sun–Thu, 10.30–01.00 Fri–Sat. Offering a rare change from the usual Macedonian fare & pizzas, this excellent Thai restaurant recently relocated to new premises south of the town centre, near the Hotel Salida. Such is the reputation of the genuine Thai chef, regulars come here all the way from Skopje. Not to be missed. $$

✕ Cafe Stara Charshija Ilinden St; m 070 356 377. Sprawling out on to a pedestrianised alley in the Old Bazaar, this popular traditional restaurant serves good inexpensive grills & is famed for its giant Macedonian burgers. $$

✕ Di Caprio Bake & Cake Town square; ⏰ noon–midnight Sun–Thu, noon–01.00 Fri–Sat. This place has nice upstairs & terrace seating on the main square, & a balcony overlooking the old town. $$

✕ Pizza Bar Academy Kuzman Josifovski St; ✆ 500 500; ✕ @PizzaBarAcademy. Swish modern Italian restaurant with attractive décor & appealing menu of pizza, pasta, salads & other Italian dishes. $$

✕ Pizzeria Leone Goce Delčev; ✆ 418 282; ⏰ 08.00–01.00 daily. Longstanding & popular restaurant serving the best pizza in town. $$

* **✕ Aura Veggie Bar** General Vasko Karangjeleski St; m 077 875 959; ✕ @aurasnackbar. Sprawling across 2 floors, this colourfully decorated place with 1st-floor balcony seating has a hippyish vibe. The alluring & very inexpensive selection of vegetarian fare – fruit & vegetable smoothies, pizza, falafel & veggie burgers, & filled naan & tortillas – is complimented by sangria, wine & beer for those who want to make an evening of it. $

🖵 Image Cafe Town square; ✆ 422 777; ✕ @imagecafe2006. Cheerful central terrace café serving excellent coffee & the cheapest pint of draught in town. $

🖵 La Strada Goce Delčev; ✆ 414 212; ⏰ 11.00–midnight Sun–Thu, 10.00–01.00 Fri–Sat. A happening bar with a raised balcony off the street. $

WHAT TO SEE AND DO
Central and suburban Prilep The old Turkish centre of Prilep is small and can be walked around in about 10 minutes. It borders on the pedestrian area of Metodi Šatarov Šarlo, and towering over the old town is the **clock tower**, next to which are the **ruins of an old mosque**, and the one remaining wall of another can be found in **Metodi Andonov Park**. West of the shopping centre is the **Memorial Museum 11 Oktomvri 1941** (Ilinden St; ✆ 401 090; m 075 240 948; e muzejprilep@yahoo.com; w muzejprilep.org.mk; ⏰ 10.00–13.00 Tue–Sun; entry 150MKD), commemorating the partisan fight against fascist forces during World War II. Prilep's memorial to the fallen of the war is at **Mogila Park**, 1km south of the town centre. While the arrangement of metre-high modern-art fists is nothing spectacular, the park itself is pretty and relatively clean. A ruined **German cemetery** is at Penka Koteska Street, behind what is known as the old cemetery (*stari grobišta*), containing the graves of 1,683 German soldiers from World War I, 156 other foreign soldiers from World War I and almost 50 German soldiers from World War II.

North of the city centre, the **Memorial Museum of Kuzman Kosifoski-Pitu** (Mara Josifovski 20; ✆ 401 090; w muzejprilep.org.mk; ⏰ by appointment; entry 120MKD) is dedicated to its namesake, a key Prilep agitator in the fight against fascism, and stands on a street named after one of his sisters.

There are two churches near Prilep's centre, though neither are particularly noteworthy. Near the library is the fairly modern **Church of Sv Kiril i Metodi**, which dates from 1926 and has no frescoes. Located opposite the **green market** on Kej 9th Septemvri, the **Church of Xram Preobražnie**, built in 1871, is dark, no frills and mostly locked, although you can look through the glass doors. The courtyard, however, provides a welcome place to sit down and there are taps here for water.

Prilep Beer Festival (w pivofestival.mk) Fast becoming the biggest event in Macedonia, the Prilep Beer Festival or Pivofest is a four-day event that attracts up to 100,000 people on its last night. Music groups from all over the region play every night, and it is thus starting to rival similar events in the rest of the Balkans. It usually takes place on the second weekend in July and is the only time when trains to Prilep will be full. Although wild camping is technically illegal in Macedonia, it is the only way in which Prilep can cope with the overload of people.

Marko's Towers (Markovi Kuli) Boasting a prominent hilltop setting about 2km northwest of central Prilep, the Fortress Tower of Marko (Markovi Kuli) is named after King Marko (see box, below), the last Macedonian king, who died fighting the Turks. Archaeological findings show that parts of the fortress date back to the Iron Age, the 3rd and 4th centuries BC and later periods during the Ottoman Empire. Most of what remains to be seen today is from medieval times and is mostly in ruins, but still well worth the hike, and the views from the top over the ruins and beyond are magnificent.

To get here from the centre of town take Ulica Markovska uphill and turn off to the right after about 1km where the road levels off, just after a small pharmacy and a car mechanic shop, opposite some conference halls. Keep going uphill until you get to the back of the houses that will lead you to the gravel road to the towers. The road passes the famous stone called Slon, meaning 'the elephant', which marks the beginning of the Markovi Kuli site and continues in a blaze of white crushed marble (Prilep is also a marble-quarrying town) around the back of the hill. This is the easy route up, suitable for a high-clearance vehicle, although whether you will find a parking space at the top on a busy weekend is another thing.

Alternatively, you could take on a frontal assault of the towers and go straight up the middle of the rocks. A path eventually forms itself if you bear right of the

MARKO, THE LAST ORTHODOX KING OF MACEDONIA

After the death of Serbian Tsar Dušan in 1355, a mere ten years after he had been crowned king in Skopje, the Serb kingdom started to fall apart at the seams. Tsar Uroš took over, helped by the Mrnjavčevič brothers, Volkašin and Ugleša. They headed feudal kingdoms within the empire, and in 1365 Volkašin proclaimed himself co-tsar and ruler of the western side of the empire with its seat of power at Prilep.

Volkašin had four sons and several daughters by his wife Elena. Marko, the eldest, was born in 1335. Thirty-six years later in 1371, when Volkašin and his brother were killed fighting against the Ottomans in Thrace, Greece, the crown of the empire passed to Marko, as neither Tsar Uroš nor Volkašin's brother Ugleša had any heirs. Even though he was of Serb origin, King Marko is often viewed by the Macedonians as the stepping stone for Macedonian nationhood between Tsar Samoil (967–1014) and the ten-day Kruševo Republic of 1903.

Marko's kingdom reached from the Šar Mountains in the northwest down the western bank of the River Vardar to Kastoria (in present-day Greece) in the south. It rarely also included Skopje or Ohrid. Prilep was centrally placed within Marko's realm, and the fortress that overlooks the town is named after the king, though it eventually fell to the Ottomans in 1394. A year later King Marko was killed in Romania while forced to fight for the Ottomans against the Vlachs.

entrance. It must have been suicidal as a foot soldier, even with armour and weapons, to attack the towers from this direction: hard work all the way up and raining arrows. Bring plenty of water with you, at least half a litre per person on a hot day, as there is none at the top and thirst would spoil an otherwise lovely gambol among the rocks.

The frontal assault and parts of the towers are steep, require some scrambling and have no handrails, so this is not advisable for those who are prone to vertigo. A watchtower has been recreated at the eastern end of the rocks using concrete, and it looks decidedly out of place. The highest part of the rock formation is marked by a metal-girder cross, similar to the one in Skopje but smaller.

From the top it is also possible to hike 8km north to Zlatovrv, where Treskavec Monastery lies (page 266).

Monastery of Sv Michael the Archangel
Perched on the southeastern edge of the rocky hill dominated by Marko's Towers, this medieval monastery, which still houses a few nuns, looks out to the northwestern suburb of Varoš and the Pelagonia plains. The monastery is entered via a 5th-century iron doorway, and although little remains of the original 12th-century church, two partial remains of frescoes and some of the old walls can be seen in the vaults.

The church now standing in the monastery courtyard is made up of two parts built during medieval times and of three classical period marble columns, which were found by the monks who built the monastery. The second-oldest Cyrillic inscription to be found in Macedonia is carved at eye level into the far-right pillar as you stand in the exonarthex (the oldest inscription is the epitaph dedicated to Tsar Samoil's mother and father). The remaining housing for the nuns was erected in the 19th century. Underneath the main inn is a deep well that is entered via a small doorway.

Allegedly there were once 77 churches in the Prilep area, but only six were left standing after the Ottoman Empire moved in. One of these was the **Church of Sv Atanas**, which no longer has a roof, and can be seen on the way to Sv Michael's Monastery.

To get to Varoš take Gorče Petrov out of town past the turning to Markovi Kuli. At this point the road turns into Orle Čopela, and very quickly you'll come to a bust of Orle Čopela on the right at the top of the rise. Just before this monument, take the unsignposted right turn on to Borke Dopačot. Follow this asphalt road northeast for about 600m until you see Sv Atanas to your right. Just after the church, a 300m road to the right winds uphill to the Monastery of Sv Michael the Archangel.

AROUND PRILEP

PRILEP TOBACCO MUSEUM (Kruševsko Đadeč bb; ☎ 401 090; e muzejzatutun@ mail.com.mk; ⊕ by appointment only during the week) Housed in the grounds of the Tutun Tobacco Institute 4km northwest of the town centre, the Prilep Tobacco Museum was opened in 1973 to celebrate the centenary of the tobacco factory that now houses both the institute and museum. Especially for the occasion, Tito ordered the purchase of over 750 items for display in the museum ranging from German tobacco pots, Chinese cigarette cases, Russian snuffboxes and Ottoman pipes, to intriguing cigar cutters and ornate *nargilehs* (water pipes) for both scented tobacco and opium. The room housing the exhibits seems an anticlimax on first entry, but a closer look at the carved faces and scenes on the artefacts reveals an exquisite craftsmanship that is fascinating and compelling, even if you don't agree with smoking (and smoking had been banned in 1634 by a decree from the Ottoman sultan). Artefacts made from a variety of woods, bone, ivory, silver, gold inlay, pearl lacquer, silver filigree, silver nitrate inlay, semi-precious stone and glazed enamels

MARKO'S TOWERS TO TRESKAVEC MONASTERY ON FOOT

Distance	6.5km
Altitude	Prilep town centre 640m, Markovi Kuli 945m, Treskavec Monastery 1,260m
Rating	Easy to moderate
Timing	2½ hours
Circular trail	Possible
Map	1:25,000 SAGW Map Sheet Prilep 782-1-3, January 2007

ROUTE DESCRIPTION There are three routes to the monastery.

Route 1: By foot from Markovi Kuli (for directions to Markovi Kuli, see page 264) This is the easiest route and is well trodden and relatively well marked by red-and-white hiking marks, paintings of saints, and a spring just over halfway along the route. Part of the hike is along some steep rocks, but the way is aided by a steel rope. The rocks along all three routes are what make Prilep's scenery famous.

Route 2: By foot along the old cobbled road from Dabnica This route is only 4.5km if you take a taxi through the disgracefully neglected Roma slums of Prilep to within 1km of Dabnica. It is steeper over the shorter distance, however. Your hike begins when the road is no longer fenced off on the left and comes to the obvious opening on to the foothills of Zlatovrv. At the end of the fence there is another dirt track to the left leading to a nearby house. The cobbled path you require, which is not obvious at first, heads straight up the ridge of the spur leading up to Zlatovrv. It lies directly between where the dirt track divides and, if you have a compass, set it to 6,000 mils or 340° and follow this bearing until you come across the obvious path uphill. After an hour, the path, with large chunks of cobbling still intact, starts to wind back and forth and comes upon a water fountain. From the fountain the path is practically straight until you get to the back gate of the monastery. Follow the path around to the left and to the front of the monastery. If you drive yourself to the start point of the hike, head west through the Roma settlement (ask for Dabnica).

Route 3: By 4x4 or foot along an asphalt road to the southwest To reach the dirt track head out of Prilep on Marksova and Orde Čopela, past the Tobacco Museum, and turn towards the town cemetery 5km from the centre of town. Follow the road left around to the back of the cemetery. At the junction where you lose the tarmac (500m from the main road) is a small sign, marked Monastir Sveta Bogorodica, Treskavec, pointing the way straight ahead. After another 2.5km turn right when you join another track through the valley, then left after another 250m. Follow this road uphill to the monastery in about 3km.

are all on display. Sadly, very little information is available in Macedonian or English, although many of the stories behind the pieces can be told by the museum curator Aleksandar Tretkoski if he is available.

TRESKAVEC MONASTERY Some 8km outside Prilep under the summit of the impressive Zlatovrv, this remote monastery is a magnificent old complex of significant historical and cultural value that is in urgent need of renovation. The site is of such worth that it made the World Monument Fund's 2006 top 100 most endangered sites. In addition to the value of the site itself, its remote setting is beautiful and earned itself a central role in Mančevski's film *Before the Rain*.

The monastery is built on the ancient town of Kolobaise, which existed from the 3rd century BC until the 7th century AD and whose name is written in a long inscription cut into a stone used as the base of the cross on top of the central dome of the church. There are also other inscriptions around the church that date back to the 1st century BC, when a temple to Apollo and Artemis was first built on this site.

Further remnants of the town under Roman rule can be found in the present 14th-century Church of Sv Bogorodica, which was built on the foundations of the original 6th-century basilica. There is a baptism font on the left of the narthex as you enter, and the walls of the narthex have a number of stone carvings and sculptures. As there are few lights in the church, it is a good idea to bring a torch with you or a lighter for the candles so that you can see the artefacts. The narthex goes around to the right, covering two sides of the church, at the end of which is a separate confessional room that is interesting for its fresco depicting the donors who paid to have the church built: the two old men dedicated their life to God and are shown, as is typical of frescoes of the original church donors, holding the church between them.

There is a secondary narthex before entering the nave, and from this narthex are some steps on the right that lead into a small chamber. Inside the cupola there is one of the few frescoes of Christ as a young boy (there is another in the Monastery of Sv Eleusa, also in the right-hand chamber). The church has a number of 16th-century frescoes with the typical greenish sheen on the face of the figures that was the hallmark of Macedonian rather than Greek artists. Also in the nave is a casket of the skulls of seven monks from the monastery who were executed, along with almost 200 other monks who lived here at the time, by the Ottomans.

To the right of the entrance into the monastery is the old dining hall. It contains the old stone tables and Roman jars and vats, but it is in a terrible state of repair, and the last fresco at the end of the hall is in dire need of help if it is to remain intact on the wall. The chips in it show that it is an older fresco that was deliberately chipped in order to apply plaster for a new one, which has long since gone.

Despite its former glory in the early Ottoman period, only one monk currently runs the monastery. Father Kališt, who speaks very good English, welcomes visitors and especially to the Sunday service held at 11.00. It is forbidden to enter the monastery scantily clad, so make sure you bring coverings for shoulders and legs before you get all the way there only to find you are improperly dressed and refused entry.

Outside the monastery are ancient graves cut into the rock. Water wells are encased in the stone wall to the left of the monastery main gate which leads to the ancient graves. There are also caves and monks' cells up on Zlatovrv. The stone outcrops and the views are intriguing, and there are thought to be 77 animal and human forms that one can find in the rocks, such as lions, people talking to each other, a sphinx, a frog and eagles.

There is comparatively little money to do much-needed renovation work at this remote monastery, and there is no charge to stay in the inns, so maybe give generously at the altar when you visit the church. State-run excavation work is ongoing around the monastery, after which Father Kališt hopes to start with renovation. For route descriptions see box, opposite.

MARIOVO To the southeast of Prilep towards the border with Greece is the region of Mariovo, a rugged, beautiful area straddling the River Crna, which is flooded to the north (forming the manmade Tikveš Lake), and to the south comes from Pelister National Park through Bitola and the ancient Paeonian city of Lynk, whose exact location is still not known. The river must have been an important one to the ancient Paeons, for outside the small village of Monastir is one of the finest examples of what little remains of their ancient cities. Built out of finely cut limestone blocks using what has become known as Cyclopean masonry (ie: a masonry technique which uses no mortar, but precision cuts and the size of the blocks to keep a construction together), these fortified cities date back to Aneolithic times.

Evidence of other such cities has been found at Prosek in Demir Kapija, Vajtos near Ohrid, Debar, Tetovo, Prilep and Skopje among other places, usually in high locations that are easy to defend. The site at Mariovo is unusual for being in the river valley, and archaeologists are still researching the site to see if they can find clues as to why it was located here.

To get to the site, take the road south out of Prilep towards Bitola and turn off southeast towards the town of Vitolište (signposted). After 5km the road passes Štavica, a picturesque village used by Mančevski in *Before the Rain*, and another 25km later it crosses the River Crna at a new bridge that replaced the old Ottoman bridge of Hasin Bey. The river crossing is popular with picnickers and fishermen, and parts of the old bridge can still be seen. After another kilometre, the old road to Monastir village is signposted from the opposite direction. Turn south to follow the dirt track (4x4 only or walk) upstream for 4km towards the village of Monastir. The site of large old limestone blocks can be seen from this track, but if you want to see for yourself the closest thing you'll get to Cyclopean masonry built by the Paeons, then let your imagination build the rest of the city for you. The new road to Monastir, 4km from the bridge, does not allow a vantage point on to this site.

STIBERA RUINS West of the highway between Prilep and Bitola, between the villages of Trojkrsti and Čepigovo, are the barely uncovered ruins of the Roman town of Stibera. It was once a prominent urban centre in ancient Macedonia, and the last Macedonian king, Perseus, had his military headquarters here, from where he conducted his campaigns against the Romans in 169BC. The Greek historian and geographer Strabo, writing in the 1st century BC, refers to Stibera by its ancient name of Stymbara as being one of three cities located along the River Erigon (today's Crna), in the ancient Paeonian region of Derriopos and Pelagonia. The archaeological remains in Stibera range in date from the 3rd century BC to the 3rd century AD, and among the remarkable finds are more than 30 marble statues and busts, many exquisitely carved, and about 20 pediments and inscriptions. Barely cordoned off, overlooking the confluence of the Blato and Crna rivers, are the Temple of Tyche (the Greek goddess of fortune) and the town school.

AROUND MAKEDONSKI BROD Another interesting monastery, halfway between Prilep and Kičevo, is the **Monastery of Zrze**, near the village of the same name. Quite spectacular to see from the approach, it is set into the cliffside as if it hangs there only by the will of God. The monks' cells are built precariously into the cliff walls under the monastery, and the inns and church are built at the site of an earlier Christian basilica, whose foundations can still be seen, along with a number of marble pillars and other artefacts.

The church dedicated to **Saints Petar and Pavle** contains frescoes from the 14th century and an additional nave, known as the Shepherd's Church, to the left of the main nave. The main church is famous for its icons, which show the Virgin Mary in profile rather than face on, and on the right of Jesus rather than the left. Legend says that when the icons first came to the church they were placed, as is usual, with Mary on the left of Jesus, but every morning the church's monks would come for morning prayers to find the icons reversed. Bewildered by this phenomenon the father prayed to Mary for enlightenment on the issue, and she apparently told him that she had to be placed on the right of Jesus because otherwise her profile depiction would turn her back rather than her face to her son, which she would never do. The depiction of Mary in profile is unusual in Macedonia, but common in Russia. There are also the graves of two Russian nuns in the grounds of the monastery (recognisable by the Russian Orthodox-style gravestones), and so it is believed that these icons originally came from Russia with the nuns.

To get here, turn off the road to Kičevo from Prilep at the village of Ropotovo, signposted for Peštalevo. Go through these next two villages until you reach the first left turn in the village of Kostinci at what appears to be the mayor's house. There is a hand water pump at this corner. Here the road turns into a dirt track and leads only to the village of Zrze and straight on to the monastery, which you'll be able to see long before you come to the village. The last turn before the monastery is very rutted, so park at the corner unless you have a 4x4.

Just before Makedonski Brod is the turn-off to **Modrište**. This area of Macedonia, like Matka and Lesnovo, is riddled with caves and underground tunnels. At the end of the road at Belica are Golubarnik, Momiček and Laprnik **caves**. Near Slatina are several more caves accessible only with equipment. However, very visible on the way to Lokvica is the entrance to **Pešna Cave**, where medieval remnants of former occupation still exist. The cave goes back a long way through the mouth of a small tunnel at the back of the main cavernous entrance.

In Makedonski Brod itself there is the **Church of Sv Nikola,** which used to be a Bektaši teke (monastery of the Muslim order of the Bektaši), and some pleasant walks along the river.

 Where to stay and eat In nearby **Plasnica**, an ethnic Turkish village, the local restaurant is renowned for its excellent fish dishes straight from the River Treška. On the outskirts of the village of Devič is **Mak Viking** (045 275 606; m 071 371 169; e makviking@t-home.mk). Owner of a small ostrich ranch, the restaurant serves ostrich steak and omelettes (among other dishes), and offers seven rooms at €25 for a double. Unfortunately, the ostriches themselves are not kept near the hotel. It's a 20-minute walk from the hotel to Devna Kula, an old ruined fortress which used to house the sister of Krali Marko (see box, page 264).

KRUŠEVO *Telephone code 048*

Macedonians rave about Kruševo. Aside from being the place of Macedonian uprising against the Ottoman Empire in 1903, it is a very quaint Vlach town and thoroughly pleasant, with a village-like feel belying the fact it supports a population of around 5,000. Kruševo is also the home town of Toše Proeski, Macedonia's once very promising and still very popular pop singer who died in a car crash on 16 October 2007, aged 26. At 1,350m, the town is the highest in Macedonia and one of the loftiest anywhere in the Balkans. It is also a ski resort in its own right, with a double-chair ski lift connecting the western side of the town to the surrounding slopes and three more lifts from there, as well as a popular base for paragliding in the surrounding mountains.

On 2 August 1903, the holy day of Sv Ilija, the Internal Macedonian Revolutionary Organisation (VMRO) rose up all over Macedonia to fight for independence from the Ottoman Empire. This day is known as Ilinden, literally *Ilija den* or 'Ilija's day'.

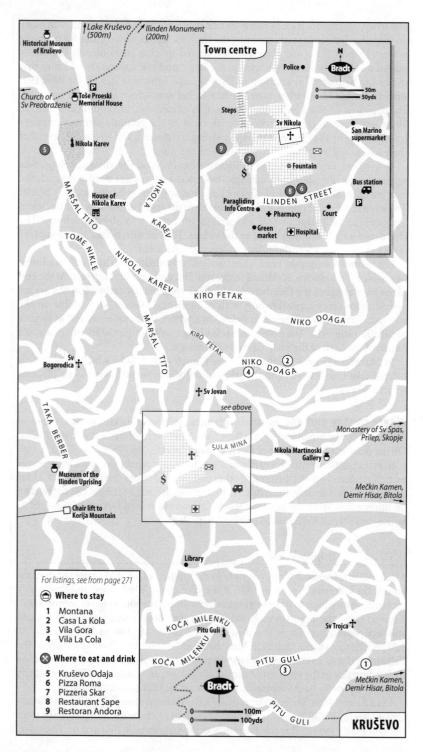

Town centre

Police

Steps

Sv Nikola

San Marino supermarket

9

7

$

Fountain

8 6

ILINDEN STREET

Bus station

Paragliding Info Centre

Pharmacy

Court

Green market

Hospital

N

0 — 50m
0 — 50yds

Bradt

Historical Museum of Kruševo

↑Lake Kruševo (500m)

↗Ilinden Monument (200m)

←Church of Sv Preobraženie

Toše Proeski Memorial House

Nikola Karev

5

House of Nikola Karev

NIKOLA KAREV

MARŠAL TITO

TOME NIKLE

NIKOLA KAREV

MARŠAL TITO

KIRO FETAK

KIRO FETAK

NIKO DOAGA

Sv Bogorodica

NIKO DOAGA

2

4

Sv Jovan

see above

TAKA BERBER

Museum of the Ilinden Uprising

Chair lift to Korija Mountain

ŠULA MINA

Nikola Martinoski Gallery

Monastery of Sv Spas, Prilep, Skopje

Mečkin Kamen, Demir Hisar, Bitola

Library

For listings, see from page 271

⌂ **Where to stay**
1 Montana
2 Casa La Kola
3 Vila Gora
4 Vila La Cola

✖ **Where to eat and drink**
5 Kruševo Odaja
6 Pizza Roma
7 Pizzeria Skar
8 Restaurant Sape
9 Restoran Andora

KOČA MILENKU

Pitu Guli

KOČA MILENKU

Sv Trojca

PITU GULI

3

1

PITU GULI

Mečkin Kamen, Demir Hisar, Bitola

N

Bradt

0 — 100m
0 — 100yds

KRUŠEVO

After fierce fighting, Kruševo succeeded in wresting power from the Ottomans and on 3 August the new government of Dinu Vangeli announced the independence of the Republic of Kruševo to a population of 14,000 (today there are only 10,000 in the municipality of Kruševo). Nikola Karev was made president. It lasted only ten days, however, before the Ottomans brought the new government to its knees and the Republic of Kruševo was no more. In 2003, the celebrations commemorating the centenary of independence (even though Macedonia has been shackled for most of the intervening years) were of the utmost national and cultural significance. For the Macedonians, 2 August is like 4 July for the Americans or 14 July for the French, although much more solemn. A re-enactment of the uprising now takes place every 2 August, and is a massive attraction.

GETTING THERE AND AWAY Kruševo is located almost equidistant between Kičevo, Bitola and Prilep and in a private vehicle it can be accessed from any of these three towns in less than an hour. Coming from Skopje, the fastest way to get here by car is via Prilep, which takes about 2½ hours. Using public transport, four direct buses run daily in either direction between Skopje and Kruševo, and there are also half a dozen buses daily to/from Prilep. Coming from anywhere else, first get yourself to Prilep, then pick up a bus to Kruševo from there. The low-key bus station (✆477 102) lies on Ilinden Street – the main road to Prilep and Bitola – 100m downhill from the central square.

 WHERE TO STAY *Map, opposite*
Family-run accommodation in Kruševo is increasing, and some of these can be found at w macedonian-hotels.mk/hotels/krusevo. Most new places are in the dedicated hotel zone at the top of Pitu Guli Street.

Hotel Montana (77 rooms) Pitu Guli; ✆477 121; m 076 444 102; e info@montanapalace.com; w montanapalace.com. Towers over the town & is well signposted: head left when the main road through town forks just after the centre. Rooms in the newer part of the hotel includes b/fast & jacuzzi bath. **$$$**

※ **Vila/Casa La Kola** (9/3 rooms) Niko Doaga 21/70; m 075 318 7789, 070 379 246; e vilalakola@yahoo.com; w lakola.mk. Refurbished old houses in the heart of the town.

Vila La Kola is the more downmarket & cheaper of the 2, but still has a traditional seating nook & b/fast area downstairs with some stone exposed wall. Casa La Kola is more upmarket, renovated with lots of traditional dark wood & a fireplace. **$$**

Vila Gora (12 rooms) Pitu Guli 53a; m 075 841 253; e info@vilagora.com; w vilagora.com. A newer building in the hotel zone, with well-equipped rooms & apts, including a dedicated children's playroom. **$$**

 WHERE TO EAT AND DRINK *Map, opposite*
For a town of relatively modest proportions, Kruševo boasts a surprising choice of restaurants, most of which are focused around the main square and central Church of Sv Nikola, an area that can be very lively at night.

※ **Kruševo Odaja Restaurant** Off Maršal Tito St; m 075 421 946. Situated uphill from the town centre, opposite Nikola Karev Park, this traditional restaurant serves a huge variety of local stews & grills. Set in a wood-dominated building that might be transplanted from Bavaria, the interior is heated by an old-fashioned coal stove

& decorated with traditional costumes, & there is also a wide terrace facing the park. **$$$**

※ **Pizzeria Skar** Town square; ✆476 602; m 070 252 517; e skarkrusevo@gmail.com; w www.pizzaskar.mk. Established in 1997, this vibey terrace restaurant has comfortable seating in the shadow of the Church of Sv Nikola. The

6

Italian menu includes pizza, pasta & lasagne but is also good on local specialities such as Kruševo pie (pastry with leek & cheese). $$$

✖ **Pizza Roma** Ilinden St; ☏476 519; m 070 536 891; w pizzaromakrusevo.com. With a rather bland interior salvaged by the pleasant 1st-floor terrace seating, this place serves a good selection of traditional fare & pizzas. $$

✖ **Restoran Andora** Takija Berber; ☏477 450. Unpretentious central pizzeria & grill serving large tasty portions in a pleasant shaded courtyard. $$

✖ **Restaurant Sape** Ilinden St; ☏477 809; m 078 377 580; ☐ @restorn.sape.krusevo. Traditional Macedonian fare in an atmospheric ground-floor setting in the same building as Pizza Roma. Good value. $$

WHAT TO SEE AND DO Even if you do not make it here for the main event of the re-enactment of the Ilinden Uprising, Kruševo has plenty to offer on all the other days of the year. Aside from taking in the architectural beauty of the old houses, the main attraction is the **Ilinden Monument** (☉ 09.00–16.00 daily; entry 60MKD), which was inaugurated in 1974, marking the 71st anniversary of the Ilinden Uprising and the 30th anniversary of Kruševo's liberation from Nazi occupation. Set in green 5ha grounds about 1km north and uphill of the central square, its centrepiece is the Makedonium, a rather surreal ball-shaped hilltop construction adorned with several protruding stained-glass oval windows and containing the tomb of Nikola Karev, who served as president of the short-lived Kruševo Republic in August 1903. The entrance fee to the monument also allows you access to the neighbouring **Historical Museum of Kruševo** (also known as the Museum of the National Liberation War), which houses displays relating to the Kruševo Republic as well as to local events during World War II. A few hundred metres west of the Ilinden Monument, you could divert to the small but pretty **Lake Kruševo**, which is set below green hills and encircled by a footpath.

Next to the car park that also serves the Ilinden Monument, the **Toše Proeski Memorial House** (☏477 888; m 070 395 085; ☉ 09.00–16.00 Tue–Sun; entry 100MKD) is a large modern cruciform building dedicated to the life and works of this once very promising young singer. When he died at the age of 26, Toše Proeski was already an ambassador for UNICEF and had started an annual concert, the money from which went to the poor of Macedonia and to improving education.

Situated on the east side of the main road up to the Ilinden Monument, the two-storey **house of Nikola Karev** is marked with an indistinct plaque but no longer now preserved as a museum. Even from the outside, it is clear that Nikola, like most of the intellectuals who made up the VMRO, was not from a poor background. A more central site of interest is the **Museum of the Ilinden Uprising** (Taka Berber 44a; ☏477 177, 476 756), although it was closed indefinitely for renovations in 2018. Also worth a visit is the **Nikola Martinoski Gallery** (Ilinden St), which exhibits 62 paintings donated by Nikola Martinoski (1903–73), an avant-garde painter often regarded to be the father of contemporary Macedonian art, at his former house in Kruševo.

On the spiritual front, the **Monastery of Sv Spas** in Trstenik, on the outskirts of Kruševo, is relatively young by Macedonian standards, having been built in 1836. It stands out on the hill as you approach Kruševo from Prilep, but the turn-off for the monastery (signposted) is low down in the valley before you start climbing up into Kruševo on the main road. In town, churches include the **Church of Sv Jovan**, built in 1904, which houses a collection of old icons from Kruševo; the **Church of Sv Nikola** in the centre, which was built in 1905 during the restoration of Kruševo after the Ilinden Uprising; and finally the youngest, the **Church of Sv Bogorodica**, built in 1967.

An hour's hike uphill from the Hotel Montana is **Mečkin Kamen**, the site of one of the battles for independence, where Macedonians gather on 2 August every year to pay homage to the early revolutionaries. There is a large statue here of a fighter throwing an extremely large boulder. For more active travellers, Mečkin Kamen is also regarded to be Macedonia's prime paragliding site, and tandem flights can be arranged through the new Paragliding Info Centre (Ilinden St, opposite Pizza Roma) or Paragliding Macedonia (m 070 333 859, 071 261 398; w paraglidingmacedonia.com).

Further afield, halfway between Bitola and Kruševo, is the small town of **Demir Hisar**. Although there is not much worth stopping for in the town itself, there are some historical villages and monasteries of worth nearby. Four kilometres to the west, outside the village of Slepče, is the monastery dedicated to **Sv Jovan Preteča** and established in the 14th century, although a newer church, dedicated to **Sv Nikola**, was built in 1672. Further south into the Plakenska Mountains is the village of **Smilevo** where, at the Congress of Smilevo, the decision was taken to carry out the Ilinden Uprising that brought about the ten-day Republic of Kruševo. The small Smilevo Kongres Museum built in 2004 displays the event. Just north of Demir Hisar is the **Nunnery and Monastery of Žurče**, near the village of the same name. Its church, dedicated to Sv Atanas Aleksandriski, was originally built in 1121, but the current frescoes are from 1671. The iconostasis was put in a century later.

Near Smilevo is the Vlach museum village of **Gopeš**, practically in ruins and barely lived in now, but home to what was the biggest church in Macedonia 200 years ago.

7

The Lower Vardar & Tikveš Winelands

Southeast of Skopje, the River Vardar bisects the ancient town of Veles before flowing on to Demir Kapija through the rich Tikveš Plain, an area renowned for its wines. Kavadarci is Macedonia's wine capital, where the country's biggest vineyard, Tikveš Wines, is based, but is rivalled by neighbouring Negotino, home to several smaller vineyards. Demir Kapija is home to the old royal Yugoslav winery, as well as the imposing Popova Kula tower, in a vineyard specialising in many indigenous varieties of wine. The climate is mild, the area being only 45m above sea level at the lowest point of the River Vardar at the border town of Gevgelija. Although Macedonian wines are little known, they easily rival better-

RAKIJA – MACEDONIA'S ELIXIR OF LIFE
Eric Manton, rakija connoisseur

As in most Balkan countries, rakija (pronounced 'RAK-eeyah') is the national drink of Macedonia. While rakijas in the surrounding countries may be made from fruits such as plums (*slivovice*), pears (*viljemovka*), grapes (*loza*) or herbs (*travarica*), Macedonian rakija is made exclusively from grapes. Macedonia's bountiful wine region, especially in the Povardarie region of the Tikveš Valley, has supplied great rakija for centuries.

The term rakija applies to all distilled spirits, similar to the terms *palinka* or brandy. The term likely comes from the Turkish *raki*, which in turn came from the Arabic term *arak* meaning 'condensation'. Distillation of alcohol supposedly started with alchemists, originating in North Africa and the Middle East and spreading to Europe in the Middle Ages through Spain, Italy and the Balkans. Alchemists used distillation for medicinal and scientific purposes in order to discover the essence of various materials. Once identified, these essences would be extracted for their curative powers. Alcohol was the preservative agent that also allowed for easier consumption. Even today in Macedonia rakija is also considered a medicine, and is called the 'elixir of life'.

In Macedonia, most people have a relative who makes their own *domašna* or homemade rakija. These private producers make their rakija the way it has been done for centuries. The fundamental ingredient is grapes; some people make rakija through the grappa method (using the leftovers from the winemaking process) or in the style of cognac (just using the juice or wine from the grapes); however, the majority of producers use the whole grape – excluding the stems, but including the juice, skins and seeds. While this type of rakija is initially slightly less smooth, the skins bring a fuller flavour.

After the grapes are crushed, they are left to ferment for three to four weeks as the natural sugars in the grapes turn into alcohol. The resulting mush is then

known wines from the Balkans, and vineyard visits and wine tastings are a great way to get to know them.

Given that the south of Macedonia was well populated by the Romans, this area is also rich in Roman remains, such as at the town of Stobi on the crossroads of the Axios and Diagonal ways. Other worthwhile sights include the tectonic Lake Dojran, rock climbing at the Iron Gate and the scenic Devil's Wall near Sv Nikole, as well as the usual assortment of monasteries, good hiking and pleasant swimming holes. It's also the home of the Saloniki Front of World War I, which runs along the entire southern border from Dojran, through Gevgelija, and a dedication to the fallen of 22 Division (UK) at Devil's Eye commemorates the 90th anniversary of the end of World War I.

VELES *Telephone code 043*

Once an important Roman settlement going by the name of Vilazora, unassuming Veles, situated just 50km southeast of Skopje along the A1, is barely more than an industrial transit town today. It was known as Köprülü (written Kuprili in some English texts) to the Ottomans, after the Albanian noble dynasty started by Köprülü Mehmed Pasha, who was born in Veles around 1580 (Köprülü means 'from Köprü', which is a village in Anatolia in Turkey). Köprülü Mehmed Pasha went on to become Grand Vizier of the Ottoman Empire from 1656 until his death

distilled or burnt in traditional copper *kazans* or pot stills of around 100 litres capacity. Using these stills as opposed to the column stills used in large-scale commercial distilleries allows for much better quality and a more refined product since the copper pot stills extract many of the more harmful types of alcohol released during distillation. The fresh rakija is then put into glass or wood barrels for ageing.

Most Macedonians prefer the *žolta* (yellow) rakija, which signifies that it has been wood aged. *Bela* rakija, or white, is less common. Aside from standard oak barrels, Macedonians also use the wood from acacia and mulberry trees. These give a different colour and flavour. For a good quality rakija, it needs to age 6–12 months in wood, or 18 months to three years in glass. Recently some commercial producers have been slipping in syrups and extracts that add artificial aroma, colour and flavour.

Another variety of rakija called mastika infuses the grape brandy with a combination of up to 27 herbs and spices, with the main flavours being mastic and aniseed similar to Greek ouzo. Macedonian mastika is highly regarded in former Yugoslav countries.

For many years, there were only a few brands of commercially produced rakija from the large wineries, Tikveš and Povardarie. Most of these rakijas are made of a mix of grape varieties. Their flavour mainly comes from the wood that is used to age them or from artificial flavouring. In recent years, several specialised distilleries have appeared. These include Altan (w altan.com.mk), Antika (produced by the Davino distillery), Bovin (w bovin.com.mk/brandies) and Skovin (w skovin.mk), the latter being renowned for its Markov Manastir, a rakija made from special vineyards from around the eponymous monastery on the opposite side of Vodno Hill to Skopje, and its yellow žolta.

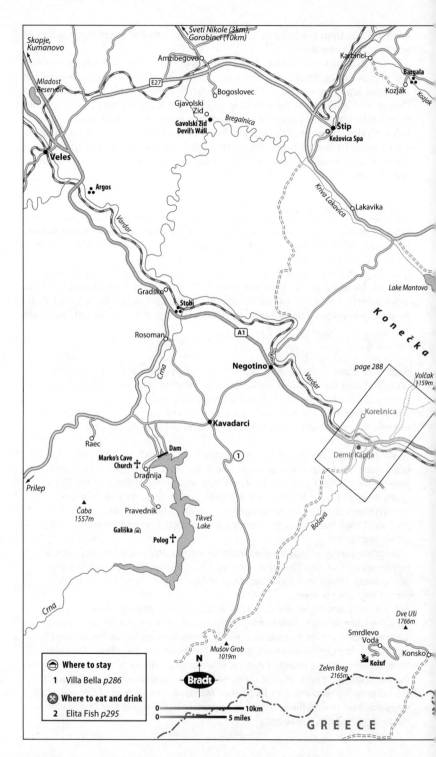

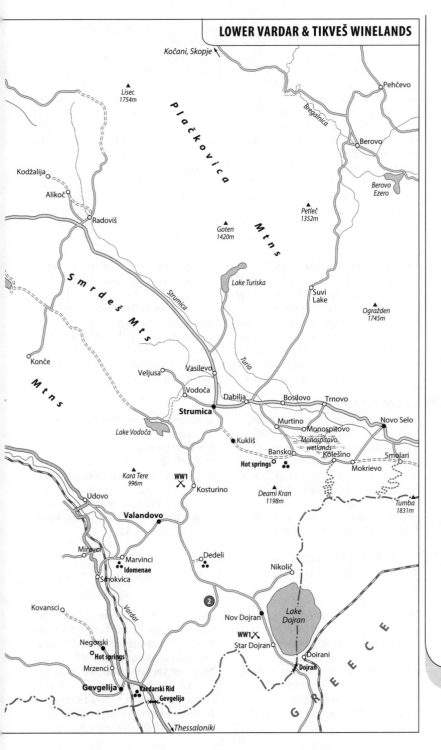

Kočani, Skopje

Lisec
1754m

Pehčevo

Bregalnica

Berovo

Kodžalija

Alikoč

Berovo
Ezero

Radoviš

P l a č k o v i c a

Petleč
1352m

Goten
1420m

M t n s

Lake Turiska

S m r d e š   M t s

Strumica

Suvi
Lake

Ogražden
1745m

Konče

Turia

M t n s

Veljusa

Vasilevo

Vodoča

Dabilja

Bosilovo

Trnovo

Novo Selo

Strumica

Murtino

Monospitovo

Lake Vodoča

Kukliš

Monospitovo
wetlands

Bansko

Kolešino

Smolari

Hot springs

Mokrievo

Kara Tere
996m

WW1

Kosturino

Deami Kran
1198m

Tumba
1831m

Udovo

Valandovo

Miravci

Marvinci

Dedeli

Idomenae

Nikolič

Smokvica

Kovansci

Vardar

2

Nov Dojran

Lake
Dojran

G
R
E
E
C
E

Negorski

WW1

Hot springs

Star Dojran

Doirani

Mrzenci

Dojran

Gevgelija

Vardarski Rid

Gevgelija

Thessaloniki

in 1661, when he was succeeded by his son Köprülü Fazil Ahmet Pasha (also born in Veles) who held the office of Grand Vizier until 1676.

Lying on the strategic route between the Kačanik Pass (in Kosovo) and the pass of Demir Kapija, Veles has long been a key defence point southeast of Skopje on the way to Solun. After World War II, it was renamed Titov Veles, in reference to the Yugoslav president Josip Tito, but the title 'Titov' was dropped in 1996. Now, it has a quaint old town and a few cultural sites worth a wander past, and local trails have been upgraded. Despite this, slag from a nearby zinc and lead smelting factory led to the World Health Organization naming Veles one of the world's most polluted towns in 2001. The factory closed in 2003, however, and the local environmental NGO Vila Zora (page 12) has been running projects to remediate local soil pollution, and while this is good news on the health side, it has damaged the town's economy. The Macedonian movie *I'm from Titov Veles* (*Jas sum od Titov Veles*) is a harrowing tale that gives an idea of what life here has been like for some, who in addition were kicked out of Aegean Macedonia during the Greek civil war in the late 1940s. Veles has moved on – albeit slowly.

GETTING THERE AND AROUND Veles has a regular **train** service to and from Skopje, with more than a dozen services daily leaving between 04.15 and 22.40. Some of these trains continue southeast through the Tikveš Plain to the Greek border town of Gevgelija, while others run southwest to Prilep and Bitola. The train station (✆231 033) is 1km northwest of the centre. **Buses** run frequently between Skopje, Veles and other parts of the country, starting at 06.00 from the capital; the last bus to Veles from Skopje is at 21.00. Veles bus station (✆234 550, 211 431) is centrally located on the east bank of the Vardar below the main bridge across it. **Taxi** companies include Bambi Drim (✆(043) 1591) and Taksi Združenje (✆(043) 1593).

WHERE TO STAY *Map, opposite*

⌂ **Hotel Romantik** (26 rooms) Lake Veles, 9km from Veles; ✆212 999; m 078 400 036; e info@hotelromantik.com.mk; w hotelromantik. com.mk. Located outside Veles itself, this place has a good restaurant, fireside bar, pool & private beach on the lake. A daily rate (09.00–17.00) is available for €20. **$$$**

⌂ **Brod Panini** (13 rooms) Lake Veles, 9km from Veles; ✆211 444; e info@brodpanini.com;

w www.brodpanini.com. You're guaranteed a lake view from this boat hotel. **$$**

⌂ **Motel Epicentrum** (7 rooms) Ilindenska; m 078 231 303; e mail@epicentrum.com; w epicentrum.com.mk. Veles's most central hotel offers small but spotless cell-like rooms with AC & TV on the 2nd floor of a block next to the main bridge, & only 200m from the bus station. A good restaurant is attached. **$$**

WHERE TO EAT AND DRINK *Map, opposite*

The main street, Blagoj Gorčev, is alive with café-bars in the evening as people stroll up and down.

✗ **Baže Piti** Alekso Demnievski 7 (opposite the post office); ✆234 056; ⏰ 11.00–23.00 daily. Serves good pizzas, piti (Macedonian layered pies), pastrmajlija & skara. **$$**

✗ **Brod Panini** Lake Veles; ✆211 444; w www. brodpanini.com; ⏰ noon–23.00 daily. Terrace restaurant beside the hotel-boat on lake. **$$**

✗ **Da Vinci's Pub** Blagoj Gorčev 99; ✆211 155. A restaurant as much as a pub, this is perhaps the

pick of a dozen or so terrace eateries that line the main road opposite the church of Sv Kiril & Metodi. It serves a predominantly Italian menu of pasta & other mains, as well as draught beer. **$$**

✗ **Epicentrum Cafe-Restaurant** Ilindenska; m 078 231 303; w epicentrum.com.mk. Attached to the eponymous motel, this bright & modern 1st-floor restaurant serves a varied selection of pizzas, pastas, risottos & Macedonian grills & stews. It has

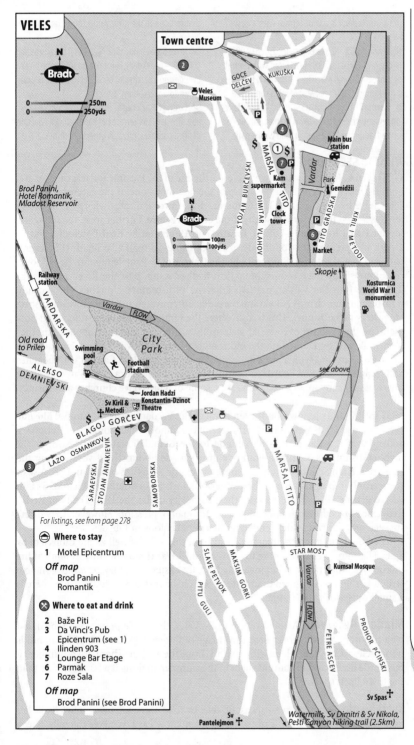

a well-stocked bar & a wide terrace with a view over town. $$

✖ Ilinden 903 Nikola Orovcanec 2; 📞612 903; ⏰ noon–23.00 daily. Cosy restaurant with central location, traditional Macedonian dishes & live music in the form of traditional Macedonian songs. $$

✖ Parmak Tito Gradska; ⏰ 10.00–23.00 daily. Conveniently close to the town market, this place serves traditional Macedonian food with a patio

that spills on to the River Vardar. Best skara in town by far. $$

✖ Roze Sala Ilindenska; 📞225 541; 📘 @rozesala; ⏰ 08.00–01.00 daily. Large restaurant tucked away overlooking a parking lot behind Epicentrum; popular for wedding receptions. $$

🍷 Lounge Bar Etage Blagoj Gorčev 59; 📞612 654. This 1st-floor terrace bar has music & a selection of filled pancakes, pizzas & other light dishes. $$

WHAT TO SEE AND DO

West bank Although the town was once the site of the Paeonic fortress of Vilazora, nothing remains to be seen now despite the fact that some of the extensive Roman ruins have been excavated. The Ottoman **clock tower** indicates where the centre of the town used to be, further south of the current centre. Further west, the imposing **Jordan Hadži Konstantin-Džinot Theatre** and **Church of Sv Kiril i Metodi** stand in a park-like area on the south side of Blagoj Gjorev, a road also lined with several bars and casual eateries. Built in 1840, the **Church of Sv Pantelejmon** in the old town rises imposingly over Veles. About 1km further south, past the River Topolka, as it empties into the Vardar, are two adjacent 14th-century churches: the recently refurbished **Church of Sv Nikola** and the older, unrenovated and thus more interesting **Monastery of Sv Dimitri**. This is also where the Ottoman Kale once stood, and now there are the remains of four old watermills scattered along the Topolka. Another 3km walk past Sv Dimitri on the old road is where the River Babuna empties into the Vardar, around which are a handful of trails up into **Pešti Canyon** with benches and multilingual panel boards indicating local fauna and flora. The 4km hike along the river and canyon is dotted with caves, some of which have churches and shrines.

East bank The old town on the left bank of the Vardar boasts the **Kumsal Mosque** (White Mosque) as well as the birthplace of the famous Macedonian revolutionary and poet, Kočo Racin. It is also home to the **Gemidžii statue**, consisting of 12 involuted sun rays, commemorating a group made up mostly of youths from the Bulgarian High School in Veles. Also known as the Assassins of Saloniki because of the terror bombing campaign they undertook in 1903 in Solun, the Gemidžii's aim was to get the Great Powers to use their authority under the 1878 Treaty of Berlin to oversee Macedonia and put an end to Ottoman oppression. However, they didn't succeed and the ringleaders ended up in a penal colony in Libya.

The bus station and the market are also on this side, as well as the **Church of Sv Spas**. High up, overlooking the town, is a **World War II monument** and **tomb of the unknown soldier** (*kosturnica*, meaning literally 'ossuary'), a blazing white concrete structure that was designed to imitate an Axis helmet struck in four. Inside, there is a small museum of the battle.

Mladost Reservoir Also known as Lake Veles, this is the poor man's Ohrid, fed by a tributary of the Vardar near the village of Otovitsa 9km north of town, but is nonetheless a popular place with visitors from the region. There are a number of busy little hotels and restaurants here in the summer, making it a far nicer base than the town itself (page 278).

Sveti Nikole Some 35km northeast of Veles by road, the small town of Sv Nikole lies on top of a hill in the middle of the fertile plain known as Ovče Pole (literally 'Sheep

Field'). Taking its name from the church built by Serbian king Milutin in 1313, the church stands prominently on top of the hill and can be seen on the approach to the town. It is enclosed within the monastery grounds, which are often closed, so ask in the town for the key if you would like to have a look around. The surrounding plain, now an important centre of sheep farming, has been inhabited since Neolithic times; remains have been found in the vicinity of the town, mostly around the villages of Amzibegovo to the south of Sveti Nikole, and Gorobinci to the northwest on the road back to Skopje. Many such items are on display at the National Museum of Sveti Nikole (Ploštad Ilinden 18; \443 610), which stands in a handsome protected two-storey house and is easily recognised by the large pots and other artefacts on the pavement outside.

To get here from Veles, take the A3 east towards Štip. After about 25km, you'll reach a large interchange where you need to turn left on to the A4 and continue north for another 11km to Sv Nikole.

Gjavolski Zid
Easily visited in conjunction with Sveti Nicole, Gjavolski Zid (literally, 'the Devil's Wall') is an amazing rock feature on the River Bregalnica some 28km east of Veles. Over 1km long, the wall is several metres high for most of its length and is made of enormous stone blocks. Nobody is sure whether it is manmade or natural, although some say it was built by Alexander the Great. Its name comes from a local legend that the devil (*gavol*) created the wall to dam the River Bregalnica and in doing so drown the nearby village of Bogoslovec (whose name means 'joy to God').

The junction south for Bogoslovec lies on the A3 about 2km west of the junction with the A4 to Sv Nikole. You arrive in Bogoslovec after 4km, and must then turn right on to a dirt track heading southwest skirting around the hill Sveti Jovanski Rid. After 3km you'll round the hill and see the start of the wall. The wall (⊕ 8440 2319) lies across two maps: 1:25,000 SAGW Map Sheets Erdželija 733-1-3 and Dobrošani 733-3-1.

Babuna Mountains
A very pretty 65km back road runs from Veles to Prilep through this range. The mountain section is not paved, and a lot of the original cobbling from over a century ago can still be seen, as well as the original distance markers. This is the old military road on which Serbian forces famously defeated Ottoman forces in the First Balkan War of 1912 and then went on to take Prilep. In speaking to Crawfurd Price, London *Times* war correspondent at the time, soldiers attributed their success against almighty odds in an uphill attack to seeing both Sv Sava and the resurrected King Marko of Prilep at their head. It had been legend for centuries that King Marko, who was thought to be buried in a cave in the region, would rise again to lead the Serbs against their Ottoman oppressors.

The road out of Veles is not signposted, so can be a little hard to find. Taking the second exit into Veles from Skopje (or the third if you are approaching from the south), cross the bridge into the centre of town and take the second right off the double roundabout. Follow the road around through the north of the town, and take the next left after the sign for the hospital (*bolnica*) and the railway station (*Železnička stanica*). Keep going straight until the T-junction with Blagoj Gorčev high street and then turn right. This will take you through the one-way system to pop out at the end of the high street.

The road follows the railway line to Prilep until shortly before Izvor, when the road takes a sharp turn to the left over a picturesque old bridge into Izvor itself. Meaning 'water spring', **Izvor** does indeed have a large built-up spring right next to the main road, from which all the locals take their drinking water – you might want to fill up any spare water bottles too as the water is very good. After Izvor, the road rises sharply into the Babuna Mountains and at mile marker 144, just after the water fountain and the sheep pens, is the turn-off to the monasteries of **Sv Stepanci** and **Sv Dimitri**. Watch out for turtles crossing the road here as they are not used to cars. After this, hairpin bends snake all the way around the **Pig's Head** (Svinska Glava) and, just before the pass at 1,134m above sea level, is the dirt track turn-off to the local mountaineering lodge. A couple of kilometres later stop at the **Monastery of Sv Gjorgi** for a good view of the descent to Prilep.

STOBI RUINS

(↖251 026; w stobi.mk; ⊕ May–Oct 08.00–20.00 daily, Nov–Apr 08.00–16.00 daily; entry 120MKD) To the northwest of Negotino and just south of Gradsko, nestled into the crook of the Black River and the Vardar River, lie the ruins of the ancient

WINES FROM THE TIKVEŠ PLAIN

The entire course of the Vardar Valley from Veles all the way south to Thessaloniki is fertile grape-growing country, and within Macedonia the Tikveš Plain around Negotino, Kavadarci and Demir Kapija produces some of the country's best wines. There are more than 50 small private wineries in Macedonia and the number is growing, as is the quality. A visit to one of the vineyards in September and October or around Sv Trifun Day in February is always well worth the time if you'd like to try out the season's newest, or the best of last year's stock.

Near Demir Kapija, the former boutique vineyard Popova Kula (page 287) is well worth a visit or overnight stay at any time of year, and you might also want to pop into the historic Royal Winery Queen Maria (page 287). Kavadarci is home to the massive Tikveš Winery, while Negotino boasts nine vineyards in its vicinity. There are also vineyards further north around Skopje, and you'll find the local wines of smaller vineyards served in plastic bottles and cardboard cartons at local petrol stations and stores.

Macedonian wines are unique in Europe for being made with very little, if any, additional sugar or sulphite preservatives. They are preserved, therefore, mostly by the grapes' own natural sugars and it is for this reason that almost all Macedonian wines are dry rather than sweet, and why you won't get such a big hangover the next day after drinking a bottle of T'ga za Jug (Longing for the South) or Alexandria.

Macedonian wines are little known outside of its borders for two reasons: most of it is still exported in bulk for use in your local supermarket chain's own-label wine; secondly, Macedonia's name dispute with Greece also affects wine exports, although this might change as a result of the name change.

Many of the usual varieties of grape found elsewhere are also grown in Macedonia, such as Chardonnay, Merlot, Pinot and Sauvignon. There are many indigenous varieties, however, and some of the grape varieties which you might be familiar with at home have a different name on a Macedonian wine bottle. Here is a guide:

Belan	Grenache. A grape which grows easily; herbaceous flavour.
Kratošija	A common indigenous red, similar to Vranec but not as full bodied.

Roman city of Stobi. Although many Macedonians would rate the ancient city of Heraklea Linkestis (page 249) near Bitola higher than Stobi, in my opinion Stobi is nicer to wander around. The cities were founded at the same time and both flourished under the Roman Empire, Heraklea becoming the capital of the region. With views of the surrounding mountains and rivers, it is easy to stand on the site and imagine the hustle and bustle of the ancient city, with its numerous travelling traders plying their wares and telling their tales of far-off lands. Stobi has a good little information centre and café.

HISTORY The ancient city of Stobi was founded at the confluence of the rivers Crna (the ancient River Erigon) and Vardar (ancient Axios), at the crossing point of the Via Egnatia, the Via Axia and the Via Diagonale. The original settlement, slightly to the north of the current archaeological site, is thought to be Bronze Age in origin, dating to around 1900BC. Bronze objects from the classical and archaic periods

Muscat(el)	This name covers a wide variety of grapes, both red and white, which have a characteristic sweet musky perfume. A semi-sweet to sweet wine, often a dessert wine.
Prokupec	A light yet nutty indigenous red, with dry fruit tones.
R'kacitel	From the Georgian *rkatsiteli*, meaning 'red stem'. Originating from Georgia, it is a very old white variety, similar to Riesling.
Smederevka	Peculiar to Macedonia and Serbia, the cultivation of this grape dates back to Roman times. Has a bitter acidic taste, best as a spritzer.
Stanušina	A refreshing semi-sweet red, usually made into a rosé or dark rosé.
Temjanika	Deriving its name from *temjanuška*, meaning 'violet' or 'pansy', this floral scented semi-sweet white is a variety of Muscat.
Teran	An imported variety from Istria, which is sourish red, very high in iron derived from the red soil it requires to grow. Its medicinal properties are valued for combating anaemia, stimulating appetite and aiding digestion. Does not age well.
Traminec	A variant of Gewürztraminer, and akin to a semi-sweet Riesling. Unstable and difficult to age.
Vranec	This is the bulls' blood of the Balkans, deepest red, dry and intense.
Žilavka	A light, refreshing and fruity indigenous white, reflecting apple, pear and peach flavours.

Few restaurants offer more than Tikveš or maybe Bovin, but supermarkets sell an increasing range and you can order online for delivery to destinations in Macedonia from w wine.mk. **Stobi** also now markets its wines in the UK – see w stobi.co.uk/stockists. Elsewhere in the world try ordering through w snooth. com.

Tours to the wineries themselves are an easy way to sample many of these grape varieties, and these are becoming more frequent in Macedonia. Go Macedonia (page 64) offer a day tour out of Skopje including lunch, travel and drinks, costing in the region of €35–45.

have been found here along with pottery from the Neolithic period and the Iron Age. The later Hellenistic city was established in the 4th century BC.

Excavation in the newer, central part of the city has revealed archaeological stratigraphy dating to the 2nd and 3rd centuries BC. Its heyday, however, came following the Roman victory in the third Macedonian war in 168BC, when Macedonia was divided into four regions, and Stobi became one of the major urban centres in one of them. The Goths destroyed the town when they invaded Macedonia in AD479 and, although it was rebuilt shortly afterwards, the earthquake of AD518 damaged the town further. Rebuilt again, further earthquakes took their toll on the town, and by the end of the 13th century the town was completely abandoned in favour of towns such as Veles further north along the Vardar, and Negotino further south.

GETTING THERE AND AWAY Stobi is just south of the town of Gradsko, accessible (and signposted) right off the Skopje–Negotino highway on the east side. Travelling south take the first exit some 3km after Gradsko, and go underneath the highway into the car park.

There is no public transport to the site, but you could take a **bus** or **train** to Gradsko or a bus to Rosoman and then a **taxi** for about 250MKD, or **walk** from Gradsko south alongside the railway for about 3km until you reach the ruins. Along the walk on the southern outskirts of Gradsko is a cemetery with German graves from World War I.

WHERE TO STAY AND EAT The **café** doesn't serve much more than tea and coffee, but Gradsko has a larger shop. **Rosoman**, 7km from the ruins, has a few small places to eat, or go on to Kavadarci (page 286) or Veles (page 278), both of which also have hotels.

WHAT TO SEE AND DO Stobi was first discovered in 1861, but excavation did not start until 1924, and even today only a fraction of the city has been uncovered. The site is not very big and can easily be explored in a couple of hours. Aside from the ruins themselves, most of the pottery, jewellery and sculptures are found in the museums of Skopje and Veles, while two of the most famous pieces, a pair of bronze satyrs, are in Belgrade's city museum.

There are numerous main buildings and town roads in Stobi. A **2nd-century amphitheatre**, which was later turned into a gladiatorial ring, has the names of family holders engraved on some of the seats. There are at least five basilicae: a northern basilica, a civilian basilica, a central basilica and synagogue, an extramural basilica, and the **Episcopal basilica**. The latter was built in the 5th century AD in a Hellenistic manner with an atrium, narthex (with a mosaic floor) and an exonarthex with a double apse, the seat of the bishop Philip. On the south of the basilica is the baptistery with a magnificent mosaic composition. There is a set of small baths (*thermae minores* or *balneum*) and a set of large baths (*thermae*), complete with three earthenware vats (*pithoses*).

The **House of the Psalms** is a sumptuous urban villa or *domus* with a large reception room or *tablinium* with exceptional mosaics, as well as a colonnaded peristyle/atrium and central *triclinium* with an apse. Several other houses that have been identified include the House of Peristeria, the House of Parthenius and the episcopal residence. The **Palace of Theodosius** is one of the biggest buildings with a floor of marble plates, a *peristilus* with mosaics and marble pedestal platforms on which statues once stood. **Domus Fullonica** was a house with a fullery for treating leather or retting cloth.

The roads of Stobi include the Via Axia, Via Principalis Inferior, Via Theodosia, Via Principalis Superior and Via Sacra. Finally, there is also a semicircular *plataea* (public open space), and the city well.

NEGOTINO *Telephone code 043*

Although it can in many ways still be described as a one-horse town, tiny Negotino is the heart of Macedonia's wine land. The town dates back to the 3rd century BC when it was called Antigona after its founder, the Macedonian king Antigon Gonat (277–240BC), and today rivals Kavadarci as the wine capital of the country. Negotino celebrates Sv Trifun Day (14 February) with a parade and wine competition, while the town museum (Maršal Tito 119; ✆ 361 712) also has the country's only wine history exhibition. Scattered around the outskirts and hills of the town are no fewer than nine wineries, among them Bovin (✆ 365 322; e bovin@t.mk; w bovin.com.mk), Dudin (✆ 368 506; e dudinwinery. com.mk; w dudinwinery.com.mk) and Pivka (✆ 371 418; e pivka@t-home.mk; w winerypivka.com.mk).

GETTING THERE AND AWAY There are a dozen **buses** a day to Negotino from Skopje between 06.00 and 10.15, as well as services from Kavadarci, Veles, Bitola and Ohrid. The bus station (Industriska bb; ✆ 361 744) is 10 minutes from the centre. A **taxi** company in the town is Radio Taxi Start (✆ (043/070) 370 300).

WHERE TO STAY AND EAT

Pamela (23 rooms) Maršal Tito 4; ✆ 361 105; m 076 337 750; e info@pamela.mk; w hotelpamela.mk. Modern hotel on the edge of town at the petrol station just after you come off the highway. Includes sgl, dbl & trpl rooms, all with AC & Wi-Fi. **$$**

Park (54 rooms) Partizanski 1; ✆ 370 960/1. Basic & run-down accommodation on a hill at the edge of town. **$$**

KAVADARCI *Telephone code 043*

A large, sprawling and rather industrial-looking town, Kavadarci is set in the heart of the winelands around 10km west of the main A1 highway and Negotino. It was founded in the late Roman period, but many relicts from this era are buried beneath Tikveš Lake, a manmade lake constructed about 5km to the southwest in 1968 to provide irrigation and hydro-electricity to the surrounding area.

Kavadarci is renowned as the home of the **Tikveš Winery** (29 Noemvri 5; ✆ 447 500; e wtikves@tikves.com.mk; w tikves.com.mk/en), which was founded by Pane Velkov in 1885 and produced its first labelled product under the custody of his son Aleksandar in 1912. Tikveš is now the largest winery in southeast Europe and it is well worth dining at the world-class Restaurant Vinery located in its wine vault, which is situated on the main road on the western outskirts of town. Reservations are a must for evenings and weekends, but they might be able to serve you impromptu for lunch during the week.

To celebrate the start of the winemaking season, Kavadarci holds an annual **Grape Harvest Festival** in late August or early September, which includes grape-crushing barefoot and a masked parade. This is followed on the third Saturday of November with the **Tikveš Young Wine Festival** when Tikveš Winery opens its doors for people to taste the first wines of that year's harvest.

7

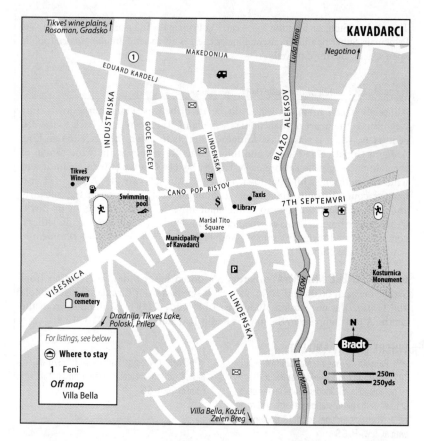

Map labels:
Tikveš wine plains, Rosoman, Gradsko
MAKEDONIJA
Negotino
EDUARD KARDELJ
Luda Mara
BLAŽO ALEKSOV
INDUSTRISKA
GOCE DELČEV
ILINDENSKA
Tikveš Winery
Swimming pool
ČANO POP RISTOV
Taxis
Library
7TH SEPTEMVRI
Maršal Tito Square
Municipality of Kavadarci
Kosturnica Monument
VIŠEŠNICA
Town cemetery
Dradnija, Tikveš Lake, Poloski, Prilep
ILINDENSKA
FLOW
Luda Mara

For listings, see below
🛏 Where to stay
1 Feni
Off map
Villa Bella

N
Bradt
0 ——— 250m
0 ——— 250yds

Villa Bella, Kožuf, Zelen Breg

Aside from wine, there are also two interesting churches in the area: **Marko's Cave Church** in Dradnija, 4km west of the Tikveš Lake Dam, and the 14th-century **Monastery of Polog** in the village of Poloski on the cliffs of Tikveš Lake. The church there, dedicated to Sv Gjorgi, is practically windowless, despite the number of window arches built into the walls, and the vaults of the church are claimed to hold the remains of Dragutin, the brother of the Serbian king Dušan. The monastery is accessible only by boat, or a 10km hike overland from the village of Pravednik.

GETTING THERE AND AWAY A dozen **buses** a day connect Kavadarci to Skopje between 06.00 and 22.15, and there are also services to Negotino, Veles, Bitola and Ohrid. **Taxi** companies include Taxi Vednas (✆ 416 001), Ekstra (✆ 400 300) and Vinozito (✆ 400 400).

🏠 WHERE TO STAY AND EAT

🏠 **Feni** [map, above] (47 rooms) Eduard Kardelj; ✆ 412 244; m 075 412 244; e maak_homes@yahoo.com.au; w hotelfeni.com. Adequate rooms & friendly attentive staff at this place 1km from the city centre. **$$**

🏠 **Villa Bella** [map, page 276] (8 rooms) 5km south of town; ✆ 522 557; m 071 221 551; e info@villabella-mk.com; w villabella-mk.com. Built in 2012, this family-run hotel is far nicer & better value than anything in town. It has modern spacious rooms, & a restaurant, swimming pool & garden. **$$**

From Veles via Stobi the southerly flow of the River Vardar takes it through the plains of the Tikveš region. The valley then narrows to a gap of barely 50m across where the surrounding mountains force the river through a mountain gorge known as Demir Kapija (meaning 'iron gate' in Turkish). Beyond this the valley sides remain steep for another 20km, and this geographical formation has forced centuries of invaders into upper Macedonia through this narrow corridor. They are effectively funnelled into a killing zone on exiting the Iron Gate into the Tikveš Plain – hence the ominous name of the rock feature.

The train ride from the north through Demir Kapija to Gevgelija is pretty, although the drive is probably more so because of the stopping place on the road between two rock towers. Barely big enough for half a dozen cars, this stopping place gives the appearance of being in an open-topped cave.

The gateway to Demir Kapija is the small town that shares its name with the gorge a short distance to its east. Pretty much everything of interest in Demir Kapija – the railway station and museum, an ATM, and a straggle of supermarkets, bars and unpretentious local eateries – flanks a two-block-long pedestrian-only stretch of Maršal Tito that curves parallel to the railway track.

GETTING THERE AND AWAY There are three **buses** a day to Demir Kapija from Skopje leaving the capital at 08.30, 15.00 and 17.30. Demir Kapija is also a stop on the main line between Skopje and Gevgelija; trains from Skopje leave at 04.45, 06.20 and 16.55. From the train station (✆367 230), it is 2km to Popova Kula winery. Taxis wait outside the train station, and Astor Taxi can be called on ✆366 252.

WHERE TO STAY, EAT AND DRINK *Map, page 288*

Hotel Moderna (20 rooms) m 078 346 436; e modernahotel@gmail.com. Situated about 1km out of town, this new place lacks the character & class of Popova Kula, but the rooms are comfortable enough & come with a bright décor, AC, TV & balcony. The ground-floor restaurant has a terrace with a view. **$$$**

Popova Kula Winery (28 rooms) Bd na vinoto 1; ✆367 400; m 076 432 640; e reservation@popovakula.com.mk; w popovakula.com.mk; see ad, 2nd colour section. In the hills behind Demir Kapija, this boutique vineyard is far & away the most appealing place to stay in the winelands, & not as expensive as you might expect. It commands an impressive view from the rooms & restaurant tower, which is worth the visit alone. Beautiful rooms come with AC, & check out their wine-tasting venue in the tower, with over 20 wines from 11 types of grape. Vineyard tours are available, & wine-tasting sessions take

place in the restaurant tower every evening at 18.00. Popova Kula specialises in indigenous grape varieties such as Stanušina & Žilavka, as well as the usual regional varieties. **$$$**

Royal Winery Queen Maria Just outside Demir Kapija; ✆446 500; e admin@wineryqueenmaria.com; w wineryqueenmaria.com. Founded in 1928 by King Aleksandar Karadjordjevic of Yugoslavia, this impressive estate was formerly known as Elenov, & still comes complete with peacocks. If you can get on a tour you will see all the old wooden wine barrels still in use as well as some of the old presses (no longer in use). The former queen's house is a listed building & now operates as a restaurant & tasting centre. **$$$**

Urban Grill Maršal Tito. The pick of a few central eateries, this pleasant owner-managed place has shady outdoor seating next to the railway line & serves the usual inexpensive chicken & meat grills, plus beer, wine & coffee. **$–$$**

WHAT TO SEE AND DO Aside from winery visits, there is plenty of **hiking** to be done in the hills to local caves and villages, including to the site of the ancient fortress **Prosek**, which can be seen from Popova Kula restaurant at the telecommunications tower

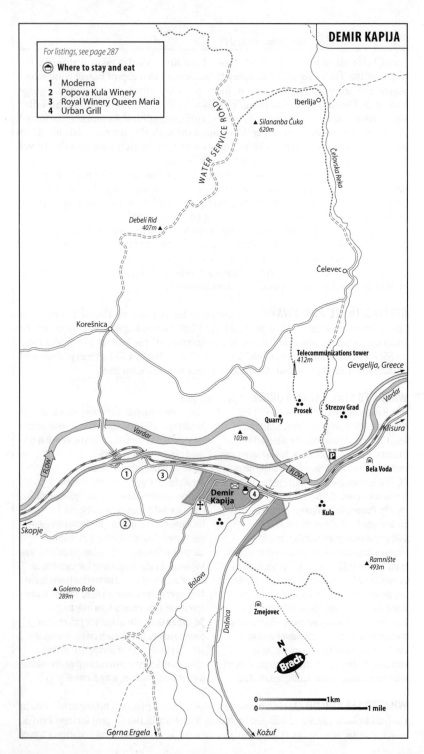

DEMIR KAPIJA

For listings, see page 287

⊖ **Where to stay and eat**

1 Moderna
2 Popova Kula Winery
3 Royal Winery Queen Maria
4 Urban Grill

WATER SERVICE ROAD

Iberlija○

▲ Silananba Čuka
620m

Čelovška Reka

Debeli Rid
407m ▲

Čelevec ○

Korešnica ○

Telecommunications tower
412m

Gevgelija, Greece

Vardar

Vardar

Prosek
Strezov Grad

Quarry

Klisura

▲ 103m

P

FLOW

FLOW

Bela Voda

① ③

Demir
Kapija

④

Skopje

②

Kula

▲ Golemo Brdo
289m

Bošava

Ramnište
493m ▲

Došnica

Zmejovec

N

Bradt

0 ————— 1km
0 ————— 1 mile

Gorna Ergela ↓

Kožuf ↓

Distance	12km
Altitude	Demir Kapija 110m, Silananba Čuka 620m
Rating	Easy to moderate: short, steep wooded section at the summit
Timing	5–6 hours
In reverse	Possible, but more difficult to get a taxi back to Demir Kapija
Map	1:25,000 SAGW Map Sheets Demir Kapija West 783-1-2 and Demir Kapija East 783-2-1, January 2007

ROUTE DESCRIPTION This is a pleasant hike to enjoy in the summer, directly from the stopping place between the two rock towers of Demir Kapija Tunnel. The path goes along the canyon stream that created the rock feature and flows between them into the River Vardar. The sides are almost vertical and offer good shade in the hot summer. The path through the canyon is easy to follow but requires fording the stream several times in the first kilometre, so shoes that have good grip in water are advisable. Thereafter the path and stream come into a more open area where the path is wider and used by farm vehicles from Čelevec village (just over an hour from trail head).

The path continues northeast alongside big boulders in the ever smaller stream and leads up to the mountain village of **Iberlija** (✪ 0821 8997, 2 hours from trail head). A couple of very old babas still tend sheep and tobacco leaves here, but most of the houses have long been abandoned. At Iberlija, go through the village and follow the track round to the west and up a steep narrow ravine. As the trickle of water and the path seem to run out (✪ 0759 9040), keep heading up the hill and in 30–40 minutes from Iberlija you will pop out of the brush at the service road (✪ 0674 9045, dirt track) for the water pipes feeding Korešnica village. A few hundred metres southeast is the trig point Silananba Čuka (620m), while the service road back to Korešnica heads off to the southwest. Some 2–3 hours gently downhill will lead you to the village shop where you can get refreshments and phone for a taxi to take you back to Demir Kapija (page 287).

on the hill to the east over the valley. To the southeast of Demir Kapija, towards the new Kožuf ski resort on the border with Greece, are some of Macedonia's many **caves** including the beautiful Golem Zmejovec (Large Dragon) and Mal Zmejovec (Small Dragon). Hiking the old road and railway on the right bank of the Vardar is also pleasant. The Demir Kapija canyon is home to some localised birds of prey including griffon vulture, Egyptian vulture, golden eagle, short-toed snake eagle, long-legged buzzard, peregrine falcon and lesser kestrel. Popova Kula can also arrange guided hikes; and see the box above for a river hike from the Iron Gate itself.

The towering rock faces of Demir Kapija (accessible from the stopping place in the middle of the tunnel through the gorge on the main road) are favourites for **rock climbing** (routes are marked, and displayed on the very informative map of Demir Kapija available in the town).

The local **museum** (Maršal Tito; **m** 077 764 290, 078 493 893; **e** museumdk@ gmail.com; **w** museumdk.mk; ⊕ 08.00–16.00 Tue–Sun; entry 50MKD), which is opposite the train station, opened in 2010 to cater for public interest in the growing

The Lower Vardar & Tikveš Winelands   DEMIR KAPIJA

7

archaeological excavations in the area, and to continue the theme of Macedonia's history in wine, as other museums are doing.

VALANDOVO

Situated 11km east of the A1 on the road running to Strumica and Lake Dojran, Valandovo is renowned for its pomegranates and for the many Roman ruins in the vicinity. These include the necropolis at Dedeli and the lost town of **Idomenae** outside the village of Marvinci, where Aleksandar III of Macedon is thought to have his burial chambers. The earliest incarnation of the city, spread over some 5,000m² within the circuit of a defensive wall, dates to the Hellenistic period (323–168BC). The visible architectural remains relate mainly to private buildings and dwellings, but there are also the remains of a pottery workshop to be seen. Although the site is not presented for the public and can be somewhat arduous to visit, several public buildings can be seen, among which is a temple dedicated to Emperor Commodus (AD180–92) in the form of the Greek god Hercules. Commodus, the son of the warrior philosopher Emperor Marcus Aurelius, called himself the Roman Hercules and famously partook in the gladiatorial arena (played by Joaquin Phoenix in the film *Gladiator*).

Valandovo was also the site of fighting during World War I between the Irish 10th Regiment and the Central Powers of Germany and Turkey, and a small graveyard to the fallen of the Irish can be found on the outskirts of the town. Other sights in the vicinity include the 14th-century **tower of King Marko** just to the west of the town, and to the north is the **Monastery of Sv Gjorgi** in the hills above Valandovo. The town also holds Macedonia's yearly competition, the Rakijada, when local people compete in mid-October to make the best rakija.

 WHERE TO STAY AND EAT

Hotel Izvor 11 rooms; m 070 410 969. About 1km north of Valandovo, this an attractive enough place built in wood & stone, among leafy surroundings outside the city centre. The wood-furnished rooms have AC & private bathrooms, & there's a restaurant serving local fish specialities & other dishes, & an enormous swimming pool with a separate area for kids. **$$**

GEVGELIJA *Telephone code 034*

As part of the defensive line of medieval Byzantium, and of the World War I Salonika Front, Gevgelija is an archaeological treasure. Once a sleepy little border town, it now sports several casinos predominantly serving Greek visitors, who also form the main market for what it claims (credibly) to be the largest concentration of dentists in the Balkans. For local tourists, Gevgelija is also the main town serving Kožuf ski resort. The town has an interesting legend attached to its name. It allegedly derives from the Turkish *gel geri*, meaning 'come again', which was called to a dervish monk who had been banished by the locals. The monk had only stopped to rest overnight when he expressed his desire to stay because it was such a nice place, but the locals of non-dervish religion took umbrage with the statement and made it very clear that neither he nor his religion were welcome. As he left, the locals feared that the monk's god might take vengeance on them for banishing the monk and so they called after him, '*Gel geri, gel geri.*' No-one knows if he ever did return.

GETTING THERE AND AWAY Gevgelija is probably Macedonia's busiest border crossing, although **trains** to Greece had stopped at the time of writing – the only way to continue a train journey on to Thessaloniki would be to go over to the Greek

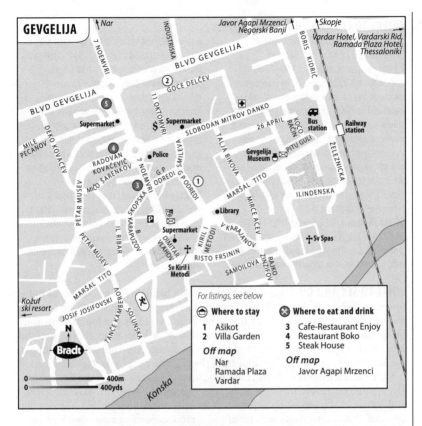

GEVGELIJA

For listings, see below	
🏠 **Where to stay**	🍴 **Where to eat and drink**
1 Ašikot	3 Cafe-Restaurant Enjoy
2 Villa Garden	4 Restaurant Boko
	5 Steak House
Off map	
Nar	*Off map*
Ramada Plaza	Javor Agapi Mrzenci
Vardar	

town of Dojran, 25km to the east. Gevgelija train station (☎212 033) is just outside town, and three trains a day connect it to Skopje (leaving at 04.45, 06.20 and 16.55), taking almost 3 hours, returning at 04.43, 16.55 and 19.48.

Gevgelija lies around 150km southeast of Skopje along the A1 via Veles and there are 11 **buses** daily from Skopje, leaving between 06.00 and 19.00. The bus station (7th Noemvri bb; ☎212 315) in the centre of town also serves the rest of Macedonia, as well as to Thessaloniki. **Taxis** can also cross the border to Greece – try Radio Taxi As (☎213 614).

🏠 **WHERE TO STAY** *Map, above*

✴ 🏠 **Ramada Plaza** (131 rooms) Bogorodica border crossing; ☎219 500; e info@rpgevgelija.com; w rpgevgelija.com. A truly international-standard luxury 5-star hotel affiliated to a reliable & well-known chain. Amenities include an indoor pool, spa, fitness centre, restaurants & nightclub. **$$$$**

🏠 **Nar Hotel** (33 rooms) Mrzenski Pat; ☎216 314. Modern hotel just outside town. All rooms with AC. Restaurant, spa. **$$$**

🏠 **Ašikot** (16 rooms) Gevgelski Partizanski Odredi 2; ☎212 238. A little down-at-heel, but fair value for money for the centre of town. **$$**

🏠 **Vardar** (24 rooms) Round the back of Vardarski Rid archaeological site; ☎213 267; 🇫 @motelvardar. Basic but quiet. **$$**

✴ 🏠 **Villa Garden** (3 rooms) Goce Delčev 70; m 075 285 335; e info@villagarden.mk; w villagarden.mk. Top-notch owner-managed B&B set in small but pretty garden on a quiet road close to the centre. Modern rooms are brightly decorated, spacious & clean, & come with all mod cons (flat-screen TV, writing desk, AC). Excellent value at €20 plus €3pp b/fast. **$$**

✖ WHERE TO EAT AND DRINK *Map, page 291*

✖ **Javor Agapi Mrzenci** 3km outside Gevgelija; ☎212 290; m 071 384 100; f @javoragapimrzenci; ⊕ 11.00–23.00 daily. Although quite expensive by Macedonian standards, the cuisine is truly outstanding for traditional Macedonian fare, serving particularly mouth-watering spit-roast lamb. The restaurant receives a lot of Greek visitors who seem to be meeting their Macedonian cousins. To get here turn off the main highway into Gevgelija & take the 2nd right heading north towards Negorci & Mrzenci. The restaurant stands out on the right before the small bridge. $$$

✖ **Steak House** Bd Gevgelija 1; ☎611 114; m 072 613 123; f @steakhousegevgelija. Smart central fish & grill restaurant with enthusiastic staff, well-stocked bar, attractive wooden interior & semi-enclosed terrace. Offers the usual grills as well as a great salad selection ($$) & significantly pricier steak & whole grilled fish ($$$$).

✖ **Restaurant Boko** Radovan Kovačevič 4; ☎211 890. Established in 1989, this stylish modern restaurant with rather formal AC interior is the most upmarket & probably the best in town. Serves the usual inexpensive grills ($$) supplemented by homemade pasta & relatively imaginative selection of chicken & pork ($$$) or fish, lamb & beef ($$$$) mains.

✖ **Cafe-Restaurant Enjoy** 7-mi Noemvri 41; ☎211 007; f @caferestaurantEnjoy. Smart bistro-like set-up with slick AC interior, wide terrace & a varied menu of pizza, pasta, salads, grills & a few relatively sophisticated Continental selections. $$

WHAT TO SEE AND DO Located on the small hill behind the city, **Vardarski Rid** is the site of a Bronze Age settlement called Gortynia, which was of some standing during the 2nd millennium BC. It was only discovered as the foundations were being laid for a monument to the National War of Liberation, ie: the partisan uprising. Gortynia is first mentioned by the Greek historian Thucydides, writing in the 5th century BC. The oldest finds from the site date back to the Neolithic period but the earliest evidence of structural remains dates to the end of the Bronze Age. Occupation continued throughout the Iron Age and the town thrived between 800 and 500BC, characterised by rich finds of jewellery and the so-called 'Macedonian Bronzes' (bronze pendants with ritual and symbolic meaning associated with an as yet unknown cult).

The city played an important regional role between the 2nd and 3rd centuries BC, and numerous buildings have been discovered from this period, along with a rich hoard of over 500 coins from the Antigonid dynasty (294–168BC). This dynasty, descended from one of Alexander's generals, Antigonese the One-Eyed, ruled over the ancient Kingdom of Macedonia and the Greek city-states. The **Gevgelija Museum** (Maršal Tito 26; ☎213 660; w muzejgevgelija.mk; ⊕ 09.00–15.00 Tue–Sun; entry 100MKD) mostly displays finds from Vardarski Rid as well as other local finds of pottery and money.

Another 1.5km along this road from Mrzenci are the hot springs of **Negorski Banji** and three recently rehabilitated hotels under the same private management (☎231 174; e info@negorskibanji.com.mk; w negorskibanji.com.mk; $$$). These baths are well kept compared with some of the others in the country, as they are mostly used for medicinal purposes. Male and female baths are separate, and there are additional rooms for massage and therapies as prescribed by the resident doctor. Public entry into the hot springs alone is 50MKD.

KOŽUF SKI RESORT

Centred on the mountain range bordering Greece, Kožuf (Gevgelija office, Maršal Tito 124; ☎034 214 441; m 071 869 999; e skikozuf@t-home.mk; w skikozuf.com) is the country's newest ski resort. Going up to 2,200m and covering an area of 2,000ha, with a chair-lift rising over 500m and some 65km of ski trails graded from beginners to advanced, it boasts being the highest and best ski resort in the region, after Bankso in Bulgaria. Like Popova Šapka, its height can make it prone to wind, but the skiing opportunities are considerably greater than at Mavrovo. At the time of writing it was still in its early days, with overnight facilities limited to 16 chalet-style wooden cabins, but a new asphalt road has been laid allowing for two-way traffic. A day pass is only 900/700MKD at weekends/weekdays, or 450/350MKD for children aged 8–14, free for children aged seven and under.

There are plans to re-mark the mountain trails in the range, including the 85km ridge trail from Kožuf to Kajmakčalan (near Bitola). One- or two-day hiking trips can be arranged, with an overnight stay in a shepherd's hut. Paragliding and rock climbing are also possible.

To get to Kožuf, take the train or bus to Gevgelija and then a taxi to Smrdliva Voda (25km; 600MKD), passing through the mountain village of Konsko on the way. At Smrdliva Voda (meaning 'smelly water' due to the sulphurous hot springs there) the Skikožuf *kombe* (minibus) (m 070 801 801) ferries people up the 18km to Kožuf at 08.30 (and back down at 16.00) for 100MKD each way. There are plans to tarmac the dirt road from Demir Kapija to Kožuf, but this may not materialise for a few years.

LAKE DOJRAN   *Telephone code 034*

Extending over 43km² along the Greek border, Dojran is Macedonia's third-largest tectonic lake after Ohrid and Prespa, having formed as a result of shifts in the Earth's land plates four million years ago. It is by far the shallowest of the three lakes, being no more than 10m deep at its fullest. At the turn of the millennium, Dojran had shrunk to about a third of its normal size, revealing around 50 islands, as a result of agricultural overuse of water, not only from the lake itself but also from the streams that feed it, on both sides of the border. At the time, there were fears it might dry up entirely, but it has since been rescued from near extinction by the combination of concerted government efforts and good rainfall. Nevertheless, there is still some way to go to restore the lake's full biological and ecological diversity.

Two small towns, imaginatively known as Star (Old) Dojran and Nov (New) Dojran, are sited about 5km apart on the lake's Macedonian shore. Prior to the temporary retreat of the lake waters, Star Dojran in particular was a popular resort known for its beauty, its curative reedy waters (for healing skin ailments) and its very good air quality. The town fell into decline at the turn of the millennium, but it has since seen a revival in fortune as a resort. Catering mainly to the domestic weekender market, it is a pretty little town, shaded by abundant plane trees, and it boasts good amenities including a generous scattering of hotels, holiday apartment complexes, grills, fish restaurants and boutique shops.

Dojran was designated a Ramsar Wetland of International Importance in 2007, and the shoreline is still teeming with wildlife. On a sunny spring day you can see more frogs than you can shake a stick at, water snakes eating tadpoles, a host of birds, butterflies and insects, and possibly even some fish. The lakeshore foot and cycle path that links Star Dojran to the altogether less appealing Nov Dojran provides a great opportunity to explore the lake on the foot, and it is also a nice spot for a jog.

GETTING THERE AND AWAY   Entering Macedonia from Greece via the Greek village of Dojran is a simple affair, and is in fact a shorter route from Thessaloniki than

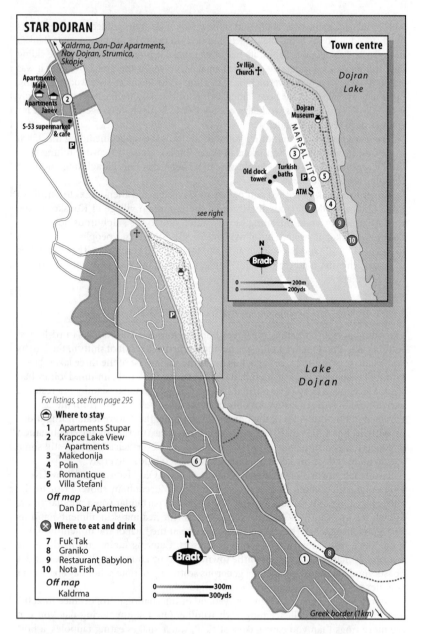

STAR DOJRAN

Kaldrma, Dan-Dar Apartments,
Nov Dojran, Strumica,
Skopje

Apartments
Maja

Apartments
Janev

2

S-53 supermarket
& cafe

P

see right

Town centre

Sv Ilija
Church ✝

*Dojran
Lake*

Dojran
Museum 🏛

MARŠAL TITO

3

Old clock
tower •

Turkish
baths

P

5

ATM $

7

4

9

10

N

Bradt

| 0 | | 200m |
| 0 | | 200yds |

✝

P

*Lake
Dojran*

For listings, see from page 295

🛏 **Where to stay**

1 Apartments Stupar
2 Krapce Lake View
  Apartments
3 Makedonija
4 Polin
5 Romantique
6 Villa Stefani

Off map
  Dan Dar Apartments

✖ **Where to eat and drink**

7 Fuk Tak
8 Graniko
9 Restaurant Babylon
10 Nota Fish

Off map
  Kaldrma

6

N

Bradt

| 0 | | 300m |
| 0 | | 300yds |

1

8

Greek border (1km)

using the highway at Gevgelija, with less traffic. The small border control station is usually very quick compared with the main Gevgelija crossing.

Star Dojran lies 175km southwest of Skopje, a drive that should take less than 3 hours in a private vehicle. Four **buses** a day connect Skopje to Star Dojran via Nov Dojran, with the first leaving at 06.00 and the last at 16.00. Seven more buses from Skopje serve nearby Bogdanci, from where you can take a **taxi** the remaining 18/23km to Nov/Star Dojran. Ask at your hotel for returning bus times as there is no dedicated bus station at either Nov or Star Dojran. A partial timetable including to Gevgelija (from where it's easier to get to other parts of the country) is at w dojran-info.com. Two buses every morning run along the 40km road between Strumica and Star Dojran. A taxi from Strumica will cost around 900MKD.

TOUR OPERATOR

Salonika Battlefield Tours m 077 904 675; e director@salonikabattlefieldtour.com; w salonikabattlefieldtour.com. Provides knowledgeable English-speaking guides who, for about €100/day, can take you around the extensive

battlefield, conduct research, provide mapping & photos, arrange cemetery visits, & book your accommodation & food. Director Romeo Drobarov is a former border policeman from the area & is well informed & very helpful.

 **WHERE TO STAY** *Map, opposite*

Apartments Stupar (20 rooms) Maršal Tito 128; m 071 346 665; e apartmanistupar@yahoo.com; f @ApartmaniStupar. Simply furnished rooms, 1.3km from the town centre on the road to the Greek border. Most rooms have balconies & own bathroom. **$$**

Dan Dar Apartments (31 rooms) Maršal Tito; m 075 222 932; e kontakt@apartmanidan-dar.com.mk; w apartmanidan-dar.com.mk. Comprising an older style building & a new build, this complex just off the main road before coming into Nov Dojran has an outdoor pool & traditional restaurant. Excellent value for money. **$$**

Hotel Makedonija (50 rooms) Maršal Tito; ☏ 225 003. Standard accommodation, right in the centre of Star Dojran on the main road. A common meeting place due to the large car park in front & the huge Macedonian flag marking the centre. **$$**

Hotel Polin (43 rooms) Maršal Tito; ☏ 225 770; e hotel_polin@hotmail.com. This is one of

the few hotels on the lake side of the main road, & has an outdoor pool as well as access to the public beachfront. It also offers lake mud spa treatments, but can be noisy in the summer due to proximity to café-bars on the beach. **$$**

Hotel Romantique (37 rooms) Maršal Tito 19; ☏ 225 050; e reservations@hotelrp.mk; w hotelrp.mk. Opened in 2013, this modern hotel is in the centre of town & has a swimming pool & its own restaurant. **$$**

Villa Stefani (6 rooms) Ilindenska 9; m 078 218 662/4; w vilastefani.com. Clean, brightly decorated tiled rooms with private balcony on a rise overlooking the town centre & lake. **$$**

Krapce Lake View Apartments (8 rooms) Maršal Tito; m 071 385 830. Neat & well-equipped studios with kitchen, writing table, fridge & private balcony. Great location next to a well-stocked supermarket & café about 1km from Star Dojran along the lakeside road to Nov Dojran. Top value. **$**

✕ WHERE TO EAT AND DRINK *Map, opposite, unless otherwise stated*

Nota Fish Restaurant Maršal Tito; m 070 238 558. Superb fish restaurant with cosy indoor or lakeshore terrace seating. 6 types of fish are available, along with the usual grills. Plenty of choice in the **$$** range but the pricier fish are **$$$$**.

Elita Fish Restaurant [map, page 277] 7km from Nov Dojran on the Gevgelija Rd; ☏ 213 701; m 070 881 146; e elita_ribnik@yahoo.com; ⊕ 10.00–midnight daily. Situated on little Lake Bolovan, the setting is relaxing, the fishing good & the food delicious. **$$**

Fuk Tak Maršal Tito 15; ☏ 255 320; ⊕ 11.00–23.00 daily. Although this small restaurant can't boast views overlooking the lake, it is the oldest & most famous in Star Dojran (& well known across all Macedonia), dating back

to the days of Macedonia's struggle to overthrow Ottoman rule. On the wall just inside the main entrance hang original photos of 8 of the founders of VMRO (Revolutionary Organisation for an Independent Macedonia). Opened just after the new train line through (now Greek) Dojran, the restaurant is named after the sound that the train engine makes: 'fuk-tak, fuk-tak, fuk-tak'. The menu offers the usual Macedonian fare, & the freshly caught carp from the lake is exquisite, extremely tender with no trace of a muddy taste at all – undoubtedly, the best carp you'll find anywhere. After 20.30 at w/ends there is live music. **$$**

Graniko At the far end of Star Dojran; m 071 251 246; ⊕ 11.00–23.00 daily. With a lovely terrace overlooking the lake, offering traditional food. **$$**

✕ Kaldrma Just past the road sign for Nov Dojran on the Star Dojran side of town; ☏ 227 122; ⏱ 11.00–23.00 daily. Serving basic local food & a variety of lake fish, this place has an upstairs dining area that commands great views of the lake & the mountains. If you like crunchy deep-fried fish, try the *perkija* (red-fin). $$

✕ Restaurant Babylon Maršal Tito. Perhaps the pick of several lakeshore terrace eateries serving well-priced pizzas & grills. $$

WHAT TO SEE AND DO Star Dojran was largely destroyed during World War I (hence why Nov Dojran sprang up), although the **old clock tower** and the **Turkish baths** can still be seen in the backstreets of the town. At the northern end of

WINNING THE DEVIL'S EYE

Abridged text from the panel boards at Kale Tepe memorial site.

The World War I Salonica Front stretched from the Gulf of Orfano in the east to Ohrid in the west, traversing variously Dojran, Strumica, Gevgelija, Prilep, Kruševo and even touching Skopje. The British offensive lay at Dojran from 1915 to 1918, with the decisive battle of September 1918 fought by the 22 Division (UK) and the Serres Division (GR) on the Allied side. Most of 22 Division was drafted from Wales and northern England, with a few chance volunteers from elsewhere. After tragic losses, 22 Division survivors erected a memorial to their fallen comrades shortly after the war at the strong point and observation position they fought so hard to attain, which was known then as the Devil's Eye on top of Kale Tepe, or the Grand Couronne.

OPEN TO THE PUBLIC The original memorial was rediscovered among thick undergrowth and vegetation in 2007. To mark the 90th anniversary of the end of World War I, the British Embassy in Skopje, in conjunction with the Municipality of Dojran, placed a replica memorial, inspired by the original, on the site. After sweeping for unexploded ordnance by the Directorate for Protection and Rescue, the area around the memorial was cleared of undergrowth and a path and benches prepared by the Dojran Municipality. Panel boards depicting the battle at Dojran have been erected, and the original memorial can still be seen, with the new memorial above it.

The hollow in front of the 22 Division memorial represents part of a large bunker that has been demolished. Other bunkers and positions stood to the east and north, parts of which can be seen today. The bunker complex at the memorial site served a supply and command system of trenches and defences. It was known to the Bulgarians as the Ferdinand and was so named to commemorate the Bulgarian victory of 1915. Images from the time clearly show the memorial fountain, which is passed on entering the newly reopened site. Dugouts and other strong points can also be seen from there.

WHAT HAPPENED AT DOJRAN In 1914, what was later to become the territory of the Republic of Macedonia was part of Serbia and was allied to Britain and France. Austro-Hungarian and German military divisions found Serbia more difficult to conquer than they had imagined, and by early 1915 they were encouraging Bulgaria, with the promise of territorial gains, to join them. On 21 September 1915 Bulgaria mobilised its forces on the border. On 11 October 1915 the Bulgarian army began their drive towards Skopje, splitting the Serbian army in two, part of which began to retreat towards Albania and the west and part of which began to retreat towards Greece and the south.

Star Dojran are the tall ruins of the **Sv Ilija Church**, which was almost completely destroyed in World War I but now has a new roof and is slowly undergoing renovation. The **Dojran Museum** (✆ 225 277/8; e infocentar@dojran-info.com; w dojran-info.com), specialising in the flora, fauna and structure of Lake Dojran, is in the tiny town hall opposite the Hotel Makedonija. The **lake** itself, with its abundant wildlife, can be enjoyed from both villages.

The **World War I Dojran battlefield** on Pip Ridge above Star Dojran is the area's main attraction for military buffs. Macedonia is mostly associated today with the Yugoslav conflict of the 1990s, and few now remember its part in the World

In order to support Serbia and try to stem the retreat, the French and British landed in Salonica (Thessaloniki) and marched north. French forces marched up the Vardar Valley as far as Veles, while the British 10 (Irish) Division marched towards Strumica forming a defensive line between Kosturino and Prstan. The amassed, well-trained Bulgarian, Austrian and German forces were unstoppable and forced the French on to the defensive to cover the retreat of the Serbs. Meanwhile, 10 Division fought fiercely in the east in a series of battles between 7 and 10 December 1915 to cover the eastern flanks of the Serbian and French withdrawal.

The Bulgarian army, in pursuit of the British and French, then occupied the southern border area and proceeded to dig in. They fortified the hills above Dojran with a well-planned system of redoubts, concrete observation positions, bunkers and machine-gun nests, the remains of which are clearly visible today.

There were two main battles in the hills above Dojran; the first in the spring of 1917 was a failure. The second battle of Dojran took place on 18 and 19 September 1918 as part of a co-ordinated assault, and succeeded in tying down Bulgarian reserves so that they could not be deployed to fight the French and Serbians to the west. Following the successful breakthrough by the French and the Serbs to the west, the Bulgarian forces above Dojran retreated, leaving their positions here deserted save for British troops moving up in pursuit.

AN ICOFORT SITE There is growing international concern about the preservation and conservation of both military archaeology and what are known as 'landscapes of conflict'. In 2005 the International Council on Monuments and Sites (ICOMOS) created a subcommittee, the International Scientific Committee on Fortifications and Military Heritage (IcoFort), specifically tasked with dealing with the preservation of military archaeology and advising UNESCO. Much of what is termed military archaeology is encompassed by existing international conventions and European treaties on archaeology and heritage, and in principle they are afforded the same status for preservation as would older remains, such as historic places of worship, historic buildings and other archaeological sites.

Macedonia is rich in landscapes of conflict from the mid 19th century through to World War II. Dojran itself was not only a site of conflict, but also part of the physical remains of a momentous point in European and world history, one which led, ultimately, to the creation of modern Europe. It is part of a wider and very well-preserved landscape of conflict across the entire Salonica Front, with trenches and redoubts, bunkers and machine-gun nests, foxholes and shell craters all still visible in the undergrowth and largely untouched by modern-day development.

The Lower Vardar & Tikveš Winelands   LAKE DOJRAN

7

War I Salonica Front, also known as the Macedonia Front, and even at the time better known as the 'forgotten front'. 'Muckydonia', as it was known in a theatre performance held by British troops in the Balkans during the war, was too small for the headline news, yet troops on the Salonika Front suffered the fog of war as much as troops in Flanders, the Somme or Verdun. Casualties were born from poor communications, malaria was endemic and life behind the lines (unlike in France and Belgium) was woefully unexciting. From 1915 to 1918, the British were held up in trenches to the southeast of Dojran while the Germans and Bulgarians held the northwest (see box, page 296). In addition to almost 10,000 men dying in combat (the majority of whom were British), many men died of malaria in the much marshier conditions of a century ago.

It's a 90-minute hike to the memorial at the Grand Couronne, unless the weather is dry enough to take a jeep (which it is not most of the year, and the track is too muddy even for a 4x4). Stone and rock trenches and old bunkers line the hills above the memorial, which is fittingly dotted with poppies (also Macedonia's national flower) in the summer. In addition to the UK memorial to 22 Division, there is a Bulgarian water fountain dedicated to their fallen at this site.

Although Dojran Municipality opened up the battlefield in 2008, it remains a difficult site to access. Even with a 1:25,000 map (sheet 784-3-2 available from w katastar.gov.mk) and excellent navigation skills it is easy to get lost on Pip Ridge (as many did in World War I). In addition, walking restrictions are often imposed in the summer due to the risk of wildfires (which sweep through the area most summers), and illegal loggers and their pursuant forestry patrol can cause the unannounced hiker considerable hassle. For a stress-free and informative day, mountain guides Gele and Bingo of Strumica-based Salonika Battlefield Tours (page 295) can arrange a guided tour for approximately €25 per person (excluding travel and subsistence, and depending on any research requests you may have). More information on the Salonika Campaign can be found at w salonikacampaignsociety.org.uk (which also offers tours), as well as in the books and web resources listed on page 357.

8

Štip, Strumica and the Southeast

> We wound our way up the mountains, past horses and carts, through a village and on to the top where we found the monastery of Veljuša with its jewel of a tiny thirteenth-century church whose foundations were seven centuries older. It stood, remarkable and unlikely as a Tardis, between a dark-furrowed vegetable patch and some recently refurbished but already tatty monastery buildings.
>
> Victoria Clark, *Why Angels Fall*, 2000

Interspersed by a series of mountain ranges with a northwest–southeast orientation, the valleys of the southeast boast an abundance of rivers and streams, hot springs and rice paddy fields, and form the wheat basket of Macedonia. The region is bisected by the Bregalnica River, which is Macedonia's second longest, rising close to the town of Berovo, then arching northwards and westwards via Delčevo, Kočani and Štip to its confluence with the Vardar near the ancient Roman town of Stobi. In ancient times, the course of the Bregalnica was followed by the Diagonal Way, the road that connected the Roman towns of Heraklea (now Bitola) and Stobi to the valley of the River Struma near Pautalija (now Kustendil in Bulgaria). Another ancient route through the region ran from Ovče Pole in the north to Serres (now in Greece) via Štip, Radoviš and Strumica. The two roads crossed at Štip, which was an important trading town in times of old.

The southeast sees relatively little tourism, but it is a pretty area, studded with historic towns. Most popular with domestic tourists is Berovo, which has a lake setting and offers forest hiking in the cool mountains. Other important settlements include Strumica (the largest in the region, and base for exploring the bird-rich Monospitovo Wetlands), Štip, Delčevo and Kočani.

ŠTIP   *Telephone code 032*

Despite the fact that Štip is still seen as the capital of the east of Macedonia, it is a relatively sleepy town, worth a stop on the way to places further east, but possibly not an overnight stay unless you are coming for the Makfest international music festival in October. The town is associated with two older names, that of Astibo from during the Kingdom of Macedonia, and Stipion from the early Byzantine era. In the 14th century, prior to the Ottoman Empire taking over the whole of Macedonia, five important churches were built in and around the town: the Church of Sv Archangel Michael, the Church of Sv Jovan, the Church of Sv Nikola, the Church of Sv Spas and the Church of Sv Basilius. In 1689, large parts of the town were burnt down during the Karpoš Uprising.

Like many Macedonian towns, Štip has claims to its own crucial role in forming a consciousness of independence in the minds of Macedonians and in so doing contributing to the struggle for that independence. Three hundred years after

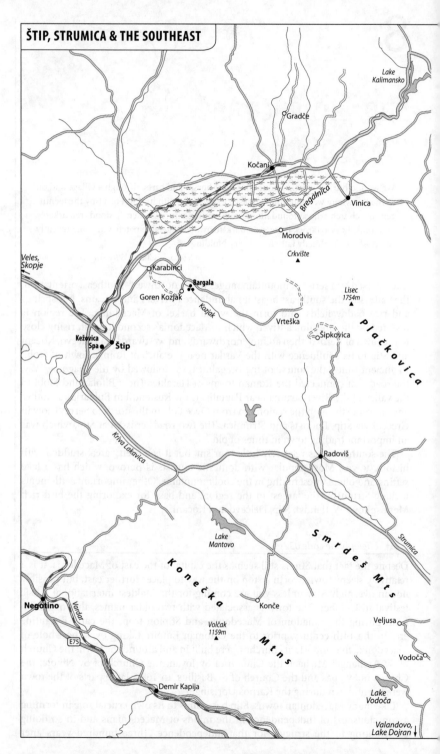

ŠTIP, STRUMICA & THE SOUTHEAST

Lake Kalimansko

Gradče

Kočani

Bregalnica

Vinica

Morodvis

Crkvište

Veles, Skopje

Karabinci

Bargala

Goren Kozjak

Kozjak

Lisec 1754m

Vrteška

Plačkovica

Šipkovica

Kežovica Spa

Štip

Kriva Lokavica

Radoviš

Smrdeš Mts

Strumica

Lake Mantovo

Konečka

Mtns

Konče

Veljusa

Negotino

Vardar

E75

Volčak 1159m

Vodoča

Demir Kapija

Lake Vodoča

Valandovo, Lake Dojran

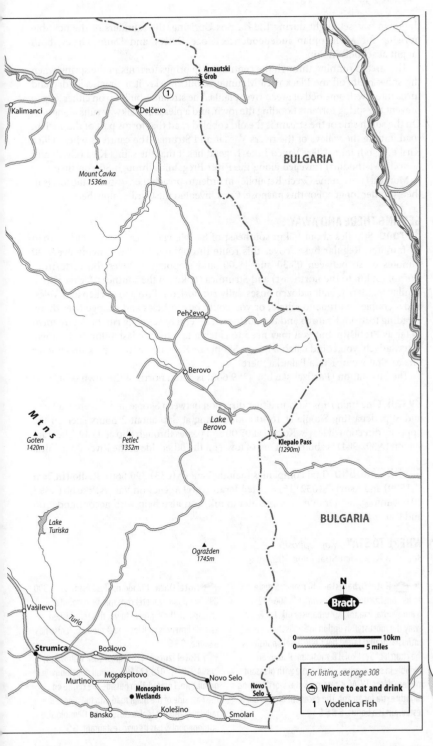

For listing, see page 308

🏠 Where to eat and drink

1   Vodenica Fish

the town was set alight during the Karpoš Uprising, the founders of the next big uprising for Macedonian independence, Goce Delčev and Dame Gruev, both taught at schools in Štip.

The stream running through the centre of Štip brings torrents in the spring when the snow melts off the Plačkovica Mountains, but by May it is practically dry and turns into a welcome bed of green river plants. The stream is built up on either side to prevent the spring torrents flooding the town, and a pleasant walkway runs alongside. On the south side of the stream is the old cobbled road that forms part of the ancient road joining the valleys of the rivers Vardar and Struma. The centre is where Ulica Kiril i Metodi joins Ulica Vančo Prke. Legend has it that the saints Kiril (Cyril) and Metodi (Methodius) travelled along the River Bregalnica through Štip on their way to Moravia (now in the Czech Republic) in order to preach the Gospel to the locals in their mother tongue. For this purpose, Cyril invented the Cyrillic alphabet.

GETTING THERE AND AWAY

By road Štip lies about 90km southeast of Skopje via Veles, a drive of less than 90 minutes. Regular buses cover this route throughout the day, leaving every 30 minutes or so between 05.30 and 18.00, and stopping at Veles. Buses to/from Kočani (30km to the northeast) and Strumica (65km to the southeast) leave with a similar regularity. Half a dozen buses daily run to/from Bitola via Prilep and Veles, and a couple continue to Ohrid, or you could bus to Veles and change over there. Heading to/from Kratovo and the northeast, several buses daily run back and forth as far as Probištip, but you may need to catch a taxi for the last 18km to Kratovo. Alternatively you could catch a bus to Skopje or Kumanovo, then pick up another one to Kratovo or Kriva Palanka there.

The bus station (Partizanska bb; ✆389 600) is 500m north of the town centre.

By rail One train runs daily in either direction between Skopje and Kočani via Veles and Štip, departing Skopje at 16.40 and arriving at Štip about 2 hours later. In the opposite direction, it leaves Kočani at 05.00 and passes through Štip at 05.49. The train station (✆392 904) is about 1km out of town on the other side of the River Bregalnica.

GETTING AROUND Taxi companies include **Vani** (✆(033) 390 860), **Radio Hit Taxi** (✆1599) and **Asovi** (✆(032) 1578). **Mediteran Travel Agency** on Vančo Prke bb (✆397 001; e info@mediteran.mk; w mediteran.mk) can also help with accommodation and transport.

 WHERE TO STAY *Map, opposite*
See also Kežovica Spa, page 305.

✳ 🏠 **Hotel Urbanista** (10 rooms, 5 more under construction) Vasil Glavinov; ✆606 112; e info@urbanista.mk; w urbanista.mk. Far & away the most stylish option in Štip is this new & enthusiastically staffed boutique hotel opposite the church of Sv Nikolai & museum. Rooms are variable in size & price but all come with pleasant modern décor, TV, AC & terrace, & it is worth paying slightly extra for an apt. The excellent terrace bar & restaurant is a bonus. **$$$$**

🏠 **Hotel Oaza** (37 rooms) Toso Arsov 32; ✆390 899; e info@oazahotel.com.mk; w oazahotel. com.mk. In the centre of town, this refurbished establishment is well located & modern. It also has a sauna. **$$$**

🏠 **Hotel Izgrev** (16 rooms) Vasil Vlahovikj 1; ✆394 919; m 078 322 698; e emil.popadinov@ gmail.com. Located 1km outside the centre on the east side of the main road into town near the railway station. It is also close to the Olympic-size outdoor pool & has its own restaurant. **$$**

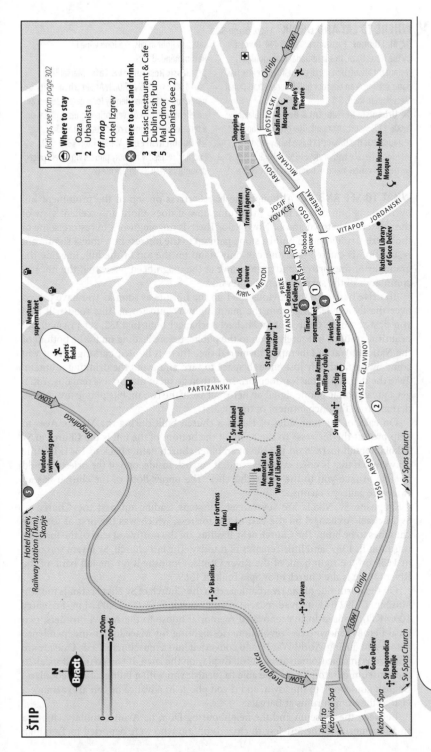

ŠTIP

N

Bradt

0   200m
0   200yds

For listings, see from page 302

Where to stay
1 Oaza
2 Urbanista

Off map
Hotel Izgrev

Where to eat and drink
3 Classic Restaurant & Cafe
4 Dublin Irish Pub
5 Mal Odmor
   Urbanista (see 2)

Hotel Izgrev,
Railway station (1km),
Skopje

Neptune
supermarket

Outdoor
swimming pool

Sports
field

Bregalnica

FLOW

Shopping
centre

Mediteran
Travel Agency

Clock
tower

KIRIL I METODI

JOSIF
KOVACEV

APOSTOLSKI
Kadin Ana
Mosque

People's
Theatre

Otinja

FLOW

ARSOV

MICHAEL

GENERAL

TOSO

VITAPOP JORDANSKI

Pasha Husa-Meda
Mosque

St Archangel
Glavatov

VANCO PRKE
Bezisten
Art Gallery

MARSAL TITO

Sloboda
Square

National Library
of Goce Delcev

Tinex
supermarket

Dom na Armija
(military club)

Štip
Museum

Jewish
memorial

Sv Nikola

PARTIZANSKI

Sv Michael
Archangel

Isar Fortress
(ruins)

Memorial to
the National
War of Liberation

Sv Basilius

Sv Jovan

VASIL GLAVINOV

TOSO ARSOV

Sv Spas Church

Otinja

FLOW

Bregalnica

FLOW

Path to
Kezovica Spa

Kezovica Spa

Goce Delcev

Sv Bogorodica
Uspenje

Sv Spas Church

X Mal Odmor Partizanski; 608 444. Owned by the Hotel Oaza, this traditional Macedonian restaurant about 1km north of the town centre has patio seating & an outdoor grill & serves traditional Macedonian food. $$

X Urbanista Restaurant & Bar Vasil Glavinov; 606 112; w urbanista.mk. The ground-floor restaurant at the Urbanista has a funky modern interior, a terrace with a view to Sv Nikolai & Isar Fortress, a varied menu of burgers, sandwiches, salads & light meals, & a long wine list. Recommended. $$

X Classic Restaurant & Cafe Maršal Tito; 614 000; m 078 257 061. As old school as its name suggests, this friendly local eatery serves an excellent selection of well-priced grills & pizzas on a terrace overlooking a concrete square. $

Dublin Irish Pub Maršal Tito; 391 099. Popular, relaxed & friendly pub serving well-priced draught as well as simple meals.

WHAT TO SEE AND DO Although the **Isar Fortress** on top of the prominent hill overlooking Štip is little more than ruins now, it does afford an excellent view of the modern-day town and of Novo Selo. There is ongoing work to restore some of the fortress ruins and to build a stone path up to the fortress but, unless significant restoration is carried out, one can only stand on the top of the hill, imagine the grandeur of the fortress and gaze in awe at the magnificent view that the hill still commands of the surrounding countryside.

To drive here take the obvious road up the hillside as soon as you have passed over the flyover leading from the main highway into town. This road will lead you past the little **Church of Sv Michael Archangel** built in 1332, set in small but beautiful grounds but rarely open to the public, before leading on to the bottom of the **National War of Liberation memorial** site. There is limited parking here if you come by car, and only just enough space to turn and avoid the drinking fountain. Take the steps up to the war memorial and then go on to the fortress remains. You'll get a great mobile phone signal up here, but sadly the two mobile phone towers also detract from the enchantment of the site.

On each of the four sides of Isar is a church built during the Middle Ages to help protect the fortress. To the south at the bottom of the hill is the **Church of Sv Nikola**, rebuilt in 1876 on the site of an older church dating back to 1341. It is the only church that is open every day and, if you ask inside, one of the priests should be able to take you to the other churches. The upper floor of the church has an extensive gallery of icons.

Opposite Sv Nikola are several sets of steps leading up past the Church of Sv Michael Archangel on the east of the fortress, which was the first of the four churches to be built. The **Church of Sv Basilius**, on the northwest side of the fortress, was built in 1337, and little remains of it today. The last church, **Sv Jovan**, was built in 1350 on the right bank of the River Otinja. Opposite it on the left bank of the River Otinja is the **Church of Sv Spas** built in 1369.

On the north side of the riverbank next to the Church of Sv Nikola stands the **Štip Museum** (392 044; e zovadimusejstip@mt.net.mk, ✆ 09.00–15.00 Mon–Fri; entry 100MKD), housed in the renovated memorial house to the Arsovi brothers, two local heroes renowned as revolutionaries fighting for Macedonian independence before and during World War II, and converted into a museum in 1955. Outside are numerous marble Roman artefacts on display on the lawn. If you go in and speak to the museum curator, he may be able to furnish you with a bilingual Macedonian–English guidebook to the town, and if you phone in advance he can also arrange a visit to the Roman ruins at Bargala.

Between the museum and the neighbouring Dom na Armija military club is a small **memorial** to the 561 Jewish citizens of Štip who were deported to Treblinka in Poland on 11 March 1943. Like many towns in Macedonia, Štip had a thriving Jewish community prior to the war and, though the lives of these citizens are well documented, little remains to be seen of their influence now.

Behind the Oaza Hotel, the **Bezisten Art Gallery** (⊕ 09.00–noon & 17.00–19.00 Tue–Thu & Sat, 09.00–13.00 Fri, 10.00–noon Sun) is housed in the town's most architecturally interesting building, an unadorned three-tiered stone construction that probably dates to the 16th or 17th century and originally served as a covered market. Štip's two mosques are south of the River Otinja. The **Kadin Ana Mosque**, built in the mid 19th century, is by the river next to the brightly coloured **People's Theatre**, which was built in 1951. It is unclear when the older **Mosque of Pasha Husa-Meda** just off Vitapop Jordanski Hill was built; while some say as early as the 14th century, others say not until the 16th. What is clear, however, is that it was constructed on the foundations of the much older Church of Sv Ilija. Within the grounds of the mosque is the turbeh containing the remains of the mosque's architect.

Festivals Štip hosts a number of events and festivals throughout the year. The UNESCO-listed **Feast of the Holy Forty Martyrs** takes place on the first day of spring (22 March), when Štipites walk up to Isar Fortress, gathering 40 pebbles and greeting 40 acquaintances, as well as 40 flowers or twigs from the surrounding almond trees, on their way up. Once at the top they throw 39 of the pebbles off the top of the hill and make a wish for the future. The remaining pebble is kept, to be placed under their pillow before going to sleep. July sees the Štip **International Film Festival** come to town, while November is **Makfest** (w makfest.mk), a highly popular festival featuring a variety of world music (book a room early if you want to stay over for it). For more exact information on festival artists and films contact Mediteran Travel Agency (page 302).

AROUND ŠTIP
Kežovica Spa (☎308 560) The spa is located just off the River Bregalnica past Novo Selo. The water emerges at the L'gji Spring at a temperature of 66.8°C, and is then mixed with cold water before it enters the baths. The baths themselves are separated for men and women, and are relatively pleasant and spacious. Entrance to the baths is 50MKD per person, and showers are an extra 50MKD. The baths are open 06.00–20.00 every day, except on Monday when the women's bath is closed for cleaning until 09.00, and on Friday when the men's bath opens at 09.00. A procurement bid has gone out to modernise and partially privatise the baths, so there is hope in the next few years that it might become the long overdue modern spa attraction it could be.

Aside from 100 beds for those booked in for physical therapy and treatment, the spa also offers 40 beds in 15 rooms to those wishing to stay overnight. Although the rooms are extremely basic and cheap at 350MKD per person per night, the spa setting alongside the River Bregalnica is very tranquil, and makes a good base for those on a shoestring budget to explore other places in the region. The spa also offers limited buffet facilities, but you are better off eating in town. It's a 3km walk from the spa along the river through Novo Selo to the centre of Štip.

Bargala Ruins The remains of the Roman city of Bargala can be found in the foothills of the Plačkovica Mountains near the village of Goren Kozjak, 18km northeast of Štip. The city itself was one of the major urban centres, along with the now lost cities of Kelenidin, Armonia and Zapara, of the Roman Province of Macedonia Salutaris. Though the first written references to Bargala date from late antiquity (around the 4th century BC), archaeological finds from the ruins suggest that the site itself was inhabited from a much earlier date. The city thrived into the 6th century AD before being overrun by the Avars. During its heyday it was enclosed in fortified walls some 300m by 150m, whose main entrance in the northwest wall can still be partly seen. Of the many antique and Roman structures to be discovered in the city, the most impressive are those of the antique bathhouse, which had a number of baths of differing temperatures as well as a sauna, and also the early Christian Church of Sv Gjorgi. The monumental three-naved basilica and associated complex is still visible, with its impressive entrance and its eight tiers of stairs leading to a room adorned with luxurious marble columns. Such architectural grandeur reflects the importance that the city held up until the 6th century AD. The associated complex housed the bishop's palace with its wide porch and colonnaded walkways. Bargala later became a bishopric in the Byzantine Empire.

PLAČKOVICA MOUNTAINS These offer a whole host of hiking opportunities and beautiful scenery. Take the Kozjak road from Karabinci to access the Plačkovica summit of Lisec (1,754m), Crkvište peak (1,689m) and the mountain villages of Šipkovica and Vrteška. At the latter village you can stay at the mountain hut **Vrteška** (64 beds; open by appointment; contact 'Lisec' hiking club in Štip: m 070 210 063).

KOČANI *Telephone code 033*

From Štip, the A3 follows the River Bregalnica to Kočani. There is not much in the town itself as, until communist industrialisation, it had mostly been a farming settlement since the time of Aleksandar III of Macedon. Around 330BC, Aleksandar sent back rice from India, which was planted in the fertile fields that are still worked today, many by hand, that provide most of Macedonia's rice. Surrounding Kočani are the archaeological sites of Morobyzdon and Vinica, and several hot springs.

GETTING THERE AND AWAY
By road Kočani lies 120km southeast of Skopje via Veles and Štip, a drive that usually takes less than 2 hours. Around 15 buses a day cover this route, leaving between 05.20 and 18.55, and stopping at Veles and Štip en route. The bus station (✆272 206) is centrally located at Pavlina Belanova.

By rail Kočani is the terminus of a railway line that runs southeast from Skopje via Veles and Štip, and is serviced by one train daily in either direction, a trip of roughly 3 hours. The train leaves Skopje at 16.40 and Kočani at 05.00. The train station (✆274 075) is located next to the bus station.

GETTING AROUND
Taxi companies include Radio Taxi Hit (✆(033) 1599). The minimum fare is 40MKD plus 20MKD/km.

🏠 WHERE TO STAY AND EAT *Map, opposite*

✳ 🏠 **Hotel Gradče** (25 rooms) 6km north of Kočani; ✆612 222; e info@eurohotelgradche.com; w eurohotelgradche.com. Well worth the winding drive for its nice rooms & tranquil setting on the western shore of Lake Gradče in the pine-swathed Osogovo Mountains. **$$**

🏠 **Hotel Leder** (12 rooms) Braka Stavrevi 19; ✆272 828; m 077 676 768. The only central option in Kočani is this 4-storey hotel overlooking a park. The brightly decorated rooms are adequate but nothing to write home about. **$$**

🏠 **Hotel Šagal** (16 rooms) 6km outside Kočani, before the turn-off to Vinica; ✆361 151/165; e sagalhotel@gmail.com. This functional hotel has indoor & outdoor restaurants, a fitness centre, sauna & tennis courts. **$$**

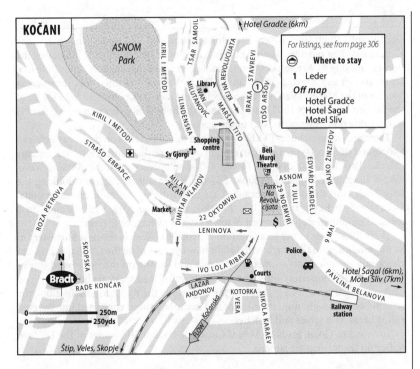

For listings, see from page 306

KOČANI

ASNOM Park

Hotel Gradče (6km)

For listings, see from page 306

⊖ **Where to stay**

1 Leder

Off map
   Hotel Gradče
   Hotel Šagal
   Motel Sliv

Library

Shopping centre

Sv Gjorgi †

Beli Murgi Theatre

ASNOM Park Na Revolucijata

Market

22 OKTOMVRI

LENINOVA

Police

IVO LOLA RIBAR

Courts

LAZAR ANDONOV

KOTORKA VERA

Hotel Šagal (6km), Motel Sliv (7km)

Railway station

N

Bradt

RADE KONČAR

0 ___ 250m
0 ___ 250yds

Štip, Veles, Skopje

🏠 **Motel Sliv** (30 rooms) Less than 1km on the turn-off to Vinica from the Kočani to Delčevo road; 📞 362 502; e motelsliv@yahoo.com. Nice restaurant, outdoor swimming pool & plenty of greenery. **$$**

WHAT TO SEE AND DO The more important town in the region in the 5th and 6th centuries AD was the religious complex of Morobyzdon near present-day **Morodvis**, 7km almost directly south of Kočani on the south side of the River Bregalnica. The site spans the late Roman period (4th century AD) to the 10th century AD and is one of the most significant in the Kočani region. The visible architectural remains of a monumental basilica date from the 5th and 6th centuries; it was furnished with a luxurious marble floor, massive columns and capitals. A large tomb, lavishly decorated in a multitude of colours, is incorporated into the basilica. Kočani became a bishopric in the 10th century under the Byzantine emperor Basilius the Great. Later, a small church, dating to the 13th century, was built over the earlier basilica. This town was probably on the ancient Diagonal Way, as was the neighbouring town of Vinica.

Vinica, named after its renown in Byzantine times for wine growing, is famous for the remarkable and unique terracotta icons found at the old fortress on the hill above the town. Archaeological finds from the fortress date to the Neolithic period. The site itself saw its heyday between the 4th and 6th centuries AD and is closely associated with the dawn of Christianity in Macedonia. The Vinica terracottas found here are ceramic tiles depicting Christian scenes in relief of traditional saints and betray an artistic style atypical of the region. The scattered pottery, stone and tile on the ground are all from the late antique settlement beneath the soil and point to the hidden city beneath your feet. The terracotta icons themselves are on display at the National Museum of Macedonia in Skopje. When the Bregalnica was dammed at **Kalimansko Ezero** in early communist times, Vinica gave up wine growing for rice and tobacco. From Vinica, the road east-southeast leads along the River Osojnica to Berovo.

Štip, Strumica and the Southeast KOČANI

8

Continuing along the River Bregalnica, Highway 27 passes the manmade Kalimansko Ezero before reaching the small town of Delčevo, just 10km before the border crossing of Arnautski Grob (meaning 'grave of the Arnauts') into Bulgaria. Once known as Carevo Selo, meaning 'Tsar's Village', the town was renamed in honour of the Macedonian revolutionary leader Goce Delčev in 1950. As a leader of the Ilinden Uprising of 1903, he is resoundingly honoured every year with a festival in his name on 2 August, the day of the uprising.

There are frequent buses (\413 684) in and out of Delčevo on their way between Skopje and Berovo. If you want to overnight or eat here, the central Hotel Makedonija (Maršal Tito 30; \410 288; m 076 483 480; e recepcija@hotelmakedonijadelcevo. mk; w hotelmakedonijadelcevo.mk; **$$**) has a pleasant location overlooking the Bregalnica, and a decent restaurant. A far better dining option is the exceptional Vodenica Fish Restaurant (m 076 250 886; map, page 301), which stands on a forested mountain slope 5km east of town near the village of Dzvegor.

Three kilometres to the southwest on the road to Golak is the new **Monastery of Sv Bogorodica**, a small church with bright new frescoes of all the familiar saints, but check out the new dance moves of Sv Eleusa and Sv Ana on the right-hand side as you go in. The monastery inns have been left unfinished for years but, even if you can't overnight here, it's a great place for a picnic as the rock formations along the stream bed are a sight unto themselves and many have been converted into covered eating areas with tables and benches.

The road to Golak leads to Mount Čavka, at 1,536m. The views of the Delčevo Valley on the way up are superb.

BEROVO   *Telephone code 033*

Turning south at Delčevo, following the River Bregalnica part way, the road comes to the quaint eastern village of Berovo. Unlike most settlements in Macedonia, this one does not hark back to Roman, medieval or Byzantine times, as it only first resembled something like a village in the late 19th century, barely 150 years ago. It got its name from the Macedonian word *bere* meaning 'to gather', probably because outsiders were so surprised that anyone would gather in a place where there wasn't already a significant settlement.

Today, people come here because of the outstanding beauty of the mountains and for the cool, refreshing mountain air. At almost 900m above sea level, Berovo lies in the Maleševo Valley of the upper reaches of the Bregalnica River. Sheltered by mountains, this valley records the coldest average temperatures in winter, and it is fairly cool here in the summer too, rarely getting into the high 20°Cs. It is an excellent getaway from the scorching heat of Skopje in June, July and August, but bring an extra sweater for the evenings. The useful municipality website is w berovo.gov.mk.

GETTING THERE AND AROUND   Berovo lies 170km southeast of Skopje via Veles, Štip, Kočani and Vinica, a drive of around 2½ hours in a private vehicle and 3½ hours by bus. This route is reasonably well served by public transport, with around a dozen buses plying back and forth in either direction daily, most using the direct route to Vinica but some diverting to Delčevo. There are also a couple of buses daily to Strumica, a 55km drive along a fabulously scenic montane road that can take up to 90 minutes to cover if you get stuck behind trucks. The bus station (Kej JNA; \471 139) is right in the centre of town next to 23 Avgust Bridge.

At the **taxi** stand opposite the bus station, Central (✆ (033) 1590) and Slivka (✆ (033) 1596) run for a minimum fare of 50MKD plus 30MKD/km.

A **map** of the town and of hiking in the area is available commercially in Skopje and in Berovo.

🏠 **WHERE TO STAY** For bed-and-breakfast options in the area try **Atlantis Travel Agency** in Strumica (✆034 345 212; w atlantis.mk), or search on w berovobooking. com.mk. Prices are around 750MKD per person per night.

🏠 **Aurora Resort & Spa** (31 rooms) Berovsko Ezero; ✆550 965; m 078 421 498; e booking@ auroraresort.mk; w auroraresort.mk. Perched at an altitude of 1,100m on a ridge overlooking Lake Berovo, this relatively smart resort offers pleasant rooms, good views & varied amenities including an outdoor swimming pool, small shop, travel agency, children's playground & animal farm. Organised hiking, biking & horseriding trips run from the resort. **$$$**

🏠 **Hotel Manastir** (36 rooms) Kiril i Metodi 6; ✆279 000; m 070 275 322; e info@hotelmanastir. com.mk; www.hotelmanastir.com.mk. This comfortable hotel stands next to Sv Michael the Archangel Monastery a few hundred metres south

of the town centre alongside the road to the lake. It offers apt-type rooms in a quaint setting, a popular restaurant serving good Macedonian food & a small spa. Decent value. **$$$**

🏠 **House Poli** (3 rooms) Zadasska 1; m 078 230 767. This 3-bedroom flat sleeping up to 8 is a little run-down but very conveniently located & great value at around €10 for the whole place. The family who run it are very helpful, too. **$**

🏠 **Motel Idila** (16 rooms) 20km southeast of Pehčevo; m 070 233 720. A beautiful location almost on the border with Bulgaria, this trout farm has an outdoor pool & nice rooms. Good little restaurant. **$**

🍴 **WHERE TO EAT AND DRINK** Several cafés and restaurants are clustered around the main pedestrianised square on Maršal Tito, and the restaurant at the Hotel Manastir is recommended for local food.

🍴 **Restaurant MRS** Maršal Tito 130; ✆471 101; m 078 454 771. Celebrating 50 years of service in 2018, Berovo's top eatery is a superior grillhouse with a homely brick-&-wood interior, seating on a

wooden terrace, & a long & varied menu of grilled meats & other local specialities. Very reasonably priced, too. **$$**

WHAT TO SEE AND DO Bisected by the Bregalnica River, Berovo is an attractive town whose focal point, the pedestrianised **Dimitar Berovski Square**, is lined with pavement cafés and overlooked by a striking church built in 1972 around a distinctive domed belltower that dates to 1930. The main urban point of interest is the **Monastery of Sv Michael the Archangel**, which predates the town by less than half a century, and stands at its southern edge. The monastery was originally built in order to train teachers in Macedonian, away from the watchful eyes of their Ottoman rulers, who feared that the development of Macedonian language and literature would lead to revolt. A famous Macedonian literary figure, Joakim Kršovski, taught here. The monastery is surrounded by a couple of inns where the nuns live and has a small informative museum, although you will need to phone the museum keeper (✆472 733), if you want to look inside, as it is usually shut.

Further afield, aside from **hiking** in the beautiful mountains, there is **skiing** in the winter from the Maleševo Recreation Centre, and **fishing** in the summer in **Lake Berovo**. The lake itself is artificial, and a lakeshore footpath leads from the car park here to the dam on the River Klepalska, which is closed off behind a locked gate. The water stays cold all year round as it is drawn from the surrounding mountains. To reach the lake, take the turning downhill at the junction for the Aurora Resort and Spa.

An alternative to taking the downhill road towards the lake is to follow the high road that runs along the forested slopes above its northeastern shore. Offering fabulous views through the trees to the lake below, the road leads after 4km to a junction where you can turn right and walk for a few hundred metres to the point where the River Klepalska enters the lake. Past here, the road continues for another scenic 7.5km to the Bulgarian border at Klepalo, although the Bulgarian side has not yet reciprocated the desire to open the border, so all you will find on the Macedonian side is an empty border and customs building.

Nine kilometres north of Berovo is the village of **Pehčevo**, which started out as an iron-mining town in Roman times and continued to produce iron ore throughout Ottoman rule. Remains of the mine at the foot of Mount Bukovik can still be found. Hiking in the vicinity is a popular pastime and there are a number of rooms for accommodation along the River Ravna.

STRUMICA *Telephone code 034*

Between the Belasica and Ogražden mountain ranges is the town of Strumica (also transliterated as Strumitsa), which lies in a little-visited area that is teeming with history, sites and natural beauty. The town itself is one of the oldest in Macedonia to have remained in its original location and not be moved by earthquake or ransacked by marauding invaders. Neolithic remains have been found on the hill above the town, and a fortress has existed there since at least the 4th century AD. Archaeological excavation there continues and is well worth a visit.

Strumica is commonly thought to be the site of the ancient city of Doberos, mentioned by Thucydides in the 5th century BC in his tales of the exploits of King Sitalcus, an ally of the Athenians in the Peloponnesian War against the Paeonians and Macedonians. Later in the 2nd century BC, the town came under the name

AN AMERICAN HOSTAGE FREES MACEDONIA

In 1878, the Treaty of Berlin returned Macedonia to Ottoman control, thus dividing what had become Bulgaria under the Treaty of Stefano earlier that year. The people of Bulgaria tried, without success, to reunite, and many from Macedonia fled north of the border to the free municipality of Bulgaria. There they formed the Supreme Committee, with the explicit aim of reuniting the former 'Greater Bulgaria'.

Within Macedonia, a faction of the Supreme Committee was established, named the Internal Macedonian Revolutionary Organisation (today's VMRO). The poorer sibling of the Supreme Committee, it settled for the more practical aim of Macedonian independence rather than reunification with Bulgaria, as reunification clearly did not appeal to the Great Powers at the time. Money and munitions for this 'lesser' aim were not forthcoming from the Supreme Committee, however, so in 1901 the VMRO drew up a number of plans to 'raise' funds.

The idea to kidnap Miss Ellen Stone, an American missionary working in Bankso (in today's Bulgaria) came from Jane Sandanski (many streets in Macedonia are named after him). Although the local Bansko VMRO committee eventually bought into the idea, the top VMRO leadership, including Goce Delčev, did not. Sandanski went ahead nevertheless. The act of the kidnap itself on 3 September 1901 went relatively smoothly, with nobody hurt. Sandanski was not to know at the time though, that Mrs Katerina Tsilka, taken along with Miss Stone to act as chaperone in regard to Victorian values, was pregnant with her second child.

Astraion, meaning 'city of stars' and named after the Astrai tribe of the Strumica Valley. In Roman times the town was called Tiveriopolis after its first Roman patron, Tiberius Claudius Menon. The arrival of Slavic tribes in the 7th century AD gave the town its current name.

In 1902, Strumica hit world headlines when America's first international hostage incident ended with the missionary Ellen Stone walking into the town (see box, below). Later, she discovered that she had been held for some of her captivity in a house in Nivičino village, just north of Strumica.

GETTING THERE AND AROUND Strumica lies about 155km southeast of Skopje, a 2-hour drive using the most direct route via Veles and Štip, and 250km east of Ohrid via Bitola and Prilep. It is served by **buses** from all over the country. A dozen run back and forth between Skopje and Strumica via Veles and Štip daily, leaving between 06.00 and 20.30, and there are also around ten buses a day in either direction between Strumica and Gevgelija. Transport west to Prilep, Bitola and Ohrid is limited to a few morning buses daily, but you could also bus through to Veles and pick up onward transport there. More locally, there are only two buses a day in either direction to Berovo, 55km to the northeast, and Star Dojran, 40km to the south. The bus station [313 G1] (✆346 030) is on Ulica Kliment Ohridski on the northeast side of town. A clean **taxi** company in Strumica is Super Taxi (✆(034) 1595), with white branded cars. The minimum fare for taxis in Strumica is 50MKD plus 30MKD/km.

TOUR OPERATOR

Atlantis [312 B4] Dimitar Vlahov 18; ✆345 212; e manager@atlantis.com.mk, ace@atlantis. com.mk; w atlantisdm.mk. Helpful friendly staff.

Informative map of Strumica & the local region available.

It took five months of negotiation for the original sum of US$110,000 to be whittled down to US$63,000, raised from the American public through a huge nationwide campaign, and for the 95kg of gold bricks to be smuggled past Turkish and Bulgarian officials into the hands of the revolutionaries. In the meantime, baby Elenchie was born on 4 January 1902 in a hut near the village of Troskovo (today in Bulgaria, some 30km northeast of Berovo). After the money was 'deposited', it took another three weeks of traipsing through the mountains before Miss Stone, Mrs Tsilka and baby Elenchie were finally left by the revolutionaries outside Strumica.

America's first modern hostage crisis had all the hallmarks of modern-day diplomacy, intelligence conundrums, public relations scandals, the terrorist versus the freedom fighter, personal advancement in the halls of power, escape and evasion. Reaching the desk of the US president Theodore Roosevelt, there was no question of setting a dangerous precedent by paying the kidnappers from state or federal funds, but every diplomatic means, including the implied threat of US warships to the Black Sea, was applied. Teresa Carpenter's excellent book, *The Miss Stone Affair* (2003), delves into all these angles and sets the incident out in a page-turner worth reading of its own accord.

In the end, the money helped to fuel the Ilinden Uprising of 2 August 1903 (page 24), but it was almost another 90 years before VMRO's dream of an independent Macedonia finally came to fruition.

8

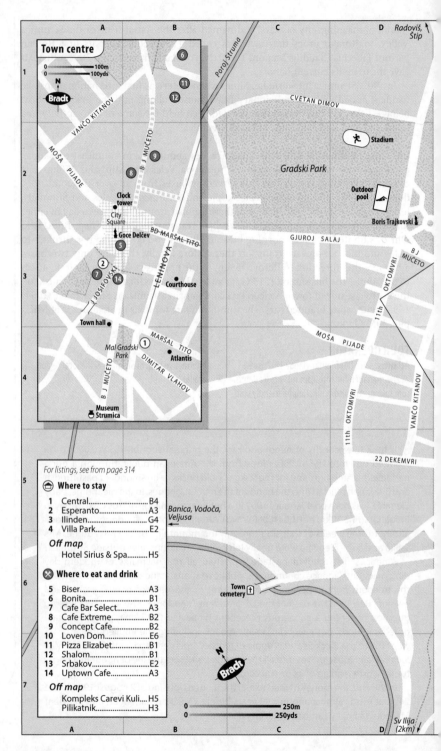

Town centre

0 ————— 100m
0 ————— 100yds

N
Bradt

Radoviš, Štip

Labels on map:

VANČO KITANOV
MOŠA PIJADE
B J MUĆETO
Clock tower
City Square
Goce Delčev
BD MARŠAL TITO
LENINOVA
JOSIFOVSKI
Courthouse
Town hall
Mal Gradski Park
MARŠAL TITO
Atlantis
DIMITAR VLAHOV
B J MUĆETO
Museum Strumica

CVETAN DIMOV
Stadium
Gradski Park
Outdoor pool
Boris Trajkovski
GJUROJ SALAJ
B J MUĆETO
11th OKTOMVRI
MOŠA PIJADE
VANČO KITANOV
11th OKTOMVRI
22 DEKEMVRI

Poroj Struma

Banica, Vodoča, Veljusa

Town cemetery

N
Bradt

Sv Ilija (2km)

0 ————— 250m
0 ————— 250yds

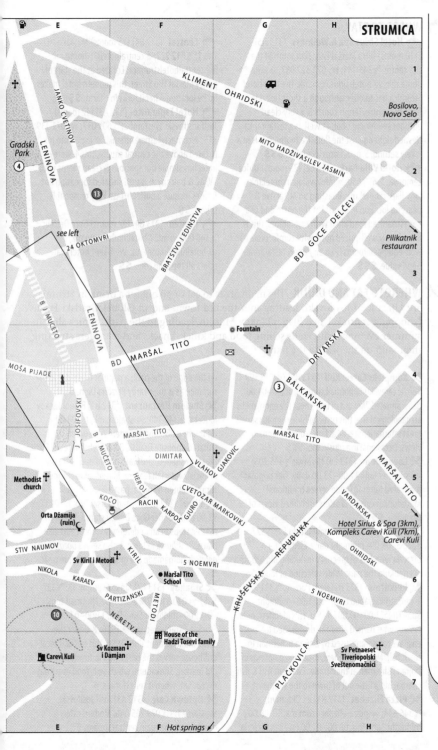

STRUMICA

WHERE TO STAY

🏠 **Hotel Sirius Spa & Wellness** [313 H5] (116 rooms) Ulica Maršal Tito, 3km south of the city centre; ✆345 141; 📱 071 322 987; 🔌 sirius@t-home.mk; 🌐 hotel-sirius.com.mk. The best hotel Strumica has to offer, although a short taxi ride from the centre. Tennis courts & a very clean outdoor swimming pool, as well as a restaurant. Nestled right against the Belasica foothills, it is in a lovely setting. 5-bed dorms available. **$$$**

🏠 **Hotel Villa Park** [313 E2] (25 rooms) Ulrica Leninova; ✆609 650; 🔌 info@villaparkhotel.mk; 🌐 villaparkhotel.mk. Boasting an attractive & peaceful location in Gradski at the north end of a pedestrianised road lined with restaurants, this is a modern & well-priced hotel with comfortable well-equipped rooms & an airy bar & restaurant. Good value. **$$$**

🏠 **Central** [312 B4] (25 rooms) Maršal Tito 1; ✆612 222; 🔌 centralhotel@t-home.mk; 🔲 centralhotelstrumica. Located at the start of pretty Maršal Tito Street, this modern hotel makes up by location what it lacks in charm. **$$**

🏠 **Hotel Esperanto** [312 A3] (42 rooms) Josif Josifovski Svestarot 2; ✆609 017; 📱 071 339 315; 🔌 contact@esperanto.mk; 🌐 esperanto.mk. Located above the central square, this 4-storey hotel has simple but spacious & clean rooms with TV, AC & balcony. It is well situated for eating out & rates include a buffet b/fast. Very reasonably priced. **$$**

🏠 **Ilinden** [313 G4] (27 rooms) Goce Delčev; ✆348 000; 🔌 info@hotelilinden.com.mk; 🌐 hotelilinden.com.mk. Well-kept hotel that offers all the mod cons. **$$**

✗ WHERE TO EAT AND DRINK
The main areas to eat or go out for a drink in Strumica are Ulica Josif Josifovski, leading into the old town, and in Global Gradski Pazar (shopping centre). Ulica Blagoj Jankov Mučeto, leading to the park, comes alive in summer evenings with stalls selling food and knick-knacks and teenagers strutting their stuff on the way to the park.

✗ **Kompleks Carevi Kuli** [313 H5] 📱 075 499 188; 🔌 carevi.kuli@hotmail.com; ⏱ 10.00–01.00 daily. Situated 7km out of town near the eponymous archaeological site, this rustic hillside complex serves great international & local fare & offers stunning views. Occasional live music, too. **$$$**

✗ **Loven Dom** [313 E6] Neretva; ✆345 206; ⏱ summer only 11.00–23.00 daily. This popular renovated hunting lodge serves traditional Macedonian cuisine & offers unrivalled views of the town. **$$$**

✗ **Bonita** [312 B1] Blagoj Mučeto 54; ✆327 122; ⏱ 08.00–midnight daily. Elegant for a pizzeria with lots of greenery including big terrace overlooking the park. Wide selection of food. **$$**

✗ **Pilikatnik** [313 H3] Boro Pockov; ✆331 926; 🔌 pilikatnik@yahoo.com; ⏱ 11.00–midnight Sun–Thu, 11.00–01.00 Fri–Sat. This Mediterranean restaurant is named after the device used to ensnare cormorants used by Dojran fisherman to catch fish. Nice atmosphere, including paintings of Dojran fishermen at their trade. Excellent fish & fish chorba, but a little out of town to the southeast. **$$**

✗ **Pizza Elizabet** [312 B1] 24 Oktomvri; ✆346 644; 🌐 pizza-elizabet.com.mk; ⏱ 08.00–midnight Sun–Thu, 08.00–01.00 Fri–Sat. Pizzeria on the edge of the park; a popular hang-out in the summer, as is the nearby Pizzeria Dion. **$$**

✗ **Shalom Restaurant** [312 B1] Blagoj Jankov Mučeto; ✆340 340; 🌐 shalom.mk; ⏱ 08.00–midnight daily. Smart modern restaurant situated opposite Gradski Park. Stylish interior & pleasant shaded courtyard dominated by a large artificial waterfall feature. Macedonian cuisine supplemented by pizza, pasta & salads. **$$**

✗ **Biser** [312 A3] Ploštad Maršal Tito; ⏱ 08.00–23.00 daily. Under Goce Delčev statue, follow the marble steps to an underground food-court-like place. Best *burek* in town & also serves *boza*. Their *gelato* is homemade & a great summertime treat. **$**

✗ **Srbakov** [313 E2] Janko Cvetinov 33; ✆327 585; 📱 070 310 578; 🔌 srbakov@hotmail.com; ⏱ 11.00–midnight Sun–Thu, 11.00–01.00 Fri–Sat. Established in the 1920s & under the same management since 1994, this popular local grillhouse serves the best *čorba* in town. Near the old market, Shukadum, which sells food every day except Sat, when it sells clothes. **$**

✗ **Uptown Cafe** [312 A3] Josif Josifovski Svestarot 1; 📱 079 265 046. Modern café overlooking the main central square. **$**

♀ **Cafe Bar Select** [312 A3] Leninova; m 070 310 013; w select.com.mk; ☉ noon–01.00 daily. The most popular bar/café in the old town. Live music, DJs. Modern, techno.

♀ **Cafe Extreme** [312 B2] Blagoj Jankov Mučeto; ☉ 10.00–midnight daily. Despite the name, is actually quite relaxed. Midway towards the park, it's well frequented in the summer.

☕ **Concept Cafe** [312 B2] Blagoj Jankov Mučeto 30; e conceptcafestrumica@gmail.com. This hip café serves snacks, smoothies, coffee, cocktails, beer & wine to a predominantly young crowd. Regular themed DJ nights.

WHAT TO SEE AND DO Strumica is a charming little town in itself and there are a whole host of things in the vicinity to keep you occupied for a good few days. The old town does not take long to get around and leads up to the restored **Loven Dom** [313 E6] ('hunter's lodge'; now a swish town-style restaurant more than a rural inn) boasting the best view over the town, for which the steep climb is also worth an expensive coffee. On the way up, Kiril i Metodi Street passes the **Church of Sv Kiril i Metodi** [313 F6], completed in 1912; Maršal Tito School [313 F6], built in the early 1900s; the disused court building; and the beautiful old house of the **Hadzi Tosevi family** [313 F7], which is in dire need of preservation.

The **Museum Strumica** [312 A4] (27th Mart 2; ☎345 925; **f** @MuseumStrumica; ☉ 09.00–16.00 Mon–Fri; entry free) is a smart building, housing a very manageable collection of prehistoric, ancient, medieval, Ottoman period and early 20th-century artefacts gathered from around Strumica. Unique to the town is an early 20th-century printing press and an exhibition dedicated to America's first international hostage incident, the Miss Stone case (see box, page 310). Among the photographs of the incident is one of the house in the village of Nežilovo, north of Strumica, where she was held for a while. To get to the museum from Kiril i Metodi Street, take the steps leading down to 27th Mart Street. The museum ethnologist, Ilijas, is proud to use his English and will give you a quick tour around.

The heart of Strumica is dominated by a huge pedestrian centre (cars travel underneath it) and a larger-than-life-size **statue of Goce Delčev** [312 A3], commemorated for his part played in the Ilinden Uprising in 1903 against the Ottomans. To the north is the pedestrian street dedicated to the Strumica hero Blagoj Jankov Mučeto, which is known as the Strumica **Korzo** – the place to see and be seen. The Korzo leads to the well-kept **Gradski Park** [312 D2] with its stadium and outdoor public pool, Aquarius. The park also has a bust of the late President Trajkovski, who was born in Strumica and died in a plane crash in 2004 over Bosnia.

From the southern end of Blagoj Jankov Mučeto is **Ulica Maršal Tito** (as opposed to the main boulevard further north) running east–west. Once the old high street, it is lined with picturesque buildings from the early 20th century; it's like a miniature Širok Sokok in Bitola, and people come here to shop and meander. At the east end is the imposing **town hall** [312 A3] overlooking the **Mal Gradski Park**. On Stiv Naumov Street is the abandoned **Orta Džamija** [313 E5]. A national monument itself, it is plain on the inside, and is not the main point of interest here; rather it is the **11th-century church** underneath. Although little is known about the true significance of the church, its size indicates a certain importance for the region, especially coupled with the medieval Carevi Kuli (page 316) and what is likely to have been a sizeable medieval walled town at the time. The necropolis complete with skeletons is still being excavated, and some of the findings from the church are housed in the Strumica Museum.

In the very poor Turkish part of town (sadly with little Turkish architecture) is the **Church of Sv Petnaeset Tiveriopolski Sveštenomačnici** [313 H7] (Holy 15 Martyrs of Tiveriopol) (Ul Slavčo Stojmenski bb), where 15 Christians, who fled from Nicea (now Iznik in today's Turkey) during the persecution of Christians in the mid 4th century, are buried. Much of the lower half of the church has been uncovered, including 16 vaults and some large mosaics, all of which can be seen. Underneath the new church, built to one side in the last century, is the **icon gallery** (⊕ 10.00–19.00 Tue–Sun; entry 100MKD) housing some 50 icons ranging from the medieval period to the late 19th century.

On the top of the hill overlooking the town are the **Carevi Kuli** (Tsar's Towers) of Strumica Fortress [313 E7]. Although this site has been fortified since at least

---

TURKS UNRECOGNISED   *KUD Kardešlik*

In the Strumica region, an ethnic Turkish population goes about its business, working as farmers or field labourers, wood cutters, manual labourers, and whatever it takes to pay the bills. Their work is largely seasonal, with fathers and mothers working and living in shelters several hours from home in order to save enough money to send their children to school in the autumn, and to pay for firewood for the ensuing winter. Although some estimates place the Turkish population in Strumica at approximately 8,500–9,000, they are mostly unrecognised within Macedonia, and are mistakenly confused with the Roma population, which itself may be an additional 5,000 in Strumica. (However, statistical information is difficult to come by, hence there is room for disagreement.) The Turkish dialect here is known as Balkan Turkish, and while understood by the Turkish in Turkey, is comparable to the differences between French proper and the French spoken in Canada, or the Spanish spoken in Spain and that of South America.

Here in the Strumica area, inter-ethnic marriage between the Roma and Turkish does occur more frequently than in Skopje, although it is certainly not widespread. Turkish and Roma children are educated in the same classrooms in the Turkish language by Turkish teachers in the primary schools, grade levels 1–4. Many ethnic Macedonians do not know the linguistic or cultural differences between the two ethnicities, and use skin colour as a rough – though highly inaccurate – proxy to determine ethnicity.

There is no doubt that these Turks love all things Turkish: Atatürk, the Children's Day (a *bayram* celebrated within Turkey and among the Turkish diaspora), meze platters of food, colourful headscarves and, of course, Turkish folklore dances. Within the past several years, festivals have been increasingly organised around traditional folklore dancing, attracting both ethnic Turks and a broad international audience. For example, the Day of Spring Festival is celebrated annually for a few days around 6 May (the holiday of Gurgovden) in the small village of Čalikli. Here, dancers and performers from all ethnicities (Bosnian, Azerbaijan Greek, Albanian, Turkish from Turkey, Turkish from Macedonia, Kosovo, etc) perform their unique dances that are peculiar to each particular city and ethnicity. Though the ethnic Turks have little, their love of music, dance and tradition allows for a spectacular sight to behold.

To learn more about the ethnic Turks, their lives, customs and culture, or how you can help send Turkish and Roma children to school, visit KUD Kardešlik's website (**w** kudkardeslik.wordpress.com).

KUD Kardešlik, of Strumica, is a cultural NGO that also provides educational, health and social services to the ethnic Turks and Roma throughout Macedonia.

Roman times, the current structure dates from Tsar Samoil's time early in the 11th century. Expansive excavation has restarted in recent years, and there are plans to rebuild the entire structure. Noticeboards in English and Macedonian dot the site. To get here, you can take a steep 20-minute hike along very narrow paths above Loven Dom, or, for a much more enjoyable approach, hike from Sv Ilija Monastery (see below) to join the newly tarmacked road that comes around the back of the mountain through Raborci and Popčevo villages.

A nice little walk from the centre of Strumica is the 1-hour hike to the small **Sv Ilija Monastery** (2km from Loven Dom). Once at Loven Dom the trail is a wide path leading behind it along the valley. A shortcut up to Carevi Kuli starts halfway along the path behind some benches, but is steep and narrow. The church is open only on Sundays, but outside seating and grill pits are used throughout the week in the summer, and outdoor pit toilets can be found at the start of the path behind the monastery inns. To continue to Carevi Kuli, take the path behind the monastery for 15 minutes (it descends slightly to the valley stream before rising again) to the saddle at the top of the stream. There the path joins the asphalt road from Popčevo village directly to the fortress – an easy half-hour walk from the saddle. It is a steep and narrow 15-minute descent from the northern end of the fortress to Loven Dom. Note that a reader reported they were assaulted along this route so safest not to do it alone or carry valuables.

For the first three days (*trimeri*) of Orthodox Lent (usually in March), Strumica holds a colourful and friendly **carnival**, which includes a special children's carnival as well as the main event and a masked ball.

AROUND STRUMICA

VODOČA Out to the west of town through the Roma village of Banica is the very small settlement of Vodoča, famous for the defeat of Tsar Samoil's army in 1014 by the army of Emperor Basilius II (see box, page 20). The 15,000 troops left of Samoil's army after their defeat on Belasica Mountain were brought here where they had their eyes gouged out, and only one man in every 100 was left with one eye to lead the remaining blinded troops back to Tsar Samoil in Prilep. Hence the name – the Macedonian *vadi oči* means 'gouged eyes'.

There is no monument here explaining this piece of Macedonian history, but a monastery was built a few years after the defeat of Tsar Samoil's empire. The present **Monastery of Sv Leonthius** is a newer construction, but right next to the church dedicated to Sv Leonthius are the ruins of the original church, which was of an early basilica style including marble columns. The columns were later moved to the Church of the Holy 15 Martyrs of Tiberiopolis, in Strumica. An earthquake in 1931 destroyed the vaults of the church but these were finally restored in 1995 with the restoration of monastery life throughout Macedonia. Lead flashing, which can be seen on the outside of the church walls, marks where the old walls lie. After the church was completed, the monks, who had originally been living in the Monastery of Veljusa (page 318), moved into the inns here.

The reconstructed church is now a wonderfully simple, high-domed affair showing the beautiful patterns of the original brickwork, with the remnants of a few frescoes. It is very unfussy compared with a lot of Macedonian churches from later periods and it instils a sense of calm. Some of the frescoes, such as those of Sv Isavrij and Sv Pantelejmon, are now on display in the National Museum of Macedonia. Still remaining in the vaults of the church, however, are believed to be the relics of the wife and son of Sv Kiril. It is very unusual for a woman to have a burial place in a church, and was especially so during those times. It is also just as unusual that Kiril's son should be buried with the mother rather than the father.

As for Sv Leonthius, to whom the church is dedicated, he was martyred in the year AD320 for refusing to renounce Christianity. This imposition of the Roman emperors and their pagan gods earned him and 40 other martyrs the right to die by freezing in Lake Sebaste in eastern Turkey. By some unfathomable connection, the Day of the Newlyweds, 22 March, is dedicated to the martyrs and is also the festival day of the Church of Sv Leonthius.

A footpath along the River Vodočnica at the back of the monastery leads up to Lake Vodoča, sometimes called Lake Strumica. The 5km hike is shaded and cool and, once at the lake, gives a good view of the valley.

VELJUSA Continuing along the same road from Vodoča, you'll come to the fairly large village of Veljusa, which rises up into the hills and has two more churches as well as the church at the **Monastery of the Holy Mother of God – Eleusa**. The grounds of this monastery are extremely well kept and look out over the village and the plain of Strumica. The church was originally built in 1080, although the exonarthex was built in the 14th century. It is a small church that suffered two fires in the last century, one in 1913 and the other in 1968. Soot marks can still be seen over some of the frescoes, many of which have been destroyed over time, but some still remain, the most interesting of which is that of Jesus at the age of 12 in the ceiling of the eastern cupola. The floor of the church shows the original mosaic construction although some of it has been renovated over the years. Some of the original marblework of the church was taken to Bulgaria during World War I and is now kept in the Archaeological Museum of Bulgaria in Sofia. Copies in marble have been made since and are now in place in the church above the entrance to the nave.

Since 1996, when the monks moved down to the Monastery of Sv Leonthius, this monastery has housed nuns.

BANSKO Bansko, 12km southeast of Strumica, is the hot springs capital of Macedonia. It may not appear to be much when you first arrive, but the potential is there. Aside from the rehabilitation baths for those with disabilities (w zavodbansko.com.mk), and the medicinal baths at the large and rather timeworn Car Samuil Hotel (✆377 210; entrance for non-lodgers 70MKD), there are also the Turkish baths (currently closed) and the ruins of a Roman bathhouse, which dates from the 3rd and 4th centuries AD. Some ten rooms, most with vaulted ceilings, are still visible covering an area of 1,000m², and several of these rooms are almost totally preserved. As a museum of hot spring baths throughout the ages, from Roman to Turkish to communist, all that remains to be added is a swish first-class modern outdoor complex complete with sauna, massage rooms and a restaurant serving the latest health salads and smoothies. While we wait for that to arrive, the Roman baths are being renovated.

To get to Bansko there are several buses a day from Strumica bus station, or you can drive out towards the Bulgarian border and turn off to Murtino and Bansko. If you have a 4x4 it is possible to drive directly from the Hotel Sirius by turning right out of the hotel through the village of Kukliš.

MONOSPITOVO WETLANDS Monospitovo Blato (see box, opposite) lies between Bansko and Kolešino in the municipality of Bosilovo. To get here take the road to Bansko and Murtino, and at Murtino turn east towards Monospitovo village; the entrance to the wetlands lies to the south of the village. In Bosilovo itself, a good place to eat is at **Pizzeria Park** (📞371 379; ⓕ Picerija-Park-198146633883988; ⏱ 08.00–midnight daily), which is famous for its *bosilanka* deep-pan pizza, made with pork, or with chicken and vegetables, and served with a delicious tomato sauce on the side.

KOLEŠINO The road from Bansko continues on through the pretty villages of Kolešino, which boasts a beautiful 36m waterfall (*vodopad*), before reaching

HOME OF THE FISH-EATING SPIDER   *Kyungah Suk*

For an authentic off-the-beaten-track experience, make a stop at the Monospitovo Blato near Monospitovo village, itself an authentic rural village where time seems to have stood still. The Blato, as it's affectionately known by its nearby residents, is a marsh, purported to be one of the last and biggest in Macedonia. It lies sprawled at the base of Mount Belasica, 17km southeast of Strumica, and has been officially designated as an environmentally protected site, conferring upon it the status 'monument of nature'.

Currently, the Blato covers approximately 400ha. It encompassed a much greater area in the past but how much bigger depends on who you talk to. (The marsh is said to have been drained and destroyed in part during Yugoslavian times due to a malaria epidemic, which did affect World War I soldiers fighting in the area, although mysteriously there are no local hospital records of this epidemic.) Regardless, the Blato continues to be a rich haven for biodiversity with abundant vegetation and wildlife.

In 2007, the Municipality of Bosilovo applied for and received a grant from the European Union to develop the Blato as an eco-rural tourism site. The grant provided funds to develop a structure within the marsh that could be used by tourists, recreational hunters and fishermen, local village people and nature enthusiasts. The structure consists of a wooden boardwalk that extends in three directions of approximately 1km in length, in total. The boardwalk further branches out so that there are seven extensions. At the end of each extension stands a thatched wooden hut built for resting and observing the biodiversity in the Blato.

The Blato also boasts two wooden birdwatching towers from the top of which one has a breath-taking panoramic view of the marsh and the land that stretches beyond it, with the majestic Mount Belasica mountain range as its backdrop. Academic and amateur nature enthusiasts have been known to spend the night at the birdwatching towers so that they can catalogue the cacophony of sounds made by the teeming wildlife in the marsh. Depending on the season, the marsh is filled with water or covered in rich vegetation.

An ecological study of the Blato was also conducted by experts from the Macedonian Ecological Society as part of the project. There is a published text containing a catalogue of flora and fauna, some of them extremely rare, found in the Blato, although unfortunately the text is in Macedonian only. Nevertheless, it details over 130 species of resident and migratory birds, including little bittern, water rail, Eurasian marsh harrier, grey heron, little egret, Northern lapwing and many others. The marsh also contains a varied flora and numerous fish, lizard, amphibian, butterfly and other insect species. Some of the wildlife is rare or on the endangered or protected lists, including the black stork, European otter, and the great raft spider, which can be up to 7cm long and whose diet includes small fish.

Mokrievo and Mokrino, where the asphalt road ends. Mokrino springs (Mokrinski izvori), a popular visit with locals, has been given a new lease of life with maintenance and signage making it a pleasant and easy spot to visit.

This part of Macedonia clearly lies in an area influenced by Methodism. The main evangelical Methodist church is in Kolešino, but there are also lots of others around, some converted back to Orthodoxy, but they are given away by their church towers which, unlike Orthodox churches, are attached directly to the church or stand over the narthex.

A popular national restaurant and inn in the area is **Podgorski An** ✳ (10 rooms; \034 351 100; e podgorski-an@hotmail.com; $$) on the western entry to Kolešino village. Taking advantage of a local watermill, the restaurant is a welcome respite and, amusingly, the restaurant chairs sport wagon wheels, making them seem a little like wheelchairs. It serves excellent traditional food and Macedonian wine, making it worth the long taxi ride from Strumica. If you want to overnight, rooms are basic but have TV, bath, air conditioning and balcony. It's a good place to come for lunch and a walk to the nearby Smolari Waterfall.

SMOLARI In a corner of Macedonia equidistant from the borders of Bulgaria and Greece is the village of Smolari, above which is the 40m drop of the **Smolari Waterfall**. Although it is a small site, it is set in beautiful surroundings, and the half-hour hike to get here is along well-maintained grounds. There are a couple of makeshift cafés on the way serving skara, beer and soft drinks, and many people bring their own picnics.

There are several buses a day from Strumica bus station to the waterfall, or Atlantis travel agency (page 311) can arrange a special bus if there is a big enough group. To drive here, head towards the Bulgarian border and after Novo Selo turn off for Smolari. Take the first right turn at the edge of the village, which is marked 'Vodopad' (waterfall), then take the next left after the village shop which will take you to a car park. Follow the path at the side of the stream uphill for about half an hour to reach the waterfall.

9

Kumanovo and the Northeast Highlands

> Some archaeological findings suggest that the site was used in the first half of the second millennium BC as a 'holy mountain' where probably more than one cult were celebrated among which the cult of the Great Mother Goddess …
>
> Information brochure on Kokino ancient observatory, 2006

Accessed via the workaday town of Kumanovo 35km northeast of Skopje, Macedonia's little-visited northeast is a land of rolling hills traversed by practically empty but well-kept roads offering wide vistas seemingly unhindered by traffic, roadworks and busy town life. If you like driving, this is the place for you. The northeast also offers its fair share of pretty churches and monasteries, hot springs and some very interesting rock formations, while its tallest mountains are in the Osogovski range, which rises to an altitude of 2,252m at the border with Bulgaria.

The most-visited site in this part of the country, at least by Orthodox Macedonians, is the Monastery of Sv Joakim Osogovski outside Kriva Palanka. Less well-known, but equally important for containing the country's first of four rare iconostases, is the Monastery of Gavril Lesnovski.

Not to be missed is the scenic small town of Kratovo, which is nestled in an extinct volcanic crater, and attractions in the vicinity include rock art, large volcanic droplets, Stone Doll rock formations at Kuklica, cave dwellings near Konjuh and a megalithic sacrificial observatory at Cocev Kamen. Closer to Kumanovo is another alleged Aneolithic observatory. Although there are fewer uncovered Roman ruins in the north of Macedonia than in the south, a Roman amphitheatre was unearthed near Klečovce in August 2003, adding to the list of important Roman ruins already found in the region at Vinica and Bargala.

KUMANOVO *Telephone code 031*

The third-largest metropolitan area in Macedonia after Skopje and Bitola is Kumanovo, with around 105,000 inhabitants. It is not an especially historically significant town, as it lies in the upper reaches of Macedonia, which did not see much development in Roman times and only saw a settlement of any size when the Kumani tribe settled here in the Middle Ages, hence its name. Straddling the banks of the River Kumanovka around 35km northeast of Skopje, the town could be regarded as the gateway to the far northeast. In practical terms, however, there is no need to make a special stop at Kumanovo, since it is bypassed by the highway heading towards the Bulgarian border, and most buses heading to the likes of Kriva Palanka and Kratovo originate in Skopje.

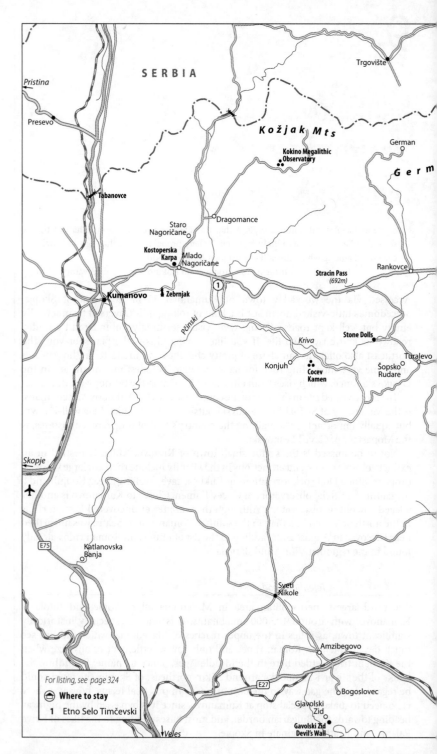

For listing, see page 324

Where to stay
1 Etno Selo Timčevski

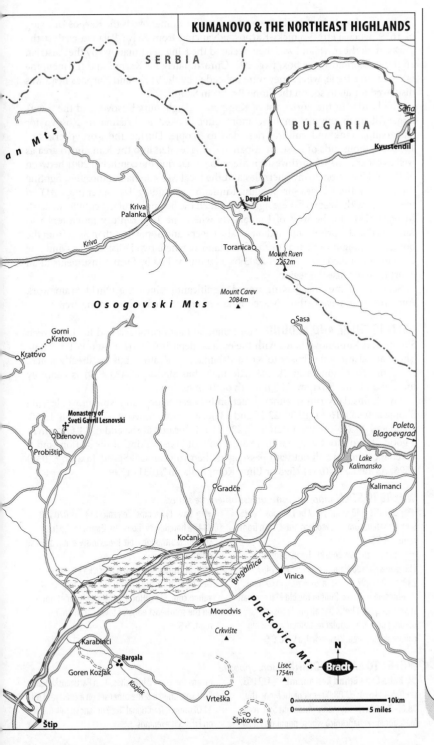

SERBIA

BULGARIA

Sofia

Kyustendil

a n M t s

Deve Bair

Kriva
Palanka

Kriva

Toranica

Mount Ruen
2252m

Mount Carev
2084m

O s o g o v s k i   M t s

Sasa

Gorni
Kratovo

Kratovo

Monastery of
Sveti Gavril Lesnovski

Drenovo

Probištip

Poleto,
Blagoevgrad

Lake
Kalimansko

Gradče

Kalimanci

Kočani

Bregalnica

Vinica

Morodvis

P l a č k o v i c a   M t s

Karabinci

Crkvište

Bargala

Goren Kozjak

Kozjak

Lisec
1754m

N

Bradt

Vrteška

0   10km
0   5 miles

Šipkovica

Štip

One incident in history that does stand out for Kumanovo is the Karpoš Uprising of 1689, when Petre Vojnički-Karpoš, advancing from Kriva Palanka against the Turks, took the town and was then declared the King of Kumanovo by the Austrian emperor Leopold I (see box, page 22). Unfortunately for Karpoš and his men, the tale ends in Skopje, where they were beheaded by the Turks and Karpoš's head was displayed for all to see on the Stone Bridge in Skopje.

The border to the northwest of Kumanovo neighbours Kosovo, and the town's large Albanian population have more often looked to Priština in Kosovo for leadership, trade and cultural ties than to Skopje. During the Kosovo crisis of 1998–99, thousands of Kosovar Albanian refugees fled into the Kumanovo area as well as other parts of northwestern Macedonia. During the conflict of 2001 between National Liberation Army guerrillas and the local Macedonian authorities, fighting broke out in the villages surrounding Kumanovo including Tanuševci (page 31) on the border with Kosovo, where fighting marked the beginning of the conflict of 2001; Matejče 17km to the west of Kumanovo, where the 14th-century monastery was ransacked and reprisals inflicted on local villagers; and Sopot, less than 3km from the border crossing into Serbia north of Kumanovo, where two Polish soldiers and one civilian were killed on 4 March 2003 by a landmine laid by former insurgents in an effort to destabilise the region.

Security in the area has improved significantly since the Ohrid Framework Agreement, and even ethnic Macedonians have returned to hike in the area.

GETTING THERE AND AROUND More than 50 **buses** run back and forth between Skopje and Kumanovo daily, with the earliest departure at 04.00 and last at 21.30. There are also regular buses to Kriva Palanka and Kratovo but, as already noted, these mostly originate in Skopje. The main bus station (\ 423 610) is centrally located on Done Božinov, 200m north of the museum.

Five **trains** daily run in either direction between Skopje and Kumanovo, leaving Skopje at 06.30, 16.34, 19.00, 22.19 and 23.00, and Kumanovo at 05.27, 07.58, 15.50, 20.00 and 20.27. The train station (\ 423 310) is located at the end of 11 Oktomvri, a good 2km out of town, but there are plenty of taxis waiting at the station, and if perchance they are all out with passengers then you can call Speed Taxi on \ (031) 1596, As Taxi on \ (031) 1598 or Bima Kompanija on \ (031) 1599.

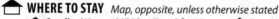

WHERE TO STAY *Map, opposite, unless otherwise stated*

Satelit (40 rooms) Ul 2 br 1 Karpoš; \ 475 999; w satelit.com.mk. Modern hotel, 2km from centre. **$$$**

Etno Selo Timčevski [map, page 322] (13 rooms) Mlado Nagoričane village; \ 497 749; m 075 497 749; e info@etnoselo.com.mk; w etnoselo.com.mk. Built in the old Macedonian style, this quaint hotel has all mod cons, an outdoor pool & a popular restaurant with a big children's play area. Well worth a visit. **$$**

Lav (17 rooms) Železnički 13; m 070 298 444; e hotellav@yahoo.com. Opposite the train station, & although a bit 1980s in style, it is at least quiet. **$$**

Mimoza (8 rooms) Nikšička bb, Goce Delčev district; \ 413 232; e hotel_mimoza@ yahoo.com, @HotelLuxMimoza. Quiet hotel on the southeast edge of town off the main road. **$$**

WHERE TO EAT AND DRINK *Map, opposite*

Baba Čana Ethno Restaurant \ 412 003; m 075 484 573; ⊕ 08.00–midnight Mon–Thu, 08.00–01.00 Fri–Sat, noon–midnight Sun. A cosy Macedonian kebapcilnica whose popularity now means there are 2 branches: 1 on Partizanski near Sv Nikola Church & the other set on a courtyard off 11 Oktomvri. Traditional live Kumanovo folk music on Fri & Sat evenings. **$$**

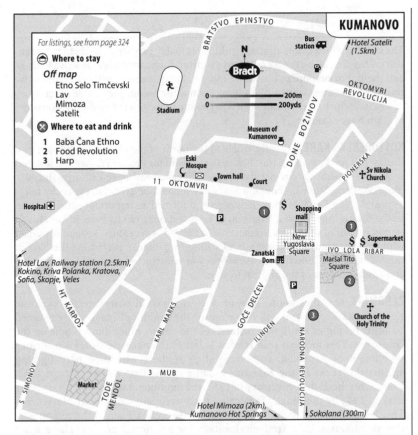

For listings, see from page 324

⊕ **Where to stay**

Off map
  Etno Selo Timčevski
  Lav
  Mimoza
  Satelit

✖ **Where to eat and drink**
  1 Baba Čana Ethno
  2 Food Revolution
  3 Harp

KUMANOVO

Bus station
Hotel Satelit (1.5km)

OKTOMVRI REVOLUCIJA

Museum of Kumanovo

DONE BOŽINOV

PIONERSKA

Sv Nikola Church

Eski Mosque

Town hall

Court

11 OKTOMVRI

Stadium

BRATSTVO EPINSTVO

Hospital

Shopping mall

New Yugoslavia Square

Zanatski Dom

Supermarket

IVO LOLA RIBAR

Maršal Tito Square

Hotel Lav, Railway station (2.5km), Kokino, Kriva Polanka, Kratova, Sofia, Skopje, Veles

HT KARPOŠ

KARL MARKS

GOCE DELČEV

ILINDEN

NARODNA REVOLUCIJA

Church of the Holy Trinity

3 MUB

Market

TODE MENDOL

S SIMONOV

Hotel Mimoza (2km), Kumanovo Hot Springs

Sokolana (300m)

✖ **Food Revolution** Maršal Tito Sq; 454 540. This tiered restaurant on the south side of the main square combines an industrial modern feel with an exceptionally varied menu of grills, pizzas, salads & burgers. Cheap beer on draught. $$

✖ **Harp** Narodna Revolucija; 418 123, 611 010; e irishpubkumanovo@gmail.com; @irishpubharp; ⏰ 08.00–midnight. 100% Irish-owned Irish pub, serving good food & cheer. $$

WHAT TO SEE AND DO Kumanovo is a pleasant enough town with a bustling centre and some impressive 19th-century buildings, such as the **Zanatski Dom** and **Sokolana**. The **Museum of Modern Art** opposite the town hall looked to have closed its doors in 2018, but the small **Museum of Kumanovo** (Done Božinov; 422 495/511), set in a garden studded with ancient Roman and other inscribed tablets, is interesting enough if you can read Macedonian and can get the curators to let you in.

The city's oldest place of worship is probably the **Eski Mosque** (11 Oktomvri), an Ottoman building that dates to 1532 but was partly reconstructed in 1751 and 2008. The central **Church of Sv Nikola** (Cnr Leninova & Pionerska), built in 1851 on the site of an earlier temple, houses icons from many other older churches in the Kumanovo region, while the more southerly marshmallow-pink **Church of the Holy Trinity** (off Tane Gergiev) was built in 1901 by Orthodox Serbs who were refused access to Sv Nikola by the Bulgarian Exarchate.

The sites described below all stand within reasonably easy striking distance for self-drivers heading along the A2 as it runs east from Kumanovo towards Kriva Palanka and the Bulgarian border, but rather more difficult of access to those using public transport. The most worthwhile among them is the unique megalithic observatory of Kokino, which can be easily visited in combination with the medieval Monastery of Staro Nagoričane.

KOSTOPERSKA KARPA Clearly visible to the north of the highway some 8km past the last exit for Kumanovo (just before the turn-off for Prohor Pčinski and Kokino) is an almost perfectly circular flat-topped hill called Kostoperska Karpa (literally, 'Bone Washing Stone'). Though it looks like it could be artificial, the rocky hill is a natural feature and, as its name suggests, it formed an important ritual location in the Bronze Age, when a large village extended out from its base. It was also an important burial site under Roman rule in the 3rd–4th century AD, and is riddled with underground niches and spaces dating to a similar period. At the base of the hill, the tiny Church of Sv Paraskeva was constructed over 1626–28 and still contains fragments of the original frescoes.

ZEBRNJAK On the south side of the highway almost directly opposite Kostoperska Karpa, you will make out in the middle distance a large ruined building on top of a hill, which stands out for many miles like a nipple on the landscape. This modern ruin is what is left of the once six-storey Kosturnica monument of Zebrnjak, commemorating soldiers who died here fighting against the Turks in the Kumanovo battle of the first Balkan War of 1912. Erected on the 25th anniversary in 1937, the monument was blown up six years later in 1943 by the Bulgarians during their occupation of Vardar Macedonia. The 360° view from the monument across the Pčinja Plain is the reason why this point was such a strategic location for occupying armies. There is no signage leading you to the monument, but you can get here by turning south off the E871 at a large white house almost 4km after the start of the E871. Turn left past the house for 1km and take the first right. This road leads straight to the monument.

MONASTERY OF STARO NAGORIČANE Situated in the village of the same name about 4km north of the highway, this monastery houses the Church of Sv Gjorgi built in 1313 by the Serbian king Milutin on the foundations of an 11th-century predecessor. The church's frescoes are almost completely intact, but the narthex has been destroyed. The monastery is surrounded by a low stone wall and has no inns. The yard, containing a few old graveyards, is unkempt and the site is usually locked, although you can get the key by asking at the small police station opposite the church where officers will contact the church warden, who should be able to come over with the key in a few minutes. Note that photography inside the church requires permission.

To get to the site, take the Prohor Pčinski exit off the E871 (Highway 2) a few hundred metres past Kostoperska Karpa, then head north. After 100m, turn left at the T-junction and then immediately right, signposted for Prohor Pčinski. Follow this road north for 2.5km, and at the top of a small hill take the new road left to the village of Staro Nagoričane. You will come across the monastery in a few hundred metres at the edge of the village.

KOKINO MEGALITHIC OBSERVATORY (w kokinoobservatory.mk; entry 120MKD) Often referred to as the Stonehenge of Macedonia, this impressive archaeological site comprises a natural rock outcrop modified by humans. It is on the summit of the large neo-volcanic peak (called Taticev Kamen, ✪ 7906 8036 near the village of Kokino) that dominates the surrounding area at a height of 1,013m above sea level. While it might look little more than an interesting rock feature, it was ranked on the NASA website in 2005 as the fourth-oldest observatory in the world, although nobody from NASA has actually visited Kokino to confirm that.

The tendency of the volcanic rock to split and form geometric cracks has resulted in this remarkable natural feature, though two flat surfaces, orientated from west to east and with a difference in height of 15m, have certainly had their tops levelled by tools. The lower platform to the west preserves the traces of several stone seats (thrones), which are aligned from north to south, so that anyone seated on them would face towards the east and the rising sun.

A series of stone markers visible from the centre of the observatory mark the positions variously of the sunrise during the summer and winter solstices, the moon in its maximal and minimal declines in winter and summer, and the sun on the day of the vernal and autumn equinoxes. The use of the location as a primitive research station to track the sun through the year goes back, therefore, almost 4,000 years. Artefacts dating back to 1815BC have been found here.

The site lies about 30km outside Kumanovo and 65km from Skopje. As with Staro Nagoričane, you need to take the Prohor Pčinski exit off the E871 (Highway 2), then head north. After 7km, you will come to the turning for Dragomance, which you should take northeast for another 14.6km along a road that is pot-holed in parts, but still navigable in any car. At the rise of a hill is a sign for the observatory. Turn north on to the dirt road for 100m and the observatory is the obvious rock feature 300m to the west (unless it is foggy and then you won't see it at all, but if you keep heading uphill you will get there). There are no facilities at the site, not even a toilet, nor is it accessible on public transport, but most operators in Skopje can organise day trips there.

KONJUH AND SURROUNDS Forgotten in the delta of the River Kriva near the village of Konjuh (w konjuh.mk; best accessed by 4x4 or a 6km hike) are an ancient cave village and a Roman rotunda from the 6th century. The place makes for an interesting half-day out and, unlike Kokino observatory, there are lots of obvious manmade rooms, waterholes, stairs and windows. To get here continue another 15.1km on Highway 2 (E871) beyond the exit to Prohor Pčinski to ✪ 8024 6729 where a dirt-track road heads south. At 4.8km, just after the tunnel under the yet-to-be-constructed railway, take the turning to the south across the River Pčinski. The rock formation on the left after the river is the cave settlement (✪ 8016 6211), while the barely visible rotunda is another 100m to the southwest, and the old Church of Sv George is 200m to the southeast of the settlement.

There are probably a hundred more Roman ruins in this valley, which was once the route linking Skupi to Kustendil. In August 2003, a Roman amphitheatre was unearthed near the village of Klečovce. The Kumanovo Hot Springs, also popular in Roman times, are near the village of Proevce, 4km southeast of Kumanovo.

KRIVA PALANKA *Telephone code 031*

Situated close to the Bulgarian border 100km east of Skopje, the pretty riverside town of Kriva Palanka is now most famous for the 12th-century monastery dedicated to

9

Sv Joakim Osogovski, 3km to its east. The town is named after the river it straddles, the Kriva, which is the Slavic translation of the name first given to the town when it was founded by the Ottomans in 1633 when it was called Egri Dere, meaning 'winding river'. The town was originally built as an important stronghold for the Ottomans on the road from Üsküb to Istanbul but, despite its supposed impregnability, it was taken by Karpoš (later given the title of King of Kumanovo, see box, page 22) during the Karpoš Uprising of 1689. When Karpoš and his men were captured and beheaded six weeks later, the town returned to Ottoman rule.

GETTING THERE AND AWAY The **bus** station (✆375 033) is north of the centre of town behind the police station. There are 11 buses a day to/from Skopje, starting at 07.00 until the last bus at 19.20. Buses to Strumica via Kratovo, Probištip and Štip leave on Monday, Wednesday and Friday at 05.30. **Taxi** companies include ✆(031) 1591 and 1592.

🏠 WHERE TO STAY

🏠 **Villa Ana Marija** (5 rooms) Duračka Reka, 8km from Kriva Palanka; w vilaanamarija. blogspot.com. Set in a traditionally styled house in the forested hills southeast of town, this owner-managed guesthouse has pleasant rooms & stands close to the excellent Vodenica Restaurant. **$$**

🏠 **Monastir Sveti Joakim Osogovski** (100 beds) 3km northeast of Kriva Palanka; ✆375 063/5; w mpc.org.mk. By far & away the best place to stay in the vicinity, this monastery set into Mount Osogovski offers beautiful views. The

monastery is well frequented & often full, so book a few days ahead during daylight hrs as monastery life closes down after evening prayers. Ask to speak to the innkeeper, Velin, as he deals with all the bookings. Bring your own food to cook in the indoor kitchens or the outdoor grill. A small shop/café sells a few soft drinks, tea & coffee. The monastery is popular with locals as a site for Sun b/fast before church. Old inns are cheaper than the new inns. Bathroom on each floor. No TV. **$**

✖ WHERE TO EAT AND DRINK

There's no shortage of restaurants, cafés and bars in the town centre, but the best places to eat are further afield.

✖ **Park Ginovci** Ginovci village, 18km before Kriva Palanka; ✆383 033; m 078 243 944; ⊕ 10.00–midnight daily. This traditional restaurant is very family oriented with a playground, small petting zoo of farmed animals (including ostriches) & little walks around a lake. Excellent food. Worth the drive. **$$**

✖ **Vodenica** Duračka Reka ✆373 800, 374 800; m 070 306 647, 070 525 455; ⊕ 11.00–midnight daily. This is a great family-friendly traditional restaurant complete with children's playground & a small water wheel (*vodenica*) to water the fishpond. **$$**

WHAT TO SEE AND DO

Sveti Joakim Osogovski This probably takes number one position as the most visited monastery in Macedonia. The location was first sought out as a monastery during the middle of the 12th century, and now houses two churches, the older one dedicated to the Virgin Mary (Sv Bogorodica), and the new church of the mid 19th century is dedicated to Sv Joakim Osogovski himself (see box, page 335).

The monastery was founded in the middle of the 12th century by the priest Teodor from Ovče Polje who decided to dedicate his life to God at this spot after the death of his wife. Located on a major thoroughfare to Constantinople (Carigrad, or Town of the Tsar in Macedonian), the monastery was frequented and honoured by Muslims as well as Christians. In 1585 the bey of Kriva Palanka received permission to renovate the dilapidated buildings. The old church was first converted into a mosque and then later a church. Some of the original 12th-century walls and 14th-century frescoes still exist, although most of the church is now being completely re-frescoed.

During the Austro–Ottoman War, led in Serbia and Macedonia by General Piccolomini in 1690, the monastery buildings and original church suffered extensive damage, and the Ottomans even ordered it to be destroyed as a punishment against local Macedonians who had sided with the Austrian general. Legend claims that on arrival at the monastery, the Ottomans were so overpowered by its spiritual force that they turned back, leaving the buildings undamaged. One of them, however, had taken a bone out of the tomb of Sv Joakim Osogovski, which proceeded to make the thief more nauseous the further he took it from the monastery. The thief soon realised that, for his own well-being, he needed to take the bone back to its rightful resting place, and so he returned it. The sultan was so overwhelmed by this account when he heard it that he ordered a protective marker of stone to be delivered to the monastery, which would signify to all Ottomans, Turks and Muslims that this monastery was not to be harmed in any way. The stone still stands on the wall near the new church, to the right as you enter the exonarthex, and is usually blessed by the residing Turkish ambassador to Macedonia at least once during his term in office.

The new church is an intricate complex with 12 cupolas in the main nave, two further naves and an exonarthex on two sides of the church. The 12 cupolas represent the 12 apostles, and each one contains a fresco of an apostle. The remainder of the main nave is brimming with well-kept frescoes. Frescoes of Sv Joakim and his three brothers (see box, page 335) can be found, as well as of the church donors, and on the outside wall to the right of the main entrance are some interesting frescoes of hell and Satan. In the base of the belfry, on the western side of the new church, is the ossuary of the senior monks and priests.

Near the monastery is an ancient milk pipeline, which used to transport milk from the surrounding mountains to the monastery dairy. The pipe is no longer used, and Pop Dobri, the father of the monastery, requests that visitors refrain from visiting it as the pipeline requires some renovation to prevent further damage by careless visitors. Pop Dobri is happy to talk to visitors about the monastery although he can't always be found here as he lives in Kriva Palanka. The only monastic inhabitant is Sister Igoumina.

During the summer, the monastery holds a young artists' convention, usually in late July or early August. The church's saints' days are on 28 August, dedicated to Sv Bogorodica (the Virgin Mary), and 29 August dedicated to Sv Joakim, when several thousand visitors come to pay their respects. Their generous offerings have allowed almost €5 million to be invested in the church since the revival of monastic life in Macedonia in 1995.

Osogovski mountain range Starting from the entrance to the monastery is the hiking path up to **Mount Carev** (2,084m), the highest point in this range completely in Macedonia, which has an excellent all-round view at the summit. An almost 20km hike from the monastery, it is not to be attempted in a single day, and even in two days only by the fit. For the less fit with a 4x4 the last turning before the Bulgarian border, towards Toranica village, turns into a fair-weather dirt track which comes to within 6km of the summit and then makes its way back down the other side of the mountain via the **Sasa Zinc Mine** and on to Highway 27 at Lake Kalimansko. The same road also comes within 4km of **Mount Ruen** (2,252m) on the border with Bulgaria. The road takes you above the treeline so the views of the surrounding mountains and into Bulgaria are extensive. It is a popular place for wild berry pickers in the summer.

If you do take this road, you may need to present identification to the mine wardens at either Toranica or Sasa where the road is gated. From Toranica gates, make sure you turn off left on to the dirt track (unsignposted) after almost 3km, just before an old building on the left and a white building on the right. For those with GPS, this is at ✪ 2290 7039. Do not continue on the tarmac until it becomes dirt road as this simply takes you into a logging maze. The dirt track becomes tarmac 1km before Sasa mine-works.

KRATOVO *Telephone code 031*

Midway between the start of the E871 (Highway 2) at Kumanovo and Kriva Palanka is the turn-off for Kratovo and Probištip, which joins Highway 2 to Highway 27. On this road, deep in the belly of an ancient and burnt-out volcanic crater, is the small village of Kratovo, a great base to explore this little-visited but fascinating region of Macedonia.

In Roman times this mining town was known as Kratiskara, meaning 'crater', and variations of its name, Koriton and Koritos in Byzantine times, have centred around this meaning. The crater-like hollow of the village has demanded high-arched bridges to cross the river and ingenious architecture to scale the steep ravine. The difficulty of getting to Kratovo has also left the town relatively free of communist concrete. Six defensive towers hark back to the time of King Karpoš. At its commercial peak in the 19th century, Kratovo was reputedly the only town in Macedonia to support distinct but harmonious Orthodox, Catholic, Muslim and Jewish communities, each of which had its own quarter – these are still recognised today, though boundaries have blurred in recent decades.

GETTING THERE AND AWAY Seven **buses** a day in either direction cover the 85km between Skopje and Kratovo, taking around 2 hours in either direction. These leave from Skopje at 07.30, 13.00, 14.00, 15.30, 16.00, 16.40 and 19.30, and from Kratovo at 05.00, 05.58, 06.30, 14.58, 17.00 and 19.00. Transport south from Kratovo is very scarce. On Monday and Friday at 06.20, the bus from Kriva Palanka to Probištip, Štip and Strumica stops in Kratovo. On other days you may need to charter a **taxi** south for the 50km to Štip and then pick up a bus onwards from there. Local taxis wait on the corner of the far side of the bridge near the Hotel Kratis. One taxi service is Džemi (Jimi) (**m** 071 322 502).

TOURIST INFORMATION The one-stop office for information on all things Kratovo is the **Rock Art Centre** (Planinski 1; **m** 070 975 684, 070 512 882; **e** stevcedonevkratovo@ yahoo.com, kratovskakuka@yahoo.com; ⊕ 08.00–20.00 Mon–Sat, 09.00–16.00 Sun), run by the friendly and incredibly helpful Stevče Donevski, who also runs Ethno House Shancheva (see below). As well as arranging local tours, they can organise degustations and slow food tastings, including the local speciality, Kratovski sol (Kratovo 'salt'), made with dried herbs and spices pounded together and served as an accompaniment with bread or other food (a degustation with sol, slatko and local honey is €1; rakija tasting is also €1). Stevče Donevski and his wife Valentina are a mine of information and thoroughly dedicated to the town, but be aware that they speak no English. The Rock Art Centre also sells souvenirs, rakija, maps of Kratovo and postcards.

 WHERE TO STAY *Map, opposite*

✳ 🏠 **Ethno House Shancheva** (4 rooms)
Skopska 9; **m** 070 975 684; **e** kratovskakuka@

yahoo.com; **w** etnohouse.mk. Beautifully renovated traditional 300-year-old house,

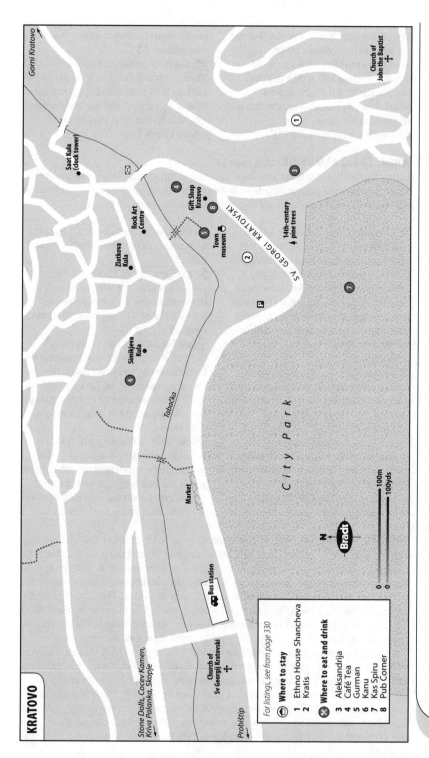

KRATOVO

Gorni Kratovo

Church of
John the Baptist ✝

Saat Kula
(clock tower) ●

⊠

③

④

Gift Shop
Kratovo ●

⑧

Rock Art
Centre ●

SV GEORGI KRATOVSKI

14th-century
pine trees

⑤

Town
museum ◧

②

Zlatkova
Kula ●

P

⑦

Simikjeva
Kula ●

⑥

Tabačka

*Stone Dolls, Cocev Kamen,
Kriva Palanka, Skopje*

City   Park

Market

⊞ Bus station

Church of
Sv Georgij Kratovski ✝

Probištip

N
Bradt

0 ——— 100m
0 ——— 100yds

For listings, see from page 330

⚪ **Where to stay**
1 Ethno House Shancheva
2 Kratis

✖ **Where to eat and drink**
3 Aleksandrija
4 Café Tea
5 Gurman
6 Kanu
7 Kas Spiru
8 Pub Corner

where genial hosts Stevče & Valentina Donevski will make you feel genuinely welcome. Stevče runs a small tour office & souvenir shop in town (page 330), is the local slow-food ambassador, & is the driving force behind promoting local grass-roots tourism in Kratovo & the surrounding region. The 4 rooms sleep up to 7 ppl in total.

Lunch & dinner available on request. Highly recommended. **$$**

🏠 **Kratis** (25 rooms) Sv Georgi Kratovski; ☎ 481 201; e info@hotelkratis.mk; w hotelkratis.mk. The only hotel in the centre commanding a high price for what it has to offer. Much nicer accommodation is available at Ethno House Shancheva. Has its own restaurant & pub. **$$**

✖ WHERE TO EAT AND DRINK Map, page 331

Eating establishments line the village square and run along Ulica Partizanska. The Kratovo version of pastrmajlija is *pastrmajka*; *mantijas* (small square meat pasties) and *mezelek* (offal casserole) are also special Kratovo dishes.

✖ **Aleksandrija** Josip Daskalov 35; ☎ 481 289; m 070 494 393; ⏰ 10.00–midnight daily. This modern restaurant, tucked up an alleyway beneath the tower of Hadži Kostova, hides one of the entrances to the old tunnel system connecting the feudal towers. The entrance is behind a closet door in the kitchen, & can be viewed for free if you dine there, or for €1 if you don't. Serious contender for the best pastrmajka in Macedonia. Good wine. Live bands at w/ends. **$$**

✖ **Gurman** Off Sv Georgi Kratovski. Superb traditional restaurant with low dark-wood ceilings, photos of old Kratovo on the walls, smart décor & a varied menu of Macedonian dishes. **$$**

✖ **Kanu** Goce Delčev 20; ☎ 482 954; m 078 599 225; ⏰ 08.00–midnight daily. Housed in an imposing factory-like building, it would be easy to pass this restaurant by. But once inside the Kratovo Academy of Science & Art (Kratovska akademija na naukite i umetnoctite: KANU for short & a tease on the real thing in Skopje) it oozes charm with its

attention to detail, bygone artefacts & typical old-town architecture. Good food, friendly attentive staff. **$$**

✖ **Kas Spiru** m 077 706 108. Set in an urban patch of pine forest alive with jays & magpies, this peaceful eatery has screened-off terrace seating & a varied & inexpensive menu of snacks & grills. **$**

🍷 **Café Tea** Maršal Tito 10; m 078 292 080; ⏰ 09.00–midnight daily. One of the original café-bars before it was joined on this popular street by the summer contestants, this has a cosy inside area for the winter overlooking the old Turkish trading street. Relaxed atmosphere amid competing music in the summer.

🍷 **Pub Corner** Sv Georgi Kratovski; ☎ 483 401. Resembling an English pub with its dark-wood interior, albeit with walls hung with vintage French posters, this place serves 30 different draught & bottled beers, & a full range of other drinks, as well as burgers, pizzas & grills.

WHAT TO SEE AND DO Several rivers run deep at the bottom of this old volcanic crater town. Three of the **stone bridges** across the River Tabačka – the Jokčiski, Čaršiski and Gročanski – date from the early Ottoman period. A wander around the **stone streets** of the town reveals more of the Atlantic-style houses than the traditional overhanging Macedonian houses seen in Ohrid. Take to some of the streets further back from the river to get a better feel for the meanderings and steep hills. A good place to start is up the little alleyway perpendicular to the entrance to the Rock Art Centre, which will take you up to the quiet backstreets.

Of the 13 original defensive **stone towers** (see box, opposite), six remain standing, of which three are open to the public. **Saat Kula**, the clock tower, has excellent exhibitions on old life in the town, and the very top floor has been made into a small bar and drinks area, although it might not be serving. There is a precarious tiny wooden balcony here from which to view the town – not for vertigo sufferers. The clock was installed in 1921; the tower itself, like several others, dates from the 14th century. The four-storey **Simikjeva Kula** has a more sinister feel to it. The

TOWERS WITHOUT STAIRS

Originally there were 13 towers in Kratovo from Ottoman times. Their original use was defensive, but between times they were used by the local mine owners to store iron ore. Each of the towers is connected by underground tunnels, and it is possible to view these if you take a paid tour (enquire at the Rock Art Centre, page 330). It was the miners of Kratovo who first rallied to Karpoš's call in 1689 (see box, page 22) when he went to fight on the side of the Austrians against the Ottomans.

Now only six towers remain: Saat (meaning 'clock'); Simikjeva; Krsteva; Emin-beg; Zlatkova; and the sixth, the Hadži Kostova tower, which was last damaged in 1929 and rebuilt in 1957. The two most impressive towers, Saat and Simikjeva, have recently been restored thanks to an EU cultural grant.

Many of the towers originally had no stairs, following an architectural trait also seen in similar defensive towers in the Caucasus, so that access to higher levels was only by ladder. If enemy forces attacked the town, then villagers could hide in the upper levels of the tower and drag the ladder up with them. If the enemy succeeded in blowing the floor of a lower level then the villagers could again ascend to a higher level, from which they would normally defend themselves by throwing projectiles, using weapons or pouring hot oil. Note the round stone at the apex of the roof of some towers, symbolic of the chief architect's head which was lopped off after he'd completed his work so the secrets of the tower and how best to attack it could never be disclosed.

doors are tiny and the steps more foreboding, with displays of weaponry from the 19th century. The top floor has a fabulous collection of postcards from World War I. If these floors are not open, ask at the museum or the Rock Art Centre. The 6.35m-high **Zlatkova Kula**, situated between the above two towers, was built in 1365, but its name refers to its most recent owner Georgi Zlatkov, and it was recently restored with US funding.

Several **churches** are scattered around Kratovo, the most interesting of which is dedicated to John the Baptist and stands a short distance uphill of Ethno House Shancheva. Founded in medieval times, it was most recently rebuilt in 1835 and it incorporates several frescoes from that period as well as an icon of the Virgin Mary dated to 1636.

The **town museum** (482 015; 08.00–15.00 Mon–Fri, 10.00–14.00 Sat–Sun; entry free) is in the former bey's house and later inn, Saraj, an attractive building close to the old Ottoman prison. It has the usual collection of local artefacts and a display of children's art. There is no sign outside and it usually looks shut, even when the museum curator is in his office. Cross the bridge south of the museum and you'll see a small urban pine forest that shrouds the Kas Spiru restaurant. The two most impressive trees here are reputedly the only survivors of a quintet planted by settlers from what is now Germany back in the 14th century.

Drop into the Kratovo **Rock Art Centre** at Planinski 1 (page 330) to sample the Bitola Slow Food programme (w slowfood.mk/bitola) promoting local and organic specialities, and to ask about the town, its surroundings and the rock art found in the area.

The town's **ethno museum** is the private collection of the Donevski family from the Rock Art Centre (page 330), a compact exhibition of what were once everyday

9

items mostly from the last 150 years, but with a few rare older pieces, ranging from kitchenware to musical instruments and World War I helmets. The collection is kept in the cellar of the Donevskis' old town house, Ethno House Shancheva (page 330). For non-guests it costs €1 to visit, including a complimentary rakija or homemade wine. Just before the last rickety metal bridge on Planinski is a two-storey house where Milaka Kocevska hand weaves **wool pile carpets** and *kilims* (flat tapestry-woven rugs often used as prayer mats). It is fascinating to see her massive looms and the beautiful designs in her cramped little workshop on the edge of the town (m 07987 49910; visits cost €1 & can be also be arranged through the Rock Art Centre). Her work can be ordered through the Rock Art Centre. Also worth mentioning is local painter Stojance Andonov, whose works are available for sale (m 070 436 225; e dito_art@yahoo.com; w ditoandonov.com), plus the Gift Shop Kratovo (m 075 444 792), which stands opposite Pub Corner and sells a variety of locally produced souvenirs.

AROUND KRATOVO

GORNI KRATOVO A lovely hike (3km; 50mins) from the centre of Kratovo up the River Kratovska takes you to the old village of Gorni Kratovo. Taking Planinska street along the River Tabačka, after the last bridge there is a short steep section before the wide path plateaus out to a gentle hike along the middle height of the valley. Gorni Kratovo itself is made up of just a few houses, including an old abandoned schoolhouse that has a welcome spring below it. Veering off the path shortly after the old school, follow the Kratovska into the exposed belly of the old volcano for another 700m and look out for the medicine ball-sized volcanic droplets wedged in the mud. Back on the main path, this continues above the village and narrows to an old Roman cobbled road above the escarpment beyond the village.

PROBIŠTIP On the edge of this tiny town is **Aquapark** (Plavica bb; 032 480 080; e aquapark@aquaparkmacedonia.mk; w aquaparkmacedonia.mk; ⊕ 10.00–18.00 daily; entry 350MKD adults, 300MKD 2–14 years, under 2 years free). The first one of its kind in Macedonia, it exemplifies the trend that if the Macedonians can't have a seaside, they'll just bring some inland: summer only, all outdoors. A great little place to eat if you've had enough of the crowded Aquapark restaurant is **Kaj Zoki** (m 078 302 186) at the end of the marketplace in the centre of town. Ask for their *manastirski ručak* for a full three-course traditional meal including local aperitif, monastery wine and a coffee for only 590MKD. It is also worth popping into Salon Hahi Tia, which sells organic honey, wine and tea.

COCEV KAMEN Some 15km directly west of Kratovo (⊕ 8211 6044 on map 682-4-4 (Pezovo)) is Cocev Kamen, a Palaeolithic (early Stone Age, some 12,000 years ago) sacrificial megalithic observatory. Unlike Kokino (page 327) there are still megaliths scattered around the site, and there are very obvious signs of human use, including hewn steps, an amphitheatre, sacrificial chamber and constructed entry path, as well as the necessary seat or throne from which to divine star charts, sun and moon movements, and time of year. The site is possibly the oldest in the Balkans and had been used over many centuries. Its rock art dates possibly from the Iron Age and has the only find of a painting of a human figure on rock in Macedonia. Some say the site is on a par with Stonehenge in the UK.

The site is hotly disputed by the current government for being in competition with Kokino (which only raises the question why there can't be two sites for people to visit). As a result the panel boards previously erected with World Bank funding in 1999 have been pulled down and the site is now somewhat overgrown with brambles. It is free to visit, but bring stout walking shoes.

To get here take the road towards Kratovo from the north. At the village of Turalevo (✪ 9368 6049), 5km before Kratovo, turn south before the large factory towards the village itself (signposted) and Šopsko Rudare. Follow the main road southwest for almost 10km until the village of Sekulica (✪ 8769 5632). At the T-junction in the village, there is a signpost to Cocev Kamen: turn right and take the road north following a northwesterly direction for another 6km past the Dobra Voda water bottling plant until you reach a right turn (if you miss the turn you'll end up less than 1km later up a hill in a dead-end hamlet with a church). Take this and continue north another 2km (towards the villages of Donja Maala and Gornja Maala and Konjuh) until you get to a crossroads (✪ 8309 6057). At the crossroads, turn right heading southwest for 1.8km to the hamlet of Šopsko Rudare. At the crossroads here turn north for 0.5km to the houses of Cocevi, after which the road becomes a dirt track continuing north towards Cocev Kamen for 300m before heading off west-northwest. It's a 300m walk from the dirt track over a usually dry stream bed to Cocev Kamen, which is an obvious rock formation 600m directly north of the village of Cocevi.

MONASTERY OF SVETI GAVRIL LESNOVSKI This monastery south of Kratovo near the village of Lesnovo was built in 1341 by the feudal lord Tyrant Oliver, and is well worth visiting. It is one of only three to contain an iconostasis by the famous woodcarvers Makarije Frčkovski and the brothers Filipovski (the other two are in the monasteries of Sv Jovan Bigorski near Debar, and the Church of Sv Spas in Skopje; a fourth in Kruševo was burnt after the Ilinden Uprising). The detail of the carving is phenomenal. The church stands on the foundations of an earlier 11th-century church, whose mosaic floor is still the floor of the present church, and contains many outstanding frescoes from the time it was built. The donor fresco of Tyrant Oliver holding the church is still in good condition to the left in front of the chancel, and frescoes of King Dušan, his wife and Tsar Uroš can be found on the left wall of the narthex above the baptism basin. Unfortunately, the fresco of Tsar Uroš has been practically lost. To the right on the ceiling of the narthex are frescoes of the sun and the moon and 12 animals or people seen in the night sky. Despite their amazing likeness to the zodiac signs, the friar will tell you that these are not designed to depict them.

THE BROTHERS OSOGOVSKI, PČINSKI, LESNOVSKI AND RILSKI

Sketchy details going back to the 10th and 11th centuries claim that the four brothers Joakim Osogovski, Prohor Pčinski, Gavril Lesnovksi and Jovan Rilski were among God's most dedicated monks. In order to serve God better, they all decided to follow a hermit's life and so they went the four directions of the compass, to found the monasteries named after each of them. Today, the beautifully painted Rilski Monastery is in Bulgaria, the Pčinski Monastery is in Serbia just over the border from Kumanovo, the Lesnovski Monastery containing the third iconostasis of Frčkovski and the Filipovski brothers is in the village of Lesnovo near Probištip (see opposite), and Osogovski Monastery is near Kriva Palanka.

Although the four are said to have been brothers, historical data show that Rilski lived at least a century earlier than the others.

A strict dress code is adhered to in the monastery: men must wear long trousers and women must wear ankle-length skirts. Spare clothing is provided at the door if you forget to bring such items with you.

To get here, head for Drenovo and ask there for the turning for Lesnovo. The Lesnovo road winds up the mountain and, at a fork in the asphalt road, follow the road to the right going up to get to the monastery rather than down to the village of Lesnovo. This will take you past some interesting rock outcrops and the entrances to some old rock mines where millstones used to be cut. With a torch you can see where half-hewn millstones are still visible in the rock.

STONE DOLLS Halfway back to Highway 2 from Kratovo are the *kukla* or Stone Doll natural rock formations near the village of Kuklica. Formed from the weathering of porous volcanic rock (as in the more familiar landscapes of Cappadocia in Turkey), large stones teeter on top of tall columns and create imaginary animals and human forms in the rock. Several hundred stone figures are scattered over three sites. Legend says the figures are the result of a petrified wedding: once upon a time a young man from the village of Kuklica decided to marry both his sweetheart from Upper Kuklica and his sweetheart from Lower Kuklica. On the day of the wedding, when the brides saw each other, one was so jealous that she cursed the entire wedding party, turning them to stone. There is an obvious pair of stone dolls at the site, who do look indeed as if they might be going through a wedding ceremony.

The site was formally developed for tourism with UN funding in 2007 and is scattered with several semi-derelict structures associated with the project. It is now unmanned but the 4km dirt feeder road is still well signposted from the turn-off, which lies on the west side of the road about halfway between the E871 highway and Kratovo (about 10km from either point). The stone formations (⊕ 870 628) cover over 1km² so have a good look around. The surrounding area is very pretty and, should you get peckish, you can dine at the under-utilised Kuklica Etno Restaurant (031 481 888; **m** 070 579 810; @KuklicaEtno; **$$**) about 1km from the site.

SEND US YOUR SNAPS!

We'd love to follow your adventures using our *North Macedonia* guide – why not tag us in your photos and stories via Twitter (@BradtGuides) and Instagram (@bradtguides)? Alternatively, you can upload your photos directly to the gallery on the North Macedonia destination page via our website (**w** bradtguides.com/northmacedonia).

Appendix 1

LANGUAGE

MACEDONIAN
Pronunciation and transliteration Like most languages (English being the prime exception) Macedonian is pronounced (almost!) exactly as it is written, so once you have mastered the sounds of each letter it is fairly straightforward to pronounce. Verbs are conjugated, but thankfully, unlike Serbian, nouns are not declined. There is no indefinite article so the word for 'one' is used instead, and the definite article is added at the end of the noun (or adjective if one precedes the noun). There is a formal and informal conjugation of 'you' singular, as in French or Old English, and in this appendix the informal conjugation follows the formal where applicable. There are male, female and neuter genders for nouns, adjectives and verbal conjugations. For more information on the rules of the Macedonian language see Christina Kramer's excellent language book (full reference is on page 357).

Finally, a tip on sounding the correct stress on Macedonian words: with the exception of words of foreign origin, stress falls on the antepenultimate (third last) syllable. The stress in words of fewer than three syllables falls on the first or only syllable. The stress in words of foreign origin tends to fall as it would in the native language.

As it is usually too difficult for short-term visitors to learn a new alphabet like Cyrillic, it is not used in this book, but the standard transliteration is. Cyrillic, transliteration and pronunciation are given in the table below.

А	A	as in f<u>a</u>ther	М	M	as in <u>m</u>ade
Б	B	as in b<u>e</u>d	Н	N	as in <u>n</u>ot
В	V	as in <u>v</u>ery	æ	Nj	as in ca<u>ny</u>on
Г	G	as in good	О	O	as in l<u>o</u>t
Д	D	as in <u>d</u>oor	П	P	as in <u>p</u>ut
Æ	Gj	as in Ma<u>gy</u>ar	Р	R	as in ma<u>r</u>k
Е	E	as in b<u>e</u>t	С	S	as in <u>s</u>it
Ж	Ž	as in plea<u>s</u>ure	Т	T	as in <u>t</u>able
З	Z	as in <u>z</u>oo	Õ	Kj	as in <u>c</u>ute
Ѕ	Dz	as in ad<u>ds</u>	У	U	as in t<u>oo</u>k
И	I	as in f<u>ee</u>t	Ф	F	as in <u>f</u>arm
Ј	J	as in <u>y</u>oung	Х	H	as in lo<u>ch</u>
К	K	as in <u>k</u>it	Ц	C	as in ca<u>ts</u>
Л	L	as in <u>l</u>og	Ч	Č	as in <u>ch</u>ur<u>ch</u>
ãı	Lj	as in Anato<u>li</u>a; soft l pronounced at the back of the mouth	/	Dž	as in e<u>dg</u>e
			Ш	Š	as in <u>sh</u>ovel

337

Words and phrases
Courtesies

Hello	*Zdravo*	I'm fine	*Dobro/super*
Goodbye	*Prijatno/čao*	Pleased to meet you	*Milo mi e što se zapoznavme*
Please	*Ve/te molam*		
Thank you	*Blagodaram/fala*	My pleasure	*Milo mi e*
Good morning	*Dobro utro*	Excuse me	*Izvenete*
Good afternoon	*Dobar den*	You're welcome/	*Povelete*
Good evening	*Dobra večer*	help yourself	
Good night	*Dobra nokj*	Welcome!	*Dobredojde!*
How are you?	*Kako ste/si?*		

Basics

yes/no	*da/ne*	excellent/terrible	*odlično/lošo*
OK	*može/važi*	hot/cold	*toplo/ladno*
maybe	*možebi*	toilet	*toalet/WC*
large/small	*golemo/malo*		(pronounced *ve-tse*)
more/less	*povekje/pomalku*	men/women	*maž/žena*
good/bad	*dobro/lošo*		

Basic questions

How?	*Kako?*	Who?	*Koj?*
How do you say in Macedonian?	*Kako se vika na makedonski?*	Why?	*Zošto?*
What?	*Što?*	Do you speak English?	*Zboruvate-li angliski?*
What is that?	*Što e toa?*	Do you understand French/German?	*Razbirate-li francuski/germanski?*
When?	*Koga?*	I do not understand Macedonian	*Ne razbiram makedonski*
When does the shop open/close?	*Koga otvora/zatvora prodavnicata?*	How much does it cost?	*Kolku čini?*
Where?	*Kade?*	What time is it?	*Kolku e saat?*
Where is there a telephone?	*Kade ima telefon?*	Which?	*Koj/koja/koe?*
The bill please?	*Smetkata molam?*		

Essentials

My name is …	*Jas se vikam/Jas sum …*
What is your name?	*Kako se vikaš?*
I am from … Britain/America/Australia	*Jas sum od … Anglija/Amerika/Avstralija*
Please would you speak more slowly	*Ve molam zboruvajte pisporo*
What is your telephone number?	*Koj e vašiot telefonski broj?*
What is your address?	*Koja e vašata adresa?*
My address in Britain/America is …	*Mojata adresa vo Velika Britanija/ Amerika e …*
I want to change dollars to denar	*Sakam da smenam dolari vo denari*
How many denar for US$1?	*Kolku denari za eden dolar?*
I need a telephone	*Mi treba telefon*

Numbers

0	*nula*	3	*tri*
1	*eden*	4	*četiri*
2	*dva*	5	*pet*

6	šest	50	pedeset
7	sedum	60	šeeset
8	osum	70	sedumdeset
9	devet	80	osumdeset
10	deset	90	devedeset
11	edinaeset	100	sto
12	dvanaest	200	dvesta
13	trinaeset	300	trista
14	četirinaeset	400	četiristo(tini)
15	petnaeset	500	petsto(tini)
16	šesnaeset	one thousand	iljada
17	sedumnaeset	two thousand	dve iljadi
18	osumnaeset	one million	milion
19	devetnaeset	two million	dva milioni
20	dvaeset	quarter	četvrt
21	dvaeset i eden	half	pola/polovina
30	trieset	three-quarters	tri četvrtini
40	četirieset		

Time

hour	čas/saat	yesterday	včera
minute	minuta	morning	utro
week	nedela/sedmica	afternoon	popladne
day	den	evening	večer
year	godina	night	nokj
month	mesec	already	vekje
today	denes	soon	naskoro
tonight	večerva	now	sega
tomorrow	utre	this week	ovaa nedela
next week	slednata nedela	last week	minatata nedela
in the morning	sabaile	tonight	večerva

Monday	ponedelnik	Friday	petok
Tuesday	vtornik	Saturday	sabota
Wednesday	sreda	Sunday	nedela
Thursday	četvrtok		

January	Januari	July	Juli
February	Fevruari	August	Avgust
March	Mart	September	Septemvri
April	April	October	Oktomvri
May	Maj	November	Noemvri
June	Juni	December	Dekemvri

spring	prolet	autumn	esen
summer	leto	winter	zima

Getting around
Public transport

I'd like …	Sakam …	I want to go to …	Sakam da odam …
a one-way ticket	billet vo eden pravec	How much is it?	Kolku pari čini?
a return ticket	povraten billet	What time is it now?	Kolku e časot?

What time does it leave?	*Vo kolku časot trgnuva?*	bus	*avtobus*
The train has been	*Vozot ...*	train	*voz*
... delayed	*... docni*	plane	*avion*
... cancelled	*... e otkažan*	boat	*brod*
first class	*prva klasa*	ferry	*feribrod*
second class	*vtora klasa*	car	*avtomobil/kola*
sleeper	*vagon za spienje*	4x4	*pogon na četiri trkala/džip*
platform	*peron*	taxi	*taksi*
ticket office	*biletara*	minibus	*minibus/kombe*
timetable	*vozen red*	motobike/moped	*motor/moped*
from	*od*	bicycle	*velosiped*
to	*do*	arrival/departure	*pristignuvanje/ trgnuvanje*
airport	*aerodrom*		
port	*pristanište*	bon voyage!	*srekjen pat!*

Private transport

Is this the road to ...?	*Dali e ova patot za ...?*
Where is the service station?	*Kade e benziskata stanica?*
Please fill it up	*Ve molam napolnete do gore*
I'd like ... litres	*Sakam ... litri*
diesel	*dizel*
leaded petrol	*benzin*
unleaded petrol	*bezoloven benzin*
I have broken down	*Mi se rasipa avtomobilot/kolata*

Road signs

give way	*prednost za premin*	toll	*patarina*
danger	*opasnost*	no entry	*zabranet vlez*
entry	*vlez*	exit	*izlez*
detour	*skršnuvanje*	keep clear	*zabraneto parkiranje*
one way	*ednonasočna*		

Directions

Where is it?	*Kade e?*
Which way is the ...?	*Na kade e ...?*
mosque/church	*džamija/crkva*
fortress/museum	*zamok (kale)/museum*
archaeological site/hotel	*arxeologska naogjalište/xotel*
cave/bridge	*peštera/most*
Go straight ahead	*Odi pravo*
turn left	*svrti levo*
turn right	*svrti desno*
... at the traffic lights	*... na semaforite*
... at the roundabout	*... kaj obikolnicata*
behind	*pozadi*
in front of	*pred*
near	*blisku*
opposite	*sproti*
here/there	*tuka/tamu*
on the left/right	*na levo/na desno*

straight on	pravo
forward/behind	napred/nazas
east/west	istok/zapad
north/south	sever/jug
Where is there a ...?	Kade ima ...?
taxi rank/travel agency	taksi stanica/putovanje agencija
bus station/train station	avtobus stanica/železnička stanica
doctor/hospital	doktor/bolnica
police station/bank	policiska stanica/banka
restaurant/shop	restoran/prodavnica
town/village	grad/selo
house/flat	kukja/stan
cinema/theatre	kino/teatar
When does the train arrive/leave?	Koga stignuva/poagja vozot?

Street signs

entrance	vlez	toilets –	toalet –
exit	izlez	men/women	maži/ženi
open	otvoreno	information	informacija
closed	zatvoreno		

Accommodation

Where is a cheap/good hotel?	Kade možam da najdam eftin/dobar hotel?
Could you please write the address?	Ve molam napišete ja adresata
Do you have any rooms available?	Dali imate slobodni sobi?
I'd like ...	Bi sakal ...
a single room	ednokrevetna soba
a double room	soba so francuski krevet
a room with two beds	soba so dva kreveta
a room with a bathroom	soba so kupatilo
to share a dorm	da delam soba
How much it is per night/person?	Kolku čini za edna nokj/eden čovek?
Where is the toilet?	Kade e toaletot?
Where is the bathroom?	Kade e kupatiloto?
Is there hot water?	Dali ima topla voda?
Is there electricity?	Dali ima struja?
Is breakfast included?	Dali e vklučen doručekot?
I am leaving today	Zaminuvam deneska

Food

Do you have a table for ... people?	Dali imate masa za ... lugje?
... a children's menu?	... detsko meni?
I am a vegetarian	Jas sum vegetarijanec
Do you have any vegetarian dishes?	Dali imate vegetarijanska hrana?
Please bring me ...	Ve molam donesete mi ...
a fork/knife/spoon	viljuška/nož/lažica
Please may I have the bill?	Ve molam donesete ja smetkata?
What do you have to drink?	Što imate za pienje?
I would like to drink ...	Sakam da pijam ...
water/juice	voda/sok
sparkling/non-sparkling	gazirane/negazirane

tea/coffee	čaj/kafe
Turkish coffee medium sweet/bitter	tursko kafe sredno/gorko
without sugar/milk	bez šeker/mleko
with lemon/honey	so limun/med
milkshake/milk	frape/mleko
white coffee	kafe so mleko
red/white wine	crno/belo vino
beer/*rakija*	pivo/rakija
mulled wine	vareno vino
What do you have to eat?	Što imate za jadenje?
I want some bread, please	Sakam malku leb, ve molam
I want …	Sakam …
fish/meat	riba/meso
trout/eel	pastrmka/jagula
soup/salad	supa/salata
yellow cheese/white cheese	kaškaval/sirenje
tomatoes/eggs	partližani/jajca
vegetables/fruit	zelenčuk/ovošje
rice/potatoes	oriz/kompir
apples/oranges	jabolko/portokal
pears/grapes	kruška/grozje
figs/apricots	smokva/kaijsija
sugar/honey	šeker/med
hazelnuts/walnuts	lešnici/orevi
ice cream/pancakes	sladoled/palačinke
I don't eat meat/fish/flour	Ne jadem meso/riba/brašno

Shopping

I'd like to buy …	Bi sakal/ a da kupam …
How much is it?	Kolku čini?
I don't like it	Ne mi se dopagja
I'm just looking	Samo razgleduvam
It's too expensive	Premnogu e skapo
I'll take it	Kje go kupam
Please may I have …	Ve molam dali može …

Do you accept …?	Dali primate …?
credit cards	kreditni kartički
travellers' cheques	čekovi
more	povekje
less	pomalku
smaller	pomalo
bigger	pogolemo

Communications

I am looking for …	Baram …
bank	banka
post office	pošta
church	crkva

embassy	ambasada
exchange office	menuvačnica
telephone centre	telefonska govornica
tourist office	turističko biro

Health

diarrhoea	dijarea
nausea	mi se loši
doctor	doktor
prescription	recept
pharmacy	apteka
paracetamol	paracetamol

antibiotics	antibiotici
antiseptic	antiseptik
tampons	tamponi
condoms	kondomi
contraceptive	kontracepcija
sunblock	zaštiten faktor

Help!	*Pomoš!*	fire	*požar*
Call a doctor!	*Povikajte doktor!*	ambulance	*ambulantna*
There's been an	*Se sluči nesreḱa*		*kola*
accident		thief	*kradec*
I'm lost	*Se izgubiv*	hospital	*bolnica*
Go away!	*Odi si!*	I am ill	*Bolen sum/*
police	*policija*		*bolna sum*

I am …	*Jas sum …*	penicillin	*penicillin*
asthmatic	*astmatičar*	nuts – walnuts,	*orevi,*
epileptic	*epileptičar*	hazelnuts, almonds	*lešnici, bademi*
diabetic	*dijabetičar*	bees	*pčeli*
I'm allergic to …	*aleričen sum na …*	wheat	*pšenica/brašno*

Travel with children

Is there a …?	*Dali ima …?*
baby changing room?	*soba za presoblekuvanje bebinja?*
a children's menu?	*detsko meni?*
Do you have …?	*Dali imate …?*
infant milk formula?	*deštačko mleko za bebinja?*
nappies	*peleni*
potty	*nokšir*
babysitter	*bebisiter*
high chair	*stolče za bebinja*
Are children allowed?	*Dali e dozvoleno za deca?*

Other

my/mine/ours/yours	*moj/moe/naše/vaše*	good/bad	*dobro/lošo*
and/some/but	*i/nekoi/no, osven, tuku*	early/late	*rano/kasno*
this/that	*ova/toa*	hot/cold	*toplo/ladno*
expensive/cheap	*skapo/eftino*	difficult/easy	*teško/lesno*
beautiful/ugly	*ubavo/neubavo*	boring/interesting	*dosadno/interesno*
old/new	*staro/novo*		

Basic verbs

to be	*da se bide*		
I am	*jas sum*	we are	*nie sme*
you are	*ti si*	you are	*vie ste*
he/she/it is	*toj/taa/toa e*	they are	*tie se*

to have	*ima*		
I have	*imam*	we have	*imame*
you have	*imas*	you have	*imate*
he/she/it has	*ima*	they have	*imaat*

to want/like/love	*saka*		
I want	*sakam*	we want	*sakame*
you want	*sakaš*	you want	*sakate*
he/she/it wants	*saka*	they want	*sakaat*

ALBANIAN

Pronunciation Albanian nouns are declined and they are either feminine or masculine. There is no neuter, except in certain set phrases. The indefinite and definite articles are used, the latter being added to the end of the noun, as in Macedonian. Verbs are conjugated, and there is a formal and informal conjugation of 'you' singular, as in French or Old English. Here the informal conjugation follows the formal where applicable, and 'they' is translated as in standard representation with the masculine version first, followed by the feminine version. Unlike English, Albanian spelling is completely phonetic, so once you have mastered the sounds, you shouldn't have too much trouble with pronunciation. Good luck!

A	as in father	N	as in not
B	as in bed	Nj	as in canyon
C	as in cats	O	as in lot
Ç	as in church	P	as in put
D	as in door	Q	as in cute
Dh	as in the	R	as in mark
E	as in bet	Rr	as in burrito; pronounced with a
Ë	as in along; it is often not		resonant roll
	pronounced at all	S	as in sit
F	as in farm	Sh	as in shovel
G	as in good	T	as in table
Gj	as in Magyar	Th	as in thin
H	as in hit	U	as in took
I	as in feet	V	as in very
J	as in young	X	as in adds
K	as in kit	Xh	as in jam
L	as in log	Y	as in mural
Ll	as in fall; pronounced at the back	Z	as in zoo
	of the mouth	Zh	as in pleasure
M	as in made		

Words and phrases
Courtesies

Hello	*Tungjatjeta*	How are you?	*Si jeni/si je?*
Goodbye	*Mirupafshim*	I'm fine	*Jam mirë*
Please	*Ju lutem/të lutem*	Pleased to meet you	*Më vjen mirë*
Thank you	*Faleminderit*	My pleasure	*Kënaqësia është e imja*
Good morning	*Mirëmëngjes*	Excuse me	*Më fal*
Good afternoon	*Mirëdita*	You're welcome	*S'ka përse*
Good evening	*Mirëmbrëma*	Help yourself	*Shëbehuni vetë*
Good night	*Natën e mirë*	Welcome!	*Mirëseardhët!*

Basics

yes/no	*po/jo*	good/bad	*mirë/keq*
OK	*mire/në regull*	hot/cold	*nxehtë/ftohtë*
maybe	*mundqë/mundet*	toilet	*nevojtore*
large/small	*madhe/vogël*	men/women	*mashkull/femër*
more/less	*më shumë/më pak*		

Basic questions

How?	*Si?*

344

How do you say in Albanian?	*Si thuhet në shqip?*
What?	*Çfarë?*
What is that?	*Çfarë është ajo?*
When?	*Kur?*
When does the shop open/close?	*Kur hapet/mbyullet shitorja?*
Where?	*Ku?*
Where is a public telephone?	*Kuka telefon publik?*
Who?	*Kush?*
Why?	*Pse?*
Which?	*Cili?*
Do you speak English?	*A flisni anglisht?*
Do you understand French/German?	*A kuptoni frëngjisht/gjermanisht?*
I do not understand Albanian	*Unë nuk kuptoj shqip*
How much does it cost?	*Sa kushton?*
What time is it?	*Sa është ora?*
The bill please?	*Llogarinë ju lutem?*

Essentials

My name is …	*Unë quhem …*
What is your name?	*Si quheni?*
I am from … Britain/America/Australia	*Unë jam nga … Anglia/Amerika/Australia*
Please would you speak more slowly	*Ju lutem, mund të flisni më ngadal*
What is your telephone number?	*Cili është numri i telefonit tënd/të juaj?*
What is your address?	*Cila është adresa tënde juaje?*
My address in Britain/America is …	*Adresa ime në Angli/Amerikë është …*
I want to change dollars to lek (the currency in Albania)	*Dua të këmbej dollarë për lekë*
How many leks will you give me for US$1?	*Sa lekë do më japish për një dollar?*
I need to make a telephone call	*Duhet të marr në telefon*

Numbers

0	zero	14	katërmbëdhjetë
1	një	15	pesëmbëdhjetë
2	dy	16	gjashtëmbëdhjetë
3	tre	17	shtatëmbëdhjetë
4	katër	18	tetëmbëdhjetë
5	pesë	19	nëntëmbëdhjetë
6	gjashtë	20	njëzet
7	shtatë	21	njëzet e një
8	tetë	30	tridhjet
9	nëntë	40	dyzet
10	dhjetë	50	pesëdhjet
11	njëmbëdhjetë	60	gjashtëdhjet
12	dymbëdhjetë	70	shtatëdhjet
13	trembëdhjetë	80	tetëdhjet

GESTURES

Hand gestures in Macedonia are the same as in the rest of Europe, but do not offer your left hand to Muslims, or show them the soles of your feet or shoes.

90	nëntëdhjet	two thousand	dy mijë
100	njëqind	one million	një miljon
200	dyqind	two million	dy miljonë
300	treqind	quarter	çerek
400	katërqind	half	gjysmë
500	pesëqind	three-quarters	tre çerekë
one thousand	një mijë		

Time

hour	orë	yesterday	dje
minute	minutë	morning	mëngjes
week	javë	afternoon	pas dite
day	ditë	evening	mbrëmje
year	vit	night	natë
month	muaj	already	veç më
today	sot	soon	së shpejti
tonight	sonte	now	tani
tomorrow	nesër	this week	këtë javë
next week	javën e ardhshme	last week	javën e kaluar

Monday	e hënë	Friday	e premte
Tuesday	e martë	Saturday	e shtunë
Wednesday	e mërkurë	Sunday	e dielë
Thursday	e ejte		

January	Janar	July	Korrik
February	Shkurt	August	Gusht
March	Mars	September	Shtator
April	Prill	October	Tetor
May	Maj	November	Nëntor
June	Qershor	December	Dhjetor

| spring | pranverë | autumn | vjeshtë |
| summer | verë | winter | dimër |

Getting around
Public transport

I'd like …	Dua …
a one-way ticket	një biletë njëdrejtimshe
a return ticket	një biletë kthyese
I want to go to …	Dua të shkoj në …
How much is it?	Sa kushton?
What time does it leave?	Kur niset?
What time is it now?	Sa është ora tani?
The train has been …	Treni do të …
delayed	vonohet
cancelled	anulohet

first class	klasa e parë	platform	platformë
second class	Klasa e dytë	ticket office	sportel
sleeper	vagon-shtrat	timetable	orar

from	*prej*	car	*veturë*
to	*gjer*	4x4	*foristadë*
airport	*aeroport*	taxi	*taksi*
port	*liman*	minibus	*minibus*
bus	*autobus*	motobike/moped	*motoçikletë*
train	*tren*	bicycle	*biçikletë*
plane	*aeroplan*	arrival/departure	*ardhje/nisje*
boat	*anije*	bon voyage!	*rrugën e mbarë!*
ferry	*ferribot*		

Private transport

Is this the road to …?	*A është kjo rruga për …?*
Where is the service station?	*Ku është pikë furnizimi?*
Please fill it up	*Ju lutem, mund ta mbushni plot?*
I'd like … litres	*Dua … litra*
diesel	*dizel/naftë*
leaded petrol	*benzin me plumb*
unleaded petrol	*benzin pa plumb*
I have broken down	*mu prish makina*

Road signs

give way	*jep përparësi*	toll	*tarifë*
danger	*rrezik*	no entry	*ndalohet hyrja*
entry	*hyrje*	exit	*dalje*
detour	*rrugë e tërthortë*	keep clear	*mos ndalo*
one way	*njëkahshe*		

Directions

Where is it?	*Ku është?*
Which way is the …?	*Nga është rruga për në …?*
mosque/church	*xhami/kishë*
castle/museum	*kala/muzeum*
archaeological site/hotel	*vend arkeologjike/hotel*
cave/bridge	*shpellë/urë*
Go straight ahead	*Shko drejt*
turn left	*kthe në të majtë*
turn right	*kthe në të djathtë*
… at the traffic lights	*… te semafori*
… at the roundabout	*… te qarkorja*
behind	*prapa*
in front of	*përpara*
near	*afër*
opposite	*përballë*
here/there	*këtu/atje*
on the left/right	*në të majtë/djathtë*
straight on	*drejt*
forward/behind	*përpara/mbrapa*
east/west	*lindje/perëndim*
north/south	*veri/jug*
Where is …?	*Ku është …?*
taxi rank/travel agency	*vendqëndrim i taksive/agjensioni turistik*

train station	stacioni i trenit
bus station	stacion i autobusave
ferry/train	target/tren
doctor/hospital	doktor/spital
police station/bank	stacioni policior/bankë
restaurant/shop	restorant/shitore
town/village	qytet/fshat
house/flat	shtëpi/apartament
cinema/theatre	kinema/teatër
When does the train arrive/leave?	Kur arin/niset treni?

Street signs

entrance	hyrje	closed	mbyllur
exit	dalje	toilets – men/women	tualet – burra/gra
open	hapur	information	informacion

Accommodation

Where is a cheap/good hotel?	Ku ka një hotel të lirë/mire?
Could you please write the address?	A mund ta shkruani adresën ju lutem?
Do you have any rooms available?	A keni dhoma të lira?
I'd like ...	Dua ...
a single room	një dhomë njëkrevatshe
a double room	një dhomë me krevat dopio
a room with two beds	një dhomë me dy krevatë
a room with a bathroom	një dhomë me banjo
to share a dorm	të ndaj dhomën me dikë
How much it is per night/person?	Sa kushton për një natë/person?
Where is the toilet?	Ku është tualeti?
Where is the bathroom?	Ku është banjoja?
Is there hot water?	A ka ujë të nxehtë?
Is there electricity?	A ka rymë elektrike?
Is breakfast included?	A është mëngjesi i përfshirë?
I am leaving today	Unë shkoj sot

Food

Do you have a table for ... people?	A keni një tavolinë për ... persona?
... a children's menu?	... meny për fëmijë?
I am a vegetarian	Unë jam vegjetarian
Do you have any vegetarian dishes?	A keni ndonjë ushqim vegjetarian?
Please bring me ...	Ju lutem më sillni ...
a fork/knife/spoon	një pirun/thikë/lugë
Please may I have the bill?	Ju lutem, mund ta sillni llogarinë?
What do you have to drink?	Çfarë ka për të pirë?
I would like to drink ...	Do të doja të pi ...
water/juice	ujë/lëng
sparkling/non-sparkling	i gazuar/i pa gazuar
tea/coffee	çaj/kafe
hot chocolate/milk	çokollatë e nxehtë/qumësht i nxehtë
white coffee	kafe me qumësht
red/white wine	verë e kuqe/bardhë
beer/rakija	birrë/raki

mulled wine	*verë e nxehtë*
What do you have to eat?	*Çfarë ka për të ngrënë?*
I want some bread, please	*Dua pak bukë, ju lutem*
I want …	*Dua …*
fish/meat	*peshk/mish*
(Ohrid) trout/eel	*troftë/ngjalë*
soup/salad	*supë/sallatë*
cheese	*djathë*
tomatoes/eggs	*domate/vezë*
vegetables/fruit	*zarzavate/fruta*
rice/potatoes	*oriz/patate*
apples/oranges	*mollë/portokaj*
pears/grapes	*dardha/rrush*
figs/apricots	*fiq/kajsi*
sugar/honey	*sheqer/mjaltë*
hazelnuts/walnuts	*lajthi/arra*
ice cream/pancakes	*akullore/petulla*
I don't eat meat/fish/wheat products	*Unë nuk ha mish/peshk/produkte të grurit*

Shopping

I'd like to buy …	*Dua të blej …*	Do you accept …?	*A pranoni …?*
How much is it?	*Sa kushton?*	credit cards	*kartela kreditore*
I don't like it	*Nuk më pëlqen*	travellers' cheques	*çeqje udhëtarësh*
I'm just looking	*Vetëm shoh*	more	*më shumë*
It's too expensive	*Është shumë shtrenjtë*	less	*më pak*
I'll take it	*Do ta marr*	smaller	*më e/i vogël*
Please may I have …	*Ju lutem, mund të ma jepni …*	bigger	*më e/i madh*

Communications

I am looking for …	*Kërkoj …*		
bank	*bankë*	exchange office	*këmbimore valutash*
post office	*postë*	telephone centre	*qendër telefonike*
church	*kishë*	tourist office	*zyrë turistike*
embassy	*ambasadë*		

Health

diarrhoea	*diarre*	sunblock	*mbrojtje nga dielli*
nausea	*të përzier*	I am …	*Unë jam …*
doctor	*mjek*	asthmatic	*asmatik*
prescription	*recetë*	epileptic	*epileptik*
pharmacy	*barnatore*	diabetic	*diabetik*
paracetamol	*paracetamoll*	I'm allergic to …	*Jam alergjik në …*
antibiotics	*antibiotik*	penicillin	*penicilin*
antiseptic	*antiseptik*	nuts	*lajthi, bajame, arra*
tampons	*tampona*	bees	*grera*
condoms	*prezervativ*	wheat	*miell/grurë*
contraceptive	*kontraceptiv*		

Travel with children

Is there a …	*A ka …*

A1

Help!	*Ndihmë!*	fire	*zjarr*
Call a doctor!	*Thirni mjek!*	ambulance	*ndihmë e*
There's been an	*Ka një*		*shpejtë*
accident	*aksident*	thief	*vjedhës*
I'm lost	*Kam humbur*	hospital	*spital*
Go away!	*Largohu!*	I am ill	*Jam i sëmurë*
police	*polici*		

baby changing room?	*dhomë pë të ndruar beben?*		
a children's menu?	*meny për fëmijë?*		
Do you have …?	*A keni …?*		
infant milk formula?	*qumësht pluhur për bebe?*		
nappies	*pelena*		
potty	*oturak*		
babysitter	*dado*		
high chair	*karrige për fëmijë*		
Are children allowed?	*A janë fëmijët të lejuar?*		

Other

my/mine/ours/yours	*imi/imja/jona/jotja*	good/bad	*mirë/keq*
and/some/but	*edhe/disa/por*	early/late	*shpejt/vonë*
this/that	*kjo/ajo*	hot/cold	*nxehtë/ftohtë*
expensive/cheap	*shtrenjt/lirë*	difficult/easy	*rëndë/lehtë*
beautiful/ugly	*e bukur/e keqe*	boring/interesting	*banal/interesant*
old/new	*e vjetër/e re*		

Basic verbs

to be	*të jesh*		
I am	*unë jam*	we are	*ne jemi*
you are	*ti je*	you are	*ju jeni*
he/she/it is	*ai/ajo është*	they are	*ata/ato janë*

to have	*të kesh*		
I have	*unë kam*	we have	*ne kemi*
you have	*ti ke*	you have	*ju keni*
he/she/it has	*ai/ajo ka*	they have	*ato/ata kanë*

to want	*të duash*		
I want	*unë dua*	we want	*ne duam*
you want	*ti do*	you want	*ju doni*
he/she/it wants	*ai/ajo do*	they want	*ato/ata duan*

Appendix 2

GLOSSARY

ARCHITECTURAL TERMS

acropolis	a fortified hill
amphitheatre	a Roman theatre, circular or semicircular in shape with tiered seats, used for animal or gladiatorial fights
an	an inn for travellers, usually four-sided around a well in an open courtyard, where travellers would sleep upstairs and animals and produce would be stored downstairs
apse	a semicircular recess in a wall
atrium	the inner courtyard of a Roman villa
basilica	a roofed Roman public hall, which by the 5th century BC had become a place of early Christian worship or formalised church
capital	distinctively decorated upper end of a column
cardac	a large niche in the wall on the second floor of a Turkish house
chancel	the altar end of a church; in the Orthodox Church this area is usually prohibited to women
čardak	first-floor balcony
cupola	domed roof
dolap	wardrobe or drawers for clothes
exonarthex	an open hall or lean-to built on to the side of a church
forum	a Roman marketplace or public square
hammam	Turkish baths, usually using water from natural hot springs
iconostasis	the screen dividing the chancel from the nave of a church
konak	formerly describing a large Turkish house, now used for the inns of a monastery
madrasa	a school teaching the Koran
methoses	land or estate owned by the Church
mihrab	the niche in the eastern wall of a mosque indicating the direction of Mecca
mimbar	the pulpit of a mosque, from where the sermon is preached
minaret	a thin circular or many-sided tower attached to an outside wall of a mosque
minder	cushion
minderlik	narrow fitted wooden benches with fitted cushions built into a room
mosaic	pictures usually depicting flora and fauna, people or buildings, made of small coloured tiles, usually laid as a flooring, but occasionally on a wall or ceiling

351

musandra	a built-in wardrobe for linen and bedding
narthex	the front lobby, porch or entrance hall of a church
nave	the main room of worship in a church
necropolis	a Roman graveyard
pithos	a large clay jar or jug used for storing foodstuffs
plinth	a square block of stone or marble at the bottom of a column
pòrtico	a row of columns holding up the exonarthex roof of a church or mosque
sergen	a glass cupboard or shop window
teke	the Bektaši equivalent of a monastery
turbe	a tomb usually found outside a mosque but within its grounds

ART TERMS

damp fold	painting or sculpting technique gathering folds of material to look as if wet and clinging to the body and used to emphasise depth and three-dimensionality
fresco	a wall painting
icon	portrait or likeness of a saint, often inlaid with silver and gold, and having holy and healing powers
iconoclasm	the destruction and prohibition of icons and artistic depiction of life forms, whether for religious or political reasons
scriptorium	place in a monastery for copying manuscripts; the body of written work of a monastery
zograph	title of a skilled fresco painter

NAMES As one might expect in a Balkan country as diverse as Macedonia, the names of famous people differ by language, and it can be quite confusing to figure out which names apply to which people. Here are some of the more commonly confusing names:

Aleksandar III of Macedon	as usually found in Macedonian literature; more commonly known as Alexander the Great, especially by the Greeks, or as Aleksandar Veliki by some Macedonians; known as Iskander in Albanian, Turkish and lands further east; abbreviated to Aco
Basilius II	the Byzantium emperor known as Basil II in English, Vasilius II in some renditions ('b' and 'v' are often interchangeable) and as Vasilie in Macedonia
Bogorodica	the Holy Mother of God (the Virgin Mary)
Gjorgi	George, also sometimes transliterated into English as Džordži
Jovan	John
Kliment	Clement in English
Pavle	Paul
Pantelejmon	meaning 'all merciful'; the patron saint of physicians
Skenderbeg	also Skenderbej/Skendery/Skenderbeu, meaning literally 'Lord' (bej/beg) Iskander/Alexander
Spas	the Holy Saviour

Appendix 3

FURTHER INFORMATION

BOOKS If you are new to Macedonia and want to know where to start with further reading, I suggest the works of both John Phillips and Robert Kaplan. Books written on Macedonia by Macedonians abound, only some of which have been translated into English. These are listed separately, below the more internationally available books (which can be ordered through most bookshops or Amazon, or can be borrowed from a good university library). Old, rare and out-of-print titles can often be found on w abebooks.co.uk (or .com). All the Macedonian books listed are available from Ikona, Kultura, Matica or Tabernakul bookshops in Skopje. Books specifically on ethnic Macedonians outside the Republic of Macedonia are not especially covered here, but many can be found at w www.pollitecon.com.

History/politics

Brown, Keith *The Past in Question: Modern Macedonia and the Uncertainties of Nation* Princeton University Press, 2003. Looks at Macedonia's work on historiography of the Kruševo Republic of 1903 and how this has been an effort to create an identity for a nation uncertain of itself. Engaging reading in parts.

Carpenter, Teresa *The Miss Stone Affair: America's First Modern Hostage Crisis!* Simon & Schuster, 2003. A page-turner of a book on the kidnap of the American missionary, Ellen Stone, and her pregnant chaperone, Mrs Tsilka, by Jane Sandanski, a member of the Internal Macedonian Revolutionary Organisation (VMRO).

Cartledge, Paul *Alexander the Great: The Hunt for a New Past* Pan Books, 2005. This latest book on Alexander the Great by a professor of Greek history at Oxford University gives some clarity to all those who struggle with whether Alexander/Aleksandar was Greek or Macedonian. Interesting reading.

Chiclet, Christophe and Lory, Bernard (eds) *La République de Macédoine* Editions L'Harmattan, Paris, 1998. This is a useful update (in French) on a lot of Hugh Poulton's book (page 354).

Clark, Victoria *Why Angels Fall: A Journey through Orthodox Europe from Byzantium to Kosovo* Picador, 2001. The 44 pages covering Macedonia also include Aegean Macedonia. They give an insight into the relationship between these two sides of geographical Macedonia and the role that the Church still plays.

Glenny, Misha *The Fall of Yugoslavia* (3rd edition) Penguin, London, 1996; and *The Balkans: Nationalism, War and the Great Powers, 1804–1999* Penguin, USA, 2001. Both books by this journalist are an excellent read although, depending on where you are in your knowledge of the Balkans, the books can either be too broad or too detailed! With the advantage of hindsight, the latter book has a weak ending.

Hammond, N G A *History of Macedonia*, Duckworth, 1979–88. The standard reference on the history of Macedonia up to the early 20th century. Three volumes.

Jezernik, Božidar *Wild Europe: The Balkans in the Gaze of Western Travellers* Saqi Books, 2004. An interesting critique of many of the books listed here. Good exposé of the Macedonian question in Chapter 9, 'A True Comedy of Errors'.

Kaplan, Robert D *Balkan Ghosts: A Journey through History* Vintage, New York, 1993. The one chapter on Macedonia is a fascinating read of historical and contemporary views of the country, especially considering it was written in 1990, before the country had even become independent.

Karakasidou, Anastasia *Fields of Wheat, Hills of Blood: Passages to a Nationhood in Greek Macedonia 1870–1990* University of Chicago Press, 1997. Originally banned in Greece and the source of death threats to the author, this book is a must-read for anyone wanting to understand Macedonia.

Lane Fox, Robin *Alexander the Great* Penguin, 2004. Highly readable account of the life of Alexander.

Moody, Simon and Wakefield, Alan *Under the Devil's Eye: Britain's Forgotten Army at Salonika 1915–1918* Sutton Publishing, 2004. Detailed reading taken from soldier accounts of their time on the Salonika Front, including the Battle of Dojran.

Mulley, Clare *The Woman Who Saved the Children: A Biography of Eglantyne Jebb* Oneworld Publications, 2009. Chapter 8 concentrates on Jebb's first and only trip to Macedonia and Kosovo to deliver aid to tens of thousands of refugees after the first Balkan War. The plight of children in particular spurs her to co-found Save the Children, and to author the Declaration of the Rights of the Child. A fascinating read. All book proceeds go to Save the Children.

Pekar, Harvey and Roberson, Heather *Macedonia: How Do You Stop a War?* Villard, 2007. Roberson's search to answer this question, through meetings with Macedonians as well as with foreigners working in Macedonia's many international organisations, is rendered into comic-book script and drawings by Pekar and illustrator Ed Piskor. The comic-book style leaves a lot out.

Pettifer, James (ed) *The New Macedonian Question* Palgrave, 2001. This is a collection of essays and articles covering a wide variety of topics concerning Macedonia. Extremely informative.

Phillips, John *Macedonia: Warlords and Rebels* IBTauris, 2004. This book by a reporter for *The Times* was the first to give full coverage of the 2001 conflict in English. It is insightful and balanced until the last few pages, when his attempt to catch up on the last two years when he was not reporting on the country paints far too pessimistic a picture. Excellent review of Macedonian history.

Poulton, Hugh *Who Are the Macedonians?* Indiana University Press, 1995. A somewhat dry book that explores the origins of the peoples who now occupy the Republic of Macedonia and what they may mean in terms of their identity.

Silber, Laura *et al. The Death of Yugoslavia* (revised edition) Penguin, 1996. An in-depth account of the ins and outs and minutiae that led up to the death of Yugoslavia. It is much easier to watch the BBC TV series.

Sokalski, Henryk J *An Ounce of Prevention: Macedonia and the UN Experience in Preventive Diplomacy* US Institute of Peace, Washington DC, 2003. Analysis by the head of UNPROFOR/UNPREDEP of the UN's first military mission in preventive diplomacy. Could the conflict of 2001 have been avoided if UNPROFOR had not been pulled out?

Thucydides *History of the Peloponnesian War* Penguin, 1972. This is *the* account of the wars over the Greek city-states and islands, a foundation work in political science, and describes the beginning of the decline of the classical Greek states. Paeonia and the royal house of Macedon are referred to in Book Two.

Macedonian authors

Koneska, Elizabeta *Yoruks* Museum of Macedonia, Skopje, 2004. Beautiful colour photographs by Robert Jankuloski and succinct text about the little-known Yoruk community of Macedonia.

Kumanovski, Risto *Ohrid and its Treasures* Mikena Publishing, Bitola, 2002. Gives an introduction to Ohrid's best sites, including 25 of its churches and monasteries.

Pavlovski, Jovan and Pavlovski, Mishel *Macedonia Yesterday and Today* (3rd edition) Mi-an Publishing, Skopje, 2001. A very readable, if very pro-Macedonian and anti-Bulgarian, account of Macedonia's history up until the first session of the Anti-fascist Assembly of the National Liberation of Macedonia (ASNOM) in October 1943.

Šeldarov, Nikola and Lilčikj, Viktor *Kralevite na antička Makedonija i nivnite moneti vo Republika Makedonija* (The Kings of Ancient Macedonia and their Coinage) National and University Library of Kliment Ohridski, Skopje, 1994. A good reference book on the ancient kingdom of the Macedons including maps of the kingdom, its tribes and towns, as well as drawings of many of their coins. Macedonian only.

Stojčev, Vanče *Military History of Macedonia*, Military Academy General Mihailo Apostolski, Skopje, 2004. Covering the period from 7BC through to World War II. A beautiful compendium of maps accompanies the main 777-page volume.

Natural history

Arnold, E Nicolas and Ovenden, Denys *Collins Field Guide to the Reptiles and Amphibians of Britain and Europe* HarperCollins, 2002. The best guide to the reptiles and amphibians of Europe.

Gorman, Gerard *Central and Eastern European Wildlife* Bradt Travel Guides, 2008. Although this guide does not cover Macedonia specifically, most of the animals to be found in Macedonia are covered in it, and it is a lot more affordable and easier to travel with than the Mitchell-Jones atlas below.

Hoffman, Helga and Marktanner, Thomas *Butterflies and Moths of Britain and Europe* HarperCollins, 1995. Small with a plastic cover, very handy for expeditions.

Karadelev, Mitko *Fungi Makedonci, Gabite na Makedonija* PGUP Sofija Bogdanci, Skopje, 2001. Available only in Macedonian, this is an excellent book with page-by-page descriptions and colour photos of all the mushrooms to be found in Macedonia.

Mitchell-Jones, A J *et al. The Atlas of European Mammals* Academic Press, 1999. A weighty tome with lots packed in.

Polunin, Oleg *The Concise Flowers of Europe* Oxford University Press, 1972.

Polunin, Oleg *Flowers of Greece and the Balkans: A Field Guide* Oxford University Press, 1987. Invaluable.

Svensson, Lars *Collins Bird Guide* HarperCollins, 2010.

Tolman, Tom and Lewington, Richard *Collins Butterfly Guide* Collins, 2009.

Historical travel writing

Čelebi, Evlija *Book of Travels: The Seyahatname* volumes V, VI and VIII, Brill Academic Publishers, Leiden, 1999. This is the best and often only source of what went on during the 17th century in the Ottoman Empire. Massively informative, if dense.

Lear, Edward *Journals of a Landscape Painter in Greece and Albania* Century, 1851, reprinted 1988. The more serious side of this most famous limerick writer offering sobering views.

Maclean, Fitzroy *Eastern Approaches* Penguin, 1991. An excellent account of Maclean's missions through the Balkans during World War I.

Moore, Frederick *The Balkan Trial* Smith, Elder and Co., 1906. An American journalist writes about his travels with other European travellers, including an English journalist, through Monastir (Bitola), Prilep and Üsküb (Skopje) and about the Kruševo Uprising from his time there in 1903, aged 29.

Pouqueville, F C H L (ed. James Pettifer, Classic Balkan Travel Series, 1998) *Travels in Epirus, Albania, Macedonia and Thessaly* Loizou Publications, Paris, 1820. Early 18th-century travels through Ottoman-held land; only a few pages on Vardar Macedonia.

West, Rebecca *Black Lamb and Grey Falcon* Canongate Books, Edinburgh, 1941, reprinted 1993. On the one hand it is one of the few accounts available of the Balkans in the early 20th century; on the other hand it is the account of a privileged upper-class lady with undisguised ethnocentric tendencies.

Willis, Martin P L *A Captive of the Bulgarian Brigand: An Englishman's Terrible Experiences in Macedonia* Ede Allum & Townsend, 1906. A revealing thriller, highlighting only one account of a more widespread problem debated by the Great Powers at the time.

Modern travel writing

Cho, Carol *A Hitchhiker's Guide to Macedonia ... and My Soul* Forum Publishing, 2002. Written by an Amerasian woman who spent three years living in the Macedonian community over the 2001 conflict period. Although the book mentions little of the conflict itself, it offers excellent insights into the trials and tribulations of a young woman coming to terms with her own self and with Macedonia.

Delisso, Christopher *Hidden Macedonia: The Mystic Lakes of Ohrid and Prespa* Haus Publishing, London, 2007. Delisso, a long-time Balkan-hand, brings his insights as editor of balkanalysis.com to bear on his 2006 journey through three countries around lakes Ohrid and Prespa. A short and readable introduction to the history, religions and races of the region.

Palin, Michael *New Europe* Weidenfeld & Nicolson, 2007. Palin's documentary takes him through all of New Europe, with a few days in Ohrid and Prilep.

Macedonian literature

Pavlovski, Božin *The Red Hypocrite* AEA Publishers, Australia, 2001. One of the most famous modern authors to emerge from Macedonia, who now lives in Australia. Other books by Pavlovski available in English include: *Duva and the Flea*; *Eagle Coat of Arms*; *Egyptian Dreamer*; *Home is Where the Heart is*; *Journey with my Beloved*; *Miladin from China*; *Neighbours of the Owl*; *Return to Fairy Tales*.

Miscellaneous

van Attekum, Marietta and de Bruin, Holger *Via Egnatia on Foot: A Journey into History (1: Durres to Thessaloniki)* 2014. Hiking guide to this newly waymarked, historic route, with detailed maps.

Biegman, Nicolaas *God's Lovers: A Sufi Community in Macedonia* Kegan Paul, 2007. Biegman, a former Dutch diplomat in Macedonia and an expert on Islam, has produced a masterful photographic treatise of the little-understood Sufi community.

Biegman, Nicolaas *Living Sufism: Sufi Rituals in the Middle East and the Balkans*

American University in Cairo Press, 2009. Complementing many of the gorgeous photographs from *God's Lovers*, this book compares the Sufi rituals across the Middle East and the Balkans and how they have developed over time and distance.

Biegman, Nicolaas *Oil Wrestlers*, Stylus Publishing, 2009. Close-up photography of *pelivan* wrestling in Macedonia. A male-only sport involving only a pair of sturdy breeches and total body coverage with sunflower oil.

Kornakov, Dimitar *A Guide to Macedonian Monasteries* Matica, Skopje, 2005. A guide in English to 29 of Macedonia's most revered monasteries. In-depth information on the building and reconstruction of the monastery buildings, on their frescoes and some of their history.

Kramer, Christina E *Macedonian: A Course for Beginning and Intermediate Students* University of Wisconsin Press, Madison, 1999. An extremely well-presented and comprehensive language-learning book with exercises. Explanations are in English and a separate CD-ROM can be purchased to accompany the book to listen to native Macedonian.

Kusevska, Maria and Mitovska, Liljana *Do You Speak Macedonian?* MEDIS-informatics, Skopje, 1995. This course book, accompanied by a workbook and cassette tape, is written entirely in Cyrillic Macedonian, so it is impossible to use as a beginner without the cassette tape. Vocabulary at the back is listed with English translations.

Murgoski, Zoze *Dictionary: English–Macedonian, Macedonian–English* National and University Library of Kliment Ohridski, Skopje, 1995. A handy little paperback dictionary for carrying in your back pocket or bag. The definitive *English– Macedonian Dictionary: The Unabridged Edition*, also by Murgoski, is all you will ever need for finding those awkward words such as 'sovereignty' and 'fennel'. And the equivalent Macedonian–English version is also now out.

Skopje City Walk. An excellent little guide to exploring Skopje on foot, available from w walkingmacedonia.com, in English or Dutch, as a printed booklet or a PDF download. *Ohrid City Walk* is also available.

Other eastern European guides
For a full list of titles, go to w bradtguides. com/shop.

Bostock, Andrew *Greece: the Peloponnese with Athens, Delphi and Kythira* 2019.
Gloyer, Gillian *Albania* 2018.
Kay, Annie *Bulgaria* 2015.
Mitchell, Laurence *Serbia* 2017.
Rellie, Annelisa *Montenegro* 2015.
Warrander, Gail and Knaus, Verena *Kosovo* 2017.

Health
Wilson-Howarth, Dr Jane *Essential Guide to Travel Health* Cadogan, 2009
Wilson-Howarth, Dr Jane, and Ellis, Dr Matthew *Your Child Abroad: A Travel Health Guide* Bradt Travel Guides, 2014

WEB RESOURCES
There are a lot of outdated sites on Macedonia so check when the site was last updated before acting upon any of the information. Macedonian websites are generally quite good at having information available in English, but if not Google Translate will translate entire webpages relatively accurately.

General
w bbc.co.uk/news/world-europe-17550407

w **kniga.com.mk** Where you can find most Macedonian books, maps and software. Only available in Macedonian at the time of writing.

w **macedonia.co.uk** The Macedonian Cultural and Information Centre for lots of useful information to help you get to know the country before you go.

w **macedonia-timeless.com** Offers hundreds of links to help you get to know, and get about, Macedonia.

w **manaki.com.mk** Official site dedicated to the Manaki brothers, pioneers of film and photography in Macedonia.

w **mhrmi.org** The website of the Macedonian Human Rights Movement International, based in Toronto, Canada.

w **pollitecon.com** A site offering books and views supporting the argument that there are ethnic Macedonians in Greece.

Travel and accommodation

w **airports.com.mk** Flight information for Skopje and Ohrid.

w **exploringmacedonia.com** The official tourist site for Macedonia. Very useful.

w **gomacedonia.com** An excellent site with up-to-date, accurate information on places worth visiting in Macedonia.

w **jsp.com.mk** The Skopje city bus website with map and timetables (sometimes only working in Macedonian).

w **macedonian-hotels.mk** Useful site listing a range of hotels in Macedonia, with those otherwise often elusive contact details.

w **mktransport.mk** Inter-town bus and train timetables for Macedonia.

w **mzi.mk** Train information for national and international rail travel through Macedonia.

w **sas.com.mk** The national and international bus service website.

w **unet.com.mk/oldmacedonianmaps** For all you map freaks.

w **viaegnatiafoundation.eu** Information on the Via Egnatia, including the newly marked long-distance trail following the section of its route from Durres to Thessaloniki.

Sports clubs and associations

w **amfora.com.mk** Diving centre in Ohrid.

w **eskimo-freeride.com** For the best skiing at the cheapest rates in Europe.

w **fpsm.org.mk** Macedonian Mountaineering Sports Federation (Macedonian only).

w **makedon.mk** Mountaineering and climbing club, based in Skopje.

w **sharamountainguide.com.mk** Homepage of Ljuboten mountaineering club, based in Tetovo, including hiring guides for Šar Planina hikes.

Government, media, communications, etc

w **balkaninsight.com** Reliable reporting of news coverage for the region.

w **dmwc.org.mk** Dobredojde Macedonia Welcome Centre (DMWC) is a non-governmental, non-profit organisation promoting Macedonian culture among the international community in Macedonia and abroad.

w **kultura.gov.mk** A very good site by the Ministry of Culture giving all the latest news on events and shows.

w **mia.com.mk** Macedonian Information Agency, the official independent national news agency – very informative and the most up to date.

w **sobranie.mk** Website of the Macedonian parliament.

w **telekom.mk** Homepage of Makedonski Telekomunikacija, the main mobile provider.

w **vlada.mk** For the latest from the government.

- w **yellowpages.com.mk** Macedonia's online business phone directory, with an optional English interface. Useful links to other Yellow Pages around the world.
- w **zels.org.mk** The Organisation of Local Self Government, with links to all the municipalities. These sites in turn, many of which are available in English, offer the latest information on the local area including places of interest, transportation and accommodation.

Business

- w **bbgm.co.uk** Homepage of the British Business Group Macedonia.
- w **companyformationmacedonia.com/set-up-doo-company-macedonia?** Runs you through how to actually set up a business in Macedonia.
- w **doingbusiness.org/data/exploreeconomies/macedonia-fyr** Compares countries across the globe in various sectors of efficiency in doing business. Updated yearly.
- w **investinmacedonia.com** A government-run portal.

Wines

- w **bovin.com.mk** Macedonia's most prestigious label. Bovin's award-winning Venus, Daron and Dissan red wines are distributed as far as California, while their Pinot Noir and Riesling are very recommendable, affordable wines. Bovin is open for wine tasting for groups of ten or more.
- w **chateaukamnik.com** A bijou winery, hotel and restaurant in the outskirts of Skopje. The hunting-themed restaurant has an extensive wine collection from around the world and of course is open for wine tasting.
- w **ezimitvino.com.mk** Near Veles, Ezimit is one of only four producers worldwide to receive the Honorable Panel of the Vine Knights of Austria. The award was received for their Vranac Reserve and Vranac Barrique, both of which are truly deserving of the award.
- **@fonko.wines** Based in Negotino, Fonko offers seven wines, the most prestigious of which is their 2002 special limited edition Chardonnay.
- w **popovakula.com.mk** A delightful winery with an impressive hotel/restaurant overlooking the ravine of Demir Kapija. Offers the widest variety of indigenous grape of the Tikveš region as well as more well-known varieties.
- w **popovwinery.com.mk** Popov family wines went commercial in 2001, since when they have produced several excellent wines for public consumption. Their Temjanika (the Macedonian variety of Muscat-Frontignan), Vranec-Cabernet Sauvignon, Žilavka and Rose (Pinot Noir and Stanušina) are particularly noteworthy.
- w **skovin.com.mk** Based near Skopje, Skovin produces a variety of wines including a very good Muscat and a rosé.
- w **tikves.com.mk** Tikveš is the largest winery in Macedonia, producing the iconic T'ga za Jug red Vranec. Their impressive wine-cellar restaurant is also open for lunch (preferably by reservation a day in advance).

World War I Salonika Front

- w **archive.org/stream/salonikafront00mannuoft/salonikafront00mannuoft_ djvu.txt** Online publication of *The Salonika Front* by Capt Arthur Mann, 1920.
- w **gwpda.org/memoir/Salonica/salonTC.htm#TC** Online publication of *The Story of the Salonika Army* by G Ward Price, 1918.
- w **memorabilia.homestead.com/files/Salonika_and_Macedonia_1916_18. htm** Listing of the battalions of each division who fought on the Salonika Front.
- w **salonikabattlefieldtour.com** A Strumica-based company providing informative tours of the Dojran battlefield and nearby graves.

FILMS/DOCUMENTARIES

Cvetanovski, Vlado *The Secret Book*, 2005. A thriller based on a fictional search for the legendary secret Slavic book of the Bogomil Gnostic religion of the 11th century. The book is supposed to have ended up in France, where a father and son duo take up the search in the 21st century à la *Da Vinci Code*. In French and Macedonian, available with English and Macedonian subtitles.

Einarsson, Sigurjon *A Name is a Name*, 2010. A travelogue road movie considering the thorny issue of naming a nation. Controversial.

Horne, Robert *Edward Lear: An Exile in Paradise* Lear Productions, 2008. A fascinating reproduction of Lear's travels from Greece, through Monastir (Bitola), Prilep and Üsküb (Skopje) in 1848. Lear is better known for his nonsense poetry and sketches, but this documentary does a great job of showcasing his landscape paintings of the time and how they compare to the region today.

Leder, Mimi *The Peacemaker*, 1997. Nuclear warheads get in the wrong hands between Russia and the Balkans. A couple of the scenes are set in the church on the main square in Bitola. Starring George Clooney and Nicole Kidman. Usual Hollywood stuff.

Mančevski, Milčo *Before the Rain*, 1995. Set in London and Macedonia in the 1990s, giving a chilling forecast of how inter-ethnic violence might start. English, Macedonian and Albanian with English subtitles. Gripping.

Mančevski, Milčo *Dust*, 2001. Set in New York and Macedonia at both ends of the 20th century. Wild West comes to Macedonia, starring Joseph Fiennes. Action packed.

Mančevski, Milčo *Mothers*, 2010. Set in contemporary Macedonia, two parts fiction, one part documentary, this movie looks at the nature of truth.

Mančevski, Milčo *Shadows*, 2008. A young doctor in Skopje has to lay to rest the wandering souls of several characters from bygone years. Not as 'insightful' of Macedonia per se, but a gripping drama all the same.

Mitrevski, Darko *Bal-Can-Can*, 2005. A fantastic parody of life in the Balkans at the turn of the 21st century. Available with English subtitles. Brilliant.

Mitrevski, Darko *The Third Half*, 2012. Based on true events set in World War II, when a Jewish German becomes the coach of a Macedonian football team and turns them around from failure to beating the Germans. But at what cost?

Mitrovic, Živorad *The Assassins of Salonika*, 1961. Classic feature of the fight for Macedonia at the end of the 19th century. Today's Macedonians grew up on this stuff. Macedonian and Serbo-Croat. Available with English subtitles.

Palin, Michael *New Europe* BBC documentary, 2007. Palin's documentary takes him all through New Europe, stopping for a few days in Ohrid and Prilep.

Popov, Stole *Tetoviranje*, 1994. Set in Šutka detention centre and Idrižovo prison. A man is detained for having an empty suitcase and ends up being shot by a Macedonian crack sniper. English subtitles. Perks up in parts.

Stone, Oliver *Alexander*, 2004. This movie was never going to win any Oscars, not least because it is too long with too many up-close battles, but it's a revealing rendition of a legendary figure. Starring Colin Farrell and Angelina Jolie.

Trajkov, Ivo *The Great Water*, 2004. Based on the book of the same name by Živko Cingo, this story tells of an orphan after World War II, whose experience as a young pioneer in the orphanage allegedly creates one of the greatest democratic forces in Yugoslavia. English subtitles. Average.

Wood, Michael *In the Footsteps of Alexander* BBC documentary, 1997. An informative and interesting account of Alexander the Great's conquest of Persia.

Index

Page numbers in *italics* indicate a map.

INDEX OF ADVERTISERS